Concepts of
BIOLOGY

SYLVIA S. MADER

Includes Selected Material for
FOOTHILL COLLEGE

 Learning Solutions

Boston   Burr Ridge, IL   Dubuque, IA   New York   San Francisco   St. Louis
Bangkok   Bogotá   Caracas   Lisbon   London   Madrid
Mexico City   Milan   New Delhi   Seoul   Singapore   Sydney   Taipei   Toronto

The *McGraw-Hill* Companies

Concepts of Biology, Second Edition
Includes Selected Material for Foothill College

This book is a McGraw-Hill Learning Solutions textbook and contains select material from *Concepts of Biology*, Second Edition by Sylvia S. Mader. Copyright © 2011 by The McGraw-Hill Companies, Inc. Reprinted with permission of the publisher. Many custom published texts are modified versions or adaptations of our best-selling textbooks. Some adaptations are printed in black and white to keep prices at a minimum, while others are in color.

1 2 3 4 5 6 7 8 9 0 CCC CCC 13 12 11

ISBN-13: 978-0-07-752156-1
ISBN-10: 0-07-752156-0

Learning Solutions Manager: Terri Harvey
Production Editor: Jessica Portz
Printer/Binder: Commercial Communivations

Brief Contents

Preface: What Sets Mader Apart?

Focus on Key Biological Concepts

Biology—like no other discipline—uses concepts as a way to understand ourselves and the world we live in, and an understanding of biological principles should be within the grasp of all those who decide to study biology. Sylvia Mader is motivated by the desire to help science-shy students gain a conceptual understanding of biology.

Concepts of Biology was written not only to present the major concepts of biology clearly and concisely but also to show the relationships between the concepts at various levels of complexity.

Emphasis on biological concepts begins in the introductory chapter. In this edition, the first chapter discusses the scientific process and then proceeds to an overview of the five major concepts of biology. These key concepts have become the part titles for the book:

Part I: Organisms Are Composed of Cells
Part II: Genes Control the Traits of Organisms
Part III: Organisms Are Related and Adapted to Their Environment
Part IV: Plants Are Homeostatic
Part V: Animals Are Homeostatic
Part VI: Organisms Live in Ecosystems

Mader Writing Style

Well-known for its clarity and simplicity, the Mader writing style makes the content accessible to students. Mader's writing appeals to students because it meets them where they are and helps them understand the concepts with its clear "take-home messages" and relevant examples.

"This book uses everyday language to immerse the student into the world of science." —Michael P. Mahan, *Armstrong Atlantic State University*

About the Author

Dr. Sylvia S. Mader has authored several nationally recognized biology texts published by McGraw-Hill. Educated at Bryn Mawr College, Harvard University, Tufts University, and Nova Southeastern University, she holds degrees in both Biology and Education. Over the years she has taught at University of Massachusetts, Lowell, Massachusetts Bay Community College, Suffolk University, and Nathan Mathew Seminars. Her ability to reach out to science-shy students led to the writing of her first text, *Inquiry into Life,* that is now in its thirteenth edition. Highly acclaimed for her crisp and entertaining writing style, her books have become models for others who write in the field of biology.

Although her writing schedule is always quite demanding, Dr. Mader enjoys taking time to visit and explore the various ecosystems of the biosphere. Her several trips to the Florida Everglades and Caribbean coral reefs resulted in talks she has given to various groups around the country. She has visited the tundra in Alaska, the taiga in the Canadian Rockies, the Sonoran Desert in Arizona, and tropical rain forests in South America and Australia. A photo safari to the Serengeti in Kenya resulted in a number of photographs for her texts. She was thrilled to think of walking in Darwin's steps when she journeyed to the Galápagos Islands with a group of biology educators. Dr. Mader was also a member of a group of biology educators who traveled to China to meet with their Chinese counterparts and exchange ideas about the teaching of modern-day biology.

For My Children   —Sylvia Mader

Applications

Applications are used throughout *Concepts of Biology* to show how biological concepts relate to students' lives.

- **NEW** **How Life Changes** applications emphasize evolution as the unifying theme of biology and how it pertains to students' lives.

- **How Biology Impacts Our Lives** applications examine issues that affect our health and environment.

- **How Science Progresses** applications discuss scientific research and advances that have helped us gain valuable biological knowledge.

All applications end with several Form Your Opinion questions that can serve as a basis for class discussion.

See page xxvii for a complete listing of application topics.

In the second edition, the "**Connecting the Concepts**" feature appears at the end of each chapter. This feature includes narrative and several questions to help students understand how the concepts in the present chapter are related to one another and to those in other chapters.

HOW LIFE CHANGES *Application*

13B Sometimes Mutations Are Beneficial

Imagine trying to redesign a vital mechanical part of an airplane, while still keeping that plane in flight. Sounds nearly impossible, doesn't it? This was one of the puzzles facing early evolutionary biologists. After all, mutations are the main way in which new traits and features arise during evolution, and yet most mutations cause damage. If a feature is important, how can it be altered while still allowing an organism and its offspring to survive?

Geneticists have shown one possible way mutations can accumulate without impairing present function: gene duplication (Fig. 13B.1). An extra (and possibly unused) copy of a gene may result from errors during cell division, efforts to repair breakage to DNA, or other mechanisms. The surprising idea here is that these seeming accidents actually can provide raw material for

natural selection. Particularly in plants, many examples of gene duplication have been found—for example, the wild mustard plant has undergone at least two duplications of *all* its chromosomes in the past, as well as duplication of several individual genes at various times in history.

An intriguing example of gene duplication involves the sweet-tasting proteins. Of the thousands of proteins studied so far, most have no noticeable flavor—but about half a dozen have an intensely sweet taste. These rare, sweet-tasting proteins are found in plants and plant products from several different continents: The protein "curculin" is found in the fruit of a Malaysian herb (Fig. 13B.2); "mabinlin" can be extracted from a traditional Chinese herb; "thaumatin" is found in the fruit of a West African rain forest shrub; and "brazzein" comes from a fruit that grows wild in Gabon, Cameron, and Zaire. Each of these proteins tastes sweet only to humans and certain monkeys. From the plant's point of view, the proteins likely provided an advantage: Sweeter fruits would be eaten more often and their seeds distributed

single copy of gene

FORM YOUR OPINION

1. Humans and perhaps apes and monkeys like sweet foods. How does this benefit plants containing sweet proteins?
2. Are humans influencing the evolution of plants when they propagate them? When they genetically modify them and then propagate them?
3. In what way is artificial selection harmful to the plants and animals selected to reproduce?

HOW BIOLOGY IMPACTS OUR LIVES *Application*

8B Tissues Can Be Grown in the Lab

Most people are now aware that stem cells can undergo the cell cycle and generate tissues for the cure of devastating human diseases, such as diabetes, cancer, brain disorders, and heart ailments (Fig. 8B). For many years, scientists have known about two types of stem cells: embryonic stem (ES) cells and adult stem cells.

Embryonic stem cells are simply the cells of an early embryonic stage. These cells can stay alive longer and are better at producing different tissues than adult stem cells, but to acquire

them a human embryo must be destroyed. Embryos are sometimes "left over" at fertility clinics, but even so many people reject the use of ES cells because it means the destruction of a potential human life. Adult stem cells are difficult to glean from the human body, and they do not multiply readily in the laboratory. Also, their potential to become all different types of tissues is not as great as that of ES cells. One drawback to both ES cells and adult stem cells is the danger of rejection by the recipient. Remember the many different types of proteins that occur in the plasma membrane? Some of those mark the cell as belonging to us, and if a transplanted tissue or organ carries different markers, our body works against them until they die. This is called rejection of the transplant.

Breakthrough

By now, scientists are experienced at coaxing stem cells to become specialized cells, but research would really benefit from an unlimited source of stem cells in order to achieve the goal of replacing diseased or damaged tissues in the human body. The scientific community is now hopeful that such a source has been found, thanks to a little-known Japanese scientist who worked alone for ten years in a tiny laboratory. Through patient research, Shinya Yamanaka was able to discover why ES cells are **pluripotent**—able to become any type of tissue in the body. He hypothesized that pluripotent cells produce certain proteins that specialized cells do not produce. Yamanaka worked with mouse skin cells until he knew that only four particular genes do the trick of making cells pluripotent. In 2006 he published his results in the journal *Cell*. Just five months later, United States scientists induced human skin cells to become pluripotent by supplying them with active forms of the four genes. These skin cells are termed iPS (induced pluripotent stem) cells. For every cell that became pluripotent, thousands of skin cells are treated. But the inefficiency doesn't matter because scientists have access to millions of skin cells. Such cells can even be obtained by simply swabbing the inside of a person's mouth! Researchers are still improving their technique and resolving various safety issues, but they feel confident they will be able to make tissues for human transplant. If replacement tissues are produced the patient's own skin cells, rejection should not be a problem. However, scientists hope that eventually labs can stockpile so different types of tissues, a good match will be available for every person. Because spinal cord injuries should be treated a few hours, there isn't time to use the patient's own skin to produce replacement nerve cells.

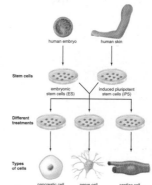

human embryo human skin Stem cells embryonic stem cells (ES) induced pluripotent stem cells (iPS) Different treatments Types of cells pancreatic cell nerve cell cardiac cell

FORM YOUR OPINION

Currently, the main safety issue with iPS cells is that they might cause cancer. If you were 75 and had Alzheimer disease, would you be willing to take the chance of cancer in order to correct this condition?

Imagine that you are a scientist who worked all alone for ten years to reach a breakthrough. Should you be allowed to patent your "invention," or should it be available to everyone?

CHAPTER 8 Cell Division and Reproduction 151

HOW SCIENCE PROGRESSES *Application*

29E Leeches, a Form of Biotherapy

Although it may seem more like an episode of a popular TV show than a real-life medical treatment, the U.S. Food and Drug Administration has approved the use of leeches as medical "devices" for treating conditions involving poor blood supply to various tissues.

Leeches are blood-sucking, aquatic creatures, whose closest living relatives are earthworms (Fig. 29E). Prior to modern times, medical practitioners frequently applied leeches to patients, mainly in an attempt to remove the bad "humors" that they thought were responsible for many diseases. This practice was abandoned, thankfully, in the nineteenth century when people realized that the "treatment" often harmed the patient.

True to their tenacious nature, however, leeches are making a comeback in twenty-first-century medicine. By applying leeches to tissues that have been injured by trauma or disease, blood supply can be

improved. When reattaching a finger, for example, it is easier to suture together the thicker-walled veins. Poorly draining blood from veins can pool in the appendage and threaten its survival. Leech saliva contains chemicals that dilate blood vessels and prevent blood from clotting by blocking the activity of thrombin. These effects can improve the circulation to the body part. Another substance in leech saliva actually anesthetizes the bite wound. In a natural setting, this allows the leech to feast on the blood supply of its victim undetected, but in a medical setting, it makes the whole experience more tolerable, at least physically. Mentally, however, the application of leeches can still be a rather unsettling experience, and patient acceptance is a major factor limiting their more widespread use.

FORM YOUR OPINION

1. Would you be willing to let leeches feast for a few minutes on your hand to improve the changes of recovering from an injury?
2. At one time, leeches were used to remove blood from a patient. How might physicians have gotten the idea that removing blood could help cure illnesses?

FIGURE 29E Leeches can attach to the body and suck out blood.

CHAPTER 29 Circulation and Cardiovascular Systems 603

CONNECTING THE CONCEPTS

Energy from the sun flows through all living things with the participation of chloroplasts and mitochondria. Through the process of photosynthesis, chloroplasts in plants and algae capture solar energy and use it to produce carbohydrates, which are broken down to carbon dioxide and water in the mitochondria of nearly all organisms. The energy released when carbohydrates (and other organic molecules) are oxidized is used to produce ATP molecules. When the cell uses ATP to do cellular work, all the captured energy dissipates as heat.

During cellular respiration, oxidation by removal of hydrogen atoms ($e^- + H^+$) from glucose or glucose products occurs during glycolysis, the prep reaction, and the Krebs cycle. The prep reaction and Krebs cycle release CO_2. The electrons are carried by NADH and $FADH_2$ to the electron transport chain (ETC) in the cristae of mitochondria. Oxygen serves as the final acceptor of electrons, and H_2O is produced. The pumping of hydrogen ions by the ETC into the intermembrane space leads to ATP production.

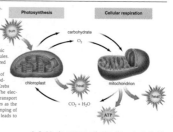

Photosynthesis Cellular respiration sun carbohydrate O_2 chloroplast heat mitochondrion heat $CO_2 + H_2O$ ATP

PUT THE PIECES TOGETHER

1. Tell how the pre-eukaryotic cell must have produced ATP. What event in the history of life would have allowed cellular respiration to evolve? Explain.
2. Explain the statement, "if chloroplasts and mitochondria are descended from a free-living common ancestor it would explain their structural similarities." What are some structural similarities?

Instructional Art

Outstanding photographs and dimensional illustrations, vibrantly colored, are featured throughout *Concepts of Biology*. Accuracy and instructional value were primary considerations in the development of each figure.

Multilevel Perspective

Illustrations depicting complex structures show macroscopic and microscopic views to help you see the relationships between increasingly detailed drawings.

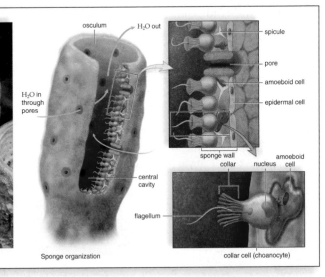

Yellow tube sponge   Sponge organization   collar cell (choanocyte)

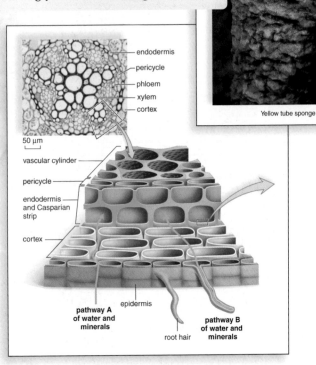

Combination Art

Drawings of structures are paired with micrographs to give you the best of both perspectives: the realism of photos and the explanatory clarity of line drawings.

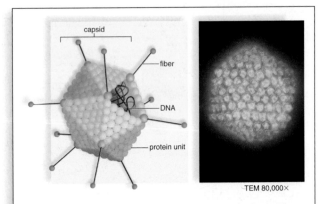

TEM 80,000×

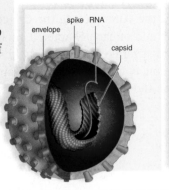

20 nm

"The illustrations support the text strongly."
—Anju Sharma, Stevens Institute of Technology

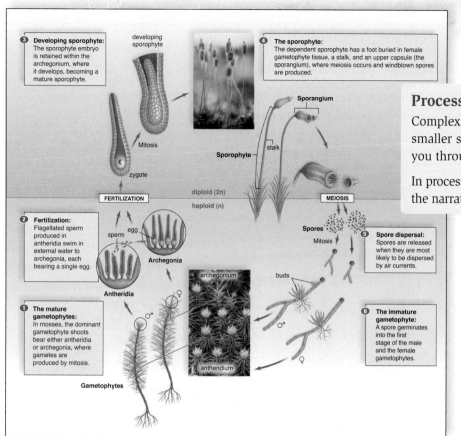

3 Developing sporophyte: The sporophyte embryo is retained within the archegonium, where it develops, becoming a mature sporophyte.

developing sporophyte

Mitosis

zygote

4 The sporophyte: The dependent sporophyte has a foot buried in female gametophyte tissue, a stalk, and an upper capsule (the sporangium), where meiosis occurs and windblown spores are produced.

Sporangium

Sporophyte

stalk

FERTILIZATION

diploid (2n)

haploid (n)

MEIOSIS

2 Fertilization: Flagellated sperm produced in antheridia swim in external water to archegonia, each bearing a single egg.

sperm egg

Archegonia

Antheridia

archegonium

antheridium

Gametophytes

Spores

Mitosis

buds

5 Spore dispersal: Spores are released when they are most likely to be dispersed by air currents.

6 The immature gametophyte: A spore germinates into the first stage of the male and the female gametophytes.

1 The mature gametophytes: In mosses, the dominant gametophyte shoots bear either antheridia or archegonia, where gametes are produced by mitosis.

Process Figures

Complex processes are broken down into a series of smaller steps that are easy to follow. Numbers guide you through the process.

In process figures, numbered steps are coordinated with the narrative for an integrated approach to learning.

10.6 During translation, polypeptide synthesis occurs one amino acid at a time

Although we often speak of protein synthesis, some proteins have more than one polypeptide, so it is more accurate to recognize that polypeptide synthesis occurs at a ribosome. Polypeptide synthesis involves three events: initiation, elongation, and termination. Enzymes are needed so that each of the three events will occur, and both initiation and elongation also require an input of energy.

Initiation During **initiation** all translation components come together. Proteins called initiation factors help assemble a small ribosomal subunit, mRNA, initiator tRNA, and a large ribosomal subunit for the start of a polypeptide synthesis.

Initiation is shown in **Figure 10.6A.** In prokaryotes, an mRNA binds to a small ribosomal subunit at the mRNA bind

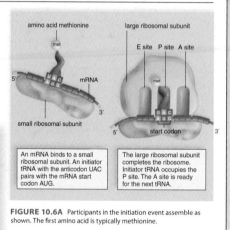

amino acid methionine

met

large ribosomal subunit

E site P site A site

met

mRNA

small ribosomal subunit

start codon

An mRNA binds to a small ribosomal subunit. An initiator tRNA with the anticodon UAC pairs with the mRNA start codon AUG.

The large ribosomal subunit completes the ribosome. Initiator tRNA occupies the P site. The A site is ready for the next tRNA.

FIGURE 10.6A Participants in the initiation event assemble as shown. The first amino acid is typically methionine.

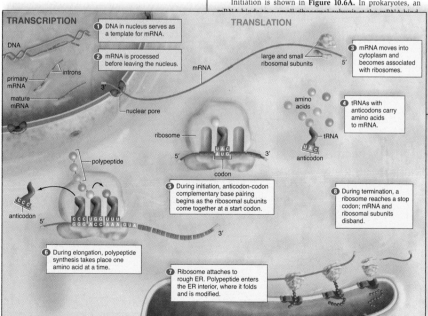

TRANSCRIPTION

DNA

1 DNA in nucleus serves as a template for mRNA.

2 mRNA is processed before leaving the nucleus.

primary mRNA

introns

mature mRNA

nuclear pore

TRANSLATION

large and small ribosomal subunits

mRNA

3 mRNA moves into cytoplasm and becomes associated with ribosomes.

amino acids

4 tRNAs with anticodons carry amino acids to mRNA.

tRNA

anticodon

ribosome

polypeptide

codon

anticodon

5 During initiation, anticodon-codon complementary base pairing begins as the ribosomal subunits come together at a start codon.

6 During elongation, polypeptide synthesis takes place one amino acid at a time.

7 Ribosome attaches to rough ER. Polypeptide enters the ER interior, where it folds and is modified.

8 During termination, a ribosome reaches a stop codon; mRNA and ribosomal subunits disband.

Color Consistency

Consistent use of color organizes information and clarifies concepts.

The Mader Learning System

Each chapter features numerous learning aids that were carefully developed to help students grasp challenging concepts.

A **Chapter Outline** lists the chapter concepts and the topics (numbered) that will be discussed in the chapter. **Applications** are also listed.

"The organization of the text around the major theories of Biology is a wise path to follow; it integrates the chapters into themes and points out the development of a theory...."
—Paul E. Wanda, Southern Illinois University, Edwardsville

Learning Outcomes are listed at the start of each major section to provide students with an overview of what they are to know.

Section Introductions orient students to concepts in a short, easy-to-understand manner.

Figure Legends have been expanded in this edition to reinforce the discussion and to improve student learning.

Check Your Progress questions at the end of each section help students assess and/or apply their understanding of a concept.

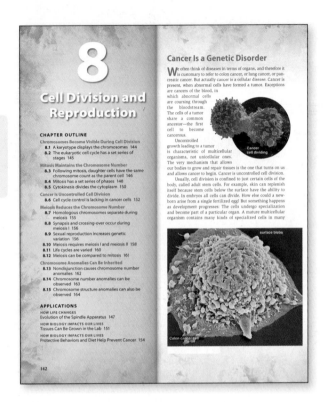

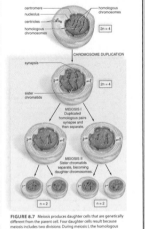

A bulleted and illustrated **Summary** is organized according to the chapter concepts and helps students review the chapter. New to this edition, the boldface terms are included in the summary as an aid to learning these terms in a nonthreatening way.

Testing Yourself offers another way to review the chapter concepts. Included are objective multiple-choice questions and Thinking Conceptually questions that ask students to apply their understanding of a concept.

"It would be fun to teach and learn using this book."
—Brian W. Schwartz,
Columbus State University

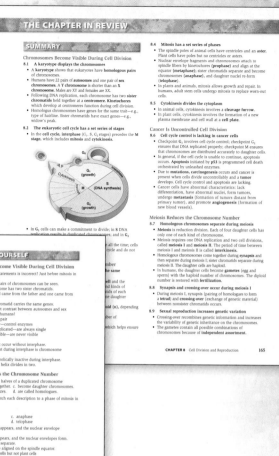

Thinking Scientifically questions end the chapter. These questions apply directly to the chapter and ask students to design an experiment or explain some part of a hypothetical experiment.

Connecting the Concepts feature at the end of the chapter shows how the concepts of the chapter are related, and how they relate to concepts in other chapters. "Put the Pieces Together" questions allow students to test their reasoning ability.

All questions are answered in the Appendix.

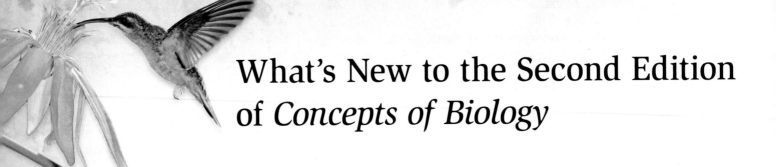

What's New to the Second Edition of *Concepts of Biology*

The second edition of *Concepts of Biology* continues to present concepts clearly and make biology relevant through the use of excellent writing, instructional art, and effective pedagogical tools. This new edition also includes

- **Significant content changes,** as outlined below.
- **Enhanced evolutionary coverage,** including extensive updates to the evolution chapters and the addition of *How Life Changes* applications.
- **Media integration,** including a robust set of teaching and learning tools through McGraw-Hill's Connect™ Biology.

Content Changes

Chapter 1, Biology, the Study of Life, was rewritten. It begins with a discussion of the scientific process and proceeds to an overview of the major concepts of biology (cell theory, gene theory, theory of evolution, theory of homeostasis, and theory of ecosystems). Basic evolutionary principles are presented, and a depiction of the Tree of Life introduces the three domains of life and the various types of eukaryotes.

Part I: Organisms Are Composed of Cells **Chapter 4,** Structure and Function of Cells, presents an improved discussion on cell structure and two new tables. Table 4.4 summarizes the differences between plant and animal cells, and Table 4.16 summarizes the eukaryotic cell structures and their functions. A new figure (Fig. 4.13) stresses that plant cells have both mitochondria and chloroplasts. **Chapter 5,** Dynamic Activities of Cells, includes sharpened energy transformation analogies with references to everyday occurrences (see Figs. 5.1, 5.3B, and 5.5A). Cell communication was stressed with the addition of a new section (Section 5.13). **Chapter 7,** Pathways of Photosynthesis, provides an improved discussion of mitochondrial structure. Changes to Figures 7.4 and 7.7B offer views from the whole cell to particles on the mitochondrial inner membrane.

Part II: Genes Control the Traits of Organisms All chapters in Part II were rewritten to present concepts at a student-friendly pace, and thereby increase student interest and learning. Modern genetics has been updated. **Chapter 11,** Regulation of Gene Activity, is now at an appropriate level and explains how humans can make do with far fewer protein-coding genes than expected. **Chapter 12,** Biotechnology and Genomics, offers a short, but complete, discussion of the human genome, including the several types of DNA sequences that are not protein-coding genes.

Part III: Organisms Are Related and Adapted to Their Environment The evolution chapters include extensive revisions. **Chapter 14,** Speciation and Evolution, now includes real-life examples of various processes that can cause speciation. The influence of regulatory genes during development helps explain how species can share the same genes but have different phenotypes. **Chapter 15,** The Evolutionary History of Life on Earth, will help instructors introduce their students to cladistics. It explains the rationale behind the replacement of Linnean classification with that of cladistics in a way that allows instructors to be up-to-date, while not overburdening beginning students. **Chapter 17,** Evolution of Protists, introduces a new evolutionary tree of protists based on molecular data. The chapter still emphasizes the biological and ecological relevance of each type of protist. **Chapter 18,** Evolution of Plants and Fungi, employs a new evolutionary tree based in part on molecular data. Land plants and stoneworts, which are charophytes, share a common green algal ancestor. All land plants protect the embryo, and thereafter each of four innovations can be associated with a particular group of land plants. **Chapter 19,** Evolution of Animals, introduces the new evolutionary tree of animals based on molecular and developmental data. The biology of each group is discussed as before. **Chapter 20,** Evolution of Humans, was rewritten to include a description and importance of the newly studied fossil *Ardipithicus ramidus.*

Part IV: Plants Are Homeostatic **Chapter 21,** Plant Organization and Homeostasis, includes a rewrite of Section 21.1 to better explain the overall organization of a plant and the functions of roots, stems, and leaves. This supports a rewrite of Section 21.8 which discusses more authoritatively how plants maintain homeostasis. **Chapter 22,** Transport and Nutrition in Plants, includes a reorganization of Sections 22.4 and 22.6 to increase student understanding of phloem structure and function, and root structure and function. **Chapter 24,** Reproduction in Plants, was reorganized and rewritten to better present an overview of the flowering plant life cycle and place it in an evolutionary context.

Part V: Animals Are Homeostatic **Chapter 26,** Coordination by Neural Signaling, was reorganized and begins with an overview of the structure and function of the human nervous system, before comparing this system to that of other animals. **Chapter 30,** Lymph Transport and Immunity, includes an updated and rewritten discussion of immunity to be consistent with current immunity literature. **Chapter 32,** Gas Exchange and Transport in Animals, provides a discussion on the transport of gases and exchange of gases that is more clearly related to external and internal respiration. **Chapter 33,** Osmoregulation and Excretion, places osmoregulation in fishes versus terrestrial animals in an evolutionary context, showing that physiology in other animals is relevant to understanding kidney function in humans. **Chapter 34,** Coordination by Hormone Signaling, was expanded to better stress the role of negative feedback in hormonal control and the role of the pituitary gland in humans.

Part VI: Organisms Live in Ecosystems **Chapter 36,** Population Ecology, was reorganized to show the relationship between growth rate, survivorship, and the age structure of a population. These same principles are more clearly applied to the human population at the end of the chapter. **Chapter 37,** Behavioral Ecology, better applies the genetic control of behavior and the process of sexual selection to behavior in general and to human behavior in particular. **Chapter 38,** Community and Ecosystem Ecology, includes an updated discussion of ecological succession to clearly show the difference between primary and secondary succession. **Chapter 40,** Conservation Biology, includes a new section on sustainability. This section stresses that it is not too late for humans to plan for and bring about sustainability so that future generations will have a comparable standard of living to our own.

Teaching and Learning Tools

McGraw-Hill Connect™ Biology

www.mhhe.com/maderconcepts2

 McGraw-Hill Connect™ Biology provides online presentation, assignment, and assessment solutions. It connects your students with the tools and resources they'll need to achieve success.

With Connect™ Biology you can deliver assignments, quizzes, and tests online. A robust set of questions and activities are presented and aligned with the textbook's learning outcomes. As an instructor, you can edit existing questions and author entirely new problems. Track individual student performance—by question, assignment, or in relation to the class overall—with detailed grade reports. Integrate grade reports easily with Learning Management Systems (LMS), such as WebCT and Blackboard. And much more.

ConnectPlus™ Biology provides students with all the advantages of Connect™ Biology, plus 24/7 online access to an eBook. This media-rich version of the book is available through the McGraw-Hill Connect™ platform and allows seamless integration of text, media, and assessments.

To learn more, visit

www.mcgrawhillconnect.com

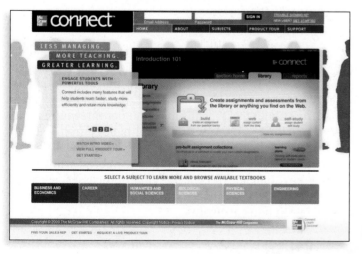

LearnSmart™

LearnSmart™ is available as an integrated feature of McGraw-Hill Connect™ Biology and provides students with a GPS (**G**uided **P**ath to **S**uccess) for your course. Using artificial intelligence, **LearnSmart™** intelligently assesses a student's knowledge of course content through a series of adaptive questions. It pinpoints concepts the student does not understand and maps out a personalized study plan for success. This innovative study tool also has features that allow instructors to see exactly what students have accomplished, and a built-in assessment tool for graded assignments.

Visit the site below for a demonstration.

www.mhlearnsmart.com

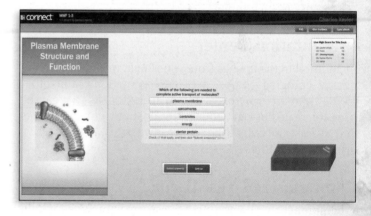

My Lectures—Tegrity

Tegrity Campus™ records and distributes your class lecture, with just a click of a button. Students can view anytime/anywhere via computer, iPod, or mobile device. It indexes as it records your PowerPoint presentations and anything shown on your computer so students can use keywords to find exactly what they want to study. Tegrity is available as an integrated feature of McGraw-Hill Connect™ Biology or as standalone.

Presentation Tools

Everything you need for outstanding presentations in one place!

www.mhhe.com/maderconcepts2

- *FlexArt Image PowerPoints*—including every piece of art that has been sized and cropped specifically for superior presentations, as well as labels that can be edited and flexible art that can be picked up and moved on key figures. Also included are tables, photographs, and unlabeled art pieces.
- *Lecture PowerPoints with Animations*—animations illustrating important processes are embedded in the lecture material.
- *Animation PowerPoints*—animations only are provided in PowerPoint.
- *Labeled Jpeg Images*—Full-color digital files of all illustrations that can be readily incorporated into presentations, exams, or custom-made classroom materials.
- *Base Art Image Files*—unlabeled digital files of all illustrations.

Chapter	Enhanced Image PPTs (includes photos, and editable art)	Lecture PPTs with Animations	Animation PowerPoints	Labeled Jpeg Images	Base Art Image Files (.jpgs, no labels or leader lines)
All Chapters	Enhanced Image PPTs (707,634 KB)	Lecture Animation PPTs (649,609 KB)	Animation PPTs (1,64,060 KB)	Labeled Images (859,337 KB)	Base Images (599,793 KB)
Ch01	Ch. 1 Enhanced Image PPTs (23,977 KB)	Ch. 1 Lecture Animation PPTs (14,860 KB)	There are no Animation PPTs correlated to this chapter.	Ch. 1 Labeled Images (28,669 KB)	Ch. 1 Base Images (21,333 KB)
Ch02	Ch. 2 Enhanced Image PPTs (9,907 KB)	Ch. 2 Lecture Animation PPTs (6,012 KB)	Ch. 2 Animation PPTs (6,794 KB)	Ch. 2 Labeled Images (15,054 KB)	Ch. 2 Base Images (8,805 KB)
Ch03	Ch. 3 Enhanced Image PPTs (16,605 KB)	Ch. 3 Lecture Animation PPTs (14,220 KB)	Ch. 3 Animation PPTs (1,833 KB)	Ch. 3 Labeled Images (18,346 KB)	Ch. 3 Base Images (14,607 KB)

Presentation Center

In addition to the images from your book, this online digital library contains photos, artwork, animations, and other media from an array of McGraw-Hill textbooks that can be used to create customized lectures, visually enhanced tests and quizzes, compelling course websites, or attractive printed support materials.

Computerized Test Bank

A comprehensive bank of test questions is provided within a computerized test bank powered by McGraw-Hill's flexible electronic testing program EZ Test Online. EZ Test Online allows you to create paper and online tests or quizzes in this easy to use program! A new tagging scheme allows you to sort questions by Bloom's difficulty level, topic, and section. Imagine being able to create and access your test or quiz anywhere, at any time, without installing the testing software. Now, with EZ Test Online, instructors can select questions from multiple McGraw-Hill test banks or author their own, and then either print the test for paper distribution or give it online.

Instructor's Manual

The instructor's manual contains chapter outlines, lecture enrichment ideas, and discussion questions.

Laboratory Manual

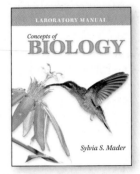

The *Concepts of Biology Laboratory Manual* is written by Dr. Sylvia Mader. With few exceptions, each chapter in the text has an accompanying laboratory exercise in the manual. Every laboratory has been written to help students learn the fundamental concepts of biology and the specific content of the chapter to which the lab relates, as well as gain a better understanding of the scientific method.

Companion Website

www.mhhe.com/maderconcepts2

The Mader: *Concepts of Biology* companion website allows students to access a variety of free digital learning tools that include:

- Chapter-level quizzing with pretest and posttest
- Bio Tutorial animations
- Vocabulary flashcards
- Virtual Labs

Biology Prep, also available on the companion website, helps students to prepare for their upcoming coursework in biology. This website enables students to perform self assessments, conduct self-study sessions with tutorials, and perform a post-assessment of their knowledge in the following areas:

- Introductory Biology Skills
- Basic Math Review I and II
- Chemistry
- Metric System
- Lab Reports and Referencing

McGraw-Hill: Biology Digitized Video Clips

ISBN (13) 978-0-312155-0
ISBN (10) 0-07-312155-X

McGraw-Hill is pleased to offer an outstanding presentation tool to text adopting instructors—digitized biology video clips on DVD! Licensed from some of the highest-quality science video producers in the world, these brief segments range from about five seconds to just under three minutes in length and cover all areas of general biology from cells to ecosystems. Engaging and informative, McGraw-Hill's digitized videos will help capture students' interest while illustrating key biological concepts and processes such as mitosis, how cilia and flagella work, and how some plants have evolved into carnivores.

Acknowledgments

Many dedicated and talented individuals assisted in the development of *Concepts of Biology*. I am very grateful for the help of so many professionals at McGraw-Hill who were involved in bringing this book to fruition. In particular, let me thank Janice Roerig-Blong and Michael Hackett, the publisher and editor who steadfastly encouraged and supported this project. The developmental editor was Rose Koos, who was very devoted, and lent her talents and advice to all those who worked on this text. The project manager, Jayne Klein, faithfully and carefully steered the book through the publication process. Tamara Maury, the marketing manager, tirelessly promoted the text and educated the sales representatives on its message.

The design of the book is the result of the creative talents of Laurie Janssen and many others who assisted in deciding the appearance of each element in the text. Electronic Publishing Services followed my guidelines as they created and reworked each illustration, emphasizing pedagogy and beauty to arrive at the best presentation on the page. Evelyn Jo Hebert and Lori Hancock did a superb job of finding just the right photographs and micrographs.

As always, my family was extremely patient with me as I remained determined to meet every deadline on the road to publication. My husband, Arthur Cohen, is also a teacher of biology. The many discussions we have about the minutest detail to the gravest concept are invaluable to me.

I am very much indebted to the contributors and reviewers whose suggestions and expertise were so valuable as I developed *Concepts of Biology*.

360° Development

McGraw-Hill's 360° Development Process is an ongoing, never-ending, market-oriented approach to building accurate and innovative print and digital products. It is dedicated to continual large-scale and incremental improvement driven by multiple customer feedback loops and checkpoints. This is initiated during the early planning stages of our new products, and intensifies during the development and production stages, then begins again upon publication in anticipation of the next edition.

This process is designed to provide a broad, comprehensive spectrum of feedback for refinement and innovation of our learning tools, for both student and instructor. The 360° Development Process includes market research, content reviews, course- and product-specific symposia, accuracy checks, and art reviews. We appreciate the expertise of the many individuals involved in this process.

Contributors

Lisa Bonneau
Metropolitan Community College—Blue River

Jane Caldwell
Washington and Jefferson College

Susan Fisher
The Ohio State University

Phil Gibson
University of Oklahoma

Jeffrey Isaacson
Nebraska Wesleyan University

Shelley Jansky
University of Wisconsin—Stevens Point

Michael Thompson
Middle Tennessee State University

Ancillary Authors

Instructor's Manual

Kimberly Lyle-Ippolito
Anderson University

Test Bank

Jo Wen Wu
Fullerton College

Stephanie Songer
North Georgia College and State University

Lecture Outlines

Brenda Leady
University of Toledo

FlexArt

Sharon Thoma
University of Wisconsin—Madison

Media Correlations

Jennifer Burtwistle
Northeast Community College

Second Edition Reviewers

Muhammad Ashraf Mian
Rust College

Ellen Baker
Santa Monica College

Mary K. Beals
Southern University A&M

Cheryl Boice
Lake City Community College

Lisa Bryant
Arkansas State University—Beebe

Kristin Byrd
Tarrant County College—Northeast

Marc DalPonte
Lake Land College

Tammy D. Dennis
Bishop State Community College

Greg Farley
Chesapeake College

Patrick Galliart
North Iowa Area Community College

Tammy R.Gamza
Arkansas State University—Beebe

Joyce Ache Gana
Chicago State University

Michaela Gazdik
Ferrum College

Sandra Gibbons
Moraine Valley Community College

Jared Gilmore
San Jacinto College—Central

James Hampton
Salt Lake Community College

Robert Harms
St. Louis Community College at Meramec

Jill Harp
Winston Salem State University

Barbara Hasek
Baton Rouge Community College

Jennifer A. Herzog
Herkimer County Community College

Ross S. Johnson
Chicago State University

Judith Kjellman
Yakima Valley Community College

Dale Lambert
Tarrant County College—Northeast

Yevgeniya Lapik
Harry S. Truman College

David Loring
Johnson County Community College

John McCastlain
ASU—Heber Springs

Melissa Meador
Arkansas State University—Beebe
Beth Miller
Pulaski Technological College
Linda Moore
Georgia Military College
Scott Murdoch
*Moraine Valley
Community College*
Rajkumar Nathaniel
Nicholls State University
Philip Pepe
Phoenix College
Crystal Pietrowicz
*Southern Maine
Community College*
Kathryn Stanley Podwall
Nassau Community College
Bob R. Pohlad
Ferrum College
Ramona Rice
Georgia Military College
Darryl Ritter
Northwest Florida State College
Roger Seeber
West Liberty State College
Juanita Sharpe
Chicago State University
Jennifer Smith
Triton College
Jim Smith
Montgomery College
Patricia Steinke
*San Jacinto College—
Central Campus*
Chad Thompson
*SUNY/Westchester
Community College*
Kip Thompson
*Ozarks Technical
Community College*
Dirk Vanderklein
Montclair State University
Elizabeth Vise
*Tarrant County College—
Northeast Campus*
Ryan Wagner
*Millersville University
of Pennsylvania*
Joe David White
Holmes Community College
Daniel Williams
Winston-Salem State University
Mary Wisgirda
San Jacinto College
Michelle Zurawski
*Moraine Valley
Community College*

First Edition Reviewers

Emily Allen
Gloucester County College
Kathy Pace Ames
Illinois Central College
Jason E. Arnold
Hopkinsville Community College
Dave Bachoon
*Georgia College and
State University*

Andrei L. Barkovskii
*Georgia College and
State University*
Lori Bean
Monroe County Community College
Mark G. Bolyard
Union University
Jason Brown
Young Harris College
Geralyn M. Caplan
*Owensboro Community
and Technical College*
Carol E. Carr
John Tyler Community College
Misty Gregg Carriger
*Northeast State
Community College*
Laurie-Ann Crawford
Hawkeye Community College
James Crowder
Brookdale Community College
Larry T. Crump
Joliet Junior College
John J. Dilustro
Chowan University
Toby Elberger
*UConn–Stamford, Sacred
Heart University*
John A. Ewing, III
Itawamba Community College
Gregory S. Farley
Chesapeake College
Teresa G. Fischer
Indian River Community College
Patricia Flower
Miramar College
Joseph D. Gar
*West Kentucky Community
and Technical College*
Nabarun Ghosh
West Texas A&M University
Jim R. Goetze
Laredo Community College
Andrew Goliszek
*North Carolina A&T
State University*
Becky C. Graham
The University of West Alabama
Cary Guffey
Our Lady of the Lake University
James R. Hampton
Salt Lake Community College
Pamela L. Hanratty
Indiana University
Stephanie G. Harvey
*Georgia Southwestern
State University*
Kendra Hill
South Dakota State University
B. K. Hull
Young Harris College
Troy W. Jesse
Broome Community College
H. Bruce Johnston
Fresno City College
Jacqueline A. Jordan
Clayton State University
Martin A. Kapper
*Central Connecticut
State University*

Arnold J. Karpoff
University of Louisville
Dawn G. Keller
Hawkeye Community College
Diane M. Kelly
Broome Community College
Natasa Kesler
*Seattle Central
Community College*
Dennis J. Kitz
*Southern Illinois University,
Edwardsville*
Peter Kobella
*Owensboro Community
and Technical College*
Anna Koshy
*Houston Community
College, Northwest*
Todd A. Kostman
University of Wisconsin–Oshkosh
Jerome A. Krueger
South Dakota State University
James J. Krupa
University of Kentucky
Steven A. Kuhl
Lander University
Janice S. Lai
*Seattle Central
Community College*
MaryLynne LaMantia
Golden West College
Thomas G. Lammers
University of Wisconsin–Oshkosh
Vic Landrum
Washburn University
Peggy Lepley
*Cincinnati State Technical
and Community College*
Fordyce G. Lux III
Lander University
Janice B. Lynn
Auburn University, Montgomery
Michael P. Mahan
*Armstrong Atlantic
State University*
Elizabeth A. Mays
Illinois Central College
TD Maze
Lander University
Jennifer Richter Maze
Lander University
Tiffany B. McFalls
*Southeastern Louisiana
University*
Debra Meuler
Cardinal Stritch University
Thomas H. Milton
Richard Bland College
Jerry W. Mimms
University of Central Arkansas
Jeanne Mitchell
Truman State University
Brenda Moore
Truman State University
Allan D. Nelson
Tarleton State University
Jonas E. Okeagu
Fayetteville State University
Nathan Okia
Auburn University—Montgomery

Frank H. Osborne
Kean University
John C. Osterman
University of Nebraska–Lincoln
Surindar Paracer
Worcester State College
Ann V. Paterson
Williams Baptist College
Jay Pitocchelli
Saint Anselm College
Ramona Crain Popplewell
Grayson County College
Rongsun Pu
Kean University
Erin Rempala
San Diego Mesa College
John E. Rinehart
Eastern Oregon University
Dan Rogers
Somerset Community College
Jason F. Schreer
*State University of New
York at Potsdam*
Gillian P. Schultz
Seattle Central Community College
Brian W. Schwartz
Columbus State University
Anju Sharma
Stevens Institute of Technology
Brian E. Smith
Black Hills State University
Maryann Smith
Brookdale Community College
Larry Szymczak
Chicago State University
Christopher Tabit
University of West Georgia
Season R. Thomson
Germanna Community College
Randall L. Tracy
Worcester State College
Anh-Hue Tu
*Georgia Southwestern
State University*
George Veomett
University of Nebraska–Lincoln
Jyoti R. Wagle
*Houston Community
College System, Central*
Ryan L. Wagner
*Millersville University
of Pennsylvania*
Paul E. Wanda
*Southern Illinois University,
Edwardsville*
Kelly J. Wessell
*Tompkins Cortland
Community College*
Virginia White
Riverside Community College
Bob Wise
University of Wisconsin–Oshkosh
Michael L. Womack
Macon State College
Lan Xu
South Dakota State University
Alan Yauck
*Middle Georgia College,
Dublin Campus*

General Biology Symposia

Every year McGraw-Hill conducts several General Biology Symposia, which are attended by instructors from across the country. These events are an opportunity for editors from McGraw-Hill to gather information about the needs and challenges of instructors teaching nonmajor-level biology courses.

It also offers a forum for the attendees to exchange ideas and experiences with colleagues they might not have otherwise met. The feedback we have received has been invaluable, and has contributed to the development of *Concepts of Biology* and its ancillaries.

Norris Armstrong
University of Georgia

David Bachoon
Georgia College and State University

Sarah Bales
Moraine Valley Community College

Lisa Bellows
North Central Texas College

Joressia Beyer
John Tyler Community College

James Bidlack
University of Central Oklahoma

Mark Bloom
Texas Christian University

Paul Bologna
Montclair University

Bradford Boyer
Suffolk County Community College

Linda Brandt
Henry Ford Community College

Marguerite Brickman
University of Georgia

Art Buikema
Virginia Polytechnic Institute

Sharon Bullock
Virginia Commonwealth University

Raymond Burton
Germanna Community College

Nancy Butler
Kutztown University of Pennsylvania

Jane Caldwell
West Virginia University

Carol Carr
John Tyler Community College

Kelly Cartwright
College of Lake County

Rex Cates
Brigham Young University

Sandra Caudle
Calhoun Community College

Genevieve Chung
Broward Community College

Jan Coles
Kansas State University

Marian Wilson Comer
Chicago State University

Renee Dawson
University of Utah

Lewis Deaton
University of Louisiana at Lafayette

Jody DeCamilo
St. Louis Community College

Jean DeSaix
University of North Carolina at Chapel Hill

JodyLee Estrada-Duek
Pima Community College, Desert Vista

Laurie Faber-Foster
Grand Rapids Community College

Susan Finazzo
Broward Community College

Theresa Fischer
Indian River Community College

Dennis Fulbright
Michigan State University

Theresa Fulcher
Pellissippi State Technical College

Steven Gabrey
Northwestern State University

Cheryl Garett
Henry Ford Community College

Farooka Gauhari
University of Nebraska–Omaha

John Geiser
Western Michigan University

Cindy Ghent
Towson University

Julie Gibbs
College of DuPage

William Glider
University of Nebraska–Lincoln

Christopher Gregg
Louisiana State University

Carla Guthridge
Cameron University

Bob Harms
St. Louis Community College–Meramec

Wendy Hartman
Palm Beach Community College

Tina Hartney
California State Polytechnic University

Kelly Hogan
University of North Carolina–Chapel Hill

Eva Horne
Kansas State University

David Huffman
Texas State University–San Marcos

Shelley Jansky
University of Wisconsin–Stevens Point

Sandra Johnson
Middle Tennessee State University

Tina Jones
Shelton State Community College

Arnold Karpoff
University of Louisville

Jeff Kaufmann
Irvine Valley College

Kyoungtae Kim
Missouri State University

Michael Koban
Morgan State University

Todd Kostman
University of Wisconsin–Oshkosh

Steven Kudravi
Georgia State University

Nicki Locascio
Marshall University

Dave Loring
Johnson County Community College

Janice Lynn
Alabama State University

Phil Mathis
Middle Tennessee State University

Mary Victoria McDonald
University of Central Arkansas

Susan Meiers
Western Illinois University

Daryl Miller
Broward Community College, South Campus

Marjorie Miller
Greenville Technical College

Meredith Norris
University of North Carolina at Charlotte

Mured Odeh
South Texas College

Nathan Olia
Auburn University–Montgomery

Rodney Olsen
Fresno City College

Alexander Olvido
Virginia State University

Clark Ovrebo
University of Central Oklahoma

Forrest Payne
University of Arkansas at Little Rock

Nancy Pencoe
University of West Georgia

Murray P. "Pat" Pendarvis
Southeastern Louisiana University

Jennie Plunkett
San Jacinto College

Scott Porteous
Fresno City College

David Pylant
Wallace State Community College

Fiona Qualls
Jones County Junior College

Eric Rabitoy
Citrus College

Karen Raines
Colorado State University

Kirsten Raines
San Jacinto College

Jill Reid
Virginia Commonwealth University

Darryl Ritter
Okaloosa-Walton College

Chris Robinson
Bronx Community College

Robin Robison
Northwest Mississippi Community College

Vickie Roettger
Missouri Southern State University

Bill Rogers
Ball State University

Vicki Rosen
Utah State University

Kim Sadler
Middle Tennessee State University

Cara Shillington
Eastern Michigan University

Greg Sievert
Emporia State University

Jimmie Sorrels
Itawamba Community College

Judy Stewart
Community College of Southern Nevada

Julie Sutherland
College of DuPage

Bill Trayler
California State University–Fresno

Linda Tyson
Santa Fe Community College

Eileen Underwood
Bowling Green State University

Heather Vance-Chalcraft
East Carolina University

Marty Vaughan
IUPUI–Indianapolis

Paul Verrell
Washington State University

Thomas Vogel
Western Illinois University

Brian Wainscott
Community College of Southern Nevada

Jennifer Warner
University of North Carolina, Charlotte

Scott Wells
Missouri Southern State University

Robin Whitekiller
University of Central Arkansas

Allison Wiedemeier
University of Illinois–Columbia

Michael Windelspecht
Appalachian State University

Mary Wisgirda
San Jacinto College, South Campus

Tom Worcester
Mount Hood Community College

Lan Xu
South Dakota State University

Frank Zhang
Kean University

Michelle Zjhra
Georgia Southern University

Victoria Zusman
Miami Dade College

Contents

PART I

Organisms Are Composed of Cells   22

2 Basic Chemistry and Cells   24

Applications

1

Biology, the Study of Life

Fire Ants Have a Good Defense

Fire ants have a red to reddish-brown color, but even so, they most likely take their name from the ability to STING. Their stinger protrudes from the rear, but in a split second, they can grab a person's skin with their mandibles and position the stinger between their legs to sting from the front. The stinger injects a toxin into the tiny wound, and the result is a burning sensation. The next day, the person has a white pustule at the site of the sting. The success of this defense mechanism is clear because most animals, including humans, try to stay away from bees, wasps, and ants—and any other animal that can sting.

Living usually in an open, grassy area, fire ants sting in order to defend their home, which is a mound of soil that they have removed from subterranean tunnels. They use the tunnels to safely travel far afield when searching for food, which they bring back to their nest mates. The queen and many worker ants live in chambers within the mound or slightly below it. The queen is much larger

Fire ant mound

than the other members of the colony, and she has only one purpose: to produce many thousands of small, white eggs. The eggs develop into cream-colored, grublike larvae, which are lavishly tended by worker ants to keep them clean and well fed. When the larvae become encased by a hard covering, they are pupae. Inside a pupa, an amazing transformation takes place, and eventually an adult ant breaks out. Most of these adults are worker ants, but in the spring, a few are winged "sexuals," which are male and female ants with the ability to reproduce. The sexuals remain inside the colony with nothing to do until the weather is cooperative enough for them to fly skyward to mate. A few of the fertilized females manage to survive the perils of an outside existence long enough to start another colony.

All of the ants in a colony have the same mother, namely the queen ant who produces the eggs. The workers are sterile, closely related sister ants. Because of their genetic relationship, we can view the members of a colony as a superorganism. The queen serves as the reproductive system, while the workers serve as the digestive and urinary systems, as well as all the other systems that keep the superorganism functioning. What fosters cooperation between the members of the superorganism? The answer is chemicals, pheromones secreted

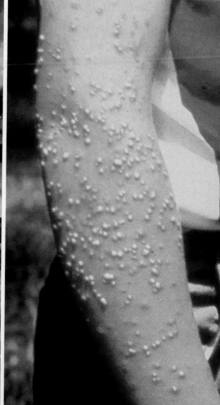

externally that influence the behavior and even the development of the ants. Fire ants, like other ants, produce several different pheromones that send messages when released into the air. The message could be "food is available" or "be alert for possible danger." The queen even releases pheromones that cause workers to attend her.

Why does it work, in a biological sense, for these sisters to spend their lives slavishly working away, raising more sterile sisters and defending the colony with little regard for their own safety? It works because the few sexual females that survive their temporary existence on the outside pass the colony's joint genes on to future generations in new and different places. Any social system that allows an organism to pass on its genes is a successful one from an evolutionary point of view.

In this chapter, we will first learn how the scientific understanding of life progresses by making observations and doing experiments. Then we will examine the five scientific theories around which this book is organized. The theory of evolution is examined in particular detail because it is the unifying theory of biology.

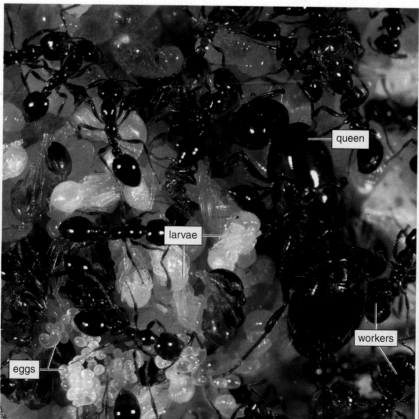

eggs

larvae

queen

workers

A fire ant colony (*Solenopsis invicta*).

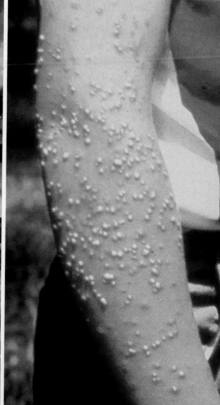

Pustules caused by fire ants.

Science Helps Us Understand the Natural World

Learning Outcomes

▶ Divide the scientific method into four steps and discuss each one. (1.1)

▶ Describe an experimental design that contains a control group. (1.2)

Biology is the scientific study of life, and therefore it is appropriate for us to first consider what we mean by science. Science is a way of making sense of the natural world around us. Religion, aesthetics, and ethics are all ways that human beings can find order in the natural world. Science, unlike these other ways of knowing is testable. It also leads to improved technology and is responsible for the modern ways in which we travel, communicate, farm, build our houses, and even how we conduct science.

1.1 Scientists use a preferred method

Despite the wide diversity of scientists and what they study (**Fig. 1.1A**), the usual four steps of the scientific method are: (1) making observations, (2) formulating a hypothesis, (3) performing experiments and making observations, and (4) coming to a conclusion (**Fig. 1.1B**).

Making Observations The scientific method begins with **observation.** We can observe with our noses that dinner is almost ready, observe with our fingertips that a surface is smooth and cold, and observe with our ears that a piano needs tuning. Scientists also extend the ability of their senses by using instruments; for example, the microscope enables them to see objects they could never see with the naked eye. Finally, scientists may expand their understanding even further by taking advantage of the knowledge and experiences of other scientists. For instance, they may look up past studies on the Internet or at the library, or they may write or speak to others who are researching similar topics.

Formulating a Hypothesis After making observations and gathering knowledge about a phenomenon, a scientist uses inductive reasoning. **Inductive reasoning** occurs whenever a person uses creative thinking to combine isolated facts into a cohesive whole. Chance alone can help a scientist arrive at an idea. The most famous case pertains to the antibiotic penicillin, which was discovered in 1928. While examining a petri dish of bacteria that had accidentally become contaminated with the mold *Penicillium,* Alexander Fleming observed an area around the mold that was free of bacteria. Fleming had long been interested in finding cures for human diseases caused by bacteria, and was very knowledgeable about antibacterial substances. So when he saw the dramatic effect of *Penicillium* mold on bacteria, he reasoned that the mold might be producing an antibacterial substance. We call such a possible explanation for a natural event a **hypothesis.** A hypothesis is based on existing knowledge, so it is much more informed than a mere guess. Fleming's hypothesis was supported by further observations. Sometimes a hypothesis is not supported, and must be either modified and subjected to additional study, or rejected.

All of a scientist's past experiences, no matter what they might be, may influence the formation of a hypothesis. But a scientist only considers hypotheses that can be tested by experiments or further observations. Moral and religious beliefs, while very important to our lives, differ between cultures and through time, and are not always testable.

FIGURE 1.1A Biologists work in a variety of settings.

Scientist in an agricultural field

Biochemist in a laboratory

Ecologist examining an artificial reef

Performing Experiments and Making Observations

Scientists often perform an **experiment**, a series of procedures to test a hypothesis. The manner in which a scientist intends to conduct an experiment is called its design. A good experimental design ensures that scientists are testing what they want to test and that their results will be meaningful. When an experiment is done in a laboratory, all conditions can be kept constant except for an **experimental variable**, which is deliberately changed. One or more **test groups** are exposed to the experimental variable, but one other group, called the **control group**, is not. If, by chance, the control group shows the same results as the test group, the experimenter knows the results are invalid.

Scientists often use a **model**, a representation of an actual object. For example, modeling occurs when scientists use software to decide how human activities will affect climate, or when they use mice instead of humans for, say, testing a new drug. Ideally, a medicine that is effective in mice should still be tested in humans. And whenever it is impossible to study the actual phenomenon, a model remains a hypothesis in need of testing. Someday, a scientist might devise a way to test it.

The results of an experiment or further observations are referred to as the **data**. Mathematical data are often displayed in the form of a graph or table. Sometimes studies rely on statistical data. Let's say an investigator wants to know if eating onions can prevent women from getting osteoporosis (weak bones). The scientist conducts a survey asking women about their onion-eating habits and then correlates these data with the condition of their bones. Other scientists critiquing this study would want to know: How many women were surveyed? How old were the women? What were their exercise habits? What criteria were used to determine the condition of their bones? And what is the probability that the data are in error? Even if the data do suggest a correlation, scientists would want to know if there is a specific ingredient in onions that has a direct biochemical or physiological effect on bones. After all, correlation does not necessarily mean causation. It could be that women who eat onions eat lots of vegetables, and have healthier diets overall than women who do not eat onions. In this way scientists are skeptics who always pressure one another to keep investigating.

Coming to a Conclusion Scientists must analyze the data in order to reach a **conclusion** about whether a hypothesis is supported or not. The data can support a hypothesis, but they do not prove it "true" because a conclusion is always subject to revision. On the other hand, it is possible to prove a hypothesis false. Because science progresses, the conclusion of one experiment can lead to the hypothesis for another experiment as represented by the return arrow in Figure 1.1B. In other words, results that do not support one hypothesis can often help a scientist formulate another hypothesis to be tested. Scientists report their findings in scientific journals so that their methodology and data are available to other scientists. Experiments and observations must be *repeatable*—that is, the reporting scientist and any scientist who repeats the experiment must get the same results, or else the data are suspect.

Scientific Theory The ultimate goal of science is to understand the natural world in terms of **scientific theories**, which

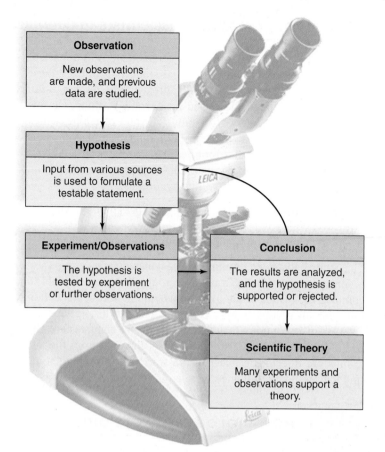

FIGURE 1.1B Flow diagram for the scientific method.

Observation
New observations are made, and previous data are studied.

Hypothesis
Input from various sources is used to formulate a testable statement.

Experiment/Observations
The hypothesis is tested by experiment or further observations.

Conclusion
The results are analyzed, and the hypothesis is supported or rejected.

Scientific Theory
Many experiments and observations support a theory.

are accepted explanations (concepts) for how the world works. The results of innumerable observations and experiments support a scientific theory. This text is organized around the following five basic theories of biology:

Theory	Concept
Cell	All organisms are composed of cells, and new cells only come from preexisting cells.
Gene	All organisms contain coded information that dictates their form, function, and behavior.
Evolution	All organisms have a common ancestor, but each is adapted to a particular way of life.
Homeostasis	All organisms have an internal environment that must stay relatively constant within a range protective of life.
Ecosystem	All organisms are members of populations that interact with each other and with the physical environment within a particular locale.

We will discuss these theories in detail later in the chapter, but right now let's turn our attention to an example of a scientific experiment.

▶ **1.1 Check Your Progress** You hypothesize that only the queen fire ant produces eggs. What type of data would allow you to come to a conclusion? What data would prove it false?

1.2 Control groups allow scientists to compare experimental results

Now that you are familiar with the common steps in the scientific method, let's consider an actual study that utilizes these steps. Because the use of synthetic nitrogen fertilizer is harmful to the environment (as described in "Organic Farming" on this page), researchers decided to study the yield of winter wheat utilizing a winter wheat/pigeon pea rotation. The pigeon pea is a **legume**, a plant that has root nodules where bacteria convert atmospheric nitrogen to a form plants such as winter wheat can use. The scientists formulated this hypothesis:

Hypothesis A winter wheat/pigeon pea rotation will cause winter wheat production to increase as well as or better than the application of synthetic nitrogen fertilizer.

This study had a good design because it included test groups and a control group. Having a control group allows researchers to compare the results of the test groups. All environmental conditions for all groups is kept constant, but the test groups are exposed to an experimental variable, the factor being tested. The use of a control group also ensures that the data from the test groups are due to the experimental variable and not to some unknown outside influence. Test groups should be as large as

possible to eliminate the influence of undetected differences in the test subjects.

The investigators decided to grow the winter wheat in pots and to have three sets of pots:

Control Pots Winter wheat was planted in clay pots of soil that received no fertilization treatment—that is, no nitrogen fertilizer and no preplanting of pigeon peas.

Test Pots I Winter wheat was grown in clay pots in soil treated with synthetic nitrogen fertilizer.

Test Pots II Winter wheat was grown in clay pots following pigeon pea plants grown in the summertime. The pigeon pea plants were then turned over in the soil.

Results **Figure 1.2** includes a color-coded bar graph that allows you to see at a glance the comparative amount of wheat obtained from each group of pots. After the first year, winter wheat yield was higher in test pots treated with nitrogen fertilizer than in the control pots. To the surprise of investigators, test

HOW BIOLOGY IMPACTS OUR LIVES

Application

1A Organic Farming

Besides being health conscious, people who buy organic may also be socially conscious. Organic farming is part of a movement to make agriculture sustainable by using farming methods that protect the health of people and ecosystems and preserve the land so that it can be productive for our generation and all future generations.

Modern agricultural methods have been dramatically successful at increasing yield, but at what price? We now know that modern farming practices lead to topsoil depletion and groundwater contamination. Without topsoil, the nutrient-rich layer that nourishes plants, agriculture is impossible, and yet modern farming practices such as tilling the land and allowing it to lie fallow (bare) allow topsoil to erode and disappear. One solution is to use a legume as a ground cover because it both protects and nourishes the soil (**Fig. 1A**). The researchers who did the study described in Section 1.2 used pigeon peas as a way to enrich the soil between winter wheat plantings.

Instead of growing legumes, farmers in recent years are accustomed to making plants bountiful by applying more and more synthetic nitrogen fertilizer. Unfortunately, nitrogen fertilizers pollute wells used for drinking water and also huge bodies of water, such as the Chesapeake Bay, the Gulf of Mexico, and the Great Lakes. Nitrates in the drinking water of infants leads to the "blue-baby" syndrome and possible death due to lack of

oxygen in the blood. In adults, nitrates are implicated in causing digestive tract cancers. Certainly they can cause an algal bloom, recognized as a green scum on the water's surface.

In response to these problems, organic farmers severely limit the use of nitrogen fertilizers and instead rely on crop rotation, alternately planting a nitrogen-providing legume and a nitrogen-requiring crop such as wheat. Organic farmers also cut way back on the use of herbicides and pesticides, and this may be the primary reason you and others buy organic. The long-term consumption of these chemicals has been associated with such health problems as birth defects, nerve damage, and cancer. Children may be especially sensitive to health risks posed by pesticides; this is the chief reason lawns sprayed with pesticides carry warning signs. We should all be aware that we too can contribute to an

FIGURE 1A
Legume plants have nodules.

organic lifestyle by limiting the use of synthetic chemicals on our lawns and gardens. In doing so, we improve our health and help preserve the environment for ourselves and future generations.

FORM YOUR OPINION

1. The United States exports its current farming technology, with all its long-range problems, to other countries. Should this be continued?
2. What circumstances might discourage a farmer from growing food organically, and how might these obstacles be overcome?

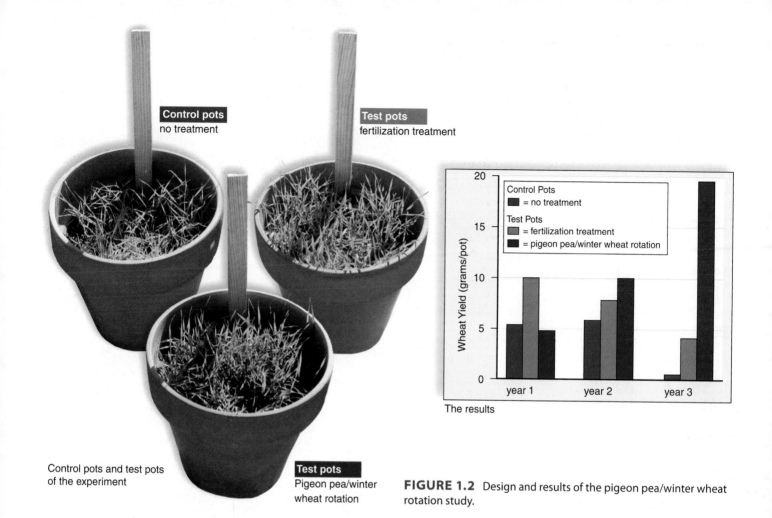

Control pots
no treatment

Test pots
fertilization treatment

Control pots and test pots
of the experiment

Test pots
Pigeon pea/winter
wheat rotation

The results

FIGURE 1.2 Design and results of the pigeon pea/winter wheat rotation study.

pots preplanted with pigeon peas did not produce as high a yield as the control pots.

Conclusion The hypothesis was not supported. Wheat yield following the growth of pigeon peas was not as great as that obtained with nitrogen fertilizer treatments.

Follow-Up Experiment and Results The researchers decided to continue the experiment, using the same design and the same pots as before, to see whether the buildup of residual soil nitrogen from pigeon peas would eventually increase wheat yield to a greater extent than the use of nitrogen fertilizer. This was their new hypothesis:

Hypothesis A sustained pigeon pea/winter wheat rotation will eventually cause an increase in winter wheat production.

They predicted that wheat yield following three years of pigeon pea/winter wheat rotation would surpass wheat yield following nitrogen fertilizer treatment.

Analysis of Results After two years, the yield from pots treated with nitrogen fertilizer was less than it had been the first year. Indeed, wheat yield in pots following a summer planting of pigeon peas was the highest of all the treatments. After three years, wheat yield in pots treated with nitrogen fertilizer was greater than in the control pots but not nearly as great as the yield in pots following summer planting of pigeon peas. Compared to the first year, wheat yield increased almost fourfold in pots having a pigeon pea/winter wheat rotation.

Conclusion The hypothesis was supported. At the end of three years, the yield of winter wheat following a pigeon pea/winter wheat rotation was much better than for the other types of test pots.

To explain their results, the researchers suggested that the soil was improved by the buildup of the organic matter in the pots as well as by the addition of nitrogen from the pigeon peas. They published their results in a scientific journal,[1] where their experimental method and results would be available to the scientific community.

▶ **1.2 Check Your Progress** What would your control group and test groups be composed of if you were testing whether a parasite could reduce the size of a fire ant colony?

[1]Bidlack, J. E., Rao, S. C., and Demezas, D. H. 2001. Nodulation, nitrogenase activity, and dry weight of chickpea and pigeon pea cultivars using different *Bradyrhizobium* strains. *Journal of Plant Nutrition* 24:549–60.

FIGURE 1.3A Levels of biological organization.

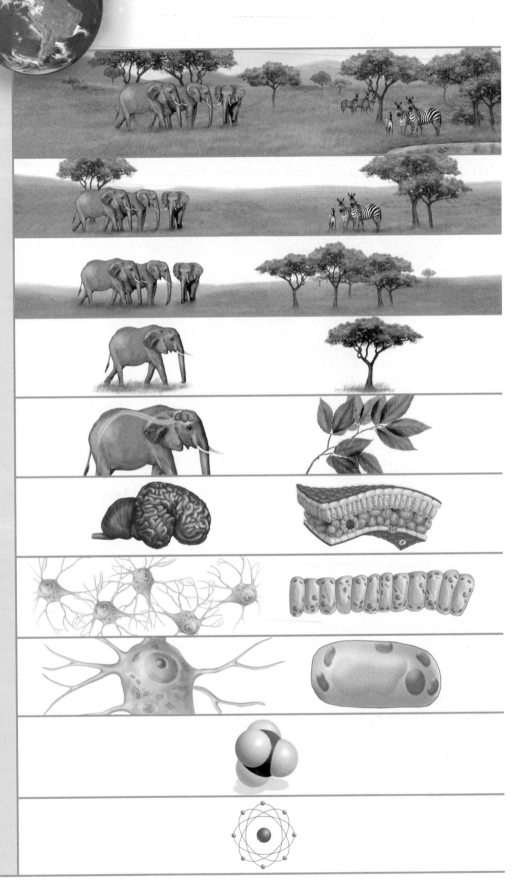

Biosphere
Regions of the Earth's crust, waters, and atmosphere inhabited by living things

↑

Ecosystem
A community plus the physical environment

↑

Community
Interacting populations in a particular area

↑

Population
Organisms of the same species in a particular area

↑

Organism
An individual; complex individuals contain organ systems

↑

Organ System
Composed of several organs working together

↑

Organ
Composed of tissues functioning together for a specific task

↑

Tissue
A group of cells with a common structure and function

↑

Cell
The structural and functional unit of all living things

↑

Molecule
Union of two or more atoms of the same or different elements

↑

Atom
Smallest unit of an element composed of electrons, protons, and neutrons

THE CELL THEORY
Organisms Are Composed of Cells

Learning Outcomes

▶ Explain the unique place of cells in biological organization. (1.3)
▶ Relate the reproduction of cells and organisms and also their need for materials and energy to the cell theory. (1.3)

From huge menacing sharks to miniscule exotic orchids, life is very diverse. Despite this diversity, biologists have concluded that life can be understood in terms of the five theories that are emphasized in this text. The first theory we will discuss is the cell theory.

1.3 Cells are the fundamental unit of living things

Figure 1.3A illustrates very well why we will first discuss the **cell theory** which says that *cells are the fundamental unit of living things.* In a cell, **atoms,** the smallest portions of an element, combine with themselves or other atoms to form **molecules.** Although cells are composed of molecules, cells, and not molecules, are alive. Some cells, such as unicellular paramecia, live independently. Other cells, such as those of the alga *Volvox,* cluster together in microscopic colonies. An elephant is a multicellular organism in which similar cells combine to form a **tissue;** one common tissue in animals is nerve tissue. Tissues make up **organs,** as when various tissues combine to form the brain. Organs work together in **organ systems;** for example, the brain works with the spinal cord and a network of nerves to form the nervous system. Organ systems are joined together to form a complete living thing, or **organism.** Only a microscope can reveal that organisms are composed of cells (**Fig. 1.3B**).

Later in this chapter, we will consider the higher levels of biological organization shown in Figure 1.3A.

Cells Come from Other Cells Cells come only from a previous cell, and organisms come only from other organisms. In other words, cells and organisms **reproduce.** Every type of living thing can reproduce, or make another organism like itself. Bacteria, protists, and other unicellular organisms simply split in two. In most multicellular organisms, the reproductive process is more complex. It begins with the pairing of a two cells—a sperm from one partner and an egg from the other partner. The union of sperm and egg, followed by many cell divisions, results in an immature stage that grows and develops through various stages to become an adult.

Cells Use Materials and Energy Cells and organisms cannot maintain their organization or carry on life's activities without an outside source of nutrients and energy. Nutrients function as building blocks or for energy. **Energy** is the capacity to do work, and it takes work to maintain the organization of the cell and the organism. When cells use nutrients to make their parts and products, they carry out a sequence of chemical reactions. Nerve cells and muscle cells also use energy as organisms move about. The term **metabolism** encompasses all the chemical reactions that occur in a cell.

The ultimate source of energy for nearly all life on Earth is the sun. Plants and certain other organisms are able to capture solar energy and carry on **photosynthesis,** a process that transforms solar energy into the chemical energy of organic nutrients. All life on Earth acquires energy by metabolizing nutrients made by photosynthesizers. This applies even to plants.

▶ **1.3 Check Your Progress** Explain (a) how life has order, (b) how it reproduces, and (c) how it acquires energy.

a.   b.   c.

FIGURE 1.3B Only micrographs (pictures taken microscopically), such as the one in **(c)**, can reveal that organisms are composed of cells.

THE GENE THEORY
Genes Control the Traits of Organisms

Learning Outcomes

▶ Relate the gene theory to the diversity of life. (1.4)
▶ Describe several applications of the gene theory. (1.4)

The cell theory studied in Section 1.3 and the gene theory are intimately connected. Genes are housed in cells, and when cells divide, they pass on genes to the next cell or organism. Genes code for proteins, and it is proteins that directly bring about the traits of organisms.

1.4 Organisms have a genetic inheritance

A nineteenth-century scientist named Gregor Mendel is often called the father of genetics because he was the first to conclude, following experimentation with pea plants, that units of heredity now called **genes** are passed from parents to offspring. Later investigators, notably James Watson and Francis Crick, discovered that genes are composed of the molecule known as **DNA** (deoxyribonucleic acid). The work of these and many other investigators allows us to state the first premise of the **gene theory**: *Genes are hereditary units composed of DNA.* Our increasing knowledge of DNA tells us that genes contain coded information that controls the structure and function of cells and organisms. The spiral staircase structure of DNA contains four different types of molecules called nucleotides, each represented by a different color (**Fig. 1.4**). DNA can **mutate** (undergo permanent changes), and each type of organism, such as those depicted in Figure 1.4, has its own particular sequence of these four nucleotides. This is called coded information because a particular nucleotide sequence codes for a particular protein. **Proteins** are cellular molecules that determine what the cell and the organism are like. The second premise of the gene theory is: *Genes control the structure and function of cells and organisms* by coding for proteins.

The gene theory has been extremely fruitful, meaning that it has led to much experimentation and many applications. Every field of biology and most aspects of our lives have changed because of the ability to analyze and manipulate DNA. Here are a few examples:

Basic Genetic Research

We can extract DNA and study metabolism at the molecular level. Therefore, we will soon know how one cell type differs from another.

We can also sequence the nucleotides in DNA and study how the metabolism of DNA is regulated. One day we will know how this makes humans different from chimpanzees, for example.

Relationship of Species

DNA technology aids in discovering the history of life on Earth— that is, who is related to whom. For example, a recent comparative study concluded that early humans did not interbreed with the archaic humans known as Neandertals. Wildlife biologists use DNA sequence data to determine how best to conserve various species.

Medicine

Genetic testing can tell us what diseases we are prone to, and doctors can use this information to prescribe drug therapy or tell us how best to protect ourselves.

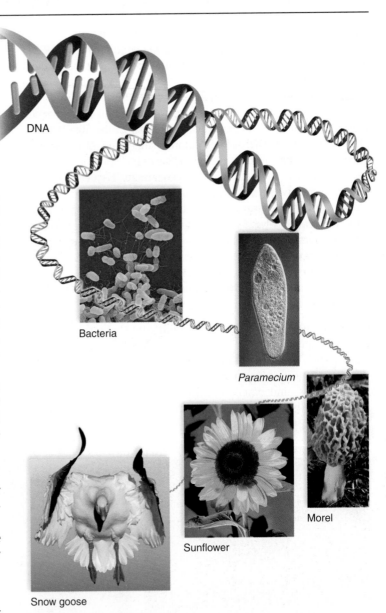

DNA

Bacteria

Paramecium

Morel

Sunflower

Snow goose

FIGURE 1.4 DNA differences account for the variety of life on Earth as exemplified by these examples.

Drugs for diabetes, blood disorders, vaccines, and many other diseases are now made by utilizing DNA technology.

▶ **1.4 Check Your Progress** Explain how genetic inheritance is a part of reproduction.

THE THEORY OF HOMEOSTASIS
Organisms Are Homeostatic

Learning Outcomes

▶ State and explain the concept of homeostasis. (1.5)
▶ Describe how an organism's ability to respond to stimuli relates to homeostasis. (1.5)

To survive, cells and organisms must maintain a state of biological balance, or **homeostasis.** For example, temperature, moisture level, acidity, and other physiological factors must remain within the tolerance range of cells.

1.5 Organisms regulate their internal environment

The **theory of homeostasis** tells us that *cells and organisms have an internal environment* and that *cells regulate this environment so that it stays fairly constant.* While individual cells are homeostatic, most examples of homeostasis involve multicellular organisms. Animals have intricate feedback and control mechanisms that do not require any conscious activity. For example, when a student is so engrossed in her textbook that she forgets to eat lunch, her liver releases stored sugar to keep her blood sugar level within normal limits. In this case, hormones regulate sugar storage and release, but in other instances, the nervous system is involved in maintaining homeostasis.

Many animals depend on behavior to regulate their internal environment. The same student may realize that she is hungry and decide to visit the local diner. Iguanas may raise their internal temperature by basking in the sun (**Fig. 1.5A**) or cool down by moving into the shade. Similarly, fire ants move upward into the mound when the warmth of the sun is needed and move back down into their cooler subterranean passageways when the sun is too hot.

We will see that plants are, to a degree, homeostatic. For example, they bend toward sunlight and have mechanisms that

FIGURE 1.5B Plants respond to light by bending toward it.

contain the damage done by hungry insects to their leaves or infections caused by bacteria and viruses.

Response to Stimuli The ability to respond to stimuli assists the homeostatic ability of organisms. For example, only because they can repond to the presence of predaceous insects can plants protect their integrity. Even unicellular organisms can respond to their environment. For some, the beating of microscopic hairs, and for others, the snapping of whiplike tails move them toward or away from light or chemicals. Multicellular organisms can manage more complex responses. A vulture can detect a carcass a mile away and soar toward dinner. A monarch butterfly can sense the approach of fall and begin its flight south where resources are still abundant.

When a plant bends toward a source of light (**Fig. 1.5B**), it acquires the energy it needs for photosynthesis, and when an animal darts safely away from danger, it lives another day. All together, daily activities are termed the behavior of the organism. Organisms display a variety of behaviors as they search and compete for energy, nutrients, shelter, and mates. Many organisms display complex communication, hunting, and defensive behaviors as well. The behavior of an organism often assists homeostasis.

FIGURE 1.5A Iguanas bask in the sun to raise their body temperature.

▶ **1.5 Check Your Progress** Explain the relationship between homeostasis and response to a stimulus.

Organisms Live in Ecosystems

Learning Outcomes

▶ Describe the various levels of biological organization beyond the organism. (1.6)
▶ Describe how an ecosystem functions. (1.6)

The organization of life extends beyond the individual to the **biosphere,** the zone of air, land, and water at the Earth's surface where living organisms are found. Individual organisms belong to a **population,** all the members of a species within a particular area. The populations within a **community** interact among themselves and with the physical environment (soil, atmosphere, etc.), thereby forming an **ecosystem.**

1.6 The biosphere is divided into ecosystems

The **theory of ecosystems** says that *organisms form units in which they interact with the biotic (living) and abiotic (nonliving) components of the environment.* One example of an ecosystem is a North American grassland, which is inhabited by populations of rabbits, hawks, and many other animals, as well as various types of grasses. These populations interact by forming food chains in which one population feeds on another. For example, rabbits feed on grasses, while hawks feed on rabbits and other organisms.

As **Figure 1.6** shows, ecosystems are characterized by *chemical cycling* and *energy flow,* both of which begin when plants, such as grasses, take in solar energy and inorganic nutrients to produce food (organic nutrients) by photosynthesis. Chemical cycling (gray arrows) occurs as chemicals move from one population to another in a food chain, until death and decomposition allow inorganic nutrients to be returned to the photosynthesizers once again. Energy (red arrows), on the other hand, flows from the sun through plants and the other members of the food chain as they feed on one another. The energy gradually dissipates and returns to the atmosphere as heat. Because energy does not cycle, ecosystems could not stay in existence without solar energy and the ability of photosynthesizers to absorb it.

The Biosphere Climate largely determines where different ecosystems are found in the biosphere. For example, deserts exist in areas of minimal rain, while forests require much rain. The two most biologically diverse ecosystems—tropical rain forests and coral reefs—occur where solar energy is most abundant. The human population tends to modify these and all ecosystems for its own purposes. Humans clear forests or grasslands in order to grow crops; later, they build houses on what was once farmland; and finally, they convert small towns into cities. As coasts are developed, humans send sediments, sewage, and other pollutants into the sea.

Tropical rain forests and coral reefs are home to many organisms. The canopy of the tropical rain forest alone supports a variety of organisms, including orchids, insects, and monkeys. Coral reefs, which are found just offshore in the Southern Hemisphere, provide a habitat for many animals, including jellyfish, sponges, snails, crabs, lobsters, sea turtles, moray eels, and some of the world's most colorful fishes. Like tropical rain forests, coral reefs are severely threatened as the human population increases in size. Aside from pollutants, overfishing and collection of coral for sale to tourists destroy the reefs.

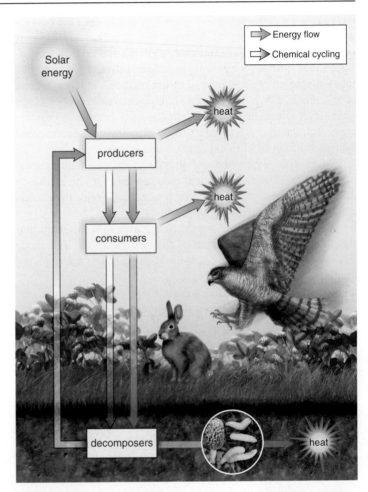

FIGURE 1.6 A grassland is a major ecosystem. Chemicals cycle because decomposers return inorganic nutrients to producers which provide organic nutrients to consumers including decomposers. With each transfer of nutrients, energy is lost as heat.

It has long been clear that human beings depend on healthy ecosystems for food, medicines, and various raw materials. We are only now beginning to realize that we depend on them even more for the services they provide. The workings of ecosystems ensure that environmental conditions are suitable for the continued existence of humans.

▶ **1.6 Check Your Progress** Give a specific example to illustrate that we depend on natural ecosystems.

Organisms Are Related and Adapted to Their Environment

Learning Outcomes

▶ Use a simple evolutionary tree to show how organisms are related. (1.7)
▶ List the major categories of classification, and explain how data are used to classify organisms. (1.8)
▶ Describe adaptation to the environment by the process of natural selection. (1.9)
▶ State seven characteristics that define life. (1.10)

Evolution explains the unity and diversity of life. All organisms share the same characteristics because they are descended from a common source. During descent, however, life changes as different forms become adapted to their environment. Evolution is the unifying concept of biology because it can explain so many aspects of life, including why organisms have shared characteristics despite their great diversity.

1.7 The ancestry of species can be determined

The **theory of evolution** says that *organisms have shared characteristics because of common descent.* Just as you and your close relatives can trace your ancestry to a particular pair of great grandparents, so species can trace their ancestry to a common source. An **evolutionary tree** is like a family tree. Just as a family tree shows how a group of people have descended from one couple, an evolutionary tree traces the ancestry of a group to a **common ancestor.** In the same way that one couple can have diverse children, a population can be a common ancestor to several other groups. Over time, diverse life-forms have arisen.

Biologists have discovered that it is possible to trace the evolution of any group—and even life itself—by using molecular data, the fossil record, the anatomy and physiology of organisms, and the embryonic development of organisms. The common ancestors for birds are known from the fossil record, and *Archaeopteryx,* an early bird, clearly has reptile characteristics (**Fig. 1.7A**). Because the evidence is so clear, birds are now classified as reptiles. Some biologists call them

flying dinosaurs. The reptiles that exist today include crocodiles, lizards, snakes, and turtles and birds! The evolutionary tree in **Figure 1.7B** traces the ancestry of *Archaeopteryx* to an early reptilian ancestor.

In Section 1.8 we will examine an evolutionary tree of life and consider how organisms are classified. Then in Section 1.9 we will show that natural selection is the mechanism that results in adaptation to the environment, such as the ability of birds to fly. One important thing to remember is that only species (types of organisms) evolve and not individual organisms. Genetics can help you understand why. The genetic makeup you inherited from your parents can mutate during your lifetime and cause cellular changes, but this does not cause your basic characteristics to change. On the other hand, mutations that show up in populations can be selected for increased representation in the next generation.

▶ **1.7 Check Your Progress** Humans are not descended from apes; they share a common ancestor with apes. Explain the difference.

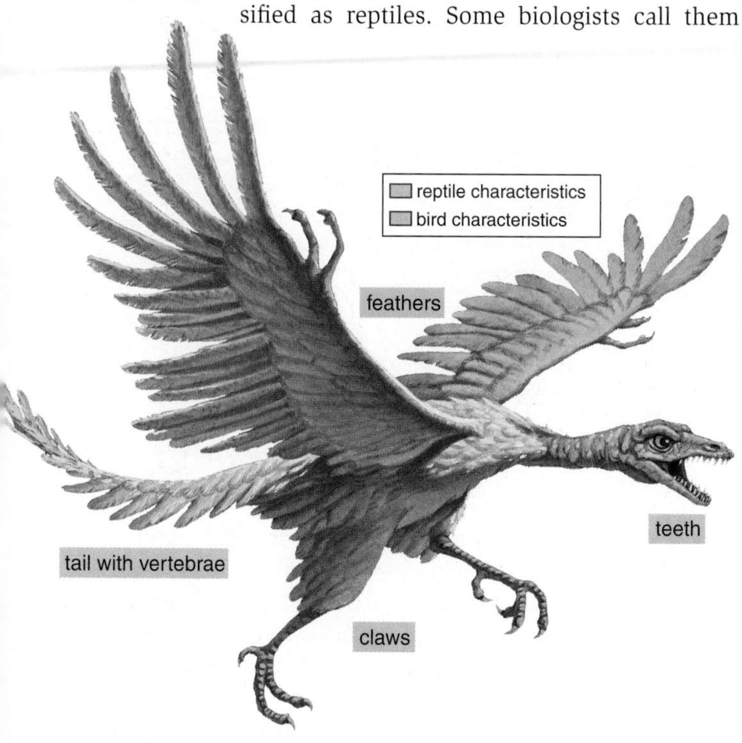

FIGURE 1.7A This depiction of *Archaeopteryx* shows its bird and reptile characteristics.

reptile characteristics
bird characteristics
feathers
tail with vertebrae
teeth
claws

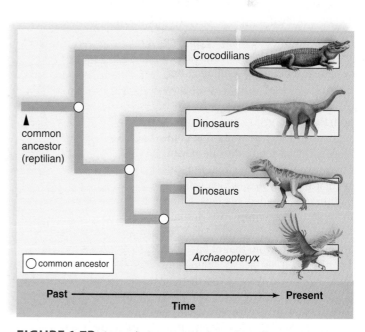

FIGURE 1.7B An evolutionary tree shows how the ancestry of *Archaeopteryx* can be traced to a common ancestor with crocodiles and dinosaurs. Each circle is an intervening common ancestor.

Crocodilians
common ancestor (reptilian)
Dinosaurs
Dinosaurs
Archaeopteryx
common ancestor
Past ———— Present
Time

1.8 Evolutionary relationships help biologists group organisms

Despite their diversity, organisms share certain characteristics, and this can be explained by evolution from a common source. For example, all forms of life are composed of cells and use DNA as their genetic material. **Figure 1.8A** is an evolutionary tree that shows how major groups of organisms are related through evolution.

Organizing Diversity Because life is so diverse, it is helpful to group organisms into categories. **Taxonomy** is the discipline of identifying and grouping organisms according to certain rules. Taxonomy makes sense out of the bewildering variety of life on Earth and is meant to provide valuable insight into evolution. As more is learned about living things, including the evolutionary relationships between species, taxonomy changes. DNA technology is now being used to revise current information and to discover previously unknown relationships between organisms.

The basic classification categories, or taxa, going from least inclusive to most inclusive, are **species, genus, family, order, class, phylum, kingdom,** and **domain (Table 1.8)**. The least inclusive category, species, is defined as a group of interbreeding individuals. Each successive classification category above species contains more types of organisms than the preceding one. Species placed within one genus share many specific characteristics and are the most closely related, while species placed in the same kingdom share only general characteristics with one another. For example, all species in the genus *Pisum* look pretty much the same—that is, like pea plants—but species in the plant kingdom can be quite varied, as is evident when we compare grasses to trees. Species placed in different domains are the most distantly related.

Domains Biochemical evidence suggests that there are only three domains: **Bacteria, Archaea,** and **Eukarya.** Figure 1.8A shows how the domains are related. Both domain Bacteria and domain Archaea evolved from the first common ancestor soon after life began. These two domains contain the unicellular **prokaryotes,** which lack the membrane-bounded nucleus found in the **eukaryotes** of domain Eukarya. However, the DNA of archaea differs from that of bacteria, and their cell surface is chemically more similar to eukaryotes than to bacteria. So, biologists have concluded that eukarya split off from the archaeal line of descent. Prokaryotes are structurally simple but metabolically complex. Archaea

TABLE 1.8	Levels of Classification	
	Human	**Corn**
Domain	Eukarya	Eukarya
Kingdom	Animalia	Plantae
Phylum	Chordata	Anthophyta
Class	Mammalia	Monocotyledones
Order	Primates	Commelinales
Family	Hominidae	Poaceae
Genus	*Homo*	*Zea*
Species*	*H. sapiens*	*Z. mays*

*To specify an organism, you must use the full binomial name, such as *Homo sapiens*.

(**Fig. 1.8B**) can live in aquatic environments that lack oxygen or are too salty, too hot, or too acidic for most other organisms. Perhaps these environments are similar to those of the primitive Earth, and archaea are the least evolved forms of life, as their name implies. Bacteria (**Fig.1.8C**) are variously adapted to living almost anywhere—in water, soil, and the atmosphere, as well as on our skin and in our mouths and large intestines.

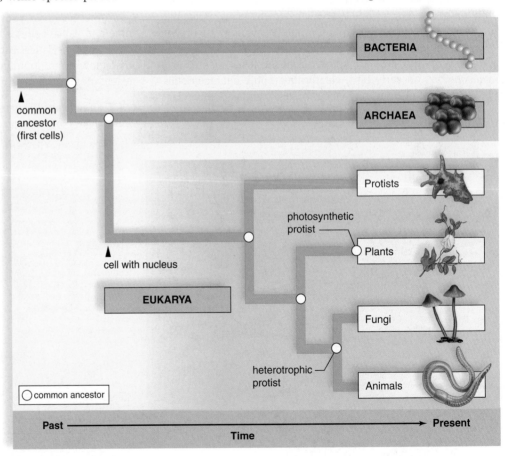

FIGURE 1.8A All species have a common ancestor that existed about four billion years ago. Domains Bacteria and Archaea were the first to appear. Domain Eukarya, which includes protists, plants, fungi, and animals, shares an ancestor with domain Archaea.

Taxonomists are in the process of deciding how to categorize the organisms within domains Archaea and Bacteria into kingdoms. Domain Eukarya, on the other hand, contains four major groups of organisms (**Fig. 1.8D**). **Protists,** which now comprise a number of kingdoms, range from unicellular forms to a few multicellular ones. Some are photosynthesizers, while others must acquire their food. Common protists include algae, the protozoans, and the water molds. Figure 1.8A shows that plants, fungi, and animals evolved from protists. **Plants** (kingdom Plantae) are multicellular photosynthetic organisms. Examples of plants include azaleas, zinnias, and pines. Among the **fungi** (kingdom Fungi) are the familiar molds and mushrooms that, along with bacteria, help decompose dead organisms. **Animals** (kingdom Animalia) are multicellular organisms that must ingest and process their food. Aardvarks, jellyfish, and zebras are representative animals.

Scientific Names Biologists use binomial nomenclature to assign each living thing a two-part name called its scientific name. For example, the scientific name for mistletoe is *Phoradendron tomentosum*. The first word is the genus, and the second word is the **specific epithet** of a species within that genus. The genus may be abbreviated (e.g., *P. tomentosum*), and if the species is unknown it may be indicated by sp. (e.g., *Phoradendron* sp.). Scientific names are universally used by biologists to avoid confusion. Common names tend to overlap and are often in the language of a particular country. Scientific names are based on Latin, a universal language that not too long ago was well known by most scholars.

▶ **1.8 Check Your Progress a.** Fire ants belong to what domain and what kingdom? **b.** What types of data did biologists use to draw the tree of life depicted in Figure 1.8A?

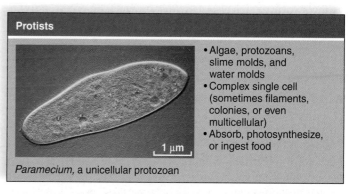

Protists

- Algae, protozoans, slime molds, and water molds
- Complex single cell (sometimes filaments, colonies, or even multicellular)
- Absorb, photosynthesize, or ingest food

1 μm

Paramecium, a unicellular protozoan

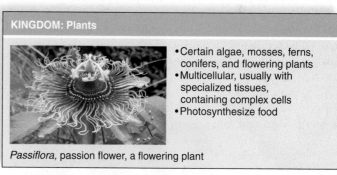

KINGDOM: Plants

- Certain algae, mosses, ferns, conifers, and flowering plants
- Multicellular, usually with specialized tissues, containing complex cells
- Photosynthesize food

Passiflora, passion flower, a flowering plant

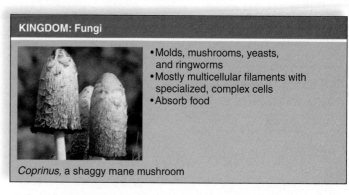

KINGDOM: Fungi

- Molds, mushrooms, yeasts, and ringworms
- Mostly multicellular filaments with specialized, complex cells
- Absorb food

Coprinus, a shaggy mane mushroom

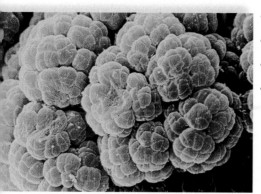

- Prokaryotic cells of various shapes
- Adaptations to extreme environments
- Absorb or chemosynthesize food
- Unique chemical characteristics

Methanosarcina mazei, an archaeon 1.6 μm

FIGURE 1.8B Domain Archaea.

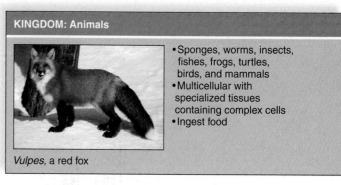

KINGDOM: Animals

- Sponges, worms, insects, fishes, frogs, turtles, birds, and mammals
- Multicellular with specialized tissues containing complex cells
- Ingest food

Vulpes, a red fox

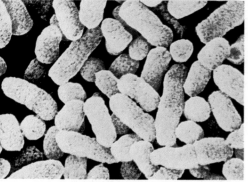

- Prokaryotic cells of various shapes
- Adaptations to all environments
- Absorb, photosynthesize, or chemosynthesize food
- Unique chemical characteristics

Escherichia coli, a bacterium 1.5 μm

FIGURE 1.8C Domain Bacteria.

FIGURE 1.8D Domain Eukarya.

1.9 Evolution through natural selection results in adaptation to the environment

The phrase "common descent with modification" sums up the process of evolution because it means that, as descent occurs from common ancestors, modifications occur that cause these organisms to be adapted (suited) to the environment. Through many observations and experiments, Charles Darwin, the father of evolution, came to the conclusion that natural selection is the process that makes modification—that is, **adaptation**—possible. In other words, the theory of evolution also states that, as evolution occurs, *natural selection brings about adaptation to the environment.* Adaptation to various environments accounts for the diversity of life.

Natural Selection During the process of natural selection, some aspect of the environment selects which traits are more apt to be passed on to the next generation. The selective agent can be an abiotic agent (part of the physical environment, such as altitude) or a biotic agent (part of the living environment, such as a deer). **Figure 1.9A** shows how deer could act as a selective agent for a particular mutant. Mutations fuel natural selection because mutations introduce variations among the members of a population. In Figure 1.9A, a plant species generally produces smooth leaves, but a mutation occurs that causes one plant's leaves to be covered with small extensions or "hairs." The plant with hairy leaves has an advantage because the deer (the selective agent) prefer to eat smooth leaves rather than hairy leaves.

Therefore, the plant with hairy leaves survives best and produces more seeds than most of its neighbors. As a result, generations later most plants of this species produce hairy leaves.

As with this example, Darwin realized that although all individuals within a population have the ability to reproduce, not all do so with the same success. Prevention of reproduction can run the gamut from an inability to capture resources, as when long-necked, but not short-necked, giraffes can reach their food source, to an inability to escape being eaten because long legs, but not short legs, can carry an animal to safety. Whatever the example, it can be seen that living things having advantageous traits can produce more offspring than those lacking them. In this way, living things change over time, and these changes are passed on from one generation to the next. Over long periods of time, the introduction of newer, more advantageous traits into a population causes a species to become adapted to an environment.

For example, rockhopper penguins (**Fig. 1.9B**) are adapted to an aquatic existence in the Antarctic. An extra layer of downy feathers is covered by short, thick feathers that form a waterproof coat. Layers of blubber also keep the birds warm in cold water. Most birds have forelimbs proportioned for flying, but penguins have stubby, flattened wings suitable for swimming. Their feet and tails serve as rudders in the water, but their flat feet also allow them to walk on land. Rockhopper penguins hop from one rock to another and have a bill adapted to eating small shellfish. Penguins also have many behavioral adaptations for living in the Antarctic. They often slide on their bellies across the snow in order to conserve energy when moving quickly. Their eggs—one, or at most two—are carried on the feet, where they are protected by a pouch of skin. This allows the birds to huddle together for warmth while standing erect and incubating eggs.

▶ **1.9 Check Your Progress** Explain how natural selection results in the adaptations of a species.

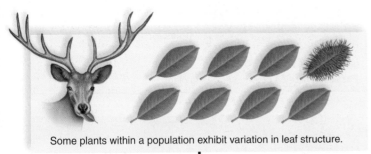
Some plants within a population exhibit variation in leaf structure.

Deer prefer a diet of smooth leaves over hairy leaves. Plants with hairy leaves reproduce more than other plants in the population.

Generations later, most plants within the population have hairy leaves, as smooth leaves are selected against.

FIGURE 1.9A Predatory deer act as a selective agent to bring about change in a plant population.

FIGURE 1.9B Rockhopper penguins are adapted to swimming in the icy waters of Antarctica.

The principles of evolution not only increase our understanding of how the world works but also help us solve practical problems that impact our lives. Many good examples can be cited in the fields of agriculture, medicine, and conservation.

Agriculture

The fruit of the wild banana plant is small and tough with large hard seeds. In contrast, the bananas we eat today are large, soft,  sweet, and for practical purposes seedless. Humans produced this type of banana by using **artificial selection;** in this case, humans were the selective agent and not the environment. Most of the vegetables we eat today, and our domesticated animals including horses, dogs, and cows, were produced in the same way.

Understanding the evolution of our agricultural plants helps us keep them healthy. For example, maize chlorotic dwarf virus (MCDV) causes an infection of young corn plants that makes them sick and reduces yield. However, it's known that our domesticated corn is derived from wild plants called teosinte, and scientists have found teosinte species in the wild that are resistant to several viral diseases, including the one caused by MCDV. This gene has been transferred to corn plants so that they too are resistant.

Farmers use pesticides to protect their crops from insects, or they grow plants that have been engineered to produce the pesticide. However, the pesticide is a selective agent for those members of the insect population that carry genes for the resistant trait. Because these insects reproduce more than nonresistant insects, a large percentage of the insect population becomes resistant. Understanding this process has caused scientists to suggest that farmers make a part of their fields pesticide free. This will allow nonresistant insects to also reproduce, and in this way the percentage of resistant insects in the next generation will be reduced.

Medicine

In the presence of an antibiotic, resistant bacteria are selected to reproduce over and over again, until the entire population of bacteria becomes resistant to the antibiotic. In 1959, a new anti-  biotic called methicillin became available to treat bacterial infections that were already resistant to penicillin. By 1997, 40% of hospital staph infections were caused by MRSA (methicillin-resistant *Staphylococcus aureus*). By now, the same bacteria can spread freely through the general population when people are in close contact. The infection is called CA-MRSA (community-acquired MRSA).

A knowledge of evolution has not only allowed scientists to understand how pathogens (e.g., bacteria and viruses) become resistant to antibiotics, but has also helped them create a process to develop new drugs to kill them. Millions of possible drugs are selected based on their ability to kill a particular pathogen. Then the best of these are tweaked chemically before this new patch of chemicals are tested for their ability to kill the pathogen. This selection process is repeated time and time again until a new drug has been developed. This drug is then tested in another mammal (e.g., mouse) or another primate (e.g., chimpanzee) that is closely related to humans through evolution. If the drug has few harmful side effects, it is prescribed to humans to cure the disease.

Conservation

A knowledge of evolution helps scientists decide which technologies can help save the environment. For example, most of us still fill the tanks of our cars with gasoline derived from oil. Yet oil is a nonrenewable resource that will eventually be depleted. What we need is a renewable resource that can be replaced over and over again. Corn is a renewable resource that can be used to produce ethanol, a fuel that substitutes for gasoline and is somewhat better for the environment. Furthermore, some scientists believe that, instead of using corn, which is food for animals and humans, billions of tons of currently unused waste materials in the United States are available for ethanol production. By mocking the natural selection process as described above for perfecting a drug, the best bacteria for changing waste to ethanol could be arrived at. Using  the natural selection process to achieve the best drug or the best bacterium or to select anything for a particular task is now described as using *directed evolution.*

A knowledge of evolution can also help us save endangered species in the wild. For example, some populations of chinook salmon are listed under the U.S. Endangered Species Act as either threatened or endangered. To save them, it is possible to build hatcheries, breed more fish, and introduce these fish into rivers where small populations of wild chinook salmon now live. However, this will not work if the captive fish have inadvertently undergone selection for reproduction in hatcheries but not in rivers. Therefore, hatcheries should mimic as much as possible the selection pressures that wild populations are exposed to. Only in that way can the introduced chinook salmon help save wild populations and our efforts will not have been wasted.

FORM YOUR OPINION

1. Give examples of how a knowledge of evolution can help humans solve practical problems that impact their lives.
2. Explain why it benefits farmers to set aside part of their fields where nonresistant insects can reproduce.
3. Give reasons why captive chinook salmon introduced into the wild need to have been exposed to the same environmental pressures as wild populations.

1.10 Evolution from a common ancestor accounts for the characteristics of life

The diversity of life has been mentioned several times by now. With so much diversity, how can we possibly define life? The best way we know to distinguish the living from the nonliving is to list the characteristics shared by all organisms. These characteristics of life must have been present in the original common ancestor or else they would not be present in all organisms.

1. **Life is organized.** The levels of biological organization extend from cells to the biosphere; see p. 8. The first living organisms were unicellular, and only later did multicellular forms arise. Once several different types of organisms arose, they interacted among themselves and became the biotic components of ecosystems.

2. **Life uses materials and energy.** The metabolic pathways that allow an organism to maintain its organization and to grow are the same in all organisms; see p. 9. We will study these metabolic pathways in future chapters because they are so critical to the lives of organisms.

3. **Life reproduces.** Unicellular organisms simply divide when they reproduce, but in multicellular forms, new life often begins with a fertilized egg that grows and develops into a new organism. When organisms reproduce, genetic differences arise that allow evolution to occur; see pp. 9–10.

4. **Life is homeostatic.** Regulatory mechanisms allow cells and organisms to keep their internal environment relatively constant; see p. 11. Homeostasis evolved because those members of a population that were homeostatic had more offspring than those that were less homeostatic.

5. **Life responds to stimuli.** Organisms respond to internal stimuli and external stimuli, and this allows them to maintain homeostasis. Response to stimuli also accounts for the behavior of organisms; see p. 11. Behavior evolves through natural selection in the same manner as do anatomical features.

6. **Life forms ecosystems.** Interactions are a hallmark of living things. Cells interact within organisms, and populations interact in ecosystems. We could not exist without food produced by plants and without bacteria and fungi that decompose dead remains; see p. 12.

7. **Life evolves.** The history of life began with a common source, but as life reproduces it passes on genes that can mutate. Through mutations, advantages arise that are suited to the environment, and through natural selection they become more prevalent in a population. Adaptation to different environments accounts for the variety of life on Earth; see pp. 13–16.

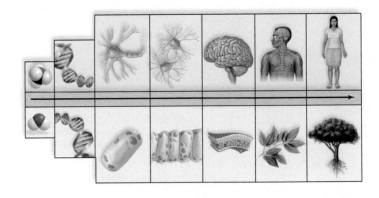

▶ **1.10 Check Your Progress** Describe how the hawk and her offspring illustrate the characteristics of life.

THE CHAPTER IN REVIEW

SUMMARY

Science Helps Us Understand the Natural World

1.1 Scientists use a preferred method
- Biology is the scientific study of life.
- The scientific method consists of four steps:
  - making **observations** using both our senses and special instruments
  - formulating a possible explanation, called a **hypothesis,** by using inductive reasoning
  - doing **experiments** that involve an **experimental variable, test groups,** and a **control group** that is not exposed to the experimental variable. Alternatively, scientists can simply make further observations. When doing experiments, scientists sometimes work with a **model.**
  - coming to a **conclusion** based on **data** as to whether the hypothesis is supported or not.
- A **scientific theory** is a major concept supported by many observations, experiments, and data.

1.2 Control groups allow scientists to compare experimental results
- In a scientific experiment involving the use of a synthetic nitrogen fertilizer versus a **legume** (pigeon pea) to enrich the soil, the control pots produced a greater yield than those utilizing the legume. After three years, however, a winter wheat/pigeon pea rotation out-performed the control pots and those that were fertilized with a synthetic nitrogen fertilizer.

Organisms Are Composed of Cells

1.3 Cells are the fundamental unit of living things
- Biological organization extends from the molecules in cells to the organism and beyond.

- The **cell theory** states that **cells,** the fundamental units of life, come from other cells as **reproduction** of cells and the organism occurs.

- In cells, **atoms** combine to form **molecules;** similar cells make up a **tissue;** and tissues compose **organs** that work together in **organ systems.** Organ systems work together in an **organism.**
- Cells and organisms acquire materials and energy from the environment to maintain their organization.
  - **Energy** is the capacity to do work.
  - **Metabolism** carries out chemical reactions.
  - **Photosynthesis** allows plants to capture solar energy and produce nutrients that sustain all organisms.

Genes Control the Traits of Organisms

1.4 Organisms have a genetic inheritance

- The **gene theory** tells us that **genes** are hereditary units composed of **DNA.**
- Genes control the structure and function of cells and organisms by coding for cellular molecules **(proteins).**
- Because genes can **mutate,** each organism has it own particular sequence of DNA nucleotides.
- The gene theory has been very fruitful, yielding many practical applications, such as those listed on page 10.

Organisms Are Homeostatic

1.5 Organisms regulate their internal environment

- The **theory of homeostasis** states that organisms and cells have mechanisms that keep the internal environment relatively constant. Only then can life continue.
- Homeostasis involves the use of sense receptors to monitor the external and internal environment.
- Organisms can respond to changes in the environment. For example, when plants turn toward sunlight, they acquire the energy they need to photosynthesize.

Organisms Live in Ecosystems

1.6 The biosphere is divided into ecosystems

- The theory of ecosystems says that within a local environment:
  - The members of each species are a population.
  - Populations form a community in which they interact with each other.
  - In a community, chemicals cycle and energy flows but does not cycle.
  - Chemical cycling requires interaction with the physical environment.

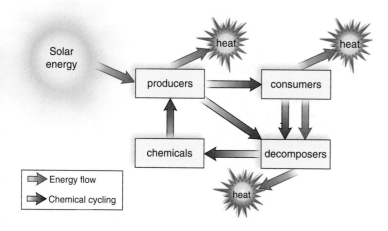

- Diverse ecosystems, including tropical rain forests and coral reefs, are being destroyed by human activities.

Organisms Are Related and Adapted to Their Environment

1.7 The ancestry of species can be determined

- The **theory of evolution** says that all species (living or extinct) can trace their ancestry to a common source.
- An **evolutionary tree** depicts the pattern of descent by way of **common ancestors.**

1.8 Evolutionary relationships help biologists group organisms

- **Taxonomy** is the classification of organisms according to the evolutionary relationships.
- The classification categories are **species** (least inclusive), **genus, family, order, class, phylum, kingdom,** and **domain** (most inclusive).
- There are three domains: **Bacteria, Archaea,** and **Eukarya.**

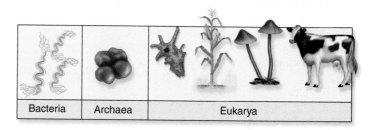

- Domain Archaea and domain Bacteria contain **prokaryotes** (organisms without a membrane-bounded nucleus).
- Domain Eukarya contains **eukaryotes** (organisms with a membrane-bounded nucleus).
- There are four major groups in domain Eukarya:
  - **Protists**—unicellular to multicellular organisms with various modes of nutrition
  - **Fungi**—molds and mushrooms
  - **Plants**—multicellular photosynthesizers
  - **Animals**—multicellular organisms that ingest food
- To classify an organism, two-part scientific names—**binomial nomenclature**—are used, consisting of the genus name and the **specific epithet.**

1.9 Evolution through natural selection results in adaptation to the environment

- The theory of evolution also says that modifications are introduced as evolution occurs, and if these modifications assist **adaptations,** they become more common through **natural selection.** The result is a wide variety of life-forms on Earth, each adapted to a different environment.

1.10 Evolution from a common ancestor accounts for the characteristics of life

- Organisms have shared characteristics because of common descent. Life is organized, uses materials and energy, reproduces, is homeostatic, responds to stimuli, forms ecosystems, and evolves.

TESTING YOURSELF

Science Helps Us Understand the Natural World

1. Which of the following words would not be part of a conclusion?
   a. proof
   b. support
   c. rejection
   d. All can be part of a conclusion.

2. Which term and definition are mismatched?
   a. data—factual information
   b. hypothesis—the idea to be tested
   c. conclusion—what the data tell us
   d. All of these are properly matched.
3. Which of these describes the control group in the pigeon pea/winter wheat experiment? The control group was
   a. planted with pigeon peas.
   b. treated with nitrogen fertilizer.
   c. not treated.
   d. not watered.
   e. Both c and d are correct.
4. **THINKING CONCEPTUALLY** What's the relationship between the scientific method and the five theories on which this book is based?

Organisms Are Composed of Cells

5. The level of organization that includes cells of similar structure and function is
   a. an organ.   c. an organ system.
   b. a tissue.   d. an organism.
6. Which sequence represents the correct order of increasing complexity in living systems?
   a. cell, molecule, organ, tissue
   b. organ, tissue, cell, molecule
   c. molecule, cell, tissue, organ
   d. cell, organ, tissue, molecule
7. All of the chemical reactions that occur in a cell are called
   a. homeostasis.   c. heterostasis.
   b. metabolism.   d. cytoplasm.
8. The process of turning solar energy into chemical energy is called
   a. work.   c. photosynthesis.
   b. metabolism.   d. respiration.

Genes Control the Traits of Organisms

9. Genes are
   a. present in eukaryotes but not in prokaryotes.
   b. composed of RNA and DNA.
   c. passed on from cell to cell and from organism to organism.
   d. All of these are correct.
10. Genes
   a. code for proteins.
   b. can mutate.
   c. are always composed of four nucleotides.
   d. All of these are correct.
11. **THINKING CONCEPTUALLY** What's the relationship between genes and the diversity of life?

Organisms Are Homeostatic

12. Which of the following are a part of homeostasis?
   a. Animals keep their internal temperature relatively constant.
   b. Your blood cell count is always about the same.
   c. Certain organs, such as the kidneys, excrete wastes.
   d. Plants are able to turn toward the sun.
   e. All of these are correct.
13. To remain homeostatic, organisms need to
   a. be multicellular.
   b. acquire material and energy from the environment.
   c. have a nervous system.
   d. respond to stimuli.
   e. Both b and d are correct.

Organisms Live in Ecosystems

14. Which sequence represents the correct order of increasing complexity?
   a. biosphere, community, ecosystem, population
   b. population, ecosystem, biosphere, community
   c. community, biosphere, population, ecosystem
   d. population, community, ecosystem, biosphere
15. In an ecosystem, energy
   a. flows and nutrients cycle.
   b. cycles and nutrients flow.
   c. and nutrients flow.
   d. and nutrients cycle.
16. An example of chemical cycling occurs when
   a. plants absorb solar energy and make their own food.
   b. energy flows through an ecosystem and becomes heat.
   c. hawks soar and nest in trees.
   d. death and decay make inorganic nutrients available to plants.
   e. we eat food and use the nutrients to grow or repair tissues.
17. Energy is brought into ecosystems by which of the following?
   a. fungi and other decomposers
   b. cows and other organisms that graze on grass
   c. meat-eating animals
   d. organisms that photosynthesize, such as plants
   e. All of these are correct.
18. **THINKING CONCEPTUALLY** How is a college campus, which is composed of buildings, students, faculty, and administrators, like an ecosystem?

Organisms Are Related and Adapted to Their Environment

19. Organisms are related because they
   a. all have the same structure and function.
   b. share the same characteristics.
   c. can all trace their ancestry to a common source.
   d. all contain genes.
20. An evolutionary tree
   a. shows common ancestors.
   b. depicts the history of a group of organisms.
   c. is based on appropriate data.
   d. shows how certain organisms are related.
   e. All of these are correct.
21. Classification of organisms reflects
   a. similarities.
   b. evolutionary history.
   c. Neither a nor b is correct.
   d. Both a and b are correct.
22. Which of these exhibits an increasingly more inclusive scheme of classification?
   a. kingdom, phylum, class, order
   b. phylum, class, order, family
   c. class, order, family, genus
   d. genus, family, order, class
23. Humans belong to the domain
   a. Archaea.   c. Eukarya.
   b. Bacteria.   d. None of these are correct.
24. In which group are you most likely to find unicellular organisms?
   a. Protists   c. Plantae
   b. Fungi   d. Animalia
25. The second word of a scientific name, such as *Homo sapiens*, is the
   a. genus.   d. species.
   b. phylum.   e. family.
   c. specific epithet.

26. Modifications that make an organism suited to its way of life are called
    a. ecosystems.   c. adaptations.
    b. populations.   d. None of these are correct.
27. **THINKING CONCEPTUALLY** Give evidence to support the phrase "Evolution is the unifying theory of biology."

For questions 28–31, match each item to a characteristic of life in the key.

KEY:

    a. is organized   d. is homeostatic
    b. uses materials   e. responds to stimuli
       and energy   f. forms ecosystems
    c. reproduces   g. evolves

28. organisms exhibit behavior
29. populations interact
30. giraffes produce only giraffes
31. common descent with modification

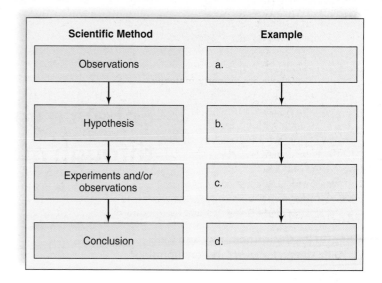

THINKING SCIENTIFICALLY

1. An investigator spills dye on a culture plate and notices that the bacteria live despite exposure to sunlight. He decides to test whether the dye is protective against ultraviolet (UV) light. He exposes to UV light one group of culture plates containing bacteria and dye and another group containing only bacteria. The bacteria on all plates die. Complete the following diagram to identify the steps of his investigation.
2. You want to grow large tomatoes and notice that a name-brand fertilizer claims to yield larger produce than a generic brand. How would you test this claim?

ONLINE RESOURCE

www.mhhe.com/maderconcepts2

Enhance your study with animations that bring concepts to life and practice tests to assess your understanding. Your instructor may also recommend the interactive eBook, individualized learning tools, and more.

CONNECTING THE CONCEPTS

The scientific method consists of making observations, formulating a hypothesis, testing the hypothesis, and coming to a conclusion on the basis of the results (data). The conclusions of many studies have allowed scientists to develop the five theories (cell theory, gene theory, theory of homeostasis, theory of ecosystems, and theory of evolution) on which this book is based. Theories are conceptual schemes that tell us how the world works. All theories of biology are related. For example, the gene theory is connected to the theory of evolution because mutations create differences between the members of a population. Better-adapted members have the opportunity through natural selection to reproduce more, and in that way a species becomes adapted to its environment.

Any two theories are related. For example, evolution is also connected to the theory of ecosystems because, as natural selection occurs, species become adapted to living in a particular ecosystem. We can connect this observation to the cell theory because, if a gazelle's nerve cells can conduct nerve impulses faster to its muscle cells than a lion's nerve cells, the gazelle is more likely to escape capture.

In exploring the theories, we have also discussed the characteristics of life. The cell theory taught us that all organisms are composed of cells and that cells are the fundamental units of life. The theory of homeostasis tells us that all organisms have mechanisms that allow them to keep their internal environment relatively constant. The gene theory tells us all organisms have genes, hereditary units that undergo mutations leading to the variety of life. Even so, all life-forms share similar characteristics because they can trace their ancestry to a common source as stated by the theory of evolution. All life-forms live in ecosystems where interactions allow them to acquire the materials and energy they need to continue their existence. Human beings are also dependent on ecosystems, and when they preserve the biosphere, they are preserving their own existence as well.

PUT THE PIECES TOGETHER

1. Give your own example (not taken from this reading) to show that two theories are related.
2. Explain in your own words how bacteria become resistant to an antibiotic.

Part I

Enhance your understanding of the cell through media and applications!

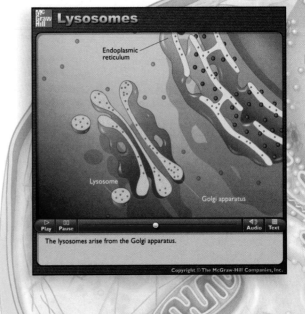

Media

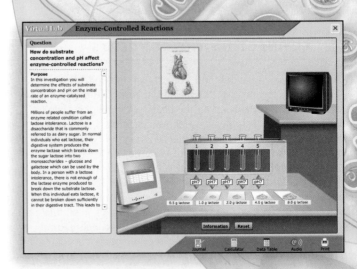

22

Organisms Are Composed of Cells

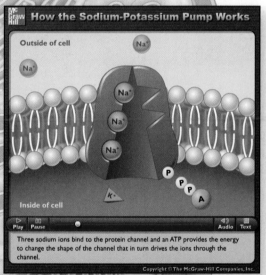

How the Sodium-Potassium Pump Works

Outside of cell

Inside of cell

Play Pause Audio Text

Three sodium ions bind to the protein channel and an ATP provides the energy to change the shape of the channel that in turn drives the ions through the channel.

Copyright © The McGraw-Hill Companies, Inc.

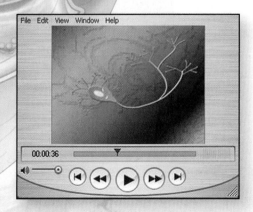

Applications

McGraw Hill **connect**™
|BIOLOGY

23

2

Basic Chemistry and Cells

Life Depends on Water

Scientists and laymen alike have often pondered the question, "Why did life arise on Earth?" It's long been thought that the answer, in part, must involve the presence of water. Three-fourths of the surface of our planet is covered by water. Water is so abundant that if the Earth's surface were absolutely smooth, it would be covered by water. Only land that projects above the seas provides a terrestrial environment.

Cells most likely arose in the oceans. Any living system is 70–90% water, a medium in which chemical reactions can easily occur. A watery environment supports and protects cells while providing an external transport system for chemicals. Homeostasis is also assisted by the ability of water to absorb and give off heat in a way that prevents rapid temperature changes. The abundance of terrestrial life correlates with the abundance of water; therefore, a limited variety of living things is found in the deserts, but much variety exists in the

Planet Earth has an abundance of water

tropics, which receive, by far, the most rain. The tropics are also warm, and water helps maintain a constant year-round temperature day and night.

Do any of the other planets have life? To answer this question, scientists first look for signs of water on a planet because life as we know it does not exist without water. NASA has long seen signs of water on Mars, and in 2008 the *Phoenix,* a robotic laboratory, landed on Mars and found ice. Also, the soil chemistry of the surrounding area suggested that the planet could have been warmer and wetter sometime within the past few million years. Now, scientists hope that evidence of life on Mars will also be found one day.

The strength of the association between water and living things is observable in that all animals, whether aquatic or terrestrial, make use of water to reproduce. Animals that live in the sea or in fresh water can simply deposit their eggs and sperm in the water, where they join to form an embryo that develops in the water. The sperm of human beings, like those of many other terrestrial animals, are deposited inside the female, where they are protected from drying out. Then, as with most other mammals, the offspring develops within a fluid, called the amniotic fluid, while contained within the uterus. Amniotic fluid cushions the embryo and protects it against possible traumas, while maintaining a constant temperature. Later, it prevents the limbs from sticking to the body and allows the fetus to move about.

This chapter discusses the properties of water that assist living things in maintaining homeostasis. It also covers the basic chemistry necessary to understanding how the cell, and therefore the organism, functions. Some chemicals alter the properties of water and, in that way, threaten the ability of organisms to maintain homeostasis.

The flagellated sperm of animals and some plants require water to swim to the egg.

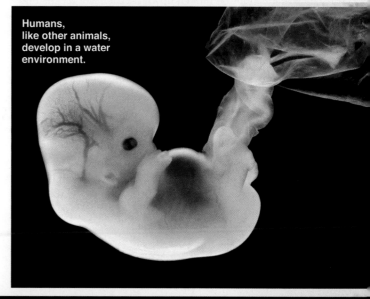

Humans, like other animals, develop in a water environment.

Mercury Venus Earth Mars Ceres Jupiter Saturn Uranus Neptune Pluto and Charon

Of all the planets, only Earth has abundant water and abundant life.

Matter Is Composed of Atoms

Learning Outcomes

▶ Name six types of atoms that are basic to life. (2.1)
▶ Describe the locations and charges of the subatomic particles. (2.2)

Cells, the smallest units of life, are composed of molecules (see Fig. 1.3A), and so it is appropriate that we begin our study of life by considering what constitutes a molecule. Our story begins with atoms because atoms join together to make a molecule.

2.1 Six types of atoms are basic to life

Both the Earth's crust and all organisms are matter. Turn a page, throw a ball, pat your dog, rake leaves; **matter** refers to anything that takes up space and has mass. Everything from the water we drink to the air we breathe is composed of matter.

Elements and Atoms It is quite remarkable that only 92 elements serve as the building blocks of matter. An **element** is a substance that cannot be broken down by chemical means into a simpler substance. However, an **atom** is the smallest unit of an element that still retains the chemical and physical properties of the element. Only six types of atoms—carbon, hydrogen, nitrogen, oxygen, phosphorus, and sulfur—are basic to life. These atoms make up about 95% of the body weight of organisms, such as the macaws in **Figure 2.1.** The macaws have gathered on a salt lick in South America. Salt contains the atoms sodium and chlorine and is a common substance sought by many forms of life.

Every atom has a name and also a symbol. The **atomic symbol** for sodium is Na because *natrium* means sodium in Latin. Chlorine, on the other hand, has the symbol Cl, which is consistent with its English name. Other atoms, however, also take their symbol from Latin. For example, the symbol for iron is Fe because *ferrum* means iron in Latin. The symbols for the six atoms basic to life are C, H, N, O, P, and S. Therefore, we can use the acronym CHNOPS to help us remember these six atoms. As we shall discover in Chapter 3, the properties of the atoms CHNOPS are essential to the uniqueness of cells and organisms. But other atoms are also important to living things, including sodium, potassium, calcium, iron, and magnesium.

▶ **2.1 Check Your Progress** Water contains the atoms hydrogen and oxygen. Which of the six atoms basic to life are missing from water?

FIGURE 2.1 Macaws at a salt lick. The table contrasts the proportion of elements in living organisms with those in the Earth's crust.

2.2 Atoms contain subatomic particles

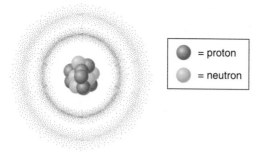

FIGURE 2.2A The stippled area shows the probable location of electrons.

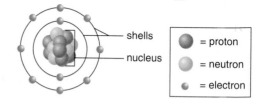

FIGURE 2.2B The shells in this atomic model represent the average location of electrons.

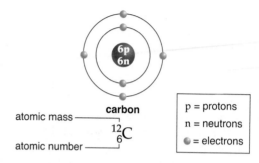

FIGURE 2.2C Atomic model of a carbon atom.

Physicists have identified a number of subatomic particles—particles that are less complex than an atom but are components of an atom. The three best-known subatomic particles are positively charged **protons,** uncharged **neutrons,** and negatively charged **electrons.** Protons and neutrons are located within the nucleus of an atom, and electrons move about the nucleus. The stippling in **Figure 2.2A** shows the probable location of the electrons in an atom that has ten electrons. In **Figure 2.2B,** the stippling has been converted to circles that represent **electron shells,** the approximate orbital paths of electrons. The inner shell has the lowest energy level and can hold two electrons. The outer shell has a higher energy level and can hold eight electrons. An atom is most stable when the outer shell has eight electrons.

In science, a model is a useful simulation of a structure or process rather than the actual structure or process. Biologists find that the model of an atom shown in Figure 2.2B is sufficient for their purposes, and you will be asked to create such atomic models. Actually, today we know that most of an atom is empty space. If an atom could be drawn the size of a football field, the nucleus would be like a gumball in the center of the field, and the electrons would be tiny specks whirling about in the upper stands. Electrons don't have to always stay within certain shells. In our analogy to a football field, the electrons might very well stray outside the stadium at times.

Atomic Number and Mass Number All atoms of an element have the same number of protons. This is called the **atomic number.** For example, the atomic number for a carbon atom is 6. The atomic number not only tells you the number of protons, but it also tells you the number of electrons when the atom is electrically neutral. The model of a carbon atom in **Figure 2.2C** shows that an electrically neutral carbon atom has 6 protons and 6 electrons. Each atom has its own specific mass. The **mass number** of an atom depends on the presence of protons and neutrons, both of which are assigned one atomic mass unit (**Table 2.2**). Electrons are so small that their mass is considered zero in most calculations.

The mass number for carbon is 12. By convention, when an atom stands alone, the atomic number is written as a subscript to the lower left of the atomic symbol. The mass number is written as a superscript to the upper left of the atomic symbol. Regardless of position, the smaller number is always the atomic number as shown in Figure 2.2C.

TABLE 2.2	Subatomic Particles		
Particle	**Electric Charge**	**Atomic Mass**	**Location**
Proton	+1	1	Nucleus
Neutron	0	1	Nucleus
Electron	−1	0	Electron shell

Isotopes **Isotopes** are atoms of a single element that differ in their number of neutrons. Isotopes have the same number of protons, but different mass numbers. For example, the element carbon has three common isotopes:

$$^{12}_{6}C \qquad ^{13}_{6}C \qquad ^{14}_{6}C*$$

$$*radioactive$$

Carbon 12 has six neutrons, carbon 13 has seven neutrons, and carbon 14 has eight neutrons. Unlike the other two isotopes, carbon 14 is unstable; it breaks down into atoms with lower atomic numbers. When it decays, it emits radiation in the form of radioactive particles, or radiant energy. Therefore, carbon 14 is called a radioactive isotope. Biologists and other scientists have found many beneficial uses for radiation. For example, Melvin Calvin and his co-workers used carbon 14 to discover the sequence of reactions that occur during the process of photosynthesis.

Atomic Mass Elements also have an **atomic mass,** the average mass of all its isotopes. The term *atomic mass* is used rather than *atomic weight,* because mass is constant, whereas weight changes according to the gravitational force of a body. The gravitational force of the Earth is greater than that of the moon; therefore, substances weigh less on the moon, even though their mass has not changed.

▶ **2.2 Check Your Progress** Draw a model for each type of atom in water.

2A The Many Medical Uses of Radioactive Isotopes

In 1860, the French physicist Antoine-Henri Becquerel discovered that a sample of uranium would produce a bright image on a photographic plate because it was radioactive. A similar method of detecting radiation is still in use today. Marie Curie, who worked with Becquerel, contributed much to the study of *radioactivity,* as she named it. Today, biologists use radiation to date objects, create images, and trace the movement of substances.

Low Levels of Radiation

In a chemical reaction, a radioactive isotope behaves the same as a stable isotope of an element. This means a radioactive isotope can act as a **tracer** to detect molecular changes. Specific tracers can also be used in imaging the body's organs and tissues. For example, after a patient drinks a solution containing a minute amount of iodine-131, it is concentrated in the thyroid gland. (The thyroid is the only organ to take up iodine, which it uses to make thyroid gland hormones.) In **Figure 2A.1,** the missing area (upper right) in the X-ray indicates the presence of a tumor that does not take up radioactive iodine.

A procedure called positron-emission tomography (PET) is a way to determine the comparative activity of tissues. Radioactively labeled glucose, which emits a subatomic particle known as a positron, is injected into the body. The radiation given off is detected by sensors and analyzed by a computer. The result is a color image that shows which tissues took up glucose and are metabolically active. In **Figure 2A.2,** the red areas surrounded by green indicate which areas of the brain are most active. Physicians use PET scans of the brain to evaluate patients who have memory disorders of an undetermined cause and suspected brain tumors or seizure disorders that could possibly benefit from surgery. PET scans of the heart can detect signs of coronary artery disease and low blood flow to the heart muscle. For this procedure, the patient is injected with a radioisotope of the metallic element thallium (thallium-201). The more thallium taken up by the heart muscle, the better the blood supply to the heart.

High Levels of Radiation

Radioactive substances in the environment can harm cells, damage DNA, and cause cancer. Marie Curie and many of her co-workers

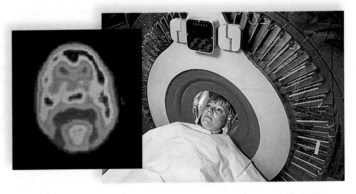

FIGURE 2A.2 Detection of brain activity by doing a PET scan.

developed cancer. The release of radioactive particles following a nuclear power plant accident can have far-reaching and long-lasting effects on human health. However, high levels of radiation can also be put to good use. Radiation from radioactive isotopes has been used for many years to sterilize medical and dental products, and in the future it may be used to sterilize the U.S. mail in order to free it of possible pathogens, such as anthrax spores.

Rapidly dividing cells are particularly sensitive to damage by radiation. For this reason, some cancerous growths can be controlled or eliminated by irradiating the area containing the growth. Radiotherapy can be administered externally, as depicted in **Figure 2A.3,** or it can be given internally. Today, internal radiotherapy allows radiation to destroy only cancer cells, with little risk to the rest of the body. For example, iodine-131 is commonly implanted to treat thyroid cancer, probably the most successful cancer treatment.

FORM YOUR OPINION

1. Since it's impossible to tell ahead of time which investigations will prove fruitful, should the government place no restrictions on its support of scientific endeavors?
2. How can the government protect individuals from the dangers of experimentation when the dangers may not be known?
3. Are you willing to be a guinea pig in experiments that might be harmful to you? Why or why not?

FIGURE 2A.3 Radiotherapy helps cure cancer.

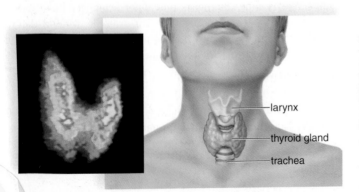

larynx

thyroid gland

trachea

IRE 2A.1 Detection of thyroid cancer by using
tive iodine.

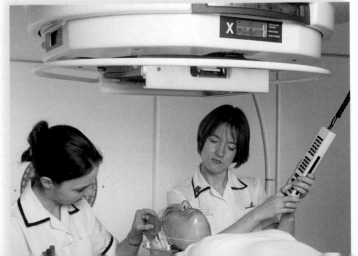

Atoms React with One Another to Form Molecules

Learning Outcomes

▶ Using the periodic table of the elements, construct some electrically neutral atoms. (2.3)
▶ Recognize and construct molecules that contain (a) an ionic bond and (b) a nonpolar and polar covalent bond. (2.4, 2.5, 2.6)
▶ Explain the properties of hydrogen bonds, and predict their presence. (2.7)

The number of electrons in an atom's outer shell largely determines its reactivity. Although some atoms do not react, the biologically important ones do tend to react, and the result is an association called a chemical bond. The two types of chemical bonds are ionic bonds and covalent bonds. When covalent bonds exhibit polarity, hydrogen bonding may occur.

2.3 After atoms react, they have a completed outer shell

Once chemists discovered a number of the elements, they arranged them in a periodic table according to their characteristics. **Figure 2.3A** shows a portion of the periodic table of the elements. The period (horizontal row) tells you how many shells an atom has, and the group (vertical column marked by a Roman numeral) tells you how many electrons an atom has in its outer shell. For example, carbon in the second period (pink) has two shells, and being in group IV, it has four electrons in the outer shell.

A model can be drawn for each of the atoms in the periodic table. **Figure 2.3B** illustrates models for the six atoms common to organisms, namely CHNOPS. For these atoms and all the others up through number 20 (calcium), each lower level is filled with electrons before the next higher level contains any electrons. The first shell (closest to the nucleus) can contain two electrons; thereafter, each additional shell can contain eight electrons.

Among CHNOPS, hydrogen is most stable when the outer shell has two electrons, and the others are most stable when the outer shell has eight electrons. Most atoms, therefore, obey the so-called **octet rule:** They will give up, accept, or share electrons in order to have eight electrons in the outer shell. Therefore, the number of electrons in an atom's outer shell, called the **valence shell,** determines its chemical reactivity. The size of an atom can also affect reactivity. Both carbon and silicon have four outer electrons, but only the smaller carbon atom often bonds to other carbon atoms and forms long-chained molecules.

Except for the atoms in group VIII, which already have eight electrons in the outer shell, atoms routinely bond with one another. For example, oxygen does not exist in nature as a single atom, O; instead, two oxygen atoms are joined to form a molecule (O_2). Other naturally occurring molecules include hydrogen (H_2) and nitrogen (N_2). When atoms of two or more elements bond together in fixed proportions, the product is called a **compound.** Water (H_2O) is a compound that contains atoms of hydrogen and oxygen. A **molecule** is the smallest part of a compound that still has the properties of that compound.

▶ **2.3 Check Your Progress a.** When hydrogen bonds with oxygen to form water, how many electrons does each hydrogen require to achieve a completed outer shell? Explain. **b.** How many electrons does oxygen require to achieve a completed outer shell? Explain.

Periods →

I							VIII
1 **H** 1.008	II	III	IV	V	VI	VII	2 **He** 4.003
3 **Li** 6.941	4 **Be** 9.012	5 **B** 10.81	6 **C** 12.01	7 **N** 14.01	8 **O** 16.00	9 **F** 19.00	10 **Ne** 20.18
11 **Na** 22.99	12 **Mg** 24.31	13 **Al** 26.98	14 **Si** 28.09	15 **P** 30.97	16 **S** 32.07	17 **Cl** 35.45	18 **Ar** 39.95
19 **K** 39.10	20 **Ca** 40.08	31 **Ga** 69.72	32 **Ge** 72.59	33 **As** 74.92	34 **Se** 78.96	35 **Br** 79.90	36 **Kr** 83.60

— Groups —

FIGURE 2.3A A portion of the periodic table of the elements. For a complete table, see Appendix C.

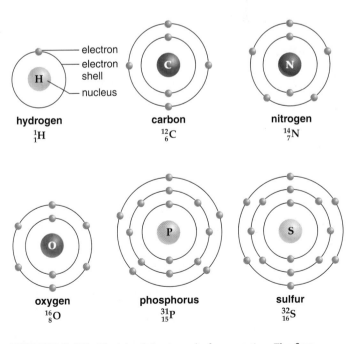

hydrogen
^1_1H

carbon
$^{12}_6C$

nitrogen
$^{14}_7N$

oxygen
$^{16}_8O$

phosphorus
$^{31}_{15}P$

sulfur
$^{32}_{16}S$

FIGURE 2.3B Models of six atoms before reacting. The first electron shell can contain up to two electrons and, in the atoms depicted, every shell after that can contain 8 electrons. Fill the first shell before filling the next.

2.4 An ionic bond occurs when electrons are transferred

When two toddlers are at play, one might take a toy from the other instead of sharing. Atoms act similarly when one takes (an) electron(s) from the other. Chlorine (Cl) is an atom that has seven electrons in its outer shell, so if it acquires one more, it has a completed outer shell. Sodium (Na), on the other hand, which has only one electron in its third shell, lets chlorine have the electron. It is an electron donor. Once the two atoms react in this way, each has eight electrons in the outer shell (**Fig. 2.4**).

The electron transfer, however, causes a charge imbalance in each atom. The sodium atom has one more proton than it has electrons; therefore, it has a net charge of $+1$ (symbolized by Na^+). The chlorine atom has one more electron than it has protons; therefore, it has a net charge of -1 (symbolized by Cl^-). Such charged particles are called **ions.**

Ionic compounds are held together by an **ionic bond,** which is an attraction between negatively and positively charged ions. When sodium reacts with chlorine, an ionic compound called sodium chloride (NaCl) results. Sodium chloride is an example of a salt; it is commonly known as table salt because it is used to season food (Fig. 2.4). **Salts** can exist as dry solids, but when salts are placed in water, they release ions as they dissolve. NaCl separates into Na^+ and Cl^-. Ionic compounds are most commonly found in this separated (dissociated) form in living things because biological systems are 70–90% water.

Sodium (Na^+) and chloride (Cl^-) are not the only biologically important ions. Some, such as potassium (K^+), are formed by the transfer of a single electron to another atom; others, such as calcium (Ca^{2+}) and magnesium (Mg^{2+}), are formed by the transfer of two electrons. Biologically important ions in the human body are listed in **Table 2.4.** The balance of these ions in the body is

TABLE 2.4	Significant Ions in the Human Body	
Name	**Symbol**	**Special Significance**
Sodium	Na^+	Found in body fluids; important in muscle contraction and nerve conduction
Chloride	Cl^-	Found in body fluids
Potassium	K^+	Found primarily inside cells; important in muscle contraction and nerve conduction
Phosphate	PO_4^{3-}	Found in bones, teeth, and the high-energy molecule ATP
Calcium	Ca^{2+}	Found in bones and teeth; important in muscle contraction and nerve conduction
Bicarbonate	HCO_3^-	Important in acid-base balance

important to our health. Too much sodium in the blood can cause high blood pressure; too much or too little potassium results in heartbeat irregularities; and not enough calcium leads to rickets (bowed legs) in children. Bicarbonate ions are involved in maintaining the acid-base balance of the body.

Ions are less likely to occur when atoms share electrons with one another, as discussed in Section 2.5.

▶ **2.4 Check Your Progress** Knowing that oxygen is able to attract an electron to a greater degree than hydrogen, supply the correct charges for the ions that result when water breaks down like this: $H_2O \longrightarrow H + OH$

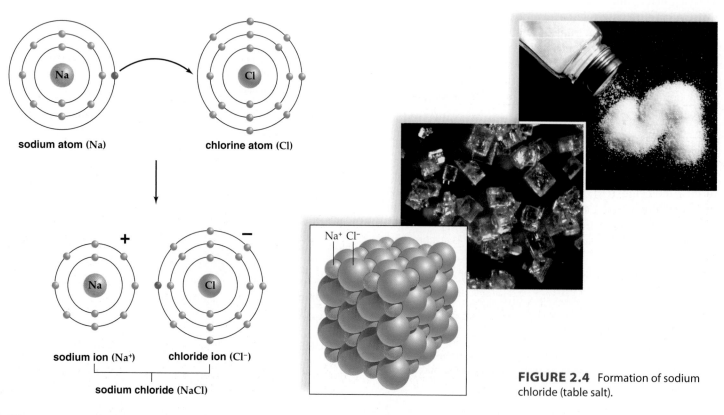

FIGURE 2.4 Formation of sodium chloride (table salt).

2.5 A covalent bond occurs when electrons are shared

Sometimes toddlers do share toys; first one has the toy and then the other. Similarly, some atoms nearly always share electrons, and both atoms are satisfied because the outer shell of each then has eight electrons (or two electrons in the case of hydrogen). In a hydrogen atom, the outer shell is complete when it contains two electrons. If hydrogen is in the presence of a strong electron acceptor, such as oxygen, it gives up its electron to become a hydrogen ion (H^+) (also called a proton because this ion has no electrons). But hydrogen can also share an electron with another atom. For example, one hydrogen atom can share with another hydrogen atom. When their two orbitals overlap, a pair of electrons is shared within a so-called **covalent bond.** Sharing is illustrated by drawing molecular models called electron models (**Fig. 2.5A**).

Bond Notations A common way to symbolize that atoms are sharing electrons is to draw a line between the two atoms, as in the structural formula H—H. In a molecular formula, the line is omitted, and the molecule is simply written as H_2 (Fig. 2.5A). Sometimes, atoms share more than one pair of electrons to complete their octets. A double covalent bond occurs when two atoms share two pairs of electrons. To show that oxygen gas (O_2) contains a double bond, the molecule can be written as O=O. It is also possible for atoms to form triple covalent bonds, as in nitrogen gas (N_2), which can be written as N≡N. Single covalent bonds between atoms are quite strong, but double and triple bonds are even stronger.

The gas methane results when carbon binds to four hydrogen atoms (CH_4). In methane, each bond actually points to one corner of a tetrahedron. A ball-and-stick model is the best way to show this arrangement, while a space-filling model comes closest to showing the actual shape of the molecule (**Fig. 2.5B**). The shapes of molecules help dictate the roles they play in organisms.

Chemical Reactions Chemical reactions, such as those in photosynthesis, are very important to organisms. An overall equation for the photosynthetic reaction indicates that some bonds are broken and others are formed:

$$6\ CO_2 \ + \ 6\ H_2O \longrightarrow C_6H_{12}O_6 \ + \ 6\ O_2$$
$$\text{carbon dioxide} \quad \text{water} \quad \text{glucose} \quad \text{oxygen}$$

This equation says that six molecules of carbon dioxide react with six molecules of water to form one glucose molecule and six molecules of oxygen. The reactants (molecules that participate in the reaction) are shown to the left of the arrow, and the products (molecules formed by the reaction) are shown to the right. Notice that the equation is "balanced"—that is, the same number of each type of atom occurs on both sides of the arrow.

Note the glucose molecule in the equation. It has six atoms of carbon, 12 atoms of hydrogen, and six atoms of oxygen bonded together to form one molecule. The structural formula for glucose is shown in Figure 3.4A.

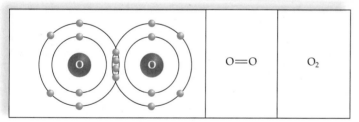

Hydrogen gas

Electron Model	Structural Formula	Molecular Formula
(Hydrogen gas)	H—H	H_2

Oxygen gas

Electron Model	Structural Formula	Molecular Formula
(Oxygen gas)	O=O	O_2

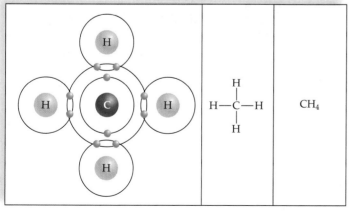

Methane

Electron Model	Structural Formula	Molecular Formula
(Methane)	H—C—H with H above and H below	CH_4

FIGURE 2.5A Electron models and formulas representing covalently bonded molecules.

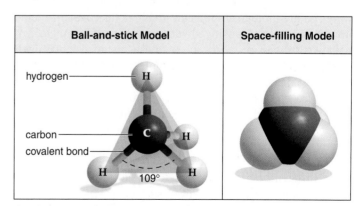

Ball-and-stick Model	Space-filling Model
hydrogen — H, carbon — C, covalent bond, H, H, H, 109°	

FIGURE 2.5B Other types of molecular models—in this case, for methane (CH_4).

▶ **2.5 Check Your Progress a.** Covalent bonds occur in water. Use overlapping atomic models to show the structure of water. **b.** Explain why water has the formula H_2O.

2.6 A covalent bond can be nonpolar or polar

When the sharing of electrons between two atoms is fairly equal, the covalent bond is said to be a **nonpolar covalent bond.** All the molecules in Figure 2.5A, including methane (CH_4), are nonpolar. However, in a water molecule (H_2O), the sharing of electrons between oxygen and each hydrogen is not completely equal. The attraction of an atom for the electrons in a covalent bond is called its **electronegativity.** The larger oxygen atom, with its greater number of protons, is more electronegative than the hydrogen atom. The oxygen atom can attract the electron pair to a greater extent than each hydrogen atom can. The shape of a water molecule allows the oxygen atom to maintain a slightly negative charge (δ^-, or "delta minus"), and allows the hydrogen atoms to maintain slightly positive charges (δ^+, or "delta plus"). The unequal sharing of electrons in a covalent bond creates a **polar covalent bond,** and in the case of water, the molecule itself is a polar molecule. **Figure 2.6** shows the electron model, the ball-and-stick model, and the space-filling model of a water molecule. The polarity of water molecules leads to the formation of hydrogen bonds, as discussed in Section 2.7.

▶ **2.6 Check Your Progress** Why is water a polar molecule?

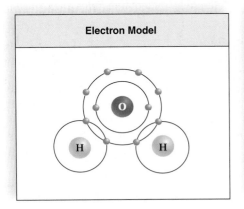

Electron Model

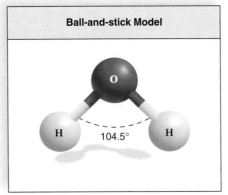

Ball-and-stick Model

104.5°

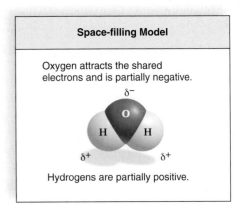

Space-filling Model

Oxygen attracts the shared electrons and is partially negative.

δ^-

O

H   H

δ^+ δ^+

Hydrogens are partially positive.

FIGURE 2.6 Three models of water.

2.7 Hydrogen bonds can occur between polar molecules

The polarity of water molecules causes the hydrogen atoms in one molecule to be attracted to the oxygen atoms in other water molecules. This attraction, which is weaker than an ionic or covalent bond, is called a **hydrogen bond.** Because a hydrogen bond is easily broken, it is often represented by a dotted line (**Fig. 2.7**). Hydrogen bonding is not unique to water. Many biological molecules have polar covalent bonds involving an electropositive hydrogen and usually an electronegative oxygen or nitrogen. In these instances, hydrogen bonds can occur within the same molecule or between different molecules.

Hydrogen bonds are a bit like Velcro: Each tiny hook and loop is weak, but when hundreds of hooks and loops come together, they are collectively strong. Continuing the analogy, a Velcro fastener is easy to pull apart when needed, and in the same way, hydrogen bonds can be disrupted.

Hydrogen bonds between cellular molecules help maintain their proper structure and function. For example, hydrogen bonds hold the two strands of DNA together. When DNA makes a copy of itself, each hydrogen bond breaks easily, allowing the DNA to unzip. On the other hand, the hydrogen bonds, acting together, add stability to the DNA molecule. As we shall see in the next part of the chapter, many of the important properties of water are the result of hydrogen bonding.

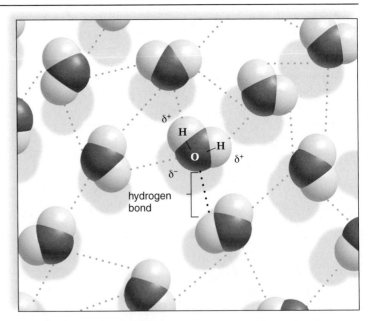

FIGURE 2.7 Hydrogen bonding between water molecules.

▶ **2.7 Check Your Progress** Like water (H_2O), ammonia (NH_3) is a polar molecule. Would you expect hydrogen bonding between ammonia molecules? Between ammonia and water molecules? Explain.

The Properties of Water Benefit Life

Learning Outcome

▶ List and describe four properties of water that benefit organisms. (2.8–2.11)

The introduction to this chapter stressed the association between water and living things. In this part of the chapter, we study four properties of water and show how these properties benefit organisms. We will see that water (1) is cohesive and adhesive, (2) changes temperature slowly, (3) dissolves other polar substances, and (4) expands as it freezes.

2.8 Water molecules stick together and to other materials

Hydrogen bonding accounts for most of the properties of water that make life possible. For example, without hydrogen bonding, frozen water would melt at −100°C, and liquid water would boil at −91°C, making most of the water on Earth steam, and life unlikely. But because of hydrogen bonding, water is a liquid at temperatures typically found on the Earth's surface. It melts at 0°C and boils at 100°C.

Water strider

Also because of hydrogen bonding, water molecules exhibit **cohesion** (they stick together) and **adhesion** (they stick to other polar materials). Diving into a pool breaks the hydrogen bonds, but they re-form behind you. Cohesion allows water to flow freely without separating. It also gives water a high surface tension so that a water strider can skip across the top of a pond, for example.

As a result of cohesion and adhesion, water is an excellent transport medium within vessels in both plants and animals.

How is it possible for water to rise to the top of even very tall trees? Water transport in plants is somewhat like sucking water through a straw—or rather, a bundle of straws. Water evaporating from leaves pulls up more water molecules from plant vessels. Cohesion keeps the water column from breaking apart, and adhesion of water molecules to vessel walls prevents the water column from falling backward (**Fig. 2.8**).

The liquid portion of our blood, which transports dissolved and suspended substances throughout the body, is 90% water. When we drink water, it eventually enters our blood vessels. The cohesion and adhesion properties of water permit blood to flow and help prevent it from falling backward, particularly in the smallest blood vessels, the capillaries (Fig. 2.8). Water prevents both plant cells and human body cells from becoming dehydrated. Plants also use water during photosynthesis, as discussed in Chapter 6.

▶ **2.8 Check Your Progress** How is hydrogen bonding related to the cohesion and adhesion properties of water?

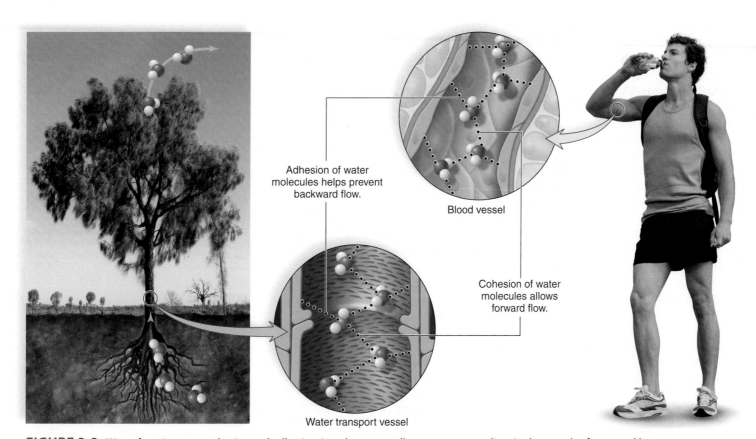

Adhesion of water molecules helps prevent backward flow.

Blood vessel

Cohesion of water molecules allows forward flow.

Water transport vessel

FIGURE 2.8 Water functions as a cohesive and adhesive, it makes an excellent transport medium in the vessels of trees and humans.

2.9 Water warms up and cools down slowly

The many hydrogen bonds that link water molecules help water absorb heat, without a great change in temperature. Because the temperature of water rises and falls slowly, organisms are better able to maintain their normal internal temperatures and are protected from rapid temperature changes.

One calorie is the amount of heat energy needed to raise the temperature of 1 gram (g) of water 1°C. In comparison, other covalently bonded liquids require input of about one-half calorie to raise the temperature 1°C. Converting 1 g of the coldest liquid water to ice requires the loss of 80 calories of heat energy. Water holds onto its heat, and its temperature falls more slowly than does that of other liquids. This property of water is important, not only for aquatic organisms, but for all living things.

Converting 1 g of the hottest water to a gas requires an input of 540 calories of heat energy. Water has a high heat of vaporization because hydrogen bonds must be broken before water boils and water molecules vaporize (evaporate into the environment). Water's high heat of vaporization gives animals in a hot environment an efficient way to release excess body heat. When an animal sweats or gets splashed, body heat is used to vaporize the water, thus cooling the animal (**Fig. 2.9**).

Because of water's high heat capacity and high heat of vaporization, the temperatures along coasts are moderate. During the summer, the ocean absorbs and stores solar heat, and during the winter, the ocean slowly releases it. In contrast, the interior regions of continents experience abrupt changes in temperature.

FIGURE 2.9 The bodies of organisms cool when their heat is used to evaporate water.

▶ **2.9 Check Your Progress** In dry climates, evaporative coolers use a fan to draw air through a water-soaked fiber pad. Why does this work?

2.10 Water dissolves other polar substances

Because of its polarity, water dissolves a great number of substances. A **solution** contains both a **solute,** usually a solid, and a **solvent,** usually a liquid. When ionic salts—for example, sodium chloride (NaCl)—are put into water, the negative ends of the water molecules are attracted to the sodium ions, and the positive ends of the water molecules are attracted to the chloride ions. This causes the sodium ions and the chloride ions to dissociate (separate) as it dissolves in water (**Fig. 2.10**). Water is also a solvent for larger molecules that contain ionized atoms or are polar. When water moves from the roots to the leaves in trees, it serves as a transport vehicle for minerals. And the transport function of blood is only possible because salts and molecules are dissolved, or suspended, in blood plasma.

Those molecules that can attract water are said to be **hydrophilic.** When ions and molecules disperse in water, they move about and collide, allowing reactions to occur. Therefore, water facilitates chemical reactions. Nonionized and nonpolar molecules that cannot attract water are said to be **hydrophobic.** Gasoline contains nonpolar molecules, and therefore it does not mix with water and is hydrophobic.

Still another property of water that benefits living organisms is discussed in Section 2.11: Ice floats on liquid water.

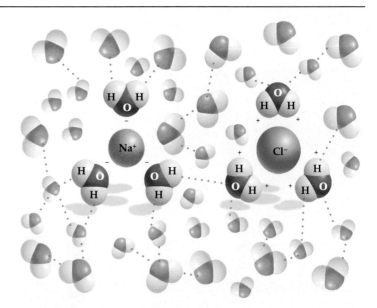

FIGURE 2.10 An ionic salt dissolves in water.

▶ **2.10 Check Your Progress** Fats are nonpolar, but they can be physically dispersed in water by combining with molecules called emulsifiers. What property do emulsifiers have that fats lack?

2.11 Frozen water is less dense than liquid water

Remarkably, water is more dense at 4°C than it is at 0°C. Most substances contract when they solidify, but water expands when it freezes. In ice, water molecules form a lattice, in which the hydrogen bonds are farther apart than they are in liquid water. This is why cans of soda burst when placed in a freezer, and why frost heaves make northern roads bumpy in the winter. It also means that ice is less dense than liquid water, and therefore ice floats (**Fig. 2.11A**).

If ice did not float on water, it would sink, and ponds, lakes, and perhaps even the ocean, would freeze solid, making life impossible in the water and also on land. Instead, bodies of water always freeze from the top down. The ice acts as an insulator to prevent the water below it from freezing and also to prevent the loss of heat to the external environment.

In a pond, the ice protects the protists, plants, and animals so that they can survive the winter (**Fig. 2.11B**). These animals, except for the otter, are ectothermic, which means they take on the temperature of the outside environment. This might seem disadvantageous; however, water remains relatively warm because of its high heat capacity. During the winter, frogs and turtles hibernate and, in this way, lower their oxygen needs. Insects survive in air pockets. Fish, as you will learn later in this text, have an efficient means of extracting oxygen from the water, and they need less oxygen than the endothermic otter, which depends on muscle activity to warm its body.

This completes our study of how the properties of water affect living things. In the next part of the chapter, we discuss chemical changes in body fluids and water sources that challenge the ability of organisms to maintain homeostasis.

▶ **2.11 Check Your Progress** Eskimos use igloos built from blocks of ice to keep warm in winter. Why does this work?

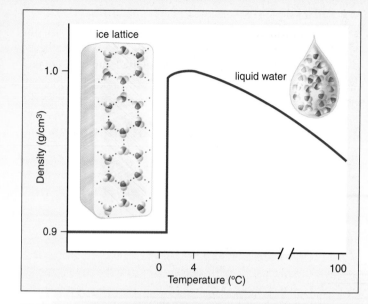

FIGURE 2.11A Ice is less dense than liquid water.

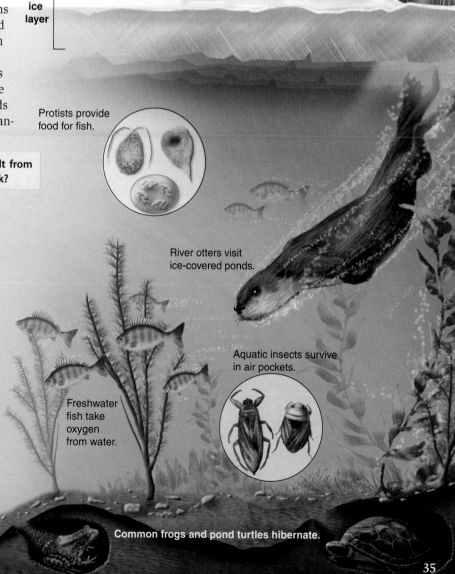

ice layer

Protists provide food for fish.

River otters visit ice-covered ponds.

Aquatic insects survive in air pockets.

Freshwater fish take oxygen from water.

FIGURE 2.11B A pond in winter.

Common frogs and pond turtles hibernate.

Living Things Require a Narrow pH Range

Learning Outcomes

▶ Distinguish between acids and bases. (2.12)

▶ Explain and use the pH scale. (2.13)

▶ Describe a buffer, and tell how buffers assist organisms. (2.14)

Living things are particularly sensitive to the hydrogen ion concentration [H⁺] of liquids. A pH scale is used to judge any changes caused by the addition of acids or bases to a fluid. Buffers assist in keeping the [H⁺] of body fluids relatively constant.

2.12 Acids and bases affect living things

FIGURE 2.12A Dissociation of water molecules.

When water dissociates, it releases an equal number of **hydrogen ions (H⁺)** and **hydroxide ions (OH⁻)**:

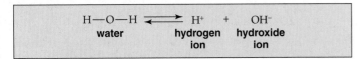

$$H\text{—}O\text{—}H \rightleftharpoons H^+ + OH^-$$

water   hydrogen   hydroxide
ion   ion

Only a few water molecules at a time dissociate. The actual number of H⁺ is $(1 \times 10^{-7}$ moles/liter$)$[1], and an equal concentration of OH⁻ at $(1 \times 10^{-7}$ moles/liter$)$ is also present (**Fig. 2.12A**).

Acids: Excess Hydrogen Ions When we eat acidic foods, our blood becomes more acidic. Lemon juice, vinegar, tomatoes, and coffee are all acidic foods. What do they have in common? **Acids** are substances that dissociate in water, releasing hydrogen ions (H⁺).[2] For example, hydrochloric acid (HCl) is an important inorganic acid that dissociates in this manner:

$$HCl \longrightarrow H^+ + Cl^-$$

Dissociation is almost complete; therefore, HCl is called a strong acid. If hydrochloric acid is added to a beaker of water, the number of hydrogen ions (H⁺) increases greatly (**Fig. 2.12B**).

Hydrochloric acid is produced in the stomach where protein is digested. Hydrochloric acid is capable of eating through most metals, and is highly toxic, burning on contact. However, a layer of mucus protects the stomach wall.

Bases: Excess Hydroxide Ions When we take in basic substances, the blood becomes more basic. Milk of magnesia and bicarbonate of soda are basic solutions familiar to most people. **Bases** are

FIGURE 2.12B Acids cause H⁺ to increase.

FIGURE 2.12C Bases cause OH⁻ to increase.

substances that either take up hydrogen ions (H⁺) or release hydroxide ions (OH⁻). For example, sodium hydroxide (NaOH) is an important inorganic base that dissociates in this manner:

$$NaOH \longrightarrow Na^+ + OH^-$$

Dissociation is almost complete; therefore, sodium hydroxide is called a strong base. If sodium hydroxide is added to a beaker of water, the number of hydroxide ions increases (**Fig. 2.12C**).

Sodium hydroxide is also known as lye or caustic soda. It is just as dangerous as a strong acid and can be used to etch aluminum. Contact with strong acids and bases should be avoided. For this reason, containers of these chemicals are marked with warning symbols.

▶ **2.12 Check Your Progress** Pure water contains an equal number of hydrogen ions (H⁺) and hydroxide ions (OH⁻). **a.** Which one, H⁺ or OH⁻, increases with acids? **b.** With bases?

---

[1]In chemistry, a mole is defined as the amount of matter that contains as many objects (atoms, molecules, ions) as the number of atoms in exactly 12 g of ¹²C.
[2]A hydrogen atom contains one electron and one proton. A hydrogen ion has only one proton, so it is often simply called a proton.

2.13 The pH scale measures acidity and basicity

The **pH scale** is used to indicate the acidity or basicity (also called alkalinity) of a solution. The pH scale ranges from 0 to 14 (**Fig. 2.13**). A pH of 7 represents a neutral state, in which the hydrogen ion concentration [H⁺] equals the hydroxide ion concentration [OH⁻]. A pH below 7 is an acidic solution because [H⁺] is greater than [OH⁻]. A pH above 7 is basic because [OH⁻] is greater than [H⁺].

Moving down the pH scale from pH 14 to pH 0, each unit has ten times the [H⁺] of the previous unit. Moving up the scale from 0 to 14, each unit has ten times the [OH⁻] of the previous unit. The pH scale eliminates the use of cumbersome numbers. For example, in the following list, hydrogen ion concentrations are on the left, and the pH is on the right:

	[H⁺] (moles per liter)	pH
0.000001	$= 1 \times 10^{-6}$	6
0.0000001	$= 1 \times 10^{-7}$	7
0.00000001	$= 1 \times 10^{-8}$	8

To further illustrate the relationship between [H⁺] and pH, consider the following question: Which of the pH values listed above indicates a higher hydrogen ion concentration [H⁺] than pH 7, and therefore would be an acidic solution? A number with a smaller negative exponent indicates a greater quantity of hydrogen ions; therefore, pH 6 is an acidic solution.

In most organisms, pH needs to be maintained within a narrow range. The pH of human blood is between 7.35 and 7.45; this is the pH at which our proteins, such as cellular enzymes, function properly. To maintain normal pH, blood is buffered.

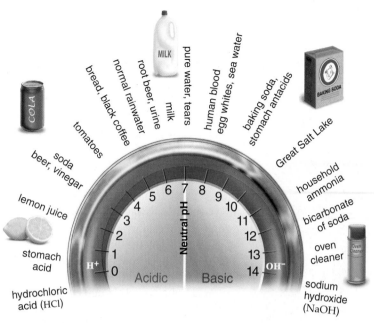

FIGURE 2.13 The pH scale.

▶ **2.13 Check Your Progress** Pure water has a pH of 7. Rainwater normally has a pH of about 5.6. **a.** Is rainwater usually acidic or usually basic? **b.** Does normal rainwater have more or less H⁺ than pure water?

2.14 Buffers help keep the pH of body fluids relatively constant

A **buffer** resists changes in pH. Many commercial products, such as aspirin, shampoos, or deodorants, are buffered as an added incentive for us to buy them. Blood and many other body fluids are buffered so the pH stays within a certain range. If blood pH rises much above pH 7.45, alkalosis is present, and if the pH lowers much below 7.35, acidosis is present. Weakness, cramping, and irritability are symptoms of alkalosis. Seizures, coma, and even death can result from acidosis. Normally, buffers take up excess hydrogen ions (H⁺) or hydroxide ions (OH⁻), thus preventing these conditions.

Usually a buffer consists of a combination of chemicals. For example, carbonic acid (H_2CO_3) and bicarbonate (HCO_3) are two chemicals present in blood that keep pH within normal limits. Carbonic acid is an acid that releases bicarbonate and H⁺ when it dissociates:

$$H_2CO_3 \rightleftharpoons HCO_3^- + H^+$$
$$\text{carbonic acid} \quad \text{bicarbonate}$$

Being a weak acid it tends not to dissociate but will do so upon the addition of a base. When bases add hydroxide ions (OH⁻) to

blood, it drives the reaction forward because the OH⁻ combines with the H⁺ from the dissociation reaction as water forms. When acids add H⁺ to blood, carbonic acid simply re-forms:

$$H^+ + HCO_3^- \longrightarrow H_2CO_3$$

In addition to buffers, breathing helps maintain pH by ridding the body of CO_2, because the more CO_2 there is in the body, the more carbonic acid there is in the blood. As powerful as the buffer and the respiration mechanisms are in maintaining pH, only the kidneys rid the body of a wide range of acidic and basic substances and otherwise adjust the pH. The kidneys are slower acting than the other two mechanisms, but they have a more powerful effect on pH. If the kidneys malfunction, alkalosis or acidosis may result.

Ecosystems are buffered, but acid deposition can overcome their buffering ability, leading to sterile lakes and dead forests as discussed in the How Biology Impacts Our Lives on page 38.

▶ **2.14 Check Your Progress** When CO_2 enters the blood, it combines with water, and carbonic acid (H_2CO_3) results. **a.** When CO_2 enters the blood, does the pH go up or down? **b.** Why?

2B Harmful Effects of Acid Rain

Normally, rainwater has a pH of about 5.6 because carbon dioxide in the air combines with water to produce a solution of carbonic acid. Acid rain or snow or dry acidic particles falling to Earth have a pH of less than 5. When fossil fuels such as coal, oil, and gasoline are burned, sulfur dioxide (SO_2) and nitrogen oxides (NO_x) are released and combine with water to produce sulfuric acid (H_2SO_4) and nitric acid (HNO_3). These pollutants are generally found eastward of where they originated because of wind patterns. The use of very tall smokestacks causes them to be carried even hundreds of miles away (**Fig. 2B.1**). For example, acid rain in southeastern Canada results from the burning of fossil fuels in factories and power plants in the midwestern United States.

Smoke stacks

FIGURE 2B.1
Smokestacks.

Acid rain adversely affects lakes, particularly in areas where the soil is thin and lacks limestone (calcium carbonate, or $CaCO_3$), a buffer to acid deposition. Acid rain leaches toxic aluminum into the soil and it eventually ends up in bodies of water. It also converts mercury deposits in lake bottom sediments to toxic methyl mercury, which accumulates in fish. People are now advised against eating fish from the Great Lakes because of high mercury levels. Hundreds of lakes are devoid of fish in Canada and New England, and thousands have suffered the same fate in the Scandinavian countries. Some of these lakes have no signs of life at all.

The leaves of plants are damaged by acid rain so that they can no longer carry on photosynthesis as before. When plants are under stress, they become susceptible to diseases and pests of all types. Forests on mountaintops receive more rain than those at lower levels; therefore, they are more affected by acid rain (**Fig. 2B.2**). Forests are also damaged when toxic chemicals such as aluminum are leached into the soil. These kill soil fungi that assist roots in acquiring the nutrients trees need. In New England, 1.3 million acres of high-elevation forests have been devastated.

A mountain forest before acid rain had an effect. | The same forest after several years of acid rain.

FIGURE 2B.2 Effect of acid rain on forests.

Humans may be affected by acid rain. Inhaling dry sulfate and nitrate particles appears to increase the occurrence of respiratory illnesses, such as asthma. Buildings and monuments made of limestone and marble break down when exposed to acid rain. The paint on homes and automobiles is likewise degraded.

FORM YOUR OPINION

1. Does it concern you that acid rain might affect the lake where you usually fish or the lumber industry that employs many workers? What about its effect on our food supply?
2. Would you be willing to drive less to help prevent acid rain? Why or why not?
3. At a time when people are stressed by the economy, should they still be concerned about environmental degradation? Why or why not?

THE CHAPTER IN REVIEW

SUMMARY

Matter Is Composed of Atoms

2.1 Six types of atoms are basic to life
- Both living and nonliving things are composed of matter.
- **Matter** takes up space; it can be a solid, a liquid, or a gas.
- All matter is composed of **elements,** substances that cannot be broken down by chemical means. An **atom** is the smallest unit of an element.
- Six atoms—carbon, hydrogen, nitrogen, oxygen, phosphorus, and sulfur—play significant roles in all organisms.
- Each type atom has an **atomic symbol.**

2.2 Atoms contain subatomic particles
- The best-known subatomic particles are **protons** (positive charge), **neutrons** (uncharged), and **electrons** (negative charge).
- Electrons are located in **electron shells** that circle the nucleus.
- The **atomic number** is the number of protons in the nucleus of an atom.

- The **mass number** is the number of protons plus the number of neutrons in the nucleus.
- The **isotopes** of an element have the same number of protons, but they differ in atomic mass due to different numbers of neutrons.
- **Atomic mass** is the average mass of an element's isotopes.

Atoms React with One Another to Form Molecules

2.3 After atoms react, they have a completed outer shell

- The **octet rule** states that atoms tend to react to achieve eight electrons in the outer shell (the most stable number) (or two electrons in the case of hydrogen).

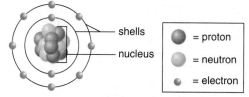

- The number of electrons in an atom's outer shell, called the **valence shell,** determines how it will react.
- A **compound** results when atoms of two or more elements are bonded together in fixed proportions.
- A **molecule** is the smallest part of a compound that has the properties of that compound.

2.4 An ionic bond occurs when electrons are transferred

- An **ionic bond** occurs when particles called **ions** are held together by the attraction between negative and positive ions.
- The negative and positive ions of **salts** dissolve in water.

2.5 A covalent bond occurs when electrons are shared

- A **covalent bond** occurs when two atoms share electrons in such a way that each atom has eight electrons in the outer shell (or two in the case of hydrogen).

2.6 A covalent bond can be nonpolar or polar

- A **nonpolar covalent bond** occurs when the sharing of electrons between atoms is fairly equal as in methane.
- The ability of an atom to attract electrons in a covalent bond is called its **electronegativity.**
- A **polar covalent bond** occurs when the sharing of electrons is not equal. Unequal sharing can result in a polar molecule (e.g., water).

2.7 Hydrogen bonds can occur between polar molecules

- A **hydrogen bond** is a weak attraction between a slightly positive hydrogen atom and a slightly negative atom of another molecule, or between atoms of the same molecule.
- Hydrogen bonds are individually weak and easily broken, but collectively strong.

The Properties of Water Benefit Life

2.8 Water molecules stick together and to other materials

- Hydrogen bonding is responsible for **cohesion** of water molecules and their **adhesion** to other polar materials.
- In living organisms (e.g., trees and humans), water serves as a transport medium.
- Hydrogen bonding causes water to have a high surface tension.

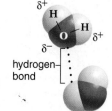

2.9 Water warms up and cools down slowly

- Hydrogen bonding causes water to have a high heat capacity and a high heat of vaporization.
- Water's high heat capacity protects living things from rapid changes in temperature.
- Water's high heat of vaporization helps organisms resist overheating.

2.10 Water dissolves other polar substances

- **Solutions** contain a **solvent** (often water) and a **solute** (dissolved substance).
- The polarity of water makes it a solvent that facilitates chemical reactions.
- **Hydrophilic** molecules (ionized and/or polar, such as salts) attract water.
- **Hydrophobic** molecules (nonionized and nonpolar, such as gasoline) do not attract water.

2.11 Frozen water is less dense than liquid water

- Frozen water expands and floats because hydrogen bonding becomes more rigid and open.
- Ice occurs at the top of ponds and lakes, protecting the water and organisms below it from freezing.

Living Things Require a Narrow pH Range

2.12 Acids and bases affect living things

- When water ionizes, it releases an equal number of **hydrogen ions (H^+)** and **hydroxide ions (OH^-).** The resulting concentration for each is 10^{-7} moles/liter.
- Acids contain excess hydrogen ions (H^+).
- Bases contain excess hydroxide ions (OH^-).

2.13 The pH scale measures acidity and basicity

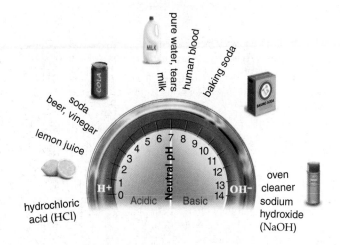

- Pure water has a neutral pH of 7.
- An acidic solution has a pH below 7: [H^+] is greater than [OH^-].
- A basic solution has a pH above 7: [OH^-] is greater than [H^+].
- Most organisms need to maintain pH within a narrow range (e.g., the pH of human blood is about 7.35–7.45).

2.14 Buffers help keep the pH of body fluids relatively constant

- A **buffer** is a chemical or combination of chemicals that resists changes in pH and helps keep pH within normal limits.
- Illness results if the pH rises much above 7.45 (alkalosis) or dips much below 7.35 (acidosis).

Matter Is Composed of Atoms

1. CHNOPS are
   a. the only atoms found in nonliving and living things.
   b. the only atoms found in living things.
   c. atoms basic to life.
   d. atoms found in rocks.
   e. Both b and c are correct.
2. Which of the following is not a component of an atom?
   a. proton   c. neutron
   b. lectons   d. electron
3. The atomic number tells you the
   a. number of neutrons in the nucleus.
   b. number of protons in the atom.
   c. atomic mass of the atom.
   d. number of its electrons if the atom has a neutral charge.
   e. Both b and d are correct.
4. Which of the subatomic particles contributes almost no weight to an atom?
   a. protons in the electron shells
   b. electrons in the nucleus
   c. neutrons in the nucleus
   d. electrons at various energy levels
5. Isotopes of the same element differ from each other only by the number of neutrons.
   a. True   b. False
6. The periodic table does not
   a. give information about the various elements.
   b. indicate the number of protons and the number of valence electrons.
   c. indicate whether an elements forms ionic or covalent bonds.
   d. play a useful role in chemistry today.

Atoms React with One Another to Form Molecules

7. The rule stating that the outer electron shell is most stable when it contains eight electrons is the
   a. stability rule.   c. octet rule.
   b. atomic rule.   d. shell rule.
8. How many electrons does nitrogen require to fill its outer shell?
   a. 0   c. 2
   b. 1   d. 3
9. When an atom gains electrons, it
   a. forms a negatively charged ion.
   b. forms a positively charged ion.
   c. forms covalent bonds.
   d. gains atomic mass.

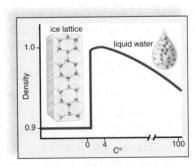

nitrogen
$^{14}_{7}N$

10. An atom that has two electrons in the outer shell, such as calcium, would most likely
    a. share to acquire a completed outer shell.
    b. lose these two electrons and become a negatively charged ion.
    c. lose these two electrons and become a positively charged ion.
    d. bind with carbon by way of hydrogen bonds.
    e. bind with another calcium atom to satisfy its energy needs.
11. Molecules held together by _____ bonds tend to dissociate in biological systems due to the water content in those systems.
    a. covalent   c. hydrogen
    b. ionic   d. nitrogen

12. Which type of bond results from the sharing of electrons between atoms?
    a. covalent   c. hydrogen
    b. ionic   d. neutral
13. In the molecule CH_4,
    a. all atoms have eight electrons in the outer shell.
    b. all atoms are sharing electrons.
    c. carbon could accept more hydrogen atoms.
    d. All of these are correct.
14. In which of these are the electrons always shared unequally?
    a. double covalent bond   d. polar covalent bond
    b. triple covalent bond   e. ionic and covalent bonds
    c. hydrogen bond
15. An example of a hydrogen bond would be the
    a. bond between a carbon atom and a hydrogen atom.
    b. bond between two carbon atoms.
    c. bond between sodium and chlorine.
    d. bond between two water molecules.
16. Explain why the correct formula for ammonia is NH_3, not NH_4.
17. **THINKING CONCEPTUALLY** Explain why you would expect an atom with two electrons in its outer shell to become an ion when it reacts with another atom.

The Properties of Water Benefit Life

18. Water flows freely, but does not separate into individual molecules because water is
    a. cohesive.   c. hydrophobic.
    b. hydrophilic.   d. adhesive.
19. Water can absorb a large amount of heat without much change in temperature, and therefore it has
    a. a high surface tension.
    b. a high heat capacity.
    c. ten times as many hydrogen ions.
    d. ten times as many hydroxide ions.
20. Which of these properties of water cannot be attributed to hydrogen bonding between water molecules?
    a. Water stabilizes temperature inside and outside the cell.
    b. Water molecules are cohesive.
    c. Water is a solvent for many molecules.
    d. Ice floats on liquid water.
    e. Both b and c are correct.

Question 21 is based on this graph:

21. This graph illustrates
    a. that ice is less dense than water.
    b. that ice is more dense than water.
    c. why ice floats on water.
    d. why water molecules form hydrogen bonds with other water molecules.
    e. Both a and c are correct.
    f. All of these are correct.

22. **THINKING CONCEPTUALLY** Explain why you would expect the blood of animals to be mostly water.

Living Things Require a Narrow pH Range

23. Acids
    a. release hydrogen ions in solution.
    b. cause the pH of a solution to rise above 7.
    c. take up sodium ions and become neutral.
    d. increase the number of water molecules.
    e. Both a and b are correct.
24. Which of these best describes the changes that occur when a solution goes from pH 5 to pH 8?
    a. The hydrogen ion concentration decreases as the solution goes from acidic to basic.
    b. The hydrogen ion concentration increases as the solution goes from basic to acidic.
    c. The hydrogen ion concentration decreases as the solution goes from basic to acidic.
25. When water dissociates, it releases
    a. equal amounts of H^+ and OH^-.
    b. more H^+ than OH^-.
    c. more OH^- than H^+.
    d. only H^+.
26. Rainwater has a pH of about 5.6; therefore, rainwater is
    a. a neutral solution.
    b. an acidic solution.
    c. a basic solution.
    d. It depends on whether the rainwater is buffered.
27. If a chemical accepted H^+ from the surrounding solution, the chemical could be
    a. a base.   d. None of these are correct.
    b. an acid.   e. Both a and c are correct.
    c. a buffer.

28. **THINKING CONCEPTUALLY** Compare a chemical buffer such as bicarbonate in the blood, the process of respiration, and kidney function with regard to how they regulate pH and how rapidly they respond to pH change.

THINKING SCIENTIFICALLY

1. Natural phenomena often require an explanation. Based on Figure 2.10 and Figure 2.11A, explain why the oceans don't freeze.
2. Melvin Calvin used radioactive carbon (as a tracer) to discover a series of molecules that form during photosynthesis. Explain why carbon behaves chemically the same, even when radioactive. (See Section 2.2.)

ONLINE RESOURCE

www.mhhe.com/maderconcepts2

Enhance your study with animations that bring concepts to life and practice tests to assess your understanding. Your instructor may also recommend the interactive eBook, individualized learning tools, and more.

CONNECTING THE CONCEPTS

It is possible to connect the concepts in this chapter to the structure and properties of the water molecule. A water molecule contains the atoms hydrogen and oxygen. Their atomic numbers are equal to the number of protons, while the mass numbers consist of the number of protons plus the number of neutrons. Because atoms of the same element have isotopes, the atomic mass of hydrogen and that of oxygen are not even numbers.

An atom of hydrogen has one electron in its outer shell, while oxygen has six electrons in its outer shell. When two hydrogens and one oxygen react, the covalent bonds in a molecule form H_2O. In water, oxygen shares a pair of electrons with each hydrogen, and in that way each hydrogen has two electrons in its outer shell while oxygen has eight electrons in its outer shell.

Because oxygen is more electronegative than a hydrogen atom, the covalent bonds in water are polar bonds. The oxygen carries a slightly negative charge, while each hydrogen carries a positive charge. Therefore, hydrogen bonds form between water molecules. Water, being a polar molecule, can dissolve other polar substances.

Hydrogen bonding leads to the other properties of water, such as cohesiveness, the tendency to change temperature slowly, and expansion when it freezes.

Water has a neutral pH, the pH preferred by organisms. If an acid is added to water, the pH decreases; if a base is added to water, the pH increases. Buffers that resist a change in pH can also be added to water.

Water is considered an inorganic substance because it doesn't contain a carbon atom. As we will learn in Chapter 3, organic molecules do contain carbon, and certain organic molecules—carbohydrates, lipids, proteins, and nucleic acids—are unique to living things.

PUT THE PIECES TOGETHER

1. Analyze the structure of methane (CH_4) by comparing it to the structure of water. Be sure to explain the formula for methane.
2. Support this statement: The structure of water accounts for its properties that are critical to life.

3

Organic Molecules and Cells

CHAPTER OUTLINE

APPLICATIONS

Plants and Animals Are the Same but Different

In what way is a plant like an animal? You're probably hard-pressed to think of ways plants and animals are alike, until you consider the lower levels of biological organization, and then it becomes obvious that plants are indeed like animals. Vegetarians have no trouble sustaining themselves as long as they include a variety of plants in their diet. That's because plants and animals generally have the same molecules in their cells—namely, carbohydrates, lipids, proteins, and nucleic acids. When we feed on plants, we digest their large biomolecules to smaller molecules, and then we use these smaller molecules to build our own types of carbohydrates, lipids, proteins, and nucleic acids.

"Same but different" will be a common theme in this chapter about the molecules of cells. For example, the genetic material for both plants and animals is the nucleic acid DNA. But each type of plant and animal has its own particular genes, even though the way genes function in cells is the same in all types of organisms.

Sameness is especially evident when animals acquire vitamins from plants and use them exactly as plants do in their own metabolism. You could go so far as to suggest that an

animal's inability to make vitamins is not disadvantageous, as long as it can get the vitamins it needs from plants. That way, an animal is not using up its own energy to make a molecule it can get otherwise. Now it has more energy to use for growth, defense, and reproduction.

Vitamins assist enzymes, the molecules in cells that speed chemical reactions. Plants and animals have to build their own enzymes, but these enzymes function similarly. The enzymes needed to extract energy from nutrient molecules and form ATP, the energy currency of all cells, are the same in plants and animals. Plant cells have many more types of enzymes than do animals because they carry on photosynthesis to form their own food. Plant cells also produce molecules that allow them to protect themselves from predators, maintain an erect posture, and in general, be more colorful than most animals. The beautiful vegetables, fruits, and flowers on this page illustrate that plants can be very pleasing to the eye indeed.

In this chapter, we continue our look at basic chemistry by considering the types of molecules unique to living things. These are the molecules that account for the structure and function of all cells in any type of organism.

43

The Variety of Organic Molecules Makes Life Diverse

Learning Outcomes

▶ List the features of carbon that result in the great variety of organic molecules. (3.1, 3.2)

▶ Tell how large biomolecules are assembled and disassembled. (3.3)

We begin our study of organic molecules by examining the chemistry of carbon, the atom that makes the variety of organic molecules in cells possible. The organic molecules made by cells are called **biomolecules.** Functional groups added to biomolecules increase their variety and allow them to play particular roles in cells. Large biomolecules are modular, and their final size is dependent on how many subunits are joined end to end.

3.1 The chemistry of carbon makes diverse molecules possible

Carbon is so versatile that an entire branch of chemistry, called **organic chemistry,** is devoted to it. What is there about carbon that makes organic molecules the same and also different? Carbon is quite small, with a total of only six electrons: two electrons in the first shell and four electrons in the outer shell. To acquire four electrons to complete its outer shell, a carbon atom almost always shares electrons with—you guessed it—CHNOPS, the elements basic to living things (see Section 2.1).

Because carbon needs four electrons to complete its outer shell, it can share with as many as four other elements, and this spells variety. But even more significant to the shape, and therefore the function, of organic molecules is the fact that carbon often shares electrons with another carbon atom. The C—C bond is quite stable and can result in carbon chains that are quite long. Hydrocarbons are chains of carbon atoms bonded exclusively to hydrogen atoms:

octane, a molecule in gasoline

Branching is possible at any carbon atom, and a hydrocarbon can also turn back on itself to form a ring compound when placed in water. One example is cyclohexane, used as an industrial solvent and in the manufacture of nylon.

Carbon can form double bonds with itself and other atoms. Double bonds restrict the movement of attached atoms, and in that way contribute to the shape of the molecule. Carbon is also capable of forming a triple bond with itself, as in acetylene, H—C≡C—H.

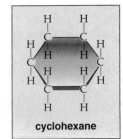

cyclohexane

Biomolecules There are only four classes of biomolecules in any living thing: carbohydrates, lipids, proteins, and nucleic acids. But despite the limited number of classes, the biomolecules in cells are quite varied. A bacterial cell contains some 5,000 different organic molecules, and a plant or animal cell has twice that number. This variety of biomolecules makes the diversity of life possible. Each of the organisms in **Figure 3.1** uses a carbohydrate as a structural molecule: A cactus uses cellulose to strengthen its cell walls, while a bacterium uses peptidoglycan for that purpose; a crab uses chitin to strengthen its shell.

Carbon is the essential ingredient in all biomolecules. Much as a salad chef first puts lettuce in a bowl, so organic molecules begin with carbon. A chef may then add other ingredients, such as cucumbers or radishes, to the lettuce to make different types of salads. So, the variety of biomolecules comes about when different groups of atoms are added to carbon.

Crab shell contains chitin.

Plant cell walls contain cellulose.

Bacteria cell walls contain peptidoglycan.

FIGURE 3.1 Each of these organisms uses a different type of structural carbohydrate.

▶ **3.1 Check Your Progress** How do you know that plant cells contain biomolecules?

3.2 Functional groups add to the variety of biomolecules

The carbon chain of a biomolecule is called its skeleton or backbone. The terminology is appropriate because just as a skeleton accounts for your shape, so does the carbon skeleton of a biomolecule account for its underlying shape. The reactivity of a biomolecule is largely dependent on the attached functional groups. A **functional group** is a specific combination of bonded atoms that always reacts in the same way, regardless of the particular carbon skeleton. As shown in **Figure 3.2A,** an *R* can be used to stand for the "rest" of the molecule because only the functional group is involved in reactions.

Notice that functional groups with a particular name and structure are found in certain types of compounds. For example, the addition of an —OH (hydroxyl group) to a carbon skeleton turns that molecule into an alcohol. When an —OH replaces one of the hydrogens in ethane, a 2-carbon hydrocarbon, it becomes ethanol, a type of alcohol that is consumable by humans. Whereas ethane, like other hydrocarbons, is **hydrophobic** (not soluble in water), ethanol is **hydrophilic** (soluble in water) because the —OH functional group is polar. Because cells are 70–90% water, the ability to interact with and be soluble in water profoundly affects the function of organic molecules in cells. Biomolecules containing carboxyl (acid) groups (—COOH) are polar, and when they ionize, they release hydrogen ions, making a solution more acidic:

$$\text{—COOH} \longrightarrow \text{—COO}^- + \text{H}^+$$

Functional groups determine the activity of a biomolecule in the body. You will see that alcohols react with carboxyl groups when a fat forms, and that carboxyl groups react with amino groups during protein formation. Notice in **Figure 3.2B** that the male sex hormone testosterone differs from the female sex hormone estrogen only by its attached groups. Yet, these molecules help bring about the characteristics that determine whether an individual is male or female.

Isomers **Isomers** are organic molecules that have identical molecular formulas but a different arrangement of atoms. In essence, isomers are variations in the architecture of a molecule. Isomers are another example of how the chemistry of carbon leads to variations in organic molecules.

The two molecules below are isomers of one another; they have the same molecular formula but different functional groups. Therefore, we would expect them to react differently in chemical reactions.

glyceraldehyde	dihydroxyacetone
H H O | | || H—C—C—C—H | | OH OH	H O H | || | H—C—C—C—H | | OH OH

▶ **3.2 Check Your Progress** Oil in salad dressing separates from the watery vinegar portion. What do the oil molecules lack?

Functional Groups		
Group	**Structure**	**Compound**
Hydroxyl	*R*—OH	Alcohol Present in sugars, some amino acids
Carbonyl	$R-C{\overset{O}{\underset{H}{}}}$	Aldehyde Present in sugars
	$R-\overset{O}{\underset{}{C}}-R$	Ketone Polar; present in sugar
Carboxyl (acidic)	$R-C{\overset{O}{\underset{OH}{}}}$	Carboxylic acid Present in fatty acids, amino acids
Amino	$R-N{\overset{H}{\underset{H}{}}}$	Amine Present in amino acids
Sulfhydryl	*R*—SH	Thiol Forms disulfide bonds Present in some amino acids
Phosphate	$R-O-\overset{O}{\underset{OH}{P}}-OH$	Organic phosphate Present in nucleotides, phospholipids

R = rest of molecule

FIGURE 3.2A Functional groups of organic molecules.

Testosterone

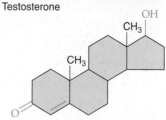

Estrogen

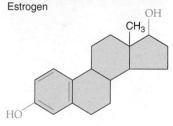

FIGURE 3.2B The functional groups in male and female sex hormones are highlighted.

3.3 Molecular subunits can be linked to form varied large biomolecules

You are very familiar with the large biomolecules called carbohydrates, lipids, proteins, because foods are known to be rich in them, as illustrated in **Figure 3.3A**. Even a late-night pizza, a quick hamburger, or an afternoon snack contains many of these large biomolecules. When you digest your food, these molecules get broken down into their subunits (**Table 3.3**). For example, digestion of bread releases monosaccharides (e.g., glucose) while digestion of meat releases amino acids. Your body then takes these subunits and builds from them the particular carbohydrates and proteins that make up your cells.

The largest of the biomolecules are called **polymers** because they are constructed by linking together a large number of the same type of subunit, called **monomers.** A protein can contain hundreds of amino acids, and a nucleic acid can contain thousands of nucleotides. How do polymers get so large? Cells use the modular approach when constructing polymers. Just as a train increases in length when boxcars are hitched together one by one, so a polymer gets longer as monomers bond to one another.

In the top part of **Figure 3.3B,** notice how synthesis (the construction) of a polymer occurs. A cell uses a **dehydration reaction** to synthesize any biomolecule that has subunits. In this reaction, the equivalent of a water molecule consisting of an —OH (hydroxyl group) and an —H (hydrogen atom) is removed as the reaction occurs. After water is removed, a bond exists between the two monomers.

In the lower part of Figure 3.3B, notice how degradation (breaking down) of a biomolecule occurs. To degrade a biomolecule, our digestive tract, or any cell, uses an opposite type of reaction. During a **hydrolysis reaction,** an —OH group from water attaches to one subunit, and an —H from water attaches

TABLE 3.3	Biomolecules	
Category	**Example**	**Subunit(s)**
Carbohydrates*	Polysaccharide	Monosaccharide
Lipids	Fat	Glycerol and fatty acids
Proteins*	Polypeptide	Amino Acid
Nucleic acids*	DNA, RNA	Nucleotide

*Polymers

to the other subunit. (*Hydro* means "water," and *lysis* means "breaking apart.") In other words, water is used to break the bond holding subunits together. Biologists frequently refer to hydrolysis, sometimes called a hydrolytic reaction, so it is a term that you will want to be familiar with.

In order for these reactions, or almost any other type of reaction, to occur in a cell, an enzyme must be present. An **enzyme** is a molecule that speeds a reaction by bringing reactants together. The enzyme may even participate in the reaction, but it is unchanged by it. Frequently, monomers must be energized before they will bind together because synthesis of a polymer requires energy. On the other hand, hydrolysis of a polymer can release energy.

▶ **3.3 Check Your Progress** Cells, including plant cells, are always carrying on both dehydration and hydrolysis reactions. Why doesn't a cell become waterlogged from dehydration reactions?

FIGURE 3.3A All foods contain carbohydrates, lipids, and proteins.

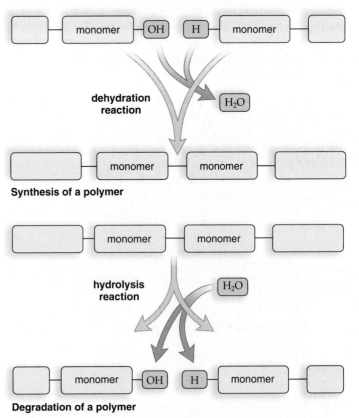

FIGURE 3.3B Synthesis and degradation of polymers.

Carbohydrates Are Energy Sources and Structural Components

Learning Outcomes

▶ Discuss the structure and function of both simple and complex carbohydrates. (3.4)

▶ Explain how some carbohydrates, despite being polymers of glucose, play a structural role in organisms. (3.5)

The majority of carbohydrates have a carbon to hydrogen to oxygen ratio of 1:2:1. The general formula (CH_2O) explains their name because it indicates that they are hydrates (water) of carbon. Some carbohydrates serve as a source of quick energy and others as energy-storage molecules. Still others are structural components of organisms (see Fig. 3.1)

3.4 Simple carbohydrates provide quick energy

Simple carbohydrates are the sweet-tasting sugars. **Monosaccharides** consist of only a single sugar molecule. A monosaccharide can have a carbon backbone of three to seven carbons. It may also have many hydroxyl groups, and this polar functional group makes it soluble in water. **Glucose,** a monosaccharide with six carbon atoms, has a molecular formula of $C_6H_{12}O_6$. Notice in **Figure 3.4A** that there are several ways to represent glucose. When the carbon atoms are included, the molecule looks crowded, so a common practice is to omit the carbon atoms, or even to simply show the hexagon shape. You are supposed to imagine the molecule as flat, with the darkened region facing you. Certain atoms bonded to carbon are above the ring, and others are below it, as indicated.

Despite the fact that glucose has several isomers, such as fructose and galactose, we usually think of $C_6H_{12}O_6$ as glucose. This sugar is the major source of cellular fuel for all living things. Glucose is transported in the blood of animals, and it is the molecule that is broken down in nearly all types of cells to release energy.

Ribose and **deoxyribose** are monosaccharides with five carbon atoms. They are significant because they are present respectively in the nucleic acids RNA and DNA, discussed later in this chapter.

A **disaccharide,** which is also a simple sugar, contains two monosaccharides that have joined during a dehydration reaction. **Figure 3.4B** shows how the disaccharide maltose (an ingredient used in brewing beer) arises when two glucose molecules bond together. When our hydrolytic digestive juices break this bond, the result is two glucose molecules. Sucrose, or table sugar, is another disaccharide of special interest because it is the form in which sugar is transported in plants. Plants transport sucrose from cells carrying on photosynthesis to other parts of their bodies. Sucrose is also the sugar we use to sweeten our food. We acquire the sugar from plants such as

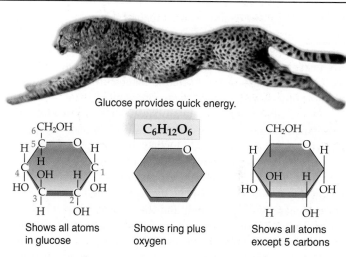

Glucose provides quick energy.

$C_6H_{12}O_6$

| Shows all atoms in glucose | Shows ring plus oxygen | Shows all atoms except 5 carbons |

FIGURE 3.4A Three ways to represent glucose, a source of quick energy for this cheetah and for all organisms.

sugarcane and sugar beets. You may also have heard of lactose, a disaccharide found in milk. Lactose is glucose combined with galactose. Individuals who are lactose intolerant cannot break this disaccharide down and therefore experience unpleasant digestive tract symptoms.

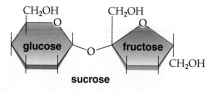

sucrose

This completes our discussion of simple carbohydrates; Section 3.5 discusses complex carbohydrates.

▶ **3.4 Check Your Progress** Plants transport sucrose, but prefer glucose for metabolism. Why would you expect a plant to be able to convert the fructose in sucrose to glucose?

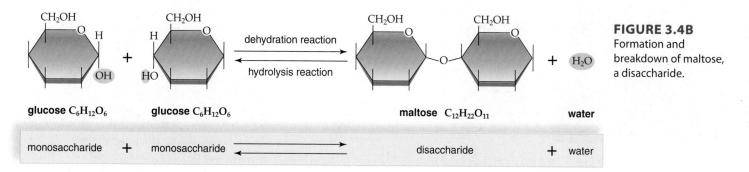

glucose $C_6H_{12}O_6$ + glucose $C_6H_{12}O_6$ → (dehydration reaction / hydrolysis reaction) → maltose $C_{12}H_{22}O_{11}$ + water H_2O

monosaccharide + monosaccharide ⇌ disaccharide + water

FIGURE 3.4B Formation and breakdown of maltose, a disaccharide.

3.5 Complex carbohydrates store energy and provide structural support

Complex carbohydrates are polymers of monosaccharides, and therefore they are **polysaccharides.** Some types of polysaccharides, such as **glycogen** in animals and **starch** in plants, function as short-term energy-storage molecules. They serve as storage molecules because they are not as soluble in water and are much larger than a simple sugar. Their large size prevents them from passing through the plasma membrane that forms a cell's boundary.

Notice in **Figure 3.5a** that glycogen is highly branched. When a polysaccharide is branched, there is no main carbon chain because new chains occur at regular intervals. In our bodies and those of other vertebrates, liver cells contain granules where glycogen is stored until needed. The storage and release of glucose from liver cells is under the control of hormones. After we eat, the release of the hormone insulin from the pancreas promotes the storage of glucose as glycogen.

Plants store glucose as starch. Starch exists in two forms—nonbranched and branched. The branched form is shown in **Figure 3.5b.** Both the nonbranched and branched forms of starch serve as glucose reservoirs in plants. The cells of a potato contain granules in which starch resides during winter until energy is needed for growth in the spring. Plants, as well as animals, can hydrolyze starch and therefore can tap into these reservoirs for energy. When an organism requires energy, polysaccharides are degraded to release sugar molecules. Their shape exposes the sugar linkages to the hydrolytic enzymes that can break them down.

Some types of polysaccharides are structural polysaccharides, such as **cellulose** in plants, **chitin** in animals and fungi, and **peptidoglycan** in bacteria (see Fig. 3.1). The cellulose monomer is simply glucose, but in chitin, the monomer has an attached amino group. The structure of peptidoglycan is more complex because each monomer also has an amino acid chain.

Cellulose is the most abundant carbohydrate and, indeed, the most abundant organic molecule on Earth (**Fig. 3.5c**). Plants produce over 100 billion tons of cellulose each year. Wood and cotton are cellulose plant products. Wood is used for construction, and cotton is used for cloth.

The majority of animals lack the necessary enzymes for digesting cellulose and using it as an energy source. But cellulose does serve as dietary fiber, which maintains regularity of elimination. Microorganisms are able to digest the bond between glucose monomers in cellulose. The protozoans in the gut of termites allow them to digest wood. In cows and other ruminants, microorganisms break down cellulose in a special stomach pouch before the "cud" is returned to the mouth for more chewing and reswallowing.

> **3.5 Check Your Progress** "Same but different" is illustrated by comparing the storage forms of glucose in plants and animals. What's the same and what's different?

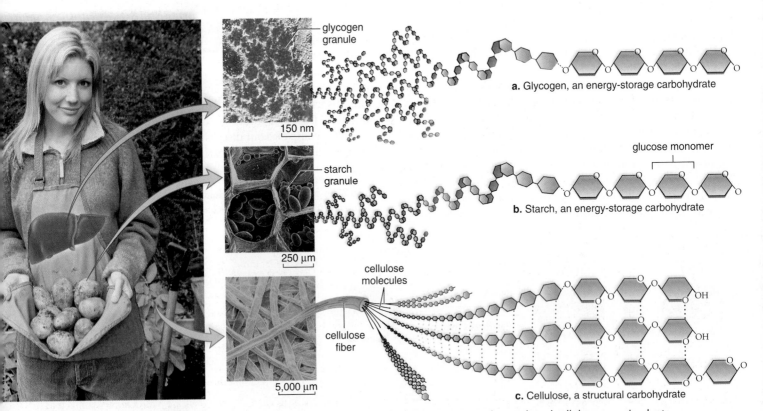

FIGURE 3.5 Some of the polysaccharides in plants and animals. Glycogen is found in animals; starch and cellulose occur in plants.

Lipids Store Energy and Have Other Functions

Learning Outcomes

▶ Relate the structure of fats and oils to their storage function in cells. (3.6)
▶ Compare the structure and function of phospholipids, steroids, and waxes. (3.7)

Most lipids are insoluble in water due to a lack of polar groups. Fats and oils, which function as long-term energy-storage molecules, are the best-known lipids. Phospholipids are constructed like fats but have a polar group that makes them soluble in water. Phospholipids are a major part of the plasma membrane that separates a cell from its environment. Steroids are a large class of lipids having a structure different from that of fats.

3.6 Fats and oils are rich energy-storage molecules

Fats and **oils** contain two types of subunit molecules: glycerol and fatty acids. **Glycerol** is a compound with three —OH groups. A **fatty acid** consists of a long hydrocarbon chain with a —COOH (acid) group at one end. When a fat or oil forms, the acid portions of three fatty acids react with the —OH groups of glycerol during a dehydration reaction (**Fig. 3.6**). Because there are three fatty acids attached to each glycerol molecule, fats and oils are sometimes called **triglycerides.** Notice that the exposed polar groups in glycerol and fatty acids no longer appear in a triglyceride, and this makes triglycerides insoluble in water. On the other hand, the many C—H bonds of fats and oils make them a richer source of chemical energy than the carbohydrates glycogen and starch.

Fatty acids are primary components of fats and oils. Most of the fatty acids in cells contain 16 or 18 carbon atoms per molecule, although smaller ones are also found. Fatty acids are either saturated or unsaturated. **Saturated fatty acids** have no double bonds between the carbon atoms. The carbon chain is saturated, so to speak, with all the hydrogens it can hold. **Unsaturated fatty acids** have double bonds (see yellow highlight in Figure 3.6) wherever the number of hydrogens in the carbon chain is less than two per carbon atom.

The double bond creates a bend in the fatty acid chain. These kinks (not shown) prevent close packing between the hydrocarbon chains and account for the fluidity of oils. On the other hand, the saturated fatty acid chains in butter can pack together tightly because they have no kinks; therefore, butter is fairly solid. **Trans fats** contain fatty acids that have been partially hydrogenated to make them more saturated, and thus more solid. Complete hydrogenation of oils causes all double bonds to become saturated. Partial hydrogenation does not saturate all bonds. It reconfigures some double bonds, and the hydrogen atoms end up on different sides of the chain. (*Trans* in Latin means across):

$$-C=C- \qquad -C-C- \qquad -C=C-$$

| **Unsaturated** (oils) | **Saturated** (butter) | **Trans fats** (hydrogenated oils) |

Trans fats are often found in processed foods—particularly margarine, baked goods, and fried foods. Saturated fats and trans fats contribute to the buildup of abnormal lipid material called plaque inside blood vessels. Unsaturated oils, particularly monounsaturated (one double bond) but also polyunsaturated (many double bonds), have been found to protect against abnormal plaque buildup.

▶ **3.6 Check Your Progress** Plants primarily store oils in seeds for use by seedlings. Why don't adult plants store long-term energy, as animals do?

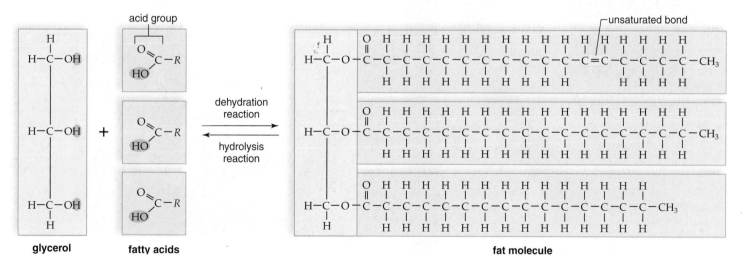

FIGURE 3.6 Formation and breakdown of a fat. The *R* (the rest of the molecule) in each fatty acid stands for the long hydrocarbon chains that are depicted in the fat molecule on the right.

3.7 Other lipids have structural, hormonal, or protective functions

The phospholipids, steroids, and waxes are also important lipids in living things (**Fig. 3.7**). Like fats, **phospholipids** contain glycerol and three groups bonded to glycerol. In phospholipids, only two of these groups are fatty acids. After bonding to glycerol, the fatty acid chains form the hydrophobic tails of the molecule. The third group contains a polar phosphate group that becomes the polar head of a phospholipid. In a watery environment, phospholipids naturally form a bilayer in which the hydrophilic heads project outward and the hydrophobic tails project inward. A cell's plasma membrane consists of a phospholipid bilayer, as will be discussed in more detail in Chapter 4. A plasma membrane is absolutely essential to the structure and function of a cell.

Steroids are lipids that have an entirely different structure from that of fat. A steroid molecule has a skeleton of four fused carbon rings. Cholesterol is the steroid that stabilizes an animal's plasma membrane. It is also the precursor of several other steroids, such as the sex hormones testosterone and estrogen (see Fig. 3.2B). Among its many effects, testosterone is responsible for the generally greater muscle development of human males. For this reason, athletes of both sexes sometimes take anabolic steroids—testosterone or steroids that resemble testosterone—in an attempt to improve their athletic performance. This use of steroids is now banned by most athletic organizations. Anabolic steroid abuse can create serious health problems involving the kidneys and the cardiovascular system, as well as changes in sexual characteristics. Females take on male characteristics, and males become feminized.

Like saturated fats, cholesterol also participates in the formation of plaque along cardiovascular walls. Plaque can restrict blood flow and result in heart attacks or strokes.

In **waxes,** long-chain fatty acids bond with long-chain alcohols. Waxes are solid at normal temperatures. Being hydrophobic, they are also waterproof and resistant to degradation. In many plants, waxes, along with other molecules, form a protective coating that retards the loss of water from all exposed parts. In many animals, waxes are involved in skin and fur maintenance. In humans, wax is produced by glands in the outer ear canal. Earwax contains cerumin, an organic compound that at the very least repels insects, and in some cases even kills them. It also traps dust and dirt, preventing them from reaching the eardrum.

Honeybees produce beeswax in glands on the underside of their abdomen. They then use this beeswax to make the six-sided cells of the comb where their honey is stored. Honey contains the sugars fructose and glucose, breakdown products of sucrose.

▶ **3.7 Check Your Progress** How is the structure of cholesterol different from that of phospholipids and wax.

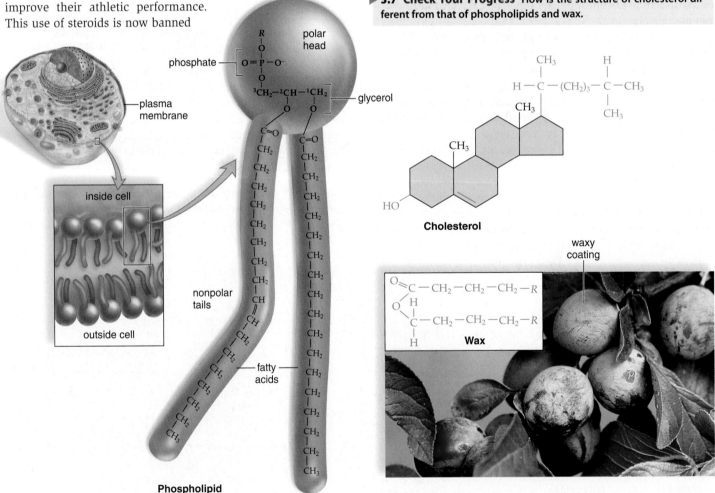

FIGURE 3.7 Structure of phospholipids, cholesterol (a steroid), and wax. In the wax molecule, *R* (rest of the molecule) stands for an extended hydrocarbon chain.

3A Controlling Obesity

Obesity, an excess accumulation of body fat, is a serious medical condition that afflicts over 30% of adults and over 16% of children and adolescents in the United States today. Obesity is judged by a person's body mass index (BMI)—weight in relation to height—as described in **Figure 3A.**

Disorders Associated with Obesity

Two serious illnesses are associated with obesity: diabetes type 2 and cardiovascular disease. When a person has diabetes type 1, the pancreas no longer produces insulin, a hormone that stimulates cells to take in glucose. When a person has diabetes type 2, the pancreas produces insulin, but the cells do not respond to it. In both instances, glucose builds up in the blood and spills over into the urine. Therefore, urinalysis detects when a person has diabetes. How might diet contribute to the occurrence of diabetes type 2? Simple sugars in foods, such as candy and ice cream, immediately enter the bloodstream, as do sugars from the digestion of starch within white bread and potatoes. When the blood glucose level rises rapidly, the pancreas produces an overload of insulin to bring the level under control. Chronically high insulin levels due to diet apparently lead to insulin resistance, a high blood fatty acid level, and diabetes type 2.

Cardiovascular disease due to arteries blocked by plaque is another condition seen in obese individuals. Plaque contains saturated fats and also cholesterol. Cholesterol is carried in the blood by two types of lipoproteins: low-density lipoprotein (LDL) and high-density lipoprotein (HDL). LDL is thought of as "bad" because it carries cholesterol from the liver to the cells, while HDL is thought of as "good" because it carries cholesterol from the cells to the liver, which takes it up and converts it to bile salts. Limiting cholesterol (present in cheese, egg yolks, shrimp, and lobster) in the diet may be helpful. Beef, dairy foods, and coconut oil are rich sources of saturated fat, which tends to raise LDL levels. Further, processed foods made with or fried in partially hydrogenated oils (e.g., vegetable shortening and stick margarine) are sources of trans fats that contribute to plaque formation.

Eating Sensibly

Before turning to more drastic measures, an overweight or obese person should first attempt to lose weight by lowering their caloric intake and increasing their caloric output through exercise. Only then will the body metabolize its stored fat for energy needs, allowing the person to lose weight. There are no quick and easy solutions for losing weight. The typical fad diet is nutritionally unbalanced and difficult to follow over the long term. Weight loss and weight maintenance require permanent lifestyle changes, such as increasing the level of physical activity and reducing portion sizes. Once body weight is under control, it needs to be maintained by continuing to eat sensibly. Complex carbohydrates, such as those in whole-grain breads and cereals, are preferable to simple carbohydrates, such as

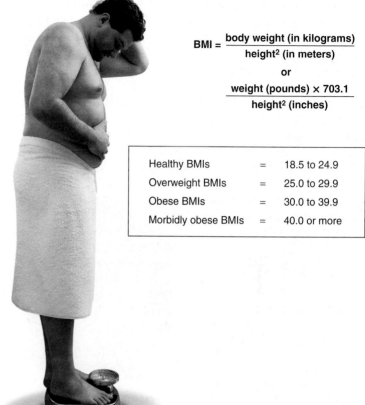

$$BMI = \frac{\text{body weight (in kilograms)}}{\text{height}^2 \text{ (in meters)}}$$

or

$$\frac{\text{weight (pounds)} \times 703.1}{\text{height}^2 \text{ (inches)}}$$

Healthy BMIs	=	18.5 to 24.9
Overweight BMIs	=	25.0 to 29.9
Obese BMIs	=	30.0 to 39.9
Morbidly obese BMIs	=	40.0 or more

FIGURE 3A You can determine your own body mass index (BMI) using either of the formulas shown here. If you are obese, you should try to reduce your BMI with diet and exercise.

candy and ice cream, because they do not cause a spike in blood insulin level and they contain dietary fiber plus vitamins and minerals. We also need to watch the type of fat in our diet. Two unsaturated fatty acids (alpha-linolenic and linoleic acids) cannot be produced in the body and therefore are called essential dietary fatty acids. Unsaturated fatty acids in olive and canola oils, most nuts, and coldwater fish tend to lower LDL-cholesterol levels. Furthermore, coldwater fish (e.g., herring, sardines, tuna, and salmon) contain polyunsaturated fatty acids and especially monounsaturated fatty acids that can reduce the risk of cardiovascular disease.

FORM YOUR OPINION

1. Today restaurants usually serve large portions of food and drinks. Should they be required to serve only smaller portions to help prevent obesity?
2. How can food manufacturers be required to consider the health effects of the ingredients they use, such as fructose sweeteners made from cornstarch, that have been implicated in childhood obesity?

Proteins Have Many Vital Functions

Learning Outcomes

▶ Describe the versatility of proteins by discussing their many functions. (3.8)

▶ Tell how amino acids and peptides are the same and how they can differ from one another. (3.9)

▶ List and discuss the four levels of a protein's structure. (3.10)

Proteins are varied in structure and function. The function of a protein is dependent on its shape, which is determined by the sequence of its amino acids. Amino acids have the same general structure, but they differ by the side chain attached to a central carbon. The particular sequence of amino acids determines the final shape of a protein.

3.8 Proteins are the most versatile of life's molecules

Proteins, which are polymers of amino acids, are of primary importance to each type of cell. As much as 50% of the dry weight of a cell consists of proteins. Presently, over 100,000 proteins have been identified. Here are some of their many functions in animals:

Support Some proteins are structural proteins. Examples include the silk protein in spider webs; keratin, the protein that makes up hair and fingernails; and collagen, the protein that lends support to skin, ligaments, and tendons.

Metabolism Some proteins are enzymes. They bring reactants together and thereby speed chemical reactions in cells. They are specific for one particular type of reaction and can function at body temperature.

Transport Channel and carrier proteins in the plasma membrane allow substances to enter and exit cells. Other proteins transport molecules in the blood of animals—for example, **hemoglobin** is a complex protein that transports oxygen.

Hair is a protein.

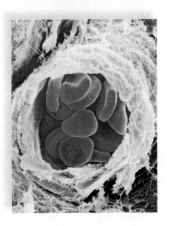

Hemoglobin is a protein.

Defense Proteins called antibodies combine with disease-causing agents to prevent them from destroying cells and upsetting homeostasis, the relative constancy of the internal environment.

Regulation Hormones are regulatory proteins. They serve as intercellular messengers that influence cell metabolism. For example, the hormone insulin regulates the content of glucose in the blood and in cells, while growth hormone determines the height of an individual.

Motion The contractile proteins actin and myosin allow parts of cells to move and cause muscles to contract. Muscle contraction enables animals to move from place to place.

Proteins are such a major part of living organisms that tissues and cells of the body can sometimes be characterized by the proteins they contain or produce. For example, muscle cells contain large amounts of actin and myosin for contraction; red blood cells are filled with hemoglobin for oxygen transport; and support tissues, such as ligaments and tendons, are composed of tough fibers made from collagen.

Muscle contains protein.

▶ **3.8 Check Your Progress** In general, why would you expect a plant cell to have more varied enzymes than an animal cell?

3.9 Each protein is a sequence of particular amino acids

The monomer of a protein is an amino acid. Amino acids have a unique carbon skeleton in which a central carbon atom bonds to a hydrogen atom, two functional groups, and a side chain, or *R* group. The name amino acid is appropriate because one of two functional groups is an —NH₂ (amino group), and another is a —COOH (acid group). The *R* group is the rest of the molecule.

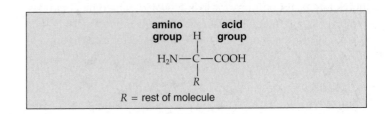

FIGURE 3.9A — A sampling of amino acids

valine (Val)
Nonpolar *R* group

methionine (Met)

phenylalanine (Phe)

cysteine (Cys)
Polar *R* group

asparagine (Asn)

serine (Ser)

glutamic acid (Glu)
Ionized (polar) *R* group

lysine (Lys)

aspartic acid (Asp)

FIGURE 3.9A A sampling of amino acids.

Amino acids differ from one another according to their particular *R* group, shaded blue in **Figure 3.9A**. The *R* groups range in complexity from a single hydrogen atom to a complicated ring compound. Some *R* groups are polar and some are not. Also, the amino acid cysteine has an *R* group that ends with a —SH group, which often connects one chain of amino acids to another by a disulfide bond, —S—S—. Several other amino acids commonly found in cells are shown in Figure 3.9A.

Peptides Proteins are large biomolecules composed of **amino acid** monomers. **Figure 3.9B** shows how two amino acids join by a dehydration reaction between the carboxyl group of one and the amino group of another. A **peptide** is two or more amino acids bonded together, and a **polypeptide** is a chain of many amino acids joined by peptide bonds. A protein may contain more than one polypeptide chain; therefore, a single protein may have a very large number of amino acids. In 1953, Frederick Sanger developed a method to determine the amino acid sequence of a polypeptide. We now know the sequences of thousands of polypeptides, and it is clear that each type of polypeptide has its own particular sequence.

The covalent bond between two amino acids is called a **peptide bond.** The atoms associated with the peptide bond share the electrons unevenly because oxygen attracts electrons more than nitrogen. Therefore, the hydrogen attached to the nitrogen has a slightly positive charge (δ^+), while the oxygen has a slightly negative charge (δ^-).

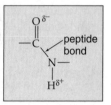

The polarity of the peptide bond means that hydrogen bonding is possible between the —CO of one amino acid and the —NH of another amino acid in a polypeptide.

▶ **3.9 Check Your Progress** Why would you expect to find the same amino acids in both plant and animal cells even though their proteins differ?

amino group

acid group

peptide bond

dehydration reaction
hydrolysis reaction

amino acid

amino acid

dipeptide

H_2O

water

FIGURE 3.9B Formation and breakdown of a peptide.

3.10 The shape of a protein is necessary to its function

The shape of a protein is suited to its function. For example, collagen has a super-coiled helical shape that allows it to lend mechanical strength to bones, tendons, and ligaments and also to support the body's tissues, including the skin. Hemoglobin has a globular shape that allows it to travel inside blood vessels as it carries oxygen throughout the body. However, environmental conditions, such as extremes of temperature and pH, can *denature* a protein—that is, alter its shape—so that it can no

longer perform its usual function. For example, cooking an egg causes the protein albumin in egg white to coagulate. Stomach acids denature any protein we ingest, including hormones, enzymes, and the muscle proteins in meat. Denaturation unravels a protein's usual shape, and it makes it more susceptible to hydrolysis by digestive enzymes.

Alcohol, including both wood alcohol (methanol) and drinking alcohol (ethanol), and the salts of heavy metals such as lead

(Pb), mercury (Hg), and silver (Ag) also denature proteins. A 70% alcohol solution is used as a disinfectant because it destroys bacteria by unraveling their proteins, and silver nitrate ($AgNO_3$) acts similarly when it is routinely used to disinfect the eyes of newborns.

The final shape of a protein is dependent on its sequence of amino acids, as discussed next.

Levels of Protein Organization

The structure of a protein has at least three levels of organization and can have four levels (**Fig. 3.10**). The first level, called the *primary structure,* can be likened to a string of beads because it is the linear sequence of the amino acids joined by peptide bonds. Each particular polypeptide has its own sequence of amino acids. Just as an alphabet of 26 letters can form the sequence of many different words, so can 20 amino acids form the sequence of many different proteins. In the next part of this chapter (p. 56), we learn that genes composed of DNA specify the sequence of amino acids in a particular protein and that genetic changes (mutations) can cause an alteration of a protein's normal shape.

The *secondary structure* of a polypeptide comes about when it takes on a certain orientation in space. As mentioned, the peptide bond is polar, and hydrogen bonding is possible between the —CO of one amino acid and the —NH of another amino acid in a polypeptide. Due to hydrogen bonding, two possible shapes can occur: a right-handed spiral, called an alpha helix, and a folding of the chain, called a pleated sheet. Fibrous proteins, such as those in hair and nails, exist as helices or pleated sheets.

Globular proteins have a *tertiary structure* as their final three-dimensional shape. In muscles, myosin molecules have a rod shape ending in globular (globe-shaped) heads. In enzymes, the polypeptide bends and twists in different ways. Invariably, the hydrophobic portions are packed mostly on the inside, and the hydrophilic portions are on the outside, where they can make contact with fluids. The tertiary shape of a polypeptide is maintained by various types of bonding between the *R* groups; covalent, ionic, and hydrogen bonding all occur.

Some proteins have only one polypeptide, and others have more than one polypeptide, each with its own primary, secondary, and tertiary structures. These separate polypeptides are arranged to give some proteins a fourth level of organization, termed the *quaternary structure.* Hemoglobin is a complex protein having a quaternary structure; most enzymes also have a quaternary structure.

▶ **3.10 Check Your Progress** Why would you expect to find globular proteins, but not fibrous proteins, in plant cells? Explain.

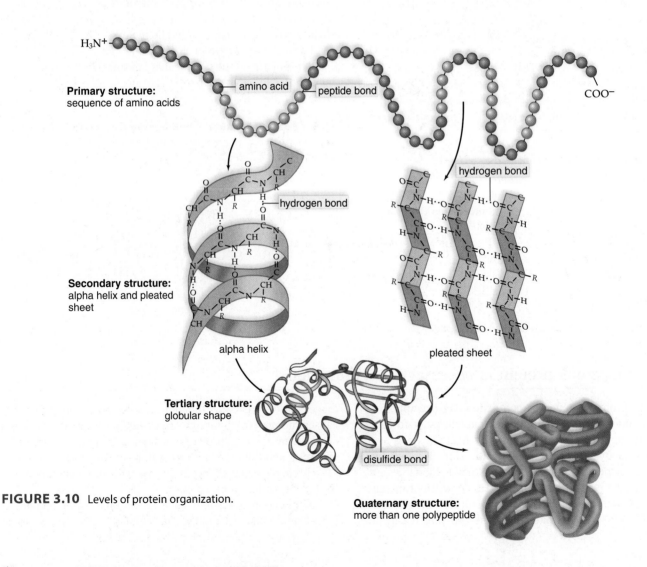

FIGURE 3.10 Levels of protein organization.

Primary structure: sequence of amino acids

Secondary structure: alpha helix and pleated sheet

alpha helix

pleated sheet

Tertiary structure: globular shape

disulfide bond

Quaternary structure: more than one polypeptide

3B Molecular Evolution—A New Endeavor

Molecular genetics has been a critical part of biology ever since Watson and Crick discovered the structure of DNA in 1959. By now, biologists have determined the nucleotide sequence in the genes of many different organisms. Comparing this information has helped us to determine how organisms are related to each other and also to decipher the history of life. The application of molecular genetics to the study of evolution has been invaluable. For example, the tree of life depicted in Figure 1.8A is based on sequence differences in both DNA and RNA. It is not a stretch to say that our knowledge of taxonomy and evolution at every level of classification has been transformed by molecular studies.

Ultimately, molecular evolutionists want to associate new gene mutations with specific advantages that are selected by the environment. The goal is to watch evolution as it proceeds from gene composition changes to population composition changes, all within an environmental context.

Bacterial Laboratory Studies

As a first step, some biologists are simply studying the occurrence of mutations in populations of bacteria. Mutations are "the raw material of evolution" because, without them, a variety of organisms would not be possible. In one study conducted by Richard Lenski at Michigan State University, bacteria were the organisms of choice because they mutate frequently due to a reproductive rate of only a few hours. In 1988, genetically identical *E. coli* bacteria were placed in 12 flasks; the environment has been held constant and no new bacteria have ever been added. By now, the original bacteria have produced 45,000 generations each. Periodically, a sample of bacteria is removed from each flask and cultured on agar in petri dishes (note the petri dishes piled up in **Figure 3B**) to detect any genetic mutations. The greatest change detected so far occurred after about 31,500 generations when some bacteria from a particular flask tested positive for the ability to digest citrate, something no other *E. coli* do. Since then, the citrate-eaters, which are considered a new species, have increased in number presumably due to a selective advantage. The student featured in Figure 3B participated in testing trillions of bacteria for their ability to eat citrate.

Pink monkey flower.

Red monkey flower.

Studies in the Wild

Another approach was undertaken by Douglas W. Schemski of Michigan State University and H.D. Bradshaw, Jr., of the University of Washington. They wanted to test a molecular evolutionary change in the wild and decided to use two species of monkey flowers as their experimental material. A species with pink flowers is mainly pollinated by bumblebees, and a species with red flowers is mainly pollinated by hummingbirds. A difference in the gene called *YUP* was found to be primarily responsible for the color difference and therefore the pollinator difference—bees prefer the pink color, and hummingbirds prefer the red color. Among

FIGURE 3B The student in the foreground is meditating after helping to plate trillions of bacteria in the petri dishes piled up behind him.

other experiments, these investigators substituted "pink" *YUP* genes for "red" *YUP* genes in certain plant embryos. When these altered embryos became plants in the wild, the gene substitutions were found to have a dramatic effect on pollinator visits. The plants had orange flowers instead of red flowers and this caused the number of bumblebee visits to increase dramatically. This experiment provides insight into how evolution can be linked to a particular gene. It is hypothesized that pink flowers originated before red flowers, so the "newly evolved" flowers produced by the investigators are a throwback.

Scientists expect that the number of molecular evolution studies seeking to link specific DNA mutations with particular adaptive changes will expand and ever increase our understanding of the evolutionary process in years to come. Stay tuned for exciting developments!

FORM YOUR OPINION

1. Sometimes major scientific advances have humble beginnings. How, then, can we judge whether a study is worthwhile?
2. Why do scientists want to give evolution a genetic basis? Is it necessary, or should we just study whole organisms?
3. Biologists know of a gene that allows tomato plants to thrive when watered with salty water. If this gene is inserted into tomato plants, have they evolved? Why or why not?

Nucleic Acids Are Information Molecules

Learning Outcomes

▶ Compare the structure and function of DNA and RNA in cells. (3.11, 3.12)
▶ Account for the role of mutations in evolution and the history of life. (3.13)
▶ Relate the structure of ATP to its function as a carrier of usable energy. (3.14)

DNA is the heredity material for all species on planet Earth, and yet life is very diverse. The structure of DNA and its relationship to RNA and proteins explain how it can be the basis for such diversity. ATP is also a unique molecule because it is the energy carrier in cells. DNA provides the information and ATP provides the energy that allow cells to build proteins, the molecules that make all humans the same and yet different.

3.11 DNA stores coded information

In Chapter 1 we learned that genes are hereditary units composed of **DNA (deoxyribonucleic acid)** and that genes control the structure and function of cells and organisms by coding for proteins. However, only by understanding DNA's structure can we understand how it functions (**Fig. 3.11**). Like a computer program whose coded information formats the appearance of text or moves cartoon figures across a screen, DNA dictates a cell's activities, even though it does not participate in those activities. For example, the particular inherited sequence of their DNA nucleotides makes the rabbit and the human different.

A **nucleotide** is a molecular complex of three types of molecules: a phosphate

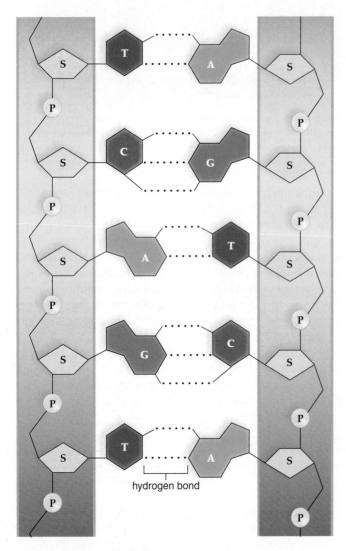

DNA: ladder configuration

DNA: double helix   DNA: space-filling model

FIGURE 3.11 DNA structure at three levels of complexity.

(phosphoric acid), a pentose (5-carbon) sugar, and a nitrogen-containing base. These molecules are called bases because their presence raises the pH of a solution. A **nucleic acid** is a polymer of nucleotides.

Both DNA and **RNA (ribonucleic acid)**, its helper, are nucleic acids. Early investigators called them nucleic acids because they were first detected in the nuclei of cells.

Structure of DNA The nucleotides in DNA contain the sugar deoxyribose, accounting for its name—deoxyribonucleic acid. DNA is double-stranded, as shown in Figure 3.11. The ladder structure of DNA is so called because the sugar and phosphate molecules make up the sides of a ladder, and **complementary paired bases** make up the rungs of the ladder. The bases are held together by hydrogen bonds represented by dotted lines. The bases can be in any order, but between strands, thymine (T) is always paired with adenine (A), and guanine (G) is always paired with cytosine (C). These are, therefore, called **complementary bases.** Every organism has a particular sequence of paired bases, and after many years of research, biologists became quite adept at determining the sequence manually. Now, equipment is available that can sequence DNA automatically and rapidly. A DNA molecule can have thousands—even millions—of bases, and a particular **gene** is only a segment of these. By now, we know the DNA base sequence of all the genes (called the **genome**) in innumerable organisms, including chickens and humans.

We will see in Chapter 10 that base pairing is absolutely essential when DNA replicates and a copy of the genome is passed from generation to generation of cells and organisms. It is also essential when RNA is synthesized.

phosphate

nitrogen-containing base

One nucleotide.

▶ **3.11 Check Your Progress** If a base sequence in part of one strand of DNA is GATCCA, what is the complementary sequence of bases in the other strand?

3.12 Genetic information flows from DNA to RNA to proteins

Figure 3.12 shows how the nucleotides are arranged in RNA, a single-stranded molecule. Notice how the sugar and phosphate molecules form the backbone of the molecule, while the bases project to the side. The 5-carbon sugar molecule is ribose, and this accounts for its name—ribonucleic acid. The bases in RNA are guanine (G), adenine (A), cytosine (C), and uracil (U) which replaces thymine in DNA (**Table 3.12**).

A molecule of RNA is synthesized next to a segment of DNA that constitutes a gene. When an RNA is synthesized, RNA nucleotides pair complementarily with those of the gene. At that time, the base uracil in RNA pairs with adenine in DNA. Several types of RNA are available in cells, but **messenger RNA (mRNA)** is of interest now because it is a copy of a gene that codes for proteins. After mRNA is synthesized, it moves to where proteins are made in the cell. The sequence of bases in RNA determines the sequence of amino acids in a protein. Therefore, genetic information flows from DNA to mRNA to protein:

DNA ⟶ mRNA ⟶ PROTEIN

Just as a monitor is needed to see the results of a computer program, so determining the proteins in a cell allows us to see the results of a cell's genetic information.

▶ **3.12 Check Your Progress** Use Figure 3.12 to point out the differences between DNA and RNA.

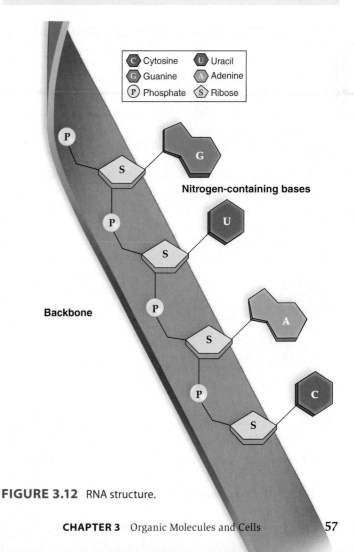

FIGURE 3.12 RNA structure.

TABLE 3.12	DNA Structure Compared to RNA Structure	
	DNA	**RNA**
Sugar	Deoxyribose	Ribose
Bases	Adenine, guanine, thymine, cytosine	Adenine, guanine, uracil, cytosine
Strands	Double-stranded with base pairing	Single-stranded
Helix	Yes	No

3.13 Genetic mutations can result in altered proteins

We now know that a **genetic mutation** is a change in the sequence of bases in a gene and a mutation can result in an altered amino acid sequence in a protein. Without mutations, evolution would be impossible because mutations can result in adaptive changes. Individuals with an adaptive change will be chosen by natural selection to reproduce to a greater extent than those without the adaptive change.

The genetic disorder sickle-cell disease exemplifies how even a seemingly harmful mutation can be adaptive. In sickle-cell disease, an individual's red blood cells are sickle-shaped because at one particular spot the amino acid valine (Val) appears in hemoglobin instead of the amino acid glutamate (Glu) (**Fig. 3.13**). When a person inherits a double mutation, red blood cells lose their normally round flexible shape and become hard and jagged. When these abnormal red blood cells go through small blood vessels, they may clog the flow of blood, causing pain, organ damage, and a low red blood cell count.

However, when a person inherits a single mutation, the red blood cells become sickle-shaped only on occasion, such as when they are invaded by a malarial parasite. The sickle shape causes the parasite to die and gives these people an advantage. This is the reason sickle-cell disease is more common among blacks who trace their ancestry to regions of Africa where malaria is prevalent.

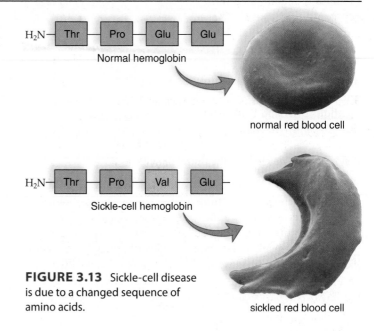

FIGURE 3.13 Sickle-cell disease is due to a changed sequence of amino acids.

▶ **3.13 Check Your Progress** Would a mutation result in an altered messenger RNA molecule? Explain.

3.14 The nucleotide ATP is the cell's energy carrier

Adenosine triphosphate (ATP) is composed of the base adenine and the sugar ribose—a compound termed **adenosine**—plus three linked phosphate groups (**Fig. 3.14A**). ATP is a high-energy molecule because the last two phosphate bonds are unstable and easily broken. In cells, the last phosphate bond is usually hydrolyzed to form **adenosine diphosphate (ADP)** and a phosphate molecule (P).

The breakdown of ATP releases energy because the products of hydrolysis, ADP and (P), are more stable than the original reactant, ATP. Cells couple the energy released by ATP breakdown to energy-requiring processes such as the synthesis of biomolecules. In muscle cells, the energy is used for muscle contraction, and in nerve cells, it is used to conduct nerve impulses. Just as you spend money when you pay for a product or a service, cells "spend" ATP when they

FIGURE 3.14B Animals convert food energy to that of ATP.

need something done. ATP is a usable energy molecule, not an energy-storage molecule as are carbohydrates and fat. Therefore, ATP is called the energy currency of cells (**Fig. 3.14B**). We will discuss more about ATP in Chapter 7.

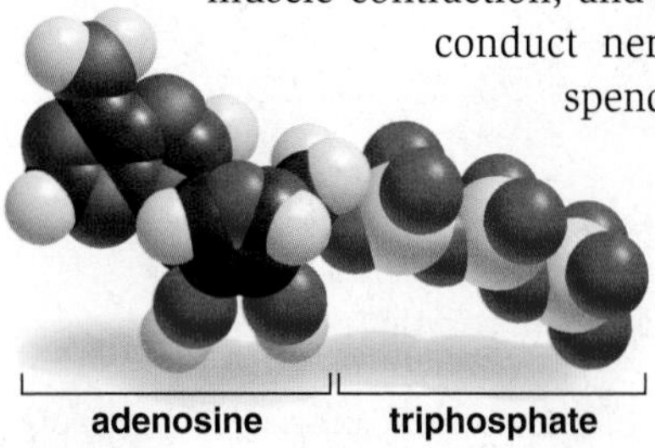

▶ **3.14 Check Your Progress** Glucose breakdown in cells leads to ATP buildup. ATP breakdown in muscle cells leads to movement. Show that your ability to move begins with the ability of plant cells to absorb solar energy.

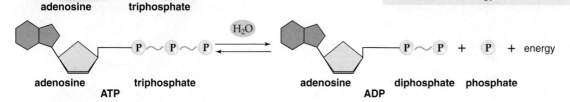

FIGURE 3.14A ATP hydrolysis releases energy.

The Variety of Organic Molecules Makes Life Diverse

3.1 The chemistry of carbon makes diverse molecules possible

- Carbon is the essential ingredient in all organic molecules, whose study is a part of **organic chemistry.**
- Carbon needs four electrons to complete its outer shell; it can share with as many as four other elements.
- The carbon—carbon bond is very stable, and so carbon chains can be very long.
- Organic molecules are usually made by living organisms and thus are called **biomolecules.**

3.2 Functional groups add to the variety of biomolecules

- **Functional groups** are a specific combination of bonded atoms that always react in the same way.
- Functional groups can make a biomolecule **hydrophobic** or **hydrophilic.**
- **Isomers** have identical molecular formulas but a different arrangement of atoms (or functional groups).
- Isomers react differently in chemical reactions.

3.3 Molecular subunits can be linked to form varied large biomolecules

- The large biomolecules in cells are carbohydrates, lipids, proteins, and nucleic acids.
- **Dehydration reactions** form **polymers** which have many subunits, called **monomers. Hydrolysis reactions** break them apart. These reactions require **enzymes.**
  - The carbohydrate monomers are monosaccharides.
  - Lipid subunits are glycerol and fatty acids.
  - The protein monomers are amino acids.
  - The nucleic acid monomers are nucleotides.

Carbohydrates Are Energy Sources and Structural Components

3.4 Simple carbohydrates provide quick energy

- **Monosaccharides** (each composed of a single sugar molecule) are simple sugars.
- **Glucose** is a simple sugar and a major source of quick energy.
- **Ribose** and **deoxyribose** are 5-carbon sugars in RNA and DNA, respectively.
- **Disaccharides** are formed from two monosaccharides joined during dehydration.
- Sucrose (table sugar) is a disaccharide.

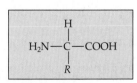

glucose

3.5 Complex carbohydrates store energy and provide structural support

- **Polysaccharides** (polymers of monosaccharides that can be broken down to sugar molecules for energy) include:
  - **glycogen** (stored glucose in animals)
  - **starch** (stored glucose in plants)
- Polysaccharides used for structural support are:
  - **cellulose** (in plants)
  - **chitin** (in animals and fungi)
  - **peptidoglycan** (in bacteria)

Lipids Store Energy and Have Other Functions

3.6 Fats and oils are rich energy-storage molecules

- **Fats** and **oils** (**triglycerides**) contain three **fatty acids** attached to a **glycerol** molecule.
- **Saturated fatty acids** (no double bonds) are characteristic of solid fats found in animals.

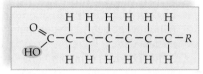

fatty acid

- **Unsaturated fatty acids** (double bonds) are characteristic of liquid oils found primarily in plant seeds.
- **Trans fats** found in processed foods contain partially hydrogenated fatty acids and are particularly harmful to our health.

3.7 Other lipids have structural, hormonal, or protective functions

- **Phospholipids** are a plasma membrane component.
- **Steroids** serve as a plasma membrane component (cholesterol) or have a hormonal function (estrogen and testosterone).
- **Waxes** prevent water loss in plants and assist in skin and fur maintenance in animals (earwax, beeswax).

Proteins Have Many Vital Functions

3.8 Proteins are the most versatile of life's molecules

- **Proteins** (polymers of amino acids) have the following functions:
  - Support (structural proteins)
  - Metabolism (speed chemical reactions)
  - Transport (**hemoglobin** transports oxygen)
  - Defense (antibodies combine with antigens to remove them)
  - Regulation (hormones)
  - Motion (muscle contraction)

3.9 Each protein is a sequence of particular amino acids

- **Amino acids** have a central carbon attached to an amino group ($-NH_2$), an acid group ($-COOH$), and an R group.

$$H_2N-C-COOH$$ with H above and R below the central C

amino acid

- Amino acids differ according to their R group.
- A **peptide** consists of two amino acids bonded together.
- A **peptide bond** is the covalent bond between two amino acids.
- A **polypeptide** is a chain of amino acids joined by peptide bonds.

3.10 The shape of a protein is necessary to its function

- The primary structure is the linear sequence of amino acids in a protein.
- The secondary structure is the particular way a polypeptide folds—alpha helix or pleated sheet.

- The tertiary structure is a globular protein's final three-dimensional shape.
- Proteins that consist of more than one polypeptide may have a quaternary structure.

Nucleic Acids Are Information Molecules

3.11 DNA stores coded information

- A **gene** is a segment of DNA that codes for a protein. The **genome** is all of an organism's genes.
- The **nucleic acids, DNA (deoxyribonucleic acid)** and **RNA (ribonucleic acid),** are polymers of nucleotides.
- A **nucleotide** is composed of a phosphate, a pentose sugar, and a nitrogen-containing base.
- The nucleotides in DNA contain the sugar deoxyribose and the bases thymine (T), adenine (A), guanine (G), and cytosine (C). DNA is double-stranded and helical.
  - In DNA, T pairs with A; G pairs with C. This is called **complementary base** pairing.

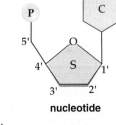

nucleotide

3.12 Genetic information flows from DNA to RNA to proteins

- In RNA, the sugar is ribose and the bases are guanine, cytosine, adenine, and uracil. RNA is single-stranded and not helical.
- When **messenger RNA** forms, DNA's coded information is passed to messenger RNA because A in RNA pairs with T in DNA. (However, A in DNA pairs with U in RNA and G in RNA pairs with C in DNA.)
- The sequence of bases in messenger RNA determines the sequence of amino acids in a protein.

3.13 Genetic mutations can result in altered proteins

- A **genetic mutation** is an altered sequence of bases, which in turn can result in an altered protein.
- Mutations are necessary to the evolutionary process and account for the diversity of life.

3.14 The nucleotide ATP is the cell's energy carrier

- **ATP (adenosine triphosphate)** is composed of adenine and ribose **(adenosine)** plus three phosphate groups **(triphosphate).**
- The last phosphate bond is hydrolyzed to form **adenosine diphosphate** (ADP) + P, and releases energy.
- Energy from ATP breakdown is used for biomolecule synthesis, muscle contraction, and nerve conduction.

TESTING YOURSELF

The Variety of Organic Molecules Makes Life Diverse

1. Which of the following is an organic molecule?
   a. CO
   b. H_2O
   c. $C_6H_{12}O_6$
   d. O_2
   e. All of these are correct.
2. Which of these is not a characteristic of carbon?
   a. forms four covalent bonds
   b. bonds with other carbon atoms
   c. is sometimes ionic
   d. can form long chains
   e. sometimes shares two pairs of electrons with another atom

3. Organic molecules containing carboxyl groups are
   a. nonpolar.
   c. basic.
   b. acidic.
   d. More than one of these is correct.
4. Monomers are attached together to create polymers when a hydroxyl group and a hydrogen atom are _____ in a _____ reaction.
   a. added, dehydration
   c. added, hydrolysis
   b. removed, dehydration
5. **THINKING CONCEPTUALLY** Based on the position of silicon in the periodic table of the elements, how is silicon like and how is it different from carbon? Explain why silicon does not form the same variety of molecules as carbon.

For questions 6–9, match the subunit with one of the biomolecules in the key.

KEY:
   a. carbohydrate   c. protein
   b. lipid   d. nucleic acid
6. Glycerol
7. Glycogen
8. Nucleotide
9. Amino acid

Carbohydrates Are Energy Sources and Structural Components

10. Which of the following is a disaccharide?
    a. glucose
    c. fructose
    b. ribose
    d. maltose
11. Plants store glucose as
    a. maltose.
    c. starch.
    b. glycogen.
    d. None of these are correct.
12. Which of these makes cellulose nondigestible in humans?
    a. a polymer of glucose subunits
    b. a fibrous protein
    c. the linkage between the glucose molecules
    d. the peptide linkage between the amino acid molecules
    e. ionization of the carboxyl groups
13. **THINKING CONCEPTUALLY** After examining Figure 3.5, give reasons why cellulose rather than starch is a structural component of plant cell walls.

Lipids Store Energy and Have Other Functions

14. A triglyceride contains
    a. glycerol and three fatty acids.
    b. glycerol and three sugars.
    c. protein and three fatty acids.
    d. protein and three sugars.
15. A fatty acid is unsaturated if it
    a. contains hydrogen.
    b. contains carbon—carbon double bonds.
    c. contains a carboxyl (acidic) group.
    d. bonds to glycogen.
    e. bonds to a nucleotide.
16. Saturated fatty acids and unsaturated fatty acids differ in
    a. the number of double bonds present.
    b. their consistency at room temperature.
    c. the number of hydrogen atoms present.
    d. All of these are correct.
17. _____ is the precursor of _____.
    a. Estrogen, cholesterol
    b. Cholesterol, glucose

c. Testosterone, cholesterol
d. Cholesterol, testosterone and estrogen
18. Which of these is not a lipid?
   a. steroid   d. wax
   b. fat   e. phospholipids
   c. polysaccharide
19. Explain why phospholipids lend themselves to forming a bilayer membrane.

Proteins Have Many Vital Functions

20. Nearly all _____ are _____.
   a. proteins, enzymes   c. enzymes, proteins
   b. sugars, monosaccharides
21. The difference between one amino acid and another is found in the
   a. amino group.   d. peptide bond.
   b. carboxyl group.   e. carbon atoms.
   c. *R* group.
22. The joining of two adjacent amino acids is called a
   a. peptide bond.   c. covalent bond.
   b. dehydration reaction. d. All of these are correct.
23. Covalent bonding between *R* groups in proteins is associated with the _____ structure.
   a. primary   c. tertiary
   b. secondary   d. None of these are correct.
24. The three-dimensional structure of a protein that contains two or more polypeptides is the
   a. primary structure.   c. tertiary structure.
   b. secondary structure. d. quaternary structure.

Nucleic Acids Are Information Molecules

25. Nucleotides
   a. are composed of a sugar, a nitrogen-containing base, and a phosphate group.
   b. are the monomers of fats and polysaccharides.
   c. join together by covalent bonding between the bases.
   d. are present in both DNA and RNA.
   e. Both a and d are correct.

26. Which of the following pertains to an RNA nucleotide, not a DNA nucleotide?
   a. contains the sugar ribose
   b. contains a nitrogen-containing base
   c. contains a phosphate molecule
   d. becomes bonded to other nucleotides by condensation
27. ATP
   a. is an amino acid.
   b. has a helical structure.
   c. is a high-energy molecule that can break down to ADP and phosphate.
   d. provides enzymes for metabolism.
28. **THINKING CONCEPTUALLY** Early chemists noted the parallel construction of a single-stranded nucleic acid and a protein. What did they mean by "parallel construction" in this context?

THINKING SCIENTIFICALLY

1. You hypothesize that the unsaturated oil content of temperate plant seeds will help them survive freezing temperatures better than the saturated oil content of tropical plant seeds. **a.** How would you test your hypothesis? **b.** Assuming your hypothesis is supported, explain why.
2. Chemical analysis reveals that an abnormal form of an enzyme contains a polar amino acid while the normal form contains a nonpolar amino acid. Formulate a hypothesis you would want to test regarding the abnormal enzyme.

ONLINE RESOURCE

CONNECTING THE CONCEPTS

The large biomolecules—carbohydrates, fats, proteins, and nucleic acids—are present in all cells and organisms, but the particular type varies with the organism. For example, while animals store carbohydrates as glycogen, plants use starch. Plants store unsaturated oils in their seeds, and animals store saturated fats in their bodies. DNA, the genetic material, has a sequence of nucleotide bases that varies according to the species and indeed even among members of the same species. The sequence of bases is coded information that determines what types of proteins will be in each organism. All cells and organisms have their particular mix of proteins, and while the function of proteins varies from species to species, proteins serve as enzymes in all organisms.

While DNA specifies the sequence of amino acids in proteins, it does not participate in the making of proteins. However, through complementary base pairing, messenger RNA receives the coded information from DNA and participates in protein synthesis so that each protein has its own sequence of amino acids, which is its primary structure. Proteins then take on a particular shape that allows them to carry out their specific function. When DNA mutates, its sequence of bases, and thus the resulting protein, changes. This is the source of the genetic variety that allows evolution to occur. ATP is unique in that it has the same structure and function in all cells.

PUT THE PIECES TOGETHER

1. Divide the biomolecules according to these categories: (1) energy storage and use, (2) genetic information storage, and (3) ongoing activities of the cell. Explain your reasoning.
2. It's currently estimated that humans have about 20,500 genes. Conceivably, then, they have at least this number of proteins. Explain how a single molecule (DNA) can code for so much variety (proteins).
3. Humans have about 210 different cell types. Concentrating just on proteins, in general how would you expect these cell types to differ?

4

Structure and Function of Cells

Cells: What Are They?

Imagine that you have never taken a biology course, and you are alone in a laboratory with a bunch of slides of plant and animal tissues and a microscope. The microscope is easy to use, and soon you are able to focus it and begin looking at the slides.

Your assignment is to define a cell. In order not to panic, you idly look at one slide after another, letting your mind wander. Was this the way Robert Hooke felt back in the seventeenth century, when he coined the word "cell"? What did he see? Actually, Hooke was using a light microscope, as you are, when he happened to look at a piece of cork. He drew what he saw like this:

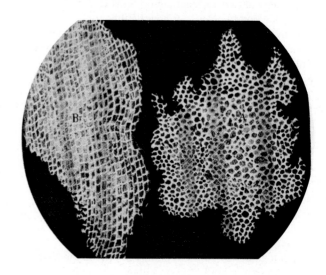

Hooke saw almost nothing except for outlines, which we know today are the cell walls of plant cells. Similarly, you can make out the demarcations between onion root cells in the micrograph on page 63. After comparing these to the nerve cells below, you might conclude that a cell is an entity, a unit of a larger whole.

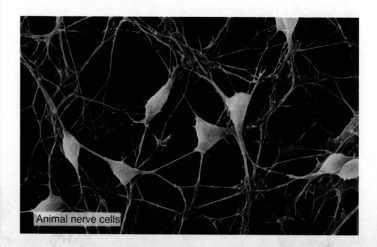

Animal nerve cells

Once you had such a definition for a cell, you might be able to conclude that cells are present in all the slides at your disposal—as in all the micrographs on these pages. But it certainly would take a gigantic leap to hypothesize that all organisms are composed of cells, and this didn't occur until almost 200 years after Hooke used the term cell. You can appreciate that science progresses slowly, little by little, and that a theory, such as the cell theory, becomes established only when an encompassing hypothesis is never found to be lacking. Indeed, it was only when Matthias Schleiden always saw cells in plant tissues, and Theodor Schwann always saw cells in animal tissues, that they concluded, respectively, in the 1830s that plants and animals are composed of cells.

This chapter begins with an explanation of the cell theory and then considers the general characteristics of cells. The cell theory was formulated before the electron microscope was invented and before the biochemical techniques now used to study cells were developed. These improvements in technology tells us how the structure of cells is suited to carrying on the functions necessary to staying alive. These activities are common to all cells, and only in later chapters do we consider the specific functions of specialized cells.

Onion root cells

Rod-shaped bacteria

Euglena, a protist

63

Cells Are the Basic Units of Life

Learning Outcomes

▶ Cite three tenets of the cell theory. (4.1)

▶ Explain why cells are so small. (4.2)

▶ Compare and contrast prokaryotic and eukaryotic cells. (4.3, 4.4)

All organisms are composed of cells, which are about the same small size whether present in an ant or a whale. Surface-to-volume relationships explain why most cells can be measured in micrometers. The two major types of cells—prokaryotic and eukaryotic—differ in complexity, but even so both contain DNA and have a cytoplasm bounded by a plasma membrane.

4.1 All organisms are composed of cells

The **cell theory** states that:

1. *A Cell Is the Basic Unit of Life* This means that nothing smaller than a cell is alive. A unicellular organism exhibits the characteristics of life we discussed in Chapter 1. No smaller unit exists that is able to reproduce, respond to stimuli, remain homeostatic, grow and develop, take in and use materials from the environment, and adapt to the environment. In short, life has a cellular nature. On this basis, we can make two other deductions.

2. *All Living Things Are Made Up of Cells* While it may be apparent that a unicellular organism is a cell, what about more complex organisms? Lilacs and rabbits as well as other visible organisms are multicellular. **Figure 4.1A** illustrates that a lilac leaf is composed of cells, and **Figure 4.1B** illustrates that the intestinal lining of a rabbit is composed of cells. Is there any tissue in these organisms that is not composed of cells? For example, you might be inclined to say that bone does not contain cells. But if you were to examine bone tissue under a microscope, you would see that it, too, is composed of cells. Cells have distinct forms—a bone cell looks quite different from a nerve cell, and they both look quite different from the cell of a lilac leaf. Although cells are specialized in structure and function, they have certain parts in common. This chapter discusses those common components.

3. *New Cells Arise Only from Preexisting Cells* This statement wasn't readily apparent to early investigators, who believed that organisms could arise from dirty rags, for example. Today, we know you cannot get a new lilac bush or a new rabbit without preexisting lilacs and rabbits. When lilacs, rabbits, or humans reproduce, a sperm cell joins with an egg cell to form a zygote, which is the first cell of a new multicellular organism.

▶ **4.1 Check Your Progress** A cell is alive, but its parts are not alive. Explain.

FIGURE 4.1B Rabbit, with a photomicrograph of its intestinal lining below.

Rabbit, an animal

Micrograph of intestine reveals cells. | 140 μm |

Lilac, a plant

Micrograph of leaf reveals cells. | 50 μm |

FIGURE 4.1A Lilac leaf, with a photomicrograph below.

4.2 Metabolically active cells are small in size

Cells tend to be quite small. A frog's egg, at about 1 millimeter (mm) in diameter, is large enough to be seen by the human eye. But most cells are far smaller than 1 mm; some are even as small as 1 micrometer (μm)—one thousandth of a millimeter. Cell structures and biomolecules that are smaller than a micrometer are measured in terms of nanometers (nm). **Figure 4.2A** outlines the visual range of the eye, the light microscope, and the electron microscope. How Science Progresses on page 66 explains why the electron microscope allows us to see so much more detail than the light microscope does.

Why are cells so small? To answer this question, consider that a cell needs a surface area large enough to allow sufficient nutrients to enter and to rid itself of wastes. Small cells, not large cells, are more likely to have this adequate surface area per volume. Consider a balloon: The air in the balloon is the volume, and the balloon's skin is its surface area. A larger balloon has more volume, as you can appreciate by trying to blow up a large balloon compared to a small balloon. How might you appreciate the amount of surface area per volume? **Figure 4.2B** shows one way because it calculates the surface area per volume for different-sized cubes. Cutting a large cube into smaller cubes provides a lot more surface area per volume. The calculations show that a 4-cm cube has a **surface-area-to-volume ratio** of only 1.5:1, whereas a 1-cm cube has a surface-area-to-volume ratio of 6:1.

We would expect, then, that actively metabolizing cells would have to remain small. A chicken's egg is several centimeters in diameter, but the egg is not actively metabolizing. Once the egg is incubated and metabolic activity begins, the egg divides repeatedly without growth. Cell division restores the amount of surface area needed for adequate exchange of materials.

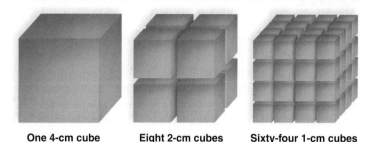

One 4-cm cube   Eight 2-cm cubes   Sixty-four 1-cm cubes

Total surface area (height × width × number of sides × number of cubes)		
96 cm^2	192 cm^2	384 cm^2
Total volume (height × width × length × number of cubes)		
64 cm^3	64 cm^3	64 cm^3
Surface-area-to-volume ratio per cube (surface area ÷ volume)		
1.5:1	3:1	6:1

FIGURE 4.2B Surface-area-to-volume relationships.

Further, cells that specialize in absorption have modifications that greatly increase the surface-area-to-volume ratio of the cell. The cells along the surface of the intestinal wall have surface foldings called microvilli (sing., microvillus) that increase their surface area. Nerve cells and some large plant cells are long and thin, and this increases the ratio of plasma membrane to cytoplasm. Nerve cells are shown on page 62.

▶ **4.2 Check Your Progress** Why is your body made up of multitudes of small cells, instead of a single large cell?

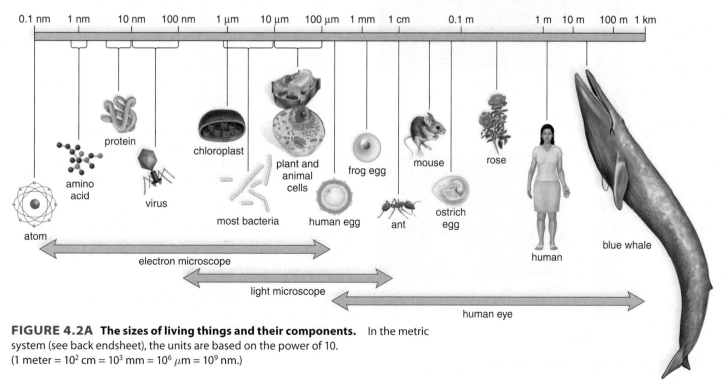

FIGURE 4.2A **The sizes of living things and their components.** In the metric system (see back endsheet), the units are based on the power of 10. (1 meter = 10^2 cm = 10^3 mm = 10^6 μm = 10^9 nm.)

4A Microscopes Allow Us to See Cells

Because cells are so small, it is best to study them microscopically. A magnifying glass containing a single lens is the simplest version of a light microscope. However, such a simple device is not powerful enough to be of much use in examining cells. The **compound light microscope** is much more suitable. It has superior magnifying power because it uses a system of multiple lenses. As you can see in **Figure 4A*a*,** a condenser lens focuses the light into a tight beam that passes through a thin specimen (such as a unicellular amoeba, a drop of blood or a thin slice of an organ). An objective lens magnifies an image of the specimen, and another lens, called the ocular lens, magnifies it yet again. It is the image from the ocular lens that is viewed with the

eye. The most commonly used compound light microscope is called a bright-field microscope, because the specimen, which is typically stained, appears dark against a light background.

The compound light microscope is widely used in research, clinical, and teaching laboratories. However, the use of light to produce an image means that the ability to view two objects as separate—the resolution—is not as good as with an electron microscope. The resolution limit of a compound light microscope is 0.2 μm, which means that objects less than 0.2 μm apart appear as a single object. Although there is no limit to the magnification that could be achieved with a compound light microscope, there is a definite limit to the resolution.

The wavelength of light is an important consideration in obtaining the best possible resolution with a compound light microscope. The shorter the wavelength of light, the better the resolution. This is why many compound light microscopes are equipped with blue filters. The shorter wavelength of blue light compared to white light improves resolution.

An electron microscope can produce finer resolution than a light microscope because, instead of using light, it fires a beam of electrons at the specimen. Electrons have a shorter wavelength than does light. The essential design of an electron microscope is similar to that of a compound light microscope, but its lenses are made of electromagnets, instead of glass. Because the human eye cannot see at the wavelengths of electrons, the images produced by electron microscopes are projected onto a screen or viewed on a television monitor.

There are two types of electron microscopes: the transmission electron microscope and the scanning electron microscope. These microscopes didn't become widely used until about 1970. A **transmission electron microscope** passes a beam of electrons through a specimen (Fig. 4A*b*). Because electrons do not have much penetrating ability, the section must be very thin—usually between 50 and 150 nm. The transmission electron microscope can discern fine details, with a limit of resolution around 1.0 nm and a magnifying power up to 200,000 times larger than the actual size. A **scanning electron microscope** does not pass a beam through a specimen; rather, it collects and focuses electrons that are scattered from the specimen's surface and generates an image with a distinctive three-dimensional appearance (Fig. 4A*c*).

Scientists often preserve microscopic images; these are referred to as micrographs. A captured image from a light microscope is termed a light micrograph (LM), or a photomicrograph. There are also transmission electron micrographs (TEM) and scanning electron micrographs (SEM). The latter two are black-and-white in their original form, but are often colorized for clarity using a computer.

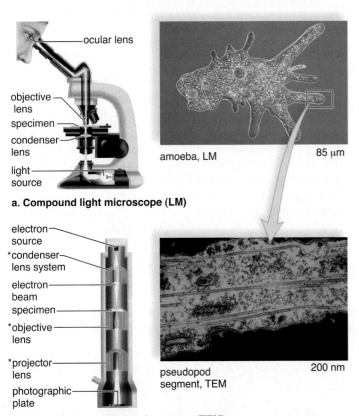

a. **Compound light microscope (LM)**

ocular lens
objective lens
specimen
condenser lens
light source

amoeba, LM   85 μm

electron source
*condenser lens system
electron beam
specimen
*objective lens
*projector lens
photographic plate

pseudopod segment, TEM   200 nm

b. **Transmission electron microscope (TEM)**

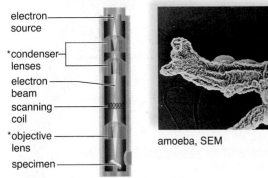

electron source
*condenser lenses
electron beam
scanning coil
*objective lens
specimen

amoeba, SEM   500 μm

c. **Scanning electron microscope (SEM)**   *electromagnetic lens

FIGURE 4A Comparison of three microscopes.

FORM YOUR OPINION

1. How would you convince a friend that what we see in micrographs actually exists?
2. TEMs are colorless but can have color added to them. Do you think color enhancement of TEMs borders on misrepresentation? Why or why not?

4.3 Prokaryotic cells evolved first

Fundamentally, two different types of cells exist. **Prokaryotic cells** (*pro*, before, and *karyon*, nucleus) are so named because they lack a membrane-bounded nucleus. The other type of cell, called a eukaryotic cell, has a nucleus. Prokaryotic cells are miniscule in size compared to eukaryotic cells (**Fig. 4.3A**). Prokaryotes are present in great numbers in the air, in bodies of water, in the soil, and also in and on other organisms.

As discussed on page 14, prokaryotic cells are divided into two groups, largely based on DNA evidence. These two groups are so biochemically different that they have been placed in separate domains, called domain **Bacteria** and domain **Archaea.** **Figure 4.3B** shows the generalized structure of a bacterium.

Like a eukaryotic cell, a bacterium is full of a semifluid substance called **cytoplasm** that is bounded by a **plasma membrane.** The plasma membrane is a phospholipid bilayer (see Fig. 3.7) with embedded proteins.

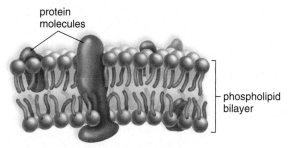

The plasma membrane has the important function of regulating the entrance and exit of substances into and out of the cytoplasm. After all, the cytoplasm has a normal composition that needs to be maintained. It contains thousands of **ribosomes** where protein synthesis ocurs. The long, looped chromosome of a prokaryotic cell is located within a region of the cytoplasm known as a **nucleoid.** Bacteria reproduce by splitting in two, and each new cell gets a copy of the chromosome. They can share DNA with other bacteria by various means. Cyanobacteria (*cyan*, blue-green) are able to photosynthesize in the same manner as plants because they have light-absorbing chlorophyll on their internal membranes.

In addition to the plasma membrane, bacteria have a **cell wall,** which helps maintain the shape of the cell. The cell wall may in turn be surrounded by a **capsule.** Many short, hollow protein rods called **pili** project through the cell wall. Pili attach the cell to solid substances and produce a slime that coats your teeth, rocks at the bottom of lakes, and the hulls of ships, for example. Motile bacteria usually have long, very thin flagella (sing., flagellum), which rotate like propellers, rapidly moving the bacterium in a fluid medium.

Bacteria are well known for causing serious diseases, such as tuberculosis, anthrax, tetanus, throat infections, and gonorrhea. However, they are important to the environment because they decompose the remains of dead organisms and contribute to the cycling of chemicals in ecosystems. Also, their great ability to synthesize molecules can be put to use for the manufacture of all sorts of products, from industrial chemicals to foodstuffs and drugs.

▶ **4.3 Check Your Progress** Why can't you define or recognize a cell by the presence of a nucleus?

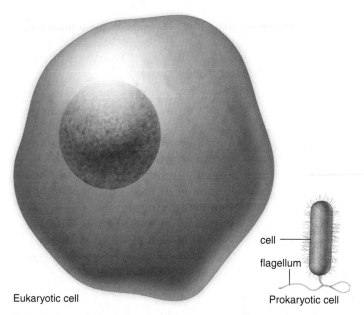

FIGURE 4.3A Eukaryotic cells are much larger than prokaryotic cells.

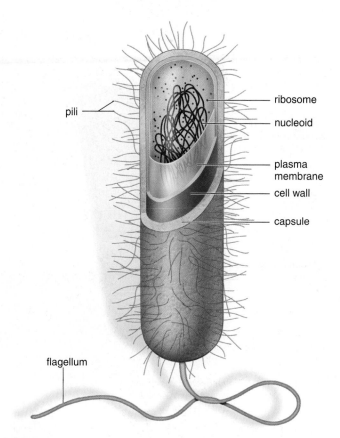

FIGURE 4.3B A prokaryotic cell is structurally simple but metabolically complex.

4.4 Eukaryotic cells contain specialized organelles: An overview

Eukaryotic cells (*eu*, true, and *karyon*, nucleus) have a membrane-bounded **nucleus,** which houses their DNA. As depicted in Figure 1.8D, protists, fungi, plants, and animals are the groups of organisms that have eukaryotic cells and are in the domain **Eukarya,** the third domain of life.

Eukaryotic cells are much larger than prokaryotic cells, and therefore they have less surface area per volume than prokaryotic cells (see Fig. 4.2B). This disadvantage has been solved because the cells are compartmentalized—they have compartments. Just like a house that has separate rooms, the compartments of a eukaryotic cell are specialized for particular functions. In the kitchen of a house are utensils, appliances, and counters necessary for preparing and serving meals, while a bedroom contains personal effects and furniture for sleeping and storing clothes. Similarly, a cell contains **organelles** (meaning "little organs") that are specialized and only perform specific functions. The organelles are located within the cytoplasm, a semifluid interior bounded by a plasma membrane. As in prokaryotic cells, the plasma membrane is a phospholipid bilayer that contains proteins, shown in the circular blow-up of **Figure 4.4A.**

Eukaryotic cells are rich in membrane, and most organelles are membranous. Originally, the term organelle referred only to membranous structures, but we will use it to include any well-defined subcellular structure. By that definition, the little particles called ribosomes are also organelles. At first it might seem difficult to learn the names and functions of all the structures in plant and animal cells. One technique that will help is to have a mental image of the structure and then discover its function. So in **figures** 4.4A and **4.4B,** first look at the structure and then follow the leader back to its name and function. A well-known truism in biology states, "Structure suits function." Why might that be? In the course of evolution, those organisms whose cells possessed organelles suited to their function were more likely to have surviving offspring, and slowly over time all organisms of that group had such cells and organelles.

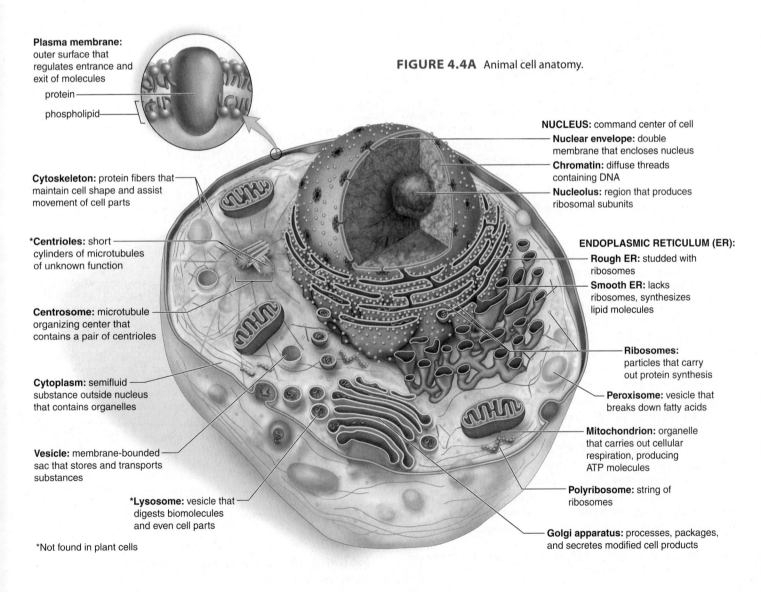

Plasma membrane: outer surface that regulates entrance and exit of molecules

protein
phospholipid

FIGURE 4.4A Animal cell anatomy.

Cytoskeleton: protein fibers that maintain cell shape and assist movement of cell parts

*Centrioles: short cylinders of microtubules of unknown function

Centrosome: microtubule organizing center that contains a pair of centrioles

Cytoplasm: semifluid substance outside nucleus that contains organelles

Vesicle: membrane-bounded sac that stores and transports substances

*Lysosome: vesicle that digests biomolecules and even cell parts

*Not found in plant cells

NUCLEUS: command center of cell
Nuclear envelope: double membrane that encloses nucleus
Chromatin: diffuse threads containing DNA
Nucleolus: region that produces ribosomal subunits

ENDOPLASMIC RETICULUM (ER):
Rough ER: studded with ribosomes
Smooth ER: lacks ribosomes, synthesizes lipid molecules

Ribosomes: particles that carry out protein synthesis

Peroxisome: vesicle that breaks down fatty acids

Mitochondrion: organelle that carries out cellular respiration, producing ATP molecules

Polyribosome: string of ribosomes

Golgi apparatus: processes, packages, and secretes modified cell products

In this chapter we are going to concentrate on aspects of structure and function common to both animal and plant cells. Both types of cells have a nucleus that houses double stranded DNA as their genetic material and ribosomes that carry on protein synthesis in the same manner, for example. The fundamental aspects of cellular organization and function do not vary between the two types of cells. Still, we have an opportunity in this chapter to point out how the two types of cells differ as listed in **Table 4.4**. The cell wall of plants is covered in chapter 5 because chapter 5 concerns the structure and function of cell surfaces. However, Table 4.4 will assist you in learning the major differences between animal and plant cells. The other cell structures (plasma membrane, nucleus, centrosome, endoplasmic reticulum, ribosomes, Golgi, peroxisomes, cytoskeleton) are present in both plant and animal cells).

The various cells in your body have the structures depicted in Figure 4.4A but many of your cells have additional structures and modifications to carry on particular functions. Similarly, the plants in your garden and the trees in your yard have cells with the structures shown in Figure 4.4B but they also have cells that are specialized in different ways. Multicellular organisms in particular have specialized cells and this leads to their diversity in form and capabilities.

It's good to keep in mind as you study cell structures and their functions that despite their small size cells display all the characteristics of life we studied in chapter 1. This chapter tells you how they can accomplish this feat.

▶ **4.4 Check Your Progress** Explain why early investigators were unable to make out the detail illustrated in Figures 4.4A and 4.4B.

TABLE 4.4	Animal and Plant Cell Differences	
Structure	**Animal Cell**	**Plant Cell**
Cell wall	No	Yes
Chloroplast	No	Yes
Lysosomes	Yes	No
Centrioles	Yes	No
Large central vacuole	No	Yes
Shape	Round	Rectangular

FIGURE 4.4B Plant cell anatomy.

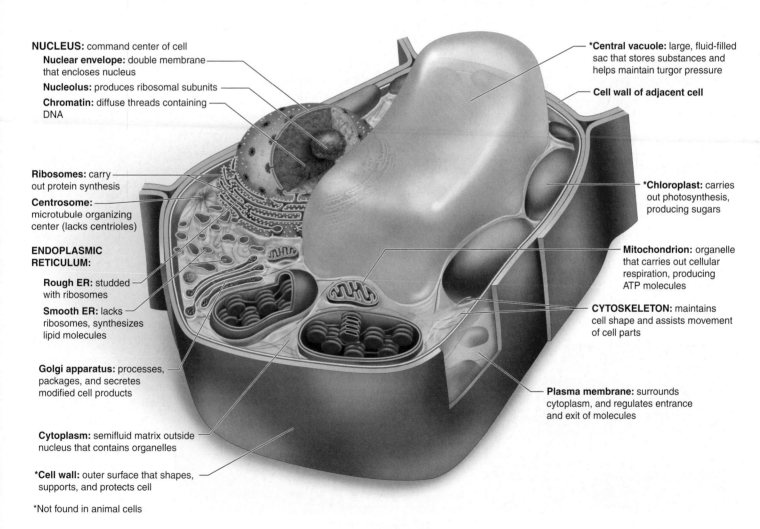

NUCLEUS: command center of cell
Nuclear envelope: double membrane that encloses nucleus
Nucleolus: produces ribosomal subunits
Chromatin: diffuse threads containing DNA

Ribosomes: carry out protein synthesis
Centrosome: microtubule organizing center (lacks centrioles)

ENDOPLASMIC RETICULUM:
Rough ER: studded with ribosomes
Smooth ER: lacks ribosomes, synthesizes lipid molecules

Golgi apparatus: processes, packages, and secretes modified cell products

Cytoplasm: semifluid matrix outside nucleus that contains organelles

*Cell wall: outer surface that shapes, supports, and protects cell

*Not found in animal cells

*Central vacuole: large, fluid-filled sac that stores substances and helps maintain turgor pressure

Cell wall of adjacent cell

*Chloroplast: carries out photosynthesis, producing sugars

Mitochondrion: organelle that carries out cellular respiration, producing ATP molecules

CYTOSKELETON: maintains cell shape and assists movement of cell parts

Plasma membrane: surrounds cytoplasm, and regulates entrance and exit of molecules

Protein Synthesis Is a Major Function of Cells

Learning Outcomes

▶ Describe the structure of the nucleus, ribosomes, endoplasmic reticulum, and Golgi apparatus. (4.5–4.8)

▶ Explain how each of these organelles participates in protein synthesis. (4.5–4.8)

This part of the chapter discusses certain organelles of eukaryotic cells, namely the nucleus, the ribosomes, the endoplasmic reticulum, and the Golgi apparatus, which are all involved in producing proteins that may serve necessary functions in the cell or may be secreted out of the cell.

4.5 The nucleus contains the cell's genetic information

The nucleus is a prominent structure, in an eukaryotic cell (**Fig. 4.5**). It generally has an oval shape and is located near the center of a cell. The nucleus contains DNA, the genetic material that is passed from cell to cell and from generation to generation. DNA dictates which proteins a cell is to synthesize and these proteins determine the cell's structure and functions; therefore, the nucleus is the command center of a cell.

At the time of cell division, DNA and proteins are organized into the several **chromosomes** of an eukaryotic cell. Following cell division, the chromosomes become extended into **chromatin,** which looks grainy, but actually is a network of fine strands. A **nucleolus** is a dark region of chromatin where the subunits of ribosomes (discussed in Section 4.6) are produced.

The nucleus is separated from the cytoplasm by a double membrane known as the **nuclear envelope.** Even so, the nucleus communicates with the cytoplasm. The nuclear envelope has **nuclear pores** of sufficient size to permit the passage of ribosomal subunits out of the nucleus into the cytoplasm, and the passage of proteins from the cytoplasm into the nucleus. High-power electron micrographs show nonmembranous components associated with the pores that form a nuclear pore complex.

▶ **4.5 Check Your Progress** Which of the photomicrographs on pages 62 and 63 are cells with nuclei? Explain.

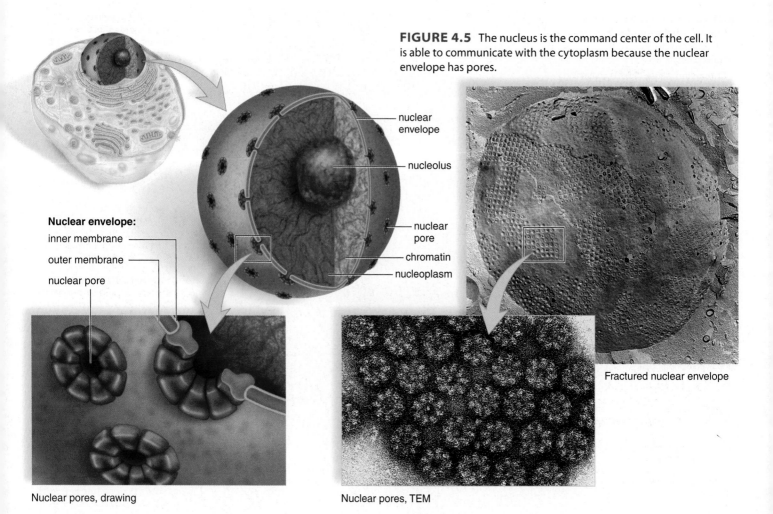

FIGURE 4.5 The nucleus is the command center of the cell. It is able to communicate with the cytoplasm because the nuclear envelope has pores.

nuclear envelope

nucleolus

nuclear pore

chromatin

nucleoplasm

Nuclear envelope:

inner membrane

outer membrane

nuclear pore

Fractured nuclear envelope

Nuclear pores, drawing

Nuclear pores, TEM

4.6 The ribosomes carry out protein synthesis

Ribosomes are non-membrane-bounded particles that are especially abundant in cells that produce plentiful proteins. When you are going to make something, you usually need a surface on which to do your work. In the same manner, a cell uses ribosomes as a workbench for producing proteins.

Ribosomes are measured in nanometers, which means they are quite small; eukaryotic ribosomes are slightly larger than those in prokaryotes. In both types of cells, ribosomes are composed of two subunits, one large and one small.

In eukaryotic cells, some ribosomes occur freely within the cytoplasm, either singly or in groups called polyribosomes. Other ribosomes are attached to the **endoplasmic reticulum (ER)**, a membranous system of flattened saccules (small sacs) and tubules, which is discussed more fully in Section 4.7.

Dressmakers usually use a pattern and directions that tell them how to make a garment. Similarly, a messenger RNA (mRNA) is a copy of a gene that tells a cell how to make the particular polypeptide of a protein at a ribosome. An mRNA leaves the nucleus by way of a nuclear pore and becomes attached to a ribosome. The mRNA copy of the gene indicates the correct sequence of amino acids for the particular polypeptide. Any slip-up in this process means the individual will have a nonworking protein and may become ill as a result!

Attachment of Ribosomes to the ER Proteins synthesized by cytoplasmic ribosomes often enter other organelles. Those synthesized by ribosomes attached to the ER end up in the interior of the ER. As shown in **Figure 4.6** ❶ after the RNA copy of the gene leaves the nucleus and enters the cytoplasm, ❷ it becomes attached to a ribosome, and polypeptide synthesis begins. ❸ The ribosome becomes attached to the ER, and the polypeptide enters the interior of the ER. ❹ The polypeptide folds into the shape of the protein inside the ER. Recall from Figure 3.10 that a protein can have up to four levels of organization. The shape of a protein is very important to its functioning appropriately.

▶ **4.6 Check Your Progress** What two functions do the nuclear pores play in protein synthesis?

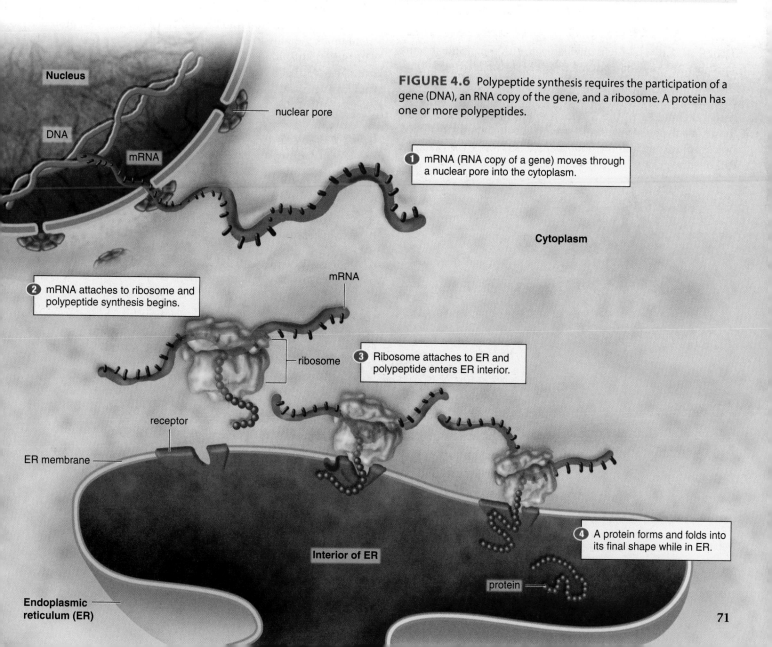

FIGURE 4.6 Polypeptide synthesis requires the participation of a gene (DNA), an RNA copy of the gene, and a ribosome. A protein has one or more polypeptides.

Nucleus

nuclear pore

DNA

mRNA

❶ mRNA (RNA copy of a gene) moves through a nuclear pore into the cytoplasm.

Cytoplasm

mRNA

❷ mRNA attaches to ribosome and polypeptide synthesis begins.

ribosome

❸ Ribosome attaches to ER and polypeptide enters ER interior.

receptor

ER membrane

❹ A protein forms and folds into its final shape while in ER.

Interior of ER

protein

Endoplasmic reticulum (ER)

4.7 The endoplasmic reticulum synthesizes and transports proteins and lipids

The term endoplasmic reticulum is a difficult one but becomes simpler if we break it down. *Endoplasmic* means "within the plasm" of the cell and *reticulum* is an elegant way of saying "network". The endoplasmic reticulum (ER) is physically continuous with the outer membrane of the nuclear envelope. It consists of membranous tubules and flattened sacs that typically account for more than half of the total membrane within an average animal cell. The membrane of the ER is continuous and encloses a single internal space. This space will be termed the interior of ER (**Fig. 4.7**). The ER twists and turns as it courses through the cytoplasm like a long snake. This structure gives the ER much more membrane than if it were simply one large sac. If you compare Figure 4.6 to Figure 4.7, you can see that Figure 4.6 shows only a small portion of the ER found in a cell.

Because many ribosomes attach themselves to the ER, it becomes the location where all the proteins are produced for the many membranes inside a eukaryotic cell as well as most of the proteins that are secreted from the cell. In humans, the protein insulin is secreted by the pancreas into the blood and then circulates about the body. Aside from proteins, the ER also produces various lipids.

Types of ER The ER is divided into the rough ER and the smooth ER. Only the **rough ER (RER)** is studded with ribosomes. The ribosomes are attached to the side of the membrane that faces the cytoplasm. Figure 4.6 shows how a polypeptide enters the interior of the ER from an attached ribosome. Once inside, a polypeptide is usually modified before it undergoes the process of folding into the final shape of a protein. For example, carbohydrate chains are often added to certain proteins.

Smooth ER (SER), which is continuous with rough ER, does not have attached ribosomes. Therefore, it has a smooth appearance in electron micrographs and more important it does not participate in polypeptide synthesis. Smooth ER is abundant in gland cells, where it synthesizes lipids of various types. For example, cells that synthesize steroid hormones from cholesterol have much SER. The SER houses the enzymes needed to make cholesterol and modify it to produce the hormones. In the liver, SER, among other functions, adds lipid to proteins, forming the lipoproteins that carry cholesterol in the blood. Also, the SER of the liver increases in quantity when a person consumes alcohol or takes barbiturates on a regular basis, because SER contains the enzymes that detoxify these molecules.

The RER and SER, working together, produce membrane, which is composed of phospholipids and various types of proteins. Because the ER produces membrane, it can form the transport vesicles by which it communicates with the Golgi apparatus. Proteins to be secreted from the cell are kept in the interior of the ER, but the ones destined to become membrane constituents become embedded in its membrane. **Transport vesicles** pinch off from the ER and carry membranes, proteins, and lipids, notably to the Golgi apparatus, where they undergo further modification. The products of the Golgi apparatus are utilized by the cell or repackaged in secretory vesicles that make their way to the plasma membrane where they are secreted (see Fig. 4.12).

▶ **4.7 Check Your Progress** Is it correct to say that *all* ribosomes reside in the cytoplasm? Explain.

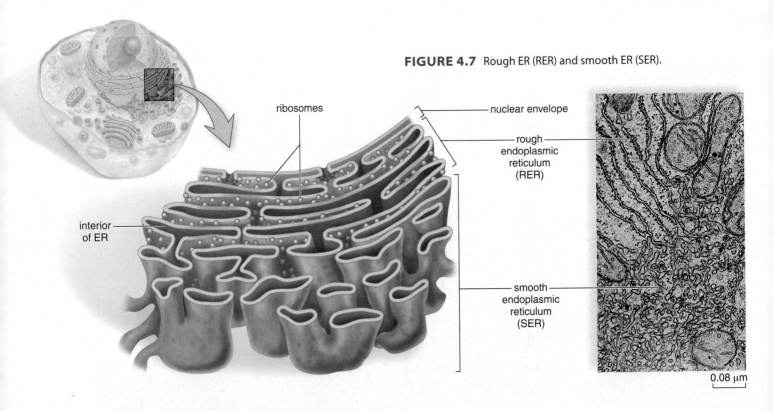

FIGURE 4.7 Rough ER (RER) and smooth ER (SER).

ribosomes

nuclear envelope

rough endoplasmic reticulum (RER)

interior of ER

smooth endoplasmic reticulum (SER)

0.08 μm

4.8 The Golgi apparatus modifies and repackages proteins for distribution

The **Golgi apparatus** is named for Camillo Golgi, who discovered its presence in cells in 1898. The Golgi apparatus, or simply the Golgi, typically consists of a stack of three to twenty slightly curved, flattened saccules whose appearance can be compared to a stack of pancakes (**Fig. 4.8**). One side of the stack is directed toward the ER, and the other side is directed toward the plasma membrane. Vesicles can frequently be seen at the edges of the saccules.

The Golgi receives, processes, and packages proteins and lipids, so that they may be sent to their final destination in the cell. In particular, it readies proteins for secretion. Protein-filled vesicles that bud from the rough ER and lipid-filled vesicles that bud from the smooth ER are received by the Golgi at its inner face. Thereafter, the Golgi alters these substances as they move through its saccules. For example, the Golgi contains enzymes that modify the carbohydrate chains first attached to proteins in the rough ER. To take an example, one sugar can be exchanged for another sugar. In some cases, the modified carbohydrate chain serves as a signal molecule that determines the protein's final destination in the cell.

The Golgi sorts and packages proteins and lipids in vesicles that depart from the outer face. In animal cells, some of these vesicles are lysosomes, which are discussed next. Secretory vesicles proceed to the plasma membrane, where they stay until a signal molecule triggers the cell to release them. Then they become part of the membrane as they discharge their contents during **secretion.** Secretion is also called *exocytosis* because the substance exits the cytoplasm.

▶ **4.8 Check Your Progress** How do proteins made by RER ribosomes become incorporated into a plasma membrane or secreted?

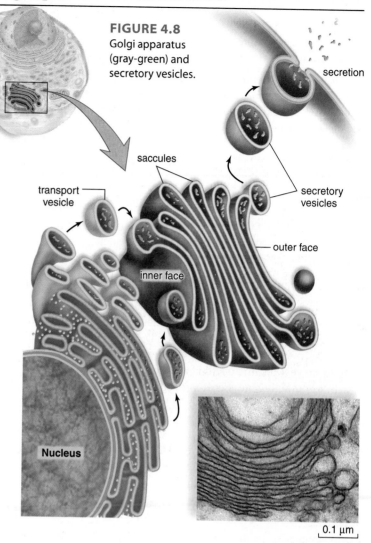

FIGURE 4.8
Golgi apparatus (gray-green) and secretory vesicles.

secretion

saccules

transport vesicle

secretory vesicles

outer face

inner face

Nucleus

0.1 μm

HOW SCIENCE PROGRESSES

Application

4B Pulse-labeling Allows Observation of the Secretory Pathway

The pathway of protein secretion was observed by George Palade and his associates using a pulse-chase technique. The rough ER was *pulse-labeled* by letting cells metabolize for a very short time with radioactive amino acids. Then the cells were given an excess of nonradioactive amino acids. This *chased* the labeled amino acids out of the ER into transport vesicles.

Electron microscopy techniques allowed these researchers to trace the fate of the labeled amino acids, as shown in **Figure 4B:** ❶ The labeled amino acids were found in the ER, then in ❷ transport vesicles, and then in ❸ the Golgi apparatus, before appearing in ❹ vesicles at the plasma membrane and finally being released.

FORM YOUR OPINION

1. Why would Palade have labeled sulfur and not carbon in the amino acids? (See Fig. 3.9A.)
2. Where else might Palade have found the labeled amino acids in the cell? (See Fig. 4.6.)

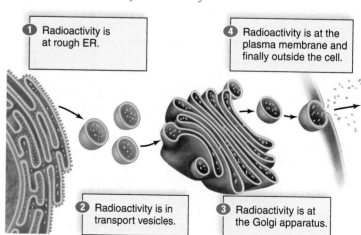

❶ Radioactivity is at rough ER.

❹ Radioactivity is at the plasma membrane and finally outside the cell.

❷ Radioactivity is in transport vesicles.

❸ Radioactivity is at the Golgi apparatus.

FIGURE 4B The secretory pathway.

Vacuoles and Vesicles Have Varied Functions

Learning Outcomes

▶ Describe the structure and function of lysosomes and peroxisomes. (4.9, 4.10)
▶ Explain the varied functions of vacuoles and vesicles in protist, plant, and animal cells. (4.11–4.12)

Cells have various membranous sacs that look the same in electron micrographs but have different functions. Lysosomes contain powerful hydrolytic enzymes that digest biomolecules, even if they form cell parts. Peroxisomes are more specialized and assist mitochondria by breaking down lipids. Some of the vacuoles in protists and plants are unique to them and not found in other eukaryotes. Vesicles allow the organelles of the endomembrane system to work together.

4.9 Lysosomes digest biomolecules and cell parts

Lysosomes are vesicles produced by the Golgi apparatus. They have a very low internal pH and contain powerful hydrolytic digestive enzymes. Lysosomes are important in recycling cellular material and digesting worn-out organelles, such as old mitochondria (**Fig. 4.9**).

Sometimes biomolecules are engulfed (brought into a cell by vesicle formation) at the plasma membrane. When a lysosome fuses with such a vesicle, its contents are digested by lysosomal enzymes into simpler subunits that then enter the cytoplasm. Some white blood cells defend the body by engulfing bacteria, which are then enclosed within vesicles. When lysosomes fuse with these vesicles, the bacteria are digested.

Lysosomal storage diseases occur when a particular lysosomal enzyme is nonfunctional. Tay Sachs disease is one such condition, in which a newborn appears healthy but then gradually becomes nonresponsive, deaf, and blind before dying within a few months. The brain cells are filled with particles containing a type of lipid that cannot be digested by lysosomes.

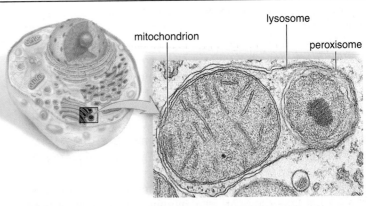

FIGURE 4.9 Lysosome fusing with and destroying spent organelles.

▶**4.9 Check Your Progress** Some white blood cells have granules, now known to be lysosomes. Why would it be beneficial for white blood cells to have lysosomes for fighting viruses and bacteria?

4.10 Peroxisomes break down long-chain fatty acids

Peroxisomes are small, membrane-bounded organelles that look very much like empty lysosomes. However, peroxisomes contain their own set of enzymes and carry out entirely different functions. Chiefly, peroxisomes bear the burden of breaking down excess quantities of long-chain fatty acids to products that can be metabolized by mitochondria for the production of ATP. In the process, they produce hydrogen peroxide (H_2O_2), a toxic molecule that is then broken down to oxygen and water.

Peroxisomes also help produce cholesterol and important phospholipids found primarily in brain and heart tissue. In germinating seeds, peroxisomes convert fatty acids and lipids to sugars. The sugars are used as a source of energy by a germinating

plant. It is fair to say that peroxisomes contribute to the energy metabolism of cells.

Normally, peroxisome size and number increase or decrease according to the needs of the cell. On rare occasions, long-chain fatty acids accumulate in cells because they are unable to enter peroxisomes for breakdown due to an inherited disorder. This leads to dramatic deterioration of the nervous system. The 1992 movie *Lorenzo's Oil* told the true story of a boy who had this condition.

▶**4.10 Check Your Progress** Why would you expect to find peroxisomes in the vicinity of mitochondria?

4.11 Vacuoles are common to plant cells

Like vesicles, **vacuoles** are membranous sacs, but vacuoles are larger than vesicles. The vacuoles of some protists are quite specialized; they include contractile vacuoles for ridding the cell of excess water and digestive vacuoles for breaking down nutrients.

Vacuoles usually store substances. Plant vacuoles contain not only water, sugars, and salts, but also water-soluble pigments and toxic molecules. The pigments are responsible for the

red, blue, or purple colors of many flowers and some leaves. The toxic substances help protect a plant from herbivorous animals.

Typically, plant cells have a large **central vacuole** that may occupy up to 90% of the volume of the cell (**Fig. 4.11**). This vacuole is filled with a watery fluid called cell sap and it gives added support to cells and in that way helps a plant stay upright, since plants don't have a bony skeleton as many animals do.

The central vacuole stores needed substances and also waste products. A system to excrete wastes never evolved in plants, most likely because their metabolism is incredibly efficient and they produce little metabolic waste. What wastes they do produce are pumped into the central vacuole and stored there permanently. As organelles age and become nonfunctional, they fuse with the vacuole, where digestive enzymes break them down. This function is carried out by lysosomes in animal cells.

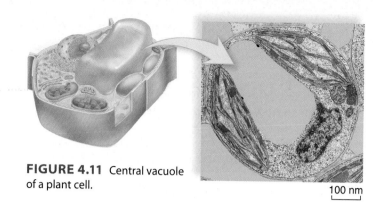

FIGURE 4.11 Central vacuole of a plant cell.

100 nm

▶ **4.11 Check Your Progress** How is the central vacuole of plant cells similar to but different from the lysosomes of animal cells?

4.12 Vesicles allow the organelles of the endomembrane system to work together

The **endomembrane system** includes various membranous organelles that work together and communicate by means of transport vesicles. It includes the endoplasmic reticulum (ER), the Golgi apparatus, lysosomes, and the transport vesicles.

Figure 4.12 shows how the components of the endomembrane system work together: ❶ Proteins, produced in the rough ER, are carried in ❷ transport vesicles to ❸ the Golgi apparatus, which sorts the proteins and packages them into vesicles that transport them to various cellular destinations.

❹ Secretory vesicles take the proteins to the plasma membrane, where they exit the cell when the vesicles fuse with the membrane. This is called secretion by exocytosis. For example, secretion into ducts occurs when the salivary glands produce

saliva or when the pancreas produces digestive enzymes. Similarly, lipids move from the smooth ER to the Golgi apparatus and can eventually be secreted.

❺ In animal cells, lysosomes produced by the Golgi apparatus ❻ fuse with incoming vesicles from the plasma membrane and digest biomolecules and debris. White blood cells are well-known for engulfing pathogens (e.g., disease-causing viruses and bacteria) that are then broken down in lysosomes.

▶ **4.12 Check Your Progress** What parts of the cell are responsible for producing and exporting the proteins found in the endomembrane system?

FIGURE 4.12 The organelles of the endomembrane system.

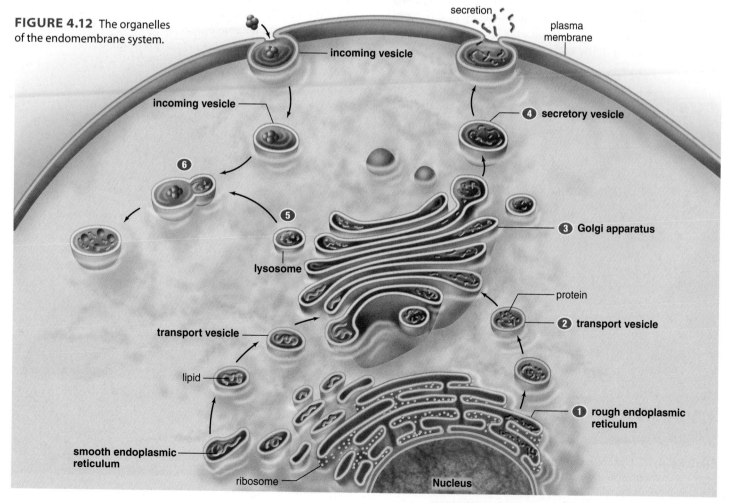

secretion

plasma membrane

incoming vesicle

incoming vesicle

❻

❹ secretory vesicle

❺

❸ Golgi apparatus

lysosome

protein

❷ transport vesicle

transport vesicle

lipid

❶ rough endoplasmic reticulum

smooth endoplasmic reticulum

ribosome

Nucleus

A Cell Carries Out Energy Transformations

Learning Outcome

▶ Compare and contrast the structure and function of chloroplasts and mitochondria. (4.13)

Chloroplasts transform solar energy into the energy of carbohydrates, which serve as organic food for themselves and all organisms in the biosphere. Mitochondria transform the energy of carbohydrates to that of ATP molecules. All cells use ATP molecules as a source of energy for metabolic reactions and processes.

4.13 Chloroplasts and mitochondria have opposite functions

We learned in Chapter 1 that all organisms must acquire energy and nutrients from their environment. Plants, however, can use solar energy and the inorganic nutrients water and carbon dioxide to make energy-rich carbohydrates during a process called photosynthesis. Carbohydrates serve as organic food for plants; therefore, we say that plants make their own food. Photosynthesis not only takes in carbon dioxide but also releases oxygen.

Plants can photosynthesize because their cells contain organelles called **chloroplasts.** Each plant cell may contain as many as 100 chloroplasts, and a square millimeter of leaf can contain up to 500,000 chloroplasts (**Fig. 4.13**). The green pigment chlorophyll as well as other pigments are responsible for the ability of chloroplasts to absorb solar energy. Within a chloroplast, chlorophyll is located in the membrane of flattened sacs called thylakoids.

Chloroplasts are of great significance to the biosphere, including humans, because they are the ultimate source of all food for living things. Consider that you either feed directly on plants or on animals that have fed on plants. Another source of food for the biosphere is carbohydrates made by cyanobacteria and algae, because they also use pigments to absorb solar energy and photosynthesize in the same manner as plants.

How would you know that chloroplasts produce carbohydrates when the sun is shining? One way is to look for starch grains to accumulate in plant cells when the sun is out. Set a plant in the dark and the starch grains disappear.

In contrast to chloroplasts, nearly all organisms and types of cells, including both plant and animal cells, contain mitochondria (Fig. 4.13). **Mitochondria** are indispensable to cells because they carry on cellular respiration, the process that transforms the energy of carbohydrates to that of ATP molecules. It's called cellular respiration because mitochondria take in oxygen and give off carbon dioxide. Because mitochondria produce ATP, they are called the powerhouse of a cell.

Cellular respiration and photosynthesis are opposite reactions:

$$\text{carbohydrate} + \text{oxygen} \rightleftharpoons \text{carbon dioxide} + \text{water} + \text{energy}$$

For cellular respiration, read left to right and replace energy with ATP. For photosynthesis, read right to left and replace energy with solar energy.

Cells use ATP, not glucose, as a direct source of metabolic energy—using a molecule of glucose would be energy-inefficient and wasteful. You use change, not a dollar bill, to buy something

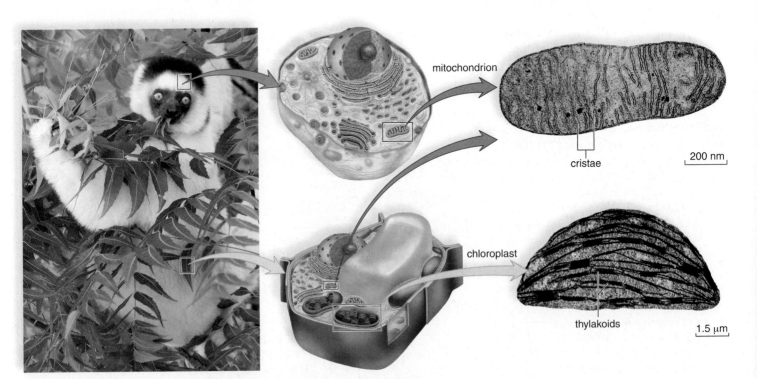

FIGURE 4.13 Plant cells carry on photosynthesis in green leaves where chloroplasts absorb solar energy because they contain the green pigment chlorophyll in thylakoid membranes. Mitochondria in plant and animal cells carry on cellular respiration, a process that produces ATP on the membranous invaginations called cristae.

that costs five cents. In the same manner, an organism converts carbohydrates to many molecules of ATP and uses them as a source of energy for individual reactions, such as linking amino acids during protein synthesis. Mitochondria are most abundant in human cells that carry out energy-intensive activities. For example, ATP provides the energy for muscle contraction and nerve conduction. Mitochondria are not as complex as chloroplasts but their inner membrane does fold back and forth, forming the cristae that act as shelves where ATP is formed. ATP exits mitochondria and enters the cytoplasm where it is utilized as an immediate energy source.

It is of great interest to scientists that both chloroplasts and mitochondria provide evidence that they were once free-living prokaryotes. For example, they have their own DNA in a nucleoid region, and they make some of their own proteins. For a more thorough discussion of this topic, see How Life Changes on this page.

▶ **4.13 Check Your Progress** In what ways are chloroplasts and mitochondria opposite, and in what ways are they similar?

HOW LIFE CHANGES

Application

4C How the Eukaryotic Cell Evolved

Life's history is written in the fossil record, which includes the remains of past life, often encased by stone (see Fig. 14A.2). The fossil record tells us that the prokaryotic cell was present about 3.5 BYA (billion years ago); the eukaryotic cell evolved in stages (**Fig. 4C**). The nuclear envelope and nucleus may have arisen around 2 BYA from an infolding of the plasma membrane, but what about the organelles such as mitochondria and chloroplasts? Much evidence supports the proposal that these organelles were once free-living prokaryotes that were either prey to or parasites of a eukaryotic cell. Their outer double membrane tells us that the eukaryotic cell engulfed them—the outer membrane is derived from the host plasma membrane, and the inner membrane was their own outer surface. By now, they are endosymbionts—organisms that live inside a host cell and are indispensable to their host, the cell that engulfed them.

Mitochondria and chloroplasts have their own DNA—circular like that of a prokaryote—and they carry on protein synthesis in the same manner as bacteria. Interestingly, chemicals that can poison and stop the metabolism in mitochondria and chloroplasts have no effect on cytoplasmic metabolism, and chemicals that poison cytoplasmic enzymes have no effect on these organelles. Then, too, they reproduce by splitting as do bacteria, and their reproduction occurs independently of host cell reproduction.

The theory of endosymbiosis explains that since all cells have mitochondria, aerobic bacteria entered the host cell first, perhaps just when oxygen began to rise in the atmosphere due to the advent of photosynthesis by free-living cyanobacteria (see page 324). A host cell with an endosymbiont that used oxygen and produced ATP molecules would have been a distinct evolutionary advantage. Later, a cyanobacterium entered certain cells, and these cells became capable of photosynthesis. Being able to make your own food does away with the need to find it elsewhere. Eventually the relationship between host cells and endosymbionts became so beneficial that by now they cannot live separately from one another!

FORM YOUR OPINION

1. Explain the phraseology "the host had an evolutionary advantage." Be sure to mention comparative number of offspring in your explanation.
2. If you compared the structure of a cyanobacterium with that of a chloroplast, what similarities would you expect to find?

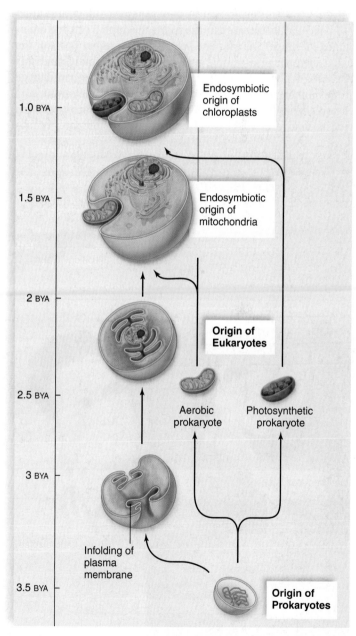

FIGURE 4C The eukaryotic cell was fully formed when a nucleated cell engulfed prokaryotes that became endosymbionts.

The Cytoskeleton Is Dynamic

Learning Outcomes

▶ Discuss the function and composition of the cytoskeleton. (4.14)
▶ Compare and contrast the structure and function of fibers making up the cytoskeleton. (4.14)
▶ Explain the structure of cilia and flagella, and give examples of their importance to the body. (4.15)

As you know, bones and muscles give an animal structure and produce movement. Similarly, the fibers of the cytoskeleton maintain cell shape and cause the cell and its organelles to move. Cilia and flagella are also instrumental in producing movement, so they are included in this part of the chapter as well.

4.14 The cytoskeleton maintains cell shape and assists movement

All eukaryotic cells have a **cytoskeleton,** a network of protein fibers within the cytoplasm. Even though both plant and animal cells have a cytoskeleton, most of our discussion pertains to an animal cell. The cytoskeleton supports the animal cell and determines its shape. Remarkably, however, the protein fibers of the cytoskeleton can assemble and disassemble rapidly, and this accounts for why the shape of some animal cells can change from moment to moment. Similarly, the cytoskeleton anchors the organelles in place but can also allow them to move, as when a vesicle moves from the Golgi to the plasma membrane. Because

the cytoskeleton has the dual function of support and movement, it is appropriately described as the "skeleton and muscles" of an animal cell.

If you could look closely at the cytoskeleton in an animal cell, you would note three types of fibers: actin filaments, intermediate filaments, and microtubules. Because you can't see these fibers with a light microscope, scientists prepare fluorescent antibodies, each of which attaches to only one type of fiber and then they photograph the cells under fluorescent light (**Fig. 4.14A**).

Much has been learned about the structure and function of each component of the cytoskeleton. The **actin filaments** are so named because they contain two twisted strands of actin, a fibrous protein. Bundles of actin filaments support the plasma membrane and other structures, such as the microvilli (short projections) of intestinal cells. However, you can primarily associate actin filaments with movement. For example, actin interacts with another protein, myosin, when muscle contraction occurs. Myosin is a motor molecule that functions just as you do when participating in a tug of war: Myosin heads attach, detach, and reattach further along the actin filament, and this pulls the actin filament along:

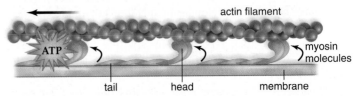

Also in conjunction with myosin, actin acts like purse strings to pinch off and separate cells during cell division. On the other hand, actin is working alone when white blood cells crawl along and their projections (called pseudopods) engulf disease-causing agents such as viruses and bacteria.

Intermediate filaments are intermediate in size between actin filaments and microtubules. Although the specific protein composition varies with the type of cell, intermediate filaments always have a ropelike structure that provides mechanical strength. Some intermediate filaments support the nuclear envelope, whereas others support the plasma membrane and take part in the formation of cell-to-cell junctions. Intermediate filaments made of the protein keratin strengthen skin cells.

Microtubules, as their name implies, are short, cylindrical structures composed of 13 rows of a protein called tubulin. Assembly is under the control of a microtubule organizing center (MTOC) located in the **centrosome** (see Fig. 4.4A). Microtubules radiate from the centrosome, helping to maintain the shape of

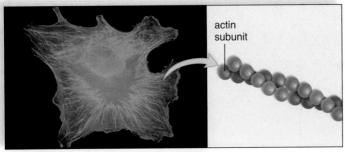

Actin filaments

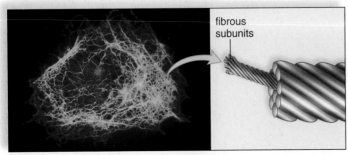

Intermediate filaments

Microtubules

FIGURE 4.14A The cytoskeleton contains these three types of fibers that support the cell.

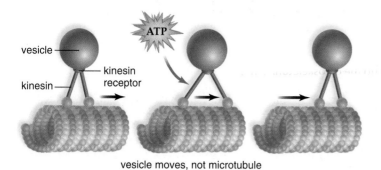

FIGURE 4.14B The motor molecule kinesin is moving a vesicle along a microtubule track.

the cell and acting as tracks along which organelles can move (**Fig. 4.14B**). The motor molecules kinesin and dynein are associated with microtubules.

Before a cell divides, microtubules disassemble and then reassemble into a structure called a spindle, which distributes chromosomes in an orderly manner. Plants have evolved various types of poisons that help prevent them from being eaten by herbivores. One of these, called colchicine, is a chemical that binds to tubulin and blocks the assembly of microtubules so that cell division is impossible.

▶ **4.14 Check Your Progress** A cell is dynamic. In general, what accounts for the ability of cell contents to move?

4.15 Cilia and flagella permit movement

Cilia and flagella (sing., cilium, flagellum) are whiplike projections of cells. **Cilia** move stiffly, like an oar, and **flagella** move in an undulating, snakelike fashion. Cilia are short (2–10 μm), and flagella are longer (usually no more than 200 μm). Unicellular protists utilize cilia or flagella to move about. In our bodies, ciliated cells are critical to respiratory health and our ability to reproduce. The ciliated cells that line our respiratory tract sweep debris trapped within mucus back up into the throat, which helps keep the lungs clean. Similarly, ciliated cells move an egg along the oviduct, where it can be fertilized by a flagellated sperm cell.

A cilium and a flagellum have the same organization of microtubules within a plasma membrane covering (**Fig. 4.15**, *right*). Attached motor molecules, powered by ATP, allow the microtubules in cilia and flagella to interact and bend, and thereby to move.

A particular genetic disorder illustrates the importance of normal cilia and flagella (**Fig. 4.15**, *left*). Some individuals have an inherited defect that leads to malformed microtubules in cilia and flagella. Not surprisingly, they suffer from recurrent and severe respiratory infections, because the ciliated cells lining their respiratory passages fail to keep their lungs clean. They are also infertile due to the lack of ciliary action to move the egg in a female, or the lack of flagellar action by sperm in a male.

FIGURE 4.15 (*right*) The presence of microtubules and motor molecules (dynein) allows a flagellum to move. (*left*) Micrograph of cilia and flagella.

Flagellated sperm in oviduct lined by ciliated cells

Centrioles Located in the centrosome, **centrioles** are short, barrel-shaped organelles composed of microtubules. It's possible that centrioles give rise to **basal bodies,** which lie at the base of and are believed to organize the microtubules in cilia and flagella. It's also possible that centrioles help organize the spindle, mentioned earlier, which is so necessary to cell division.

We have completed our study of eukaryotic organelles. In the next part of the chapter, we review how cell structures work together.

▶ **4.15 Check Your Progress** How do cilia and flagella differ in structure and movement?

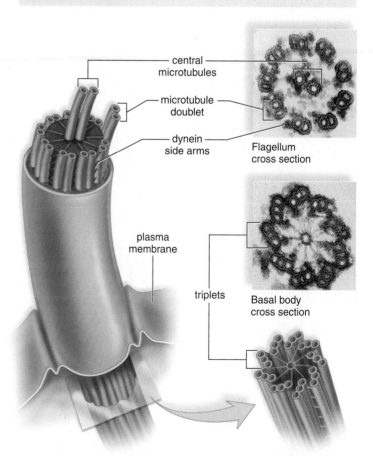

Flagellum

Basal body

Cell Structures Work Together

Learning Outcome

▶ Discuss the function of cell parts according to four categories: protein synthesis and modification; storage, transport, and digestion; energy transformations; and cell shape and movement.

Cell structures can be grouped into four categories according to their functions. Understanding how these structures function together for the benefit of the cell facilitates learning them.

TABLE 4.16	Eukaryotic Cell Structures			
Function	**Cell Structure**		**Description**	**Function**
Protein Synthesis and Modification	Nucleus		Bounded by nuclear envelope with pores; contains DNA within chromosomes and nucleolus	Acts as control center of cell; specifies protein synthesis
	Ribosomes		Small particles, each with two subunits	Are sites of protein synthesis
	Endoplasmic reticulum (ER)		Network of membranous tubules and flattened sacs	
			Rough ER: studded with ribosomes	Carries out protein synthesis and modification; forms transport vesicles
			Smooth ER: lacks ribosomes	Carries out lipid synthesis; forms transport vesicles
	Golgi apparatus		Stack of flattened saccules	Carries out processing and packaging of proteins and lipids; forms secretory vesicles
Storage, Transport, and Digestion	Vesicle		Tiny membranous sac	Stores and transports proteins and lipids
	Vacuole		Small to large membranous sac	In plants, a large vacuole stores substances including wastes
	Lysosome		A type of vesicle	Digests biomolecules and cell parts
	Peroxisome		A type of vesicle	Assists with lipid metabolism, breakdown of poisons
Energy Transformations	Chloroplast		Bounded by a double membrane	Carries on photosynthesis and produces carbohydrate
	Mitochondrion		Bounded by a double membrane; inner membrane forms cristae	Carries on cellular respiration and produces ATP molecules
Cell Shape and Movement	Plasma membrane		Phospholipid bilayer with embedded proteins	Regulates entrance and exit of molecules into and out of cell
	Cell wall		In plant cells, outer layer of cellulose	Helps maintain shape of cell, protects and supports
	Cytoskeleton		Network of protein fibers	Supports organelles, assists movement of cell and its parts
	Flagella and cilia		Microtubule-containing cellular extensions	Move the cell or move substances along its surface

SUMMARY

Cells Are the Basic Units of Life

4.1 All organisms are composed of cells

- The **cell theory** states the following:
  - A cell is the basic unit of life.
  - All living things are made up of cells.
  - New cells arise only from preexisting cells.

4.2 Metabolically active cells are small in size

- Cells must remain small in order to have an adequate **surface-area-to-volume ratio.**

4.3 Prokaryotic cells evolved first

- **Prokaryotic cells** have the following characteristics:
  - Lack a membrane-bounded nucleus; the chromosome is in a region called the **nucleoid.**
  - Have a **plasma membrane** surrounding the **cytoplasm** (semifluid interior contains **ribosomes**), which in turn is bounded by a **cell wall** and a **capsule. Pili** allow the cell to attach to solid substances.
  - Are simpler and much smaller than eukaryotic cells.
  - Are members of domains **Archaea** and **Bacteria.**

4.4 Eukaryotic cells contain specialized organelles: An overview

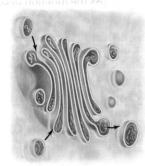

- Organisms in the domain **Eukarya,** have **eukaryotic cells** with the following characteristics:
  - A membrane-bounded **nucleus.**
  - **Organelles,** structures specialized to perform specific functions.
  - Compartmentalization through the presence of membranous organelles, allowing a eukaryotic cell to be larger than a prokaryotic cell.

Protein Synthesis Is a Major Function of Cells

4.5 The nucleus contains the cell's genetic information

- Genes, composed of DNA, are located within **chromatin** that become organized as **chromosomes** when nuclear division occurs.
- **Nuclear pores** in the **nuclear envelope** permit communication between the nucleus and the cytoplasm.
- The **nucleolus** produces ribosomal subunits.

4.6 The ribosomes carry out protein synthesis

- Ribosomes in the cytoplasm and on the **endoplasmic reticulum (ER)** synthesize proteins.
- The proteins synthesized at the ribosomes enter the interior of the ER where the protein takes on its final shape.

4.7 The endoplasmic reticulum synthesizes and transports proteins and lipids

- The ER produces proteins **(rough ER)** and lipids **(smooth ER)** that become incorporated in membrane or are secreted from the cell.
- **Transport vesicles** from the ER carry proteins and lipids to the Golgi apparatus.

4.8 The Golgi apparatus modifies and repackages proteins for distribution

- Enzymes modify carbohydrate chains attached to proteins.
- Vesicles leave the **Golgi apparatus** and travel to the plasma membrane, where **secretion** occurs.

Vacuoles and Vesicles Have Varied Functions

4.9 Lysosomes digest biomolecules and cell parts

- **Lysosomes,** which are vesicles produced by the Golgi apparatus, contain hydrolytic digestive enzymes.

4.10 Peroxisomes break down long-chain fatty acids

- **Peroxisomes,** which are vesicles resembling lysosomes, break down long-chain fatty acids.

4.11 Vacuoles are common to plant cells

- **Vacuoles,** like vesicles, are membranous sacs.
- Vacuoles are larger than vesicles and usually store substances.
- Plant cells have a large **central vacuole** that stores watery cell sap and maintains turgor pressure.

4.12 Vesicles allow the organelles of the endomembrane system to work together

- The ER, Golgi apparatus, lysosomes, and transport vesicles make up the **endomembrane system.**

A Cell Carries Out Energy Transformations

4.13 Chloroplasts and mitochondria have opposite functions

- **Chloroplasts** carry on photosynthesis and produce carbohydrates.
- In chloroplasts, thylakoids (containing chlorophyll) capture solar energy.
- **Mitochondria** carry on cellular respiration and break down carbohydrates.
- In mitochondria, the cristae produce ATP, and therefore they are the power house of the cell.

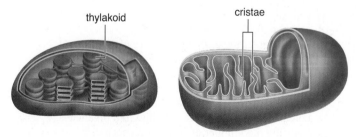

thylakoid   cristae

The Cytoskeleton Is Dynamic

4.14 The cytoskeleton maintains cell shape and assists movement

- **Actin filaments** are organized in bundles or networks.
- **Intermediate filaments** are ropelike assemblies of polypeptides.
- **Microtubules** are made of the globular protein tubulin. They act as tracks for organelle movement.

- The microtubule organizing center (MTOC) regulates microtubule assembly and is located in the **centrosome.**

4.15 Cilia and flagella permit movement
- **Cilia** (short) and **flagella** (long) are projections from the cell that allow the cell to move.
- Cilia and flagella grow from **basal bodies,** perhaps derived from **centrioles.**

Cell Structures Work Together
- See Table 4.16.

TESTING YOURSELF

Cells Are the Basic Units of Life

1. The cell theory states
   a. cells form as organelles and molecules become grouped together in an organized manner.
   b. the normal functioning of an organism depends on its individual cells.
   c. the cell is the basic unit of life.
   d. only eukaryotic organisms are made of cells.
2. When you examine a cell using a light microscope, which might you be able to see?
   a. the nucleus only
   b. the nucleus and the nucleolus
   c. the nucleus, the nucleolus, and the threads of chromatin
   d. all of these plus the DNA double helix
3. The small size of cells best correlates with
   a. their ability to reproduce.
   b. their prokaryotic versus eukaryotic nature.
   c. an adequate surface area for exchange of materials.
   d. their vast versatility.
   e. All of these are correct.
4. Which size relationship is incorrect?
   a. The Golgi apparatus is smaller than a mitochondrion.
   b. The nucleus is smaller than a chloroplast.
   c. The entire endoplasmic reticulum is larger than the cell.
   d. The area of the plasma membrane is larger than that of the cytoskeleton.
   e. All of these are incorrect.
5. Which of the following structures are found in both plant and animal cells?
   a. centrioles
   b. chloroplasts
   c. cell wall
   d. mitochondria
   e. All of these are found in both types of cells.
6. Eukaryotic cells compensate for a low surface-to-volume ratio by
   a. taking up materials from the environment more efficiently.
   b. lowering their rate of metabolism.
   c. compartmentalizing their activities into organelles.
   d. reducing the number of activities in each cell.
7. The cell wall and capsule of bacteria
   a. are located inside the plasma membrane.
   b. compensate for the lack of a plasma membrane.
   c. provide easy access to the cytoplasm.
   d. have projections called pili.
   e. Both b and c are correct.
8. **THINKING CONCEPTUALLY** What evidence would best convince you that bacteria are on your skin?

Protein Synthesis Is a Major Function of Cells

9. What is synthesized by the nucleolus?
   a. mitochondria   c. transfer RNA
   b. ribosomal subunits d. DNA
10. Ribosomes are found
    a. at the Golgi apparatus.
    b. in the cytoplasm and on the rough endoplasmic reticulum.
    c. in the nucleus and nucleolus.
    d. at the plasma membrane releasing proteins.
    e. All of these are correct.
11. The organelle that can modify a protein and determine its destination in the cell is the
    a. ribosome.   c. Golgi apparatus.
    b. vacuole.   d. lysosome.
12. Which of these is not involved in protein synthesis and secretion?
    a. smooth ER   c. plasma membrane
    b. nucleus   d. All of these are correct.
13. **THINKING CONCEPTUALLY** Communication is critical in cells. How does the nucleus communicate with the cytoplasm, and how does the rough ER communicate with the Golgi?

Vacuoles and Vesicles Have Varied Functions

14. The central vacuole of plant cells may contain
    a. flower color pigments.
    b. toxins that protect plants against herbivorous animals.
    c. sugars.
    d. All of these are correct.
15. _____ are produced by the Golgi apparatus and contain _____.
    a. Lysosomes, DNA
    b. Mitochondria, DNA
    c. Lysosomes, enzymes
    d. Nuclei, DNA
16. Vesicles from the ER most likely are on their way to
    a. the rough ER.
    b. the lysosomes.
    c. the Golgi apparatus.
    d. the plant cell vacuole only.
    e. the location suitable to their size.
17. Which organelle in the endomembrane system is incorrectly matched with its function?
    a. Nucleus—contains genetic information regarding the sequence of amino acids in proteins
    b. Transport vesicles—the way the nucleus communicates with the ER
    c. Golgi apparatus—involved in modification and packaging of proteins
    d. Lysosomes—digest biomolecules and cell parts
    e. All of these associations are correct.
18. **THINKING CONCEPTUALLY** A concept is an encompassing idea tested by the scientific method. The concept of the endomembrane system is based on what data?

A Cell Carries Out Energy Transformations

19. Mitochondria
    a. are involved in cellular respiration.
    b. break down ATP to release energy for cells.
    c. contain stacks of thylakoid membranes.
    d. are present in animal cells but not in plant cells.
    e. All of these are correct.

20. The products of photosynthesis are
    a. glucose and oxygen.
    b. oxygen and water.
    c. carbon dioxide and water.
    d. glucose and water.
21. Why are mitochondria but not chloroplasts called the powerhouses of the cell?
    a. Mitochondria form glucose, but chloroplasts break it down.
    b. Mitochondria but not chloroplasts have their own genetic material.
    c. Mitochondria but not chloroplasts capture solar energy.
    d. Mitochondria but not chloroplasts directly provide ATP to the cell.
    e. Both a and b are correct.
22. **THINKING CONCEPTUALLY** Both chloroplasts and mitochondria are critical to your existence. How so?

The Cytoskeleton Is Dynamic

23. Which of these are involved in movement of the cell or the cell contents?
    a. actin filaments   c. basal bodies
    b. microtubules   d. All of these are correct.
24. Which of these statements is not true?
    a. Actin filaments are found in muscle cells.
    b. Microtubules radiate from the ER.
    c. Intermediate filaments sometimes contain keratin.
    d. Motor molecules that are moving organelles use microtubules as tracks.
25. Plant cells lack centrioles, and this correlates with their lack of
    a. mitochondria.   c. a large central vacuole.
    b. flagella.   d. All of these are correct

Cell Structures Work Together

For questions 26–30, match the functions to the organelles in the key.

KEY:
    a. endoplasmic reticulum and Golgi apparatus
    b. peroxisomes and lysosomes
    c. chloroplast and mitochondria
    d. centrosome and microtubules
    e. nucleus and ribosomes
26. Carbohydrate metabolism resulting in ATP formation
27. Contain enzymes for breaking down substances
28. Protein formation and secretion
29. Protein production as DNA dictates
30. Movement of the cell and its parts

THINKING SCIENTIFICALLY

1. Utilizing Palade's procedure, described on page 73, you decide to label and trace the base uracil. What type of molecule are you labeling, and where do you expect to find it in Figure 4B?
2. After publishing your study from question 1, you are criticized for failing to trace uracil from mitochondria. Why might you have looked for uracil in mitochondria, and what comparative difference between the nuclear envelope and the mitochondrial double membrane might justify your study as is?

ONLINE RESOURCE

www.mhhe.com/maderconcepts2

Enhance your study with animations that bring concepts to life and practice tests to assess your understanding. Your instructor may also recommend the interactive eBook, individualized learning tools, and more.

CONNECTING THE CONCEPTS

Our knowledge of cell anatomy has been gathered by studying micrographs of cells. This has allowed cytologists (biologists who study cells) to arrive at a generalized picture of cells, such as those depicted for an animal and a plant cell in Section 4.4. Eukaryotic cells, taken as a whole, contain several types of organelles, and the learning outcomes for the chapter suggest that you should know the structure and function of each one. A concept to keep in mind is that "structure suits function." For example, ribosomal subunits move from the nucleus to the cytoplasm; therefore, it seems reasonable that the nuclear envelope has pores. Finding relationships between structure and function will give you a deeper understanding of the cell and boost your memory capabilities.

Also, realizing that the organelles work together is helpful. If you wanted to describe the involvement of cell parts to make a protein, you would start with the nucleus because chromosomes contain DNA, which specifies the order of amino acids in a particular protein. From there, you would mention the ribosomes at the rough endoplasmic reticulum (RER), transport vesicles, the Golgi apparatus, and a possible final destination for the protein. Analogies can help. For example, the endomembrane system can be compared to a post office: Proteins (the letters) are deposited into the RER (the local post office), which sends them to a Golgi (the regional sorting center) from which they are sent to their correct destinations. The pulse-labeling technique, described in Section 4B, provides evidence to support this analogy.

Table 4.16 shows you other ways to group the organelles. Lysosomes and peroxisomes are vesicles with digestive functions: Lysosomes digest various biomolecules while peroxisomes break down lipids.

The origin of the eukaryotic cell links together what you know about the structure of prokaryotic and eukaryotic cells because the endosymbiotic theory says that mitochondria and chloroplasts were once free-living prokaryotes.

In Chapter 5, we continue our general study of the cell by considering some of the functions common to all cells. For example, all cells exchange substances across the plasma membrane, and they also carry out enzymatic metabolic reactions, which either release or require energy.

PUT THE PIECES TOGETHER

1. Use the structure of the prokaryotic cell to support the endosymbiotic theory.
2. Explain how the structure of the endoplasmic reticulum suits its function.
3. Microtubules are a part of the cytoskeleton and are found in cilia and flagella. What function of the cytoskeleton is consistent with the presence of microtubules in these structures?

5

Dynamic Activities of Cells

Life's Energy Comes from the Sun

Life on Earth is dependent on a flow of energy, and this flow begins with the sun. The sun is a huge cloud of hot gases where thermonuclear reactions occur between hydrogen and helium atoms. These thermonuclear reactions are the source of the energy that supports the biosphere.

Solar radiation travels through the immense amount of space that separates us from the sun. If not for this distance, the Earth would be too hot for life to exist. Even so, every hour, more solar energy reaches the Earth than the entire world's population consumes in a year.

We all enjoy the warmth of the sun, and most solar energy does become heat that is absorbed by the Earth or reradiated back into space. Less than 1% of the solar energy that strikes the Earth is taken up by photosynthesizers, which include plants, algae, and cyanobacteria. Like all photosynthesizers, grasses have the ability to convert solar energy into the chemical energy of organic molecules. The organic molecules allow grasses to grow and serve as food for animals, such as impalas on the African plain. Food provides the building blocks and energy that impalas need just to exist. Impalas also use energy to take off at high speed when they are trying to evade a predator, such as a cheetah. Eating impalas provides cheetahs with

Hot gasses surrounding the surface of the sun

Cheetah chasing an impala

the food they need to maintain themselves and to be quick enough to catch impalas! Notice that we have just described a flow of energy that proceeds like this: from the sun, to grasses, to impalas, and finally to cheetahs.

The illustrations on this page give another example of energy flow. Do you get it? It goes like this: from the sun, to corn plants, to cattle, to humans out for a run with their dog. Your gnawing stomach makes you aware of the need to eat food every day, but you may not realize why, like all living things, humans are dependent on a constant flow of energy from the sun. The answer is: "Energy dissipates." When muscle contraction is over, energy escapes into the body of an animal and then into the environment. The heat given off when your muscles contract is put to good use. It keeps you warm, but it is no longer usable by photosynthesizers for chemical reactions. It is too diffuse. However, solar energy is concentrated enough to allow plants to keep on photosynthesizing and, in that way, provide the biosphere with organic food.

This introduction gives you an overview of how organisms use energy, the first topic we consider in this chapter. Energy is an important part of metabolism, and so are enzymes, the proteins that speed chemical reactions. Without enzymes, you would not be able to make use of energy to maintain your body and to carry on such activities as muscle contraction. Metabolism is a cellular affair, and cells can't keep on metabolizing unless substances cross the plasma membrane. Therefore, we will be considering how molecules get into and out of the many cells that make up your body.

Sunrise over a cornfield

Beef
cattle

Cheetah eating an impala

Living Things Transform Energy

Learning Outcomes

▶ Explain the difference between potential energy and kinetic energy. (5.1)
▶ State two energy laws and apply them to energy transformations. (5.2)
▶ Give reasons why ATP is called the energy currency of cells. (5.3)
▶ Give examples to show how ATP hydrolysis is coupled to energy-requiring reactions. (5.4)

Cells readily convert—that is, transform—one form of energy into another, but even so they need a continual supply of energy. Two energy laws will be used to explain this paradox. The preferred form of immediate energy in cells is ATP. ATP is called the "energy currency" of cells because when cells do any kind of work, they "spend" ATP.

5.1 Energy makes things happen

Living organisms are highly ordered, and energy is needed to maintain this order. Organisms acquire energy, store energy, and release energy, and only by transforming one form of energy into another form can organisms continue to stay alive. Despite its importance to living things and society, energy is a commodity that cannot be seen. Energy is indeed merely conceptual. Most authorities define **energy** as the capacity to do work—to make things happen.

Potential energy is stored energy of position or configuration

Kinetic energy is energy of motion

Potential energy is being converted to kinetic energy

Diving Board

FIGURE 5.1 Food has stored potential energy and a nourishing lunch supplied this diver with the chemical energy she is using to mount the steps to a diving board. Climbing steps is energy of motion or kinetic energy. At the diving board this diver possesses the stored energy of position, a form of potential energy. Potential energy is converted to kinetic energy once she dives.

There are five specific forms of energy: radiant, chemical, mechanical, electrical, and nuclear. In this book, we are particularly interested in radiant energy, chemical energy, and mechanical energy. Radiant energy, in the form of solar energy, can be captured by plants to make food for themselves and for the biosphere. Chemical energy is present in organic molecules, and therefore, food is a source of chemical energy. Food is a high-quality source of energy because the energy in it is available to do work. Mechanical energy is represented by any type of motion—the motion of a diver, as well as the motion of atoms, ions, or molecules. The latter is better known as **heat.** Heat is low-quality energy because it is too dispersed to do useful work. Usually heat is used to warm something, such as the human body, but we learned in Chapter 2 that excess heat can evaporate sweat, and in that way, lower the temperature of the body.

All the specific types of energy we have been discussing are either potential energy or kinetic energy. **Potential energy** is stored energy, and **kinetic energy** is energy in action. Potential energy is constantly being converted to kinetic energy, and vice versa.

Let's look at the example in **Figure 5.1.** The chemical energy in the food a diver had for lunch contains potential energy of configuration. Energy is in the bonds and the relationships between atoms. When the diver climbs the ladder to the diving board, the potential energy of food is converted to the kinetic energy of motion. Once she reaches the diving board, kinetic energy has been converted to the potential energy of location (greater altitude). As she makes her dive, this potential energy is converted to kinetic energy again. The diver could not continue this cycle for long without a new supply of chemical energy. Chemical energy supplies the potential energy that organisms need to stay in existence and to perform work.

Both potential and kinetic energy are important to living things because cells constantly store energy and then gradually release it to do work. To take an example, liver cells store energy as glycogen, and then they break down glycogen in order to make ATP molecules, which carry on the work of the cell.

It is important to have a way to measure energy. A **calorie** is the amount of heat required to raise the temperature of 1 g of water by 1° Celsius. This isn't much energy, so the caloric value of food is listed in nutrition labels and in diet charts in terms of **kilocalories** (1,000 calories). In this text, we use Calorie (C) to mean 1,000 calories.

▶ **5.1 Check Your Progress a.** Does ATP represent kinetic energy or potential energy? Explain. **b.** Muscle movement driven by ATP is what type of energy?

5.2 Two laws apply to energy and its use

Two laws, called the laws of thermodynamics, govern the use of energy. These laws were formulated by early researchers who studied energy relationships and exchanges. Neither nonliving nor living things can circumvent these laws.

> The first law of thermodynamics—the law of conservation of energy—states that energy cannot be created or destroyed, but it can be changed from one form to another.

Figure 5.2 shows how this law applies to living things. Grass is able to convert solar energy to chemical energy, and a horse, like all animals including humans, is able to convert chemical energy into the energy of motion. However, notice that with every energy transformation, some energy is lost as heat. The word "lost" recognizes that when energy has become heat, it is no longer usable to perform work.

> The second law of thermodynamics states that energy cannot be changed from one form to another without a loss of usable energy.

Let's look at Figure 5.2 in a bit more detail. When grass photosynthesizes, it uses solar energy to form carbohydrate molecules from carbon dioxide and water. (Carbohydrates are energy-rich molecules, while carbon dioxide and water are energy-poor molecules.) Not all of the captured solar energy becomes carbohydrates; some becomes heat:

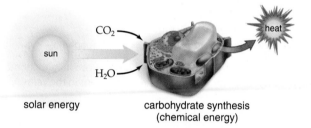

solar energy   carbohydrate synthesis
(chemical energy)

Plant cells do not create or destroy energy in this process—the sun is the energy source, and the unusable heat is still a form of energy. Similarly, as a horse uses the energy derived from carbohydrates to power its muscles, none is destroyed, but some becomes heat, which dissipates into the environment:

carbohydrate   muscle contraction
(chemical energy)   (mechanical energy)

With transformation upon transformation, eventually all of the captured solar energy becomes heat that is lost to the environment. Therefore, we say that energy flows through living things and does not cycle. Therefore, all living things are dependent on a constant supply of solar energy because photosynthesizers use solar energy to synthesize organic molecules.

The second law of thermodynamics tells us that as energy conversions occur, disorder increases because it is difficult to use heat to perform more work. The word **entropy** is often used to describe this disorder. Energy transformations can occur, but they always increase entropy because no conversion of energy is ever 100% efficient. For example, the gasoline engine in an automobile is between 20% and 30% efficient in converting chemical energy into mechanical energy. The majority of energy is lost as heat. Cells are capable of about 40% efficiency, with the remaining energy given off to the surroundings as heat.

▶ **5.2 Check Your Progress** If you take a walk on the beach with your dog, does entropy increase? Explain.

FIGURE 5.2 The grass converts solar energy to the chemical energy of nutrient molecules. The horse converts a portion of this chemical energy to the mechanical energy of motion. Eventually, all solar energy absorbed by the plant dissipates as heat. (This is an Icelandic horse, native to Iceland.)

5.3 Cellular work is powered by ATP

Many of the appliances in your kitchen, such as the dishwasher, stove, and refrigerator, are powered by electricity. Cells, as mentioned earlier, use ATP (adenosine triphosphate) to power reactions. ATP is often called the energy currency of cells. Just as you use cash to purchase all sorts of products, a cell uses ATP to carry out nearly all of its activities, including synthesizing biomolecules, transporting ions across plasma membranes, and causing organelles and cilia to move.

ATP is a nucleotide, the type of molecule that serves as a monomer for the construction of DNA and RNA. Its name, adenosine triphosphate, means that it contains the sugar ribose, the nitrogen-containing base adenine, and three phosphate groups (**Fig. 5.3A**). The three phosphate groups are negatively charged and repel one another. It takes energy to overcome their repulsion, and thus these phosphate groups make the molecule unstable.

ATP easily loses the last phosphate group because the breakdown products, ADP (adenosine diphosphate) and a separate phosphate group symbolized as P, are more stable than ATP. This reaction is written as: ATP⟶ADP + P. ADP can also lose a phosphate group to become AMP (adenosine monophosphate).

The continual breakdown and regeneration of ATP is known as the ATP cycle (Fig. 5.3A). As soon as ATP forms, it is used in a reaction that requires energy. Then ATP is rebuilt from ADP + P. Each ATP molecule undergoes about 10,000 cycles of synthesis and breakdown every day. Our bodies use some 40 kg (about 88 lb) of ATP daily, and the amount on hand at any one moment is sufficiently high to meet only current metabolic needs.

ATP's instability, the very feature that makes it an effective energy donor, keeps it from being an energy-storage molecule. Instead, the many H—C bonds of carbohydrates and fats make them the energy-storage molecules of choice. Their energy is extracted during cellular respiration and used to rebuild ATP, mostly within mitochondria. Cellular respiration, during which glucose is broken down, is called an **exergonic reaction** because this process gives up energy. In other words, energy *exits* from cellular respiration and is used to build up ATP. However, only 40% of the potential energy of glucose is converted to the potential energy of ATP; the rest is lost as heat. The production of ATP is still worthwhile for the following reasons:

1. ATP is suitable for use in many different types of cellular reactions that only occur if energy is supplied. Such reactions are called **endergonic reactions.** In other words, energy must *enter* in order for these reactions to occur.

2. When ATP becomes ADP + P, the amount of energy released is more than the amount needed for a biological purpose, but not overly wasteful. Section 5.4 explains how cells capture the energy of ATP breakdown to perform work.

Figure 5.3B Illustrates how exergonic reactions can drive endergonic reactions so that energy can be capture for a particular purpose. To bring about a structure such as a building or an organism, energy must be capture.

> **5.3 Check Your Progress** Humans store little ATP, but they can work for an entire day. Why?

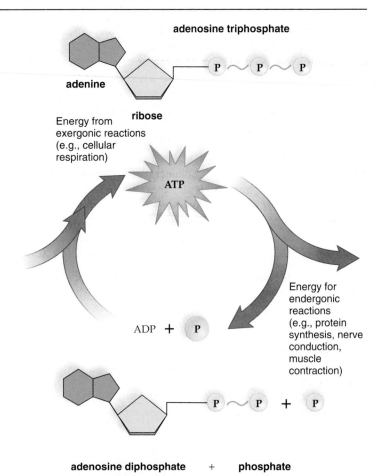

FIGURE 5.3A ATP cycle. First, ATP is produced in mitochondria, and then it is used for energy-requiring reactions in the cell.

FIGURE 5.3B This person is working and releasing energy (exergonic) and constructing a building which is energy requiring (endergonic). Similarly there are also exergonic and endergonic reactions.

5.4 ATP breakdown is coupled to energy-requiring reactions

How can the energy released by ATP hydrolysis be transferred to a reaction that requires energy so that the reaction will occur? In other words, how does ATP act as a carrier of chemical energy? The answer is that ATP breakdown is coupled to the energy-requiring reaction. **Coupled reactions** are reactions that occur in the same place, at the same time, and in such a way that an energy-releasing (exergonic) reaction drives an energy-requiring (endergonic) reaction. Usually the energy-releasing reaction is the hydrolysis of ATP. Because the cleavage of ATP's phosphate group releases more energy than the amount consumed by the energy-requiring reaction, entropy increases, and both reactions proceed. The simplest way to represent a coupled reaction is like this:

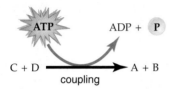

This reaction tells you that coupling occurs, but it does not show how coupling is achieved. A cell has two main ways to couple ATP hydrolysis to an energy-requiring reaction: ATP is used to energize a reactant, or ATP is used to change the shape of a reactant. Both can be achieved by transferring a phosphate group to the reactant.

For example, when iodine collects inside a thyroid cell, ATP is hydrolyzed, and instead of the last phosphate group floating away, an enzyme attaches it to a protein. This causes the protein to undergo a change in shape that allows it to move more iodine into the cell. As a contrasting example, when a polypeptide is synthesized at a ribosome, an enzyme transfers a phosphate group from ATP to each amino acid in turn, and this transfer supplies the energy that allows an amino acid to bond with another amino acid.

Figure 5.4 shows how ATP hydrolysis provides the necessary energy for muscle contraction. During muscle contraction, myosin filaments pull actin filaments to the center of the cell, and the muscle shortens. ❶ A myosin head at the end of a filament combines with ATP (three connected green triangles) and takes on its resting shape. ❷ When the ATP breaks down to ADP (two green triangles) plus Ⓟ, the myosin head attaches to actin. ❸ The release of ADP plus Ⓟ from the myosin head causes it to change shape and pull on the actin filament. The cycle begins again at ❶, when a myosin head combines with ATP and takes on its resting shape once more. During this cycle, chemical energy has been transformed to mechanical energy, and entropy has increased.

Through coupled reactions, ATP drives forward energetically unfavorable processes that must occur if the high degree of order essential for life is maintained. Biomolecules must be made and organized to form cells and tissues; the internal composition of the cell and the organism must be sustained; and movement of cellular organelles and the organism must occur if life is to continue.

This completes our discussion of energy transformations in cells. In the next part of the chapter, we will study metabolism in general.

▶ **5.4 Check Your Progress** The ability of impalas to dash across the African plain obeys the second law of thermodynamics. How so?

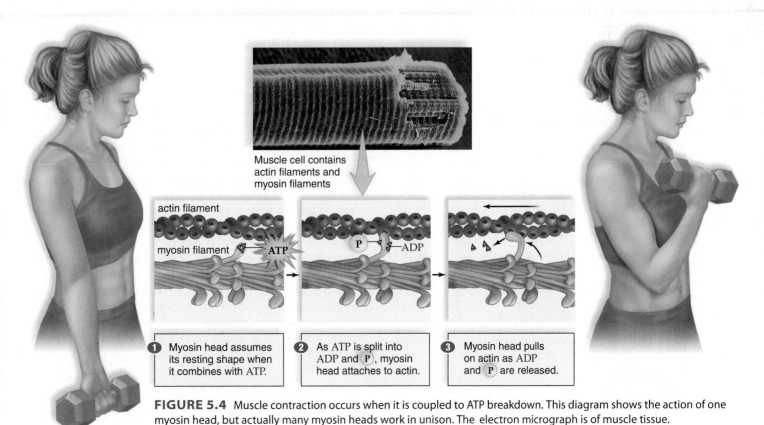

Muscle cell contains actin filaments and myosin filaments

actin filament

myosin filament — ATP

P — ADP

❶ Myosin head assumes its resting shape when it combines with ATP.

❷ As ATP is split into ADP and Ⓟ, myosin head attaches to actin.

❸ Myosin head pulls on actin as ADP and Ⓟ are released.

FIGURE 5.4 Muscle contraction occurs when it is coupled to ATP breakdown. This diagram shows the action of one myosin head, but actually many myosin heads work in unison. The electron micrograph is of muscle tissue.

Enzymes Speed Chemical Reactions

Learning Outcomes

▶ Explain how enzymes speed chemical reactions. (5.5)
▶ List conditions that affect enzyme speed. (5.6)
▶ Explain two ways an inhibitor of enzymes can function. (5.7)

The metabolism of a cell is governed by the enzymes present, because few reactions occur in a cell unless an enzyme is present. Enzymes lower the energy of activation by bringing specific reactants together in a way that causes them to react. Therefore, the study of metabolism involves a study of enzymes and how their activity is regulated by local conditions and by the influence of inhibitors.

5.5 Enzymes speed reactions by lowering activation barriers

The food on your dinner plate doesn't break down into nutrient molecules until it enters your digestive tract, where it encounters enzymes. An **enzyme** is typically a protein molecule that functions as an organic catalyst to speed a chemical reaction without itself being affected by the reaction. Just like your digestive tract, cells contain many types of enzymes. Regardless of where they are, enzymes cause reactions to occur. However, enzymes can only speed reactions that would occur anyway, not energetically unfavorable reactions.

Imagine the graph in **Figure 5.5A** as a roller coaster ride. To get the ride started, you have to push the car (the reactants) to the top of an incline. Then, just as the car will naturally fall, the reaction will occur. In the lab, heat is often used to increase the effective collisions between molecules so that the reaction can occur. When an enzyme is present, the **energy of activation** (E_a) is lower than it would be without the enzyme.

Enzymes lower the energy of activation by bringing reactants together in an effective way *at body temperature*. Each enzyme is specific to the reaction it speeds. That is why a cell needs so many different enzymes. The reactants in an enzymatic reaction are called the enzyme's **substrate(s)**. Substrates are specific to a particular enzyme because they bind with an enzyme, forming an enzyme-substrate complex. Only one small part of the enzyme, called the **active site**, binds with the substrate(s) to form an enzyme-substrate

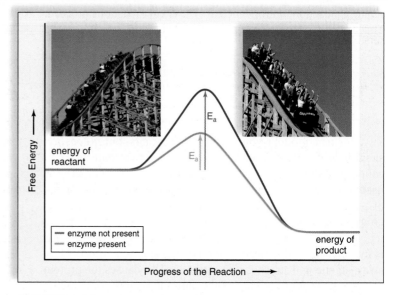

FIGURE 5.5A The energy of activation (E_a) (as when a roller coaster rises) allows the reaction to take place (roller coaster descends).

complex. In (**Fig. 5.5B**) the enzyme is digesting a polypeptide to dipeptides, the product. This reaction can symbolized as:

$$\underset{\text{enzyme}}{E} + \underset{\text{substrate}}{S} \longrightarrow \underset{\substack{\text{enzyme-substrate} \\ \text{complex}}}{ES} + \underset{\text{enzyme}}{E} + \underset{\text{product}}{P}$$

At one time, biologists thought that an enzyme and a substrate fit together like a key fits a lock, but now we know that the active site undergoes a slight change in shape to accommodate the substrate(s). This is called the **induced fit model** because the enzyme is induced to undergo a slight alteration to achieve optimum fit. The change in shape of the active site facilitates the reaction that now occurs. After the reaction has been completed, the product is released, and the active site returns to its original state, ready to bind to another substrate molecule. A cell needs only a small amount of enzyme because enzymes are not used up by the reaction; instead, they are used over and over again.

Some enzymes do more than simply bind with their substrate(s); they participate in the reaction. For example, trypsin digests protein by breaking peptide bonds. The active site of trypsin contains three amino acids with *R* groups that actually interact with members of the peptide bond—first to break the bond and then to introduce the components of water.

▶ **5.5 Check Your Progress** Every enzyme has an active site. How does the active site of one enzyme differ from another?

FIGURE 5.5B An enzyme is not altered by the reaction it speeds.

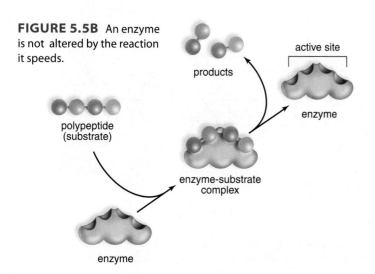

5.6 Enzyme speed is affected by local conditions

The rate of a reaction is the amount of product produced per unit time. Generally, enzymes work quickly, and in some instances they can increase the reaction rate more than 10 million times. To achieve the maximum rate, enough substrate should be available to fill the active sites of all enzyme molecules most of the time. Increasing the amount of substrate, and providing an adequate temperature and optimal pH, also increase the rate of an enzymatic reaction.

Substrate Concentration Molecules must come together in order to react. Generally, enzyme activity increases as substrate concentration increases because there are more chance encounters between substrate molecules and the enzyme. As more substrate molecules fill active sites, more product results per unit time. But when the enzyme's active sites are filled almost continuously with substrate, the enzyme's rate of activity cannot increase any more. Maximum rate has been reached.

Just as the amount of substrate can increase or limit the rate of an enzymatic reaction, so the amount of active enzyme can also increase or limit the rate of an enzymatic reaction.

Temperature Typically, as temperature rises, enzyme activity increases (**Fig. 5.6A**). This occurs because warmer temperatures cause more effective encounters between enzyme and substrate.

The body temperature of an animal seems to affect whether it is normally active or inactive. It has been suggested that the often cold temperature of a reptile's body (**Fig. 5.6B**) hinders metabolic reactions and may account for why mammals are more prevalent today. The generally warm temperature of a mammal's body (**Fig. 5.6C**) allows its enzymes to work at a rapid rate despite a cold outside temperature.

In the laboratory, if the temperature rises beyond a certain point, enzyme activity eventually levels out and then declines rapidly because the enzyme has been **denatured.** An enzyme's shape changes during denaturation, and then it can no longer bind its substrate(s) efficiently. Nevertheless, some prokaryotes can live in hot springs because their enzymes do not denature.

pH Each enzyme also has an optimal pH at which the rate of the reaction is highest. At this pH value, these enzymes have their normal configurations. The globular structure of an enzyme is dependent on interactions, such as hydrogen bonding, between R groups.

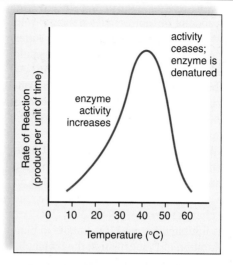

FIGURE 5.6A
Temperature affects the rate of an enzymatic reaction.

A change in pH can alter the ionization of these side chains and disrupt normal interactions; under extreme conditions of pH, denaturation eventually occurs. Again, the enzyme's shape has been altered so that it is unable to combine efficiently with its substrate.

Cofactors Many enzymes require the presence of an inorganic ion, or a nonprotein organic molecule, in order to be active; these necessary ions or molecules are called **cofactors.** The inorganic ions are metals such as copper, zinc, or iron. The nonprotein organic molecules are called **coenzymes.** These cofactors assist the enzyme and may even accept or contribute atoms to the reactions.

Vitamins are relatively small organic molecules that are required in trace amounts in the diets of humans and other animals for synthesis of coenzymes. The vitamin becomes part of a coenzyme's molecular structure. If a vitamin is not available, enzymatic activity decreases, and the result is a vitamin-deficiency disorder. For example, niacin deficiency results in a skin disease called pellagra, and riboflavin deficiency results in cracks at the corners of the mouth.

Inhibitors, discussed in Section 5.7, reduce the amount of product produced by an enzyme per unit time.

▶ **5.6 Check Your Progress** A pH of 1–2 is optimal for pepsin, a digestive enzyme. But like all human enzymes, pepsin works best at body temperature. Explain.

FIGURE 5.6B If body temperature tends to be cold, as in reptiles, reaction rates are slow.

FIGURE 5.6C If body temperature tends to be warm, as in mammals, reaction rates increase.

5.7 Enzymes can be inhibited noncompetitively and competitively

Figure 5.7 shows that reactions do not occur haphazardly in cells; they are usually part of ❶ a **metabolic pathway,** a series of linked reactions. Enzyme inhibition occurs when a molecule (the inhibitor) binds to an enzyme and decreases its activity. As shown, the inhibitor can be the end product of a metabolic pathway. This is beneficial because once sufficient end product of a metabolic pathway is present, it is best to inhibit further production to conserve raw materials and energy.

❷ Figure 5.7 also illustrates **noncompetitive inhibition** because the inhibitor (F, the end product) binds to the enzyme E_1 at a location other than the active site. The site is called an allosteric site. When an inhibitor is at the allosteric site, the active site of the enzyme changes shape.

❸ The enzyme E_1 is inhibited because it is unable to bind to A, its substrate. The inhibition of E_1 means that the metabolic pathway is inhibited and no more end product will be produced.

In contrast to noncompetitive inhibition, **competitive inhibition** occurs when an inhibitor and the substrate compete for the active site of an enzyme. Product forms only when the substrate, not the inhibitor, is at the active site. In this way, the amount of product is regulated.

Normally, enzyme inhibition is reversible, and the enzyme is not damaged by being inhibited. When enzyme inhibition is irreversible, the inhibitor permanently inactivates or destroys an enzyme. As discussed in How Biology Impacts Our Lives on this page, many metabolic poisons are irreversible enzyme inhibitors.

▶ **5.7 Check Your Progress** Enzyme inhibition can be dangerous, and yet it is used in the cell to regulate enzymes. Explain.

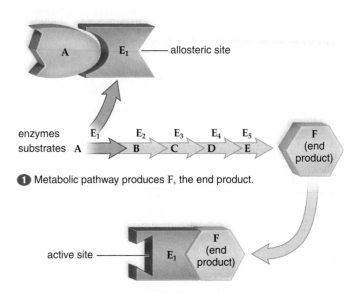

❶ Metabolic pathway produces F, the end product.

❷ F binds to allosteric site and the active site of E_1 changes shape.

❸ A cannot bind to E_1; the enzyme has been inhibited by F.

FIGURE 5.7 Metabolic pathways and noncompetitive inhibition. In the pathway, A–E are substrates, E_1–E_5 are enzymes, and F is the end product of the pathway.

HOW BIOLOGY IMPACTS OUR LIVES *Application*

5A Enzyme Inhibitors Can Spell Death

Cyanide gas was formerly used to execute people. How did it work? Cyanide can be fatal because it binds to a mitochondrial enzyme necessary for the production of ATP. MPTP (1-methyl-4-phenyl-1,2,3.6-tetrahydropyridine) is another enzyme inhibitor that stops mitochondria from producing ATP. The toxic nature of MPTP was discovered in the early 1980s, when a group of intravenous drug users in California suddenly developed symptoms of Parkinson disease, including uncontrollable tremors and rigidity. All of the drug users had injected a synthetic form of heroin that was contaminated with MPTP. Parkinson disease is characterized by the death of brain cells, the very ones that are also destroyed by MPTP.

Sarin is a chemical that inhibits an enzyme at neuromuscular junctions, where nerves stimulate muscles. When the enzyme is inhibited, the signal for muscle contraction cannot be turned off, so the muscles are unable to relax and become paralyzed. Sarin can be fatal if the muscles needed for breathing become paralyzed. In 1995, terrorists released sarin gas on a subway in Japan. Although many people developed symptoms, only 17 died (**Fig. 5A**).

A fungus that contaminates and causes spoilage of sweet clover produces a chemical called warfarin. Cattle that eat the spoiled feed

die from internal bleeding because warfarin inhibits a crucial enzyme for blood clotting. Today, warfarin is widely used as a rat poison. Unfortunately, it is not uncommon for warfarin to be mistakenly eaten by pets and even very small children, with tragic results.

Many people are prescribed a medicine called Coumadin to prevent inappropriate blood clotting. For example, those who have received an artificial heart valve need such a medication. Coumadin contains a nonlethal dose of warfarin.

FORM YOUR OPINION

1. Should all poisons be banned, or are they a necessary evil?
2. Should countries have poison detectors to warn people of a biological attack before they get sick? Why or why not?

FIGURE 5A The aftermath when sarin, a nerve gas that results in the inability to breathe, was released by terrorists in a Japanese subway in 1995.

The Plasma Membrane Has Many and Various Functions

Learning Outcomes

▶ Describe the structure of a plasma membrane in terms of the fluid-mosaic model. (5.8)

▶ List six types of proteins in the plasma membrane and discuss their functions. (5.9)

In this part of chapter, we will study the structure of the plasma membrane and the functions of the many types of proteins found within it. The plasma membrane is not a passive boundary for the cell. Rather, it has many varied functions that are often dependent on the many proteins present in the membrane.

5.8 The plasma membrane is a phospholipid bilayer with embedded proteins

The plasma membrane marks the boundary between the outside and the inside of a cell. Its integrity and function are necessary to the life of the cell. Not only does it serve as the boundary of the cell, but it also regulates the passage of molecules into and out of the cell, and it allows the cell to communicate with its neighbors.

In both bacteria and eukaryotes, the plasma membrane is a **phospholipid bilayer** that has the consistency of olive oil. Recall that the polar head of a phospholipid is hydrophilic, while the nonpolar tails are hydrophobic. The polar heads of the phospholipids face toward the outside of the cell and toward the inside of the cell, where there is a watery medium. The nonpolar tails face inward toward each other, where there is no water.

The membrane contains embedded proteins that lie within it and peripheral proteins that lie along the inside. The embedded proteins have a hydrophobic region within the membrane and hydrophilic regions that extend beyond the surface of the membrane. The presence of these regions prevents embedded proteins from flipping, but they can move laterally.

The **fluid-mosaic model** states that the protein molecules embedded in the membrane have a pattern (form a mosaic) within the fluid phospholipid bilayer (**Fig. 5.8**). The pattern varies according to the particular membrane and also within the same membrane at different times. **Cholesterol** molecules are steroids that lend support to the membrane; other steroids perform this function in the plasma membranes of plants.

Both phospholipids and proteins can have attached carbohydrate (sugar) chains. Molecules carrying such chains are called **glycolipids** and **glycoproteins,** respectively. Since the carbohydrate chains occur only on the outside surface, and since peripheral proteins occur only on the inner surface of the membrane, the two sides of the membrane are not identical.

In animal cells, the carbohydrate chains project into the extracellular matrix (ECM) shown and discussed in Section 5.13. The ECM protects the cell and has various other functions. For example, it facilitates adhesion between cells and the reception of signaling molecules that influence the behavior of the cell.

▶ **5.8 Check Your Progress** A mosaic floor is made of small tiles of different colors, cemented in place. How is the structure of the plasma membrane similar to, but different from, a mosaic floor?

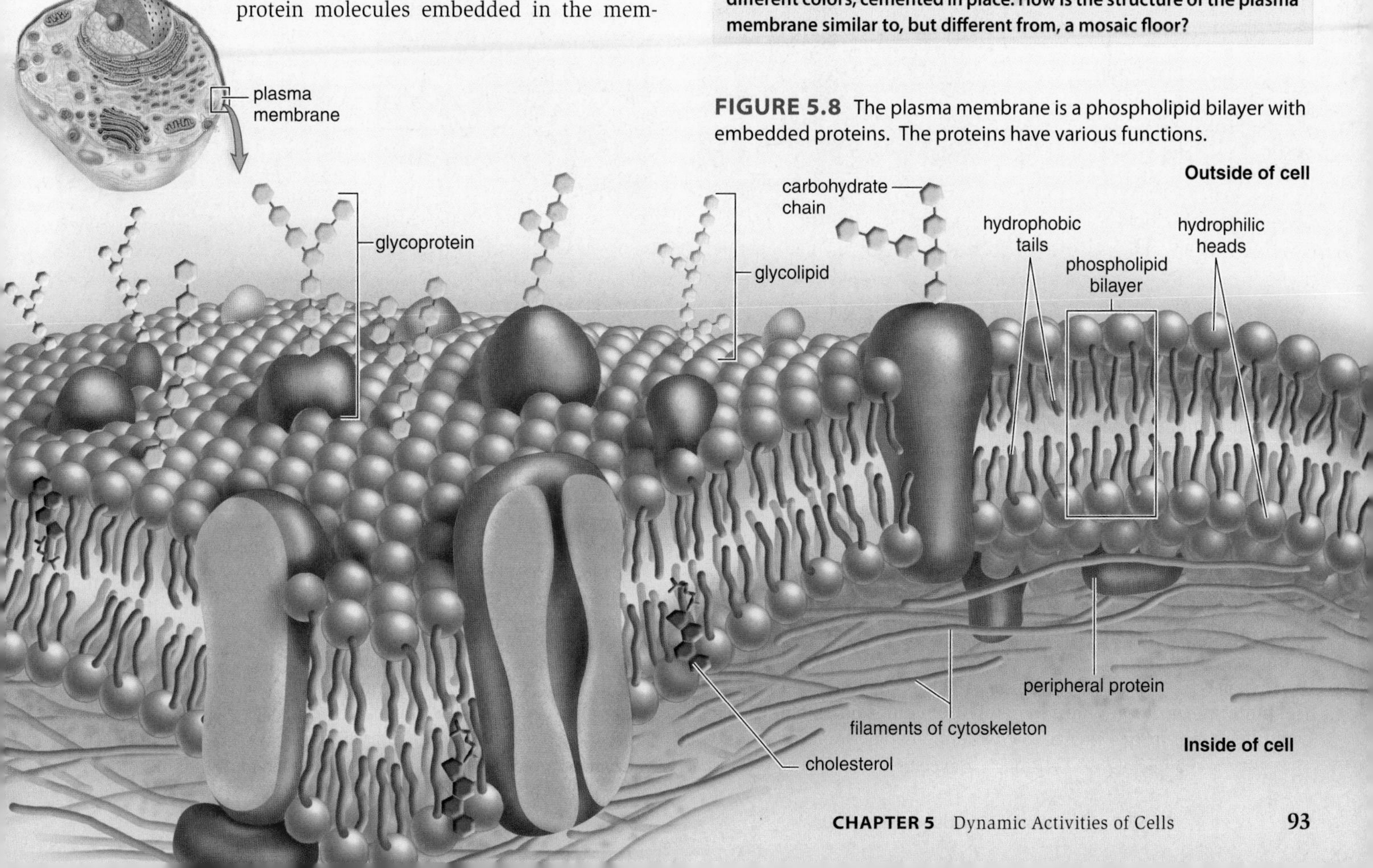

FIGURE 5.8 The plasma membrane is a phospholipid bilayer with embedded proteins. The proteins have various functions.

plasma membrane

Outside of cell

carbohydrate chain

hydrophobic tails

hydrophilic heads

glycoprotein

glycolipid

phospholipid bilayer

peripheral protein

filaments of cytoskeleton

cholesterol

Inside of cell

5.9 Proteins in the plasma membrane have numerous functions

The plasma membranes of different cells and the membranes of various organelles each have their own particular collections of these specific types of embedded proteins. The six types of embedded proteins described here and depicted in **Figure 5.9** help a membrane fulfill its functions. Decide whether each of these proteins helps the membrane regulate the passage of molecules into and out of the cell or helps the cell communicate with its environment and/or its neighbors:

Channel proteins Channel proteins have a channel that, when open, allows molecules to simply move across the membrane. For example, a channel protein allows hydrogen ions to flow across the inner mitochondrial membrane. Without this movement of hydrogen ions, ATP would never be produced.

Carrier proteins Carrier proteins are different from channel proteins because they combine with a substance and help it move across the membrane. For example, a carrier protein transports sodium and potassium ions across a nerve cell membrane. Without this carrier protein, nerve conduction would be impossible.

Cell recognition proteins Cell recognition proteins are glycoproteins. Foreign cells bear their own glycoproteins that enable the immune system to recognize them and mount a defense. Without this recognition, harmful organisms (pathogens) would be able to freely invade the body.

Receptor proteins Receptor proteins have a binding site for a specific molecule. The binding of this molecule causes the protein to change its shape and, thereby, bring about a cellular response. The coordination of the body's organs is totally dependent on signaling molecules that bind to receptors. For example, the liver stores glucose after it is signaled to do so by insulin.

Enzymatic proteins Some plasma membrane proteins are enzymatic proteins that carry out metabolic reactions directly. Without the presence of enzymes, some of which are attached to the various membranes of the cell, a cell would never be able to perform the metabolic reactions necessary for its proper function.

Junction proteins As discussed in Section 5.13, proteins are also involved in forming various types of junctions between cells. The junctions assist cell-to-cell communication.

▶ **5.9 Check Your Progress** Which types of plasma membrane proteins are directly involved in allowing substances to enter or exit the cell?

FIGURE 5.9 The proteins in a membrane have many varied functions.

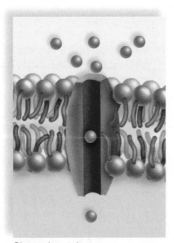
Channel protein

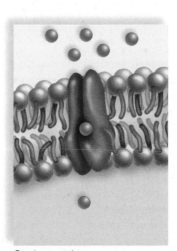
Carrier protein

Cell recognition protein

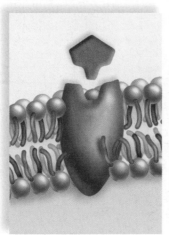
Receptor protein

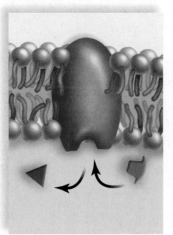
Enzymatic protein

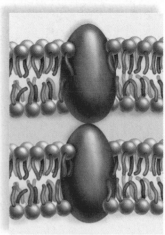
Junction proteins

Suppose you went to the doctor for a particular medical condition. Would you expect to hear that your condition was due to your plasma membrane? That is what might happen with certain illnesses. Take diabetes type 2, for example.

Diabetes Type 2

The typical diabetes type 2 patient is somewhat, or even grossly, overweight. The symptoms include unusual hunger and/or thirst, excessive fatigue, blurred vision, sores that do not heal, and frequent urination, especially at night. The doctor does a urinalysis and finds sugar in the urine, and yet the blood test shows insulin in the blood. Usually when we eat sugar, the pancreas, a gland that lies near the stomach, releases the hormone insulin into the bloodstream, and it travels to the cells, where it binds to its receptor protein. The binding of insulin signals a cell to send carrier proteins to the plasma membrane that will transport glucose into the cells. In the case of diabetes type 2, the insulin binds to its receptor protein, but the number of carrier proteins sent to the plasma membrane for glucose is not enough. The result is too much glucose in the blood, which spills over into the urine.

Patients can prevent, or at least control, diabetes type 2 by switching to a healthy diet and engaging in daily exercise. In addition to the symptoms mentioned, diabetics are at risk for blindness, kidney disease, and cardiovascular disease.

Color Blindness

If you have ever found yourself accidentally wearing socks of two different colors, you may have endured a little teasing about being color blind. Color vision is dependent on the action of cone cells present in the retina, the part of the eye that allows us to see. People with normal color vision have three types of cones: blue, green, and red, each activated by different wavelengths of visible light. The perception of color requires activation of a combination of these three types of cone cells.

When a cone cell receives the wavelength of light to which its particular photopigment is sensitive, a signal is sent to close sodium ion channels in its plasma membrane. However, some people, mostly males, have inherited a mutation that results in a lack of functional red or green photopigment proteins and therefore an inability to close sodium ion channels in the plasma membrane. Such individuals have what is termed "red-green color blindness" and have difficulty distinguishing these two colors. In a much less common situation, both red and green photopigments are missing; such people may lack all color vision and see a monochromatic world.

Cystic Fibrosis (CF)

The typical CF patient is a child, usually younger than three years of age, who has experienced repeated lung infections or poor growth. The doctor orders a test that measures the amount of salt (NaCl) in the child's sweat, because children with CF have more salt in their sweat than normal children. Usually, chloride ions (Cl^-) pass easily through a plasma membrane channel protein, but when their passage is not properly regulated, a thick mucus appears in the lungs and pancreas (**Fig. 5B***a*). The mucus clogs

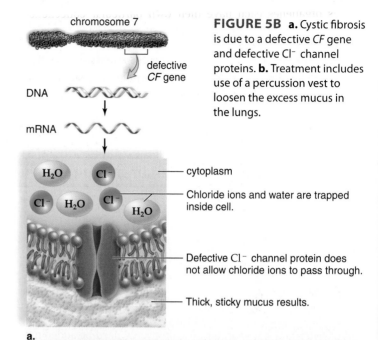

FIGURE 5B a. Cystic fibrosis is due to a defective *CF* gene and defective Cl^- channel proteins. **b.** Treatment includes use of a percussion vest to loosen the excess mucus in the lungs.

chromosome 7

defective *CF* gene

DNA

mRNA

H_2O Cl^-

Cl^- H_2O Cl^-

H_2O

— cytoplasm

— Chloride ions and water are trapped inside cell.

— Defective Cl^- channel protein does not allow chloride ions to pass through.

— Thick, sticky mucus results.

a.

b.

the lungs, causing breathing problems. It also provides fertile ground for bacterial growth. The result is frequent lung infections, which eventually damage the lungs and contribute to an early death. Also, thick digestive fluids may clog ducts leading from the pancreas to the small intestine. This prevents enzymes from reaching the small intestine, where they are needed to digest food. Digestive problems and slow growth result. Various treatments have been devised to extend the lives of CF patients (Fig. 5B*b*).

CF can be confirmed by doing a genetic test for the gene that causes CF. Genetic defects result in a defective protein—in this instance, an abnormal channel protein for chloride in the plasma membrane.

FORM YOUR OPINION

1. How can you convince people that they can prevent diabetes type 2 with good nutrition and exercise?
2. Should textbooks use strong contrasts in color—even ones jarring to other people—because color-blind individuals cannot otherwise see a contrast?

The Plasma Membrane Regulates the Passage of Molecules Into and Out of Cells

Learning Outcomes

▶ Compare and contrast passive ways (energy not required) and active ways (energy required) for substances to cross the plasma membrane. (5.10–5.12)

▶ Predict the effect of osmotic conditions on animal versus plant cells. (5.10)

The plasma membrane is **differentially permeable,** meaning that only certain substances can freely diffuse across the membrane and others cannot. For the latter, a transporter and/or energy are involved (**Table 5.10**). Facilitated diffusion moves substances toward a lower concentration, a transporter is required but no energy. Active transport moves substances toward a higher concentration and both a transporter and energy are required. Bulk transport which moves substances by vesicle formation is not affected by concentration gradients.

5.10 Diffusion across a membrane requires no energy

During **diffusion,** a molecule moves from a high concentration to a low concentration until it is distributed equally. In other words, the molecule follows its **concentration gradient** until the gradient disappears. Diffusion is a physical process that can be observed with any type of molecule, any place. For example, if you release a perfume in one corner of a room, the scent spreads out into all corners by diffusion.

Diffusion occurs because molecules are in motion, and it is a *passive* form of transport because no energy need be added for it to happen. Diffusion can take place across a membrane if the substance is able to cross the membrane. In **Figure 5.10A,** a red dye is added to water on one side of the membrane. The dye particles are able to cross the membrane, and while they move in both directions, the net movement is toward the opposite side of the membrane (long arrow). Eventually, the dye is dispersed, with no net movement of dye in either direction.

Very few molecules can simply diffuse through the hydrophobic portion of the plasma membrane. Alcohols, being lipid soluble, can diffuse across, and so can gases such as oxygen (O_2) and carbon dioxide (CO_2). Diffusion allows O_2 to enter the blood from the air sacs of the lungs, and CO_2 to move in the opposite direction. No energy is required because the gases are simply following their concentration gradient. Similarly, cellular respiration in cells sets up favorable concentrations for gas exchange to occur by diffusion.

Facilitated Diffusion Certain molecules (e.g., water, glucose, and amino acids) and ions (Na^+, Cl^-, Ca^{2+}) cross plasma membranes at a rate faster than expected based on their size and polarity because their passage is facilitated. **Facilitated diffusion**

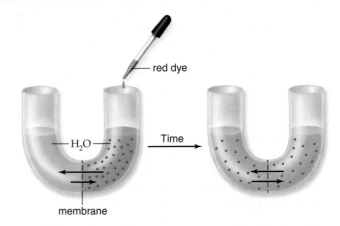

FIGURE 5.10A Some molecules can move freely by simply diffusing across a membrane.

(also called facilitated transport) requires a transporter but no energy because the molecule or ion is moving down its concentration gradient in the same direction it would tend to move anyway. The transporter can be a carrier protein or a channel protein, but each is *specific* because it assists the passage of only its own particular substance.

A carrier protein is slower acting than a channel protein because it combines with a molecule and then deposits it on the other side (**Fig. 5.10B**). A carrier protein is highly specific, and the abundance of glucose transporters accounts for why glucose can cross the membrane hundreds of times faster than other sugars of the same size and polarity. After a carrier has assisted

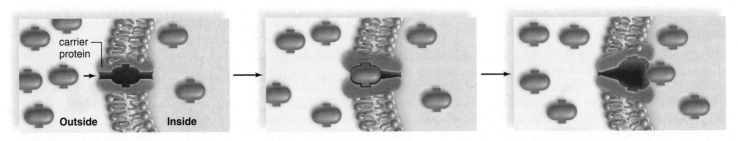

FIGURE 5.10B During this type of facilitated diffusion, a carrier protein combines with and assists solute movement across the membrane.

the movement of its molecule to the other side of the membrane, it is free to assist the passage of another one.

Channel proteins allow ions and water to enter a cell if they are open (see Fig. 5.9). Channel proteins open when they are signaled to do so by an external or internal signal. As discussed in "Malfunctioning Plasma Membrane Proteins" on page 95, cystic fibrosis is due to the inability of a Cl⁻ channel to open. A channel protein is faster acting than a carrier protein because the substance simply flows through it. Thousands of millions of water molecules per second pass through a single channel protein, named an **aquaporin** because of its specificity.

Osmosis The diffusion of water across the plasma membrane due to concentration differences is called **osmosis.** When osmosis occurs, the solute is unable to cross the plasma membrane whereas water, the solvent, is able to freely cross the membrane. Which way the water moves is dependent on the solute versus water concentration on both sides of the membrane. In the laboratory, cells are normally placed in **isotonic solutions** (*iso,* same as) in which the cell neither gains nor loses water because the concentration of solute versus water is the same on both sides of the membrane (**Fig. 5.10C**). In medical settings, a 0.9% solution of sodium chloride (NaCl) is known to be isotonic to red blood cells; therefore, intravenous solutions usually have this concentration.

Cells placed in a **hypotonic** (*hypo,* less than) **solution** cause the cell to gain water. Outside the cell, the concentration of solute is less, and the concentration of water is greater, than inside the cell. Animal cells placed in a hypotonic solution expand and sometimes burst. The term *lysis* refers to disrupted cells; *hemolysis,* then, is disruption of red blood cells (*hemo,* blood). Organisms that live in fresh water have to prevent their internal environment from gaining too much water. Many protozoans, such as paramecia, have contractile vacuoles that rid the body of excess water. Freshwater fishes excrete a large volume of dilute urine and take in salts at their gills, ensuring that their internal fluids don't become hypotonic to their cells.

When a plant cell is placed in a hypotonic solution, the large central vacuole gains water, and the plasma membrane pushes against the rigid cell wall as the plant cell becomes *turgid.* The plant cell does not burst because the cell wall does not give way. **Turgor pressure** in plant cells is extremely important in maintaining the plant's erect position. If you forget to water your plants, they wilt due to decreased turgor pressure.

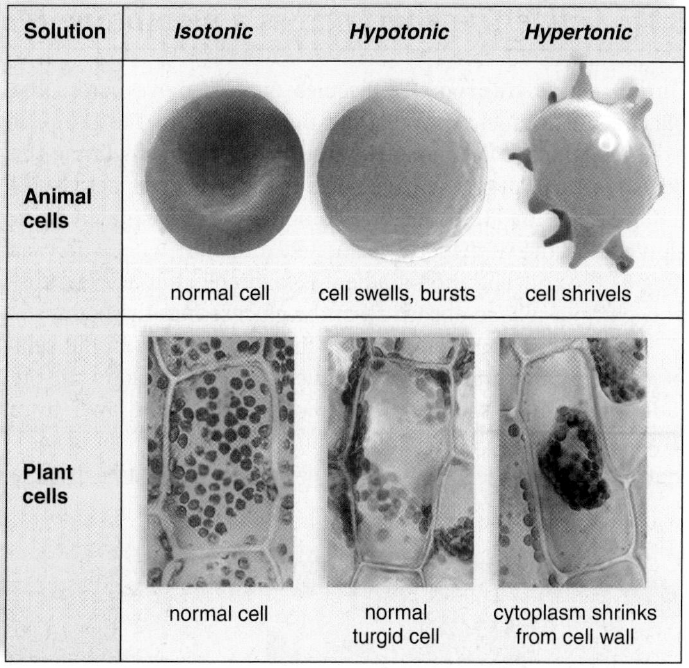

Solution	*Isotonic*	*Hypotonic*	*Hypertonic*
Animal cells	normal cell	cell swells, bursts	cell shrivels
Plant cells	normal cell	normal turgid cell	cytoplasm shrinks from cell wall

FIGURE 5.10C When cells are in an isotonic solution, they remain normal. When cells are in a hypotonic solution, they gain water, and when they are in a hypertonic solution, they lose water to the environment.

Cells placed in a **hypertonic** (*hyper,* more than) **solution** lose water. Outside the cell, the concentration of solute is more, and the concentration of water is less, than inside the cell. Animal cells placed in a hypertonic solution shrink. Marine fishes prevent their internal environment from becoming hypertonic to their cells by excreting salts across their gills. Hypertonicity can be put to good use. For example, meats are sometimes preserved by being salted. Bacteria are killed, not by the salt, but by the lack of water in the meat.

When a plant cell is placed in a hypertonic solution, the plasma membrane pulls away from the cell wall as the large central vacuole loses water. This is an example of *plasmolysis,* shrinking of the cytoplasm due to osmosis.

▶ **5.10 Check Your Progress** Why will letting a dishcloth dry out help disinfect it?

TABLE 5.10		Passage of Molecules Into and Out of the Cell		
	Name	**Direction**	**Requirements**	**Examples**
Energy Not Required	Diffusion	Toward lower concentration	No transporter, no energy	Lipid-soluble molecules, and gases
	Facilitated diffusion	Toward lower concentration	Transporter, no energy	Some sugars, amino acids
Energy Required	Active transport	Toward higher concentration	Transporter, energy	Sugars, amino acids, ions
	Bulk transport		Vesicle formation	Macromolecules

5.11 Active transport across a membrane requires a transporter and energy

During **active transport,** molecules or ions move across the plasma membrane, accumulating on one side of the cell. For example, glucose is completely absorbed by the cells lining the digestive tract after you have eaten. Glucose moves across the lining of the small intestine by a combination of facilitated diffusion and active transport. Facilitated diffusion works only as long as the concentration gradient is favorable, but active transport permits cells to absorb all of the glucose into the body.

Most of the iodine that enters the body collects in the cells of the thyroid gland for the production of a hormone. In the kidneys, sodium can be almost completely withdrawn from urine by cells lining the kidney tubules. The movement of molecules against their concentration gradients requires both a carrier protein and ATP (**Fig. 5.11**). Therefore, cells involved in active transport, such as kidney cells, have a large number of mitochondria near their plasma membranes to generate ATP.

Proteins engaged in active transport are often called *pumps.* The **sodium-potassium pump,** vitally important to nerve function, undergoes a change in shape when it combines with ATP, and this allows it to combine alternately with sodium ions and potassium ions to move them across the membrane.

▶ **5.11 Check Your Progress** How is a carrier protein for active transport like a turnstile that allows people to move into an area after they have paid?

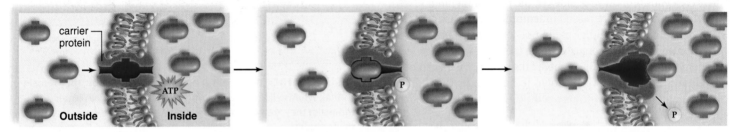

FIGURE 5.11 During active transport, a protein carrier assists solute movement toward a higher concentration, and energy is required.

5.12 Bulk transport involves the use of vesicles

Bulk transport occurs when fluid or particles are brought into a cell by vesicle formation, called **endocytosis** (**Fig. 5.12**), or out of a cell by evagination, called **exocytosis.** To imagine exocytosis, reverse the arrows in Figure 5.12.

Macromolecules, such as polypeptides, polysaccharides, or polynucleotides, are too large to be moved by carrier proteins. Instead, endocytosis takes them into a cell, and exocytosis takes them out. If the material taken in is large, such as a food particle or another cell, the process is called **phagocytosis.** Phagocytosis is common in unicellular organisms, such as amoebas. It also occurs in humans. Certain types of human white blood cells are amoeboid—that is, they are mobile like an amoeba, and are able to engulf debris such as worn-out red blood cells or bacteria. When an endocytic vesicle fuses with a lysosome in the cell, digestion occurs (see Fig. 4.9).

Pinocytosis occurs when vesicles form around a liquid or around very small particles. Cells that use pinocytosis to ingest substances include white blood cells, cells that line the kidney tubules and the intestinal wall, and plant root cells.

During **receptor-mediated endocytosis,** receptors for particular substances are found at one location in the plasma membrane. This location is called a coated pit because there is a layer of protein on its intracellular side. Receptor-mediated endocytosis is selective and much more efficient than ordinary pinocytosis. It is involved when substances move from maternal blood into fetal blood at the placenta, for example.

In contrast to endocytosis, digestive enzymes and hormones are transported out of the cell by exocytosis. In cells that synthesize

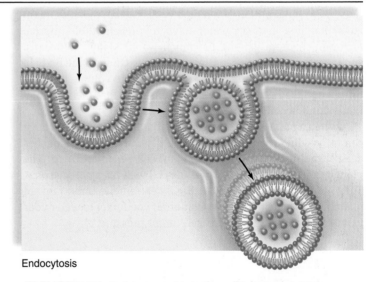

Endocytosis

FIGURE 5.12 Bulk transport into the cell is by endocytosis.

these products, secretory vesicles accumulate near the plasma membrane. The vesicles release their contents only when the cell is stimulated by a signal received at the plasma membrane, a process called regulated secretion.

▶ **5.12 Check Your Progress** Receptor-mediated endocytosis allows cholesterol to enter cells (along with the lipoprotein that transports cholesterol in the blood). If the receptor is faulty, cardiovascular disease results. Why?

18. **THINKING CONCEPTUALLY** Human blood always has a greater concentration of solutes than does tissue fluid. Why is that important to blood's transport function?

For questions 19–22, match the items to the transport methods in the key. Each question may have more than one answer.

KEY:
   a. simple diffusion
   b. facilitated diffusion
   c. osmosis
   d. active transport

19. Movement of molecules, from high concentration to low concentration.
20. Requires a membrane.
21. Requires energy input.
22. Requires a transporter.

In Multicellular Organisms, Cells Communicate

23. Which type of junction holds neighboring cells together so tightly that fluids cannot pass between them?
   a. anchoring   c. plasmodesmata
   b. gap   d. tight
24. Communication between cells often involves
   a. cell signaling.
   b. a transduction pathway.
   c. only enzymes and energy.
   d. the passage of molecules by channel proteins.
   e. Both a and b are correct.

CONNECTING THE CONCEPTS

Energy is the ability to do work, to bring about change, and to make things happen, whether it's a leaf growing or a human running. A cell is dynamic because it carries out enzymatic reactions, many of which release or require energy. Exchanges across the plasma membrane allow the cell to continue to perform its usual reactions. Few reactions occur in a cell without the presence of an enzyme because enzymes lower the energy of activation by bringing substrates together. Enzymes are proteins, and as such they are sensitive to environmental conditions, including pH, temperature, and any inhibitors present. In a cell, noncompetitive inhibition regulates the activity of an enzyme.

ATP, the universal energy "currency" of life, makes energy-requiring (endergonic) reactions go. Most often in cells, the exergonic breakdown of carbohydrates drives the buildup of ATP molecules. The metabolic pathways inside cells use the chemical energy of ATP to synthesize molecules, to cause muscle contraction, and even to allow you to read these words.

The plasma membrane is quite appropriately called the gatekeeper of the cell because its numerous proteins allow certain substances to enter or exit. Also, its glycoproteins and glycolipids mark the cell as belonging to the organism. In a person who has diabetes, cystic fibrosis, or high cholesterol, knowing that the plasma membrane within a cell is malfunctioning is a first step toward curing the condition.

Multicellular organisms require mechanisms to join their cells and allow them to communicate. The plasma membrane excretes materials that support cells and also function in cell-to-cell communication.

In Chapter 6, we will see how photosynthesis inside chloroplasts transforms solar energy into the chemical energy of carbohydrates. Then, in Chapter 7, we will discuss how carbohydrate products are broken down in mitochondria as ATP is built up. Chloroplasts and mitochondria are the cellular organelles that permit energy to flow from the sun through all living things.

PUT THE PIECES TOGETHER

1. How does enzyme structure result in a lowering of activation barriers?
2. In a cell, what environmental conditions must be met for an endergonic reaction such as polypeptide synthesis to occur?
3. Which types of proteins in the plasma membrane are involved in cell-to-cell communication?

6

Pathways of Photosynthesis

CHAPTER OUTLINE

Color It Green

It's easy to show that plants do not use green light for photosynthesis. Simply put a sprig of the plant elodea in a glass jar, fill it with water (elodea lives in water), and shine a green light on it. NOTHING HAPPENS. But switch to a bright white light, and watch the bubbling. Bubbling is caused by oxygen gas escaping from the water. That's your evidence that photosynthesis is occurring. Plants always give off oxygen when they photosynthesize, for which we humans are mightily thankful.

White light, the visible light that shines down on us every day, contains different colors of light, from violet to blue, green, yellow, orange, and finally red. Plants use all the colors except green—and that's why we see them as green! Red algae are protists that live in the ocean, and like all the other types of algae, they photosynthesize. Despite their name, some forms of red algae are

dark-colored, almost black, which means that they are able to use all the different colors in white light for photosynthesis. Does this mean that if plants weren't so wasteful and used green light for photosynthesis, in addition to all the other colors, they would appear black to us? Yes, it does. Look out the window and imagine that all the plants you see are black instead of green. Aren't we glad that photosynthesis on land is inefficient and wasteful of green light, making our world a sea of green!

How did it happen that plants do not use green light for photosynthesis? During the evolution of organisms, photosynthesizing bacteria floating in the oceans above the sediments possessed a pigment that could absorb and use green light. Natural selection, therefore, favored the evolution of a pigment that absorbed only blue and red light. The green pigment chlorophyll, which absorbs the blue and red ranges of light, evolved and became the

photosynthetic pigment of plants. The inefficiency of chlorophyll doesn't matter on land, where light is readily available, so no plants on land ever evolved a more efficient pigment than chlorophyll. Plants are green and our world is beautiful because their primary photosynthetic pigment doesn't absorb green light!

Green leaves and variously colored eukaryotic algae carry on photosynthesis in chloroplasts, as discussed in this chapter. Photosynthesis, which produces food in the form of a carbohydrate and also oxygen for the biosphere, consists of two connected types of metabolic pathways: the light reactions and the Calvin cycle reactions. We will see how the absorption of solar energy during the light reactions drives the Calvin cycle reactions, that produce a carbohydrate, the end product of photosynthesis. This chapter also shows that the process of photosynthesis is adapted to different environmental conditions.

Photosynthesis Produces Food and Releases Oxygen

Learning Outcomes

▶ List the types of organisms that carry on photosynthesis. (6.1)
▶ Identify the main parts of a chloroplast, a eukaryotic organelle. (6.2)
▶ Write a redox equation for photosynthesis that shows both the reactants and the products. (6.3)
▶ Divide photosynthesis into two sets of reactions—one set that captures solar energy and the other that reduces carbon dioxide. (6.3)

Photosynthesizers not only produce food for the biosphere, but they are also the source of the fossil fuel our society burns to maintain its standard of living. The overall equation for photosynthesis shows the starting reactants and the end products. But we will see that, in actuality, photosynthesis requires two metabolic pathways: the light reactions that occur in thylakoid membranes and the Calvin cycle reactions that occur in the stroma of a chloroplast.

6.1 Photosynthesizers are autotrophs that produce their own food

Photosynthesis converts solar energy into the chemical energy of a carbohydrate. Photosynthetic organisms, including plants, algae, and cyanobacteria, are called **autotrophs** because they produce their own organic food (**Fig. 6.1**). Photosynthesis produces an enormous amount of carbohydrate. So much that, if it could be instantly converted to coal and the coal loaded into standard railroad cars (each car holding about 50 tons), the photosynthesizers of the biosphere would fill more than 100 cars with coal *per second.*

No wonder photosynthetic organisms are able to sustain themselves and all other living things on Earth. With few exceptions, it is possible to trace any food chain back to plants and algae. In other words, producers, which have the ability to synthesize carbohydrates, feed not only themselves but also consumers, which must take in preformed organic molecules.

Collectively, consumers are called **heterotrophs.** Both autotrophs and heterotrophs use organic molecules produced by photosynthesis as a source of building blocks for growth and repair and as a source of chemical energy for cellular work.

Our analogy about photosynthetic products becoming coal is apt because the bodies of many ancient plants became the coal we burn today. This process began several hundred million years ago, and that is why coal is called a fossil fuel. Today we use coal in large part to produce electricity. In the future, it's possible not only agricultural crops (e.g., corn), but also grasses, algae, and wastes, such as wood chips, will be used to produce biofuels (alcohols, methane, or diesel gas) and these will run power plants or your car.

▶ **6.1 Check Your Progress** It might seem as if plants are self-sustainable, as long as solar energy is available. Why?

FIGURE 6.1 Photosynthetic organisms include cyanobacteria, algae, and plants.

Euglena, a protist

kelp, a protist

trees, deciduous and evergreen

Gloeocapsa, a cyanobacterium   diatom, a protist

sunflower, a garden plant

moss, a plant

6.2 In eukaryotes, chloroplasts carry out photosynthesis

Chloroplasts occur in algae and plants. Photosynthesis takes place in the green portions of plants, particularly the leaves (**Fig. 6.2**). ❶ The leaves of a plant contain mesophyll tissue in which cells are specialized for photosynthesis. The raw materials for photosynthesis are water and carbon dioxide. The roots of a plant absorb water, which then moves in vascular tissue up the stem to a leaf where it is distributed by way of ❷ the leaf veins. ❸ Carbon dioxide in the air enters a leaf through small openings called **stomata** (sing., stoma).

After entering a leaf cell, carbon dioxide and water diffuse into **chloroplasts,** the organelles that carry on photosynthesis. ❹ A double membrane surrounds a chloroplast and its fluid-filled interior, called the ❺ **stroma.** A different membrane system within the stroma forms flattened sacs called **thylakoids,** which in some places are stacked to form ❻ **grana** (sing., granum), so called because they looked like piles of seeds to early microscopists.

❼ The space of each thylakoid is thought to be connected to the space of every other thylakoid within a chloroplast, thereby forming an inner compartment within chloroplasts called the thylakoid space. The thylakoid membrane contains **chlorophyll** and other pigments that are capable of absorbing solar energy. This is the energy that drives photosynthesis. The stroma contains a metabolic pathway where carbon dioxide is first attached to an organic compound and then converted to a carbohydrate. Therefore, it is proper to associate the absorption of solar energy with the thylakoid membranes making up the grana and to associate the conversion of carbon dioxide to a carbohydrate with the stroma of a chloroplast.

Human beings, and indeed nearly all organisms, release carbon dioxide into the air. This is some of the same carbon dioxide that enters a leaf through the stomata and is converted to a carbohydrate. Carbohydrate, in the form of glucose, is the chief energy source for most organisms.

▶ **6.2 Check Your Progress** Which part of a chloroplast absorbs solar energy? Explain. Which part forms a carbohydrate? Explain.

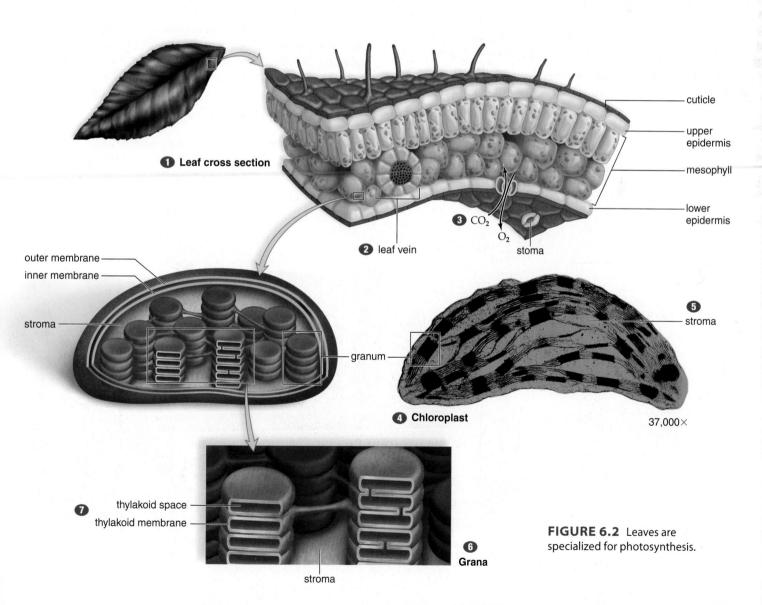

❶ **Leaf cross section**

cuticle

upper epidermis

mesophyll

lower epidermis

❸ CO_2

O_2

stoma

❷ leaf vein

outer membrane
inner membrane

stroma

granum

❺ stroma

❹ **Chloroplast**

37,000×

❼ thylakoid space
thylakoid membrane

stroma

❻ **Grana**

FIGURE 6.2 Leaves are specialized for photosynthesis.

6.3 Photosynthesis involves two sets of reactions: the light reactions and the Calvin cycle reactions

During photosynthesis, hydrogen atoms are transferred from water to carbon dioxide with the release of O_2 and the formation of glucose:

$$CO_2 + H_2O \xrightarrow[\text{Oxidation}]{\substack{\text{Reduction} \\ \text{solar energy}}} (CH_2O) + O_2$$

In chemistry, **oxidation** is the loss of electrons, and **reduction** is the gain of electrons. In cells, oxidation is instead the loss of hydrogen atoms, and reduction is the gain of hydrogen atoms. This difference is easily explained because a hydrogen atom contains one electron and one hydrogen ion ($e^- + H^+$); when a molecule loses a hydrogen atom, it has lost an electron, and when a molecule gains a hydrogen atom, it has gained an electron. Therefore, photosynthesis is indeed an oxidation-reduction, usually shortened to a **redox reaction.**

Even though we often use the overall reaction for photosynthesis, researchers have known for some time that photosynthesis involves two sets of reactions. These two sets of reactions can be associated with the two parts of a chloroplast—namely, the stacks of thylakoids (grana) and the stroma, as shown in **Figure 6.3.**

Light Reactions The **light reactions** (sometimes called the light-dependent reactions) are so named because they only occur when solar energy is available (during the daylight hours). At that time, the chlorophyll molecules and other pigment molecules located within the thylakoid membranes absorb solar energy and use it to energize electrons taken from water, which splits, releasing oxygen:

$$H_2O \longrightarrow e^- + 2H^+ + \tfrac{1}{2} O_2$$

The energy of these electrons empowered by the sun is captured and later used for ATP production.

Energized electrons are also taken up by a coenzyme called $NADP^+$ (nicotinamide adenine dinucleotide phosphate). After $NADP^+$ accepts electrons, it combines with an H^+ derived from water. The reaction that reduces $NADP^+$ is:

$$NADP^+ + 2\ e^- + H^+ \longrightarrow NADPH$$

The lower set of red arrows in Figure 6.3 show that the NADPH and ATP produced by the light reactions are sent to the Calvin cycle reactions.

Calvin Cycle Reactions The Calvin cycle reactions (sometimes called the light-independent reactions because they can occur both day and night) are named for Marvin Calvin who discovered them and their cyclical arrangement. The enzymatic reactions of the Calvin cycle occur in the stroma of a chloroplast. During the Calvin cycle, CO_2 is taken up and then reduced to a carbohydrate that can be used to form glucose. Reduction of CO_2 to a carbohydrate (CH_2O) requires hydrogen atoms supplied by NADPH and energy supplied by ATP, both molecules provided by the light reactions.

The upper set of red arrows in Figure 6.3 show that after the Calvin cycle reactions are complete, ADP + ⓟ and $NADP^+$ are sent back to the light reactions.

▶ **6.3 Check Your Progress** What two molecules form a "bridge" linking the light reactions with the Calvin cycle reactions, and what molecules function similarly in the opposite direction?

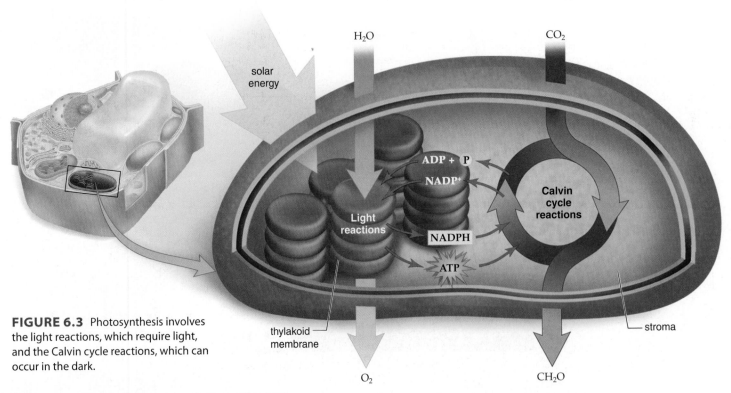

FIGURE 6.3 Photosynthesis involves the light reactions, which require light, and the Calvin cycle reactions, which can occur in the dark.

The Light Reactions Capture Solar Energy

Learning Outcomes

▸ Explain why leaves are green, with reference to the electromagnetic spectrum. (6.4)

▸ Explain how solar energy is converted to that of ATP during photosynthesis. (6.5–6.6)

▸ Trace the path of excited electrons, from the absorption of solar energy to the production of ATP and NADPH. (6.7)

▸ Explain how the thylakoid is organized to produce ATP and NADPH. (6.8)

The light reactions begin when pigments in the thylakoid membrane absorb certain wavelengths of light. The thylakoid membrane is highly organized for absorbing solar energy and producing ATP and NADPH, needed by the Calvin cycle reactions to reduce carbon dioxide to a carbohydrate in the stroma.

6.4 Solar energy is absorbed by pigments

Solar energy (radiant energy from the sun) can be described in terms of its wavelength and its energy content. **Figure 6.4A** lists the different types of radiant energy, from the shortest wavelength, gamma rays, to the longest, radio waves. We are most interested in white light, or *visible light*, because it is the type of radiation used for photosynthesis and for vision.

When visible light is passed through a prism, we can observe that it is made up of various colors. (Actually, of course, our brain interprets these wavelengths as colors.) The colors in visible light range from violet (the shortest wavelength) to blue, green, yellow, orange, and red (the longest wavelength). The energy content is highest for violet light and lowest for red light.

The pigments within most types of photosynthesizing cells are **chlorophylls *a*** and ***b*** and **carotenoids.** These pigments are capable of absorbing various portions of visible light. The absorption spectrum for these pigments is shown in **Figure 6.4B**. Both chlorophyll *a* and chlorophyll *b* absorb violet, blue, and red light better than the light of other colors. Because green light is reflected and only minimally absorbed, leaves appear green to us. The yellow or orange carotenoids are able to absorb light in the violet-blue-green range. Only in the fall is it obvious that pigments other than chlorophyll assist in absorbing solar energy. In the spring and summer, plant cells mask the instability of chlorophyll by using ATP molecules to rebuild it. As the hours of sunlight lessen in the fall, sufficient energy to rebuild chlorophyll is not available. Further, enzymes are working at a reduced speed because of the lower temperatures. Therefore, the amount of chlorophyll in leaves slowly disintegrates. When that happens, we begin to see yellow and orange pigments in the leaves.

In some trees, such as maples, certain pigments accumulate in acidic vacuoles, leading to a brilliant red color. The brown color of certain oak leaves is due to wastes left in the leaves.

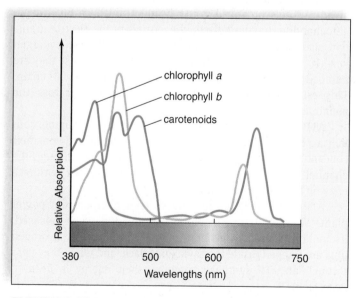

▸ **6.4 Check Your Progress** Why do leaves appear green to us as long as the weather remains warm?

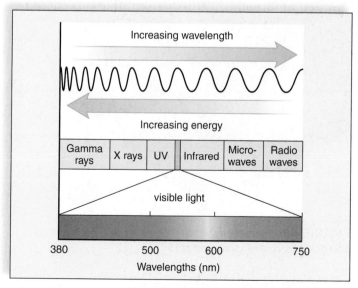

FIGURE 6.4A The electromagnetic spectrum includes visible light, which drives photosynthesis. Here, visible light is expanded to show its component colors.

FIGURE 6.4B Absorption spectrum of photosynthetic pigments. Notice that these pigments do not absorb green light—that's why the leaves of plants appear green to us.

6.5 Solar energy boosts electrons to a higher energy level

In the thylakoid membrane, photosystems contain (1) a pigment complex that absorbs solar energy and (2) an electron-acceptor molecule (**Fig. 6.5**). Each pigment complex consists of antenna molecules and a reaction center. Antenna molecules are light-absorbing pigments, such as chlorophyll *a* and *b* and carotenoid pigments. They are called antenna molecules because they absorb light energy just as a radio antenna absorbs radio waves. The antenna molecules pass all their energy on to the reaction center, which contains a particular chlorophyll *a* molecule. The reaction center, chlorophyll excites electrons and sends them on to the electron acceptor. Remember the old-fashioned "use a mallet to ring the bell, win a prize" carnival game? Similarly, solar energy has been used to launch electrons from the reaction center all the way up to the energy level of the electron acceptor.

Two types of photosystems, called **photosystem I (PS I)** and **photosystem II (PS II),** participate in the light reactions. The reaction center in PS I absorbs light with a wavelength of 700 nm, and the one in PS II absorbs light with a wavelength of 680 nm.

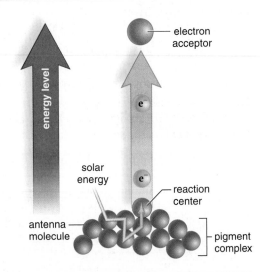

FIGURE 6.5 A general model of a photosystem.

electron acceptor

energy level

solar energy

reaction center

antenna molecule

pigment complex

▶ **6.5 Check Your Progress** What is the function of antenna molecules in the pigment complex of a photosystem?

6.6 Electrons release their energy as ATP forms

Chloroplasts use electrons energized by solar energy to generate ATP. They do this by way of an **electron transport chain (ETC),** a series of membrane-bound carriers that pass electrons from one to another. High-energy electrons (e⁻) are delivered to the chain, and low-energy electrons leave it. Every time electrons are transferred to a new carrier, energy is released; this energy is ultimately used to produce ATP molecules (**Fig. 6.6**).

For many years, scientists did not know how ATP synthesis was coupled to the electron transport chain. Peter Mitchell, a British biochemist, received a Nobel Prize in 1978 for his model of how ATP is produced not only in chloroplasts but also in mitochondria. In chloroplasts, the carriers of the electron transport chain are located within a thylakoid membrane. Hydrogen ions (H⁺) collect on one side of the membrane because they are pumped there by certain carriers of the electron transport chain. This establishes a *hydrogen ion (H⁺) gradient* across the membrane.

ATP synthase complexes, which span the membrane, contain a channel that allows hydrogen ions to flow down their concentration gradient. The flow of hydrogen ions through the channel provides the energy needed for the ATP synthase enzyme to produce ATP from ADP + Ⓟ.

ATP production is comparable to a hydroelectric power plant. Water is trapped behind a dam, and when released, its motion is used to generate electricity. Similarly, hydrogen ions are trapped inside the thylakoid space, and when they pass through an ATP synthase complex, their energy is used to generate ATP.

Section 6.7 pulls everything together to show you how the different parts of the light reactions generate both ATP and NADPH.

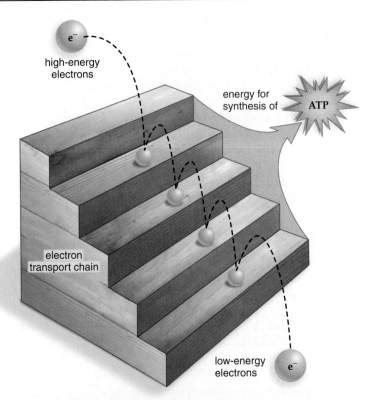

high-energy electrons

energy for synthesis of ATP

electron transport chain

low-energy electrons

FIGURE 6.6 High-energy electrons (e⁻) release energy as they pass down an electron transport chain.

▶ **6.6 Check Your Progress** What kind of energy is the flow of hydrogen ions down their concentration gradient through an ATP synthase?

6.7 A noncyclic flow of electrons produces ATP and NADPH

During the light reactions in the thylakoid membrane, electrons follow a *noncyclic pathway* that begins with PS II (**Fig. 6.7**). (PS II was discovered second and it also happens to be the second photosystem to evolve.) ❶ The absorbed solar energy in PS II is passed from one pigment to the other in the pigment complex, until it is concentrated in the reaction center, which contains a special chlorophyll *a* molecule. ❷ Electrons (e⁻) in the reaction center become so energized that they escape from the reaction center and ❸ move to a nearby electron-acceptor molecule.

PS II would disintegrate without replacement electrons; thus, ❹ electrons are removed from water, which splits, releasing oxygen to the atmosphere. Notice that with the loss of electrons, water has been oxidized, and that indeed, the ❺ oxygen released during photosynthesis comes from water. The oxygen escapes into the spongy mesophyll of a leaf and exits into the atmosphere by way of the stomata (see Fig. 6.2). ❻ However, the hydrogen ions (H⁺) are trapped in the thylakoid space.

❼ The electron acceptor sends the energized electrons down an electron transport chain and ATP is produced. (We now know that as the electrons pass from one carrier to the next, certain carriers pump hydrogen ions from the stroma into the thylakoid space. In this way, energy is captured and stored in the form of a hydrogen ion (H⁺) concentration gradient. Later, as H⁺ flows down this gradient (from the thylakoid space into the stroma, ATP is produced.)

When the PS I pigment complex absorbs solar energy, energized electrons leave its reaction center and are captured by a different ❽ electron acceptor. (Low-energy electrons from the electron transport chain adjacent to PS II replace those lost by PS I.) This electron acceptor passes its electrons on to ❾ NADP⁺ molecules. ❿ Each NADP⁺ molecule accepts two electrons and an H⁺ to become a reduced form of the molecule—that is, NADPH. ATP and NADPH from the light reactions are used by the Calvin cycle reactions to reduce carbon dioxide to a carbohydrate.

▶ **6.7 Check Your Progress** What molecule supplies the noncyclic electron pathway with electrons so it can keep going, and what molecule is at the end of the pathway?

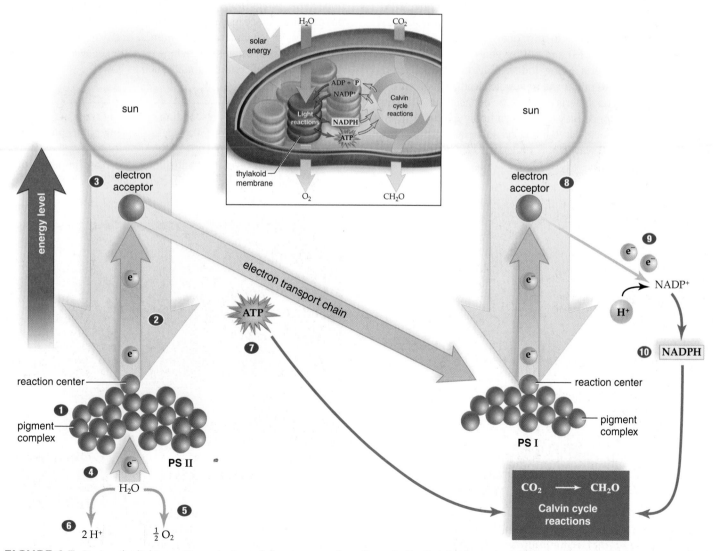

FIGURE 6.7 During the light reactions, electrons follow a noncyclic pathway in the thylakoid membrane; electrons move from water to NADP⁺.

6A Photosystem I Evolved Before Photosystem II

Most types of bacteria are heterotrophs, but among the photosynthesizing bacteria, a few can produce their own food even though they contain only photosystem I. This means that they do not utilize the noncyclic flow of electrons we have just described and instead make use of a cyclic flow of electrons, as illustrated in **Figure 6A.1.** The cyclic electron pathway begins when the antenna complex of PS I absorbs solar energy and energized electrons are taken up by an electron acceptor molecule. The acceptor molecule sends the electrons down a transport chain, and ATP is produced. The pathway is cyclic because the electrons return to PS I, where they are energized once more. Notice that the cyclic electron pathway produces ATP but no NADPH. To reduce carbon dioxide to a carbohydrate, both ATP and hydrogen atoms are required.

Oxygen-releasing photosynthesis, which involves PS II, is able to take electrons from water and in that way also use water as a hydrogen source (see Fig. 6.8). PS I cannot split water because it absorbs solar energy at a lower level than PS II (680 nm compared to 700 nm). However, the early atmosphere had many hydrogen sources, such as hydrogen sulfide (H_2S). Living bacteria that only use the cyclic electron pathway also use H_2S as a hydrogen source to produce their own food. They release elemental sulfur (S) and not oxygen.

Among the bacteria living today, only the cyanobacteria (**Fig. 6A.2**) are able to utilize the noncyclic electron pathway and release oxygen. Cyanobacteria are the type of bacterium that gave rise to chloroplasts once they were taken up by a pre-eukaryotic cell. Interestingly enough, free-living cyanobacteria can revert to a cyclic electron pathway when necessary. When they revert,

they use hydrogen sulfide (H_2S) as a hydrogen source to reduce carbon dioxide just like the other bacterial groups that can produce their own food.

The cyanobacteria have a complex structure; they contain thylakoids flattened membranous sacs arranged adjacent to the surface of the cell. We can speculate that the evolution of thylakoids made the evolution of the noncyclic electron flow possible. Just as you need a place to set up your electronic hardware, so oxygen-releasing prokaryotic photosynthesizers needed a location for the noncyclic electron pathway. Thylakoid membrane provided this location.

Scientists tell us with confidence that cyanobacteria were the first organisms to release oxygen into the atmosphere. We tend to think of oxygen as a gift to living things because most organisms alive today, including ourselves, make use of oxygen in mitochondria to produce ATP. However, this mindset is not completely accurate. Oxygen is a poison to organisms because it damages organic molecules. Organisms get rid of oxygen by reducing it to water during cellular respiration. So, let's give thanks to the cyanobacteria, which not only release oxygen into the atmosphere but can also reduce its supply by using it to produce ATP. Obligate anaerobes, which cannot use oxygen in this way, live only in the mudflats of lake bottoms, decaying vegetation of swamps, and the digestive tracts of certain animals such as cows!

FORM YOUR OPINION

1. Evolution proceeds by "adding on" rather than starting over. How is the evolution of oxygen-releasing photosynthesis an example of this concept?
2. Often during evolution, attributes are "lost." Today, what ability do free-living cyanobacteria have that chloroplasts do not have?

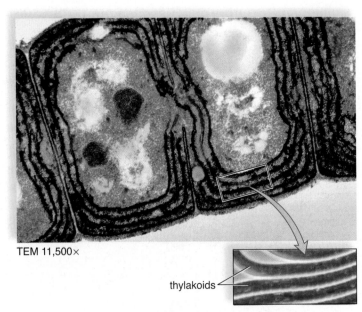

TEM 11,500×

thylakoids

FIGURE 6A.1 Photosynthesis evolved in stages. Scientists hypothesize that a cyclic electron pathway utilizing only PS I evolved before the noncyclic electron pathway shown in Figure 6.7.

FIGURE 6A.2 Cyanobacteria, such as *Oscillatoria,* contain thylakoids and can photosynthesize in the same manner as plants even though they are prokaryotes.

6.8 A thylakoid is highly organized for its task

Let's divide the molecular complexes in the thylakoid membrane (**Fig. 6.8**) into those that "get ready" and those that represent the "payoff."

Get Ready

1 PS II consists of a pigment complex that absorbs solar energy and passes electrons on to an electron-acceptor molecule. **2** PS II receives replacement electrons from water, which splits, releasing H^+ and oxygen (O_2).

3 The electron transport chain, consisting of a series of electron carriers such as cytochrome complexes, passes electrons from PS II to PS I. (Notice, therefore, that PS I receives replacement electrons from the electron transport chain.) **4** Members of the electron transport chain also pump H^+ from the stroma into the thylakoid space. Eventually, an electron gradient is present: The thylakoid space contains much more H^+ than the stroma.

5 PS I consists of a pigment complex that absorbs solar energy and sends excited electrons on to an electron-acceptor mol-

ecule, which passes them to an enzyme called $NADP^+$ reductase.

Payoff

6 $NADP^+$ reductase, an enzyme, receives electrons and reduces $NADP^+$. $NADP^+$ combines with H^+ and becomes **7** NADPH.

8 H^+ flows down its concentration gradient through a channel in an ATP synthase complex. This complex contains an enzyme that then enzymatically binds ADP to P, producing **9** ATP.

This method of producing ATP is called **chemiosmosis** because ATP production is tied to an H^+ gradient across a membrane.

We have now concluded our study of the light reactions. In the next part of the chapter, we will study the Calvin cycle reactions.

▶ **6.8 Check Your Progress** What is the end result of the "get ready" phase, and what is the end result of the "payoff" phase of the light reactions?

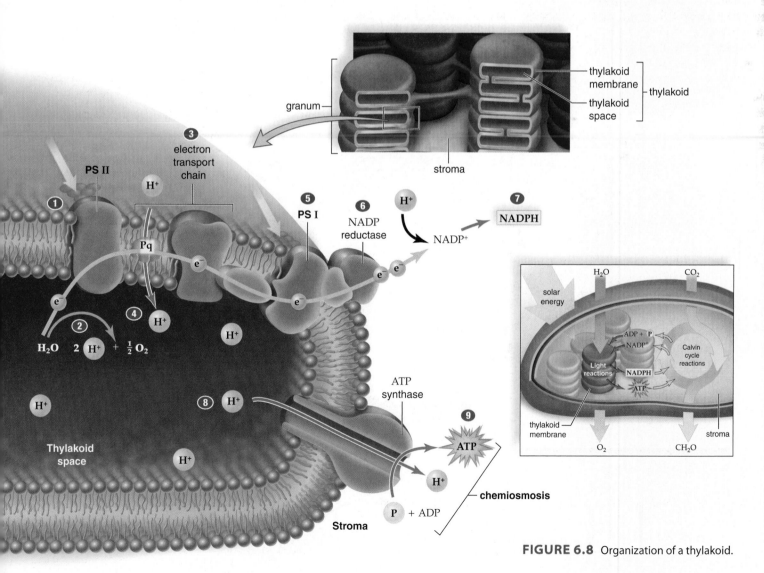

FIGURE 6.8 Organization of a thylakoid.

The Calvin Cycle Reactions Synthesize Carbohydrates

Learning Outcomes

▶ Describe the three phases of the Calvin cycle, and indicate when ATP and/or NADPH are involved. (6.9)
▶ Draw a diagram showing that G3P is a pivotal molecule in a plant's metabolic pathway. (6.10)

From the overall equation for photosynthesis, associate carbon dioxide and carbohydrate (CH_2O) with the Calvin cycle reactions. The Calvin cycle reactions are light-independent because they can occur in the light or the dark, but even so they could not occur without the ATP and NADPH from the light reactions because they are needed to reduce CO_2 to a carbohydrate.

6.9 ATP and NADPH from the light-dependent reactions are needed to produce a carbohydrate

The Calvin cycle is a series of reactions that produces carbohydrate before returning to the starting point once more (**Fig. 6.9**). Melvin Calvin and his colleagues used the radioactive isotope ^{14}C as a tracer to discover its many reactions. The reactions can be divided into these phases: CO_2 fixation, CO_2 reduction, and finally regeneration of RuBP, the molecule that combines with and fixes CO_2 from the atmosphere. The steps in the Calvin cycle are multiplied by three for reasons that will be explained.

CO_2 Fixation ❶ During the first phase of the Calvin cycle, CO_2 from the atmosphere combines with RuBP, a 5-carbon molecule, and a C_6 (6-carbon) molecule results. The enzyme that speeds this reaction, called **RuBP carboxylase,** is a protein that makes up 20–50% of the protein content in chloroplasts. The reason for its abundance may be that it is unusually slow (it processes only a few molecules of substrate per second compared to thousands per second for a typical enzyme), and so there has to be a lot of it to keep the Calvin cycle going.

FIGURE 6.9 During the Calvin cycle, carbon dioxide is reduced to a carbohydrate (G3P). It takes two molecules of G3P to form glucose.

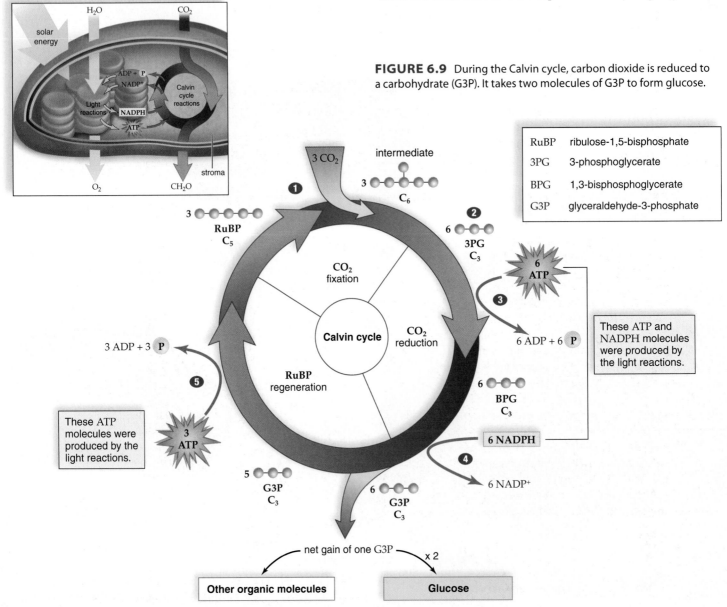

RuBP	ribulose-1,5-bisphosphate
3PG	3-phosphoglycerate
BPG	1,3-bisphosphoglycerate
G3P	glyceraldehyde-3-phosphate

② The C_6 molecule immediately splits into two C_3 molecules. (Remember that all molecules are multiplied by three in Figure 6.9.) This C_3 molecule is called 3PG.

CO₂ Reduction **③** and **④** Each of the 3PG molecules undergoes reduction to G3P in two steps:

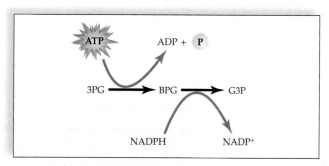

During this phase, CO_2 is reduced to a carbohydrate because R—CO_2 (3PG) has become R—CH_2O (G3P). Energy and electrons are needed for this reduction reaction, and these are supplied by ATP and NADPH, which become ADP + Ⓟ, and $NADP^+$, respectively.

RuBP Regeneration The reactions in Figure 6.9 are multiplied by three because it takes three turns of the Calvin cycle to allow one G3P to exit. Why? Because, for every three turns of the Calvin cycle, five molecules of G3P are used to re-form three molecules of RuBP, and the cycle continues. Notice that 5×3 (carbons in G3P) $= 3 \times 5$ (carbons in RuBP):

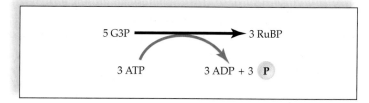

⑤ As this ATP produced by the light reactions breaks down, ADP + Ⓟ results.

The ADP + Ⓟ and $NADP^+$ that result from the Calvin cycle return to the light reactions so that they can continue to produce ATP and NADPH for the light-independent reactions.

▶ **6.9 Check Your Progress** Justify the use of the expression light-independent reactions for the Calvin cycle even though it is still very much dependent on solar energy. Explain.

6.10 In photosynthesizers, a carbohydrate is the starting point for other molecules

G3P (glyceraldehyde-3-phosphate) is the product of the Calvin cycle that can be converted to all sorts of organic molecules. Compared to animal cells, algae and plants have enormous biochemical capabilities. They use G3P for the purposes described in **Figure 6.10**.

① Notice that glucose phosphate is among the organic molecules that result from G3P metabolism. This is of interest to us because glucose is the molecule that plants and other organisms most often metabolize to produce the ATP molecules they require. Glucose is blood sugar in human beings.

Glucose can be combined with **②** fructose (with the removal of phosphates) to form **③** sucrose, the transport form of sugar in plants.

④ Glucose phosphate is also the starting point for the synthesis of **⑤** starch and **⑥** cellulose. Starch is the storage form of glucose. Some starch is stored in chloroplasts, but most starch is stored in roots. Cellulose is a structural component of plant cell walls and becomes fiber in our diet because we are unable to digest it.

⑦ A plant can use the hydrocarbon skeleton of G3P to form fatty acids and glycerol, which are combined in plant oils such as the corn oil, sunflower oil, and olive oil and used in cooking. **⑧** Also, when nitrogen is added to the hydrocarbon skeleton derived from G3P, amino acids form.

▶ **6.10 Check Your Progress** Glucose phosphate produced by a plant can be converted to what other molecules?

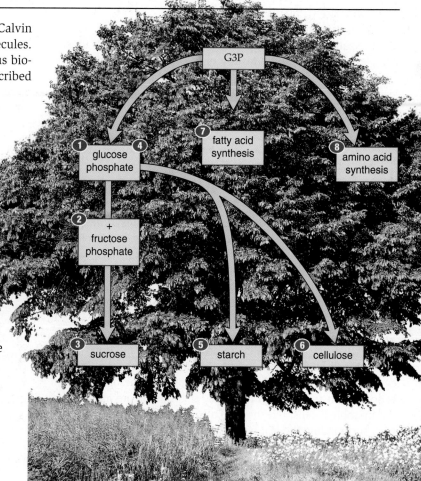

FIGURE 6.10 Trees and all photosynthesizers have the metabolic pathways that are able to convert G3P to all the molecules noted.

C₃, C₄, and CAM Photosynthesis Thrive Under Different Conditions

Learning Outcome

▶ Compare and contrast three modes of photosynthesis. (6.11–6.13)

Thus far, we have been observing C_3 photosynthesis, named for the number of carbons in the first observable molecule following the uptake of CO_2. In contrast, C_4 photosynthesis is more advantageous when the weather is warm and CO_2 is in short supply inside leaves, due to closure of stomata. CAM, a third type of photosynthesis, was first observed in desert plants, which need to conserve water.

6.11 C₃ photosynthesis is negatively affected by the presence of oxygen

In regions where temperature and rainfall tend to be moderate, plants carry on **C_3 photosynthesis,** and are therefore called C_3 plants. In a C_3 plant, the first detectable molecule after CO_2 fixation is a C_3 molecule, namely 3PG (**Fig. 6.11**). Look again at the Calvin cycle (see Fig. 6.9), and notice that the original C_6 molecule formed when RuBP carboxylase combines with carbon dioxide immediately breaks down to two 3PG, a C_3 molecule. It would be necessary to use a radioactive tracer, as Melvin Calvin did, to determine that this molecule is the first detectable one following CO_2 uptake by RuBP carboxylase.

When stomata close due to lack of water, CO_2 decreases in leaf spaces and O_2 increases. In C_3 plants, this O_2 competes with CO_2 for the active site of RuBP carboxylase, the first enzyme of the Calvin cycle, and less C_3 is produced. Such decreases in yield are of concern to humans because many food crops are C_3 plants.

What can explain this apparent drawback in the efficiency of RuBP carboxylase? The Calvin cycle, and therefore RuBP, most likely evolved early in the history of life on Earth. At that time, oxygen was in limited supply, and the ability of RuBP carboxylase to combine with oxygen would not have been a problem. Photosynthesis itself later caused O_2 to rise in the atmosphere, and now a plant has an advantage if it can prevent RuBP from

FIGURE 6.11 Carbon dioxide fixation in C_3 plants as exemplified by these wildflowers.

combining with O_2. As we shall see in Section 6.12, C_4 plants have such an advantage when the weather is warm.

▶ **6.11 Check Your Progress** Explain the term C_3 photosynthesis.

6.12 C₄ photosynthesis boosts CO₂ concentration for RuBP carboxylase

A modification of C_3 photosynthesis, called **C_4 photosynthesis,** is more efficient when CO_2 is scarce inside leaf spaces. In a C_4 plant, the first detectable molecule following CO_2 fixation is a C_4 molecule having four carbon atoms. C_4 plants are able to avoid the uptake of O_2 by RuBP carboxylase by minimizing the amount of O_2 and maximizing the amount of CO_2 available to the enzyme. Let's explore how C_4 plants do this.

The anatomy of a C_4 plant is different from that of a C_3 plant. In a C_3 leaf, mesophyll cells are arranged in parallel rows and contain well-formed chloroplasts (**Fig. 6.12A,** *left*). The Calvin cycle reactions occur in the chloroplasts of these mesophyll cells exposed to leaf spaces. In a C_4 leaf, chloroplasts are located in the mesophyll cells, but they are also located in bundle sheath cells surrounding the leaf vein. Further, the mesophyll cells are arranged concentrically around the bundle sheath cells preventing any exposure to O_2 in leaf spaces (Fig. 6.12A, *right*).

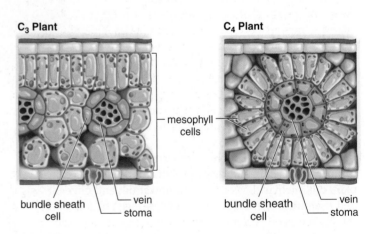

FIGURE 6.12A Anatomy of a C_3 plant compared to a C_4 plant.

In C_4 plants, the Calvin cycle reactions occur in the bundle sheath cells and not in the mesophyll cells. Therefore, CO_2 from the air is not fixed by the Calvin cycle. Instead, CO_2 is fixed by a C_3 molecule, and the C_4 that results is modified and then pumped into the bundle sheath cells (**Fig. 6.12B**). Now the C_4 molecule releases CO_2 to the Calvin cycle. This represents **partitioning** (of pathways) **in space.**

It takes energy to pump molecules, and you would expect the C_4 pathway outlined in Figure 6.12B to be disadvantageous. Yet, in warm climates when stomata close and CO_2 is in limited supply inside leaves, the net photosynthetic rate of C_4 plants (e.g., sugarcane, corn, and Bermuda grass) is two to three times that of C_3 plants (e.g., wheat, rice, and oats). Why do C_4 plants enjoy such an advantage? The answer is that RuBP carboxylase located in bundle sheath cells always combines with CO_2 and does not combine with O_2.

When the weather is moderate, C_3 plants ordinarily have the advantage, but when the weather becomes warm C_4 plants have their chance to take over, and we can expect them to predominate. In the early summer, C_3 plants such as Kentucky bluegrass and creeping bent grass are predominant in lawns in the cooler parts of the United States, but by midsummer, crabgrass, a C_4 plant, begins to take over.

FIGURE 6.12B Carbon dioxide fixation in C_4 plants as exemplified by corn.

Section 6.13 discusses still another form of photosynthesis, called CAM photosynthesis, which is prevalent in desert plants.

▶ **6.12 Check Your Progress** Structure suits function. How do C_4 plants prevent exposure of the RuBP carboxylase enzyme to oxygen?

6.13 CAM photosynthesis is another alternative to C_3 photosynthesis

CAM, which stands for crassulacean-acid metabolism, is an alternative to C_3 photosynthesis when the weather is hot and dry, as in a desert. **CAM photosynthesis** gets its name from the Crassulaceae, a family of flowering succulent (water-containing) plants that live in hot, arid regions of the world. CAM was first discovered in these plants, but now it is also known to be prevalent among most other succulent plants that grow in desert environments, including cactuses.

Whereas a C_4 plant represents partitioning in space—that is, carbon dioxide fixation occurs in mesophyll cells, and the Calvin cycle reactions occur in bundle sheath cells—CAM is **partitioning in time.** During the night, CAM plants use a C_3 molecule to fix some CO_2, forming C_4 molecules. These molecules are stored in large vacuoles in mesophyll cells. During the day, the C_4 molecules release CO_2 to the Calvin cycle when NADPH and ATP are available from the light reactions (**Fig. 6.13**).

Again, the primary advantage of this partitioning relates to the conservation of water. Because CAM plants open their stomata only at night, only then is atmospheric CO_2 available. During the day, the stomata are closed. This conserves water, but prevents more CO_2 from entering the plant.

Photosynthesis in a CAM plant is minimal because a limited amount of CO_2 is fixed at night. However, this amount of CO_2 fixation does allow CAM plants to live under stressful conditions. Whenever water and carbon dioxide are plentiful, C_3 plants can compete well. But when temperatures are warmer and CO_2 is scarce inside leaves, C_4 plants become the better competitors.

FIGURE 6.13 Carbon dioxide fixation in CAM plants as exemplified by pineapple.

Where the climate is hot and dry (deserts), stomata close up during the day and CAM plants become competitive also.

The occurrence of climate change is accompanied by an increased level of CO_2. How Science Progresses on page 118 discusses how tropical rain forests can help prevent any further rise in atmospheric CO_2.

▶ **6.13 Check Your Progress** How is CAM photosynthesis partitioned by the use of time?

6B Tropical Rain Forests and Global Climate Change

Tropical rain forests occur near the equator, wherever temperatures are above 26°C and rainfall is regular and heavy (100–200 cm per year). Huge trees with buttressed trunks and broad, undivided, dark-green leaves predominate. Nearly all of the plants in a tropical rain forest are woody, and woody vines are also abundant. There is no undergrowth except at clearings. Instead, orchids, ferns, and bromeliads live in the branches of the trees.

Despite the fact that tropical rain forests have dwindled from an original 14% to 6% of land surface today, they still make a substantial contribution to global CO_2 fixation. Taking into account all ecosystems, marine and terrestrial, photosynthesis produces organic matter that is 300 to 600 times the mass of the people currently living on Earth. Tropical rain forests contribute greatly to the uptake of CO_2 and the productivity of photosynthesis because they are the most efficient of all terrestrial ecosystems.

We have learned that organic matter produced by photosynthesizers feeds all living things and that photosynthesis releases oxygen (O_2), a gas needed to complete the process of cellular respiration. Does photosynthesis by tropical rain forests provide any other service that has significant worldwide importance? **Figure 6B** projects a rise in the average global temperature during the twenty-first century due to the introduction of certain gases, chiefly carbon dioxide, into the atmosphere. The process of photosynthesis and also the oceans act as a sink for carbon dioxide. For at least a thousand years prior to 1850, atmospheric CO_2 levels remained fairly constant at 0.028%. Since the 1850s, when industrialization began, the amount of CO_2 in the atmosphere has increased to 0.038%.

Much like the panes of a greenhouse, CO_2 in our atmosphere traps radiant heat from the sun and warms the world. Therefore, CO_2 and other gases that act similarly are called *greenhouse gases*. Without any greenhouse gases, Earth's temperature would be about 33°C cooler than it is now. Therefore, it is hypothesized that increasing the concentration of these gases will cause an increase in global temperatures that will disrupt climate patterns recognizable by such events as heatwaves, droughts, and storms including an increased number of hurricanes and tornadoes.

Burning fossil fuels adds CO_2 to the atmosphere. Have any other factors contributed to an increase in atmospheric CO_2? Between 10 and 30 million hectares of rain forests are lost every year to ranching, logging, mining, and other means of developing forests for human needs. The clearing of forests often involves burning them, which is double trouble for global climate change. Each year, deforestation of tropical rain forests accounts for 20–30% of all the carbon dioxide in the atmosphere. At the same time, burning removes trees that would ordinarily absorb CO_2.

Some investigators hypothesized that an increased amount of CO_2 in the atmosphere will cause photosynthesis to increase in the remaining portion of the forest. To study this possibility, they measured atmospheric CO_2 levels, daily temperature levels, and tree girth in La Selva, Costa Rica, for 16 years. The data collected demonstrated relatively *lower* forest productivity at higher temperatures. These findings suggest that, if temperatures rise, tropical rain forests may add to ongoing atmospheric CO_2 accumulation rather than the reverse.

Some countries have programs to combat the problem of deforestation. In the mid-1970s, Costa Rica established a system of national parks and reserves to protect the country's land area from degradation. At present over 25% of Costa Rica is composed of protected forests. Similar efforts in other countries may help slow the threat of climate change.

FORM YOUR OPINION

1. What are some other advantages to preserving tropical rain forests aside from helping to prevent any further rise in CO_2?
2. What can the countries of the world that have no tropical rain forests do to help preserve them?

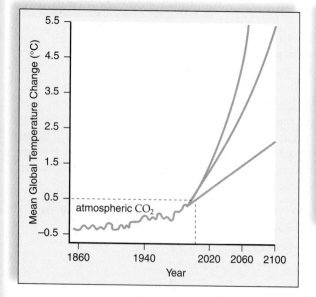

FIGURE 6B This graph shows how atmospheric CO_2 is expected to affect global temperature. As shown the global temperature is now 0.05°C higher world wide than in the 20th century. Burning forests adds to atmospheric CO_2.

SUMMARY

Photosynthesis Produces Food and Releases Oxygen

6.1   Photosynthesizers are autotrophs that produce their own food

- **Photosynthesis** converts solar energy to the chemical energy of a carbohydrate.
- Producers **(autotrophs)** produce food for themselves and for consumers **(heterotrophs).**

6.2   In eukaryotes, chloroplasts carry out photosynthesis

- Photosynthesis occurs in the **chloroplasts** of leaf cells.
- CO_2 enters a leaf through small openings called **stomata.**
- **Chlorophyll** and other pigments within the thylakoid membranes of thylakoids within a **granum** absorb solar energy.
- Conversion of CO_2 to a carbohydrate occurs in the **stroma,** the enzyme-containing interior of chloroplasts.

6.3   Photosynthesis involves two sets of reactions: The light reactions and the Calvin cycle reactions

- **Oxidation** occurs when a molecule loses electrons (hydrogen atoms), and **reduction** occurs when a molecule gains electrons (hydrogen atoms).
- The overall reaction for photosynthesis shows that CO_2 is reduced and water is oxidized, resulting in a carbohydrate and oxygen. This is a **redox reaction:**

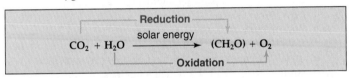

- The **light reactions** only occur in thylakoids during the day when solar energy is available.
- The light reactions split water, releasing O_2, and send NADPH and ATP to the light reactions.
- The **Calvin cycle reactions** are enzymatic reactions that occur in the stroma anytime, day or night.
- The Calvin cycle reactions use the NADPH and ATP from the light reactions to reduce CO_2 to a carbohydrate (CH_2O).

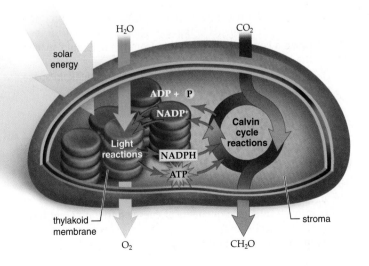

The Calvin Cycle Reactions Capture Solar Energy

6.4   Solar energy is absorbed by pigments

- **Chlorophylls *a* and *b*** and **carotenoids** absorb violet, blue, and red light better than other portions of visible light.
- Because these pigments don't absorb green light, leaves appear green to us.

6.5   Solar energy boosts electrons to a higher energy level

- Within thylakoid membranes, pigment complexes in **photosystem I (PS I)** and **photosystem II (PS II)** absorb solar energy.
- Energized electrons are passed by a reaction center chlorophyll *a* molecule to an electron acceptor.

6.6   Electrons release their energy as ATP forms

- An electron acceptor sends energized electrons down an **electron transport chain (ETC),** a series of membrane-bound electron carriers.
- As electrons are passed from carrier to carrier, they give up energy.
- Some carriers of an electron transport chain use this energy to pump H^+ across a membrane. In chloroplasts, H^+ collects in the thylakoid space.
- When the hydrogen ions flow down their electrochemical gradient, through an **ATP synthase complex,** ATP forms.

6.7   A noncyclic flow of electrons produces ATP and NADPH

- During a noncyclic electron pathway, electrons move from PS II down an electron transport chain to PS I and on to $NADP^+$.
  - Replacement electrons are removed from water, which splits, releasing O_2 and H^+.
  - An electron transport chain between PS II and PS I stores energy in the form of an H^+ gradient and then this gradient helps generate ATP.
  - $NADP^+$ receives e^- and H^+ and becomes NADPH.
- The light reactions send NADPH and ATP to the Calvin cycle reactions.

6.8   A thylakoid is highly organized for its task

- Get-ready phase:
  - PS II: Pigment complex plus electron acceptor. Water splits, releasing H^+ and O_2.
  - Members of the electron transport chain pump H^+ from the stroma to the thylakoid space; H^+ gradient results.
  - PS I absorbs solar energy, and electrons are picked up by $NADP^+$ reductase.
- Payoff phase:
  - $NADP^+$ reductase passes electrons to $NADP^+$, and NADPH results.
  - **Chemiosmosis:** H^+ flows down its concentration gradient through the ATP synthase complex; ADP binds to P; ATP are produced.

The Calvin Cycle Reactions Synthesize Carbohydrates

6.9   ATP and NADPH from the light reactions are needed to produce a carbohydrate

- CO_2 fixation: The enzyme **RuBP carboxylase** fixes CO_2 to RuBP, producing a C_6 molecule that immediately splits into two C_3 molecules (3PG).

- CO_2 reduction: Each 3PG is reduced to a G3P molecule. This step requires ATP and NADPH:

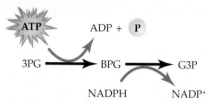

$$3PG \longrightarrow BPG \longrightarrow G3P$$

- RuBP regeneration: During three turns of the Calvin cycle, five molecules of G3P are used to re-form three molecules of RuBP. This step requires ATP energy.

6.10 In photosynthesizers, a carbohydrate is the starting point for other molecules

- **G3P** (phosphoglyceraldehyde-3-phosphate) can be converted to all organic molecules needed by a plant.
- It takes two G3P molecules to make one glucose molecule.

C_3, C_4, and CAM Photosynthesis Thrive Under Different Conditions

6.11 C_3 photosynthesis is negatively affected by the presence of oxygen

- **C_3 photosynthesis** occurs under conditions of moderate temperature and rainfall.
- RuBP carboxylase combines with O_2 when CO_2 supply is low, due to stomata closure, and this reduces yield.

6.12 C_4 photosynthesis boosts CO_2 concentration for RuBP carboxylase

- **C4 photosynthesis,** which occurs when the climate is warm, prevents RuBP from combining with O_2.
- **Partitioning in space:** CO_2 fixation first occurs in mesophyll; the Calvin cycle occurs in bundle sheath cells, where RuBP is not exposed to O_2.

6.13 CAM photosynthesis is another alternative to C_3 photosynthesis

- During **CAM photosynthesis,** common in desert plants, stomata are closed during the day, and this conserves water.
- **Partitioning in time:** CO_2 is fixed at night; does not enter the Calvin cycle until the next day.

TESTING YOURSELF

Photosynthesis Produces Food and Releases Oxygen

1. The raw materials for photosynthesis are
   a. oxygen and water.
   b. oxygen and carbon dioxide.
   c. carbon dioxide and water.
   d. carbohydrates and water.
   e. carbohydrates and carbon dioxide.
2. During photosynthesis, _____ is reduced to _____.
   a. CO_2, oxygen
   b. oxygen, CO_2
   c. water, oxygen
   d. CO_2, a carbohydrate
3. The light reactions
   a. take place in the stroma.
   b. consist of the Calvin cycle.
   c. Both a and b are correct.
   d. Neither a nor b is correct.
4. The function of the light reactions is to
   a. obtain CO_2.
   b. make carbohydrate.

c. convert light energy into usable forms of chemical energy.
   d. regenerate RuBP.
5. Label the following diagram of a chloroplast.

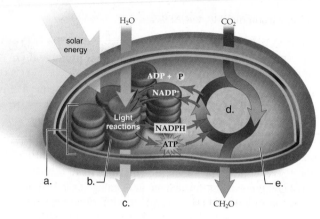

6. **THINKING CONCEPTUALLY** In order for the biosphere to have animal life, some animals must eat plants. Explain.

The Light Reactions Capture Solar Energy

7. When leaves change color in the fall, _____ light is not absorbed for photosynthesis.
   a. orange range
   b. red range
   c. violet-blue-green range
   d. None of these are correct.
8. A photosystem contains
   a. pigments, a reaction center, and an electron receiver.
   b. ADP, (P), and hydrogen ions (H^+).
   c. protons, photons, and pigments.
   d. cytochromes only.
   e. Both b and c are correct.
9. PS I, PS II, and the electron transport chain are located in the
   a. thylakoid membrane.
   b. stroma.
   c. outer chloroplast membrane.
   d. cell's nucleus.
10. The final acceptor of electrons during the noncyclic electron pathway is
    a. PS I.
    b. PS II.
    c. water.
    d. ATP.
    e. $NADP^+$.
11. When electrons in the reaction center of PS II are passed to an electron acceptor, they are replaced by electrons that come from
    a. oxygen.
    b. glucose.
    c. carbon dioxide.
    d. water.
12. During the light reactions of photosynthesis, ATP is produced when hydrogen ions (H^+) move
    a. down a concentration gradient from the thylakoid space to the stroma.
    b. against a concentration gradient from the thylakoid space to the stroma.
    c. down a concentration gradient from the stroma to the thylakoid space.

The Calvin Cycle Reactions Synthesize Carbohydrates

13. The Calvin cycle reactions
    a. produce carbohydrates.
    b. convert one form of chemical energy into a different form of chemical energy.
    c. regenerate more RuBP.

d. use the products of the light reactions.
    e. All of these are correct.
14. The Calvin cycle requires _____ from the light reactions.
    a. carbon dioxide and water   d. ATP and water
    b. ATP and NADPH   e. NADH and water
    c. carbon dioxide and ATP
15. **THINKING CONCEPTUALLY** The overall equation for photosynthesis doesn't include ATP. Why is ATP needed?

C_3, C_4, and CAM Photosynthesis Thrive Under Different Conditions

16. C_4 photosynthesis
    a. occurs in plants whose bundle sheath cells contain chloroplasts.
    b. takes place in plants such as wheat, rice, and oats.
    c. is an advantage when the weather is warm.
    d. Both a and c are correct.
17. CAM photosynthesis
    a. is the same as C_4 photosynthesis.
    b. is an adaptation to cold environments in the Southern Hemisphere.
    c. is prevalent in desert plants that close their stomata during the day.
    d. stands for chloroplasts and mitochondria.

18. The different types of photosynthesis are dependent upon the timing and location of
    a. CO_2 fixation.   c. H_2O fixation.
    b. nitrogen fixation.   d. All of these are correct.

THINKING SCIENTIFICALLY

1. Elodea, a plant that lives in the water, is in a beaker of water. Bubbling occurs with white light, but not green. Why do environmental conditions have to be kept constant, and suggest a control for this experiment.
2. The process of photosynthesis supports the cell theory. How?

ONLINE RESOURCE

www.mhhe.com/maderconcepts2

Enhance your study with animations that bring concepts to life and practice tests to assess your understanding. Your instructor may also recommend the interactive eBook, individualized learning tools, and more.

CONNECTING THE CONCEPTS

The overall equation for photosynthesis $CO_2 + H_2O \longrightarrow (CH_2O) + O_2$ takes place in chloroplasts. This equation does not reflect that photosynthesis requires two separate sets of reactions: the light reactions (take place in thylakoid membrane) and the Calvin cycle reactions (take place in stroma).

The light reactions absorb solar energy and convert it into chemical forms of energy that drive the Calvin cycle reactions. As a result of the noncyclic flow of electrons, NADPH carries electrons, and ATP provides energy to reduce carbon dioxide to a carbohydrate during the Calvin cycle.

Photosystem I, which is capable of a cyclic flow of electrons, evolved before photosystem II. Some photosynthesizing bacteria today utilize only photosystem I. They must live under anaerobic conditions because they die in the presence of oxygen released by photosynthesizers who utilize both photosystem I and photosystem II. Cyanobacteria do utilize both photosystems, and they carry on cellular respiration, which soaks up oxygen.

C_3 photosynthesis was the first form of photosynthesis to evolve. We can tell it evolved when oxygen was in limited supply because RuBP carboxylase is inefficient in the presence of oxygen. By now, two other forms of photosynthesis have evolved—C_4 photosynthesis (partitioning in space) and CAM photosynthesis (partitioning in

time). Both of the alternative forms of photosynthesis are means of supplying RuBP carboxylase with CO_2, while limiting its exposure to oxygen produced by the plant.

The details of photosynthesis should not cause us to lose sight of its great contribution to the biosphere. It keeps the biosphere functioning because it supplies energy, in the form of carbohydrates, to all organisms. Most organisms have a way to tap into the energy provided by carbohydrates. It's called cellular respiration and is the subject of our next chapter. Cellular respiration is completed within mitochondria. Mitochondria are called the powerhouses of the cell because they convert the energy of carbohydrates (and other organic molecules) to that of ATP molecules, the energy currency of cells.

PUT THE PIECES TOGETHER

1. What is the significance of cyanobacteria in the history of life?
2. Prepare an overview of photosynthesis that includes a simplified version of the light reactions (Fig. 6.7) and the Calvin cycle reactions (Fig. 6.9). Compare your diagram to that produced by another group and critique both diagrams.
3. Why would you predict that C_4 photosynthesis evolved after C_3 photosynthesis?

Part II

Enhance your understanding of genetics through media and applications!

Media

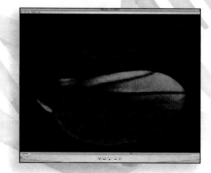

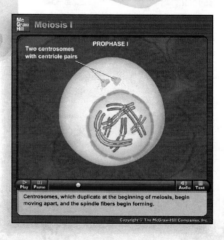

Genes Control the Traits of Organisms

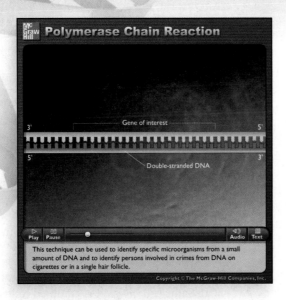

Polymerase Chain Reaction

3'   Gene of interest   5'

5'   Double-stranded DNA   3'

▷ Play   ⏸ Pause   ◁) Audio   ▤ Text

This technique can be used to identify specific microorganisms from a small amount of DNA and to identify persons involved in crimes from DNA on cigarettes or in a single hair follicle.

Copyright © The McGraw-Hill Companies, Inc.

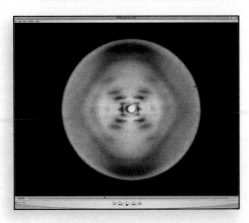

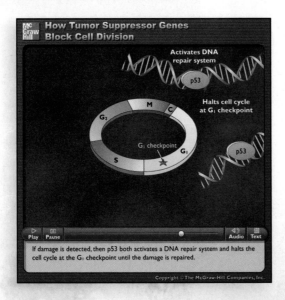

How Tumor Suppressor Genes Block Cell Division

Activates DNA repair system

p53

Halts cell cycle at G₁ checkpoint

M   C
G₂
G₁ checkpoint   G₁
S

p53

▷ Play   ⏸ Pause   ◁) Audio   ▤ Text

If damage is detected, then p53 both activates a DNA repair system and halts the cell cycle at the G₁ checkpoint until the damage is repaired.

Copyright © The McGraw-Hill Companies, Inc.

Applications

McGraw Hill **connect**™ | BIOLOGY

8

Cell Division and Reproduction

CHAPTER OUTLINE

Cancer Is a Genetic Disorder

We often think of diseases in terms of organs, and therefore it is customary to refer to colon cancer, or lung cancer, or pancreatic cancer. But actually cancer is a cellular disease. Cancer is present when abnormal cells have formed a tumor. Exceptions are cancers of the blood, in which abnormal cells are coursing through the bloodstream. The cells of a tumor share a common ancestor—the first cell to become cancerous.

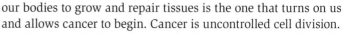

Uncontrolled growth leading to a tumor is characteristic of multicellular organisms, not unicellular ones. The very mechanism that allows our bodies to grow and repair tissues is the one that turns on us and allows cancer to begin. Cancer is uncontrolled cell division.

Usually, cell division is confined to just certain cells of the body, called adult stem cells. For example, skin can replenish itself because stem cells below the surface have the ability to divide. In embryos all cells can divide. How else could a newborn arise from a single fertilized egg? But something happens as development progresses: The cells undergo specialization and become part of a particular organ. A mature multicellular organism contains many kinds of specialized cells in many

Cancer cell dividing

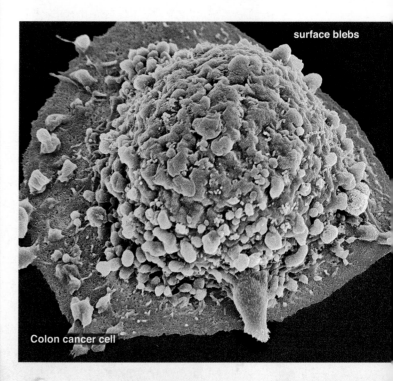

surface blebs

Colon cancer cell

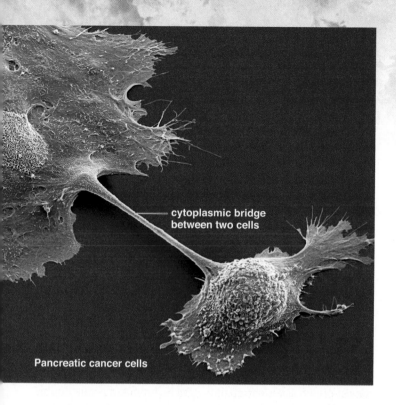

cytoplasmic bridge
between two cells

Pancreatic cancer cells

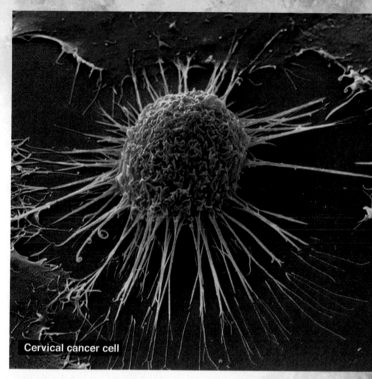

Cervical cancer cell

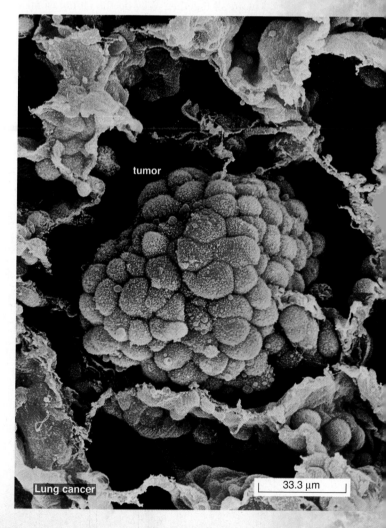

tumor

Lung cancer

33.3 μm

different organs. Normally, these cells listen to their neighbors and participate in the operation of the organ. But when a cell becomes cancerous, it loses its specialization and becomes youthful again—it starts to divide and divide, until a tumor exists. The tumor interferes with the operation of the organ.

Each cell in a multicellular organism has a copy of the genetic instructions the organism received from its parents. During cell division, the instructions were passed to the millions and millions of cells making up the body. Some of these genes call a halt to cell division, a necessary step if cells are to mature and become specialized. Without control of cell division, a multicellular organism would be a bunch of embryonic cells with no particular purpose. When cell division genes mutate, uncontrolled division so characteristic of cancer becomes possible. Therefore, cancer is a genetic disorder. Research tells us that cancer-causing mutations may be induced, for example, by chemicals or radiation that damage DNA; viruses that carry mutated genes into cells; or random errors that occur during DNA synthesis. A series of mutations is required before cells begin to grow abnormally and eventually become a tumor. In these cells, genetic alteration is obvious: Some chromosomes are present in three or four copies, rather than the usual two, and other chromosomes have been rearranged in various ways.

In this chapter, we will study cell division and how it is normally controlled, before examining the characteristics of cancer cells. We will also see how a special type of cell division contributes to the formation of the egg and sperm, which fuse during sexual reproduction. If abnormalities occur during the production of the egg and sperm, the offspring will have a chromosome anomaly. We will examine a few of such anomalies in this chapter.

Chromosomes Become Visible During Cell Division

Learning Outcomes

▶ Describe the arrangement and appearance of the chromosomes in a human karyotype. (8.1)

▶ List and describe the stages of the eukaryotic cell cycle. (8.2)

Before a cell can divide, chromatin must condense into chromosomes. At that time the chromosomes are duplicated and consist of two identical parts, called sister chromatids. Also, the organelles must duplicate so that each new cell can receive its share. During the cell cycle, the cell gets ready for the process of cell division before it divides

8.1 A karyotype displays the chromosomes

We have already observed that the nucleus of a eukaryotic cell contains chromatin, which is a network of fine threads composed of DNA (the genes) and various proteins, including histone proteins that are especially involved in keeping chromatin organized. When a cell is about to divide, chromatin becomes highly coiled and condensed into the chromosomes. At that time it's possible to stop cell division and view the chromosomes. Staining causes the chromosomes to have dark and light cross-bands, which can be used in addition to size and shape to distinguish one chromosome from the other. A display of the chromosomes is called a **karyotype; Figure 8.1** is the karyotype of a human male.

This karyotype shows that humans have 23 pairs of chromosomes, for a total of 46 all together. Why do the chromosomes come in pairs? Because one member of each pair was donated by the mother and the other member was donated by the father. Also, it should be noted that 22 pairs of chromosomes, called **autosomes,** have nothing to do with the gender of the individual, while one pair called the **sex chromosomes,** determines gender. In human males, the sex chromosomes have a different appearance and are called an **X** and a **Y.** In females, the sex chromosomes are two X chromosomes.

We will be discussing the sex chromosomes in more detail later. Just now, let's continue our discussion of the autosomal chromosomes. Each pair of autosomal chromosomes is called a

homologous pair because not only do they look alike, but they also carry genes for the same traits, such as type of hairline, length of fingers, or type of earlobe. Their genes need not be exactly alike, however. Therefore, one homologous chromosome (from the father) could call for a continuous hairline, and the other homologous chromosome (from the mother) could call for a widow's peak.

Each chromosome in a karyotype has two parts, called **sister chromatids.** This is because one important event prior to cell division is replication of the DNA. Following DNA replication, the chromosomes have duplicated in the sense that they then consist of two sister chromatids. (Each chromatid is one double helix.) Because the sister chromatids are duplicates of each other their genes are exactly alike. For example, the sister chromatids would call for the same type hairline. Sister chromatids are held together at a constricted region called the **centromere.** After cell division has begun, protein complexes called **kinetochores** assemble at the centromeres, one for each sister chromatid. A kinetochore allows a chromatid to attach to a spindle fiber as is described in Section 8.4.

▶ **8.1 Check Your Progress** Any cell in the body can be the source of chromosomes for a karyotype. Would the karyotype of a cancer cell be normal or abnormal? Explain.

FIGURE 8.1 This karyotype of a normal male shows 23 pairs of homologous chromosomes. These chromosomes are duplicated, and each one is composed of two sister chromatids.

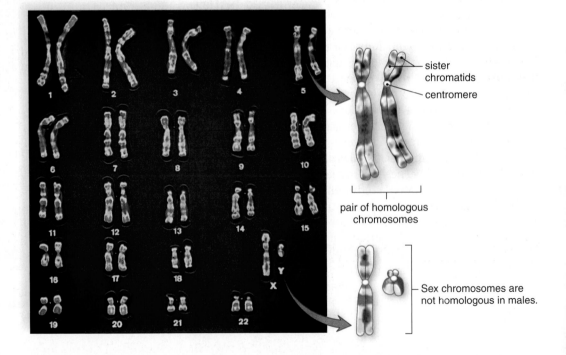

sister chromatids

centromere

pair of homologous chromosomes

Sex chromosomes are not homologous in males.

8.2 The eukaryotic cell cycle has a set series of stages

Cell division is only a small part of the **cell cycle,** an orderly set of stages that take place between the time a eukaryotic cell divides and the time the resulting daughter cells also divide (**Fig. 8.2A**). The amount of time it takes for a cell to complete the cycle varies widely, but adult mammalian cells can usually finish the cell cycle in about 24 hours.

Interphase For most of the cell cycle, the cell is in **interphase,** defined as the period of time between cell divisions. During interphase, a cell is performing its normal work of communicating with other cells, secreting substances, and carrying out cellular respiration. In addition, the cell may be preparing for cell division.

Interphase has three stages: G_1, S, and G_2. Years ago, when cell biologists picked the terms G_1, S, and G_2, they said that G stood for "gap", but this now seems inappropriate because the cell is actually busy during both G phases. So today, it is better to think of G as standing for "growth." Protein synthesis is very much a part of these growth stages.

During the **G_1 stage,** the cell first recovers from the previous division. Then it may make a commitment to divide again. If not, a cell can enter **G_0,** which is a substage of the G_1 stage. During G_0, a cell continues to perform normal everyday processes, but no preparations are being made for cell division. However, cells can exit the G_0 stage upon receiving proper signals from other cells and other parts of the body. Some types of cells, such as nerve and muscle cells, are more apt to be in G_0 than other types of cells. Embryonic cells and also adult stem cells do not enter G_0. **Adult stem cells** are relatively nonspecialized cells whose job is to divide and produce cells that will become mature. In red bone marrow, the division of stem cells gives rise to all the types of blood cells in the body.

As soon as a cell makes a commitment to divide, during G_1 it increases in size, doubles its organelles (such as mitochondria and ribosomes), and accumulates molecules that will be used for DNA synthesis.

The **S stage** of interphase follows the G_1 stage. The "S" stands for synthesis, and certainly DNA synthesis occurs as DNA replicates. At the end of the S stage, each chromosome is composed of two identical *sister chromatids.* Another way of expressing these events is to say that DNA replication results in duplicated chromosomes.

The **G_2 stage** follows the S stage. The G_2 stage extends from the completion of DNA replication to the onset of cell division. Organelle replication continues during this stage, and the cell synthesizes proteins that will assist cell division. For example, it makes the proteins that form microtubules. Microtubules are used during the mitotic stage to form a spindle apparatus that helps nuclear division occur.

M Stage Cell division occurs during the **M stage,** which encompasses both division of the nucleus and division of the cytoplasm. Just now, we can say that the M stands for mitosis because this is the type of nuclear division we discuss in the next section. **Mitosis** maintains the chromosome number because the daughter cells have the same number of chromosomes as the parent cell

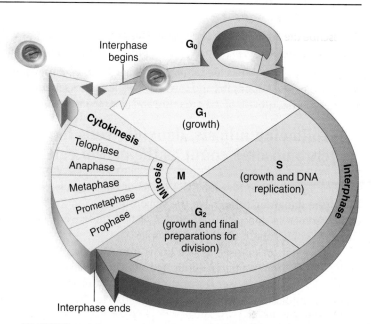

FIGURE 8.2A The cell cycle is a series of events that can occur over and over again. Interphase includes G_1, S, and G_2. The M stage of the cell cycle includes mitosis and cytokinesis.

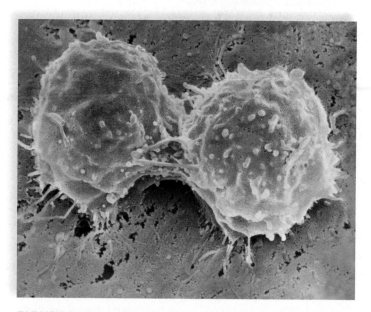

FIGURE 8.2B Cytokinesis (shown here) is a noticeable part of the cell cycle because division of the cytoplasm occurs.

had. Division of the cytoplasm, which starts even before mitosis is finished, is called **cytokinesis (Fig. 8.2B).**

▶ **8.2 Check Your Progress** Which part of the cell cycle—interphase or the M stage—would you expect to be curtailed in cancer cells? Why?

Mitosis Maintains the Chromosome Number

Learning Outcomes

▶ Give an overview of mitosis to illustrate how mitosis maintains the chromosome number. (8.3)
▶ Describe the phases of mitosis and the process of cytokinesis in animal and plant cells. (8.4–8.5)

Every cell in your body has the same number and kinds of chromosomes. The cell cycle ensures that this will happen because the chromosomes first duplicate, and then the identical parts separate during mitosis and go into the daughter nuclei. Without a cell cycle that includes mitosis, growth of the organism and also repair of tissues would be impossible.

8.3 Following mitosis, daughter cells have the same chromosome count as the parent cell

Mitosis is duplication division. The nuclei of the two new cells, called the **daughter cells,** have the same number and kinds of chromosomes as the cell that divides, called the **parent cell.** How this comes about is relatively simple.

At the start of mitosis, as you know from studying the cell cycle, each chromosome is duplicated and composed of two identical parts, called sister chromatids. This diagram shows you how one duplicated chromosome can give rise to two identical chromosomes:

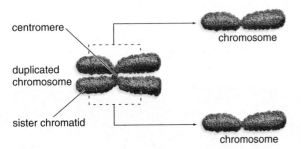

It is important when studying cell division to determine the number of chromosomes by counting the number of independent centromeres. For example, you can tell that all the cells in **Figure 8.3** have the same number of chromosomes because they have the same number of centromeres. Since the chromosomes occur in pairs, the cells are **diploid,** symbolized as **2n.** Pairs are determined by shape and size; therefore the cells in Figure 8.3 have two pairs—one pair is long and the other is short. The difference in color signifies that one of each pair (e.g., blue) was inherited from the father and the other (e.g., red) was inherited from the mother. If the chromosomes are not in pairs, the cell is **haploid,** symbolized as **n.** In animal cells, the cell is diploid, but in many protists and fungi, the cell is haploid before and after mitosis.

The Spindle Apparatus A **centrosome** is the microtubule organizing center of the cell, and as shown in Figure 8.3, the centrosome divides at the start of a nuclear division. The daughter centrosomes produce the spindle fibers of the **spindle apparatus,** which assists the separation of the chromatids as they move toward the opposite poles of the spindle. As soon as the chromatids separate, they are called daughter chromosomes.

In animal cells, the centrioles are short cylinders of microtubules located in centrosomes. It seems doubtful that centrioles help form the spindle, because plant cells don't have centrioles but they do have a spindle apparatus. How Life Changes on the next page discusses how the spindle fibers function and how the spindle may have evolved.

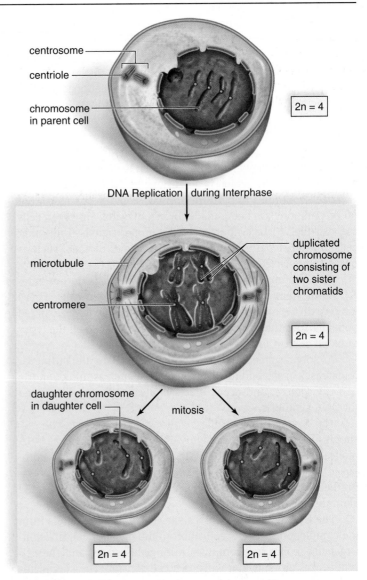

FIGURE 8.3 DNA replication precedes mitosis. During mitosis, the parent cell divides to produce two daughter cells with the same number and kinds of chromosomes as the parent cell. The parent cell and the daughter cells are also genetically identical.

▶ **8.3 Check Your Progress** In general explain how mitosis can result in daughter cells with the same number of chromosomes as the parent cell.

8A Evolution of the Spindle Apparatus

In plant and animal cells, mitosis involves a spindle apparatus composed of microtubules organized into spindle fibers of two types: kinetochore fibers and polar fibers. The nuclear envelope has fragmented and the spindle takes up the entire cell (**Fig. 8A**, *top, center*).

During mitosis, each chromatid has a kinetochore (a special assembly of proteins) in the region of the centromere. You can think of a kinetochore as an engine that runs along a train track, where the train track is a kinetochore spindle fiber. As the kinetochore moves up the fiber, the fiber disassembles. In this way, the daughter chromosomes are seemingly pulled apart (*top, left*). The spindle apparatus also contains polar fibers that overlap at the equator of the spindle. When the polar spindle fibers lengthen, the poles are pushed apart (*top, right*). It's said that the daughter chromosomes separate by a push-pull system.

The origin of the spindle apparatus is an evolutionary puzzle that researchers have been investigating for quite some time. When bacteria, which lacks a nucleus, reproduce, the daughter chromosomes are attached to a plasma membrane site, and they separate as the cell elongates. No microtubules are involved in this process, which is called binary fission (*bottom, left*). In some way, mitosis must have evolved from binary fission, but it is unlikely that mitosis developed in a straight-line manner. Instead, the evolution of the spindle apparatus must have involved numerous dead ends and variations that finally resulted in the spindle used by animals, plants, and most fungi. The fossil record is unlikely to help discover the evolutionary

pathway because soft, pliable cells don't make good fossils. Therefore, researchers studying the origin of the spindle apparatus have turned to living unicellular protists and eukaryotes to see how the spindle may have evolved. Two significant groups of unicellular organisms offer clues:

1. In dinoflagellates (*bottom, center*), the nuclear envelope does not fragment, and microtubules merely stabilize the nuclear envelope when mitosis occurs. The daughter chromosomes are attached to the nuclear envelope as the nucleus elongates and divides.
2. In diatoms and yeast cells (*bottom, right*), the nuclear envelope does not fragment; the spindle forms inside the nucleus and functions as in plant and animal cells.

These studies result in a hypothesis that once the eukaryotic cell arose, spindle fibers became more and more involved in the process of chromosome separation so that today the nuclear envelope fragments and the spindle apparatus fills the cell during mitosis (*top, center*).

FORM YOUR OPINION

1. Bacteria make a protein related to tubulin which is found in eukaryotic microtubules. In what way does this help trace the evolution of the spindle?
2. An opportunistic person makes use of any benefits that come their way. Why could it be said that evolution is opportunistic?

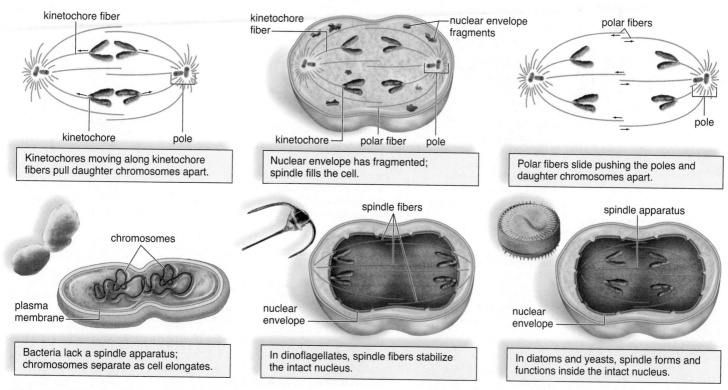

FIGURE 8A Organisms range from having no need of a spindle apparatus to complete reliance on a spindle apparatus (as in top center) to separate the daughter chromosomes.

8.4 Mitosis has a set series of phases

Figure 8.4A describes mitosis in animal cells (*top*) and in plant cells (*bottom*). The poles of animal cells are prominent because short spindle fibers, called an **aster,** radiate from the pair of centrioles located within each centrosome. Plant cells don't have centrioles or an aster.

Mitosis is one stage of the cell cycle; however, it is composed of a number of phases simplified as **propase, metaphase, anaphase,** and **telophase.** Each phase can be further divided into "early" and/or "late". Because you count the number of centromeres to determine the number of chromosomes, all the cells in Figure 8.4A have four chromosomes. During mitosis, kinetochores develop in the region of centromeres and these facilitate attachment of chromosomes to the spindle apparatus. Keep in mind that, although mitosis is divided into phases, it is a continuous process.

The process of mitosis ensures that all the cells of an individual have the same chromosomes and the same genes. All living cells require a copy of the same genes that allow them to carry out their normal activities, such as protein synthesis, cellular respiration, and yes, to divide. The daughter cells of mitosis enter the G_1 phase of the cell cycle, and if they make a commitment to divide, the chromosomes duplicate once more.

FIGURE 8.4A Phases of mitosis in animal cells and plant cells.

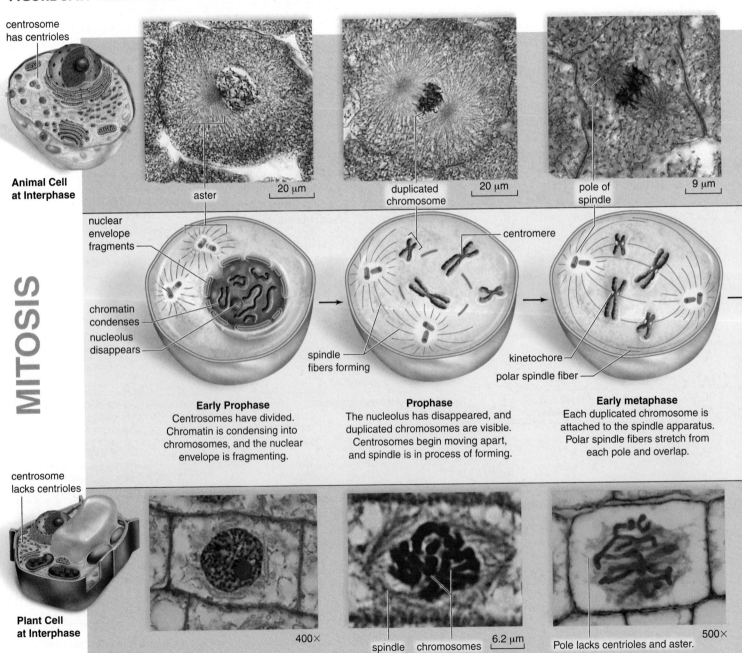

centrosome has centrioles

Animal Cell at Interphase

aster — 20 μm

duplicated chromosome — 20 μm

pole of spindle — 9 μm

MITOSIS

nuclear envelope fragments

chromatin condenses

nucleolus disappears

centromere

spindle fibers forming

kinetochore

polar spindle fiber

Early Prophase
Centrosomes have divided. Chromatin is condensing into chromosomes, and the nuclear envelope is fragmenting.

Prophase
The nucleolus has disappeared, and duplicated chromosomes are visible. Centrosomes begin moving apart, and spindle is in process of forming.

Early metaphase
Each duplicated chromosome is attached to the spindle apparatus. Polar spindle fibers stretch from each pole and overlap.

centrosome lacks centrioles

Plant Cell at Interphase

400×

spindle   chromosomes   6.2 μm

Pole lacks centrioles and aster.   500×

Contribution of the Cell Cycle to Human Health In both animals and plants, mitosis permits growth and repair. In human beings, mitosis is necessary as a fertilized egg develops into a newborn. Mitosis also occurs after birth as a child becomes an adult. Throughout life, mitosis allows a cut to heal or a broken bone to mend (**Fig. 8.4B**).

Mitosis also allows adult stem cells to re-supply the body with cells that will become specialized.

For example, stem cells in skin undergo mitosis and these new cells replace the skin cells that are continually shed from the surface of the body.

▶ **8.4 Check Your Progress** Tell a friend how you will be able to recognize drawings of the various phases of mitosis.

Children grow.

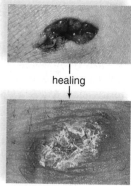
healing

Tissues undergo repair.

FIGURE 8.4B The cell cycle, including mitosis, occurs when humans grow and when tissues undergo repair.

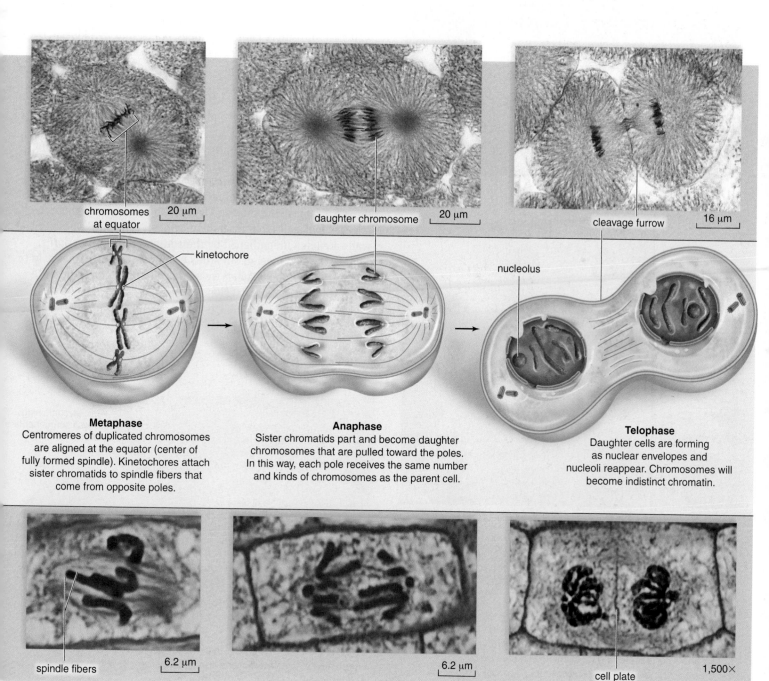

chromosomes at equator   20 μm

daughter chromosome   20 μm

cleavage furrow   16 μm

kinetochore

nucleolus

Metaphase
Centromeres of duplicated chromosomes are aligned at the equator (center of fully formed spindle). Kinetochores attach sister chromatids to spindle fibers that come from opposite poles.

Anaphase
Sister chromatids part and become daughter chromosomes that are pulled toward the poles. In this way, each pole receives the same number and kinds of chromosomes as the parent cell.

Telophase
Daughter cells are forming as nuclear envelopes and nucleoli reappear. Chromosomes will become indistinct chromatin.

spindle fibers   6.2 μm

6.2 μm

cell plate   1,500×

8.5 Cytokinesis divides the cytoplasm

We should always remember that mitosis means nuclear division and that cell division involves not only division of the nucleus but also division of the cytoplasm. Cytokinesis, meaning division of the cytoplasm, follows mitosis in most cells, but not all of them. When mitosis occurs but cytokinesis does not occur, the result is a multinucleated cell. For example, you will see later in this book that skeletal muscle cells in vertebrate animals and, at one point, the embryo sac in a flowering plant are multinucleated.

Ordinarily, cytokinesis begins during telophase and continues after the nuclei have formed until there are two daughter cells.

Animal Cell Cytokinesis In animal cells, a **cleavage furrow,** which is an indentation of the membrane between the two daughter nuclei, begins at the start of telophase. The cleavage furrow deepens when a band of actin filaments, called the contractile ring, slowly forms a circular constriction between the two daughter cells. The action of the contractile ring can be likened to pulling a drawstring ever tighter about the middle of a balloon. A narrow bridge between the two cells is visible during telophase, and then the contractile ring continues to separate the cytoplasm until there are two independent daughter cells. First, the cleavage furrow appears, and then the contractile ring tightens the constriction (**Fig. 8.5A**).

Plant Cell Cytokinesis In plant cells, cytokinesis occurs by a process different from that seen in animal cells. The rigid cell wall that surrounds plant cells does not permit cytokinesis by furrowing. Instead, cytokinesis in plant cells involves the building of new plasma membranes and cell walls between the daughter cells.

Cytokinesis is apparent when a small, flattened disk appears between the two daughter plant cells. Electron micrographs reveal that the disk is composed of vesicles (**Fig. 8.5B**). The Golgi apparatus produces these vesicles, which move along microtubules to the region of the disk. As more vesicles arrive and fuse, a cell plate can be seen. The **cell plate** is simply newly formed plasma membrane that expands outward until it reaches the old plasma membrane and fuses with it. The new membrane releases molecules that form the new plant cell walls. These cell walls are later strengthened by the addition of cellulose fibrils.

We have completed our study of mitosis and cytokinesis. In the next part of the chapter, we study cell cycle control, because when it falters, cancer develops.

▶ **8.5 Check Your Progress** Cytokinesis in plant cells is more complex than in animal cells. Why?

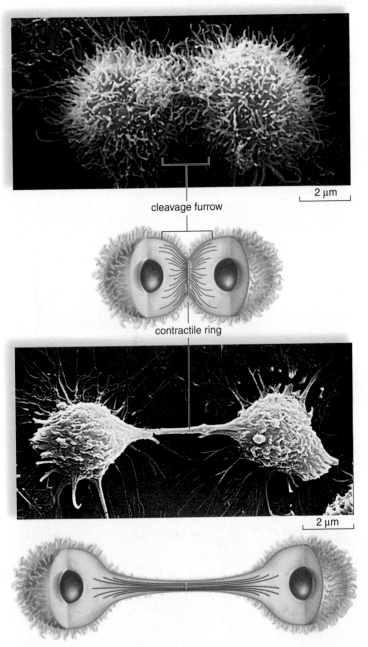

FIGURE 8.5A Cytokinesis in an animal cell involves a cleavage furrow and a contractile ring that pinches off the two cells.

© R. G. Kessel and C. Y. Shih, *Scanning Electron Microscopy in Biology. A Student's Atlas on Biological Organization,* 1974 Springer-Verlag, New York.

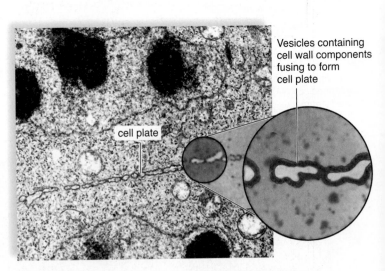

FIGURE 8.5B Cytokinesis in plant cells involves a cell plate where new plasma membrane and cell wall form between the two daughter cells.

8B Tissues Can Be Grown in the Lab

Most people are now aware that stem cells can undergo the cell cycle and generate tissues for the cure of devastating human diseases, such as diabetes, cancer, brain disorders, and heart ailments (**Fig. 8B**). For many years, scientists have known about two types of stem cells: embryonic stem (ES) cells and adult stem cells.

Embryonic stem cells are simply the cells of an early embryonic stage. These cells can stay alive longer and are better at producing different tissues than adult stem cells, but to acquire them a human embryo must be destroyed. Embryos are sometimes "left over" at fertility clinics, but even so many people reject the use of ES cells because it means the destruction of a potential human life. Adult stem cells are difficult to glean from the human body, and they do not multiply readily in the laboratory. Also, their potential to become all different types of tissues is not as great as that of ES cells. One drawback to both ES cells and adult stem cells is the danger of rejection by the recipient. Remember the many different types of proteins that occur in the plasma membrane? Some of those mark the cell as belonging to us, and if a transplanted tissue or organ carries different markers, our body works against them until they die. This is called rejection of the transplant.

Breakthrough

By now, scientists are experienced at coaxing stem cells to become specialized cells, but research would really benefit from an unlimited source of stem cells in order to achieve the goal of replacing diseased or damaged tissues in the human body. The scientific community is now hopeful that such a source has been found, thanks to a little-known Japanese scientist who worked alone for ten years in a tiny laboratory. Through patient research, Shinya Yamanaka was able to discover why ES cells are **pluripotent**—able to become any type of tissue in the body. He hypothesized that pluripotent cells produce certain proteins that specialized cells do not produce. Yamanaka worked with mouse skin cells until he knew that only four particular genes do the trick of making cells pluripotent. In 2006 he published his results in the journal *Cell*. Just five months later, United States scientists induced human skin cells to become pluripotent by supplying them with active forms of the four genes. These skin cells are termed iPS (induced pluripotent stem) cells. For every cell that became pluripotent, thousands of skin cells are treated. But the inefficiency doesn't matter because scientists have access to millions of skin cells. Such cells can even be obtained by simply swabbing the inside of a person's mouth! Researchers are still improving their technique and resolving various safety issues, but they feel confident they will be able to make tissues for human transplant. If replacement tissues are produced using the patient's own skin cells, rejection should not be a problem. However, scientists hope that eventually labs can stockpile so many different types of tissues, a good match will be available for most every person. Because spinal cord injuries should be treated within a few hours, there isn't time to use the patient's own skin cells to produce replacement nerve cells.

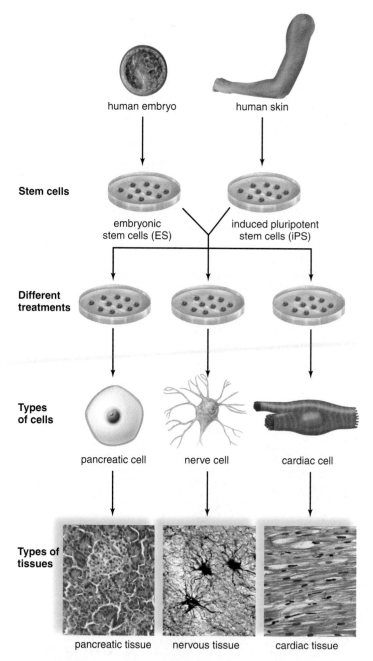

FIGURE 8B ES (embryonic stem) cells and iPS (induced pleuripotent stem) cells both produce many different types of specialized cells and tissues in the lab. Safety issues need to be resolved, but eventually scientists believe that iPS tissues will be available to cure human ills.

FORM YOUR OPINION

1. Currently, the main safety issue with iPS cells is that they might cause cancer. If you were 75 and had Alzheimer disease, would you be willing to take the chance of cancer in order to correct this condition?

2. Imagine that you are a scientist who worked all alone for ten years to reach a breakthrough. Should you be allowed to patent your "invention," or should it be available to everyone?

Cancer Is Uncontrolled Cell Division

Learning Outcomes

▶ Explain how various checkpoints control the cell cycle. (8.6)
▶ Relate the characteristics of cancer cells to a cell cycle out of control. (8.6)

The cell cycle's control system ensures that the cell cycle occurs in an orderly manner. Cancer develops when the cell cycle control system is not functioning as it should. A cell cycle out of control accounts for the abnormal characteristics of cancer cells.

8.6 Cell cycle control is lacking in cancer cells

In order for the body to remain healthy, the cell cycle must be controlled. The method of cell cycle control can be understood by comparing it to the events that occur in an automatic washing machine. The washer's control system starts to wash only when the tub is full of water, does not spin until the water has been emptied, delays the most vigorous spin until rinsing has occurred, and so forth. Similarly, the cell cycle's control system ensures that the G_1, S, G_2, and M stages occur in order and only when the previous stage has been successfully completed. The cell cycle has checkpoints that can delay the cycle until all is well. The cell cycle has many checkpoints, but we will consider only three: G_1, G_2, and M (mitotic) (**Fig. 8.6A**).

❶ The G_1 checkpoint is especially significant, because if the cell cycle passes this checkpoint, the cell is committed to divide. If the cell does not pass this checkpoint, it can enter G_0, during which it performs specialized functions but does not divide. If the DNA is damaged beyond repair, the internal signaling protein **p53** can stop the cycle at this checkpoint. First, p53 attempts to initiate DNA repair, but if that is not possible, it brings about the death of the cell by **apoptosis,** defined as programmed cell death.

❷ The cell cycle hesitates at the G_2 checkpoint, ensuring that DNA has replicated. This prevents the initiation of the M stage unless the chromosomes are duplicated. Also, if DNA is damaged, as from exposure to solar radiation or X-rays, arresting the cell cycle at this checkpoint allows time for the damage to be repaired, so that it is not passed on to daughter cells. If repair is not possible, apoptosis occurs.

❸ The M checkpoint occurs during the mitotic stage. The cycle hesitates at the M checkpoint to make sure the chromosomes are going to be distributed accurately to the daughter cells. The cell cycle does not continue until every duplicated chromosome is ready for the chromatids to separate.

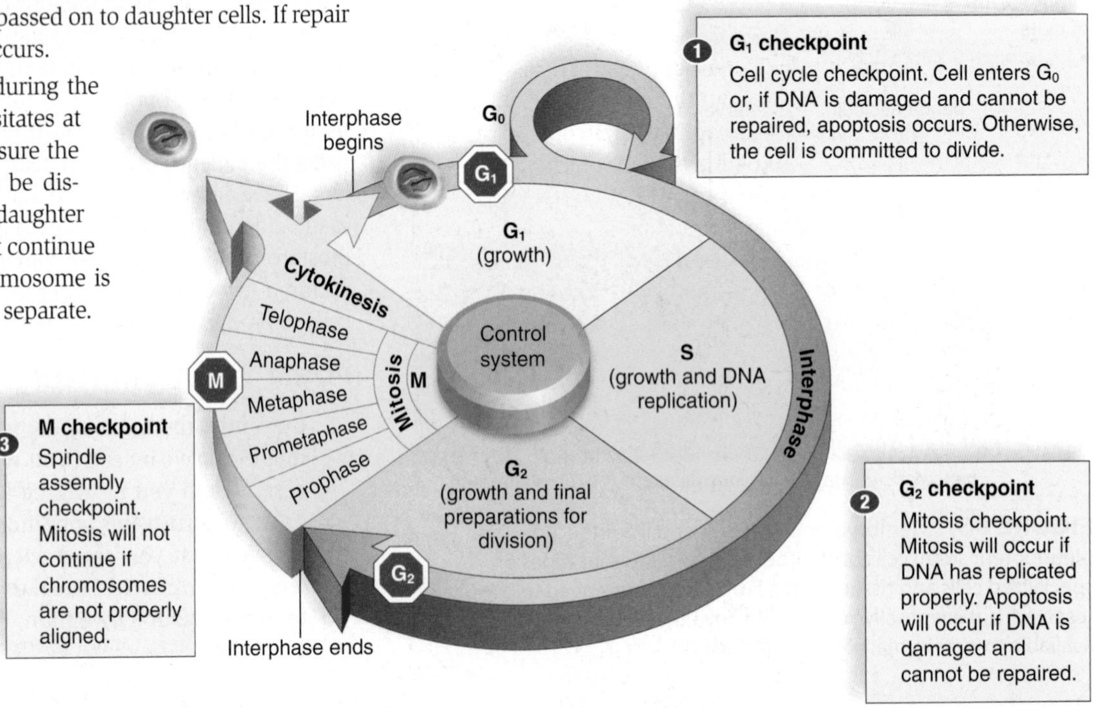

Apoptosis During apoptosis, the cell progresses through a typical series of events that bring about its destruction. The cell rounds up and loses contact with its neighbors. The nucleus fragments, and the plasma membrane develops blisters. Finally, the cell breaks into fragments, and its bits and pieces are engulfed by white blood cells and/or neighboring cells. A remarkable finding in the past few years is that cells routinely harbor the enzymes, now called *caspases,* that bring about apoptosis. These enzymes are ordinarily held in check by inhibitors, but are unleashed by either internal or external signals.

Cell division and apoptosis are two opposing processes that keep the number of cells in the body at an appropriate level. They are normal parts of growth and development. An organism begins as a single cell that repeatedly undergoes the cell cycle to produce many cells, but eventually some cells must die in order for the organism to take shape. For example, when a tadpole becomes a frog, the tail disappears as apoptosis occurs. In humans, the fingers and toes of an embryo are at first webbed, but later the webbing disappears as a result of apoptosis, and the fingers are freed from one another. Apoptosis is also helpful if an abnormal cell that could become cancerous appears. Otherwise, a tumor might develop.

Development of Cancer As explained in the introduction to this chapter, **mutations** (DNA changes) due to different environmental

FIGURE 8.6A
Checkpoints control and keep the cell cycle occurring normally.

❶ **G_1 checkpoint**
Cell cycle checkpoint. Cell enters G_0 or, if DNA is damaged and cannot be repaired, apoptosis occurs. Otherwise, the cell is committed to divide.

❸ **M checkpoint**
Spindle assembly checkpoint. Mitosis will not continue if chromosomes are not properly aligned.

❷ **G_2 checkpoint**
Mitosis checkpoint. Mitosis will occur if DNA has replicated properly. Apoptosis will occur if DNA is damaged and cannot be repaired.

Interphase begins

G_0

G_1

G_1 (growth)

Cytokinesis

Telophase

Anaphase

Metaphase

Prometaphase

Prophase

Mitosis

M

Control system

S (growth and DNA replication)

Interphase

G_2 (growth and final preparations for division)

G_2

Interphase ends

assaults can result in abnormal growth of cells and eventually cancer. Any tissue that already has a high rate of cell division is inherently more susceptible to **carcinogenesis,** the development of cancer, because division gives cells the opportunity to undergo a series of genetic mutations, each one making the next generation of cells more abnormal. Once the cell cycle is out of control, its checkpoints are not working and apoptosis is not occurring. Yet, the cells live on and keep dividing even though they are abnormal.

Cancers are classified according to tissue of origin. *Carcinomas* are cancers of the tissue type that lines organs; *sarcomas* are cancers arising in muscle or bone and cartilage; and *leukemias* are cancers of the blood. In general, cancer cells have the following characteristics:

Cancer cells lack differentiation Cancer cells are nonspecialized and do not contribute to the functioning of a body part. A cancer cell does not look like a specialized skin, muscle, nerve, or liver cell; instead, it looks distinctly abnormal. Normal cells enter the cell cycle about 70 times, and then they die. Cancer cells can enter the cell cycle repeatedly, and in this way they are immortal.

Cancer cells have abnormal nuclei The nuclei of cancer cells are enlarged and may contain an abnormal number of chromosomes. For example, the nuclei of the cervical cancer cells shown in **Figure 8.6B** have increased to the point that they take up most of the cell. The chromosomes are also abnormal; some parts may be duplicated, or some may be deleted. In addition, gene amplification (extra copies of specific genes) is seen much more frequently in cancer cells than in normal cells.

Cancer cells form tumors Normal cells anchor themselves to a substrate and/or adhere to their neighbors. Then they exhibit contact inhibition and stop dividing. But when cancer is present, cells have lost all restraint; they pile on top of one another and grow in multiple layers, forming a **tumor.** Normal cells respond to signals from their neighbors telling them when to grow and when to stop growing. Cancer cells have no need for stimulatory signals, and they do not respond to inhibitory signals. As cancer develops, the most aggressive cell becomes the dominant cell of the tumor.

Cancer cells undergo angiogenesis and metastasis To grow larger than a million cells (about the size of a pea), a tumor must have a well-developed capillary network to bring it nutrients and oxygen. **Angiogenesis** is the formation of new blood vessels. The low oxygen content in the middle of a tumor may turn on genes for secretions that diffuse into the nearby tissues and cause new vessels to form. Due to mutations, cancer cells tend to be motile because they have a disorganized internal cytoskeleton and lack intact actin filament bundles. To metastasize, cancer cells must make their way across the extracellular matrix and invade a blood vessel or lymphatic vessel. Invasive cancer cells are odd-shaped (see Fig. 8.6B) and don't look at all like normal cells. Cancer cells produce proteinase enzymes that degrade the membrane and allow them to invade underlying tissues. When these cells begin new tumors far from the primary tumor, **metastasis** has occurred. Not many cancer cells achieve this feat (maybe 1 in 10,000), but those that successfully metastasize spread the cancer throughout the body.

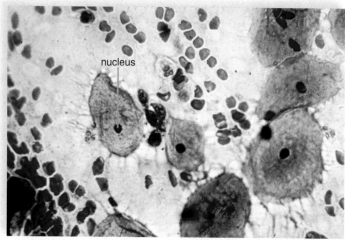

Normal cervical cells
50 μm

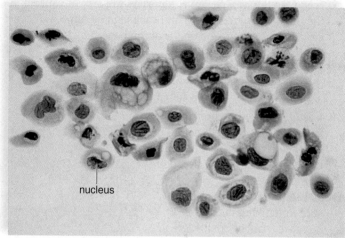

Precancerous cervical cells
100 μm

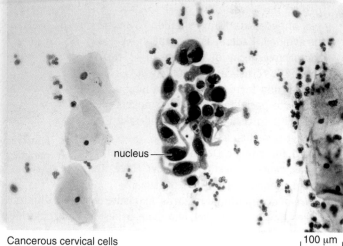

Cancerous cervical cells
100 μm

FIGURE 8.6B These micrographs show a progression toward cancer of the cervix in a female. Cervical cancer is often caused by the human papillomavirus (HPV), a sexually transmitted virus. Therefore, all young women should be vaccinated to protect themselves against any new HPV infections.

▶ **8.6 Check Your Progress** *a.* Which characteristics of cancer cells can be associated with loss of cell cycle control? *b.* Which are abnormalities that go beyond the loss of cell cycle control?

8C Protective Behaviors and Diet Help Prevent Cancer

Evidence suggests that the risk of certain types of cancer can be reduced by adopting protective behaviors and the right diet.

Protective Behaviors

The following behaviors help prevent cancer:

Don't smoke Cigarette smoking accounts for about 30% of all cancer deaths. Smoking is responsible for 90% of lung cancer cases among men and 79% among women—about 87% altogether. People who smoke two or more packs of cigarettes per day have lung cancer mortality rates 15–25 times greater than those of nonsmokers. Smokeless tobacco (chewing tobacco or snuff) increases the risk of cancers of the mouth, larynx, throat, and esophagus. Chances of cancer increase when smoking is accompanied by heavy alcohol use.

Use sunscreen Almost all cases of skin cancer are considered sun-related. Use a sunscreen with a sun protection factor (SPF) of at least 15, and wear protective clothing if you are going to be out during the brightest part of the day. Don't sunbathe on the beach or in a tanning salon.

Avoid radiation Excessive exposure to ionizing radiation can increase cancer risk. Even though most medical and dental X-rays are adjusted to deliver the lowest dose possible, unnecessary X-rays should be avoided. Radon gas from the radioactive decay of uranium in the Earth's crust can accumulate in houses and increase the risk of lung cancer, especially in cigarette smokers. It is best to test your home and take the proper remedial actions.

Be tested for cancer Do the shower check for breast cancer or testicular cancer. Have other exams done regularly by a physician.

Be aware of occupational hazards Exposure to several different industrial agents (nickel, chromate, asbestos, vinyl chloride, etc.) and/or radiation increases the risk of various cancers. The risk from asbestos is greatly increased when combined with cigarette smoking.

Carefully consider hormone therapy A new study conducted by the Women's Health Initiative found that combined estrogen-progestin therapy prescribed to ease the symptoms of menopause increased the incidence of breast cancer. Also, the risk outweighed the possible decrease in the number of colorectal cancer cases sometimes attributed to hormone therapy.

Sunscreen with SPF 15 minimizes skin cancer.

The Right Diet

Statistical studies have suggested that people who follow the following dietary guidelines are less likely to have cancer.

Increase consumption of foods rich in vitamins A and C Beta-carotene, a precursor of vitamin A, is found in carrots, fruits, and dark-green, leafy vegetables. Vitamin C is present in citrus fruits. These vitamins are called antioxidants because in cells they prevent the formation of free radicals (organic ions having an unpaired electron) that can possibly damage DNA. Vitamin C also prevents the conversion of nitrates and nitrites into carcinogenic nitrosamines in the digestive tract.

Limit consumption of salt-cured, smoked, or nitrite-cured foods Consuming salt-cured or pickled foods may increase the risk of stomach and esophageal cancers. Smoked foods, such as ham and sausage, contain chemical carcinogens similar to those in tobacco smoke. Nitrites, sometimes added to processed meats (e.g., hot dogs and cold cuts) and other foods to protect them from spoilage, are associated with the development of cancer.

Include vegetables from the cabbage family in the diet The cabbage family includes cabbage, broccoli, brussels sprouts, kohlrabi, and cauliflower. These vegetables may reduce the risk of gastrointestinal and respiratory tract cancers.

Be moderate in the consumption of alcohol The risks of cancer development rise as the level of alcohol intake increases. The strongest associations are with oral, pharyngeal, esophageal, and laryngeal cancer, but cancer of the breast and liver are also implicated. People who both drink and smoke greatly increase their risk for developing cancer.

Maintain a healthy weight The risk of cancer (especially colon, breast, and uterine cancers) is 55% greater among obese women, and the risk of colon cancer is 33% greater among obese men, compared to people of normal weight.

FORM YOUR OPINION

1. What mental processes might cause people to sunbathe even when they know skin cancer could result from this behavior? What could you say to change their mind? Are these the same mental processes that cause people to smoke and drink?
2. It can take years to acquire cancer by neglecting this list of do's and don'ts. How much does that affect people's behavior today?

Meiosis Reduces the Chromosome Number

Learning Outcomes

▶ Describe three ways genetic variation is ensured in the next generation. (8.7–8.9)

▶ Describe the phases of meiosis, and compare the occurrence of meiosis in the life cycle of various organisms. (8.10–8.11)

▶ Compare the process and the result of meiosis to those of mitosis. (8.12)

Meiosis is necessary to sexual reproduction, the type of reproduction that requires two parents. In animals, the two parents are called a male and a female. The results of meiosis cause the offspring to be different from each other and from either parent. Exactly where meiosis occurs in the life cycle of organisms determines the adult chromosome number. Even though meiosis is different from mitosis, the two processes bear certain similarities.

8.7 Homologous chromosomes separate during meiosis

Meiosis is reduction division. Because meiosis involves two divisions, four daughter cells result. Each of these daughter cells has one of each kind of chromosome and, therefore, half as many chromosomes as the parent cell.

In **Figure 8.7,** the diploid (2n) number of chromosomes is four, and there are two pairs of chromosomes. The short chromosomes are one pair, and the long chromosomes are another. They are homologous chromosomes (also called **homologues**) because they look alike and carry genes for the same traits, such as finger length. However, one homologue could call for short fingers and the other for long fingers.

Prior to the first division, called **meiosis I,** DNA replication has occurred, and the chromosomes are duplicated. During meiosis I, the homologous chromosomes come together and line up side by side. This so-called **synapsis** results in an association of four chromatids that stay in close proximity during the first two phases of meiosis I. Also, because of synapsis, there are pairs of homologous chromosomes at the equator during meiosis I. (Keep in mind that only during meiosis I is it possible to observe paired chromosomes at the equator.) Synapsis leads to a reduction in the chromosome number because it permits orderly separation of homologous chromosomes. The daughter nuclei are haploid because they receive only one member of each pair. The haploid (n) nature of each daughter cell can be verified by counting its centromeres. Each chromosome, however, is still duplicated, and no replication of DNA occurs between meiosis I and meiosis II. The period of time between meiosis I and meiosis II is called **interkinesis.**

During **meiosis II,** the sister chromatids of each chromosome separate, becoming daughter chromosomes that are distributed to daughter nuclei. In the end, each of four daughter cells has the n, or haploid, number of chromosomes, and each chromosome consists of one chromatid.

In humans, the daughter cells mature into **gametes** (sex cells—sperm and egg) that fuse during fertilization. **Fertilization** restores the diploid number of chromosomes in the zygote, the first cell of the new individual. If the gametes carried the diploid instead of the haploid number of chromosomes, the chromosome number would double with each fertilization. After several generations, the zygote would be nothing but chromosomes.

▶ **8.7 Check Your Progress** At the completion of meiosis I, are the cells diploid (2n) or haploid (n)? Explain.

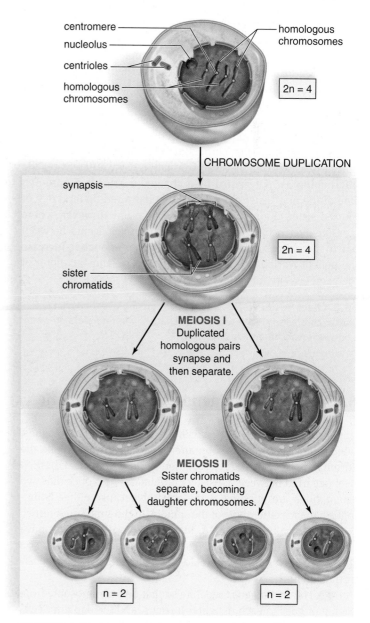

FIGURE 8.7 Meiosis produces daughter cells that are genetically different from the parent cell. Four daughter cells result because meiosis includes two divisions: During meiosis I, the homologous chromosomes separate, and during meiosis II the chromatids separate, becoming daughter chromosomes.

8.8 Synapsis and crossing-over occur during meiosis I

During meiosis I, two events occur that are not seen in mitosis: synapsis and crossing-over. As you know, prior to meiosis I, the chromosomes have duplicated, and each consists of two sister chromatids held together at the centromere.

Synapsis The homologous chromosomes come together and line up side by side, much like two dancing partners who will stay together until the dance ends. The homologues are held in place by a protein lattice that develops between them. Because each homologue has two sister chromatids, four chromatids are in close association. Each set of four chromatids is called a **tetrad.**

Crossing-over During synapsis, the homologues sometimes exchange genetic material, an event called **crossing-over.** To be specific, as **Figure 8.8** shows, the nonsister chromatids are involved in crossing-over events. The homologues carry genetic information for certain traits, such as finger length, type of hair-line, and any number of other traits. The genetic information of nonsister chromatids can differ because they belong to the other homologue. For example, one set of nonsister chromatids could call for short fingers, and the other set could call for long fingers.

After the nonsister chromatids exchange genetic material during crossing-over, the sister chromatids carry different genetic information as represented by a change in color in Figure 8.8: One of the blue sister chromatids now has a red tip, and one of the red sister chromatids now has a blue tip. However, where crossing-over occurs is random. Crossing-over occurs between one to three times per chromosome, which is enough to increase the genetic variability of the daughter cells—and therefore, of the gametes—in animals.

▶ **8.8 Check Your Progress** Why does crossing-over between non-sister chromatids increase genetic variation, whereas crossing-over between sister chromatids would not?

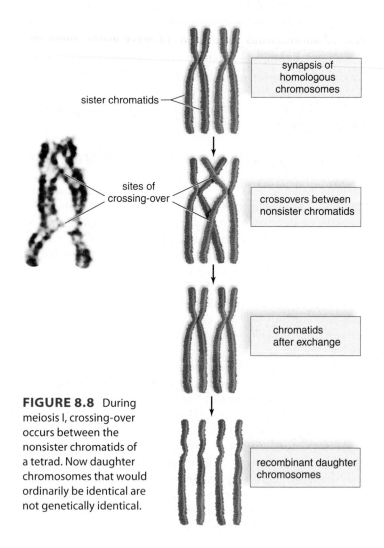

FIGURE 8.8 During meiosis I, crossing-over occurs between the nonsister chromatids of a tetrad. Now daughter chromosomes that would ordinarily be identical are not genetically identical.

8.9 Sexual reproduction increases genetic variation

In **Figure 8.9A,** ❶ the parent cell has two pairs of homologues, which undergo synapsis soon after meiosis I begins. While the chromatids were in close association during synapsis, crossing-over occurred between nonsister chromatids. ❷ Notice that two orientations are possible at the equator because either homologue can face either pole of the spindle. In the simplest of terms, with reference to Figure 8.9A, the red chromosomes don't have to be on the left, and the blue chromosomes don't have to be on the right. Therefore, the homologous pairs *align independently* at the equator.

❸ The homologues separate so that one chromosome from each pair goes to each daughter nucleus, and the daughter cells are haploid. ❹ All possible combinations of chromosomes can occur among the gametes. Therefore, **independent assortment** of homologues occurs during meiosis. In the simplest of terms, any short chromosome (blue or red) can be with any long chromosome (blue or red). The genetic variation brought about by independent assortment of chromosomes is increased by crossing-over.

Fertilization The union of male and female gametes during fertilization produces a zygote, the first cell of the new individual. As we have seen, the gametes produced by individuals, such as humans, have the same number of chromosomes, but the chromosomes may carry different genetic information due to independent assortment and crossing-over. In humans, each gamete has 23 chromosomes. Considering the fusion of unlike gametes due to independent assortment, it means that $(2^{23})^2$, or 70,368,744,000,000, chromosomally different zygotes are possible, even assuming no crossing-over. If crossing-over occurs once, then $(4^{23})^2$, or 4,951,760,200,000,000,000,000,000,000, genetically different zygotes are possible for every couple. Keep in mind that crossing-over can occur several times between homologues.

Advantages of Genetic Variation The process of sexual reproduction brings about genetic variation among members of a population. Therefore, if the environment changes, genetic variability among offspring, introduced by sexual reproduction, may be advantageous (**Fig. 8.9B**). In other words, some off-spring may have a better chance of survival and reproductive success than others in a population. For example, suppose the ambient temperature were to rise due to global climate change. A dog with genes for the least amount of fur may have an advantage over other dogs of its generation.

In a changing environment, sexual reproduction, with its reshuffling of genetic information due to meiosis and fertilization, is expected to give at least a few offspring a better chance of survival when environmental conditions change.

▶ **8.9 Check Your Progress** The mating of relatives reduces possible variations. Why?

FIGURE 8.9B The puppies in this litter differ in appearance because crossing-over and independent assortment occurred during meiosis, and fertilization brought different gametes together.

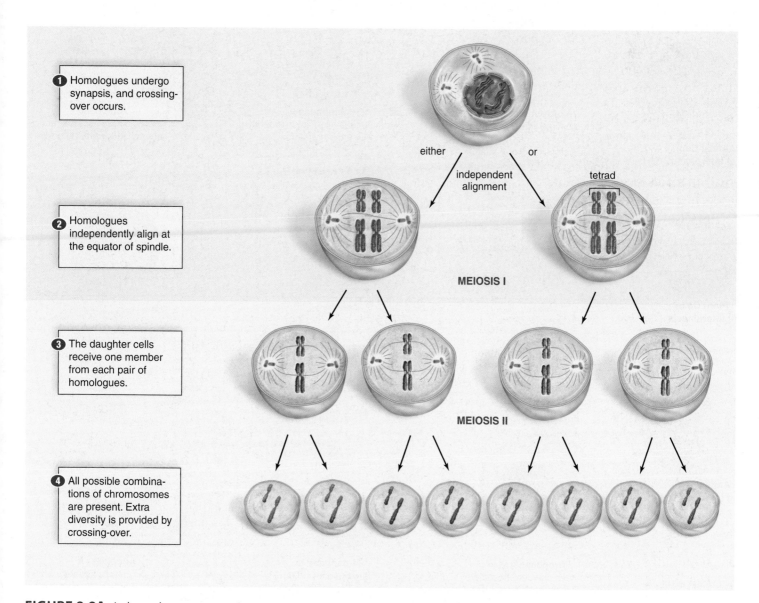

❶ Homologues undergo synapsis, and crossing-over occurs.

❷ Homologues independently align at the equator of spindle.

❸ The daughter cells receive one member from each pair of homologues.

❹ All possible combinations of chromosomes are present. Extra diversity is provided by crossing-over.

either

or

independent alignment

tetrad

MEIOSIS I

MEIOSIS II

FIGURE 8.9A Independent assortment increases genetic variation. Blue background = 2n; tan background = n.

8.10 Meiosis requires meiosis I and meiosis II

The same four phases of mitosis—prophase, metaphase, anaphase, and telophase—occur during both meiosis I (**Fig. 8.10A**) and meiosis II (**Fig. 8.10B**). During **prophase I**, the nuclear envelope fragments, the nucleolus disappears as the spindle appears, and the condensing homologues undergo synapsis. The formation of tetrads helps prepare the homologous chromosomes for separation; it also allows crossing-over to occur between nonsis-

ter chromatids. During **metaphase I**, tetrads are present and homologues align independently at the spindle equator. Following separation of the homologues during **anaphase I** and reformation of the nuclear envelopes during **telophase I**, the daughter nuclei are haploid: Each daughter cell contains only one chromosome from each pair of homologues. The chromosomes are duplicated, and each still has two sister chromatids.

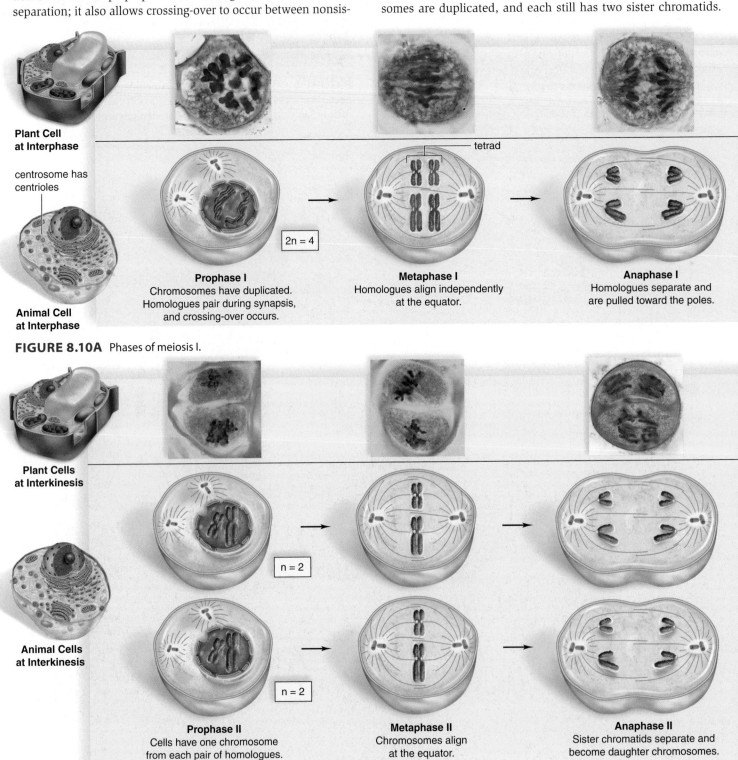

Plant Cell at Interphase

centrosome has centrioles

Animal Cell at Interphase

tetrad

2n = 4

Prophase I
Chromosomes have duplicated. Homologues pair during synapsis, and crossing-over occurs.

Metaphase I
Homologues align independently at the equator.

Anaphase I
Homologues separate and are pulled toward the poles.

FIGURE 8.10A Phases of meiosis I.

Plant Cells at Interkinesis

Animal Cells at Interkinesis

n = 2

n = 2

Prophase II
Cells have one chromosome from each pair of homologues.

Metaphase II
Chromosomes align at the equator.

Anaphase II
Sister chromatids separate and become daughter chromosomes.

FIGURE 8.10B Phases of meiosis II. Blue background = 2n; tan background = n.

No replication of DNA occurs during a period of time called **interkinesis.**

When you think about it, the events of meiosis II are the same as those for mitosis, except the cells are haploid. At the beginning of prophase II, a spindle appears, while the nuclear envelope fragments and the nucleolus disappears. Duplicated chromosomes (one from each pair of homologous chromosomes) are present, and each attaches to the spindle. During metaphase II, the duplicated chromosomes line up at the spindle equator. During anaphase II, sister chromatids separate and move toward the poles. Each pole receives the same number and kinds of chromosomes. In telophase II, the spindle disappears as nuclear envelopes form.

Now that we have a good working knowledge of meiosis, Section 8.11 discusses when it occurs in the life cycle of various types of organisms.

▶ **8.10 Check Your Progress** How would you recognize a diagram of plant cell meiosis?

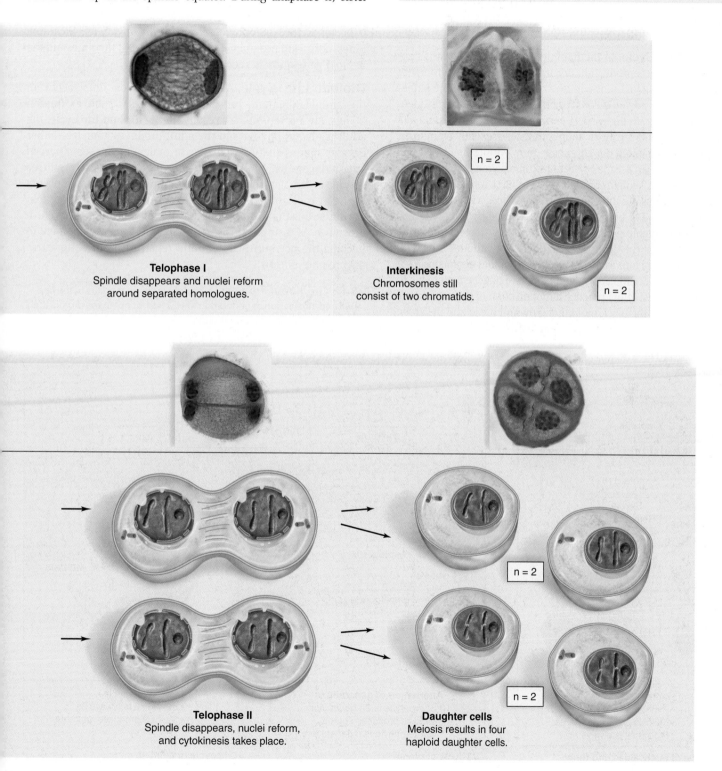

Telophase I
Spindle disappears and nuclei reform around separated homologues.

Interkinesis
Chromosomes still consist of two chromatids.

n = 2

n = 2

Telophase II
Spindle disappears, nuclei reform, and cytokinesis takes place.

Daughter cells
Meiosis results in four haploid daughter cells.

n = 2

n = 2

8.11 Life cycles are varied

A **life cycle** includes the reproductive events that occur from one generation to the next. Prokaryotes and a few protists reproduce asexually by means of binary fission. During **asexual reproduction,** there is only one parent, and the offspring are genetically identical to that parent. Sexual exchange does occur among prokaryotic, however, as will be discussed in chapter 16. Eukaryotes can usually reproduce sexually. **Sexual reproduction** usually requires two parents and the life cycle involves both meiosis and mitosis; among eukaryotes, three possible life cycles are known.

Haploid Life Cycle In the **haploid life cycle,** the adult is haploid, and asexual reproduction occurs as long as the environment is stable. This is consistent with the observation that if the parent is doing well it is advantageous for offspring to be genetically identical to the parent. In **Figure 8.11** *bottom,* an alga called *Chlamydomonas* is a haploid organism and reproduces asexually by mitosis. As many as 16 haploid daughter cells form within the cell wall of the parent and then escape by secreting an enzyme that digests the parent cell wall. Sexual reproduction (**Fig. 8.11** *top*) occurs when growth conditions are unfavorable and produces a zygote that can survive bad weather because it has a protective covering. Meiosis occurs as the zygote germinates and produces haploid spores. A spore is a cell that can give rise to an organism without fusing with another cell. More importantly, since these haploid organisms have different genetic compositions, some of them may be better able to survive bad times. Fungi practice a modification of the haploid life cycle. Therefore, the black mold that grows on bread and the green scum (algae) that floats on a pond are both haploid.

Alternation of Generations Life Cycle Plants have various means of reproducing asexually. As an example, the "eye" of a sweet potato will produce an entire plant. But, in general, plants practice sexual reproduction in a life cycle known as **alternation of generations.** The diploid sporophyte produces haploid spores by meiosis; mitosis occurs as spores become haploid gametophytes. The gametophyte produces haploid gametes. Fusion of gametes produces a zygote that undergoes mitosis as it becomes the sporophyte. The majority of plants, including pines, corn, and pea plants, are diploid most of the time, and the haploid generation is short-lived.

Diploid Life Cycle Asexual reproduction does occur in the animal kingdom, but complex animals, such as human beings, always reproduce sexually. In the **diploid life cycle,** the adult is always diploid and the adult produces gametes (either eggs or sperm) that are haploid. In males, meiosis is a part of spermatogenesis, which occurs in the testes and produces sperm. In females, meiosis is a part of oogenesis, which occurs in the ovaries and produces eggs. After the sperm and egg join during fertilization, the zygote has the diploid number of chromosomes. Mitosis occurs as a zygote undergoes development to become the newborn. Growth and repair of tissues after birth also require mitosis.

▶ **8.11 Check Your Progress** A haploid individual occurs in the haploid and alternation of generation life cycles but not in the diploid life cycles. What accounts for this difference in the cycles?

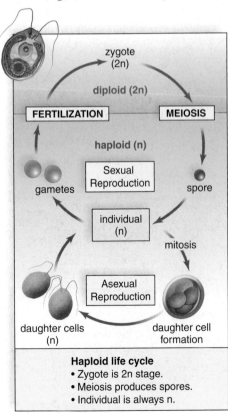

Haploid life cycle
- Zygote is 2n stage.
- Meiosis produces spores.
- Individual is always n.

Life cycle of many algae and fungi

Alternation of generations
- Sporophyte is 2n generation.
- Meiosis produces spores.
- Gametophyte is n generation.

Life cycle of plants

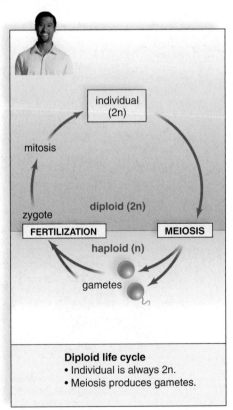

Diploid life cycle
- Individual is always 2n.
- Meiosis produces gametes.

Life cycle of animals

FIGURE 8.11 Common life cycles.

8.12 Meiosis can be compared to mitosis

Figure 8.12 compares meiosis to mitosis. Notice that:

- Meiosis requires two nuclear divisions, but mitosis requires only one nuclear division.
- Meiosis results in four daughter cells. Mitosis results in two daughter cells.
- Following meiosis, the four daughter cells are haploid, meaning that they have half the chromosome number of the parent cell. Following mitosis, the daughter cells are diploid, having the same chromosome number as the parent cell.
- Following meiosis, the daughter cells are genetically dissimilar to each other and to the parent cell. Following mitosis, the daughter cells are genetically identical to each other and to the parent cell.

These differences between meiosis and mitosis are due to certain events:

- During meiosis I, tetrads form, and crossing-over occurs during prophase I. These events do not occur during mitosis.

- During metaphase I of meiosis, tetrads are at the equator. The homologues align at the spindle equator independently. During metaphase in mitosis, duplicated chromosomes align at the spindle equator.
- During anaphase I of meiosis, homologues separate, and duplicated chromosomes (with centromeres intact) move to opposite poles. During anaphase of mitosis, sister chromatids separate, becoming daughter chromosomes that move to opposite poles.

The events of meiosis II are just like those of mitosis except that in meiosis II, the daughter cells have the haploid number of chromosomes. Could abnormal meiosis cause the inheritance of a chromosome anomaly? Section 8.13 shows how this is possible.

▶ **8.12 Check Your Progress** How are meiosis I and II like but different from mitosis?

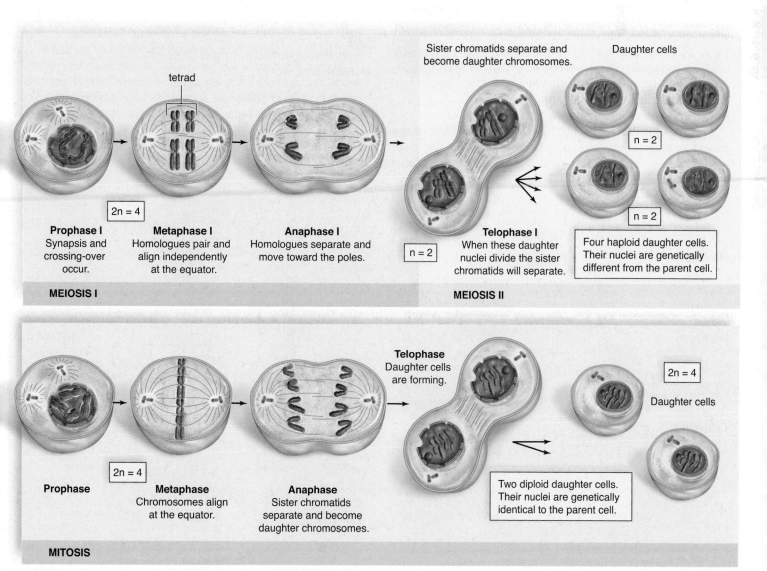

FIGURE 8.12 Meiosis (*top*) compared to mitosis (*bottom*).

Chromosome Anomalies Can Be Inherited

Learning Outcomes

▸ Relate polyploidy to oversized flowers and fruits and aneuploidy to nondisjunction. (8.13)

▸ Describe Down syndrome, Turner syndrome, and Klinefelter syndrome, including their unusual chromosome number. (8.14)

▸ Describe four anomalies in chromosome structure and relate each to human disorders. (8.15)

Chromosome mutations fall into two categories: change in chromosome number and change in chromosome structure. The presence of more than two sets of chromosomes (polyploidy) is common in plants. The gain or loss of a single chromosome (aneuploidy) occurs because of nondisjunction during meiosis. Changes in chromosome structure include deletion, duplication, inversion, and translocation.

8.13 Nondisjunction causes chromosome number anomalies

Changes in chromosome number also increase the amount of genetic variation among individuals.

Changes in the chromosome number include polyploidy and aneuploidy. When a eukaryote has three or more complete sets of chromosomes, it is called a **polyploid.** More specifically, triploids (3n) have three of each kind of chromosome, tetraploids (4n) have four sets, pentaploids (5n) have five sets, and so on. Although polyploidy is not often seen in animals, it is a major evolutionary mechanism in plants, including many of our most important crops— wheat, corn, cotton, and sugarcane, as well as fruits such as watermelons, strawberries, bananas, and apples. The strawberry on the left is an octaploid and much larger than the diploid one on the right. Also, many attractive flowers, including chrysanthemums and daylilies, are polyploids.

An organism that does not have an exact multiple of the diploid number of chromosomes is an **aneuploid.** When an individual has only one of a particular type of chromosome, monosomy (2n − 1) occurs. When an individual has three of a particular type of chromosome (2n + 1), **trisomy** occurs. The usual cause of monosomy and trisomy is nondisjunction during meiosis. **Nondisjunction** occurs during meiosis I when homologues fail to separate and both homologues go into the same daughter cell (**Fig. 8.13A**), or during meiosis II when the sister chromatids fail to separate and both daughter chromosomes go into the same gamete (**Fig. 8.13B**).

Monosomy and trisomy occur in both plants and animals. In animals, autosomal monosomies and trisomies are generally lethal, but a trisomic individual is more likely to survive than a monosomic one. The survivors are characterized by a distinctive set of physical and mental anomalies, as in the human condition called trisomy 21 (see Section 8.14). Sex chromosome aneuploids have a better chance of producing survivors than do autosomal aneuploids.

▸ **8.13 Check Your Progress** Why might problems arise if a person were to inherit three copies, instead of two copies, of a chromosome?

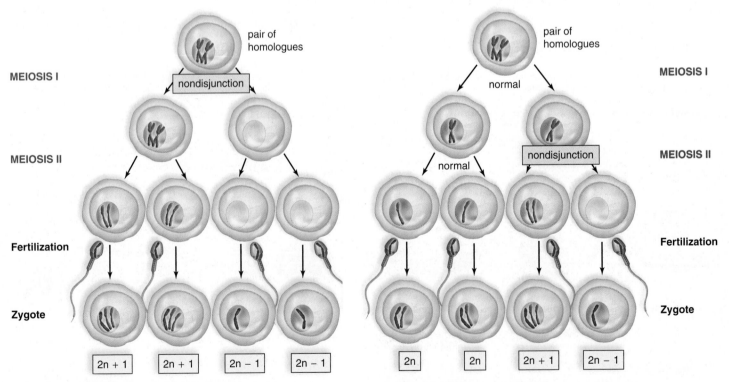

FIGURE 8.13A Nondisjunction of chromosomes during meiosis I of oogenesis, followed by fertilization with normal sperm.

FIGURE 8.13B Nondisjunction of chromosomes during meiosis II of oogenesis, followed by fertilization with normal sperm.

8.14 Chromosome number anomalies can be observed

When an individual inherits an aneuploidy, certain characteristics commonly appear that together are called a **syndrome**. Despite these characteristics, early intervention and ongoing support can enable many people with syndromes to lead normal, healthy, and productive lives.

Trisomy 21 (Down Syndrome) The most common autosomal trisomy among humans is trisomy 21, also called Down syndrome. This syndrome is easily recognized by these characteristics: short stature, eyelid fold, flat face, stubby fingers, wide gap between the first and second toes, large, fissured tongue, round head, distinctive palm crease, heart problems, and mental retardation, which can sometimes be severe (**Fig. 8.14**). In addition, these individuals have an increased chance of developing Alzheimer disease later in life.

Over 90% of individuals with Down syndrome have three copies of chromosome 21. Usually, two copies are contributed by the egg; however, recent studies indicate that in 23% of the cases studied, the sperm contributed the extra chromosome. The chances of a woman having a child with Down syndrome increase rapidly with age. In women age 20–30, 1 in 1,400 births have Down syndrome, while in women 30–35, about 1 in 750 births have Down syndrome. It is thought the longer oocytes are dormant in the ovaries, the greater the chances of a nondisjunction event.

Although an older woman is more likely to have a Down syndrome child, most babies with Down syndrome are born to women younger than age 40 because this is the age group having the most babies. A karyotype of the individual's chromosomes can detect a Down syndrome child. However, young women are not routinely encouraged to undergo the procedures necessary to get a sample of fetal cells because the risk of complications is greater than the risk of having a Down syndrome child. Fortunately, a test based on substances in maternal blood can help identify fetuses who may need to be karyotyped.

TABLE 8.14	Aneuploidy in Humans	
Chromosomes	**Syndrome**	**Frequency**
Autosomes		
Trisomy 21	Down	1/700
Trisomy 13[†]	Patau	1/5,000
Trisomy 18[†]	Edwards	1/10,000
Sex chromosomes, females		
XO, monosomy	Turner	1/5,000
XXX, trisomy[††]		1/700
Sex chromosomes, males		
XYY, trisomy	Normal	1/10,000
XXY, trisomy[††]	Klinefelter	1/500

[†]Structural anomalies usually result in early death.
[††]A greater number of X chromosomes is possible.

Sex Chromosome Number Anomalies Newborns with an X chromosome number anomaly are more likely to survive than those with an autosome number anomaly, because both males and females have only one functioning X chromosome. Any others become an inactive mass called a Barr body (after Murray Barr, the person who discovered it; see Section 11.3).

Turner syndrome females have only a single X chromosome. They tend to be short, with a broad chest and widely spaced nipples. These individuals also have a low posterior hairline and neck webbing. Their ovaries, oviducts, and uterus are very small and underdeveloped. Turner females do not undergo puberty or menstruate, and their breasts do not develop. However, some have given birth following in vitro fertilization using donor eggs.

About 1 in every 700 females has an extra X chromosome, but they lack symptoms, because all but one of the X chromosomes is inactivated as discussed in Section 11.3, page 214.

A male with **Klinefelter syndrome** has two or more X chromosomes in addition to a Y chromosome. The extra X chromosomes become inactivated. In Klinefelter males, the testes and prostate gland are underdeveloped, and facial hair is lacking. There may be some breast development. Affected individuals have large hands and feet and very long arms and legs. They are usually slow to learn but not mentally retarded, unless they inherit more than two X chromosomes. No matter how many X chromosomes are present, an individual with a Y chromosome is a male.

Certain human syndromes known to result from aneuploidy can lead to early death because of the imbalance of genetic material (Table 8.14). Chromosome structural changes can also cause syndromes. Some of these are examined in Section 8.15.

FIGURE 8.14 Down syndrome is due to three copies of chromosome 21, shown in circle.

▶ **8.14 Check Your Progress** When a male is XYY, did nondisjunction occur during meiosis I or meiosis II?

8.15 Chromosome structure anomalies can also be observed

Changes in chromosome structure occur in humans and lead to various syndromes, many of which are just now being discovered. Various agents in the environment, such as radiation, certain organic chemicals, or even viruses, can cause chromosomes to break. Ordinarily, when breaks occur in chromosomes, the two broken ends reunite and retain the same sequence of genes. Sometimes, however, the broken ends of one or more chromosomes do not rejoin in the same pattern as before, and the result can be various types of chromosomal rearrangements.

Changes in chromosome structure include deletions, duplications, inversions, and translocations of chromosome segments (**Fig. 8.15**). A **deletion** occurs when an end of a chromosome breaks off or when two simultaneous breaks lead to the loss of an internal segment. Even when only one member of a pair of chromosomes is affected, a deletion often cause a syndrome.

A **duplication** is the presence of a particular chromosome segment more than once in the same chromosome. An **inversion** has occurred when a segment of a chromosome is turned 180 degrees. This reversed sequence of genes can lead to altered gene activities and to deletions and duplications during meiosis.

A **translocation** is the movement of a chromosome segment from one chromosome to another, nonhomologous chromosome.

Syndrome Examples Sometimes geneticists can detect changes in chromosome structure in humans by doing a karyotype. They may also discover such changes by studying the inheritance pattern of a disorder in a particular family.

Williams syndrome occurs when chromosome 7 loses a tiny end piece. Children who have this syndrome look like pixies, with turned-up noses, wide mouths, small chins, and large ears. Although their academic skills are poor, they exhibit excellent verbal and musical abilities. The gene that governs the production of the protein elastin is missing, and this affects the health of the cardiovascular system and causes their skin to age prematurely. Such individuals are very friendly but need an ordered life, perhaps because of the loss of a gene for a protein that is normally active in the brain.

Cri du chat (cat's cry) syndrome develops when chromosome 5 is missing an end piece. The affected individual has a small head, is mentally retarded, and has facial abnormalities. Abnormal development of the glottis and larynx results in the most characteristic symptom—the infant's cry resembles that of a cat.

A person who has both of the chromosomes involved in a translocation has the normal amount of genetic material and is healthy, unless the chromosome exchange breaks an allele into two pieces. The person who inherits only one of the translocated chromosomes has only one copy of certain alleles and three copies of certain other alleles. A genetic counselor begins to suspect a translocation has occurred when spontaneous abortions are commonplace, and when family members suffer from various syndromes.

In 5% of cases, Down syndrome occurs because of a translocation between chromosomes 21 and 14 in an ancestor. Because of the inheritance of the unusual chromosome plus two copies of chromosome 21, the individual has three copies of certain genes and manifests Down syndrome. This cause of Down syndrome runs in families and is not related to the age of the mother.

Translocations can be responsible for certain types of cancer. In the 1970s, new staining techniques showed that a translocation from a portion of chromosome 22 to chromosome 9 was responsible for chronic myelogenous leukemia. In Burkitt lymphoma, a cancer common in children in equatorial Africa, a large tumor develops from lymph glands in the region of the jaw. This disorder involves a translocation from a portion of chromosome 8 to chromosome 14.

▶ **8.15 Check Your Progress** A woman with a normal karyotype reproduces with a man who has a translocation between chromosomes 21 and 14. Could their child have a normal karyotype? Explain.

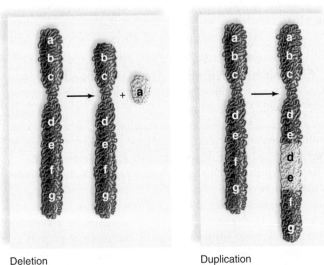

Deletion

Duplication

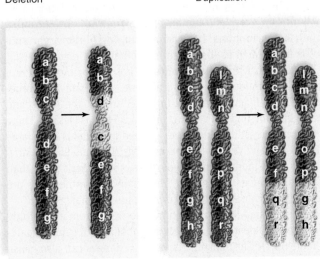

Inversion

Translocation

FIGURE 8.15 Types of chromosome structure anomalies.

SUMMARY

Chromosomes Become Visible During Cell Division

8.1 A karyotype displays the chromosomes

- A **karyotype** shows that eukaryotes have **homologous pairs** of chromosomes.
- Humans have 22 pairs of **autosomes** and one pair of **sex chromosomes.** A **Y chromosome** is shorter than an **X chromosome.** Males are XY and females are XX.
- Following DNA replication, each chromosome has two **sister chromatids** held together at a **centromere. Kinetochores** which develop at centromeres function during cell division.
- Homologus chromosomes have genes for the same trait—e.g., type of hairline. Sister chromatids have exact genes—e.g., widow's peak.

8.2 The eukaryotic cell cycle has a set series of stages

- In the **cell cycle, interphase** (G_1, S, G_2 stages) precedes the **M stage,** which includes **mitosis** and **cytokinesis.**

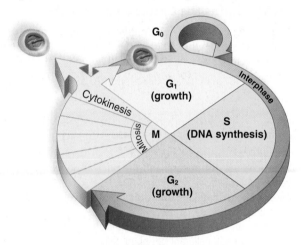

- In G_1 cells can make a commitment to divide; in **S** DNA replication results in duplicated chromosomes; and in G_2 proteins are made to form microtubules.
- Embryonic cells and **adult stem cells** divide all the time; cells in the G_0 stage have dropped out of the cell cycle and do not divide until stimulated to do so.

Mitosis Maintains the Chromosome Number

8.3 Following mitosis, daughter cells have the same chromosome count as the parent cell

- Mitosis is duplication division; the **parent cell** and the **daughter cells** all have the same number and kinds of chromosomes because the identical chromatids of each duplicated chromosome separate and become daughter chromosomes.
- The parent cell can be **diploid (2n)** or **haploid (n),** depending on the species.
- The number of centromeres equals the number of chromosomes a cell has.
- **Centrosomes** form the **spindle apparatus,** which helps ensure orderly separation of chromatids.

8.4 Mitosis has a set series of phases

- The spindle poles of animal cells have centrioles and an **aster.** Plant cells have poles but no centrioles or asters.
- Nuclear envelope fragments and chromosomes attach to spindle fibers by kinetochores **(prophase)** and align at the equator **(metaphase);** sister chromatids separate and become chromosomes **(anaphase),** and daughter nuclei re-form **(telophase).**
- In plants and animals, mitosis allows growth and repair. In humans, adult stem cells undergo mitosis to replace worn-out cells.

8.5 Cytokinesis divides the cytoplasm

- In animal cells, cytokinesis involves a **cleavage furrow.**
- In plant cells, cytokinesis involves the formation of a new plasma membrane and cell wall at a **cell plate.**

Cancer Is Uncontrolled Cell Division

8.6 Cell cycle control is lacking in cancer cells

- Checkpoint G_1 involves cell cycle control; checkpoint G_2 ensures that DNA replicated properly; checkpoint M ensures that chromosomes are distributed accurately to daughter cells.
- In general, if the cell cycle is unable to continue, apoptosis occurs. **Apoptosis** initiated by **p53** is programmed cell death orchestrated by unleashed enzymes.
- Due to **mutations, carcinogenesis** occurs and cancer is present when cells divide uncontrollably and a **tumor** develops. Cell cycle control and apoptosis are lacking.
- Cancer cells have abnormal characteristics: lack differentiation, have abnormal nuclei, form tumors, undergo **metastasis** (formation of tumors distant from primary tumor), and promote **angiogenesis** (formation of new blood vessels).

Meiosis Reduces the Chromosome Number

8.7 Homologous chromosomes separate during meiosis

- **Meiosis** is reduction division. Each of four daughter cells has only one of each kind of chromosome.
- Meiosis requires one DNA replication and two cell divisions, called **meiosis I** and **meiosis II.** The period of time between meiosis I and meiosis II is called **interkinesis.**
- Homologous chromosomes come together during **synapsis** and then separate during meiosis I; sister chromatids separate during meiosis II. The daughter cells are haploid.
- In humans, the daughter cells become **gametes** (egg and sperm) with the haploid number of chromosomes. The diploid number is restored with **fertilization.**

8.8 Synapsis and crossing-over occur during meiosis I

- During meiosis I, synapsis (pairing of homologues to form a **tetrad**) and **crossing-over** (exchange of genetic material) between nonsister chromatids occurs.

8.9 Sexual reproduction increases genetic variation

- Crossing-over recombines genetic information and increases the variability of genetic inheritance on the chromosomes.
- The gametes contain all possible combinations of chromosomes because of **independent assortment.**

- Independent assortment occurs because the paired homologous chromosomes align during meiosis I with either homologue facing either pole.
- Fertilization brings together genetically different gametes that fuse to form a **zygote.**

8.10 Meiosis requires meiosis I and meiosis II
- Meiosis I: **prophase I**—homologues pair and crossing-over occurs; **metaphase I**—homologue pairs align at equator independently; **anaphase I**—homologues separate; **telophase I**—daughter cells are haploid.
- Interkinesis is the time period between meiosis I and meiosis II. No DNA replication occurs.
- Meiosis II: During stages designated by the Roman numeral II, the chromatids of duplicated chromosomes from meiosis I separate, producing a total of four daughter cells for meiosis.

8.11 Life cycles are varied
- Asexual reproduction results in offspring that are genetically identical to the single parent.
- In the **haploid life cycle,** asexual reproduction occurs when a haploid parent produces offspring by mitosis that are also haploid. In sexual reproduction, only the zygote is diploid and undergoes meiosis to produce haploid offspring. Algae and fungi often have the haploid life cycle.
- In the **alternation of generations life cycle,** which usually occurs in plants, the diploid sporophyte produces spores by meiosis. A spore undergoes mitosis to become a gametophyte, which produces gametes. When the gametes fuse, the diploid zygote becomes a sporophyte.
- In the **diploid life cycle,** which usually takes place in animals, the diploid adult produces gametes by meiosis, which are the only haploid part of the life cycle. Mitosis is involved in growth.

8.12 Meiosis can be compared to mitosis
- See Figure 8.12 and note that homologous chromosomes only pair during metaphase I of meiosis and that four haploid daughter cells result from meiosis but not mitosis.

Chromosome Anomalies Can Be Inherited

8.13 Nondisjunction causes chromosome number anomalies
- A **polyploid** has a multiple of the haploid number of chromosomes; an **aneuploid** is a **monosomy** $(2n-1)$ or a **trisomy** $(2n+1)$.
- Aneuploidy is due to **nondisjunction** when homologues do not separate during meiosis I or when chromatids do not separate during meiosis II.

8.14 Chromosome number anomalies can be observed
- A **syndrome** is due to the inheritance of a set of physical characteristics that can be overcome with proper medical care and support.
- **Down syndrome** is an autosomal trisomy. **Turner syndrome** and **Klinefelter syndrome** result from sex chromosome anomalies.

8.15 Chromosome structure anomalies can also be observed
- **Deletion:** A segment of a chromosome is missing.
- **Duplication:** A segment occurs twice on the same chromosome.
- **Inversion:** A segment has turned 180 degrees.
- **Translocation:** Segments have moved between nonhomologous chromosomes.

TESTING YOURSELF

Chromosomes Become Visible During Cell Division

1. Which of these statements is incorrect? Just before mitosis in a eukaryotic cell,
   a. homologous pairs of chromosomes can be seen.
   b. each chromosome has two sister chromatids.
   c. one chromatid came from the father and one came from the mother.
   d. each sister chromatid carries the same genes.
2. Which is a correct contrast between autosomes and sex chromosomes in humans?
   a. 22 pairs—one pair
   b. control gender—control enzymes
   c. are always duplicated—are always single
   d. are always visible—are never visible
3. In the cell cycle,
   a. mitosis cannot occur without interphase.
   b. the single event during interphase is chromosome duplication.
   c. cells are metabolically inactive during interphase.
   d. a DNA double helix divides in two.

Mitosis Maintains the Chromosome Number

4. The two identical halves of a duplicated chromosome
   a. always stay together. c. become daughter chromosomes.
   b. are different sizes.   d. are called homologues.

For questions 5–8, match each description to a phase of mitosis in the key.

KEY:
   a. prophase   c. anaphase
   b. metaphase   d. telophase

5. The nucleolus disappears, and the nuclear envelope breaks down.
6. The spindle disappears, and the nuclear envelopes form.
7. Sister chromatids separate.
8. Chromosomes are aligned on the spindle equator.
9. Mitosis in animal cells but not plant cells
   a. maintains the chromosome number.
   b. uses a spindle apparatus.
   c. has centrioles at the poles.
   d. produces two unequal daughter cells.
10. Label this diagram of a cell in early prophase of mitosis:

a._____   _____d.
b._____
c._____

Cancer Is Uncontrolled Cell Division

11. Which of these is an incorrect statement?
   a. Checkpoints allow the cell cycle to continue if all is normal.
   b. A DNA abnormality can cause apoptosis to occur.

c. The cell cycle stages take place in the order dictated by external signals.

d. Mutations can cause the cell cycle to occur repeatedly.

12. Which of the following is typical of normal cells, but not typical of cancer cells?
    a. Cell cycle control is always present.
    b. The cells have enlarged nuclei.
    c. The cells stimulate the formation of new blood vessels.
    d. The cells are capable of traveling through blood and lymph.

Meiosis Reduces the Chromosome Number

13. Which are ways that meiosis increases genetic variation?
    a. Homologues align independently at the equator.
    b. Daughter cells always have the same combination of father and mother chromosomes.
    c. Following crossing-over, sister chromatids carry different genes.
    e. Both a and c are correct.

14. At the equator during metaphase II of meiosis, there are
    a. single chromosomes.
    b. unpaired duplicated chromosomes.
    c. homologous pairs.
    d. always 23 chromosomes.

15. During which phase of meiosis do homologous chromosomes separate?
    a. prophase II   d. anaphase I
    b. telophase I   e. anaphase II
    c. metaphase I

16. **THINKING CONCEPTUALLY** Use the events of meiosis to briefly explain why you and a sibling with the same parents have different characteristics.

17. When a haploid alga reproduces asexually by mitosis, the
    a. offspring are genetically identical to the parent.
    b. offspring undergo meiosis and become diploid.
    c. offspring number more than four.
    d. Both a and c are correct.

18. Which is an incorrect comparison between meiosis and mitosis?
    a. four daughter cells—two daughter cells
    b. crossing-over occurs—crossing-over does not occur

c. homologues separate—chromatids separate
d. daughter cells are diploid—daughter cells are haploid

Chromosome Anomalies Can Be Inherited

19. An individual can have too many or too few chromosomes as a result of
    a. nondisjunction.   d. amniocentesis.
    b. Barr bodies.   e. cell cycle control.
    c. mitosis.

20. Which of the following could cause a chromosome anomaly?
    a. inheritance of an extra chromosome 21
    b. deletion in chromosome 7
    c. the inheritance of 23 pairs of chromosomes
    d. translocation between chromosomes 2 and 20
    e. All but c are correct.

21. Turner syndrome (X0) can only result if nondisjunction occurred during
    a. mitosis.   c. meiosis II.
    b. meiosis I.   d. All of these are correct.

THINKING SCIENTIFICALLY

1. Genetic testing shows that Mary has only 46 chromosomes, but both members of one homologous pair came from her father. In which parent did nondisjunction occur? Explain.

2. Criticize the hypothesis that it would be possible to clone an individual by using an egg and a sperm with the exact genetic makeup as those that produced the individual.

ONLINE RESOURCE

www.mhhe.com/maderconcepts2 **Mc Graw Hill** **connect**

|BIOLOGY

Enhance your study with animations that bring concepts to life and practice tests to assess your understanding. Your instructor may also recommend the interactive eBook, individualized learning tools, and more.

CONNECTING THE CONCEPTS

All cells receive DNA from preexisting cells through the process of cell division. Cell division ensures that DNA is passed on to the next generation of cells and to the next generation of organisms.

The end product of ordinary cell division (i.e., mitosis) is two new cells, each with the same number and kinds of chromosomes as the parent cell. Mitosis is part of the cell cycle, and negative consequences result if the cell cycle becomes unsynchronized. Knowing how the cell cycle is regulated has contributed greatly to our knowledge of cancer and other disorders.

In contrast to mitosis, meiosis is part of the production of gametes, which have half the number of chromosomes as the parent cell. Through the mechanics of meiosis, which involves synapsis, sexually reproducing species have a greater likelihood of genetic variations among offspring than otherwise. However, meiosis brings with it the risk of chromosome anomalies.

Genetic variations are essential to the process of evolution, which is discussed in Part III. In the meantime, Chapter 9 reviews the fundamental laws of genetics established by Gregor Mendel. Although Mendel had no knowledge of chromosome behavior, modern students have the advantage of being able to apply their knowledge of meiosis to their understanding of Mendel's laws. Mendel's laws are fundamental to understanding the inheritance of particular alleles on the chromosomes.

PUT THE PIECES TOGETHER

1. Synapsis during meiosis is necessary to crossing-over and independent assortment of chromosomes. Explain.

2. What other process aside from those mentioned in question 1 result in increased variation among offspring?

3. Create a scenario by which meiosis could have evolved from mitosis.

9

Patterns of Genetic Inheritance

CHAPTER OUTLINE

Troubles With Dog Breeding

When dogs—or people—reproduce, they pass on their genes, units of heredity that determine what the offspring will be like. Dog breeders rely on this common knowledge when they choose close relatives with like characteristics to reproduce with one another. Only in this way has it been possible to produce over 150 different dog breeds from an original common ancestor.

Each breed of dogs has favored traits. Golden retrievers were bred to be beautiful, sturdy, friendly dogs with a cream- to golden-colored coat. In German shepherds, the body is longer than it is tall and has an outline of smooth curves rather than angles. Unfortunately, these two breeds of dogs are also prone to hip dysplasia, a painful condition caused by malformed hip joints. Inbreeding not only passes along desirable traits, it also is more likely to pass on undesirable traits. English bulldogs and pugs look cute, but they may develop breathing and digestive problems due to a protruding lower jaw and a shortened upper jaw.

In an effort to improve dog breeding today, reformers point out that dog breeding became especially organized and systematic in the nineteenth century and by now some pedigree

English bulldog

dog breeds are so inbred they might cease to exist. One cause of genetic diversity loss is the use of "super-sires," dogs that have won prizes at dog shows and thereafter are used through artificial insemination to produce many litters. The Kennel Club of Great Britain, which sets the standards for awarding winners of dog shows, has put 12 breeds on what it calls its "worry list." They now recognize that inbreeding limits the gene pool so that a breed loses vigor and is unable to maintain itself. Now it is up to responsible breeders to sometimes mate their dogs to unrelated dogs in order to introduce new genes that will help maintain the overall health of the breed.

As in human genetics, tracing the causes of genetic disorders in dogs is complicated, but modern genetics can help. Breeders can keep careful records of matings and the results of those matings. From these records, they should be able to determine the pattern of a disorder's inheritance and which dogs should not be used for breeding. It is also possible today to screen for many genetic diseases, so that dogs with the same but hidden (recessive) genetic faults are not mated to each other. In other words proper dog breeding can avoid producing dogs with physical deformities. Modernization can also include the successful use of gene therapy in collies and Briard sheepdogs to cure blindness, another condition resulting from continual inbreeding. Researchers injected a harmless virus carrying the corrective gene beneath the retina and waited several months. When tested, the dogs could see through the eye that was treated, but not through the eye that was not treated. The researchers hope their work will be a step toward curing blindness in humans one day.

Dog owners can also help. Researchers who have studied hip dysplasia in dogs tell us this condition is not a birth

Collie

defect. The dogs are born with what appear to be normal hips and then develop the disease later. In addition, some dogs with the genetic tendency do not develop the condition, while the degree of hip dysplasia in others can vary. It appears that multiple genetic factors, plus environmental factors, are involved in determining the degree of hip dysplasia. This is also true of many human disorders—both genes and the environment seem to play a role. Researchers have identified the possible contributing factors for hip dysplasia. A test group of Labrador retrievers, who were fed 25% less than normal, showed less hip dysplasia than a control group allowed to eat as much as they wanted. The researchers concluded that rapid weight gain can contribute to the development of hip dysplasia.

This chapter begins our study of inheritance by taking a look at the work of Gregor Mendel, who is often called the father of genetics. After discussing how genes function in peas, we will turn our attention to humans. The same laws of heredity function in plants, dogs, humans, and every other organism. By understanding these laws we can prevent and cure genetic disorders in dogs and humans.

German shepherd with hip dysplasia

Dog shows influence breeding

Gregor Mendel Deduced Laws of Inheritance

Learning Outcomes

▶ Describe the major hypothesis about genetics before Mendel began his work. (9.1)

▶ Explain why Mendel's experimental design was a good one. (9.2)

The experiments performed by Gregor Mendel with garden peas refuted the blending concept of inheritance prevalent at the time. In contrast to a blending hypothesis, Mendel's work showed that inheritance is particulate and, therefore, that traits such as tall or short height always reoccur in future generations.

9.1 A blending model of inheritance existed prior to Mendel

Like begets like—zebras always produce zebras, never camels; pumpkins always produce seeds for pumpkins, never watermelons. It is apparent to anyone who observes such phenomena that parents pass hereditary information to their offspring. However, an offspring can be markedly different from either parent. For example, black-coated mice occasionally produce white-coated mice. The science of genetics founded by Gregor Mendel, an Austrian monk (**Fig. 9.1**), provides explanations about not only the stability of inheritance, but also the variations observed between generations and among organisms.

Various hypotheses about heredity had been proposed before Mendel began his experiments in the 1860s. In particular, investigators had been trying to support a blending concept of inheritance. Most plant and animal breeders acknowledged that both sexes contribute equally to a new individual, and they felt that parents of contrasting appearance always produce offspring of intermediate appearance. According to this blending concept, a cross between plants with red flowers and plants with white flowers would yield only plants with pink flowers. When red and white flowers reappeared in future generations, the breeders mistakenly attributed this to an instability in the genetic material.

The blending model of inheritance had offered little help to Charles Darwin, the father of evolution. If populations contained only intermediate individuals and normally lacked variations,

how could diverse forms evolve? However, Mendel's theory of inheritance does account for the presence of variations among the members of a population, generation after generation.

Although Darwin was a contemporary of Mendel, Darwin never learned of Mendel's work and it went unrecognized until 1900. Therefore, Darwin was never able to make use of Mendel's research to support his theory of evolution, and his treatise on natural selection lacked a strong genetic basis.

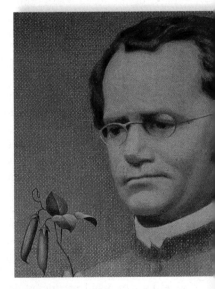

FIGURE 9.1 Gregor Mendel examining a pea plant.

▶ **9.1 Check Your Progress** Inbreeding in dogs supports the genetic basis of inheritance and also the concept of evolution. Explain.

9.2 Mendel designed his experiments well

Mendel had a background suitable to his task. Previously, he had studied science and mathematics at the University of Vienna, and at the time of his genetic research, he was a substitute natural science teacher at a local high school. Aside from theoretical knowledge, Mendel knew how to cultivate plants. Most likely, his knowledge of mathematics prompted him to use a statistical basis for his breeding experiments. He prepared for his experiments carefully and conducted preliminary studies with various animals and plants. He then chose to work with the garden pea, *Pisum sativum.*

The garden pea was a good choice. The plants are easy to cultivate, have a short generation time, and produce many offspring. A pea plant normally self-pollinates because the reproductive organs in the flower are completely enclosed by petals (**Fig. 9.2A**), ❶ As in all flowering plants, the reproductive organs in peas are the stamen and the carpel. A stamen produces sperm-bearing pollen in the anther, and the carpel produces egg-bearing ovules in the ovary. When Mendel wanted the plants to

self-fertilize, he covered the flowers with a bag to ensure that only the pollen of that flower would reach the carpel of that flower. Even though pea plants normally self-fertilize, they can be cross-pollinated by an experimenter who manually transfers pollen from an anther to the carpel. ❷ Mendel prevented self-fertilization by cutting away the anthers before they produced any pollen. ❸ Then he dusted that flower's carpel with pollen from another plant. ❹ Afterwards, the carpel developed into a pod containing peas. In the cross illustrated here, pollen from a plant that normally produces yellow peas was used to fertilize the eggs of a plant that normally produces green peas. These plants produced only yellow peas. In the next, or F_2, generation, a few peas were green again.

Many varieties of pea plants were available, and Mendel chose 22 of them for his experiments. When these varieties self-fertilized, they were *true-breeding,* meaning that the offspring were like the parent plants and like each other. In contrast to his predecessors, Mendel studied the inheritance of relatively

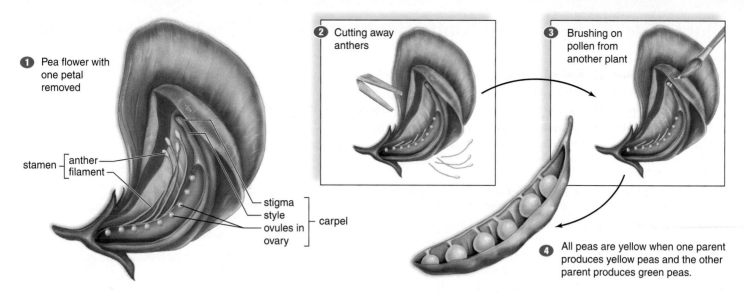

FIGURE 9.2A Garden pea anatomy and the cross-pollination procedure Mendel used.

simple, clear-cut, and easily detected traits, such as seed shape, seed color, and flower color, and he observed no intermediate characteristics among the offspring (**Fig. 9.2B**).

As Mendel followed the inheritance of individual traits, he kept careful records. Then he used his understanding of the mathematical laws of probability to interpret his results and to arrive at a theory that has been supported by innumerable experiments since. It is called a *particulate theory of inheritance*

because it is based on the existence of minute *particles*, or hereditary units, that we now call genes. Inheritance involves the reshuffling of the same genes from generation to generation.

Mendel clearly stated conclusions that are now considered laws of heredity which are stated in Sections 9.3 and 9.5.

▶ **9.2 Check Your Progress** Why were true-breeding pea plants a better choice than true-breeding dogs for Mendel's studies?

Trait	Characteristics			F_2 Results		
	Dominant		Recessive	Dominant	Recessive	Dominant/ Recessive Ratio
Stem length	Tall		Short	787	277	3:1
Pod shape	Inflated		Constricted	882	299	3:1
Seed shape	Round		Wrinkled	5,474	1,850	3:1
Seed color	Yellow		Green	6,022	2,001	3:1
Flower color	Purple		White	705	224	3:1
Pod color	Green		Yellow	428	152	3:1

FIGURE 9.2B Garden pea traits and crosses studied by Mendel. His F_2 results allowed him to deduce the first of his laws of heredity.

Single-Trait Crosses Reveal Units of Inheritance and the Law of Segregation

Learning Outcomes

▶ Use Mendel's law of segregation and the concept of alleles to determine the genotype (and phenotype) and the gametes of an individual in a single-trait cross. (9.3)

▶ Use Mendel's law of segregation to solve genetics problems involving single-trait crosses. (9.4)

After doing crosses that pertained to only one trait, such as height, Mendel proposed his law of segregation. The individual has two factors, today called alleles, for each trait, but the gametes have only one allele for each trait. This segregation process allows a recessive allele to be passed on to an offspring independently of the dominant allele.

9.3 Mendel's law of segregation describes how gametes pass on traits

After ensuring that his pea plants were true-breeding—for example, that his tall plants always had tall offspring and his short plants always had short offspring—Mendel was ready to perform a cross-fertilization experiment between two strains. For these initial experiments, Mendel chose varieties that differed in only one trait. If the blending theory of inheritance were correct, the cross should yield offspring with an intermediate appearance compared to the parents. For example, the offspring of a cross between a tall plant and a short plant should be intermediate in height.

Mendel called the original parents the **P generation** and the first batch of offspring the F_1 (for filial) **generation.** The final batch of offspring became the F_2 **generation.** He performed reciprocal crosses: First, he dusted the pollen of tall plants onto the stigmas of short plants, and then he dusted the pollen of short plants onto the stigmas of tall plants. In both cases, all F_1 offspring resembled the tall parent.

Certainly, these results were contrary to those predicted by the blending theory of inheritance. Rather than being intermediate, the F_1 plants resembled only one parent. Did these results mean that the other characteristic (i.e., shortness) had disappeared permanently? Apparently not, because when Mendel allowed the F_1 plants to self-pollinate, ¾ of the F_2 generation were tall, and ¼ were short, a 3:1 ratio (**Fig. 9.3**). Therefore, the F_1 plants were able to pass on a factor for shortness—it didn't just disappear.

Mendel counted many offspring. For this particular cross, he counted a total of 1,064 offspring, of which 787 were tall and 277 were short. In all the crosses he performed, he found a 3:1 ratio in the F_2 generation. The characteristic that had disappeared in the F_1 generation reappeared in ¼ of the F_2 offspring (see Fig. 9.2B).

Mendel's mathematical approach led him to interpret his results differently than previous breeders. He knew that the same ratio was obtained among the F_2 generation time and time again for the crosses he was studying. Eventually, Mendel arrived at this explanation: A 3:1 ratio among the F_2 offspring was possible if the F_1 parents contained two separate copies of each hereditary factor, one of these being dominant and the other recessive. The factors separated when the gametes were formed, and each gamete carried only one copy of each factor; random fusion of all possible gametes occurred upon fertilization. Only in this way would shortness reoccur in the F_2 generation.

After doing many F_1 crosses, called **monohybrid crosses** because they examine only one trait, Mendel arrived at the first of his laws of inheritance—the law of segregation, which is a cornerstone of his particulate theory of inheritance.

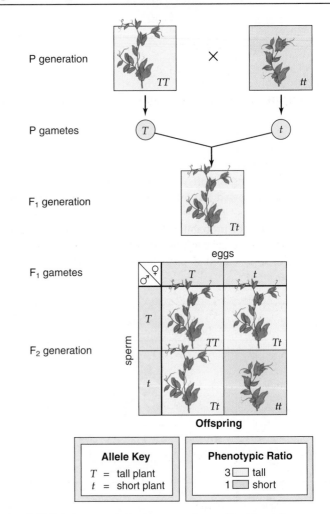

FIGURE 9.3 Monohybrid cross performed by Mendel.

The **law of segregation** states the following:
- Each individual has two factors for each trait.
- The factors segregate (separate) during the formation of the gametes.
- Each gamete contains only one factor from each pair of factors.
- Fertilization gives each new individual two factors for each trait.

▶ **9.3 Check Your Progress** Based on Mendel's study, explain why only some offspring of normal golden retrievers have hip dysplasia.

9.4 The units of inheritance are alleles of genes

Mendel said that organisms received "factors" from their parents, but today we use the term "genes." Traits are controlled by **alleles,** alternative forms of a gene. The alleles occur on homologous chromosomes at a particular **gene locus (Fig. 9.4).** The **dominant allele** is so named because of its ability to mask the expression of the other allele, called the **recessive allele.** (Therefore, dominant does not mean the normal or most frequent condition.) The dominant allele is identified by a capital letter, and the recessive allele by the same letter, but lowercase. Usually, the letter chosen has some connection to the trait itself. For example, when considering stem length in peas, the allele for tallness is T, and the allele for shortness is t.

As you learned in Chapter 8, meiosis is the type of cell division that reduces the chromosome number. During meiosis I, homologous chromosomes each having sister chromatids separate. During meiosis II, the chromatids separate. Therefore, the process of meiosis explains Mendel's law of segregation and why there is only one allele for each trait in a gamete.

In Mendel's cross (see Fig. 9.3), the original parents (P generation) were true-breeding; therefore, the tall plants had two copies of the same allele for tallness (TT), and the short plants had two copies of the same allele for shortness (tt). When an organism has two identical alleles, as these had, we say it is **homozygous.** Because the parents were homozygous, all gametes produced by the tall plant contained the allele for tallness (T), and all gametes produced by the short plant contained the allele for shortness (t).

After cross-fertilization, all the individuals in the resulting F_1 generation had one allele for tallness and one for shortness (Tt). When an organism has two different alleles at a gene locus, we say that it is **heterozygous.** Although the plants of the F_1 generation had one of each type of allele, they were all tall. The allele that is expressed in a heterozygous individual is the domi-

TABLE 9.4	Genotype Versus Phenotype
Genotype	**Phenotype**
TT, homozygous dominant	Tall plant
Tt, heterozygous	Tall plant
tt, homozygous recessive	Short plant

nant allele. The allele that is not expressed in a heterozygote is the recessive allele.

You can see that two organisms with different allelic combinations for a trait can have the same outward appearance. For example, TT and Tt pea plants are both tall. For this reason, it is necessary to distinguish between the alleles present in an organism and the appearance of that organism.

The word **genotype** refers to the alleles an individual receives at fertilization. Genotype may be indicated by letters or by short, descriptive phrases. Genotype TT is called homozygous dominant, genotype tt is called homozygous recessive, and genotype Tt is called heterozygous.

The word **phenotype** refers to the physical appearance of the individual. The homozygous dominant (TT) individual and the heterozygous (Tt) individual both show the dominant phenotype and are tall, while the homozygous recessive (tt) individual shows the recessive phenotype and is short. **Table 9.4** compares genotype with phenotype.

Continuing with the discussion of Mendel's cross (see Fig. 9.3), the F_1 plants produce gametes in which 50% have the dominant allele T and 50% have the recessive allele t. During the process of fertilization, we assume that all types of sperm (T or t) have an equal chance to fertilize all types of eggs (T or t). When this occurs, a monohybrid cross always produces a 3:1 (dominant to recessive) ratio among the offspring. Figure 9.2B gives Mendel's results for several monohybrid crosses, and you can see that the phenotypic ratio was always close to 3:1.

Linkage All of the alleles on any chromosome form a **linkage group** and will be inherited together unless crossing-over occurs. Only when we are dealing with more than one trait does linkage become a consideration, however.

▶ **9.4 Check Your Progress**

1. Choose a letter of the alphabet and give the genotype of a plant that is: **a.** homozygous for round seeds, a dominant characteristic; **b.** heterozygous for round seeds.

2. For each of the following genotypes, list all possible gametes, noting the proportion of each for the individual. **a.** WW **b.** Rr **c.** Tt **d.** TT

3. In rabbits, if B = dominant black allele and b = recessive white allele, which of these genotypes (Bb, BB, bb) could a white rabbit have?

4. If a heterozygous rabbit reproduces with one of its own kind, what phenotypic ratio would you expect among the offspring? If there are 120 rabbits, how many would you expect to be white?

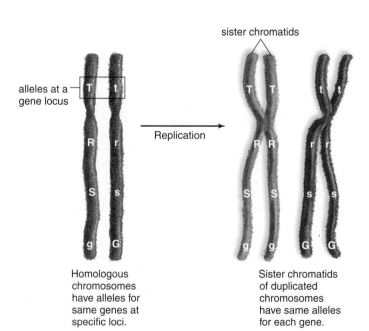

| Homologous chromosomes have alleles for same genes at specific loci. | Sister chromatids of duplicated chromosomes have same alleles for each gene. |

FIGURE 9.4 Occurrence of alleles on homologous chromosomes.

Two-Trait Crosses Support the Law of Independent Assortment

Learning Outcomes

▶ Use the law of independent assortment to determine the genotype (and phenotype) and the gametes of an individual in a two-trait cross. (9.5–9.7)

▶ Use the law of independent assortment to solve genetics problems involving two-trait crosses. (9.5–9.7)

▶ Show how two rules of probability relate to the Punnett square. (9.6)

After doing crosses that involved two traits, such as height and color of peas, Mendel proposed his law of independent assortment. This law states that only one allele for each trait can occur in a gamete, but any allele for one trait can occur with any allele for another trait. Therefore, all possible phenotypes can occur among offspring.

9.5 Mendel's law of independent assortment describes inheritance of multiple traits

Mendel performed a second series of crosses in which true-breeding plants differed in two traits. For example, he crossed tall plants having green pods with short plants having yellow pods (**Fig. 9.5**). The F_1 plants showed both dominant characteristics. As before, Mendel then allowed the F_1 plants to self-pollinate. These F_1 crosses are called **dihybrid crosses** because they are examining two traits. Mendel reasoned that two possible results could occur in the F_2 generation:

1. If the dominant factors (*TG*) always segregate into the F_1 gametes together, and the recessive factors (*tg*) always stay together, two phenotypes would occur among the F_2 plants—tall plants with green pods and short plants with yellow pods.
2. If the four factors segregate into the F_1 gametes independently, four phenotypes would occur among the F_2 plants—tall plants with green pods, tall plants with yellow pods, short plants with green pods, and short plants with yellow pods.

Figure 9.5 shows that Mendel observed four phenotypes among the F_2 plants, supporting the second hypothesis. Therefore, Mendel knew that the gametes for a dihybrid cross always consist of the two dominants (such as *TG*), the two recessives (such as *tg*), and ones that have a dominant and a recessive (such as *Tg* and *tG*). He always observed a phenotypic ratio of 9:3:3:1. This allowed him to formulate his second law of heredity—the law of independent assortment.

The **law of independent assortment** states the following:
- Each pair of factors separates (assorts) independently (without regard to how the others separate).
- All possible combinations of factors can occur in the gametes.

As long as the alleles are not linked, the process of meiosis explains why Mendel's F_1 plants produced every possible type of gamete, and therefore why four phenotypes appear among the F_2 generation of plants. As was explained in Figure 8.9A, there are no rules regarding alignment of homologues at the equator—either homologue can face either spindle pole. Because of this, the daughter cells from meiosis I (and also meiosis II) have all possible combinations of unlinked alleles.

▶ **9.5 Check Your Progress** What are the four possible genotypes of a tall pea plant with green pods?

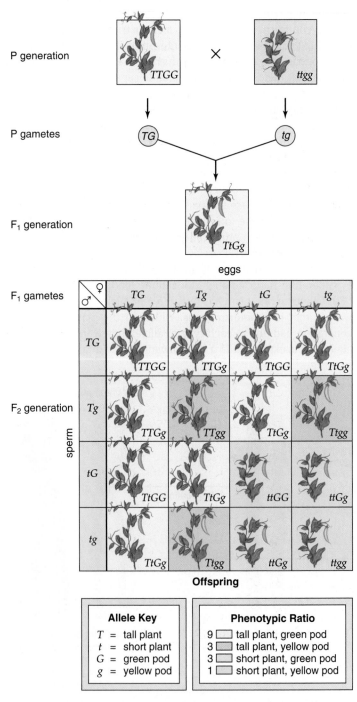

FIGURE 9.5 Dihybrid cross performed by Mendel.

9.6 Mendel's results are consistent with the rules of probability

The diagram we have been using to calculate the results of a cross is called a **Punnett square.** The Punnett square allows us to easily calculate the chances, or the probability, of genotypes and phenotypes among the offspring. Like flipping a coin each gamete (sperm or egg) in Figure 9.6 can bear an *E* or *e*. Therefore, as illustrated in the Punnett square, an offspring of the cross has a 50% (or ½) chance of receiving an *E* for unattached earlobe or an *e* for attached earlobe from each parent:

The chance of *E* = ½
The chance of *e* = ½

How likely is it that an offspring will inherit a specific set of two alleles, one from each parent? To answer this question we have to turn to the rules of probability. The product rule of probability tells us that we have to multiply the chances of independent events to get the answer:

1. The chance of *EE* = ½ × ½ = ¼
2. The chance of *Ee* = ½ × ½ = ¼
3. The chance of *eE* = ½ × ½ = ¼
4. The chance of *ee* = ½ × ½ = ¼

The Punnett square does this for us because we can easily see that each genotype occurs in ¼ of the total number of squares. How do we get the phenotypic results? The sum rule of probability tells us that when the same event can occur in more than one way, we add the results. Because 1, 2, and 3 all result in unattached earlobes, we add them up to know that the chance of unattached earlobes is ¾, or 75%. The chance of attached earlobes is ¼, or 25%. The Punnett square doesn't do this for us—we have to add the results ourselves.

Another useful concept in genetics is that "chance has no memory." This statement tells us that each child has the same chances. So, if a couple has four children, each child has a 25% chance of having attached earlobes. This may not be significant if we are considering earlobes. But it does become significant if we are considering a recessive genetic disorder, such as cystic fibrosis, a debilitating respiratory illness. If a heterozygous couple has four children, each child has a 25% chance of inheriting two recessive alleles, and all four children could have cystic fibrosis.

We can use the product rule and the sum rule of probability to predict the results of a dihybrid cross, such as the one shown in Figure 9.5. The Punnett square carries out the multiplication for us, and we add the results to find that the phenotypic ratio is 9:3:3:1. We expect these same results for each and every dihybrid cross. Therefore, it is not necessary to do a Punnett square over and over again for either a monohybrid or a dihybrid cross. *Instead, we can simply remember the probable results of 3:1 and 9:3:3:1.* But we have to remember that the 9 represents the two dominant phenotypes together, the 3's are a dominant phenotype with a recessive, and the 1 stands for the two recessive phenotypes together. This tells you the probable phenotypic ratio among the offspring, but not the chances for each possible phenotype. Because the Punnett square has 16 squares, the chances are $^9/_{16}$ for the two dominants together, $^3/_{16}$ for the dominants with each recessive, and $^1/_{16}$ for the two recessives together. To take an example, what is the chance of

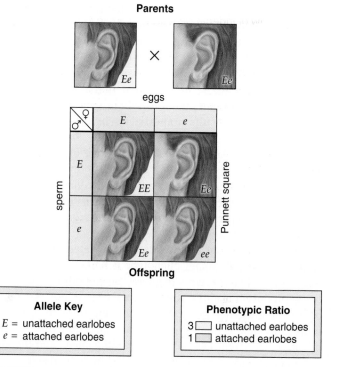

Parents

eggs

Punnett square

sperm

Offspring

Allele Key
E = unattached earlobes
e = attached earlobes

Phenotypic Ratio
3 ☐ unattached earlobes
1 ☐ attached earlobes

FIGURE 9.6 Use of a Punnett square to calculate probable results; in this case a 3:1 phenotypic ratio.

a tall plant with a yellow pod in Figure 9.5? How many possible genotypes are there for this type plant? You are correct if you answered the chances of this phenotype is $^3/_{16}$ but the number of possible genotypes is only two.

Mendel counted the results of many similar crosses to get the probable results, and in the laboratory, we too have to count the results of many individual crosses to get the probable results for a monohybrid or a dihybrid cross. Why? Consider that each time you toss a coin, you have a 50% chance of getting heads or tails. If you tossed the coin only a couple of times, you might very well have the same result both times. However, if you toss the coin many times, you are more likely to finally achieve 50% heads and 50% tails.

Section 9.7 illustrates that the results of testcrosses are consistent with Mendel's laws and have the added advantage of determining the genotype of the monohybrid or dihybrid heterozygote.

▶ 9.6 Check Your Progress

1. Give the genotype of a plant that is homozygous for round seeds and homozygous for purple flowers (see fig. 9.2). If such flowers are crossed, what phenotype will all the offspring have?

2. In humans, freckles is dominant over no freckles. A man with freckles reproduces with a woman with freckles, but the children have no freckles. What chance did each child have for freckles?

3. In fruit flies, long wings (*L*) is dominant over vestigial (short) wings (*l*), and gray body (*G*) is dominant over black body (*g*). Without doing a Punnett square, what phenotypic ratio is probable among the offspring of a dihybrid cross? What are the chances of an offspring with short wings and a black body?

9.7 Testcrosses support Mendel's laws and indicate the genotype

One-trait Testcross To confirm that the F_1 of his one-trait crosses were heterozygous, Mendel crossed his F_1 generation plants with true-breeding, short (homozygous recessive) plants. Mendel performed these so-called **testcrosses** because they allowed him to support the law of segregation. For the cross in **Figure 9.7A,** he reasoned that half the offspring should be tall and half should be short, producing a 1:1 phenotypic ratio. His results supported the hypothesis that alleles segregate when gametes are formed. In Figure 9.7A, the homozygous recessive parent can produce only one type of gamete (*t*), and so the Punnett square has only one column. The use of one column signifies that all the gametes carry a *t*. *When a heterozygous individual is crossed with one that is homozygous recessive, the probable results are always a 1:1 phenotypic ratio.*

Today, a one-trait testcross is used to determine if an individual with the dominant phenotype is homozygous dominant (e.g., *TT*) or heterozygous (e.g., *Tt*). Since both of these genotypes produce the dominant phenotype, it is not possible to determine the genotype by observation. **Figure 9.7B** shows that if the individual is homozygous dominant, all the offspring will be tall. Each parent has only one type of gamete, and therefore a Punnett square is not required to determine the results.

Two-trait Testcross When doing a two-trait testcross, an individual with the dominant phenotype is crossed with one having the recessive phenotype for both traits. Suppose you are working with fruit flies in which:

L = long wings	*G* = gray body
l = vestigial (short) wings	*g* = black body

You wouldn't know by examination whether the fly on the left was homozygous or heterozygous for wing and body color. In order to find out the genotype of the test fly, you cross it with the one on the right. You know by examination that this vestigial-winged and black-bodied fly is homozygous recessive for both traits.

If the test fly is homozygous dominant for both traits with the genotype *LLGG*, it will form only one gamete: *LG*. Therefore, all the offspring from the proposed cross will have long wings and a gray body.

However, if the test fly is heterozygous for both traits, having the genotype *LlGg*, it will form four different types of gametes:

Gametes: *LG*   *Lg*   *lG*   *lg*

and have four different offspring:

LlGg   *Llgg*   *llGg*   *llgg*

The presence of the offspring with vestigial wings and a black body shows that the test fly is heterozygous for both traits and has the genotype *LlGg*. Otherwise, it could not have this offspring. In general, you will want to remember that *when an individual*

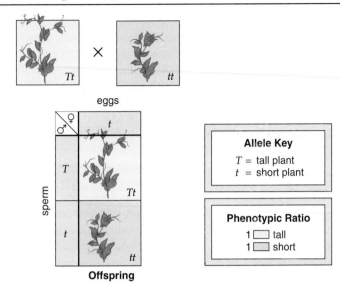

FIGURE 9.7A One-trait testcross, when the individual with the dominant phenotype is heterozygous.

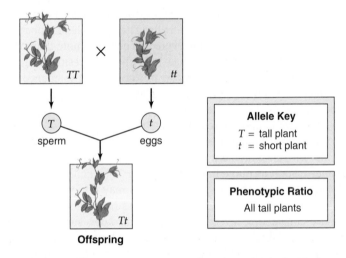

FIGURE 9.7B One-trait testcross, when the individual with the dominant phenotype is homozygous.

heterozygous for two traits is crossed with one that is recessive for the traits, the offspring have a 1:1:1:1 phenotypic ratio.

We will observe in the next part of the chapter that Mendel's laws also apply to humans.

▶ **9.7 Check Your Progress**

1. A heterozygous fruit fly (*LlGg*) is crossed with a homozygous recessive (*llgg*). What are the chances of offspring with long wings and a black body?

2. An individual with long fingers (*s*) has a father with short fingers (*S*). What is the genotype of the father?

3. In horses, trotter (*T*) is dominant over pacer (*t*). A trotter is mated to a pacer, and the offspring is a pacer. Give the genotype of both parents and their offspring.

9A The Theory of Natural Selection

It's amazing to learn that Darwin didn't know any genetics and was unaware of Mendel's studies with garden peas. Both men lived at the same time, although in different countries—Mendel in Austria and Darwin outside London, England. Mendel actually visited a London expedition in 1862 when he was 40 and Darwin was 53, but they never met. Darwin's scientific theory of natural selection was based on observations of phenotypes, such as the many different types of horses, and not on their genotype. He was very much aware, however, that traits are inherited. He even performed **artificial selection** in which the breeder selects individuals with the desired traits (**Fig. 9A.1**). Because the traits are passed from parents to offspring, the next generation has a higher proportion of the desired traits than the previous generation. Artificial selection is the way humans have produced many of the crops that sustain us today, including wheat, corn, bananas, and tomatoes.

Despite having a basic knowledge of genetics, it wasn't until the mid-twentieth century that biologists introduced the concept of alleles into Darwin's theory of natural selection in this way:

- The alleles of genes are responsible for the traits of an individual.
- As we have learned with peas, individuals pass their alleles to their offspring, and the alleles on separate chromosomes are shuffled with each generation due to the process of meiosis. (During meiosis, you'll recall, recombination of alleles occurs as a result of crossing-over, and independent assortment of chromosomes occurs because homolous pairs align at the equator independently.)
- Mutations are the raw material of evolution because they introduce new traits. Because beneficial mutations are bound to be selected, their effect is greater than neutral or

FIGURE 9A.2 Due to natural selection, the bill of a green honeycreeper can catch insects; that of an oystercatcher can pry open the shell of a mussel. The talons of an osprey are adapted to catching fish.

harmful mutations. Indeed, without beneficial mutations, new species could not arise.

- The new combination of alleles, plus any mutations, will likely make some individuals more suited to the environment and therefore better able to survive and reproduce than other members of a population (**Fig. 9A.2**). For example, a plant better able to survive drought would have an advantage over other members of a plant population in a dry environment.
- In this way, each generation becomes better adapted to the environment than the previous generation. Adaptation to the environment makes natural selection very different from artificial selection, which often does not consider adaptation. Race horses, for example, are bred for speed without considering whether the trait is useful for survival.

Darwin's theory of natural selection has stood the test of time, as is well witnessed by its consistency with the principles of Mendelian genetics as well as with those of molecular genetics, which we will study in Chapters 10–12.

FORM YOUR OPINION

1. The compatibility of the gene theory with the theory of evolution lends support to the theory of evolution. How so?
2. Why is it significant that natural selection but not artificial selection is expected to result in adaptation to the environment?
3. Why did it work for Mendel and Darwin to rely only on the phenotypes of organisms to deduce their hypotheses?

FIGURE 9A.1 Due to artificial selection, draft horses are large enough to do heavy lifting; quarter horses are agile enough to do maneuvers; thoroughbred horses are fast enough to race.

Mendel's Laws Apply to Humans

Learning Outcomes

▶ Be able to recognize and construct pedigrees pertaining to traits carried on the autosomal chromosomes. (9.8)

▶ Use a pedigree to determine whether a genetic disorder is autosomal dominant or autosomal recessive. (9.8)

▶ Describe several autosomal recessive and several autosomal dominant genetic disorders. (9.9–9.10)

Geneticists construct a family tree called a pedigree to determine a trait's pattern of inheritance. The pedigree is different for an autosomal dominant versus an autosomal recessive trait. Therefore, by constructing a pedigree we can determine whether a disorder is an autosomal dominant disorder or an autosomal recessive disorder.

9.8 Pedigrees can reveal the patterns of inheritance

Some genetic disorders are due to the inheritance of abnormal recessive or dominant alleles on **autosomal chromosomes,** which are all the chromosomes except the sex chromosomes. When a genetic disorder is autosomal recessive, only individuals with the alleles *aa* have the disorder. When a genetic disorder is autosomal dominant, an individual with the alleles *AA* or *Aa* has the disorder. Geneticists often construct **pedigrees** to determine whether a condition is recessive or dominant.

In a pedigree, males are designated by squares and females by circles. Shaded circles and squares are affected individuals. A line between a square and a circle represents a union. A vertical line going downward leads to offspring. (If there is more than one offspring, they are placed off a horizontal line.) A pedigree shows the pattern of inheritance for a particular condition. Consider these two possible patterns of inheritance:

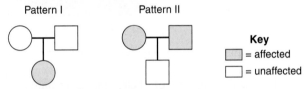

Pattern I	Pattern II	Key
		▢ = affected
		□ = unaffected

Which pattern of inheritance (I or II) do you think pertains to an autosomal dominant characteristic, and which pertains to an autosomal recessive characteristic?

In pattern I, the child is affected, but neither parent is; this can happen if the condition is recessive and the parents are *Aa*. Notice that the parents are **carriers** because they appear normal but are capable of having a child with the genetic disorder. In pattern II, the child is unaffected, but the parents are affected. This can happen if the condition is dominant and the parents are *Aa*.

Figure 9.8A shows other ways to recognize an autosomal recessive pattern of inheritance, and **Figure 9.8B** shows other ways to recognize an autosomal dominant pattern of inheritance. In these pedigrees, generations are indicated by Roman numerals placed on the left side. Notice in the third generation of Figure 9.8A that two closely related individuals have produced three children, two of whom have the affected phenotype. This illustrates that reproduction between closely related persons increases the chances of children inheriting two copies of a potentially harmful recessive allele.

The inheritance pattern of alleles on the X chromosome follows different rules than those on the autosomal chromosomes, as discussed in Section 9.16.

> ▶ **9.8 Check Your Progress** How does Figure 9.8A demonstrate that dog breeders should keep careful pedigree records?

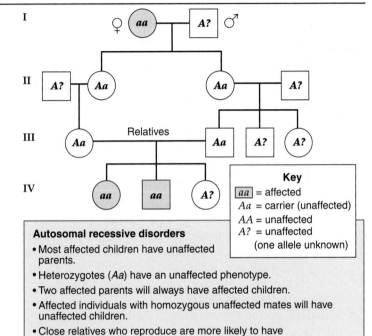

Autosomal recessive disorders

• Most affected children have unaffected parents.
• Heterozygotes (*Aa*) have an unaffected phenotype.
• Two affected parents will always have affected children.
• Affected individuals with homozygous unaffected mates will have unaffected children.
• Close relatives who reproduce are more likely to have affected children.
• Both males and females are affected with equal frequency.

FIGURE 9.8A Autosomal recessive pedigree.

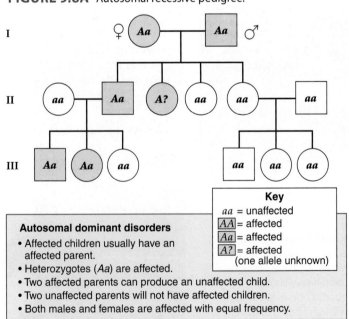

Autosomal dominant disorders

• Affected children usually have an affected parent.
• Heterozygotes (*Aa*) are affected.
• Two affected parents can produce an unaffected child.
• Two unaffected parents will not have affected children.
• Both males and females are affected with equal frequency.

FIGURE 9.8B Autosomal dominant pedigree.

9.9 Some human genetic disorders are autosomal recessive

In humans, a number of genetic disorders are controlled by a single pair of alleles. Four of the best-known autosomal recessive disorders are Tay-Sachs disease, cystic fibrosis, phenylketonuria, and sickle-cell disease. Individuals can be carriers for these diseases.

Tay-Sachs Disease In a baby with Tay-Sachs disease, development begins to slow down between 4 and 8 months of age, and neurological impairment and psychomotor difficulties then become apparent. The child gradually becomes blind and helpless, develops uncontrollable seizures, and eventually becomes paralyzed prior to dying. Tay-Sachs disease results from a lack of the lysosomal enzyme Hex A and the subsequent storage of its substrate, a lipid, in lysosomes. As the lipid builds up in the lysosomes, it crowds the organelles and impairs their function, especially in the brain.

Carriers of Tay-Sachs disease have about half the level of Hex A activity found in homozygous dominant individuals but they appear to be normal. Prenatal diagnosis of the disease is possible following either amniocentesis or chorionic villi sampling. The gene for Tay-Sachs disease is located on chromosome 15.

Cystic Fibrosis Cystic fibrosis (CF) is the most common lethal genetic disease among Caucasians in the United States. Abnormal secretions related to the chloride ion channel characterize this disorder. One of the most obvious symptoms in CF patients is extremely salty sweat. In children with CF, the mucus in the bronchial tubes and pancreatic ducts is particularly thick and viscous, interfering with the function of the lungs and pancreas. To ease breathing, the thick mucus in the lungs has to be loosened periodically, but still the lungs frequently become infected. In the past few years, new treatments, including the administration of antibiotics by means of a nebulizer and the use of a percussion vest to loosen mucus in the lungs (**Fig. 9.9**), have raised the average life expectancy for CF patients to as much as 35 years of age. Genetic testing for the recessive allele is possible if individuals want to know whether they are carriers.

PKU Phenylketonuria (PKU) is the most commonly inherited metabolic disorder that affects nervous system development. Affected individuals lack an enzyme that is needed for the normal metabolism of the amino acid phenylalanine, so an abnormal breakdown product (a phenylketone) accumulates in the urine. Newborns are routinely tested in the hospital for elevated levels of the amino acid in the blood. If elevated levels are detected, newborns are placed on a special diet, which must be continued until the brain is fully developed (around the age of 7 years), or else severe mental retardation occurs. Some doctors recommend that the diet continue for life, but in any case, a pregnant woman with PKU must be on the diet to protect her unborn child from harm. Many diet products, such as soft drinks, have warnings that the product contains the amino acid phenylalanine.

Sickle-cell Disease Sickle-cell disease occurs among people of African descent and is not usually seen among other racial groups. It is estimated that 1 in 12 African Americans are carriers for the disease. In individuals with sickle-cell disease, the red blood cells are shaped like sickles, or half-moons, instead of

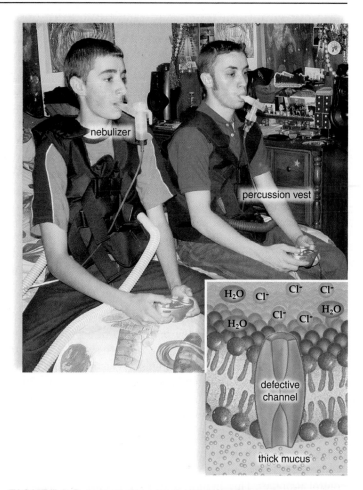

FIGURE 9.9 In cystic fibrosis a faulty channel protein fails to allow Cl^- ions to enter bronchial tubes; water will follow. Therefore, a thick mucus develops in respiratory passages. Therapy includes using a nebulizer and a percussion vest to loosen the mucus.

biconcave discs (see Fig. 9.14 B). An abnormal hemoglobin molecule (Hb^S) causes the defect. Normal hemoglobin (Hb^A) differs from Hb^S by one amino acid in the protein globin. The single change causes Hb^S to be less soluble than Hb^A.

A person with sickle-cell disease who has the genotype Hb^SHb^S exhibits a number of symptoms, ranging from severe anemia to heart failure as discussed in Section 9.14. Individuals who are Hb^AHb^S have sickle-cell trait, in which sickling of the red blood cells occurs when the oxygen content of the blood is low. Presently, prenatal diagnosis for sickle-cell disease is possible. In the future, gene therapy may be available for these patients.

Two individuals with sickle-cell trait can produce children with three possible phenotypes. The chances of producing an individual with a normal genotype (Hb^AHb^A) are 25%, with sickle-cell trait (Hb^AHb^S) 50%, and with sickle-cell disease (Hb^SHb^S) 25%. Because of the three possible phenotypes, some geneticists consider sickle-cell disease an example of incomplete dominance, an inheritance pattern to be discussed in Section 9.11.

▶ **9.9 Check Your Progress** What is the genotype of normal parents who have a child with cystic fibrosis?

9.10 Some human genetic disorders are autosomal dominant

A number of autosomal dominant disorders have been identified in humans. Three relatively common ones are neurofibromatosis, Huntington disease, and achondroplasia.

Neurofibromatosis Neurofibromatosis, sometimes called von Recklinghausen disease, is one of the most common genetic disorders and is seen equally in every racial and ethnic group throughout the world, many times in families with no history of the disorder. Once it appears in a family, it becomes a recurring trait.

At birth, or later, the affected individual may have six or more large, tan spots on the skin. Such spots may increase in size and number and get darker. Small, benign tumors (lumps) called neurofibromas, which arise from the fibrous coverings of nerves, may develop. In most cases, symptoms are mild, and patients live a normal life. In some cases, however, the effects are severe and include skeletal deformities, such as a large head, and eye and ear tumors that can lead to blindness and hearing loss. Many children with neurofibromatosis have learning disabilities and are hyperactive.

In 1990, researchers isolated the gene for neurofibromatosis and learned that it controls the production of a protein called neurofibromin, which normally blocks growth signals leading to cell division. Any number of mutations can lead to a neurofibromin that fails to block cell growth, and the result is the formation of tumors. Some mutations are caused by inserted DNA bases that do not belong in their present location.

Huntington Disease Huntington disease is a neurological disorder that leads to progressive degeneration of brain cells. **Figure 9.10A** shows that a portion of the brain involved in motor control atrophies. This, in turn, causes severe muscle spasms that worsen with time (**Fig. 9.10B**). The disease is caused by a single mutated copy of the gene for a protein called huntingtin. Most patients appear normal until they are of middle age and have already had children, who may eventually also be stricken. Occasionally, the first sign of the disease in the next generation is seen in teenagers or even younger children. There is no effective treatment, and death comes 10–15 years after the onset of symptoms.

Several years ago, researchers found that the gene for Huntington disease is located on chromosome 4. A test was devel-

FIGURE 9.10B Patients with Huntington disease have neuromuscular spasms.

oped to detect the presence of the gene, but few people want to know if they have inherited the gene because there is no cure. At least now we know that the disease stems from a mutation that causes huntingtin to have too many copies of the amino acid glutamine. The normal version of the huntingtin protein has stretches of between 10 and 25 glutamines. If the huntingtin protein has more than 36 glutamines, it changes shape and forms large clumps inside neurons. Even worse, it attracts and causes other proteins to clump with it. One of these proteins, called CBP, ordinarily helps nerve cells survive. Researchers hope they may be able to combat the disease by boosting normal CBP levels.

Another possible treatment is to transplant stem cells into the brain. Scientists hypothesize that these will replace some of the damaged neurons. Animal studies show promising results.

Achondroplasia Achondroplasia is a common form of dwarfism associated with a defect in the growth of long bones. Individuals with achondroplasia have short arms and legs and a swayback, but a normal torso and head. About 1 in 25,000 people have achondroplasia. The condition arises when a gene on chromosome 4 undergoes a spontaneous mutation. Individuals who have achondroplasia are heterozygotes (*Aa*). The homozygous recessive (*aa*) genotype yields normal-length limbs. The homozygous dominant condition (*AA*) is lethal, and death generally occurs shortly after birth.

Parents often wish to avoid having children with the disorders we have been discussing, and possible procedures to use are reviewed on the next page.

▶ **9.10 Check Your Progress** If a trait for blindness were dominant, could two blind collies have an offspring that was not blind?

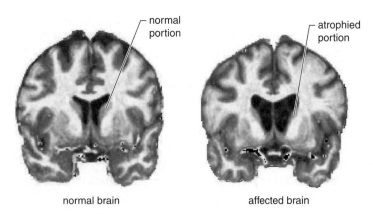

normal portion

atrophied portion

normal brain   affected brain

FIGURE 9.10A A normal brain compared to the brain of a patient affected by Huntington disease.

9B Genetic Disorders May Now Be Detected Early On

A variety of procedures are available to test for genetic disorders. Some of these involve testing after pregnancy, and others involve testing before pregnancy. It's important to realize that a woman is not pregnant until the embryo implants itself in the womb.

Testing After Implantation

During **amniocentesis,** a long needle is passed through the abdominal and uterine walls to withdraw a small amount of the fluid that surrounds the fetus and contains a few fetal cells. Thereafter, genetic tests can be done on this fluid and on fetal chromosomes from the cells. During **chorionic villi sampling (CVS),** a long, thin tube is inserted through the vagina into the uterus. Then a sampling of fetal cells is obtained by suction. The cells do not have to be cultured, as they must be following amniocentesis, and testing can be done immediately. These procedures carry a slight risk of miscarriage. If the fetus is found to have a genetic disorder it may not be acceptable for ethical, psychosocial, or religious reasons to terminate the pregnancy.

Preimplantation Genetic Diagnosis (PGD)

PGD is expected to play an ever-more-significant role in the control and prevention of genetic disease. Because it does not involve the termination of a pregnancy there is a reduced risk of miscarriage, and parents can avoid the heartbreak of having a child with a genetic disorder. The prospective parents have two choices: They can elect to test the embryo, or they can elect to test the egg.

If the embryo is to be tested (**Fig. 9B.1**), development begins in laboratory glassware through the process of in vitro fertilization (IVF). A physician obtains eggs from the prospective mother and

sperm from the prospective father, and places them in the same receptacle, where fertilization occurs. Then the zygote (fertilized egg) begins dividing. A single cell is removed from the 8-celled embryo and subjected to PGD. Removing a single cell does not affect the developing embryo. Only healthy embryos that test negative for the genetic disorders of interest are placed in the mother's uterus, where they hopefully implant and continue developing.

For testing the egg (**Fig. 9B.2**) you need to know that meiosis in females results in a single egg and at least two nonfunctional cells called **polar bodies.** Polar bodies, which later disintegrate, receive very little cytoplasm, but they do receive a haploid number of chromosomes. When a woman is heterozygous for a recessive genetic disorder, about half the polar bodies have received the mutated allele, and in these instances the egg received the normal allele. Therefore, if a polar body tests positive for a mutated allele, the egg received the normal allele. Only normal eggs are then used for IVF. Even if the sperm should happen to carry the mutation, the zygote will, at worst, be heterozygous. But the phenotype will appear normal. Testing the egg may be favored over testing the embryo because it does not involve discarding rejected embryos.

FORM YOUR OPINION

1. Do you agree that PGD is an acceptable procedure to avoid having a child with a genetic disorder, whereas terminating a pregnancy is not acceptable?
2. Is IVF acceptable to you, and if so do you prefer testing the egg over testing the embryo? Explain your reasoning.

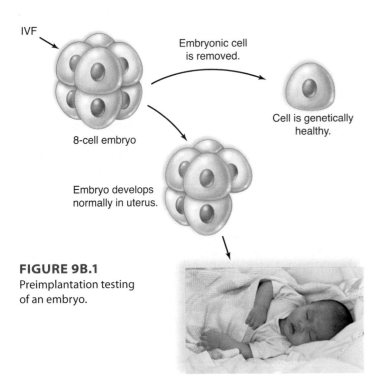

FIGURE 9B.1
Preimplantation testing of an embryo.

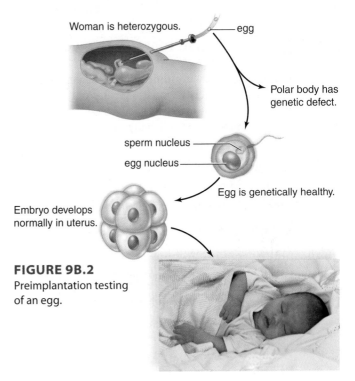

FIGURE 9B.2
Preimplantation testing of an egg.

Complex Inheritance Patterns Extend the Range of Mendelian Genetics

Learning Outcome

▶ Explain the inheritance pattern for and solve genetics problems regarding incomplete dominance, multiple alleles, polygenic inheritance, and pleiotropy. (9.11–9.14)

In this part of the chapter, we see that Mendelian genetics also applies to complex patterns of inheritance, such as incomplete dominance, multiple alleles, polygenic inheritance, and pleiotropy. You will want to recognize each of these patterns of inheritance and be able to solve genetics problems concerning them.

9.11 Incomplete dominance still follows the law of segregation

When the heterozygote has an intermediate phenotype between that of either homozygote, **incomplete dominance** is exhibited. In a cross between a true-breeding, red-flowered four-o'clock strain and a true-breeding, white-flowered strain (**Fig. 9.11**), ❶ the offspring have pink flowers. But this is not an example of the blending theory of inheritance. When the plants with pink flowers self-pollinate, ❷ the offspring have a phenotypic ratio of 1 red-flower: 2 pink-flower: 1 white-flower. The reappearance of all three phenotypes in this

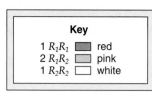

❶

R_1R_2

FIGURE 9.11
Incomplete dominance.

❷

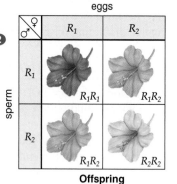

Key	
1 R_1R_1 ▮	red
2 R_1R_2 ▦	pink
1 R_2R_2 ▯	white

eggs

	R_1	R_2
R_1	R_1R_1	R_1R_2
R_2	R_1R_2	R_2R_2

sperm

Offspring

generation makes it clear that flower color in this instance is controlled by a single pair of alleles.

It would appear that in R_1R_1 individuals, a double dose of pigment results in red flowers; in R_1R_2 individuals, a single dose of pigment results in pink flowers; and because the R_2R_2 individuals produce no pigment, the flowers are white.

In humans, familial hypercholesterolemia (FH) is an example of incomplete dominance. An individual with two alleles for this disorder develops fatty deposits in the skin and tendons and may have a heart attack as a child. An individual with one normal allele and one FH allele may suffer a heart attack as a young adult, and an individual with two normal alleles does not have the disorder.

Perhaps the inheritance pattern of other human disorders should be considered as incomplete dominance. For example, to detect the carriers of cystic fibrosis and Tay-Sachs disease, it is customary to determine the amount of enzyme activity of the gene in question. When the activity is one-half that of the dominant homozygote, the individual is a carrier. In other words, at the level of gene expression, the homozygotes and heterozygotes differ in the same manner as four-o'clock plants.

▶ **9.11 Check Your Progress** If two carriers for FH conceive a baby, what are the potential phenotypes of the resulting offspring?

9.12 A gene may have more than two alleles

When a trait is controlled by **multiple alleles,** the gene exists in several allelic forms. But each person usually has only two of the possible alleles. For example, a person's ABO blood type is determined by multiple alleles. The following alleles determine the presence or absence of antigens on red blood cells:

I^A = A antigen on red blood cells

I^B = B antigen on red blood cells

i = Neither A nor B antigen on red blood cells

The possible phenotypes and genotypes for blood type are as follows:

Phenotype	Genotype
A	I^AI^A, I^Ai
B	I^BI^B, I^Bi
AB	I^AI^B
O	ii

The inheritance of the ABO blood group in humans is also an example of **codominance** because both I^A and I^B are fully expressed in the presence of the other. Therefore, a person inheriting one of each of these alleles will have type AB blood.

This inheritance pattern differs greatly from Mendel's findings, since more than one allele is fully expressed. Both I^A and I^B are dominant over i. There are two possible genotypes for type A blood and two possible genotypes for type B blood. Use a Punnett square to confirm that reproduction between a heterozygote with type A blood and a heterozygote with type B blood can result in any one of the four blood types. Such a cross makes it clear that an offspring can have a different blood type from either parent, and for this reason, DNA fingerprinting, instead of blood type, is now used to identify the parents of an individual.

▶ **9.12 Check Your Progress** A child with type O blood is born to a mother with type A blood. What is the genotype of the child? The mother? What are the possible genotypes of the father?

9.13 Several genes and the environment influence a multifactorial trait

Polygenic inheritance occurs when a trait is governed by polygenes—two or more genes or more precisely sets of alleles. The individual has a copy of all allelic pairs, possibly located on many different pairs of chromosomes. Each dominant allele has a quantitative effect on the phenotype, and these effects are additive. The result is a continuous variation of phenotypes, resulting in a distribution that resembles a bell-shaped curve. The more genes involved, the more continuous are the variations and distribution of the phenotypes. In **Figure 9.13,** a cross between the genotypes *AABBCC* and *aabbcc* yields F$_1$ hybrids with the genotype *AaBbCc.* A range of genotypes and phenotypes results in the F$_2$ generation, and therefore a bell-shaped curve. To give an easily understood example of a polygenic trait,

when a very dark person has children with a very light person, the children have medium-brown skin. If two people with medium-brown skin have children, they can range from very dark to very light skin.

Multifactorial traits are controlled by polygenes but are also subject to environmental influences. Recall that rapid weight gain possibly contributes to the occurrence of hip dysplasia in dogs, as discussed in the introduction to this chapter. In humans, skin color and disorders such as cleft lip and/or palate, clubfoot, congenital dislocations of the hip, hypertension, diabetes, schizophrenia, and even allergies and cancers are likely due to the combined action of many genes plus environmental influences. In Figure 9.13 brown shading was added to show that, for example, skin color is influenced by exposure to the sun.

Reports have surfaced in recent years that all sorts of behaviors, including alcoholism, phobias, and even suicide, can be associated with particular genes. No doubt, behavioral traits are somewhat controlled by genes, but it is impossible at this time to determine to what degree. And very few scientists would support the idea that these behavioral traits are predetermined by our genes.

The relative importance of genetic and environmental influences on the phenotype can vary, but in some instances the environment seems to have an extreme effect. One interesting study showed that cardiovascular disease is more prevalent among offspring whose biological *or adoptive* parents had cardiovascular disease. Can you suggest environmental ways that adoptive parents can bring on cardiovascular disease in their children, based on your study of Chapter 3?

These examples lend support to the belief that human traits controlled by polygenes are likely also subject to environmental influences. Therefore, many investigators are trying to determine what percentage of various traits is due to nature (inheritance) and what percentage is due to nurture (the environment). Some studies use twins separated since birth, because if identical twins in different environments share the same trait, that trait is most likely inherited. These studies suggest that identical twins are more similar in (1) intellectual talents, (2) personality traits, and (3) levels of lifelong happiness than are fraternal twins separated at birth. However, biologists conclude that all behavioral traits are partly heritable, and that genes exert their effects by acting together in complex combinations susceptible to environmental influences.

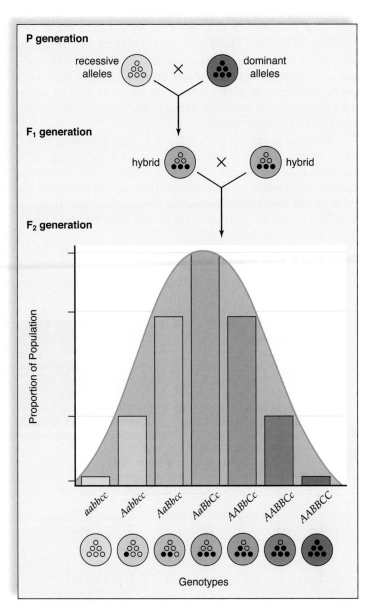

FIGURE 9.13 Polygenic inheritance: Because several dominant alleles (dark circles) contribute to the trait, the result is a continuous phenotypic variation from one extreme to the other (light blue to dark blue).

▶ 9.13 Check Your Progress

1. A polygenic trait is controlled by three different loci. Give seven genotypes among the offspring that will result in seven different phenotypes when *AaBbCc* is crossed with *AaBbCc*.

2. Investigators crossed insecticide resistant fruit flies with nonresistant fruit flies. They found that when a fly inherited its X chromosome and chromosomes 2 and 3 from its insecticide resistant parent, it had maximal insecticide resistance. What conclusion do you suggest?

3. Investigators divided cloned hens into several groups whose diet varied. They then measured the size of the eggs produced by each group. Why would this study be an approved method for studying a multifactorial trait?

9.14 One gene can influence several characteristics

Pleiotropy occurs when genes have more than one effect. For example, persons with Marfan syndrome have disproportionately long arms, legs, hands, and feet; a weakened aorta; poor eyesight; and other characteristics (**Fig. 9.14A**). All of these characteristics are due to the production of abnormal connective tissue. Marfan syndrome has been linked to a mutated gene (FBN_1) on chromosome 15 that ordinarily specifies a functional protein called fibrillin. Fibrillin is essential for the formation of elastic fibers in connective tissue. Without the structural support of normal connective tissue, the aorta can burst, particularly if the person is engaged in a strenuous sport, such as volleyball or basketball. Flo Hyman may have been the best American woman volleyball player ever, but she fell to the floor and died at the age of only 31 because her aorta gave way during a game. Now that coaches are aware of Marfan syndrome, they are on the lookout for it among very tall basketball players. Chris Weisheit, whose career was cut short after he was diagnosed with Marfan syndrome, said, "I don't want to die playing basketball."

Many other disorders, including porphyria and sickle-cell disease, are examples of pleiotropic traits. Porphyria is caused by a chemical insufficiency in the production of hemoglobin, the pigment that makes red blood cells red. The symptoms of porphyria are photosensitivity, strong abdominal pain, port-wine-colored urine, and paralysis in the arms and legs. In the late 1700s and early 1800s, many members of the British royal family suffered from this disorder, which can lead to epileptic convulsions, bizarre behavior, and coma.

In a person suffering from sickle-cell disease ($Hb^S Hb^S$), described in Section 9.9, the cells are sickle-shaped (**Fig. 9.14B**). The abnormally shaped

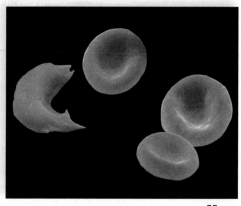

FIGURE 9.14B In persons with sickle-cell disease, the red blood cells are sickle-shaped.

.55 μm

cells slow down blood flow and clog small blood vessels. In addition, sickled red blood cells have a shorter life span than normal red blood cells. Affected individuals may exhibit a number of symptoms, including severe anemia, physical weakness, poor circulation, impaired mental function, pain, high fever, rheumatism, paralysis, spleen damage, low resistance to disease, and kidney and heart failure.

Although sickle-cell disease is a devastating disorder, it provides heterozygous individuals with a survival advantage. People who have sickle-cell trait are resistant to the protozoan parasite that causes malaria. The parasite spends part of its life cycle in red blood cells feeding on hemoglobin, but it cannot complete its life cycle when sickle-shaped cells form and break down earlier than usual.

▶ **9.14 Check Your Progress** Argue that cystic fibrosis (CF) should also be considered a pleiotropic disorder.

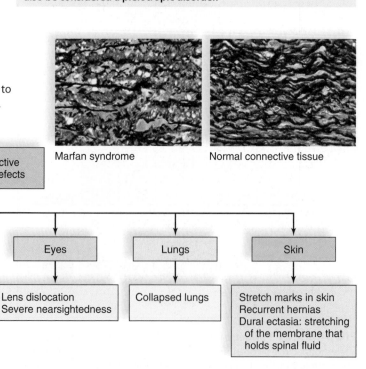

FIGURE 9.14A a. A student who has all the attributes to play basketball in college may have his or her career cut short due to Marfan syndrome. **b.** Defective connective tissue leads to the various characteristics of Marfan syndrome.

Marfan syndrome

Normal connective tissue

Connective tissue defects

| Skeleton | Heart and blood vessels | Eyes | Lungs | Skin |

Chest wall deformities
Long, thin fingers, arms, legs
Scoliosis (curvature of the spine)
Flat feet
Long, narrow face
Loose joints

Mitral valve prolapse

Enlargement of aorta

Lens dislocation
Severe nearsightedness

Collapsed lungs

Stretch marks in skin
Recurrent hernias
Dural ectasia: stretching of the membrane that holds spinal fluid

Aneurysm
Aortic wall tear

a.

b.

The Sex Chromosomes Also Carry Genes

Learning Outcomes

▶ Explain the inheritance pattern for X-linked recessive traits, and use a pedigree to detect when a disorder is X-linked. (9.15–9.16)

▶ Be able to solve genetics problems involving X-linked recessive disorders. (9.15–9.16)

The trait white eye in *Drosophila*, the fruit fly, was the first allele to be definitively assigned to a chromosome—in this case, the X chromosome. X-linked alleles have an unusual inheritance pattern because the Y chromosome does not have a corresponding allele. Some human disorders have the X-linked pattern of inheritance.

9.15 Traits transmitted via the X chromosome have a unique pattern of inheritance

By the early 1900s, investigators had noted the parallel behavior of chromosomes and genes during meiosis (see Fig. 8.9A), but they were looking for further data to support their belief that the genes were located on the chromosomes. A Columbia University group, headed by Thomas Hunt Morgan, performed the first experiments definitely linking a gene to a chromosome. This group worked with fruit flies (*Drosophila*). Fruit flies are even better subjects for genetic studies than garden peas: They can be easily and inexpensively raised in simple laboratory glassware; females mate and then lay hundreds of eggs during their lifetimes; and the generation time is short, taking only about ten days when conditions are favorable.

Drosophila flies have the same sex chromosome pattern as humans, and this facilitates our understanding of a cross performed by Morgan. Morgan took a newly discovered mutant male with white eyes and crossed it with a red-eyed female. All of the offspring had red eyes; therefore, he knew that red eyes are the dominant characteristic and white eyes are the recessive characteristic. He then crossed the F_1 flies. The F_2 generation showed the expected 3 red-eyed: 1 white-eyed ratio, but it struck Morgan as odd that all of the white-eyed flies were males:

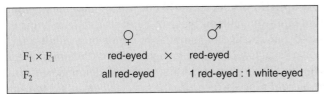

$F_1 \times F_1$	♀ red-eyed	×	♂ red-eyed
F_2	all red-eyed		1 red-eyed : 1 white-eyed

Obviously, a major difference between the male flies and the female flies was their sex chromosomes. Could it be possible that an allele for eye color was on the Y chromosome but not on the X? This idea could be quickly discarded because usually females have red eyes, and they have no Y chromosome. But perhaps an allele for eye color was on the X chromosome, and not on the Y chromosome. **Figure 9.15** indicates that this explanation matches the results obtained in the experiment. Therefore, the white-eye allele must be on the X chromosome. Once investigators had discovered a number of genes on one chromosome, they used crossing-over frequencies to determine the sequence of alleles on a chromosome, even human chromosomes. Today the accepted procedure for "mapping the chromosomes" is purely molecular (see Chapter 12).

Pattern of Inheritance Notice that X-linked alleles have a different pattern of inheritance than alleles on the autosomes because the Y chromosome is lacking for these alleles, and the

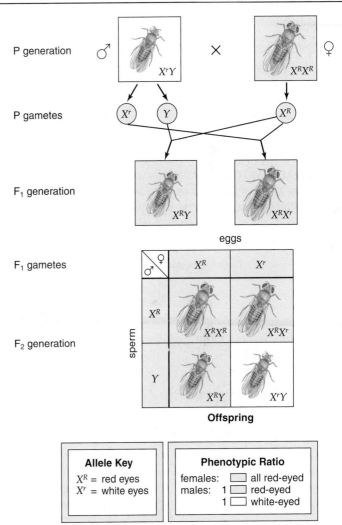

FIGURE 9.15 X-linked recessive inheritance.

inheritance of a Y chromosome cannot offset the inheritance of an X-linked recessive allele. For the same reason, affected males always receive an X-linked recessive mutant allele from the female parent—they receive the Y chromosome from the male parent (see Fig. 9.16).

▶ **9.15 Check Your Progress** Examine the karyotype for a male in Figure 8.1 and give a reason why very few Y-linked alleles have been found.

9.16 Humans have X-linked recessive disorders

Several X-linked recessive disorders occur in humans, including color blindness, muscular dystrophy, and hemophilia.

Color Blindness In humans, the receptors for color vision in the retina of the eyes are three different classes of cone cells. Only one type of pigment protein is present in each class of cone cell; there are blue-sensitive, red-sensitive, and green-sensitive cone cells. The allele for the blue-sensitive protein is autosomal, but the alleles for the red- and green-sensitive proteins are on the X chromosome. About 8% of Caucasian men have red-green color blindness. Most of them see brighter greens as tans, olive greens as browns, and reds as reddish browns. A few cannot tell reds from greens at all. They see only yellows, blues, blacks, whites, and grays.

The pedigree in **Figure 9.16** shows the usual pattern of inheritance for color blindness and, indeed, for any X-linked recessive disorder. More males than females exhibit the trait because recessive alleles on the X chromosome are expressed in males. The disorder often passes from grandfather to grandson through a carrier daughter.

Muscular Dystrophy Muscular dystrophy, as the name implies, is characterized by wasting away of the muscles. The most common form, Duchenne muscular dystrophy, is X-linked and occurs in about 1 out of every 3,600 male births. Symptoms, such as waddling gait, toe walking, frequent falls, and difficulty rising, may appear as soon as the child starts to walk. Muscle weakness intensifies until the individual is confined to a wheelchair. Death usually occurs by age 20; therefore, affected males are rarely fathers. The recessive allele remains in the population through passage from carrier mother to carrier daughter.

The allele for Duchenne muscular dystrophy has been isolated, and researchers have discovered that the absence of a protein called dystrophin causes the disorder. Much investigative work determined that dystrophin is involved in the release of calcium from the sarcoplasmic reticulum in muscle fibers. The lack of dystrophin causes calcium to leak into the cell, which promotes the action of an enzyme that dissolves muscle fibers. When the body attempts to repair the tissue, fibrous tissue forms, and this cuts off the blood supply so that more and more cells die. In the meantime, the calves of the legs enlarge.

Calves enlarge due to fibrous tissue

A test is now available to detect carriers of Duchenne muscular dystrophy. Also, various treatments have been tried. Immature muscle cells have been injected into muscles, and for every 100,000 cells injected, dystrophin production occurs in 30–40% of muscle fibers. The allele for dystrophin has been inserted into thigh muscle cells, and about 1% of these cells then produced dystrophin.

Hemophilia About 1 in 10,000 males is a hemophiliac. There are two common types of hemophilia: Hemophilia A is due to the absence or minimal presence of a clotting factor known as factor VIII, and hemophilia B (or Christmas disease) is due to the absence of clotting factor IX. Hemophilia is called the bleeder's disease because the affected person's blood either does not clot or clots very slowly. Although hemophiliacs bleed externally after an injury, they also bleed internally, particularly around joints. Hemorrhages can be stopped with transfusions of fresh blood (or plasma) or concentrates of the clotting protein. Also, clotting factors are now available as biotechnology products.

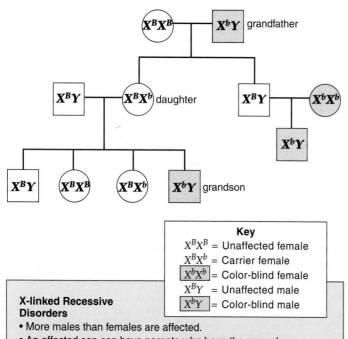

Key
$X^B X^B$ = Unaffected female
$X^B X^b$ = Carrier female
$X^b X^b$ = Color-blind female
$X^B Y$ = Unaffected male
$X^b Y$ = Color-blind male

X-linked Recessive Disorders
- More males than females are affected.
- An affected son can have parents who have the normal phenotype.
- For a female to have the characteristic, her father must also have it. Her mother must have it or be a carrier.
- The characteristic often skips a generation from the grandfather to the grandson.
- If a woman has the characteristic, all of her sons will have it.

FIGURE 9.16 X-linked recessive pedigree.

▶ **9.16 Check Your Progress**
1. Color blindness is an X-linked recessive trait. A female with normal vision and a color-blind male have a daughter who is color-blind. What are the genotypes of all the individuals involved?
2. In *Drosophila,* if a homozygous red-eyed female and a red-eyed male mated, what would be the possible genotypes of their offspring?
3. Which *Drosophila* cross would produce white-eyed males: a. $X^R X^R \times X^r Y$ or b. $X^R X^r \times X^R Y$? In what ratio?

pass genetic factors (now called alleles) to their offspring. A progression of genetic studies in the twentieth century first established that DNA is the genetic material. Then scientists discovered the structure of DNA and how it functions in a cell. Today, the emphasis is on studying the specific function of individual genes, which are segments of DNA.

Every organism has its own sequence of DNA bases, and we know the order of the bases for many organisms, including humans and *Arabidopsis*. Irradiating the seeds of *Arabidopsis* causes a mutation, a change in the normal sequence of bases. The creation of *Arabidopsis* mutants plays a significant role in revealing what each of its genes do. For example, if a mutant plant lacks stomata (openings in leaves), we know that the affected gene influences the formation of stomata.

Think of Mendel working in an abbey garden, and then think of today's laboratory, where researchers study model organisms with the aid of advanced, high-speed equipment. Amazing, too, is the recognition that, just like Mendel's peas, the work with *Arabidopsis* can assist our understanding of how human genes function. In this chapter, we begin our study of molecular genetics by examining the structure of DNA with the surety that structure suits function. Our ultimate goal is to show that DNA meets the criteria for the genetic material: (1) DNA is variable between species and able to store the information that makes species different; (2) DNA is constant within a species and able to be replicated with high fidelity during cell division; (3) DNA is able to undergo rare changes, called mutations, that provide the raw material needed for evolution to occur.

Arabidopsis flower

Mutated flower

Mutated flower

A flat of *Arabidopsis*

Lab

DNA Structure Suits Its Function

Learning Outcomes

▶ Describe how you would distinguish a **DNA (deoxyribonucleic acid)** polymer from an **RNA (ribonucleic acid)** polymer. (10.1)

▶ Describe how the structure of DNA allows it to be variable, as required for a genetic material. (10.1)

▶ Describe how the two strands of DNA are arranged in relation to one another. (10.2)

Watson and Crick deduced the structure of DNA from the data gathered by other scientists. Chemists told them that nucleic acids are polymers of nucleotides and that the bases of DNA can be in any order but the base adenine symbolized as A always paired with T (thymine) while C (cytosine) is always paired with G (guanine). X-ray diffraction told them that DNA is a double helix. The structure of DNA explains how it can have a distinctive sequence of paired bases in each species and yet replicate faithfully.

10.1 DNA and RNA are polymers of nucleotides

It wasn't until the early 1950s that James Watson, a postdoctoral student, and Francis Crick, a biophysicist, deduced the double helical structure of DNA after studying the data that had been gathered by previous scientists. They can be likened to a person who has the parts of a bicycle laid out on the grass and is trying to figure out how to put the parts together to make the bicycle run. Their achievement was to create a complete structure of DNA from knowing only its parts. Once the structure of DNA was known, biologists could determine how it functioned. What *did* Watson and Crick know when they started to build their model of DNA?

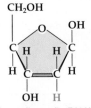

False colored EM of nucleus

DNA and RNA We want to keep in mind that the structure of DNA suits its function, and so it is fitting to point out that an early investigator found DNA in the nucleus of cells! In 1869, the Swiss physician Johann Miescher removed nuclei from pus cells and found they contained a chemical he called nuclein. Nuclein, he said, was rich in phosphorus and had no sulfur, and these properties distinguished it from protein. Later, other chemists working with nuclein found that it had acidic properties. Therefore, they decided to call the molecule **nucleic acid.**

Nucleotides Early in the 1900s, researchers discovered that nucleic acids contain only nucleotides. Each generalized **nucleotide** has three parts: a pentose sugar (5-carbon sugar), a phosphate, and a nitrogen-containing base. In this representation of a nucleotide, the carbons are numbered:

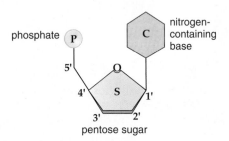

The particular sugar and base of a nucleotide can differ. For example, from **Figure 10.1A***a,* you can choose one of two sugars. If you substitute the sugar deoxyribose, you have constructed a DNA nucleotide, but if you substitute the sugar ribose, you have constructed an RNA nucleotide. To complete

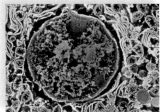

deoxyribose (in DNA)   ribose (in RNA)

a. Deoxyribose versus ribose

FIGURE 10.1A   a. A DNA nucleotide always has the sugar deoxyribose while a RNA nucleotide always has the sugar ribose. Notice that deoxyribose lacks an oxygen found in ribose. **b.** In DNA nucleotides, the four bases are symbolized as C, T, A, and G. In RNA nucleotides the four bases are C, U, A, and G. Notice that the pyrimidines have only one organic ring while the purines have two organic rings.

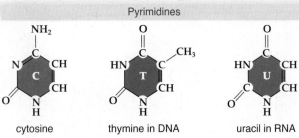

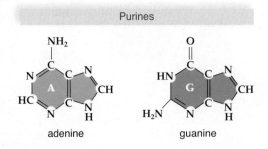

b. Pyrimidines compared to purines

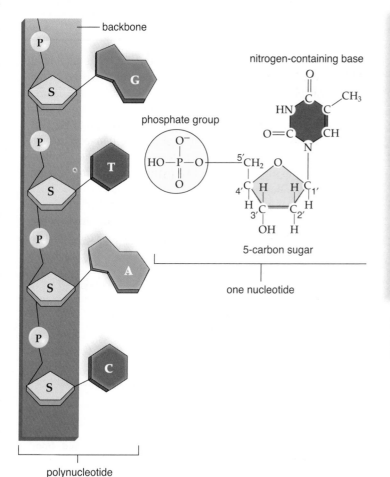

FIGURE 10.1B Nucleic acids are polynucleotides of nucleotides. The nucleotides join to produce a sugar-phosphate backbone, and the bases project to the side. The bases can be in any order.

your DNA nucleotide, you have a choice of four bases, symbolized as **C, T, A,** and **G.** An RNA nucleotide is the same except for a **U** in place of the T. If you see a T in a nucleic acid, as in **Figure 10.1B,** you know you are dealing with DNA, but if you see a U, the molecule has to be an RNA. Some bases mentioned are pyrimidines (one ring), and some are purines (two rings) (Fig. 10.1A*b*).

Polymers In a nucleic acid, the nucleotides join in a particular way. Notice in Figure 10.1B how the sugars are joined by phosphate molecules. In the backbone of both DNA and RNA polymers, a sugar group continuously alternates with a phosphate group, and the bases project to the side. The dark bar in Figure 10.1B represents the backbone of the molecule. An important feature discovered by the chemist Erwin Chargaff is that the bases can be in any order. Without this aspect of its structure, DNA wouldn't have the variability needed to be a genetic material (**Fig. 10.1C**).

Chargaff's Rules With the development of new chemical techniques in the 1940s, it became possible for Erwin Chargaff to analyze the base content of the DNA of different species. At the time, researchers thought that perhaps the four bases repeated the same in all species, like this: ATGC, ATGC, ATGC....

FIGURE 10.1C The sequence of DNA bases differs in the plants, the man, and the alligator. This is how DNA stores the genetic information that accounts for the phenotypic differences between species.

DNA Composition in Various Species (%)				
Species	**A**	**T**	**G**	**C**
Homo sapiens (human)	31.0	31.5	19.1	18.4
Drosophila melanogaster (fruit fly)	27.3	27.6	22.5	22.5
Zea mays (corn)	25.6	25.3	24.5	24.6
Neurospora crassa (fungus)	23.0	23.3	27.1	26.6
Escherichia coli (bacterium)	24.6	24.3	25.5	25.6

FIGURE 10.1D Chargaff's data showed that the DNA base composition of various species differs. For example, in humans the A and T percentages are about 31%, but in fruit flies these percentages are about 27%. However, in all organisms, the amount of A = T and the amount of G = C.

If that were the case, all species would have the same sequence of bases. But Chargaff discovered that the base composition of DNA varies between species. A sample of his data is given in **Figure 10.1D.** You can see that, while some species have approximately 25% of each type of nucleotide, most do not. Instead, the percentage of each type of nucleotide differs from species to species, as you would expect if each species has its own distinctive sequence of bases. Most important for Watson and Crick, Chargaff also discovered that, despite DNA's variability, the amount of A = T and the amount of G = C.

▶ **10.1 Check Your Progress a.** What chemical components differ between DNA and RNA? **b.** What makes one DNA molecule differ from another DNA molecule?

10.2 DNA is a double helix

In the mid-1950s, researchers were racing against each other to discover the structure of DNA. Much had already been learned. They knew that DNA is a polymer of nucleotides and, based on Chargaff's data, that the amount of base A = T and the amount of base C = G. But exactly how was the molecule put together? Watson and Crick, working at Cambridge, were much aided by the findings of Rosalind Franklin and Maurice H. F. Wilkins, who were at King's College of London.

X-ray Diffraction of DNA Franklin and Wilkins studied the structure of DNA using X-ray crystallography. Franklin found that if a concentrated, viscous solution of DNA is made, it can be separated into fibers. Under the right conditions, the fibers are enough like a crystal (a solid substance whose atoms are arranged in a definite manner) to produce an X-ray diffraction pattern (**Fig. 10.2A** *left*). The X-ray diffraction pattern of DNA suggested to Watson and Crick that DNA is a **double helix.** The helical shape is indicated by the crossed (X) pattern in the center of the photograph in Figure 10.2A *right*. The dark portions at the top and bottom of the photograph indicate that some portion of the double helix is repeated.

Watson and Crick also knew that the structure of some proteins is helical and maintained by hydrogen bonding between amino acids. This set them to thinking that DNA is a *double-stranded* helix, meaning that the two strands spiral about one another.

The Model Built by Watson and Crick As shown in **Figure 10.2B***a,* it is possible to envision DNA as a twisted ladder. The sugar-phosphate groups make up the sides of the ladder, and paired bases make up the rungs of the ladder. Mathematical measurements provided by the X-ray diffraction data told Watson and Crick there was only so much space between the two strands, and in order for the paired bases to fit the available space, a purine must be linked to a pyrimidine. Hydrogen bonding is possible between the paired bases if A pairs with T and C pairs with G as predicted by Chargaff's rules. The pairing of these bases is called **complementary base pairing.** Also, hydrogen bonding is only possible if the two strands of the molecule are antiparallel as shown here:

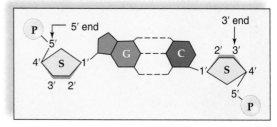

Notice in Figure 10.2B*b* that the sugars in the right strand are upside down with respect to the sugars in the left strand.

▶ **10.2 Check Your Progress** DNA from *Arabidopsis* and from humans has the same X-ray diffraction pattern. Explain.

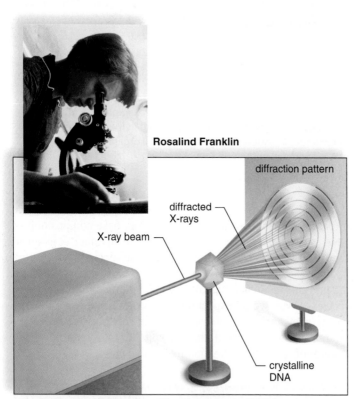

Rosalind Franklin

a. Procedure to obtain X-ray diffraction pattern of DNA

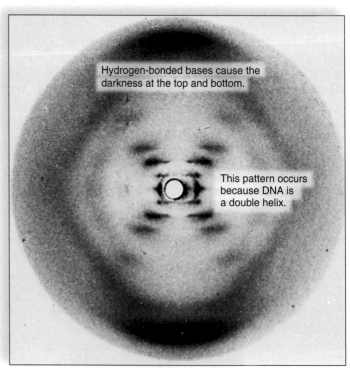

Hydrogen-bonded bases cause the darkness at the top and bottom.

This pattern occurs because DNA is a double helix.

b. Photograph of diffraction pattern

FIGURE 10.2A *(Left)* When a crystal is X-rayed, the way the beam is diffracted reflects the pattern of the molecules in the crystal. *(Right)* DNA's diffraction pattern had an X in the center, telling Watson and Crick that DNA is a helix. The dark portions at the top and bottom told them that some feature is repeated over and over. Watson and Crick determined that the feature was the hydrogen-bonded bases.

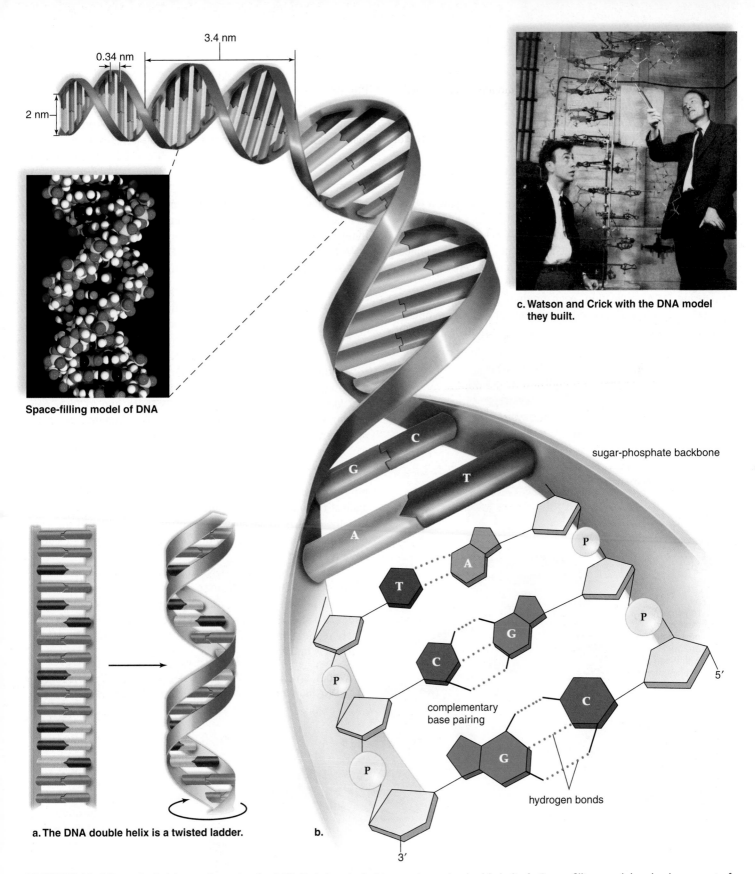

0.34 nm

3.4 nm

2 nm

Space-filling model of DNA

c. Watson and Crick with the DNA model they built.

sugar-phosphate backbone

C

G

T

A

P

T

A

G

C

P

complementary base pairing

C

G

hydrogen bonds

P

P

5′

3′

a. The DNA double helix is a twisted ladder.

b.

FIGURE 10.2B a. The ladder configuration for DNA. Twisting the ladder produces the double helix. **b.** Space-filling model and enlargement of the double helix. Each strand of the molecule has a sugar-phosphate backbone and among the bases, A is always hydrogen bonded to T, and C is always bonded to G. **c.** Watson and Crick used the X-ray diffraction pattern of DNA to build their double helix model.

DNA Replication Is a Duplication

Learning Outcomes

▶ Summarize how DNA replicates and why the process is semiconservative. (10.3)

▶ Explain why replication errors are infrequent. (10.3)

DNA replication is a duplication because it results in two double helix molecules, each exactly like the other. The process relies on complementary base pairing, and therefore each daughter DNA double helix consists of a template (old) strand and a new strand.

10.3 DNA replication is semiconservative

The term **DNA replication** refers to the process of copying a DNA molecule. Following replication, there is usually an exact copy of the DNA double helix. As soon as Watson and Crick developed their double helix model, they commented, "It has not escaped our notice that the specific pairing we have postulated immediately suggests a possible copying mechanism for the genetic material."

During DNA replication, each original DNA strand of the parental molecule (original double helix) serves as a template for a new strand in a daughter molecule. A **template** is a pattern used to produce a shape complementary to itself. DNA replication is termed **semiconservative replication** because the template, or old strand, is conserved, or present, in each daughter DNA molecule (new double helix) (**Fig. 10.3**).

Replication requires the following steps:

1. *Unwinding.* The old strands that make up the parental DNA molecule are unwound and "unzipped" (i.e., the weak hydrogen bonds between the paired bases are broken). A special enzyme called helicase unwinds the molecule.
2. *Complementary base pairing.* New complementary nucleotides, always present in the nucleus, are positioned by the process of complementary base pairing.
3. *Joining.* The complementary nucleotides join to form new strands. Each daughter DNA molecule contains a template strand, or old strand, and a new strand, but the sequence of bases in the two double helix molecules is exactly the same.

Steps 2 and 3 are carried out by an enzyme complex called **DNA polymerase.** DNA polymerase also proofreads the new strand against the old strand and detects any mismatched nucleotides; usually, each is replaced with a correct nucleotide. In the end, only about one mistake occurs for every 1 billion nucleotide pairs replicated.

While easily outlined, DNA replication is actually a complicated process. One complication is that DNA polymerase cannot start the process of replication and instead has to add nucleotides to a short sequence of RNA bases complementary to DNA where replication starts. The RNA is later removed and replaced with DNA nucleotides.

▶ **10.3 Check Your Progress** Replication produces identical DNA molecules. What critical step brings this about?

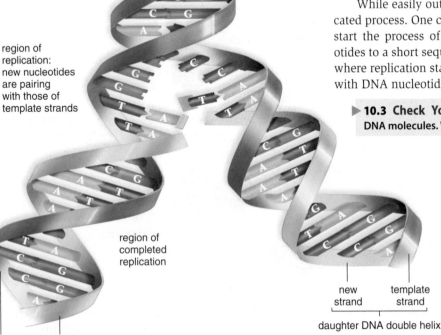

region of parental DNA double helix

region of replication: new nucleotides are pairing with those of template strands

region of completed replication

template strand | new strand

daughter DNA double helix

new strand | template strand

daughter DNA double helix

FIGURE 10.3 Semiconservative replication. Notice that each new double helix contains a template (old) strand and a new strand.

10A DNA Replication in a Test Tube

The polymerase chain reaction (PCR) is a powerful molecular way to select and copy a particular segment of DNA in a test tube (**Fig. 10A**). It's call the polymerase chain reaction because the enzyme DNA polymerase is bringing about replication of a chosen segment over and over again. Once it starts, a chain of replications occurs until there are thousands of copies of the same DNA segment. The beauty of the process is its precision in selecting only a tiny portion of DNA to be copied. The primers used can seek out and bind to a segment of viral DNA, human DNA, plant DNA—or any particular type of DNA, as long as it is in the test tube. Analysis of the copied segment produces visual results.

The expression "**DNA fingerprinting**" refers to the use of PCR to identify a specific individual. Just like a traditional fingerprint, the analytical results are unique to the individual. There is only a slight chance a genetic fingerprint will be the same for any two people. To guard against even this possibility, however, PCR is done twice, using two different target segments for replication.

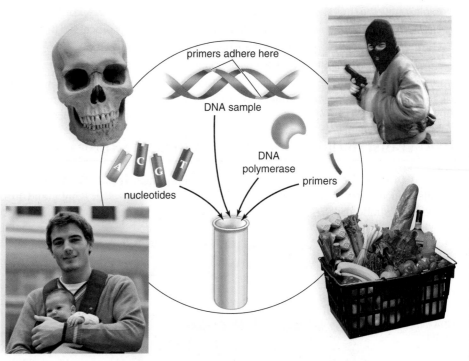

FIGURE 10A PCR requirements are minimal, but the applications are many and varied. Evolutionary relationships can be clarified, criminals can be identified, foods can be tested for contamination, and parents can be identified.

The applications for DNA fingerprinting are extremely varied, and some of them are quite dramatic. For example, Arthur Whitfield had already served 22 years for rape when DNA fingerprinting of a saved semen sample taken from the vagina of the rape victim showed he was not the rapist. On the basis of that evidence, the state of Virginia set him free. Any type of body sample, such as a drop of blood or even a single hair root from a crime scene, can be used to identify a suspect—or to clear a suspect. Investigators identified the victims of the September 11, 2001, terrorist attacks in the United States by comparing the DNA of body remains with that of a few cells taken from a personal object, such as a toothbrush. Parental testing can match an individual to close relatives. For example, the biological father of Anna Nicole Smith's daughter, Danielynn, was found to be photographer Larry Birkhead through the use of DNA fingerprinting.

Applications of PCR are limited only by our imaginations. Both vegetables and meats can be tested to detect specific bacterial or viral contamination. Medical applications are numerous. When the segment of DNA chosen for replication matches that of a virus or mutated gene, we know that a viral infection, a genetic disorder, or cancer is present. Blood typing may soon be done utilizing PCR, and PCR is already being used to test for an HIV infection. Formerly, it was necessary to wait several weeks to confirm the presence of the HIV virus, but PCR can detect the virus as soon as it enters the body. Donated blood can be screened directly for HIV, and newborns can be immediately tested. The beneficial effects of antiviral HIV treatment can also be evaluated. PCR analysis is essential to preimplantation genetic diagnosis, which requires testing a polar body or embryonic cell for a particular genetic mutation. Similarly, prospective parents can be tested for being genetic carriers, or their children can be tested for actually having a particular genetic disorder.

Biologists have also found many uses for PCR. PCR analysis can be carried out on mummies that are thousands of years old. Hair, muscle, skin, or bone samples have been used to determine the gender of mummies, for example. An open phylogenetic question is the evolutionary relationship of Neandertals to modern humans. PCR studies have begun, and so far the results indicate that Neandertal DNA is significantly different from modern humans, meaning that they are not our ancestors and we did not interbreed with them. Ecologists have found that PCR analysis of droppings can help them estimate the size of rare animal populations in a particular area and to infer the animals' eating habits.

FORM YOUR OPINION

1. The chief limitation of PCR is inadvertent contamination with stray DNA in the test tube. How could this concern be addressed, or should PCR not be used?
2. Should the DNA fingerprints of convicted felons be kept on file for easy identification in the case of future crimes?
3. Should PCR procedures be available for any and all purposes, or should they be regulated. If so, by whom?

Genes Specify the Primary Structure of a Protein

Learning Outcomes

- Explain how the sequences of bases in an RNA molecule, called mRNA, constitute a genetic code. (10.4)
- Describe how mRNA is formed during transcription and how it is processed before entering the cytoplasm. (10.4)
- List the RNA participants and explain the role of each during translation. (10.5)
- Diagram the processes of initiation and elongation in protein synthesis. (10.6–10.7)

Producing a cellular protein requires two steps: During transcription, DNA is a **template** (mold) for RNA formation, and during translation, the sequence of bases in a messenger RNA (mRNA) codes for the sequence of amino acids in a polypeptide. Transfer RNA (tRNA) and ribosomal RNA (rRNA) are also active during translation. Once a protein product is present in a cell, a gene has been expressed.

10.4 Transcription is the first step in gene expression

Figure 10.4A gives an overview of gene expression, which is complete once a new protein has been made. First, during **transcription,** a strand of RNA forms that is complementary to the DNA template strand. Transcription means to "make a faithful copy", and in this case, a sequence of nucleotides in DNA is copied into a sequence of nucleotides in mRNA. The mRNA molecule that forms is a transcript of a gene. Second, gene expression also requires the process of **translation.** Translation means "to put information into a different language". In this case, a sequence of nucleotides is translated into a sequence of amino acids. This is possible only if the bases in DNA and mRNA code for amino acids. This code is called the **genetic code.**

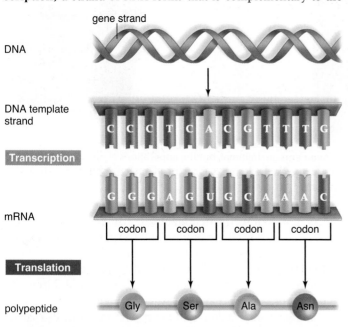

FIGURE 10.4A Transcription occurs when mRNA forms through complementary base pairing with the DNA template strand. Translation occurs when the sequence of codons in mRNA specifies the sequence of amino acids in a polypeptide.

The Genetic Code Recognizing that there must be a genetic code, investigators wanted to know how four bases (A, C, G, U) could provide enough combinations to code for 20 amino acids. If the code were a singlet code (one base standing for one amino acid), only four amino acids could be encoded. If the code were a doublet (any two bases standing for one amino acid), it would still not be possible to code for 20 amino acids. But if the code were a triplet, then the four bases could supply 64 different triplets, far more than needed to code for 20 different amino acids. It should come as no surprise then to learn that the genetic code is a **triplet code.**

Each three-letter (base) unit of an mRNA molecule is called a **codon.** The translation of all 64 mRNA codons has been determined (**Fig. 10.4B**). Sixty-one triplets correspond to a particular amino acid; the remaining three are stop codons, which signal polypeptide termination. The one codon that stands for the amino acid methionine is also a start codon, signaling polypeptide initiation. Notice, too, that most amino acids have more

FIGURE 10.4B Notice that in this chart, each of the codons is composed of three letters. As an example, find the rectangle where C is the first base and A is the second base. U, C, A, or G can be the third base. CAU and CAC are codons for the amino acid His (histidine); CAA and CAG are codons for Gln (glutamine).

First base	Second base: U	Second base: C	Second base: A	Second base: G	Third base
U	UUU, UUC – phenylalanine (Phe) UUA, UUG – leucine (Leu)	UCU, UCC, UCA, UCG – serine (Ser)	UAU, UAC – tyrosine (Tyr) UAA *stop* UAG *stop*	UGU, UGC – cysteine (Cys) UGA *stop* UGG tryptophan (Trp)	U C A G
C	CUU, CUC, CUA, CUG – leucine (Leu)	CCU, CCC, CCA, CCG – proline (Pro)	CAU, CAC – histidine (His) CAA, CAG – glutamine (Gln)	CGU, CGC, CGA, CGG – arginine (Arg)	U C A G
A	AUU, AUC, AUA – isoleucine (Ile) AUG methionine (Met) *(start)*	ACU, ACC, ACA, ACG – threonine (Thr)	AAU, AAC – asparagine (Asn) AAA, AAG – lysine (Lys)	AGU, AGC – serine (Ser) AGA, AGG – arginine (Arg)	U C A G
G	GUU, GUC, GUA, GUG – valine (Val)	GCU, GCC, GCA, GCG – alanine (Ala)	GAU, GAC – aspartic acid (Asp) GAA, GAG – glutamic acid (Glu)	GGU, GGC, GGA, GGG – glycine (Gly)	U C A G

than one codon; for example, leucine, serine, and arginine have six different codons. This offers some protection against possibly harmful mutations that change the sequence of the bases.

To crack the code, a cell-free experiment was done: Artificial RNA was added to a medium containing bacterial ribosomes and a mixture of amino acids. Comparison of the bases in the RNA with the resulting polypeptide allowed investigators to decipher the code. For example, an mRNA with a sequence of repeating guanines (GGGGGG...) would encode a string of glycine amino acids.

The genetic code is just about universal in living things. This suggests that the code dates back to the very first organisms on Earth and that all living organisms are related.

The Process of Transcription Suppose you have a wood-working encyclopedia in your bookcase and you want to make a step stool. Rather than taking the entire set of encyclopedias out to the workshop, you might copy the instructions to make a step stool onto a sheet of paper and take just that to your workshop. We can liken the DNA in a nucleus to the encyclopedia containing the instructions for all sorts of wood products (polypeptides). The sheet of paper becomes an mRNA molecule that has instructions for the step stool, which represents the particular polypeptide to be made.

During transcription, an RNA molecule is transcribed off the DNA template strand (**Fig. 10.4C**). Although all three classes of RNA are formed by transcription, we will focus on transcription to form **messenger RNA (mRNA).** Transcription begins when the enzyme RNA polymerase opens up the DNA helix just in front of it so that complementary base pairing can occur. Then RNA polymerase joins the RNA nucleotides, and an mRNA molecule results. When mRNA forms, it has a sequence of bases complementary to the DNA template strand; wherever A, T, G, or C is present in the DNA template strand, U, A, C, or G is incorporated into the mRNA molecule. Now mRNA is a faithful copy of a **gene strand.** A gene is a portion of DNA that codes for a protein product.

Processing mRNA In eukaryotes, the newly synthesized primary-mRNA must be processed before it enters the cytoplasm. During processing, which occurs in the nucleus, one end of the primary-mRNA is modified by the addition of a cap that is composed of an altered guanine nucleotide (**Fig. 10.4D**). At the other end, there is a poly-A tail, a series of adenosine nucleotides. These modifications provide stability to the mRNA; only those that have a cap and tail remain active in the cell.

Most genes in humans are interrupted by segments of DNA that do not code for protein. These portions are called **introns** because they are intervening segments. The other portions of the gene, called **exons,** contain the protein-coding portion of the gene. In primary-mRNA splicing, the introns are removed by enzymes and the exons are joined together. Only the mature mRNA molecule consisting of continuous exons is ready to be translated.

Processing can utilize all the exons of a gene. In some instances, however, only certain exons form the mature RNA transcript and are utilized. The result will be a different protein product, depending on the exons used. In other words, so-called **alternative mRNA splicing** can potentially increase the possible number of protein products that can be made from a single gene.

▶ **10.4 Check Your Progress** What is the significance of transcription and alternative mRNA splicing in gene expression?

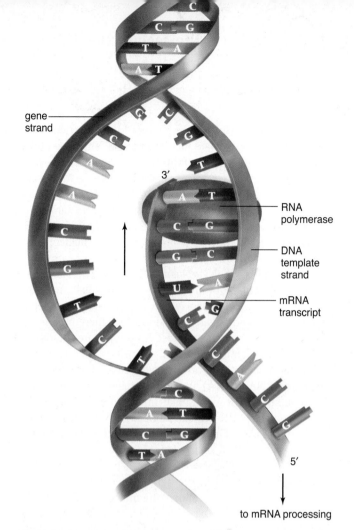

FIGURE 10.4C During transcription, complementary RNA is made off the DNA template strand. A portion of DNA unwinds and unzips at the point of attachment of RNA polymerase. A strand of mRNA is produced when complementary bases join in the order dictated by the sequence of bases in the DNA template strand.

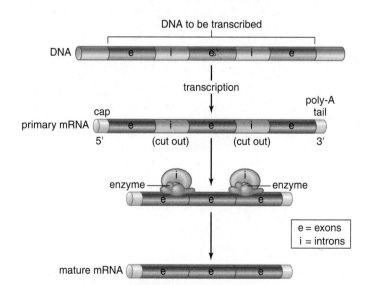

FIGURE 10.4D A cap and a poly-A tail are attached to the ends of the primary RNA transcript, and the introns are removed so that only the exons remain. This mature mRNA molecule moves into the cytoplasm of the cell, where translation occurs.

10.5 Translation is the second step in gene expression: An overview

Translation, the second step in gene expression, occurs in the cytoplasm of eukaryotic cells and requires the following types of RNA:

- **Messenger RNA (mRNA)** is produced in the nucleus where DNA serves as a template for its formation. This type of RNA carries genetic information from DNA to the cytoplasm where protein synthesis occurs. This is possible because the bases in mRNA constitute the codons, each one consisting of only three bases that code for a particular amino acid. For example, the codon CUU codes for the amino acid leucine (see Fig. 10.4B).

- **Ribosomal RNA (rRNA)** is produced in the nucleolus of a nucleus off a DNA template. Ribosomal RNA joins with proteins made in the cytoplasm to form the two subunits of ribosomes. The subunits leave the nucleus and come together in the cytoplasm when protein synthesis begins. mRNA has a binding site on a ribosome where protein synthesis specifically occurs. Most ribosomes are attached to rough endoplasmic reticulum, but ribosomes can occur freely in the cytoplasm or in clusters called polyribosomes.

- **Transfer RNA (tRNA)** is produced in the nucleus off a DNA template. However, like mRNA, tRNA functions in the cytoplasm. True to its name, tRNA transfers amino acids to the ribosomes, where the amino acids are joined, forming a protein. Like any organic molecule, the structure of tRNA can be represented by various models, each depicting a specific aspect of the actual molecule (**Fig. 10.5A**). The space-filling model shows the molecule's three-dimensional shape, but the cloverleaf model shows clearly that tRNA contains regions where intramolecular base pairing occurs. It's this pairing that gives tRNA two ends: The **acceptor end** binds to an amino acid, and the **anticodon end** binds to a codon for that amino acid. Why? Because each **anticodon** is complementary to the codon for its amino acid. For example, an anticodon for leucine would

be GAA because GAA binds to CUU, the codon for leucine. (Recall that U occurs in RNA instead of T.)

The Process of Translation In our previous analogy, DNA was a woodworking encyclopedia, and mRNA was a copy of a page for making a step stool. Continuing that comparison, a ribosome is a table in the workshop where the step stool is made. The term translation is appropriate because DNA and RNA are made of nucleotides, and polypeptides are made of amino acids. In other words, one language (nucleic acids) gets translated into another language (protein).

During translation, the sequence of codons in the mRNA at a ribosome directs the sequence of amino acids in a polypeptide. This works because the tRNA-amino acid complexes bind to the mRNAs in the order dictated by the sequence of the codons. There can be several tRNAs for each amino acid, depending on the number of codons for that amino acid (see Fig. 10.4B). As mentioned, this helps ensure that, despite changes in DNA base sequences, the sequence of amino acids will remain the same.

Let's revisit Figure 10.4B to show how translation works. If the codon sequence is ACC, GUA, and AAA, what will be the anticodons and sequence of amino acids in a portion of the polypeptide? Check your answers against the following chart.

Codon	Anticodon	Amino Acid
ACC	UGG	Threonine
GUA	CAU	Valine
AAA	UUU	Lysine

Function of a Ribosome Both prokaryotic and eukaryotic cells contain thousands of ribosomes per cell because they are needed for protein synthesis. Ribosomes have a binding site for mRNA and three binding sites for transfer RNA (tRNA) molecules (**Fig. 10.5B*a*, *above***). These binding sites are called the **A site,** the **P site,** and the **E site.** The tRNA at the A site bears only an *amino*

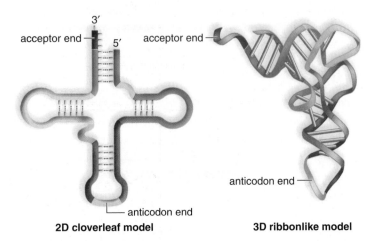
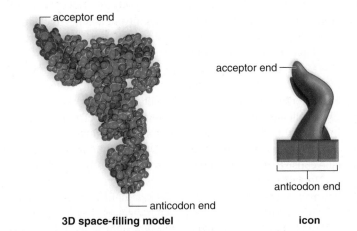

2D cloverleaf model   **3D ribbonlike model**   **3D space-filling model**   **icon**

FIGURE 10.5A In the cloverleaf model of tRNA, the base pairing within the molecule that creates the anticodon loop and the acceptor end where the amino acid attaches are obvious. The ribbonlike model gives a more realistic view of the polynucleotide chain making up the molecule. The 3D space-filling model shows the actual shape of the molecule. The icon for tRNA used in this book is based on the space-filling model.

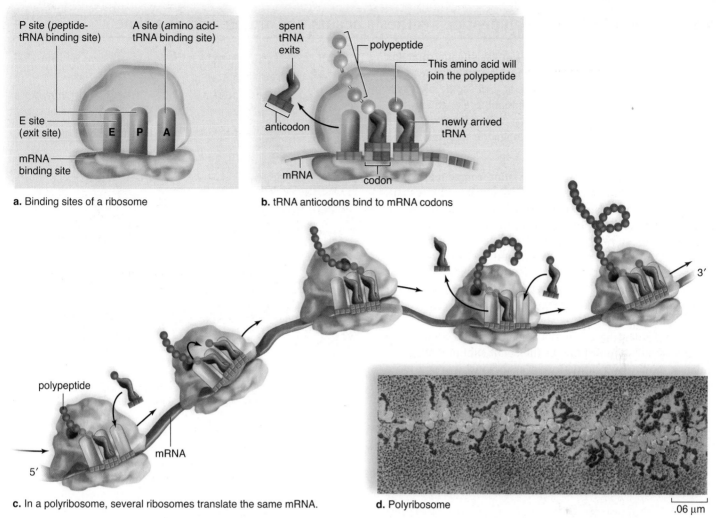

a. Binding sites of a ribosome

b. tRNA anticodons bind to mRNA codons

c. In a polyribosome, several ribosomes translate the same mRNA.

d. Polyribosome

.06 μm

FIGURE 10.5B a. A ribosome has three binding sites where **(b)** tRNA anticodons bind to codons. **c., d.** A polyribosome is a number of ribosomes all translating the same mRNA transcript. This makes translation more efficient.

acid, while the tRNA at the P site bears a *p*eptide. The tRNA that leaves the *e*xit site bears neither, and this is why it leaves the ribosome. The tRNA binding sites facilitate complementary base pairing between tRNA anticodons and mRNA codons.

Conceivably three tRNAs could momentarily be at the ribosome at the same time, but more likely an amino acid-tRNA is just coming and/or an empty tRNA is just leaving (Fig. 10.5B*b*). Just as a parent might drop off a student and wait to make sure the student joins a line-up to enter the school, so a tRNA takes an amino acid to a ribosome and leaves after the amino acid has taken its place in a growing polypeptide. The methodology to get the amino acids lined up properly in a polypeptide is discussed in Section 10.7. Also, translation begins with the start codon and terminates at a stop codon.

What is the function of ribosomes? They help ensure that the amino acids in a polypeptide are sequenced according to the order originally specified by DNA. This comes about because the anticodons of the tRNAs bind to the codons in a particular sequence.

A **polyribosome** is several ribosomes attached to and translating the same mRNA (Fig. 10.5B*c, d*). As soon as the initial

portion of mRNA has been translated by one ribosome, and the ribosome has begun to move down the mRNA, another ribosome attaches to the mRNA. A polyribosome greatly increases the efficiency of translation. The average speed of protein synthesis is 20 peptide bonds per second. But when you consider that many ribosomes may be synthesizing the same protein, the speed per protein may be much higher, even up to 2,000 identical proteins per second. Not surprisingly, it has been calculated that *E. coli* spends 90% of its energy on supplying the substrates and the means to carry out protein synthesis.

Efficient antibiotics attack a bacterium where it is most vulnerable. The antibiotic tetracycline blocks the A site of bacterial ribosomes so tRNAs cannot bind to this site, and the antibiotic streptomycin causes a misreading of the genetic code so that a faulty protein is produced. Either of these events leads to death of the bacterium.

▶ **10.5 Check Your Progress** What would be the last three amino acids in the polypeptide attached to the tRNA at the P site in Figure 10.5B*b* if their mRNA codons were CCA, UAC, and AGA?

10.6 During translation, polypeptide synthesis occurs one amino acid at a time

Although we often speak of protein synthesis, some proteins have more than one polypeptide, so it is more accurate to recognize that polypeptide synthesis occurs at a ribosome. Polypeptide synthesis involves three events: initiation, elongation, and termination. Enzymes are needed so that each of the three events will occur, and both initiation and elongation also require an input of energy.

Initiation During **initiation** all translation components come together. Proteins called initiation factors help assemble a small ribosomal subunit, mRNA, initiator tRNA, and a large ribosomal subunit for the start of a polypeptide synthesis.

Initiation is shown in **Figure 10.6A.** In prokaryotes, an mRNA binds to a small ribosomal subunit at the mRNA binding site. The start codon AUG is at the P site. The first, or initiator, tRNA pairs with this codon because its anticodon is UAC. As you can see by examining Figure 10.4B, AUG is the codon for methionine. Methionine is always the first amino acid of a polypeptide. After the small ribosomal unit has attached, a large ribosomal subunit joins to the small subunit. Although similar in many ways, initiation in eukaryotes is much more complex.

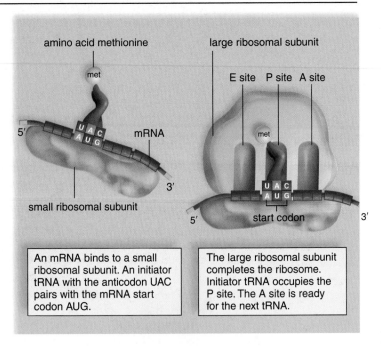

An mRNA binds to a small ribosomal subunit. An initiator tRNA with the anticodon UAC pairs with the mRNA start codon AUG.

The large ribosomal subunit completes the ribosome. Initiator tRNA occupies the P site. The A site is ready for the next tRNA.

FIGURE 10.6A Participants in the initiation event assemble as shown. The first amino acid is typically methionine.

As shown in Figure 10.6A, a ribosome has three binding sites for tRNAs. Although the second is ordinarily for a peptide-tRNA, the initiator tRNA is capable of binding to it even though it carries only the amino acid methionine. The next amino acid-tRNA binds to the A site.

Elongation During **elongation,** a polypeptide increases in length, one amino acid at a time. In addition to the participation of tRNAs, elongation requires elongation factors, which facilitate the binding of tRNA anticodons to mRNA codons at a ribosome.

Elongation is shown in **Figure 10.6B,** where ❶ a tRNA with an attached peptide is already at the P site, and a tRNA carrying its appropriate amino acid is just arriving at the A site. ❷ Once the next tRNA is in place at the A site, the peptide will be transferred to this tRNA. This transfer requires energy and a ribozyme. **Ribozymes,** located in the larger ribosomal subunit, are enzymes composed of RNA instead of protein. Ribozymes join peptides (from the P sites) to amino acids at the A sites. The bond that joins them together is a peptide bond (see Fig. 3.9B). ❸ After peptide bond formation occurs, the peptide is one amino acid longer than it was before. ❹ Finally, **translocation** occurs: The ribosome *moves forward,* and the peptide-tRNA is now at the P site of the ribosome. The used tRNA exits from the E site. A new codon is at the A site, ready to receive another tRNA. Eventually, the ribosome reaches a stop codon, and **termination** occurs, during which the polypeptide is released.

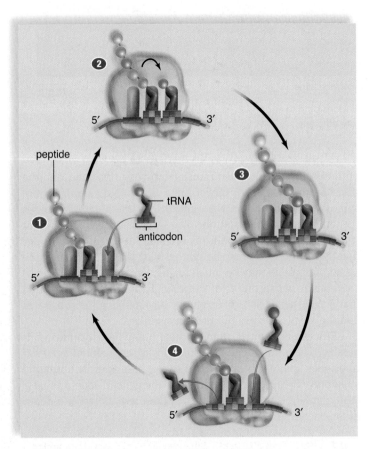

FIGURE 10.6B During elongation, a polypeptide increases by one amino acid at a time. As a result of #1 and #2, the peptide at the P site will pass to the amino acid that just arrived at the A site. Then between #3 and #4 translocation occurs: the ribosome moves forward so that the peptide-tRNA is now at the P site. The empty tRNA exits.

▶ **10.6 Check Your Progress a.** In *Arabidopsis* (or any organism), what is the significance of finding the bases TAC in DNA? **b.** With reference to Figure 10.4B, what is the significance of finding these sequences ATT, ATC, or ACT in DNA?

10.7 Let's review gene expression

Gene expression requires two steps, called transcription and translation. **Figure 10.7** shows that in a eukaryotic cell, transcription occurs in the nucleus and translation occurs in the cytoplasm. ❶ and ❷ mRNA is produced and processed before leaving the nucleus. ❸ – ❻ After mRNA becomes associated with ribosomes, polypeptide synthesis occurs one amino acid at a time. **Table 10.7** reviews the participants in gene expression.

Many ribosomes can be translating the same section of DNA at a time, and collectively these ribosomes are called a polyribosome. As discussed earlier, some ribosomes remain free in the cytoplasm, and others become attached to rough ER. ❼ After the polypeptide enters the lumen of the ER by way of a channel, it is folded and further processed by the addition of sugars, phosphates, or lipids. ❽ When the ribosome reaches a stop codon and termination occurs, ribosomal units and mRNA are separated from one another, and the polypeptide is released.

We have finished our examination of gene expression (the making of a protein). In the next part of the chapter, we will study the biochemistry of mutations.

TABLE 10.7	Participants in Gene Expression	
Name of Molecule	**Special Significance**	**Definition**
DNA	Has genetic information	Sequence of DNA bases
mRNA	Has codons	Sequence of three RNA bases complementary to DNA
tRNA	Has an anticodon	Sequence of three RNA bases complementary to codon
rRNA	Located in ribosomes	Site of protein synthesis
Amino acid	Monomer of a polypeptide	Transported to ribosome by tRNA
Polypeptide	Enzyme, structural, or secretory product	Amino acids joined in a predetermined order

▶ **10.7 Check Your Progress** What does a cell do with the genetic information stored by DNA. In your answer mention the participants involved in transcription and translation.

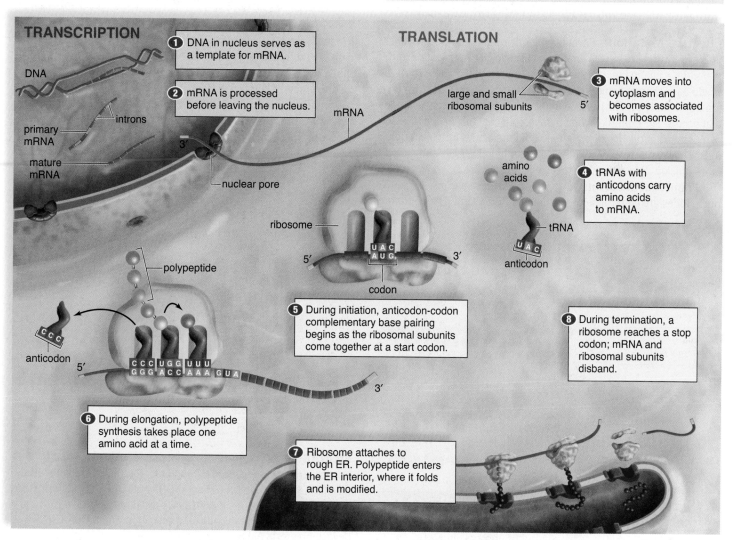

TRANSCRIPTION

TRANSLATION

❶ DNA in nucleus serves as a template for mRNA.

❷ mRNA is processed before leaving the nucleus.

❸ mRNA moves into cytoplasm and becomes associated with ribosomes.

❹ tRNAs with anticodons carry amino acids to mRNA.

❺ During initiation, anticodon-codon complementary base pairing begins as the ribosomal subunits come together at a start codon.

❻ During elongation, polypeptide synthesis takes place one amino acid at a time.

❼ Ribosome attaches to rough ER. Polypeptide enters the ER interior, where it folds and is modified.

❽ During termination, a ribosome reaches a stop codon; mRNA and ribosomal subunits disband.

DNA, introns, primary mRNA, mature mRNA, nuclear pore, polypeptide, anticodon, 5', anticodon, mRNA, ribosome, codon, large and small ribosomal subunits, amino acids, tRNA, anticodon

CCC UGG UUU / GGG ACC AAA GUA

FIGURE 10.7 Summary of gene expression in eukaryotes.

Mutations Are Changes in the Sequence of DNA Bases

Learning Outcome

▶ Give examples of the different types of mutations and their possible effects. (10.8)

In molecular terms, a gene is a sequence of DNA bases, and a genetic mutation is a change in this sequence. Frameshift mutations can result in nonfunctional proteins and have powerful effects. Even point mutations, such as those in sickle-cell hemoglobin, can be serious.

10.8 Mutations alter genetic information and expression

A **genetic mutation** is a permanent change in the sequence of bases in DNA. The effect of a DNA base sequence change on protein activity can range from no effect to complete inactivity. In general, there are two types of mutations: germ-line mutations and somatic mutations. Germ-line mutations occur in sex cells and can be passed to subsequent generations. Somatic mutations occur in body cells, and therefore they may affect only a small number of cells in a tissue. Somatic mutations are not passed on to future generations, but they can lead to the development of cancer.

Some mutations are spontaneous—they happen for no apparent reason—while others are induced by environmental influences. Induced mutations may result from exposure to toxic chemicals or radiation, as discussed in "How Biology Impacts Our Lives" on page 206.

Effect of Mutations Several types of mutations are possible. **Point mutations** involve a change in a single DNA nucleotide and, therefore, a change in a specific codon. **Figure 10.8a** shows how a single base change could have no effect—or a drastic effect (in the form of a faulty protein)—depending on the particular base change that occurs. For example, when hemoglobin contains valine instead of glutamate at one location, hemoglobin molecules form semirigid rods. The resulting sickle-shaped cells clog blood vessels and die off more quickly than normal-shaped cells (Fig. 10.8b, c).

Frameshift mutations most often occur because one or more nucleotides are either inserted or deleted from DNA. The result of

a frameshift mutation can be a completely new sequence of codons and nonfunctional proteins. Here is how this occurs: The sequence of codons is read from a specific starting point, as in this sentence, THE CAT ATE THE RAT. If the letter C is deleted from this sentence and the reading frame is shifted, we read THE ATA TET HER AT—something that doesn't make sense. Cystic fibrosis involves a frameshift mutation that results from a faulty code for a chloride ion channel protein in the plasma membrane.

A single nonfunctioning protein can have a dramatic effect on the phenotype. For example, one particular metabolic pathway in cells is as follows:

$$A \text{ (phenylalanine)} \xrightarrow{E_A} B \text{ (tyrosine)} \xrightarrow{E_B} C \text{ (melanin)}$$

If a faulty code for enzyme E_A is inherited, a person is unable to convert molecule A to molecule B. Phenylalanine builds up in the system, and the excess causes the symptoms of the genetic disorder phenylketonuria (PKU). In the same pathway, if a person inherits a faulty code for enzyme E_B, then B cannot be converted to C, and the individual is an albino lacking all color in the skin, hair, and eyes.

▶ **10.8 Check Your Progress** Why would a frameshift mutation in *Arabidopsis* affect a protein to a greater degree if it altered the base sequence early on?

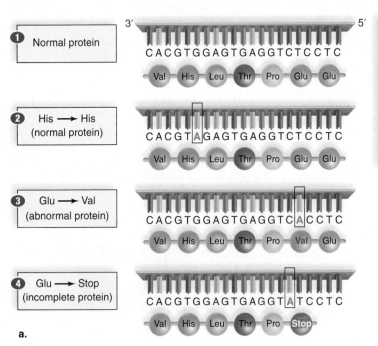

a.

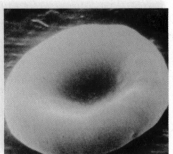

b. Normal red blood cell

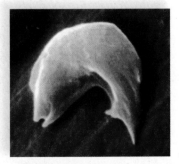

c. Sickled red blood cell

FIGURE 10.8 The effect of a point mutation can vary. **a.** ❶ Normal sequence of bases in hemoglobin. ❷ The base change has no effect. ❸ Due to a base change, DNA now codes for valine instead of glutamic acid, and the result is sickle-cell disease. ❹ A base change will cause DNA to code for termination, and the protein will be incomplete. **b.** A normal red blood cell compared to (**c**) a sickled red blood cell.

10B Transposons Cause Mutations

In 1983 Barbara McClintock, shown in **Figure 10B***a,* received a Nobel Prize in Physiology or Medicine for her work in genetics. When she began studying inheritance in corn (maize) plants, geneticists believed that each nucleotide had a fixed position on a chromosome. In the course of her studies with corn, she concluded that "controlling elements"—later called transposons—could undergo transposition and move from one location to another on the chromosome. If a transposon, now known to be a short sequence of DNA nucleotides, lands in the middle of a gene, it prevents the expression of that gene. Dr. McClintock said that because transposons are capable of suppressing gene expression, they could account for the pigment pattern of the corn strain popularly known as Indian corn (Fig. 10B*b*).

Suppose, for example, that the expression of a normal gene results in a corn kernel that is purple:

codes for
purple
pigment

What happens if transposition causes a transposon to land in the middle of this normal gene? The cells of the corn kernel are unable to produce the purple pigment, and the corn kernel is now white, instead of purple:

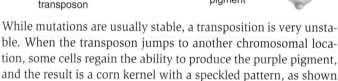

cannot
code for
purple
pigment

transposon

While mutations are usually stable, a transposition is very unstable. When the transposon jumps to another chromosomal location, some cells regain the ability to produce the purple pigment, and the result is a corn kernel with a speckled pattern, as shown in Figure 10B*b*.

When McClintock first published her results in the 1950s, the scientific community paid little attention. Years later, when molecular genetics was well established, transposons were also discovered in bacteria, yeasts, plants, fruit flies, and humans. We now know that transposons make up 45% of all the DNA in a human cell! So the study of transposons is now of tremendous importance. Unfortunately, transposons can have harmful effects:

1. Transposons cause genetic mutations when they block transcription. They are known to cause human diseases, including hemophilia and muscular dystrophy.
2. Transposons cause chromosomal mutations, including translocations, deletions, and inversions, because they often carry a copy of certain host genes with them when they jump. Transposons also cause duplications if they leave copies of themselves and certain host genes before jumping.
3. Transposons in bacteria encourage the spread of human infectious diseases because they contain one or more genes that make a bacterium resistant to antibiotics.

Because of their ability to strongly affect the genotype, transposons are thought likely to have played a significant role in

a.

b.

FIGURE 10B **a.** Barbara McClintock discovered transposons. Her experimental material was the maize (corn) plant. **b.** Transposons are responsible for the speckled or striped patterns in Indian corn.

evolution and the development of organisms. In her acceptance speech for the Nobel Prize, the 81-year-old scientist proclaimed that "it might seem unfair to reward a person for having so much pleasure over the years, asking the maize plant to solve specific problems, and then watching its responses."

FORM YOUR OPINION

1. Transposons are generally considered "selfish DNA parasites." Why is this expression warranted? In what sense is all DNA selfish?
2. One family of transposons in *Drosophila melanogaster,* called P elements, probably appeared in the twelfth century and since has spread to all populations of the *Drosophila* species. Create a scenario by which this would be possible.

10C Environmental Mutagens Can Cause Cancer

A mutagen is an environmental agent that increases the chances of a mutation. Among the best-known mutagens are radiation and organic chemicals. Many mutagens also cause cancer. Scientists use the Ames test to see if a substance is mutagenic. In the Ames test, a histidine-requiring (His−) strain of bacteria is exposed to a chemical (**Fig. 10C.1**). If the chemical is mutagenic, the bacterium regains the ability to grow without histidine. A large number of chemicals used in agriculture and industry give a positive Ames test result. Examples are ethylene dibromide (EDB), which is added to leaded gasoline (to vaporize lead deposits in the engine and send them out the exhaust), and ziram, which is used to prevent fungal disease in crops. Some drugs, such as isoniazid (used to prevent tuberculosis), are mutagenic according to the Ames test. The mutagenic potency of AF-2, a food additive once widely used in Japan, and safrole, a natural flavoring agent that used to be added to root beers, caused them to be banned. Although most testing has been done on man-made chemicals, many naturally occurring substances have been shown to be mutagenic. One of these is aflatoxin, produced in moldy grain and peanuts (and present in peanut butter at an average level of 2 parts per billion). Traces of nine different substances that give positive Ames test results have been found in fried hamburger.

Tobacco smoke contains a number of organic chemicals that are known carcinogens, and an estimated one-third of all cancer deaths are attributed to smoking. Lung cancer is the most frequent lethal cancer in the United States, and smoking is also implicated in the development of cancers of the mouth, larynx, bladder, kidneys, and pancreas. The greater the number of cigarettes smoked per day, the earlier the habit starts, and the higher the tar content, the greater chance a person has of developing cancer. When smoking is combined with drinking alcohol, the risk of these cancers increases even more.

Aside from chemicals, certain forms of radiation, such as X-rays and gamma rays used in medical procedures, can cause mutations. They are called ionizing radiation because they create free radicals, which are ionized atoms with unpaired electrons. Free radicals react with and alter the structure of other molecules, including DNA. Because of the carcinogenic effect of X-rays, it is wise to avoid unnecessary exposure. Ultraviolet (UV) radiation in sunlight is easily absorbed by the pyrimidines in DNA. Wherever two thymine molecules exist next to one another,

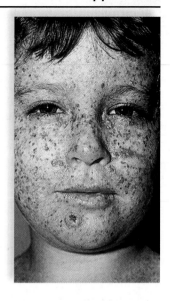

FIGURE 10C.2 In xeroderma pigmentosum, deficient DNA repair enzymes leave the skin cells vulnerable to the mutagenic effects of ultraviolet light, allowing many induced mutations to accumulate. Hundreds of skin cancers (small dark spots) appear on the skin exposed to the sun. This individual also has a tumor on the bridge of the nose.

ultraviolet radiation may cause them to bond together, forming thymine dimers. A kink in the DNA results:

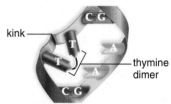

Usually, these dimers are removed from damaged DNA by repair enzymes, which constantly monitor DNA and fix any irregularities. One enzyme excises a portion of DNA that contains the dimer; another makes a new section by using the other strand as a template; and still another seals the new section in place. When skin cancer develops because of sunbathing, repair enzymes have failed. The importance of repair enzymes is exemplified by individuals with the condition known as xeroderma pigmentosum (**Fig. 10C.2**). They lack some of the repair enzymes, and as a consequence, these individuals have a high incidence of skin cancer.

FORM YOUR OPINION

1. Should people who smoke and sunbathe pay the same amount for health insurance as those who are more protective of their health?
2. Is it acceptable to rely on the results of an Ames test when it tests the effect of mutagens on bacteria?

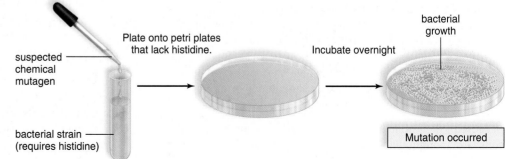

FIGURE 10C.1 During the Ames test, bacteria that require histidine to grow are exposed to a suspected chemical mutagen. If the bacteria grow on a petri dish that lacks histidine, a mutation has occurred and the chemical is an environmental mutagen.

suspected chemical mutagen

bacterial strain (requires histidine)

Plate onto petri plates that lack histidine.

Incubate overnight

bacterial growth

Mutation occurred

SUMMARY

DNA Structure Suits Its Function

10.1 DNA and RNA are polymers of nucleotides

- **Nucleotides** in the **nucleic acid DNA (deoxyribonucleic acid)** contain the sugar deoxyribose and the bases adenine (A), thymine (T), cytosine (C), and guanine (G).
- The nucleotides in **RNA (ribonucleic acid)** contain the sugar ribose and the bases A, C, G, and uracil (U) instead of T.
- Chargaff discovered that the base composition of DNA varies between species, showing that DNA does have the variability to be a genetic material.
- In all species, the percentage of A always equals the percentage of T, and the percentage of G equals the percentage of C.

10.2 DNA is a double helix

- Watson and Crick constructed the first **double helix** model of DNA, using all the data mentioned in Section 10.1 as well as Franklin and Wilkins's X-ray diffraction data.
- In the model, A pairs with T and G pairs with C. This is called **complementary base pairing.** Each species has its own sequence of bases.
- The double helix model suggests how the replication of DNA occurs.

DNA Replication Is a Duplication

10.3 DNA replication is semiconservative

- **Semiconservative replication** means that each new double helix contains an old strand that acted as a **template** and a new strand made off the template.
- The steps in replication are unwinding, complementary base pairing, and joining.
- **DNA polymerase** is used in pairing and joining.

Genes Specify the Primary Structure of a Protein

10.4 Transcription is the first step in gene expression

- Gene expression (the making of a protein) has two steps: **transcription** and **translation.**
- During transcription, a sequence of DNA nucleotides is transcribed into a sequence of RNA nucleotides. The nucleotides in a **messenger RNA (mRNA)** are complementary to those in a protein-encoding **gene.** A gene is a portion of the DNA molecule.
  - The **genetic code** is a **triplet code:** Every three bases in mRNA, called a **codon,** stands for an amino acid. The genetic code has start and stop codons, and most amino acids have more than one codon.
- In eukaryotes, an mRNA is processed before leaving the nucleus.
  - mRNA receives a cap and a tail.

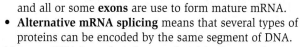

- During splicing of primary mRNA, **introns** are removed, and all or some **exons** are use to form mature mRNA.
- **Alternative mRNA splicing** means that several types of proteins can be encoded by the same segment of DNA.
- Mature mRNA is ready to be translated in the cytoplasm.

10.5 Translation is the second step in gene expression: An overview

- All three types of mRNA are involved in translation.
  - mRNA contains a sequence of codons complementary to the bases in DNA.
  - **Ribosomal RNA (rRNA)** combines with proteins to form the ribosomes, which have binding sites for mRNA, and three **transfer RNAs (tRNAs).**
  - Each tRNA brings a specific amino acid to the ribosomes.
- A tRNA has an **acceptor end** where its amino acid binds and also an **anticodon end.** The **anticodon** is a sequence of three bases that are complementary to a codon for that amino acid.
- A ribosome has binding sites for mRNA and three tRNAs at the **A site,** the **P site,** and the **E site.** An amino acid-tRNA is at the A site, and a peptide-tRNA is at the P site. A tRNA that lacks an attached amino acid exits from the E site.
- A **polyribosome** is composed of several ribosomes attached to and translating the same mRNA. This increases the efficiency of protein synthesis.

10.6 During translation, polypeptide synthesis occurs one step at a time

- During **initation** in prokaryotes, ribosomal subunits, mRNA, and initiator tRNA come together. Initiation is more complicated in eukaryotes.
- The first amino acid-tRNA is one that carries the amino acid methionine (Met)to the ribosome.
- During **elongation,** the peptide increases one amino acid at a time in this way: The peptide at the P site binds to the amino acid at the A site. A **ribozyme** speeds the formation of a peptide bond between the two.
- Now **translocation** occurs: The ribosome moves forward, and the peptide-tRNA is now at the P site. The spent tRNA exits from the E site. This process occurs over and over again.
- At **termination,** the ribosome reaches a stop codon, and the polypeptide is released.

10.7 Let's review gene expression

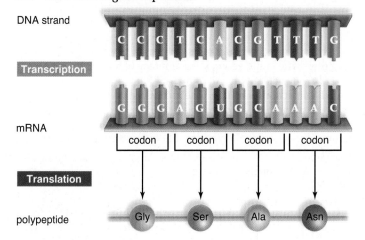

DNA strand

Transcription

mRNA

| codon | codon | codon | codon |

Translation

polypeptide   Gly   Ser   Ala   Asn

Mutations Are Changes in the Sequence of DNA Bases

10.8 Mutations alter genetic information and expression

- A **genetic mutation** is a permanent change in the sequence of DNA bases.
- Both **point mutations** and **frameshift mutations** can cause genetic disorders.

TESTING YOURSELF

DNA Structure Suits Its Function

1. If 30% of an organism's DNA is thymine, then
   a. 70% is purine.
   b. 10% is guanine.
   c. 30% is adenine.
   d. 70% is pyrimidine.
   e. Both c and d are correct.
2. In a DNA molecule, the
   a. backbone is sugar and phosphate molecules.
   b. bases are covalently bonded to the sugars.
   c. sugars are covalently bonded to the phosphates.
   d. bases are hydrogen-bonded to one another.
   e. All of these are correct.
3. Which of these characteristics of DNA is not paired with a proper explanation for that characteristic?
   a. variable between species—sequence of bases can vary
   b. store information—sugar-phosphate backbones never vary
   c. constant within a species—can be replicated by complementary base pairing
   d. able to undergo mutations—sequence of bases can change
4. Which of these statements is true concerning DNA structure?
   a. A sugar bonds to phosphate and to a base.
   b. A sugar bonds only to two phosphate groups.
   c. U is present in DNA but absent in RNA.
   d. Sugars being ring structures hydrogen bond together.

DNA Replication Is a Duplication

5. Because each daughter molecule contains one old strand of DNA, DNA replication is said to be
   a. conservative.
   b. preservative.
   c. semidiscontinuous.
   d. semiconservative.
6. During DNA replication, the parental strand ATTGGC would code for the daughter strand
   a. ATTGGC.
   b. CGGTTA.
   c. TAACCG.
   d. GCCAAT.
7. DNA polymerase carries out replication, except it cannot
   a. carry out complementary base pairing.
   b. unwind the double helix.
   c. join the nucleotides together.
   d. proofread the polymer for accuracy of base pairing.
8. **THINKING CONCEPTUALLY** AZT, the well-known medicine for HIV infection, is a DNA base analogue that hinders DNA replication. Explain why it works.

Genes Specify the Primary Structure of a Protein

For questions 9–13, match each molecule to its special significance in gene expression as listed in the key.

KEY:
   a. Stores genetic information from generation to generation
   b. Sequence of three RNA bases complementary to those in DNA
   c. Has an anticodon
   d. Located in ribosomes
   e. The gene product

9. rRNA
10. mRNA codon
11. Protein
12. DNA
13. tRNA
14. Transcription produces _____, while translation produces _____.
   a. DNA, RNA
   b. RNA, polypeptides
   c. polypeptides, RNA
   d. RNA, DNA
15. Which of the following statements does not characterize the process of transcription? Choose more than one answer if correct.
   a. During transcription, RNA nucleotides base pair to the DNA template strand.
   b. To make RNA, the base uracil pairs with adenine.
   c. The enzyme RNA polymerase synthesizes RNA.
   d. RNA is made in the cytoplasm of eukaryotic cells.
16. Because there are more codons than amino acids,
   a. some amino acids are specified by more than one codon.
   b. some codons do not specify any amino acid.
   c. some amino acids do not have codons.
   d. Both a and b are correct
17. If the sequence of bases in DNA template strand is TAGC, then the sequence of bases in RNA will be
   a. ATCG.
   b. TAGC.
   c. AUCG.
   d. GCTA.
   e. Both a and b are correct.
18. mRNA processing
   a. is the same as transcription.
   b. is an event that occurs after RNA is transcribed.
   c. is the rejection of old, worn-out RNA.
   d. pertains to the function of transfer RNA during protein synthesis.
   e. Both b and d are correct.
19. Label this diagram showing the participants in translation.

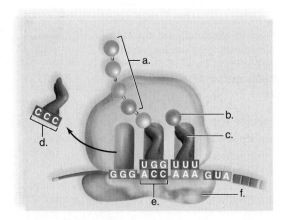

20. During protein synthesis, the anticodon of transfer RNA (tRNA) pairs with
   a. DNA nucleotide bases.
   b. ribosomal RNA (rRNA) nucleotide bases.
   c. messenger RNA (mRNA) nucleotide bases.
   d. other tRNA nucleotide bases.
   e. Any one of these pairings can occur.
21. Following is a segment of a DNA molecule. (Remember that only the template strand is transcribed.) What are (a) the

RNA codons, (b) the tRNA anticodons, and (c) the sequence of amino acids in a protein?

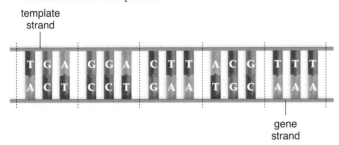

template
strand

gene
strand

22. **THINKING CONCEPTUALLY** What type information does DNA store, and how does it store the information?

Mutations Are Changes in the Sequence of DNA Bases

23. How would you know that a genetic mutation has occurred?
    a. A person has an infectious disease.
    b. A person inherits a faulty gene.
    c. Transcription and translation occur.
    d. All of these are correct.
24. A mutation involving the replacement of one DNA nucleotide base pair with another is called a
    a. frameshift mutation.
    b. point mutation.
    c. transposon.

25. Give an example of a point mutation that would have no effect on the cell. Explain.
26. **THINKING CONCEPTUALLY** Mutations can cause cancer, but on the other hand, it is important for DNA to mutate. Explain.

THINKING SCIENTIFICALLY

1. How would you test your hypothesis that the genetic condition neurofibromatosis is due to a transposon?
2. Knowing that you can clone plants from a few cells in tissue culture, how would you determine if an isolated *Arabidopsis* gene causes a particular mutation?

ONLINE RESOURCE

www.mhhe.com/maderconcepts2

Enhance your study with animations that bring concepts to life and practice tests to assess your understanding. Your instructor may also recommend the interactive eBook, individualized learning tools, and more.

CONNECTING THE CONCEPTS

A genetic material should meet three requirements: It must be variable, accounting for the differences between species; it must be able to replicate; and it must be able to undergo mutations. The ability of DNA to fulfill these requirements lies in the sequence of its bases. Furthermore, DNA contains coded information stored from one generation to the next that permits the synthesis of particular proteins, and it is the difference in proteins between species that makes one species different from another. By studying the activity of genes in cells, geneticists have confirmed that proteins are the link between genotype and phenotype. In other words, you have blue, or brown, or hazel eye pigments because of the types of enzymes (proteins) contained within your cells.

Polypeptide synthesis is a two-step process. Three types of RNA (mRNA, rRNA, and tRNA) participate in polypeptide synthesis, but only mRNA carries the coded information to the ribosomes containing the rRNA. mRNA contains a faithful copy of a gene—a portion of the DNA—and this copy is used during transcription to build a polypeptide. Just as an office saves the master copy of a form so it can always make more copies, the cell keeps its master copy of the genes safely stored in the nucleus. The tRNAs capture amino acids

and bring them to the ribosome where binding of tRNA to the correct codons ensures that the amino acids will be sequenced in the correct order.

We now know the sequence of bases in human DNA, but it turns out that humans have far fewer genes than expected. A complicated organism such as a human being can make do with fewer genes if each gene has more than one function, according to how it is regulated. Regulation of gene activity, to be discussed in Chapter 11, has become the focal point of modern-day research.

PUT THE PIECES TOGETHER

1. Show that DNA fulfills the criteria for a genetic material.
2. Mature cells are specialized for particular functions and contain their own specific set of proteins. What does this say about the activity of protein-coding genes in specialized cells?
3. Drugs are usually molecules that affect the activity of proteins in cells. Futuristic drugs might affect which part of the protein synthesis procedure?

11

Regulation of Gene Activity

CHAPTER OUTLINE

APPLICATIONS

Moth and Butterfly Wings Tell a Story

After you set an ornate moth free, all that is left on your hand is a smudge of dustlike residue. The residue is actually composed of many scales, the units of moth and butterfly wings. The multitude of scale colors and patterns in moths and butterflies is awe-inspiring. Each individual scale is a particular color and may vary completely from a neighboring scale. The color of the scales is due to the presence of particular pigments that transmit, absorb, and reflect certain colors of light.

Most specialists who study insects agree that scales evolved from the bristles of an ancestor to moths and butterflies. Over time, the bristles became wide and flat and lost any sensory function. You might think that scales have an accessory and unnecessary function, but evidence suggests otherwise. For example, the easy detachment of scales may have made it easier for ancient moths and butterflies to escape from spiderwebs and other predators. The possible protective function of scales is strengthened by their role in forming eyespots, a rounded eyelike marking on moth and butterfly wings.

Leafwing butterfly

Other animals also have eyespots. For example, eyespots can be found on the tail of a redfish, on the bodies of spiders

eyespot

Bull's-eye moth

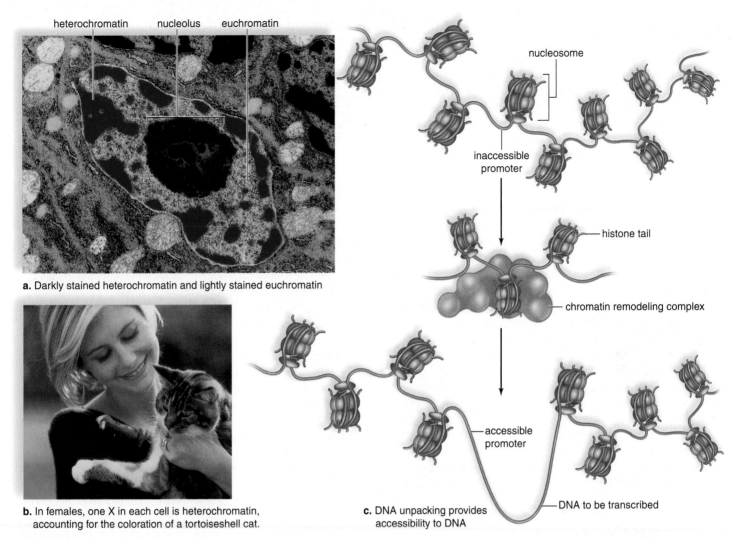

a. Darkly stained heterochromatin and lightly stained euchromatin

b. In females, one X in each cell is heterochromatin, accounting for the coloration of a tortoiseshell cat.

c. DNA unpacking provides accessibility to DNA

FIGURE 11.3B a. A nucleus contains heterochromatin which is inactive (not being transcribed) and euchromatin which is active (being transcribed). **b.** Tortoiseshell cats are females which have patches of both black and orange. Black appears when X chromosomes carrying an allele for orange are inactivated and orange appears when X chromosomes carrying an allele for black are inactivated. **c.** When euchromatin is transcribed, a chromatin remodeling complex pushes aside the histone portions of nucleosomes so that RNA polymerase and transcription factors have access to the gene to be transcribed.

increases in size and strength to make up for the defective tissue). And women who are heterozygous for X-linked hereditary absence of sweat glands have patches of skin lacking sweat glands. The female tortoiseshell cat also provides dramatic support for a difference in X-inactivation in its cells. In these cats, an allele for black coat color is on one X chromosome, and a corresponding allele for orange coat color is on the other X chromosome. The patches of black and orange in the coat can be related to which X chromosome is in the Barr bodies of the cells found in the patches (Fig. 11.3B*b*).

Euchromatin Is Transcribed Active genes in eukaryotic cells are associated with more loosely compacted euchromatin. Histones regulate accessibility to DNA, and euchromatin becomes genetically active when histones no longer bar access to DNA. When DNA in euchromatin is transcribed, a so-called

chromatin remodeling complex pushes aside the histone portion of a nucleosome so that access to DNA is not barred and transcription can begin (Fig. 13.3B*c*). After **unpacking** occurs, many decondensed loops radiate from the central axis of the chromosome. These chromosomes have been named lampbrush chromosomes because their feathery appearance resembles the brushes that were once used to clean kerosene lamps.

What regulates whether chromatin exists as euchromatin or heterochromatin? Histone molecules have tails, strings of amino acids that extend beyond the main portion of the nucleosome (Fig. 13.3B*c*). In euchromatin, the histone tails tend to have attached acetyl groups (—COCH$_3$); in heterochromatin, the histone tails tend to bear methyl groups (—CH$_4$).

▶ **11.3 Check Your Progress** Metaphase chromosomes are inactive heterochromatin. Explain "inactive" and explain "heterochromatin."

11.4 Hox proteins are DNA-binding proteins active during development

Investigators using the fruit fly or the mouse as their experimental material have begun to discover the types of genes that control development. These genes are regulatory genes that code for either signaling proteins or for transcription factors which are also proteins. As described in Figure 5B p.100, signaling proteins activate transduction pathways and a transduction pathway ends with a transcription factor that binds to DNA and affects gene expression.

Hox Genes Code for Hox Proteins The *Hox* genes function during development after the basic coordinates of the body and its various segments have been established. (Coordinates determine which end of the animal will be the head and which the tail, for example.) Segmental animals such as fruit flies, mice, and ourselves have a body divided into a set number of segments. In fruit flies, *Hox* genes determine which segments will have wings and which will have legs. *Hox* gene mutations may result in abnormalities, such as legs where antennae should be or wings where legs should be (**Fig. 11.4A**).

Hox genes can be found in many different types of organisms, and they can be recognized by the presence of a particular sequence of bases called a **homeobox** (Fig. 11.4A). The homeobox codes for a particular sequence of amino acids called a homeodomain. *Hox* genes are **master developmental regulatory genes** because they code for Hox proteins which are transcription factors that bind to and activate other regulatory genes. The homeodomain is the DNA-binding portion of the transcription factor and a variable sequence determines which target genes are affected. The target genes are directly involved in pattern formation, or what the animal will look like.

The importance of *Hox* genes is underscored by the finding that they are highly conserved, being present in the genomes of many organisms, including mammals such as mice and even humans. In both flies and mammals, the position of the *Hox* on the chromosome matches their anterior-to-posterior expression pattern in the body. The first gene clusters determine the final development of anterior segments, while those later in the

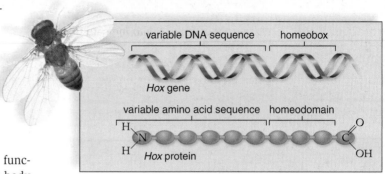

FIGURE 11.4A *Hox* genes are master developmental genes identified in many different species by the presence of a homeobox that codes for a homeodomain. If a *Hox* gene malfunctions in fruit flies, the result can be more than one pair of wings.

sequence determine the final development of posterior segments of the animal's body.

Mutations in *Hox* genes in the mammalian body have effects similar to the transformations observed in fruit flies. For instance, mutations in two adjacent *Hox* genes in the mouse result in shortened forelimbs that are missing the radius and ulna bones. In humans, mutations in a different *Hox* gene cause synpolydactyly, a rare condition characterized by extra digits (fingers and toes), some of which are fused to their neighbors.

While *Hox* genes determine the final development of a segment, other master developmental genes affect an entire region. A recent surprising finding is that a master developmental regulatory gene called *Pax6* triggers eye development in many different types of organisms, including a fly, a human, and a squid, even though the structure of their eyes is entirely different (**Fig. 11.4B**).

▶ **11.4 Check Your Progress** How does the ability of *Pax6* to trigger the development of the eye in different organisms support the theory of evolution?

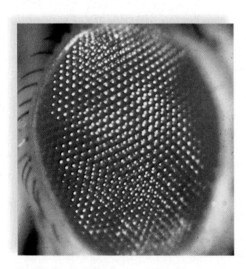
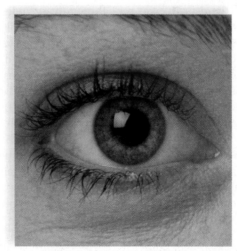
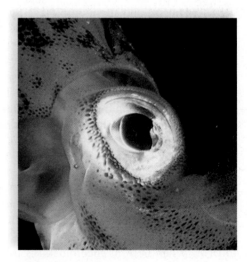

FIGURE 11.4B *Pax6* is a master developmental regulatory gene that turns on eye development in a fly, a human, and a squid.

11A Regulatory Genes and the Origin of the Genus *Homo*

Fossils of immediate ancestors to the genus **Homo** indicate that they spent part of their time climbing trees and that they retained many apelike traits. In some, the arms, like those of an ape, were long compared to the length of the legs. Then, too, our ancestors had strong wrists and long, curved fingers and toes. These traits would have served well for climbing, and these predecessors to humans probably climbed trees for the same reason that chimpanzees do today: to gather fruits and nuts in trees and to sleep aboveground at night in order to avoid predatory animals, such as lions and hyenas.

Whereas our brain is about the size of a grapefruit, that of our predecessors was about the size of an orange—and only slightly larger than that of a chimpanzee. There is no evidence that they manufactured stone tools; presumably, they were not smart enough to do so.

Several years ago, Stephen Stanley of Johns Hopkins University concluded that the genus *Homo* could not have evolved if our immediate ancestors lived in trees. The obstacle relates to the way we, members of *Homo*, develop our large brain. Unlike apes, we retain a high rate of fetal brain growth through the first year after birth. (That is why a one-year-old child has a very large head in proportion to the rest of its body.) The brain of apes grows rapidly before birth, but immediately after birth the brain grows more slowly. As a result, an adult human brain is more than three times as large as that of an adult chimpanzee.

A continuation of the high rate of fetal brain growth in our ancestors eventually allowed the genus *Homo* to evolve. But the continued brain growth is linked to underdevelopment of the body as a whole. Although the human brain eventually becomes more complex, human babies are remarkably weak and uncoordinated. Such helpless infants must be carried about and tended. Human babies are unable to cling to their mothers the way chimpanzee babies can.

The origin of the genus *Homo* entailed a great evolutionary compromise. Humans gained a large brain, but they were saddled with a long period of infantile helplessness. The positive value of a large brain must have outweighed the negative aspects of infantile helplessness, such as the inability of adults to climb trees while holding an infant, or else genus *Homo* wouldn't have evolved. Having a larger brain meant that humans were able to outsmart or ward off predators with weapons they were clever enough to manufacture.

If regulatory genes were involved, as presumably they were, very few genetic changes were required to delay maturation and produce the large brain of *Homo*. The mutation of a master developmental regulatory gene, such as a *Pax* gene, that controls one or more other genes most likely could have been all that was needed. As we learn more about the human genome, we will eventually uncover the particular gene or gene combinations that caused early *Homo* to have a large brain, and this will be a very exciting discovery. As of now, we know that changes in gene expression occur more often in other organs (such as the liver) than they do in the brain, but any changes that occurred were very dramatic in humans. This correlates with the unique

An infant chimpanzee can cling to its mother, leaving her hands free.

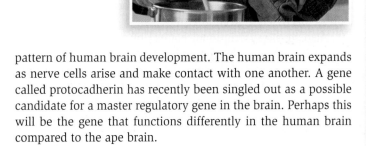

A human infant cannot cling and has to be carried.

pattern of human brain development. The human brain expands as nerve cells arise and make contact with one another. A gene called protocadherin has recently been singled out as a possible candidate for a master regulatory gene in the brain. Perhaps this will be the gene that functions differently in the human brain compared to the ape brain.

FORM YOUR OPINION

1. Should researchers spend much time and resources discovering what makes our brain different from that of the apes? Why or why not?
2. *Mosaic evolution* is a term used for evolution of one part of the body at the expense of another. Why does this term apply to the aspects of human evolution discussed in this reading?
3. During human development, life begins as a single cell that divides many times, and these cells slowly take on the shape and function of specialized tissues and organs. Does it make sense to you that regulatory genes play an important role in development? Why or why not?

RNAs Regulate Gene Expression Following Transcription

Learning Outcomes

▶ Describe how alternative mRNA splicing controls the specific protein products of a gene. (11.5)

▶ Explain the role of small RNAs in regulating the amount of a gene's product. (11.6)

The role of RNAs in gene expression is only now being recognized and given greater significance. Alternative mRNA splicing has been known for some time, but the presence and activity of small RNA sequences in regulating gene expression is a new finding. Biologists are asking: Is RNA simply DNA's helper, or is RNA the regulator that controls what the cell and the organism will be like?

11.5 Alternative mRNA splicing results in varied gene products

You'll recall that during pre-mRNA processing, introns (noncoding regions) are excised, and exons (expressed regions) are spliced together. When introns are removed, **pre-mRNA alternative splicing** of exons can occur, and this affects gene expression. For example, an exon that is normally included in an mRNA transcript may be skipped, and it is excised along with the flanking introns (**Fig. 11.5**). The resulting mature mRNA has an altered sequence, and the protein product differs. Sometimes introns remain in an mRNA transcript; when this occurs, the protein coding sequence also changes.

Examples of alternative pre-mRNA splicing abound. Both the hypothalamus and the thyroid gland produce a protein hormone called calcitonin, but the mRNA that leaves the nucleus is not the same in both types of cells. This causes the thyroid to release a slightly different version of calcitonin than the hypothalamus. Evidence of alternative mRNA splicing is also found in other cells, such as those that produce neurotransmitters, muscle regulatory proteins, and antibodies. This process allows the cells of humans and other complex organisms to recombine genes in many new and novel ways to create the great variety of proteins found in these organisms.

Researchers are busy determining how introns and other types of small RNAs can affect mRNA processing and translation as discussed in Section 11.6.

Also, posttranscriptional control of gene expression can simply be achieved by modifying the speed of transport of mRNA from the nucleus into the cytoplasm. Evidence indicates there is a difference in the length of time it takes various mRNA molecules to pass through a nuclear pore, affecting the amount of gene product realized per unit time following transcription.

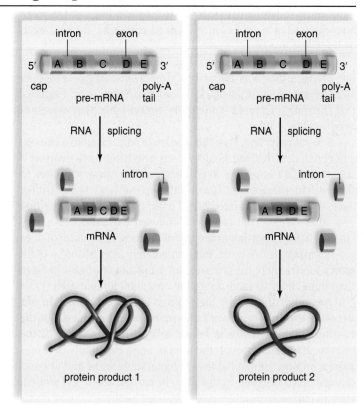

FIGURE 11.5 Because the pre-mRNAs are processed differently in these two cells, distinct proteins result. This is a form of posttranscriptional control of gene expression.

▶ **11.5 Check Your Progress** What happens to introns during mRNA processing?

11.6 Small RNAs function in several ways to affect gene expression

A new level of control has been discovered, particularly in vertebrates such as ourselves. Much of our DNA is transcribed into RNA but not into the three types of RNA (mRNA, rRNA, and tRNA) we have discussed so far. Only 1.5% of our DNA codes for protein, and yet 74% to 93% of the DNA in the nucleus is transcribed into RNA. A vast amount of DNA was formerly thought of as junk DNA because scientists didn't know its

function. But now they know that it is transcribed into RNA, and they have begun to discover its various functions.

Notice that in **Figure 11.6,** ❶ transcribed RNA can become looped and double-stranded (dsRNA) as hydrogen bonding occurs between its bases. ❷ dsRNA is diced up into **small RNAs (sRNA)** that regulate gene expression in various ways. Their effect may be just as important to gene expression as

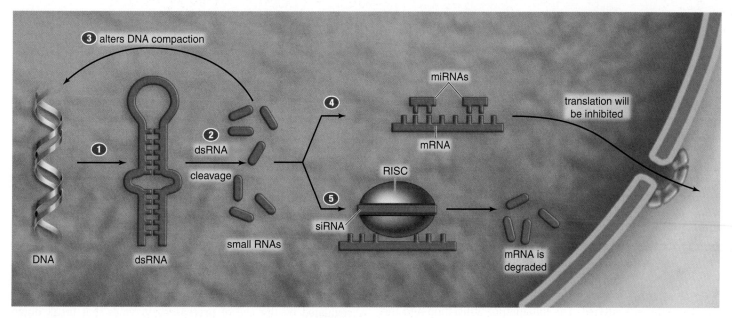

FIGURE 11.6 This flow diagram begins with DNA because ❶ transcription of DNA leads to looped and double-stranded RNA (dsRNA). ❷ Cleavage of dsRNA results in an ample supply of small RNAs. ❸ A small RNA can double-back to increase DNA compaction. A small RNA can also become an miRNA or an siRNA. ❹ When a miRNA binds to a sequence of complementary mRNA bases, the translation of this mRNA decreases. ❺ An siRNA combines with an enzyme and forms a RISC, which degrades any mRNA with a sequence of bases complementary to the siRNA.

transcription factors are. Two forms of the sRNAs don't regulate transcription; instead, their presence in the nucleus affects future translation in the cytoplasm. Three ways have been found by which small RNAs can regulate gene expression and the amount of gene product:

- Small RNAs have been known to alter the compaction of DNA so that some genes become inaccessible for transcription. See ❸

- Small RNAs are the source of **microRNAs (miRNA),** small snippets of RNA that can bind to and dampen the translation of an mRNA in the cytoplasm. In that case, the amount of gene product made is regulated. See ❹

- Small RNAs are also the source of **small interfering RNAs (siRNA)** that join with an enzyme to form a silencing complex. The complex targets certain mRNAs for breakdown. See ❺

The term **RNA interference** recognizes that small RNAs serve as a means of controling which genes produce a product and the amount they produce. Much like a dimmer switch on a light, miRNAs fine-tune gene expression because when they combine with an mRNA, translation of that mRNA in the cytoplasm is inhibited. Medical scientists have immediately turned their attention to the possibility of using miRNAs as therapeutic agents to dampen the expression of disease-causing genes. The 2006 Nobel Prize in Physiology and Medicine was awarded to Andrew Fire and Craig Mello for constructing the first artificial miRNA to suppress the expression of a specific gene.

Recent research indicates that beyond modulating gene expression, miRNAs may also be responsible for allowing organisms to respond to various environmental stimuli, and may even play a role in maintaining homeostasis. In 2006, scientists in Taiwan demonstrated that a specific miRNA allows *Arabidopsis* to respond to changing levels of inorganic phosphate in the soil. Phosphate starvation of these plants resulted in an increased number of carrier proteins for phosphate uptake from the soil. The increased number was brought about because the miRNA caused limited production of an enzyme that ordinarily degrades the carriers! This shows how an miRNA can cause an increase in one gene product over another.

Whereas miRNAs work alone, siRNA requires a partner. Small RNA combines with an enzyme to form an RNA-induced silencing complex (RISC). RISC degrades any mRNA that contains a base sequence complementary to the siRNA. Some viruses use RNA as their genetic material, and it's possible that RNA interference evolved as a way to prevent these viruses from infecting the cell. Today, RNA interference is an important way for cells to defend themselves against parasitic viruses, but by now small RNAs also function in controlling gene expression and even directing development. Because miRNAs and siRNAs are more plentiful in vertebrates than invertebrates, some researchers suggest they might be responsible for the evolution of vertebrates, including humans.

▶ **11.6 Check Your Progress** Contrast the effect of miRNA and siRNA on the translation of an mRNA.

Regulation of Gene Expression Also Occurs in the Cytoplasm

Learning Outcomes

▶ Discuss the manner in which regulation of gene expression occurs in the cytoplasm. (11.7)

▶ Summarize the types of gene expression control that occur in the nucleus and the cytoplasm. (11.8)

The stability of mRNA for translation and the protein product following translation can vary. Proteins that are old, or unused perhaps due to being incorrectly folded, are degraded by a proteasome complex. Neurogenerative diseases can arise from abnormal protein accumulations.

11.7 Both the activity of mRNA and the protein product are regulated

Recall that when a gene has been expressed, its protein product has been made and is functioning. In this section, we consider the degree to which mRNA translation occurs at a ribosome in the cytoplasm and the activity of a protein once it is formed.

Translational Control The initiation of translation and the stability of the mRNA transcript are both regulated. Translation requires the presence of various enzymes; if any one of them is absent, translation cannot begin. Translation can also be inhibited either by the presence of miRNAs attached to the mRNA or by the presence of translation repressor proteins. For example, ferritin, an iron-storing protein, is not made unless iron is present. If iron is not present, a **translation repressor protein** attaches to the beginning of the ferritin mRNA, making it impossible for mRNA to bind to a ribosome. When iron enters the cell, it combines with the repressor protein and dissociates from the ferritin mRNA. Now translation begins. Notice that, unlike the use of repressor proteins in prokaryotes, this is an example of translational control by the use of a repressor protein.

The stability of an mRNA transcript affects how long it is active and therefore the amount of protein product. Some mRNA transcripts are active for hours and others for only a few minutes. Recall that every mRNA that leaves the nucleus has a cap and a poly-A tail. If histone proteins are not needed because DNA replication is not occurring, histone mRNA is degraded within minutes due to the loss of the poly-A tail. The mRNAs for regulatory proteins become unstable due to a modification of their poly-A tail by the addition of A and U nucleotides. Nucleases in the cytoplasm digest any unstable mRNA transcripts.

Posttranslational Control Similar to mRNA, protein activity is regulated in various ways. Some proteins are not active until they have been modified by the addition of a carbohydrate chain or phosphate group or by the removal of some amino acids. For example, insulin is only active after the original polypeptide has been cleaved.

Just how long a protein remains active in a cell is usually regulated by the use of **proteases,** enzymes that break down proteins. Proteases have to be confined to a particular cellular structure because otherwise the cell itself would soon be digested. Lysosomes confine proteases, and so does a cellular organelle called a **proteasome (Fig. 11.7).** A proteasome is a barrel-shaped structure with caps on either side of a central region. The central region is where protease activity takes place.

For a protein to enter a proteasome, it has to be tagged with a signaling protein recognized by a proteasome cap. When the cap recognizes the tag, it opens and allows the protein to enter its central core where the protein is digested to peptide fragments. Proteasomes have been implicated in cancer because they digest regulatory proteins, including p53 (see p. 222), which help control the cell cyle and prevent cancer. Drugs that inhibit proteasome activity and thereby raise the level of p53 are now being investigated as a way to treat cancer. The inability of proteasomes to degrade other proteins is implicated in Alzheimer, Parkinson, and mad cow disease. Notice that proteasomes function in regulating gene expression because they help control the amount of protein product in the cytoplasm.

▶ **11.7 Check Your Progress** This section gives what evidence that regulation of gene expression involves various proteins in the cytoplasm?

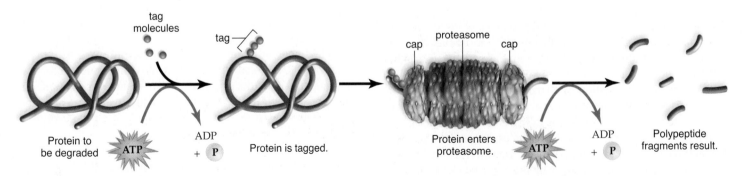

FIGURE 11.7 Proteins to be degraded are first tagged with a signaling molecule. Then they enter a proteasome, a large, cylindrical complex that contains a protease. The protease enzymes digest the protein to polypeptide fragments. The process requires energy in the form of ATP.

11.8 Let's summarize gene expression control in eukaryotes

We have observed various ways in which eukaryotes control gene expression—that is, production of a gene product **Figure 11.8**. A gene product is defined as any type of protein that functions in a cell.

1 *Chromatin structure.* Chromatin packing can keep genes turned off. If genes are not accessible to RNA polymerase and transcription factors and activators, they cannot be transcribed. Histones and small RNAs play a role in chromatin packing.

2 *Transcriptional control.* The degree to which a gene is transcribed into mRNA determines the amount of gene product. DNA-binding proteins, including transcription factors and transcription activators, determine when and if transcription begins.

3 *Posttranscriptional control.* Posttranscriptional control occurs in the nucleus. mRNA processing differences can affect gene expression by determining what protein products a cell can possibly make. Also, RISC (RNA-induced silencing complex) can degrade an mRNA, and attached miRNA snippets can dampen the degree to which it is translated once it reaches the cytoplasm. The speed with which mature mRNA enters the cytoplasm can affect the amount of gene product made.

4 *Translational control.* Translational control occurs in the cytoplasm. Various molecules in the cytoplasm determine whether translations begins. Also, the presence of the 5′ cap and the length of the 3′ poly-A tail can influence the stability of an mRNA transcript and, therefore, the amount of gene product.

5 *Posttranslational control.* Posttranslational control, which also takes place in the cytoplasm, occurs after protein synthesis. Only a functional protein is an active gene product. The polypeptide product may have to undergo additional changes before it is biologically functional. For example, some enzymes have a portion removed before they are active. Also, the cell has structures, actually giant protein complexes, called proteasomes that carry out the task of destroying proteins. The length of time before a protein is broken down by a proteasome can affect how long a gene product is active.

We have seen that regulatory proteins include transcription factors, but we should mention that the members of signal transduction pathways are also regulatory proteins. Indeed, some of these pathways often end in transcription factors. In the next part of the chapter, we will see that malfunctioning transduction pathways can result in cancer.

▶ **11.8 Check Your Progress** An active *Hox* gene **a.** has been turned on by what type factor (p. 213); **b.** is located in what type of chromatin (p. 215); **c.** its mRNA has been modified in what way (p. 218); **d.** has not been degraded by what complex in the nucleus (p. 219); and **e.** its protein will be broken down by what structure in the cytoplasm (p. 220)?

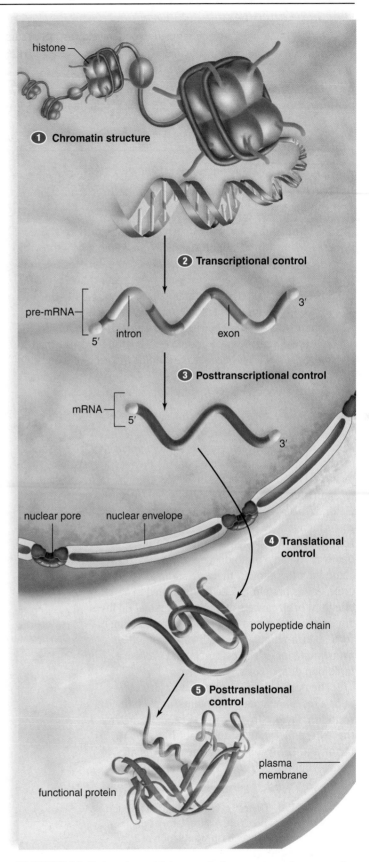

FIGURE 11.8 Levels at which control of gene expression occurs in eukaryotic cells.

Lack of Genetic Control Causes Cancer

Learning Outcomes

▶ Contrast the signal transduction pathways of proto-oncogenes and tumor suppressor genes. (11.9)
▶ Describe the development of cancer as a multistep process. (11.10)

In this part of the chapter, we study genes, called proto-oncogenes and tumor suppressor genes, that control the cell cycle. These genes are part of regulatory pathways that stretch from the plasma membrane to the nucleus where they are located. Several proteins in these pathways must malfunction before cancer develops; therefore, it takes several years for cancer to develop.

11.9 Two types of genes ordinarily control the cell cycle

Recall that the cell cycle consists of interphase followed by mitosis. Two types of genes ordinarily keep the cell cycle functioning as it should:

1. **Proto-oncogenes** code for proteins that promote the cell cycle and inhibit apoptosis. They are often likened to the gas pedal of a car because they keep the cell cycle going. When proto-oncogenes mutate, they become cancer-causing genes, called **oncogenes,** that overstimulate the cell cycle. Also apoptosis is inhibited to a greater extent.
2. **Tumor suppressor genes** code for proteins that inhibit the cell cycle and promote apoptosis. They are often likened to the brakes of a car because they inhibit the cell cycle and stop cells from dividing. When tumor suppressor genes mutate, tumors are more likely to develop and apoptosis is inhibited.

These genes are a part of signal transduction pathways that extend from the plasma membrane to the nucleus (**Fig. 11.9**). A normal stimulatory pathway ends with a proto-oncogene. The pathway consists of a stimulatory growth factor, the receptor, signaling proteins, and a transcription factor. When a growth factor binds to the receptor, the stimulatory pathway is activated. The transcription factor is necessary for turning on a proto-oncogene that codes for a protein that is part of the stimulatory pathway. For example, Ras proteins are a part of the stimulatory pathway. When a proto-oncogene mutates, the result could be a Ras protein that overstimulates the cell cycle. A Ras protein has been implicated in about one-third of all cancers in humans. A mutation in any one of the genes that code for a signaling protein in a stimulatory pathway can lead to overstimulation of the cell cycle and excessive inhibition of apoptosis.

The normal inhibitory pathway also contains a receptor signaling proteins, and a transcription factor. In this instance, however, the external signal is an inhibiting growth factor and the transcription factor turns on a tumor suppressor gene. The protein p53 is a transcription factor instrumental in stopping the cell cycle and activating chromosomal repair enzymes. If repair is impossible, the p53 protein goes on to promote apoptosis. You'll recall that apoptosis is a process by which cell death occurs due to the release of particular enzymes inside a cell; see Section 8.6, p. 152. If a tumor suppressor gene undergoes a mutation, it may code for a protein that cannot inhibit the cell cycle or cannot promote apoptosis. Lack of p53 is implicated in over half of human cancers. The retinoblastoma protein (RB) is another tumor suppressor protein that is dysfunctional in many types of cancer.

▶ **11.9 Check Your Progress a.** How is a mutated tumor suppressor gene like faulty breaks? **b.** What specifically causes this effect?

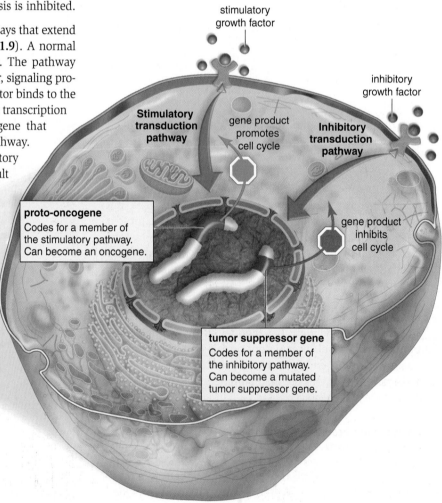

FIGURE 11.9 The cell cycle is regulated through control of gene expression. A stimulatory signal transduction pathway ends in stimulation of a proto-onocogene (green arrow) An inhibiting signal transduction pathway ends in stimulation of a tumor suppressor gene (red arrow).

stimulatory growth factor

inhibitory growth factor

Stimulatory transduction pathway

gene product promotes cell cycle

Inhibitory transduction pathway

proto-oncogene
Codes for a member of the stimulatory pathway. Can become an oncogene.

gene product inhibits cell cycle

tumor suppressor gene
Codes for a member of the inhibitory pathway. Can become a mutated tumor suppressor gene.

11.10 Cancer and malignancy develop gradually

As we have seen, two types of signal transduction pathways are of fundamental importance to normal operation of the cell cycle and control of apoptosis. Therefore, it is not surprising that inherited or acquired defects in these pathways contribute to **carcinogenesis,** the development of cancer. Some of the inherited cancer-causing genes are known:

BRCA1 and **BRCA2** In 1990, DNA linkage studies of large families in which females tended to develop breast cancer identified the first gene allele associated with breast cancer. Scientists named this gene *breast cancer 1*, or *BRCA1* (pronounced brakuh). Later, they found that breast cancer in other families was due to a faulty allele of another gene they called *BRCA2*. Both alleles are mutant tumor suppressor genes that are inherited in an autosomal recessive manner. If one mutated allele is inherited from either parent, a mutation in the other allele is required before the predisposition to cancer is increased. Because the first mutated gene is inherited, it is present in all cells of the body, and then cancer is more likely wherever the second mutation occurs. If the second mutation occurs in the breast, breast cancer may develop. If the second mutation is in the ovary, ovarian cancer may develop if additional cancer-causing mutations occur.

RB Gene The *RB* gene is also a tumor suppressor gene. It takes its name from its association with an eye tumor called a retinoblastoma, which first appears as a white mass in the retina. A tumor in one eye is most common because it takes mutations in both alleles before cancer can develop. Children who inherit a mutated allele are more likely to have tumors in both eyes.

RET Gene An abnormal allele of the *RET* gene, which predisposes a person to thyroid cancer, can be passed from parent to child. *RET* is a proto-oncogene known to be inherited in an autosomal dominant manner—only one mutated allele is needed for an increased predisposition to cancer. The remaining mutations necessary for thyroid cancer to develop are acquired (not inherited).

Figure 11.10 shows that carcinogenesis requires several mutations. First, a single cell undergoes a mutation that causes it to begin to divide repeatedly. Among the progeny of this cell, one cell mutates further and can start a tumor whose cells have further selective advantages. A tumor is present, but it is called cancer in situ because it is contained within its place of origin. To grow larger than a pea, a tumor must have a well-developed capillary network to bring it nutrients and oxygen. The tumor cells release growth factors that lead to **angiogenesis,** the formation of new blood vessels. A new investigative treatment for cancer uses drugs that break up the network of new capillaries in the vicinity of a tumor.

New mutations cause the tumor cells to have a disorganized internal cytoskeleton and to lack intact actin filament bundles. By now they are motile cells and can invade underlying tissues because they produce proteinase enzymes that degrade their extracellular matrix. Other mutations give cancer cells the ability

New mutations arise, and one cell (brown) has the ability to start a tumor.

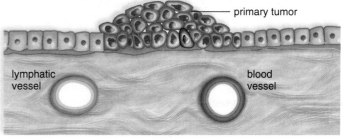

Cancer in situ. The tumor is at its place of origin. One cell (purple) mutates further.

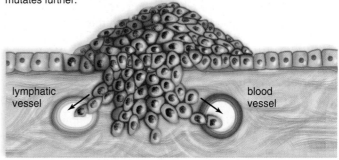

Cancer cells now have the ability to invade lymphatic and blood vessels and travel throughout the body.

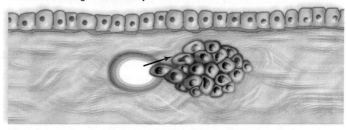

New metastatic tumors are found some distance from the primary tumor.

FIGURE 11.10 The development of cancer requires a series of mutations leading first to a localized tumor and then to metastatic tumors. With each successive step toward cancer, the most genetically altered and aggressive cell becomes the dominant type of tumor. The cells take on characteristics of embryonic cells in that they are not differentiated, and they can divide uncontrollably.

to invade lymphatic vessels and blood vessels, which take them to other parts of the body. **Malignancy** is present when cancer cells are found in nearby lymph nodes. When cancer cells initiate new tumors far from the primary tumor, **metastasis** has occurred. Not many cancer cells achieve this feat (maybe 1 in 10,000), but those that successfully metastasize make the probability of complete recovery doubtful.

▶ **11.10 Check Your Progress** Explain why a person who inherits an allele for cancer may never get cancer.

11B A *BRCA* Female Tells Her Story

I am a *BRCA1* female [as are the sisters in **Figure 11B**]. The *BRCA1* mutation manifests itself primarily as breast cancer, but it may also result in ovarian cancer. My mother, sister, and I recently underwent genetic testing and were found to carry the *BRCA1* mutation. One month after genetic testing and after speaking with a genetic counselor, I was diagnosed with stage 3C ovarian cancer at the age of 35. Five days later, I was in surgery for removal of my ovaries, oviducts, and omentum (part of the abdominal lining). The cancer had devoured the omentum, and I was carrying more than 7 liters of excess fluid in my abdomen. I lost more than 30 pounds as a result of the surgery. Three weeks later, I underwent three months of chemotherapy. I was also diagnosed with deep vein thrombosis in my left thigh and had to take Coumadin for 6 months. Recent CT scans indicate that there is still cancer in the lower omentum, but the size is trivial, and the monthly CA-125 blood test used to indicate ovarian cancer shows that I am improving.

Three weeks after my diagnosis, my younger sister was diagnosed with stage 1 breast cancer. The breast cancer was discovered when she was undergoing a routine exam before taking the precautionary measure of having an oophorectomy, the removal of her ovaries. After the discovery of the breast cancer, she also elected to have a double mastectomy and hysterectomy, followed by chemotherapy. She is now cancer-free and is investigating medications to ensure that she remains that way.

We knew we had a history of reproductive cancer in our family: My maternal grandmother and aunt both died of ovarian cancer in their 40s, and my mother was diagnosed with early stage cancer of the oviducts (a type of *BRCA1* cancer commonly mistaken for ovarian cancer) at age 46. She underwent chemotherapy, and then had additional surgery to remove her uterus and to biopsy nearby lymph nodes. It was also recommended that she have a double mastectomy. However, we were unaware that our family's experience with reproductive cancer was a result of a genetic mutation.

The psychological effects of cancer on our families resulted in helplessness, depression, sadness, and confusion. Our husbands, while very supportive, dealt with the news and treatments differently. Our children were initially shocked, but recovered quickly from the news of the cancer. They have been positive role models for the entire family and their resiliency has been inspiring. We received information from the Mayo Clinic inviting us to participate in a "Familial Breast and Ovarian Cancer Study." This is exciting news for us because participating in case studies and research groups helps us contribute to finding cures for these cancers. This particular study will help pinpoint any other contributing genetic and environmental factors regarding ovarian and breast cancer, as well as other minor cancers that may be caused by *BRCA1* or *BRCA2* gene mutations.

My sister and I now have concerns that our children may also carry the mutation. Consultation with several doctors and genetic counselors has revealed that we should make our children aware of the issues associated with the mutation, but that we should keep the information age-appropriate. It was recommended that the children have genetic counseling when they are in their late teens or early 20s, and that testing should be at their own discretion. Usually, testing can wait until age 25. By this age, woman have or know if they are going to have children and are more likely to have a relationship with a doctor and make regular gynecological appointments. Mammograms and breast MRIs should be started annually at age 30 if a person has a *BRCA1* or *BRCA2* mutation.

These revelations have also necessitated many changes in my lifestyle. I am progressing toward a healthier diet, and I have started a daily exercise routine that I hardly consider a chore any longer. I exercise 20 to 30 minutes each day and constantly try new activities to keep my interest piqued. My sister is on a stringent diet and fitness routine. In fact, she recently ran a 5K road race in under 30 minutes, her best time ever. My mother has not yet established a regular exercise routine, but she rides her bicycle several times a week with my father. The challenges my family has endured as a result of the cancer and *BRCA1* genetic mutation may seem daunting, but genetic testing, support from family, friends, and physicians, and healthy lifestyle changes have made all the difference in our attitudes toward dealing with this chronic disease.

FORM YOUR OPINION

1. Should young people be made aware that they could carry a cancer gene? Why or why not?
2. Just as all women are advised to have mammograms, should everyone be advised to be tested for cancer-causing alleles? Why or why not?

FIGURE 11B These three sisters have all had breast cancer. Genetic tests can identify women at risk for breast cancer so that they can choose to have frequent examinations to allow for early detection.

SEM of breast cancer cell

Proteins Regulate Transcription of mRNA

11.1 DNA-binding proteins usually turn genes off in prokaryotes

- The **operon** model explains gene regulation in prokaryotes.
- In prokaryotes, a **regulatory gene** codes for a **repressor,** a DNA-binding protein.
- An operon also includes a **promoter,** an **operator** (*off switch*) and s**tructural genes.** All of these are portions of DNA.
- The important concept is that a DNA-binding protein, the active repressor, ordinarily turns the structural genes off by binding to the operator. Then, RNA polymerase cannot bind to the promoter.
- In the *lac* operon, the repressor is usually active and the structural genes are usually turned off—lactose is not a preferred food. If lactose is present and needs to be digested, the repressor becomes inactive after binding to lactose.
- In the *trp* operon, the repressor must be activated by tryptophan. When tryptophan is present, the enzymes to make tryptophan (coded for by structural genes) are not needed.

11.2 DNA-binding proteins usually turn genes on in eukaryotes

- In eukaryotes, regulatory genes code for **transcription factors** and **transcription activators,** proteins that act together to turn on genes one by one.
- Transcription factors bind to the promoter and assist the binding of RNA polymerase.
- Transcription may still not begin until a transcription activator binds to an **enhancer** some distance away.
- The chromosome bends to bring the enhancer near the transcription factors.

11.3 Histones regulate accessibility of DNA for transcription

- In **nucleosomes,** DNA is wound around **histones.** Nucleosomes zigzag and then coil as chromatin condenses.

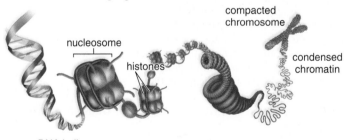

- Highly condensed **chromatin** is called **heterochromatin.**
- **Barr bodies** are inactive X chromosomes. The genes in Barr bodies are not expressed. Because one X chromosome is inactive, females are mosaics.
- **Euchromatin** consists of loosely condensed chromatin.
- Genes in euchromatin are accessible to RNA polymerase and transcription factors after a **chromatin remodeling complex** pushes aside the histones to expose the DNA. This is called **unpacking** the DNA.

11.4 Hox proteins are DNA-binding proteins active during development

- *Hox* genes are **master developmental regulatory genes** that code for **Hox proteins.**

- Hox proteins are transcription factors that turn on genes directing the development of segments.
- *Hox* genes contain a homeobox that codes for a homeodomain. The **homeobox** can be used to identify *Hox* genes and they are found in many different segmental animals.
- Other master developmental genes affect the development of an entire region. Investigators were surprised to discover *Pax6* gene, which directs the formation of an eye, in diverse animals.

RNAs Regulate Gene Expression Following Transcription

11.5 Alternative mRNA splicing results in varied gene products

- Posttranscriptional control of gene expression occurs in the nucleus and involves mRNA processing and the speed at which mRNA leaves the nucleus.
- **Pre-mRNA alternate processing** during which different introns are removed can cause the particular protein product in cells to be different.

11.6 Small RNAs function in several ways to affect gene expression

- **Small RNAs (sRNA)** are transcribed from a DNA template located in what use to be called junk DNA because it did not code for protein.
- Small RNAs can double-back to affect compaction of DNA so that some genes become inaccessible for transcription.
- Small RNAs are the source of **microRNAs (miRNA),** small snippets of RNA that can bind to and dampen the translation of an mRNA in the cytoplasm.
- Small RNAs are also the source of **small interfering RNAs (siRNA)** that join with an enzyme to form a RISC (RNA-induced silencing complex). RISC degrades any mRNA that has a base sequence complementary to that in siRNA.
- The term **RNA interference** refers to the activities of miRNAs and siRNAs, which are now known to be important for controlling gene expression especially in vertebrates.
- Translational control begins when processed mRNA reaches the cytoplasm before there is a protein product.
- Posttranslational control begins once a protein has been synthesized and becomes active.

Regulation of Gene Expression Also Occurs in the Cytoplasm

11.7 Both the activity of mRNA and the protein product are regulated

- Translation of mRNA is regulated in various ways:
  - A **translation repressor protein** attaches to the mRNA, preventing it from binding to a ribosome.
  - Removal or modification of the poly-A tail causes the mRNA to be degraded by nucleases.
- The amount of active protein product is regulated in various ways:
  - A protein may be modified by the addition of a carbohydrate chain or by being cleaved.
  - Old, unused, or misfolded proteins are usually degraded by a **proteasome,** a structure that has protease activity.

11.8 Let's summarize gene expression control in eukaryotes

- The five primary levels of gene expression control are:
  - Chromatin structure: Histones compact chromatin.
  - Transcriptional control: Transcription factors and transcription activators are needed for transcription to begin.
  - Posttranscriptional control: Alternative mRNA splicing and RNA interference involving miRNAs and siRNAs are involved.
  - Translational control: Attachment of a repressor translation protein can delay translation, or modification of the mRNA poly-A tail can cause it to be degraded.
  - Posttranslational control: Proteins have to be modified before they are active and proteins are degraded by proteasomes.

Lack of Genetic Control Causes Cancer

11.9 Two types of genes ordinarily control the cell cycle

- **Proto-oncogenes** promote the cell cycle and inhibit apoptosis.
- **Tumor suppressor genes** inhibit the cell cycle and promote apoptosis.
- A stimulatory signal transduction pathway turns on a proto-oncogene whose product stimulates the cell cycle.
  - When cancer occurs, the product of an **oncogene** leads to overstimulation of the pathway and the cell cycle and excessive inhibition of apoptosis.
- An inhibitory signal transduction pathway turns on a tumor suppressor gene whose product inhibits the cell cycle and promotes apoptosis.
  - When cancer occurs, the product of a mutated tumor suppressor gene fails to stop the cell cycle and fails to promote apoptosis.

11.10 Cancer and malignancy develop gradually

- **Carcinogenesis** refers to tumor formation due to repeated mutations.
- **Angiogenesis** (formation of new blood vessels) provides nutrients to a growing tumor.
- Motile cells invade lymphatic and blood vessels.
- **Metastasis** has occurred when a new tumor forms far from the first tumor.

TESTING YOURSELF

Proteins Regulate Transcription of mRNA

1. Label this diagram of an operon:

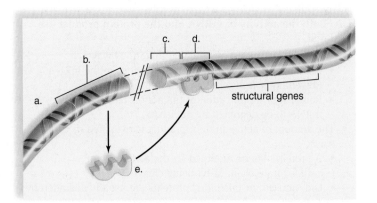

2. In operon models, the function of the promoter is to
   a. code for the repressor protein.
   b. bind with RNA polymerase.
   c. bind to the repressor.
   d. code for the regulatory gene.
3. Which of these correctly describes the function of a regulatory gene for the *lac* operon?
   a. prevents transcription from occurring
   b. a sequence of DNA that codes for the repressor
   c. prevents the repressor from binding to the operator
   d. keeps the operon off until lactose is present
   e. Both b and d are correct.
4. Which of these associations is mismatched?
   a. loosely packed chromatin—gene can be active
   b. transcription factors—gene is inactivated
   c. mRNA—translation can begin
   d. proteasomes—protein is inactive
5. The genes that determine which body parts form on each body segment of a fruit fly are called _____ genes.
   a. promoter   c. intron
   b. exon   d. *Hox*
6. Which of the following is part of a transcription factor that binds to DNA?
   a. homeobox   c. homeotic gene
   b. homeodomain   d. Bicoid protein

RNAs Regulate Gene Expression Following Transcription

7. Investigators were surprised to find that
   a. transcriptional regulation occurs.
   b. RNA interference mechanisms affect the activity of mRNA.
   c. proteasomes digest proteins.
   d. chromatin compacting occurs.
   e. All of these are correct.
8. Only
   a. miRNA binds to complementary sequences.
   b. siRNA helps degrade mRNA.
   c. miRNA is made from a DNA template.
   d. siRNA acts in the nucleus.
9. Alternative pre-mRNA splicing can
   a. produce miRNA and siRNA.
   b. result in different protein products.
   c. produce transcription factors.
   d. occur in the cytoplasm and the nucleus.

Regulation of Gene Expression Also Occurs in the Cytoplasm

10. Which of these is a true statement?
    a. Once an mRNA is made, a product always follows.
    b. Translation of mRNA can alter the protein product.
    c. Translational control can alter the amount of a protein product.
    d. Proteasomes degrade mRNA molecules.
11. Proteasomes
    a. only accept proteins that have been properly tagged.
    b. are cell structures.
    c. contain catalytic enzymes.
    d. are protein complexes.
    e. All of these are correct.

For questions 12–16, match the examples to the gene expression control mechanisms in the key. Each answer can be used more than once.

KEY:

  a. chromatin structure
  b. transcriptional control
  c. posttranscriptional control
  d. translational control
  e. posttranslational control

12. Insulin does not become active until 30 amino acids are cleaved from the middle of the molecule.
13. The mRNA for vitellin is longer-lived if it has a poly-A tail.
14. Genes in Barr bodies are inactivated.
15. Calcitonin is produced in both the hypothalamus and the thyroid gland, but in different forms due to exon splicing.
16. DNA-binding proteins are active.
17. **THINKING CONCEPTUALLY** A variety of mechanisms regulate gene expression in eukaryotic cells. What are the benefits and the drawbacks of this arrangement?

Lack of Genetic Control Causes Cancer

For questions 18–21, choose two answers for each type of gene.

KEY:

  a. Cell cycle is promoted and apoptosis is inhibited.
  b. Cell cycle is inhibited and apoptosis is promoted.
  c. Signal transduction pathway contains normal proteins.
  d. Signal transduction pathway contains abnormal proteins.

18. Tumor suppressor gene
19. Proto-oncogene
20. Mutated tumor suppressor gene
21. Oncogene
22. Sequence these events that lead to the development of cancer:
  a. Cells gain the ability to invade underlying tissues.
  b. Metastatic tumors occur.
  c. Cell division leads to a tumor.
  d. Blood vessels arise and service the tumor.

THINKING SCIENTIFICALLY

1. You receive much criticism for your conclusion that development in the mouse and fruit fly is similar because you have found several homeoboxes in the genes of both organisms. Why? See Section 11.4.
2. You are a skilled cytologist and want to show that a particular environmental pollutant causes a cell to divide uncontrollably. How will you do this? See Section 11.9.

ONLINE RESOURCE

www.mhhe.com/maderconcepts2

Enhance your study with animations that bring concepts to life and practice tests to assess your understanding. Your instructor may also recommend the interactive eBook, individualized learning tools, and more.

CONNECTING THE CONCEPTS

Gene regulation involves control at different levels. Anyone who has cooked a meal knows how important control can be if all is to go well. The meal should be balanced, and the quantity of each food should be appropriate to the number of diners. Similarly, a cell needs to make only the proteins that are immediately needed and in the amount needed. In both prokaryotes and eukaryotes, the products of regulatory genes are DNA-binding proteins that determine which genes will be transcribed. In eukaryotes, if the gene is located in euchromatin, transcription factors and transcription activators initiate transcription, and the result is a pre-mRNA molecule. This is the first step toward specialization of a cell, but the importance of posttranscriptional control is only now being recognized. Alternative pre-mRNA splicing can affect the particular protein product of cells, and small RNAs (miRNAs and siRNAs) determine which mRNAs will be translated and in what quantity. Does this mean that small RNAs have the upper hand when it comes to the protein constituency of the cell? Some scientists think so.

In the cytoplasm, gene regulation is still needed to make sure that translation is appropriately timed. After all, for protein synthesis to occur as needed, all necessary materials must be available and mRNA must be active only as long as needed. A cell couldn't continue to exist if all the proteins ever made couldn't be disposed of. Returning to our meal analogy, there are always some left overs that go into the disposal. Similarly, proteasomes keep the content of the cell up-to-date by degrading previously made proteins. You can see, then, that regulation of gene activity is an absolute necessity in cells. Also, knowledge of how genes are regulated can help explain not only the specialization of cells but also how basic genetic differences have arisen among species, such as between humans and chimpanzees.

In Chapter 12, you will see how our molecular knowledge has contributed to a biotechnology revolution. We now know how to isolate and move genes between organisms of the same species and even different species. We have sequenced the DNA of humans and have much to report about how the present state of our understanding can be used to benefit our well-being.

PUT THE PIECES TOGETHER

1. How does the evolution of the genus *Homo* warrant an understanding of regulatory genes?
2. How can a knowledge of regulation be used to cure diseases?
3. Make up an analogy to illustrate the importance of genetic regulation in cells.

12

Biotechnology and Genomics

CHAPTER OUTLINE

APPLICATIONS

Witnessing Genetic Engineering

Genetic engineering has been around since 1973, so by now many genetically modified organisms (GMOs) have been produced. Fish and cows are now expressing foreign genes that make them grow larger. Pigs have been engineered to make their organs acceptable for transplant into humans. Strawberry and potato plants don't freeze, and soybeans are resistant to viral, bacterial, and fungal pathogens—all because they have been genetically engineered. Bacteria produce human insulin as well as other important medicines. And gene therapy in humans, which is the insertion of normal human genes to make up for ones that do not function properly, is already undergoing clinical trials.

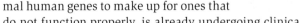

Bioluminescent dinoflagellate

With so many examples of GMOs, you might think it would be easy to "prove" to a friend that it is possible to transfer a gene from one organism to another—but how would you go about it? Well, first you need a gene that makes its appearance known visibly. How about a gene for bioluminescence? Some organisms, including fireflies, jellyfish, glowworms, beetles, and various fishes, can create their own light because they are bioluminescent. The advantages of bioluminescence are varied. Glowworms use their light to attract their prey, and fireflies use the ability to glow to attract mates. The gene for bioluminescence in jellyfish codes for a protein called green fluorescent protein (GFP), and when this gene is transferred to another organism, it glows!

The basic technique you would use to genetically engineer an organism is relatively simple. For example, to transfer the jellyfish gene for bioluminescence to a pig, first locate the gene among all the others in a jellyfish genome. Then fragment the

Bioluminescent fish

DNA, and introduce the fragment that contains the bioluminescence gene into the embryo of a pig, mouse, or rabbit, for example. The result is a "glow-in-the-dark" organism.

Genes have no difficulty crossing the species barrier. Mammalian genes work just as well in bacteria, and an invertebrate gene, such as the bioluminescence gene, has no trouble functioning in mammals. The genes of any organism are composed of DNA, and the manufacture of a protein (and indeed, the function of that protein) is similar, regardless of the DNA source. Glowing pigs, mice, and rabbits are certainly living proof that genes can be transferred and also that all cells use basically the same machinery.

Is it ethical to give a mouse a gene that makes it glow? Advocacy groups have even graver concerns about creating genetically modified organisms. Some worry that modified bacteria and plants might harm the environment. Others fear that products produced by GMOs might not be healthy for humans. Perhaps terrorists could use biotechnology to produce weapons of mass destruction. Finally, to what extent is it proper to improve the human genome? All citizens should be knowledgeable about genetics and biotechnology so that they can participate in deciding these issues.

Biotechnology is defined as the use of living organisms for the benefit of human beings, and certainly this chapter will abound with examples of how this is possible. Gene therapy occurs when humans are genetically modified in order to cure a genetic disorder. The sequencing of the human genome is finished and is expected to increase the possibility of treating and/or curing human genetic disorders. Comparative genomics is expected to shed light on our relationship to other animals. Proteomics and bioinformatics are new fields very much dependent on computer technologies. The news media said Craig Venter had created a cell when he used the computer recently to produce an entire bacterial genome in the lab. The genome worked perfectly when he inserted it into a bacterial cell cleared of its own DNA!

Bioluminescent pigs

Bioluminescent jellyfish

Bioluminescent mouse

Cloning Can Produce an Organism or Tissues

Learning Outcomes

▶ List the steps in cloning an animal and explain why the animal has the phenotype of the donor's nucleus. (12.1)
▶ Compare the end result of reproductive cloning with that of therapeutic cloning. (12.1)

Biotechnology is the use of a natural biological system to make a product or achieve some other end desired by humans. Formerly cloning meant the production of an exact copy of an organism; now it also refers to the production of tissues from the same embryonic source. In the next part of the chapter we will even consider the cloning of a gene.

12.1 A cloned product has the donor's DNA

With **reproductive cloning,** the desired end is an individual that is exactly like the original individual. Figure 12.1 shows the steps necessary to clone an animal:

1. Remove a cell from the animal to be cloned to serve as a source for a 2n nucleus.
2. Place this nucleus in an egg after its own nucleus has been removed.
3. After development begins, place the embryo in the uterus of a surrogate mother so development will continue to term.
4. The newborn animal will be a clone of the animal that donated the 2n nucleus.

Reproductive cloning shows that any 2n nucleus contains all the genes necessary to produce an organism but the genes must be turned on in order for an adult cell to "start over" and overcome its present specialization. At one time, investigators found it difficult to achieve this hurdle. But in March 1997, Scottish investigators announced they had successfully cloned a Dorset sheep, which they named Dolly. How was their procedure different from all the others that had been attempted? Again, an adult nucleus was placed in an enucleated egg cell. However, the donor cell had been starved, which caused it to stop dividing and go into a resting stage (the G_0 stage of the cell cycle) (**Fig. 12.1**). The G_0 nucleus was amenable to cytoplasmic signals for initiation of development.

Today it is common practice to clone farm animals that have desirable traits, and even to clone rare animals that might otherwise become extinct. However, the cloning of farm animals is not yet efficient. In the case of Dolly, out of 29 clones, only one was successful. Also, cloned animals may not be healthy. Dolly was put down by lethal injection in 2003 because she was suffering from lung cancer and crippling arthritis. She had lived only half the normal life span for a Dorset sheep. In the United States, no federal funds can be used for experiments to reproductively clone human beings.

You may also have heard of **therapeutic cloning.** The desired end of therapeutic cloning is not an individual organism, but mature cells of various cell types that could be used to treat human illnesses, such as diabetes, spinal cord injuries, and Parkinson disease. To carry out therapeutic cloning, a researcher might use *embryonic stem cells,* which are simply the cells of an embryo. Each cell is subjected to a treatment that causes it to develop into a particular type of cell, such as red blood cells, muscle cells, or nerve cells. Ethical concerns exist about this procedure because if the embryo had been allowed to continue development, it would have become a person. However, we now have other sources of stem cells, including *adult stem cells,* which are found in many organs of an adult's body. For example, the skin has stem cells that constantly divide and produce new skin cells, while the bone marrow has stem cells that produce new blood cells. The chances of success are better if the stem cells are from the tissue to be produced. But this is not always possible; for example, nervous stem cells must be acquired from the brain.

Recently, investigators have circumvented the need to use various types of adult stem cells by inducing ordinary skin cells to return to an embryonic state and become tissues, as discussed on page 151. Using ordinary skin cells solves any ethical issues and problems of availability.

▶ **12.1 Check Your Progress** Why does an animal clone have the traits of the nucleus donor and not the traits of the surrogate mother?

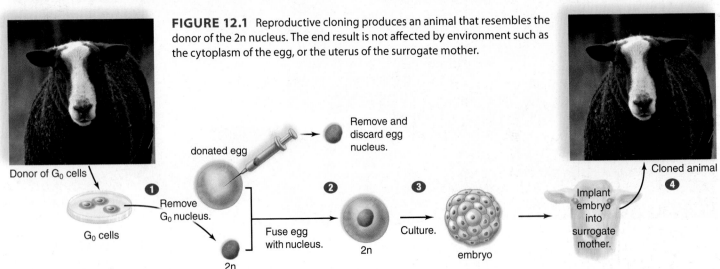

FIGURE 12.1 Reproductive cloning produces an animal that resembles the donor of the 2n nucleus. The end result is not affected by environment such as the cytoplasm of the egg, or the uterus of the surrogate mother.

Donor of G_0 cells

G_0 cells

donated egg

Remove and discard egg nucleus.

1 Remove G_0 nucleus.

2n

Fuse egg with nucleus.

2

2n

3 Culture.

embryo

Implant embryo into surrogate mother.

Cloned animal

4

12A Animal Cloning Has Benefits and Drawbacks

A number of Hollywood thrillers take advantage of the general public's lack of knowledge about cloning by portraying cloning as an evil process. In the movies, scientists clone dinosaurs, mammoths, and even saber-toothed tigers which existed long ago. Sometimes, scientists even clone evil characters in order to take over the world. If considered pure entertainment, the movies are okay. However, many people take these movies seriously, and therefore consider cloning the work of dark hearts.

As discussed in Section 12.1, reproductive cloning results in a replica of an individual. If all goes well, an identical copy of the donor animal is born at the end of the gestation period. Although this process sounds relatively simple, the failure rate is high and reproductive cloning of humans is illegal in the United States.

The first mammal to be successfully cloned was Dolly, the sheep (see Section 12.1). Since Dolly, a number of mammals have been successfully cloned, including mice, rabbits, cats, dogs, pigs, deer, horses, cattle, mules, and rhesus monkeys.

The debate regarding animal cloning is intense. Both sides present valid arguments, and both sides are capable of powerful displays of emotion. Recent surveys by CNN and *Time* showed that 66% of Americans think animal cloning is immoral, 74% think cloning is against God's will, and although 49% do not mind eating cloned plants, only 33% would eat cloned farm animals.

Opponents of reproductive cloning present several valid scientific arguments. They contend that, because the donor's mitochondrial DNA is not passed to the clone, premature aging may occur; that the mutation rate is higher in clones and the regulation of gene expression is abnormal; that clones are prone to "large offspring syndrome"; and that the process of development can result in a clone that is different from the donor. For example, pigs that have been cloned are no more alike than siblings, and the cloned cat Carbon Copy is very different from its donor, Rainbow.

Cloning is expensive. A cloned cat can cost as much as $50,000 to produce; recently, a Florida couple paid $155,000 for a cloned copy of their deceased golden Labrador. A California biotech company did the cloning using the method described in Figure 12.1. A Korean company announced they can lower the price dramatically because

Cloned pigs.

Cloned rhesus monkeys.

adult stem cells taken from fat tissue will develop into embryos they can implant in surrogate mother dogs.

Cloning of farm animals makes it possible to use them to produce pharmaceuticals (see Fig. 12.4A) but it raises ethical issues concerning animal rights and the loss of individuality.

Still animal cloning has many advocates. The process of cloning increases our knowledge of gene interactions and embryological development. Cloning may be the only way, at present, to save endangered species. For example, cloning can save a species even if there are no females remaining, and can produce offspring when animals are infertile.

FORM YOUR OPINION

1. What are the benefits of reproductive cloning?
2. Are you opposed to the reproductive cloning of animals? Of humans? Why or why not?
3. Are you opposed to therapeutic cloning if the source of the needed stem cells is an embryo? Adult stem cells? Treated skin cells? Why or why not?

Carbon Copy, the first cloned cat, and her donor, Rainbow.
Photo reproduced with permission of the Texas A&M University College of Veterinary Medicine & Biomedical Sciences.

Recombinant Technology Clones a Gene

Learning Outcomes

▶ Describe the use of recombinant DNA technology to clone a gene. (12.2)
▶ Describe how gene cloning can result in biotechnology products and genetically modified (GM) bacteria. (12.2)
▶ Explain the rationale for genetically modifying plants and animals, and give examples of the products acquired. (12.3, 12.4)
▶ Contrast ex vivo and in vivo gene therapy in humans, and give examples of each. (12.5)

Recombinant DNA technology utilizing plasmids and a donor gene allows bacteria to be genetically modified and provides genes that can be used to modify plants, animals, and humans. In humans, this use is called gene therapy.

12.2 Genes can be acquired and cloned in bacteria

Gene cloning is done to produce many identical copies of the same gene. Gene cloning requires **recombinant DNA (rDNA),** which contains DNA from two or more different sources. To create rDNA, a technician needs a **vector,** by which the gene of interest will be introduced into a host cell, which is often a bacterium. One common vector is a **plasmid,** a small accessory ring of DNA found in bacteria. The ring is not part of the bacterial chromosome and replicates on its own.

Figure 12.2A traces the steps in cloning a gene:

1 A **restriction enzyme** is used to cleave the plasmid. Hundreds of restriction enzymes occur naturally in bacteria, where they cut up any viral DNA that enters the cell. They are called restriction enzymes because they *restrict* the growth of viruses, but they also act as molecular scissors to cleave any piece of DNA at a specific site. For example, the restriction enzyme called *Eco*RI always cuts double-stranded DNA at this sequence of bases and in this manner:

Notice that there is now a gap into which a piece of foreign DNA can be placed if it begins and ends in bases complementary to those exposed by the restriction enzyme. To ensure this, it is only necessary to cleave the foreign DNA; for example, a human chromosome that contains the gene for insulin (or a jellyfish chromosome that contains the gene for green fluorescent protein [GFP]) is cleaved with the same type of restriction enzyme.

2 The enzyme **DNA ligase** is used to seal foreign DNA into the opening created in the plasmid. The single-stranded, but complementary, ends of a cleaved DNA molecule are called "sticky ends" because they can bind a piece of DNA by complementary base pairing. Sticky ends facilitate the pasting of the plasmid DNA with the DNA of the inserted gene. The use of both restriction enzymes and ligase allows researchers to cut and paste DNA strands at will. Now the vector is complete, and an rDNA molecule has been prepared.

3 Some of the bacteria take up a recombinant plasmid, especially if the bacteria have been treated to make them more permeable.

4a Gene cloning occurs as the plasmid replicates on its own. Scientists clone genes for a number of reasons. They might want to determine the base sequence of the gene and compare it to other cloned genes. Or, they might use the genes to genetically modify other organisms.

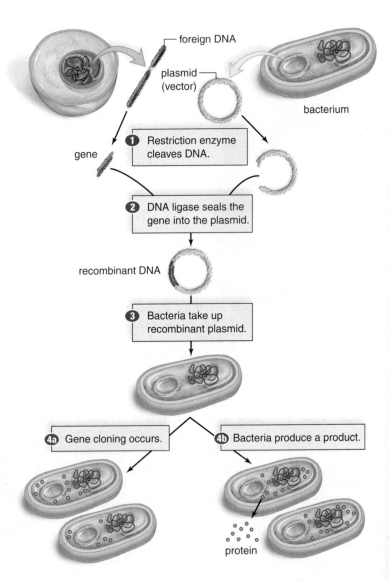

FIGURE 12.2A Cloning a gene that produces a product.

4b The bacterium has been **genetically engineered** and is a **genetically modified organism (GMO)** that can make a product (e.g., insulin or GFP) it could not make before.

The Cloned Gene and Its Product Biologists use the cloned gene for various purposes. For example, a gene that helps plants keep track of the daily cycle of light and dark was cloned and is now being studied by scientists at Scribbs Research Institute to see how it works. Similarly, scientists at the University of Toronto cloned a gene for early-onset Alzheimer disease as a first step toward studying how the gene is implicated in this condition.

Of more direct interest to you, perhaps, are the **biotechnology products** now being produced by **genetically modified (GM) bacteria.** For example, if the gene in Figure 12.2A is the one for insulin from human cells, and if the gene is expressed in the bacteria, then the protein being made by the GM bacterium is insulin. GM bacteria are grown in huge vats called bioreactors, and the gene product is collected from the medium, packaged, and sold as a commercial product.

The products featured in Figure 12.2B may be of special interest to you. GM bacteria assist in making and washing our clothes, in keeping us safe from terrorists, and in making medical biotechnology products. Aside from the insulin being injected by the young girl, GM bacteria produce other medical products such as clotting factor VIII, human growth hormone, t-PA (tissue plasminogen activator), and hepatitis B vaccine.

Not shown in figure 12.2B are several other products. For example, an eel-like fish, the ocean pout, produces a natural anti-freeze protein that is now made commercially by GM bacteria. The product is readily available to all, even ice cream manufacturers who want their product to be free of ice crystals. In the past, the cheese-making industry was dependent upon a substance called rennet, which was collected from the stomach lining of calves. With the decline in the veal industry (veal is a meat derived from calves), a rennet shortage resulted, and no satisfactory substitute could be found. The essential ingredient in rennet for making cheese is chymosin, and the cheese industry was dramatically rescued when chymosin was isolated from calf cells and cloned in bacteria.

Genetically Modified Bacteria Many uses have been found for genetically modified bacteria, aside from the production of proteins. For example, bacteria that normally live on plants and encourage the formation of ice crystals have been changed from frost-plus to frost-minus bacteria. As a result, new crops such as frost-resistant strawberries are being developed. Also, a bacterium that normally colonizes the roots of corn plants has now been endowed with genes (from another bacterium) that code for an insect toxin. The toxin protects the roots from insects.

GM bacteria can also perform various services. Bacteria can be selected for their ability to degrade a particular substance, and this ability can then be enhanced by genetic engineering. For instance, naturally occurring bacteria that eat oil can be genetically engineered to do an even better job of cleaning up beaches after oil spills. Bacteria can also remove sulfur from coal before it is burned and help clean up toxic waste dumps. One such strain was given genes that allowed it to clean up levels of toxins that would have killed other strains. Further, these bacteria were given "suicide" genes that caused them to self-destruct when the job was done.

Organic chemicals are often synthesized by having catalysts act on precursor molecules or by using bacteria to carry out the synthesis. Today, it is possible to go one step further and manipulate the genes that code for these enzymes. For instance, biochemists discovered a strain of bacteria that is especially good at producing phenylalanine, an organic chemical needed to make aspartame, the dipeptide sweetener better known as NutraSweet. They isolated, altered, and formed a vector for the appropriate genes so that various bacteria could be genetically modified to produce phenylalanine.

▶ **12.2 Check Your Progress** You have produced GM bacteria to (1) express the GFP (green fluorescent protein) gene, (2) clean up an oil spill, and then (3) self-destruct. How could you be sure the bacteria did self-destruct?

a. Help produce biodegradable dog waste bags and dye for blue jeans.

b. Produce enzymes allowing us to use less detergent.

c. Produce spider web silk.

d. Glow in dark if chemical warfare agent is present.

e. Produce vaccines.

f. Produce insulin.

FIGURE 12.2B Genetically modified bacteria have the many uses illustrated here.

12.3 Plants can be genetically modified

Corn, potato, soybean, and cotton plants have been engineered to be resistant to either insect predation or widely used herbicides. Some corn and cotton plants are now both insect- and herbicide-resistant. In 2006, GMOs were planted on more than 252 million acres worldwide, an increase of over 13% from the previous year. If crops are resistant to a broad-spectrum herbicide and weeds are not, the herbicide can be used to kill the weeds. When herbicide-resistant plants were planted, weeds were easily controlled, less tillage was needed, and soil erosion was minimized.

Crops with other improved agricultural and food-quality traits are desirable (**Fig. 12.3A***a*). For example, crop production is currently limited by the effects of salinization on about 50% of irrigated lands. Salt-tolerant crops would increase yield on this land. Salt- and also drought- and cold-tolerant crops might help provide enough food for a world population that may nearly double by 2050. A salt-tolerant tomato has already been developed (**Fig. 12.3A***b*). First, scientists identified a gene coding for a channel protein that transports Na^+ across the vacuole membrane. Sequestering the Na^+ in a vacuole prevents it from interfering with plant metabolism. Then the scientists cloned the gene and used it to genetically engineer plants that overproduce the channel protein. The modified plants thrived when watered with a salty solution.

Potato blight is the most serious potato disease in the world. About 150 years ago, it was responsible for the Irish potato famine, which caused the deaths of millions of people. By placing a gene from a naturally blight-resistant wild potato into a farmed variety, researchers have now made potato plants that are invulnerable to a range of blight strains. In **Figure 12.3B**, the B.t.t. + potato plant produces an insecticide protein and is resistant to the Colorado potato beetle.

Some progress has also been made in increasing the food quality of crops. Soybeans have been developed that mainly produce the monounsaturated fatty acid oleic acid, a change that may improve human health. Genetically modified plants requiring more than a single gene transfer are also expected to increase

FIGURE 12.3B The potato plant on the left is nonresistant to the Colorado potato beetle, while the plant on the right is resistant.

productivity. For example, stomata might be altered to take in more carbon dioxide or lose less water. The efficiency of the enzyme RuBP carboxylase, which captures carbon dioxide in plants, could be improved. A team of Japanese scientists is working on introducing the C_4 photosynthetic cycle into rice. (As discussed in Chapter 6, C_4 plants do well in warm, dry weather.)

Genetic engineering of plants has also developed many products for medical use, such as human hormones, clotting factors, and antibodies. One type of antibody made by corn can deliver radioisotopes to tumor cells, and another made by soybeans may be developed to treat genital herpes.

How Biology Impacts Our Lives on page 235 makes it clear that people have two basic concerns about genetically modified foods: food safety and environmental impact.

▶ **12.3 Check Your Progress** Surprisingly, plants can be modified to produce any type of protein, even GFP. Explain why this is possible.

GM Crops of the Future	
Improved Agricultural Traits	
Disease-protected	Wheat, corn, potatoes
Herbicide-resistant	Wheat, rice, sugar beets, canola
Salt-tolerant	Cereals, rice, sugarcane
Drought-tolerant	Cereals, rice, sugarcane
Cold-tolerant	Cereals, rice, sugarcane
Improved yield	Cereals, rice, corn, cotton
Modified wood pulp	Trees
Improved Food Quality Traits	
Fatty acid/oil content	Corn, soybeans
Protein/starch content	Cereals, potatoes, soybeans, rice, corn
Amino acid content	Corn, soybeans

a.

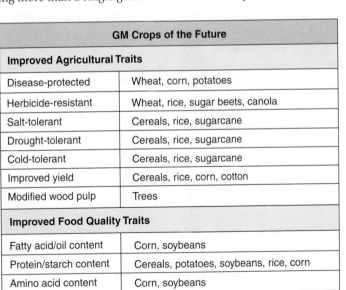

b.

FIGURE 12.3A **a.** Genetically modified crops are expected in the future. **b.** Researchers have already engineered a salt-tolerant tomato plant.

12B Are Genetically Engineered Foods Safe?

A series of focus groups conducted by the Food and Drug Administration (FDA) in 2000 showed that, although most participants believed genetically engineered foods might offer benefits, they also feared unknown long-term health consequences that might be associated with the technology. Conrad G. Brunk, a bioethicist at the University of Waterloo in Ontario, has said, "When it comes to human and environmental safety, there should be clear evidence of the absence of risks. The mere absence of evidence is not enough."

The discovery by activists that GM corn called StarLink had inadvertently made it into the food supply triggered the recall of taco shells, tortillas, and many other corn-based foodstuffs from U.S. supermarkets. Furthermore, the makers of StarLink were forced to buy back StarLink from farmers and to compensate food producers at an estimated cost of several hundred million dollars. StarLink corn is a type of "Bt" corn, so called because it contains a foreign gene taken from a common soil organism, *Bacillus thuringiensis,* whose insecticidal properties have been long known. About a dozen Bt varieties, including corn, potato (**Fig. 12B,** *top*), and even a tomato, have now been approved for human consumption. These strains contain a gene for an insecticide protein called CrylA. However, the makers of StarLink decided to use a gene for a related protein called Cry9C. They thought this molecule might slow the development of pest resistance to Bt corn. To get FDA approval for use in foods, the makers of StarLink performed the required tests. Like the other now-approved strains, StarLink wasn't poisonous to rodents, and its biochemical structure is not similar to those of most food allergens. But the Cry9C protein resisted digestion longer than the other Bt proteins when placed in simulated stomach acid and subjected to heat. Because this is a characteristic of most food allergens, StarLink was not approved for human consumption.

Scientists are now trying to devise more tests because they have not been able to determine conclusively whether Cry9C is an allergen. Also, at this point, it is unclear how resistant to digestion a protein must be in order to be an allergen, or what degree of sequence similarity to a known allergen is enough to raise concern. Other scientists are concerned about the following potential drawbacks to the planting of Bt corn: (1) resistance among populations of the target pest, (2) exchange of genetic material between the GM crop and related plant species, and (3) Bt crops' impact on nontarget species. They feel many more studies are needed before they can state for certain that Bt corn has no ecological drawbacks.

Despite controversies, the planting of GM corn has steadily increased (**Fig. 12B,** *bottom*). The public wants all genetically engineered foods to be labeled as such, but this may not be easy because, for example, most cornmeal is derived from both conventional and genetically engineered corn. So far, there has been little attempt to sort out one type of food product from the other. However, health food stores label foods that do not contain GMOs. Amid this controversy, the Union of Concerned Scientists released a 2009 report that evaluates the effect of genetic engineering on crop yields. The study, based on two dozen academic studies of corn and soybeans crops in the United States, concludes that GM crops have not contributed to increased yield and instead increased yield has been due to traditional breeding programs and improved agricultural practices.

If increased yield alone is the desired end, they believe farmers should use traditional crops and sustainable organic farming technology.

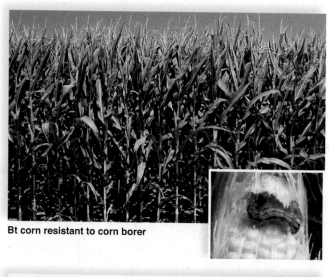

Bt corn resistant to corn borer

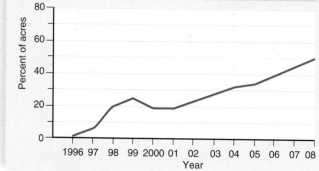

Bt corn usage since 1996

FIGURE 12B Bt corn (top) has been genetically modified to express a bacterial gene that allows the plants to resist insects such as corn borers (see insert), which decrease yield. The graph shows how the planting of Bt corn has increased over the years.

FORM YOUR OPINION

1. On what basis would it be possible to decide whether GM crops pose any harm to the consumer?
2. Are you in favor of banning GM crops—even if it means food prices would rise? Do you approve of ecoterrorists who burn GM crops and destroy biotechnology labs?
3. One GM rice has been developed that might prevent childhood blindness in less-developed countries because it provides vitamin A. Should this rice also be banned? What data would help you make this decision?

12.4 Animals can be genetically modified

Techniques have been developed to insert genes into the eggs of animals. It is possible to microinject foreign genes into eggs by hand, but another method uses vortex mixing. DNA and eggs are placed in an agitator with silicon-carbide needles. The needles make tiny holes, through which the DNA can enter. When these eggs are fertilized, the resulting offspring are transgenic animals. Using this technique, many types of animal eggs have taken up the gene for bovine growth hormone (bGH), and this has led to the production of larger fishes, cows, pigs, rabbits, and sheep.

Gene pharming, the use of transgenic animals to produce pharmaceuticals, is being pursued by a number of firms. Genes that code for therapeutic and diagnostic proteins are incorporated into an animal's DNA, and the proteins appear in the animal's milk (**Fig. 12.4A**). Plans are under way to produce medicines for the treatment of cystic fibrosis, cancer, blood diseases, and other disorders by this method. Figure 12.4A outlines the procedure for producing GM mammals. ❶ The gene of interest (in this case, for human growth hormone) is microinjected into donor eggs. ❷ Following in vitro fertilization, the zygotes are placed in host females, where they develop. ❸ After the transgenic female offspring mature, the product is secreted in their milk. Then, cloning can be used to produce many animals that produce the same product: ❹ Donor enucleated eggs are fused with 2n transgenic nuclei. The eggs are coaxed to begin development in vitro. ❺ Development continues in host females until the clones are born. ❻ The female offspring are clones that have the same product in their milk.

Many researchers are using transgenic mice for various research projects. **Figure 12.4B** shows how this technology has demonstrated that a section of DNA called *SRY* (sex-determining region of the Y chromosome) produces a male animal. The *SRY* DNA was cloned, and then one copy was injected into one-celled mouse embryos with two X chromosomes. Injected embryos developed into males, but any that were not injected developed into females. Mouse models have also been created to study human diseases. An allele such as the one that causes cystic fibrosis can be cloned and inserted into mice embryonic stem cells, and occasionally a mouse embryo homozygous for cystic fibrosis will result. This embryo develops into a mutant mouse that has a phenotype similar to that of a human with cystic fibrosis. New drugs for the treatment of cystic fibrosis can then be tested in these mice.

Xenotransplantation is the use of animal organs, instead of human organs, in transplant patients. Scientists have chosen to work with pigs because they are prolific and have long been raised as a meat source. Pigs are being genetically modified to make their organs less likely to be rejected by the human body. The hope is that one day a pig organ will be as easily accepted by the human body as a blood transfusion from a person with the same blood type.

▶ **12.4 Check Your Progress** In Figure 12.4A, only transgenic females produce milk. Why was cloning done instead of simply producing more GM animals?

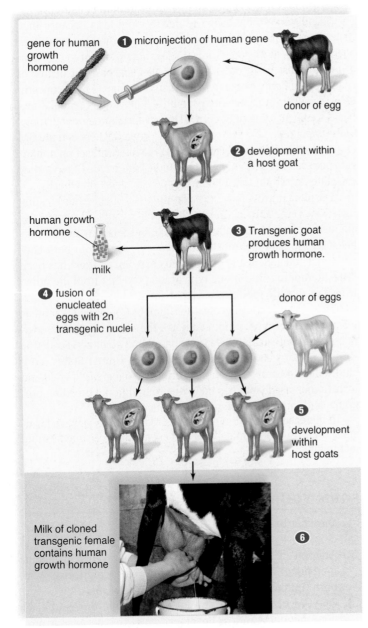

FIGURE 12.4A Procedure for producing many female clones that yield the same product.

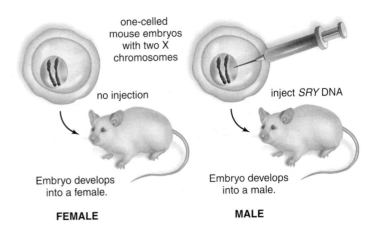

FIGURE 12.4B GM mice showed that maleness is due to *SRY* DNA.

12.5 A person's genome can be modified

The manipulation of an organism's genes can be extended to humans in a process called gene therapy. **Gene therapy** is the insertion of a foreign gene into human cells for the treatment of a disorder. Gene therapy has been used to cure inborn errors of metabolism as well as more generalized disorders, such as cardiovascular disease and cancer. *Ex vivo gene therapy* means the gene is inserted into cells that have been removed and then returned to the body while *in vivo gene therapy* means the gene is delivered directly into the body. **Figure 12.5** shows regions of the body that have received copies of normal genes by various methods of gene transfer. Viruses genetically modified to be safe can be used to ferry a normal gene into the body, and so can liposomes, which are microscopic globules of lipids specially prepared to enclose the normal gene. On the other hand, sometimes the gene is injected directly into a particular region of the body.

Ex Vivo Gene Therapy Children who have SCID (severe combined immunodeficiency) lack the enzyme ADA (adenosine deaminase), which is involved in the maturation of white blood cells. Therefore, these children are prone to constant infections and may die without treatment. To carry out gene therapy, bone marrow stem cells are removed from the bone marrow of the patient and infected with a virus that carries a normal gene for the enzyme. Then the cells are returned to the patient, where it is hoped they will divide to produce more blood cells with the same genes.

Familial hypercholesterolemia is a condition in which high levels of blood cholesterol make patients subject to fatal heart attacks at a young age. Through ex vivo gene therapy, a small portion of the liver is surgically excised and then infected with a virus containing a normal gene for the receptor before being returned to the patient. Patients are expected to experience lowered serum cholesterol levels following this procedure.

Investigators are also working on a cure for phenylketonuria (PKU), an inherited condition that can cause mental retardation. If detected early enough, the child can be placed on a special diet for the first few years of life, but this is very inconvenient. These investigators believe they will be able to inject the gene directly into the DNA of excised liver cells, which will then be returned to the patient.

In Vivo Gene Therapy Cystic fibrosis patients lack a gene that codes for the transmembrane carrier of the chloride ion. They often suffer from numerous and potentially deadly infections of the respiratory tract. In gene therapy trials, the gene needed to cure cystic fibrosis is sprayed into the nose or delivered to the lower respiratory tract by a virus or by liposomes, artificial vesicles made from phospholipids. So far, this treatment has resulted in limited success.

Genes are also being used to treat medical conditions such as poor coronary circulation. Scientists have known for some time that VEGF (vascular endothelial growth factor) can cause the growth of new blood vessels. The gene that codes for this growth factor can be injected alone or within a virus into the heart to stimulate branching of coronary blood vessels. Patients report that they have less chest pain and can run longer on a treadmill.

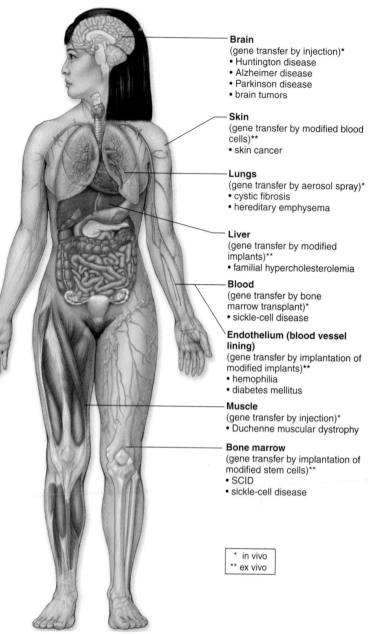

Brain
(gene transfer by injection)*
• Huntington disease
• Alzheimer disease
• Parkinson disease
• brain tumors

Skin
(gene transfer by modified blood cells)**
• skin cancer

Lungs
(gene transfer by aerosol spray)*
• cystic fibrosis
• hereditary emphysema

Liver
(gene transfer by modified implants)**
• familial hypercholesterolemia

Blood
(gene transfer by bone marrow transplant)*
• sickle-cell disease

Endothelium (blood vessel lining)
(gene transfer by implantation of modified implants)**
• hemophilia
• diabetes mellitus

Muscle
(gene transfer by injection)*
• Duchenne muscular dystrophy

Bone marrow
(gene transfer by implantation of modified stem cells)**
• SCID
• sickle-cell disease

* in vivo
** ex vivo

FIGURE 12.5 Sites of ex vivo and in vivo gene therapy to cure the conditions noted.

Gene therapy is increasingly being applied as a part of cancer therapy. Genes are used to make healthy cells more tolerant of chemotherapy and to make tumors more vulnerable to chemotherapy. The gene *p53* brings about apoptosis, and there is much interest in introducing it into cancer cells and, in that way, killing them off.

▶ **12.5 Check Your Progress** In DNA cloning (see Fig. 12.2A), a plasmid is used as a vector (carrier) for the gene. What is the vector of choice for ex vivo gene therapy?

The Human Genome Can Be Studied

Learning Outcomes

▶ State the goal of the human genome project and tell how it was achieved. (12.6)

▶ Describe the human genome in terms of coding and noncoding DNA. (12.7)

▶ Explain how microarrays can provide functional genetic information about the cell and the individual. (12.8)

▶ Discuss the relationship of proteomics to bioinformatics and compare the human genome to that of other organisms. (12.8)

A **genome** is all the DNA in a cell. Now that the human genome and the genomes of many other organisms have been base-sequenced, the field of genomics is dedicated to discovering and understanding the function of the genome and the proteins in a cell. The computer will help achieve this goal, and so will the use of microarrays. Microarrays are also of interest to the medical community in diagnosing diseases. Scientists want to compare the structure and function of the human genome to that of other organisms.

12.6 The human genome has been sequenced

In the previous century, researchers discovered the structure of DNA, how DNA replicates, and how DNA and RNA are involved in protein synthesis. Genetics in the twenty-first century concerns genomics, the study of all our DNA as well as that of other organisms. We now know the sequence of bases in the human genome and are beginning to study the function of all its genetic components.

The enormity of sequencing the human genome can be appreciated by knowing that it has approximately 3.2 billion base pairs. In order to record them all, a book would have to have 500,000 pages. It's been calculated that it would take you 60 years to read all the bases out loud, reading 5 bases a second for 8 hours a day. The feat of sequencing the bases was accomplished by the **Human Genome Project (HGP),** a 13-year effort that involved both university and private laboratories around the world.

You'll be interested to know that the task would not have been possible without the use of automated laboratory equipment, including a thermocycler that performs the **polymerase chain reaction (PCR)** and high-speed DNA sequencing machines. You'll recall that the many applications of PCR were discussed on page 197; now, we want to see how PCR assisted research scientists. Human DNA was cut into fragments by using restriction enzymes, and then PCR amplified the fragments. The thermocycler shown in **Figure 12.6A** is so-called because the temperature changes automatically. A high temperature is needed to separate DNA strands prior to the use of a DNA polymerase to copy target DNA. A DNA polymerase that can stand this high temperature

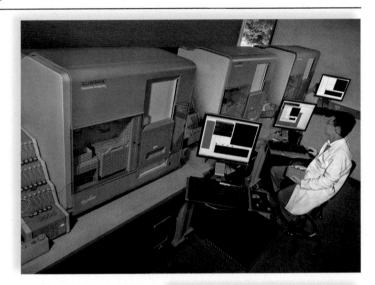

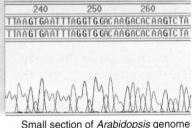

FIGURE 12.6B An automated DNA sequencer produces a pattern that can be read by a computer to tell the sequence of the bases.

Small section of *Arabidopsis* genome

was extracted from the bacterium *Thermus aquaticus,* which lives in hot springs. Therefore it is called *Taq DNA polymerase.*

Years before, investigators had perfected a manual method (requiring many copies of the same DNA) to decipher a base sequence, but naturally they began to use automated sequencers when they became available (**Fig. 12.6B**). Over the 13-year span of the HGP, DNA sequencers were constantly improved, and now modern instruments can automatically analyze up to 2 million base pairs of DNA in a 24-hour period. Where did the DNA come from? Sperm DNA was the material of choice because it has a much higher ratio of DNA to protein than other types of cells. However, white cells from the blood of female donors were also used. The DNA donors were of European, African, American (both North and South), and Asian ancestry.

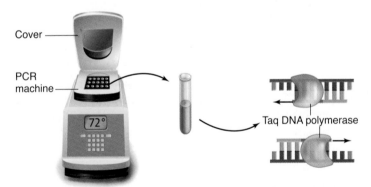

FIGURE 12.6A PCR is done in a thermocycler that changes the temperature automatically. Target DNA (purple) between the primers (green) is copied at a temperature of 72°C. Each time the target DNA is copied, the amount of target DNA doubles.

▶ **12.6 Check Your Progress** If DNA was sequenced piece by piece, what did researchers need to determine about the pieces before they knew the base sequence of the entire human genome?

12.7 The genome contains coding and noncoding DNA

Coding DNA While we often speak of protein-coding genes, **Figure 12.7** reminds us that only exons are incorporated into mRNA and go on to participate in protein synthesis at a ribosome. An amazing discovery was that only 2% of our genome consists of protein-coding exons. The number of our protein-coding genes is still being determined, but it lies between 20,000 and 25,000. A much larger number was expected, considering that the genome has 3 billion base pairs. The genome can contain more than one copy of each protein-coding gene. Multiple copies of the same gene can allow an organism to produce a great deal of product within a short time. Also, a duplicate gene doubles the possibility of a gene undergoing an advantageous mutation that could contribute to evolution. The term **pseudo-gene** is used for copies of genes that are nonfunctional because of a mutation.

Noncoding DNA The genome has a tremendous amount (98%) of noncoding DNA. You might think that noncoding DNA could vary between parent and child, but it does not. A parent passes on a haploid set of chromosomes that contains both coding and noncoding DNA in a particular order. The fact that noncoding DNA is often transcribed into RNA raises the possibility that a heretofore-overlooked regulatory network may be what allows

eukaryotes, including humans, to achieve a structural complexity far beyond anything seen in the prokaryotic world.

Among the noncoding DNA, 24% consists of **introns.** Once regarded as merely intervening sequences, introns may very well be regulators of gene expression. The presence of introns allows exons to be put together in various sequences so that different mRNAs and proteins can result from a single gene. In general, more complex organisms have more and larger introns. Introns can also be a source of small RNAs.

The rest of the noncoding DNA is colored red in Figure 12.7. Of this, **repetitive DNA** is much the larger piece (59%). This is the portion of our genome that was once specifically called "junk DNA." Although many scientists still dismiss repetitive DNA as having no function, others point out that the centromeres and the ends (telomeres) of chromosomes are composed of repetitive elements and, therefore, repetitive DNA may not be as useless as once thought. For example, repetitive elements of the centromere could possibly help with segregating the chromosomes during cell division.

Repetitive DNA can occur as tandem repeats and interspersed repeats. **Tandem repeat** means that the repeated sequences are next to each other on the chromosome. For example, ACTGACT-GACTG would be a tandem repeat. The number and types of

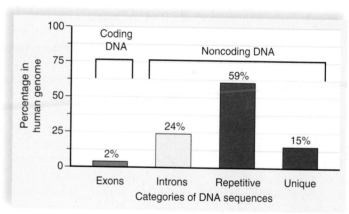

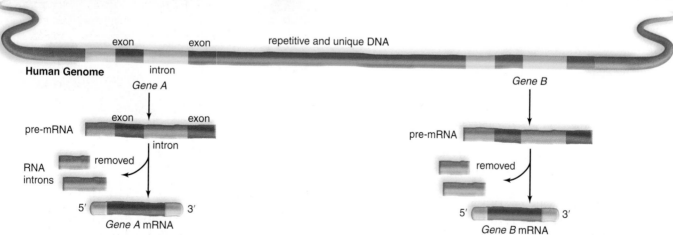

FIGURE 12.7 A genome contains protein-coding DNA (exons) and noncoding DNA, including introns (light blue) and other intergenic sequences (red). Only the exons are present in mRNA and specify protein synthesis. Children inherit both coding and noncoding DNA from their parents.

tandem repeats may vary significantly from one individual to another, making them invaluable as indicators of heritage. One type of tandem repeat sequence, referred to as short tandem repeats, or STRs, has become a standard method in forensic science for distinguishing one individual from another through DNA fingerprinting. The second type of repetitive DNA is called an **interspersed repeat**, meaning that the repetitions may be placed intermittently along a single chromosome, or across multiple chromosomes. Because of their common occurrence, interspersed repeats are thought to play a role in the evolution of new genes.

Transposons are specific repetitive DNA sequences, called elements, that have the remarkable ability to move within and between chromosomes. Because it can move, a repetitive DNA sequence known as the *Alu element* is interspersed on multiple chromosomes once per every 5,000 base pairs in human DNA. Transposons have by now been discovered in most organisms. Barbara McClintock received a Nobel Prize in 1983 for her discovery of transposons in corn (see How Science Progresses, p. 205).

The movement of transposons to a new location sometimes alters neighboring genes, particularly by decreasing their expression. In other words, a transposon sometimes acts like a regulatory gene. The movement of transposons throughout the genome is thought to be a driving force in the evolution of living things. In fact, many scientists now think that many repetitive DNA elements are or were originally derived from transposons.

Little is known about **unique noncoding DNA,** and it's possible that this region codes for the regulatory small RNAs discussed in Chapter 11. No doubt we will hear more about this mysterious 15% of our genome in the future.

▶ **12.7 Check Your Progress a. Name three types of noncoding DNA. b. Which occupies the largest percentage of the genome, and what function might it serve?**

12.8 Functional and comparative genomics are active fields of study

Since we now know the structure of the human genome, the emphasis today is on functional genomics and also on comparative genomics.

Functional Genomics The aim of **functional genomics** is to understand the exact role of the genome in cells or organisms. To that end, a new technology called **DNA microarrays** can be used to monitor the expression of thousands of genes simultaneously. In other words, the use of a microarray can tell you what genes are turned on in a specific cell or organism at a particular time and under what particular environmental circumstances. DNA microarrays contain microscopic amounts of known DNA sequences, called DNA probes, fixed onto a small glass slide or silicon chip in known locations (**Fig. 12.8A**). When tagged DNA or mRNA molecules of a cell or organism bind through complementary base pairing with the various DNA sequences, that gene is active in the cell. DNA microarrays are available that rapidly identify all the various mutations in the genome of an individual. This is called the person's **genetic profile.** The genetic profile can indicate if any genetic illnesses are likely and what type of drug therapy might be most appropriate for that individual.

Functional genomics is greatly assisted by proteomics and bioinformatics. The entire collection of a species' proteins is the **proteome.** At first, it may be surprising to learn that the proteome is larger than the genome, until we consider all the many regulatory mechanisms, such as alternative pre-mRNA splicing, that increase the number of possible proteins in an organism.

Proteomics is the study of the structure, function, and interaction of cellular proteins. Specific regulatory mechanisms differ between cells, and these differences account for the specialization of cells. One goal of proteomics is to identify and determine the function of the proteins within a particular cell type. Each cell produces thousands of different proteins that can vary between cells and within the same cell, depending on circumstances. Therefore, the goal of proteomics is an overwhelming endeavor. Microarray technology can assist with this project, and so can today's supercomputers.

Computer modeling of the three-dimensional shape of cellular proteins is also an important part of proteomics. If the primary structure of a protein is known, it should be possible to predict its final three-dimensional shape, and even the effects of DNA mutations on the protein's shape and function.

The study of protein function is viewed as essential to the discovery of new and better drugs. Also, it may be possible one day to correlate drug treatment to the particular proteome of the individual to increase efficiency and decrease side effects. Proteomics will be a critical field of endeavor for many years to come.

Bioinformatics is the application of computer technologies, specially developed software, and statistical techniques to the study of biological information, particularly databases that contain much genomic and proteomic information (**Fig. 12.8B**). New data produced by genomics and proteomics is stored in databases that are readily available to research scientists. It is called raw data

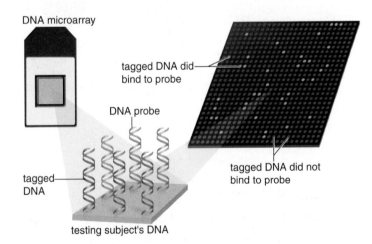

FIGURE 12.8A A DNA microarray contains many known DNA sequences, called DNA probes, bound to specific locations on a silicon chip. The subject's DNA is fluorescently tagged and whenever it binds to a probe a technician knows that the subject tests positive for that DNA probe.

FIGURE 12.8B Bioinformatics use new computer programs to make sense out of the raw data generated by genomics and proteomics.

because, as yet, it has little meaning. Functional genomics and proteomics depend on computer analysis to find significant patterns in the raw data. For example, BLAST, which stands for basic local alignment search tool, is a computer program that can identify homologous genes among the genomic sequences of model organisms. **Homologous genes** are genes that code for the same proteins, although the base sequence may be slightly different. Finding these differences can help trace the history of evolution among a group of organisms.

Bioinformatics also has various applications in human genetics. For example, researchers found the function of the protein that causes cystic fibrosis by using the computer to search for genes in model organisms that have the same sequence. Because they knew the function of this same gene in model organisms, they could deduce the function in humans. This was a necessary step toward possibly developing specific treatments for cystic fibrosis. The human genome has 3 billion known base pairs, and without the computer it would be almost impossible to make sense of these data. For example, we now know that an individual's genome often contains multiple copies of a gene. But individuals may differ in the number of copies, called copy number variations. Now it seems that the number of copies in a genome can be associated with specific diseases. The computer can help correlate genomic differences among large numbers of people with a specific disease.

It is safe to say that without bioinformatics, our progress would be extremely slow in determining the function of DNA sequences, comparing our genome to model organisms, knowing how genes and proteins interact in cells, and other investigations. Instead, with the help of bioinformatics, progress should proceed rapidly in these and other areas.

Comparative Genomics The aim of **comparative genomics** is to compare the human genome to the genome of other organisms, such as the model organisms shown in **Table 12.8**. Surprisingly, perhaps, functional genomics has also been advanced by sequencing the genome of these model organisms. Model organisms are used in genetic analysis because they have many genetic mechanisms and cellular pathways in common with each other and with humans. Much has been learned by genetically modifying mice; however, other model organisms can also sometimes be used. Scientists inserted a human gene associated with early-onset Parkinson disease into *Drosophila melanogaster,* and the flies showed symptoms similar to those seen in humans with the disorder. This suggests that we might be able to use these organisms instead of mice to test therapies for Parkinson disease.

Comparative genomics also offers a way to study changes in a genome over time because the model organisms have a shorter generation time than humans. Comparing genomes will also help us understand the evolutionary relationships between organisms. One surprising discovery is that the genomes of all vertebrates are similar. Researchers were not surprised to find that the genes of chimpanzees and humans are 98% alike, but they did not expect to learn that our sequence is also 85% like that of a mouse. Genomic comparisons will likely reveal evolutionary relationships between organisms never previously considered.

▶ **12.8 Check Your Progress** What kind of information can we learn through a. proteomics and b. bioinformatics?

TABLE 12.8	Genome Sizes of Humans and Some Model Organisms					
Organism	*Homo sapiens* (human)	*Mus musculus* (mouse)	*Drosophila melanogaster* (fruit fly)	*Arabidopsis thaliana* (flowering plant)	*Caenorhabditis elegans* (roundworm)	*Saccharomyces cerevisiae* (yeast)
Estimated Size	2,900 million bases	2,500 million bases	180 million bases	125 million bases	97 million bases	12 million bases
Estimated Number of Genes	~25,000	~30,000	13,600	25,500	19,100	6,300
Average Gene Density	1 gene per 100,000 bases	1 gene per 100,000 bases	1 gene per 9,000 bases	1 gene per 4,000 bases	1 gene per 5,000 bases	1 gene per 2,000 bases
Chromosome Number	46	40	8	10	12	32

12C We Are Closely Related to Chimpanzees

Much genetic evidence indicates that humans and chimpanzees are very closely related, despite the observation that chimpanzees have 48 chromosomes and we have only 46. At first, the difference in chromosome number was considered significant— so significant that the great apes (chimpanzees, gorillas, and orangutans) and humans were classified into different families. The apes were in family Pongidae, and humans were in family Hominidae. In 1991, however, investigators at Yale University showed that human chromosome 2 is a fusion of two chimpanzee chromosomes:

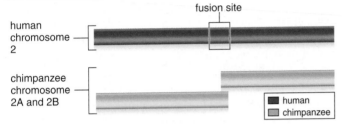

As you know, there are plentiful transposons in the human genome. Most no longer transpose and instead remain at one location. They are relics of past retrovirus infections of the genome. A retrovirus has an RNA genome and an enzyme called reverse transcriptase. This enzyme copies the viral genome into DNA before it enters the host genome. Through the course of many studies, investigators have found that humans and chimpanzees have similar patterns of transposons in their genomes. Here is an example showing how the Alu element (a transposon) inserted itself into the human genome and the chimpanzee genome in the vicinity of hemoglobin genes:

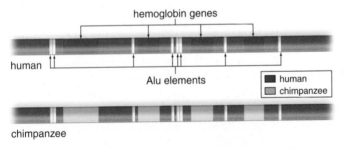

Pseudogenes are nonfunctional copies of genes that were active in the past. Pseudogenes are presently not active due to a mutation that prevents them from coding for a functional protein. The pseudogene pattern in humans is most similar to that in chimpanzee DNA and to a lesser extent to that of the other great apes. These and other studies have caused a reclassification of the primates most closely related to us. All of the great apes are now in the same family as humans; chimpanzees are in the same subfamily (Homininae).

Modern genomic data show that the base sequence of chimpanzees and humans differs only by 1.5% of their bases. By now, we take as a given that humans and chimpanzees are genetically similar, and it has become the task of geneticists to determine what genetic factors make us different from chimpanzees. Even though our base sequences are quite similar,

Now that we know chimpanzees are closely related to us, studies have shifted to finding the genetic differences that make us so anatomically different.

significant differences do exist. For example, when we compare the chimpanzee and the human genome, many DNA stretches (about 5 million) are absent in one or the other genome. We know that in the evolution of mammals there was an explosion in the amount of noncoding sequences relative to the number of coding genes. So a common mammalian ancestor may have had a larger quantity of noncoding DNA, and each mammalian species lost different DNA stretches since their lines of descent separated. Many examples tell us that noncoding DNA is not the mere junk as was largely thought only a few years ago, and so it could very well be that primate anatomical differences could be due to which stretches of noncoding DNA were retained by the particular primate. Microarray chip data support the conclusion that certain genes are not expressed in chimpanzees to the same degree as in humans. Which genes might these be? Evidence is gaining that the genes controlling the development of the brain may have been affected the most by the gaps present in the chimpanzee genome compared to the human genome. This may account for why our brains are larger than those of chimpanzees today.

FORM YOUR OPINION

1. This reading concludes that chimpanzees and humans differ most in gene regulation. Would you have expected gene regulation to account for major differences in evolution? Why or why not?

2. Would you be willing to participate in a comparative human study to determine what types of genomes are prone to what illnesses? Why or why not?

3. Would you expect your genome to differ from that of your siblings? Why or why not?

Cloning Can Produce an Organism or Tissues

12.1 A cloned product has the donor's DNA

- The desired result of **reproductive cloning** is a new individual exactly like the original individual.
- The desired result of **therapeutic cloning** is mature cells of various types for medical purposes.
- Either embryonic stem cells or adult stem cells may be used in therapeutic cloning. The use of treated skin cells for therapeutic cloning will solve ethical problems.

Recombinant Technology Clones a Gene

12.2 Genes can be acquired and cloned in bacteria

- **Gene cloning** produces identical copies of a particular gene.
- **Recombinant DNA** contains DNA from two sources.
- A **plasmid** is a **vector** that can accept a foreign gene if both the plasmid and foreign DNA are cleaved by the same **restriction enzyme.**
- **DNA ligase** seals the gene into the plasmid, which carries the foreign gene into the host cell—in this case, a bacterium.
- The bacterium has been **genetically engineered** and is a **genetically modified organism (GMO).**

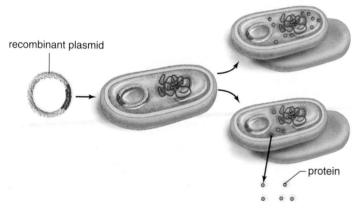

recombinant plasmid

protein

- The gene is cloned as the plasmid replicates, and the bacterium will produce a new and different product. The protein produced is a **biotechnology product,** either medical (e.g., vaccines, growth hormone, etc.) or commercial (e.g., NutraSweet, products that clean up oil spills, etc.).

12.3 Plants can be genetically modified

- Certain crops have been engineered to resist disease, insects, or herbicides.
- Genetic engineering is being used to improve the agricultural and food qualities of certain crops.
- Some plants have been engineered to manufacture medical products.

12.4 Animals can be genetically modified

- Genes can be inserted into the eggs of animals.
- Through **gene pharming,** transgenic animals produce pharmaceuticals.
- Transgenic mice are bred for research.

- **Xenotransplantation** is the use of animal organs in human transplant patients.

12.5 A person's genome can be modified

- **Gene therapy** can be done in two ways:
  - Using ex vivo therapy, cells or tissues are removed from the body, given a normal gene, and then reinserted into the body.
  - Using in vivo therapy, a gene is delivered directly into the body.

The Human Genome Can Be Studied

12.6 The human genome has been sequenced

- The **Human Genome Project (HGP)** determined the order of bases in the human **genome.**
- The **polymerase chain reaction** and automated equipment (PCR thermocycler, DNA sequencers) facilitated the project.

12.7 The genome contains coding and noncoding DNA

- Coding DNA (exons) is transcribed into mRNA that binds to a ribosome where protein synthesis occurs. Some coding genes occur in multiple copies; a **pseudogene** is a nonfunctional copy.
- Noncoding DNA contains (1) **introns**, (2) **repetitive DNA**, and (3) **unique noncoding** DNA. Surprisingly, this DNA may be transcribed into RNA, and this RNA is thought to have a regulatory function.
- Repetitive DNA contains **tandem repeats, interspersed repeats,** and **transposons.**
- The function of unique noncoding DNA is still to be discovered.

12.8 Functional and comparative genomics are active fields of study

- **Functional genomics** is aided by **DNA microarrays,** which contain DNA fragments on a silicon chip. DNA microarrays can be used to determine the genetic activity in a cell or an individual. This is called the **genetic profile** of an individual.
- **Proteomics** is the study of the structure, function, and interaction of cellular proteins.
- The human **proteome** is the complete collection of proteins that humans produce.
- **Bioinformatics** is the application of computer technologies to the study of the genome, including functional genomics.
- **Comparative genomics** focuses on determining how species are related and how their genes compare to those of humans.

Cloning Can Produce an Organism or Tissues

1. During reproductive cloning, a(n) _____ is placed into a(n) _____.
   a. enucleated egg cell, adult cell nucleus
   b. adult cell nucleus, enucleated egg cell
   c. egg cell nucleus, enucleated adult cell
   d. enucleated adult cell, egg cell nucleus

2. The major challenge to therapeutic cloning using adult stem cells is
   a. finding appropriate cell types.
   b. obtaining enough tissue.
   c. controlling gene expression.
   d. keeping cells alive in culture.
3. The product of therapeutic cloning differs from the product of reproductive cloning in that it is
   a. various mature cells, not an individual.
   b. genetically identical to the somatic cells from the donor.
   c. various mature cells with the ability to become an individual.
   d. an individual that is genetically identical to the donor of the nucleus.

Recombinant Technology Clones a Gene

4. Which of the following is not a clone?
   a. a colony of identical bacterial cells
   b. identical quintuplets
   c. a forest of identical trees
   d. eggs produced by oogenesis
   e. copies of a gene produced through PCR
5. The enzymes needed to introduce foreign DNA into a vector are
   a. DNA gyrase and DNA ligase.
   b. DNA ligase and DNA polymerase.
   c. DNA gyrase and DNA polymerase.
   d. restriction enzyme and DNA gyrase.
   e. restriction enzyme and DNA ligase.
6. Put the lettered phrases in the correct order to form a plasmid-carrying recombinant DNA.
   a. Use restriction enzymes.
   b. Use DNA ligase.
   c. Remove plasmid from parent bacterium and acquire donor eukaryotic DNA.
   d. Introduce plasmid into new host bacterium.
7. Restriction enzymes found in bacterial cells are ordinarily used
   a. during DNA replication.
   b. to degrade the bacterial cell's DNA.
   c. to degrade viral DNA that enters the cell.
   d. to attach pieces of DNA together.
8. Recombinant DNA technology is used
   a. for gene therapy.
   b. to clone a gene.
   c. to acquire GM bacteria.
   d. Both b and c are correct.
9. The restriction enzyme *Eco*RI has cut double-stranded DNA in the following manner. The piece of foreign DNA to be inserted begins and ends with what base pairs?

10. Which of these would you not expect to be a biotechnology product?
    a. phospholipid   c. modified enzyme
    b. protein hormone   d. clotting enzyme

11. The cheese industry was rescued when
    a. chymosin became a biotechnology product.
    b. insulin was produced by bacteria.
    c. plants and animals were genetically modified.
    d. it gave up making GM products.
12. Which of these are desired ends of GM plants?
    a. salt-tolerant crops
    b. drought-tolerant crops
    c. protein-enriched foods
    d. crops that can resist herbicides
    e. All of these are correct.
13. **THINKING CONCEPTUALLY** Use the ability of plants to express a human gene to support evolution of organisms from a common source.
14. Gene pharming uses
    a. genetically engineered farm animals to produce therapeutic drugs.
    b. DNA polymerase to produce many copies of targeted genes.
    c. restriction enzymes to alter bacterial genomes.
    d. All of these are correct.
15. A farmer decides to clone a GM goat that produces a GM product because
    a. it takes a lot of tries to get more GM goats from scratch.
    b. he prefers the coloration of the GM goat.
    c. it's more likely to produce GM goats than by breeding them.
    d. Both a and c are correct.
16. Gene therapy has been used to treat which of the following conditions?
    a. cystic fibrosis
    b. familial hypercholesterolemia
    c. severe combined immunodeficiency
    d. All of these are correct.
17. The use of both ex vivo and in vivo gene therapy shows that
    a. only one type of therapy will be successful.
    b. there is more than one way to introduce beneficial genes into the body.
    c. human cells will take up beneficial genes directly or by using a viral vector.
    d. researchers can't make up their minds.
    e. Both b and c are correct.
18. **THINKING CONCEPTUALLY** Explain why gene therapy researchers prefer to genetically modify the stem cells of white blood cells, as opposed to the white blood cells themselves.

The Human Genome Can Be Studied

19. Which of the following is not required for the polymerase chain reaction?
    a. DNA polymerase   c. a DNA sample
    b. RNA polymerase   d. nucleotides
20. Today, the polymerase chain reaction (PCR)
    a. uses RNA polymerase.
    b. takes place in huge bioreactors.
    c. uses a heat-tolerant enzyme.
    d. makes lots of nonidentical copies of DNA.
21. DNA amplified by PCR could come from
    a. any diploid or haploid cell.
    b. only white blood cells that have been karyotyped.
    c. only skin cells after they are dead.
    d. only purified animal cells.
    e. Both b and d are correct.

22. **THINKING CONCEPTUALLY** You have 30 dinosaur genes. Explain why it would be impossible to create a dinosaur, even by using PCR to increase the quantity of each gene.
23. Because of the Human Genome Project, we know
    a. the sequence of the base pairs of our DNA.
    b. the sequence of all genes along the human chromosomes.
    c. all the mutations that lead to genetic disorders.
    d. All of these are correct.
    e. Only a and c are correct.
24. Which of these pairs is mismatched?
    a. repetitive DNA—tandem repeats and interspersed repeats
    b. tandem repeats—ACGACGACG
    c. transposons—jumping genes
    d. introns—same as exons
    e. Both a and c are mismatched.
25. Repetitive DNA could
    a. be the source of small RNAs that play a regulatory role in cells.
    b. account for an RNA network necessary to our complexity.
    c. be more important than formerly thought.
    d. All of these are correct.
26. Which of these pairs is mismatched?
    a. genome—all the genes of an individual
    b. proteome—all the proteins in an individual
    c. bioinformatics—all the genetic information present in the organism
    d. genetic profile—includes the mutations of an individual
27. The field of comparative genomics is not concerned with
    a. the function of gene products.
    b. the number of genes in various organisms.
    c. who is related to whom.
    d. how to cure human genetic diseases.

28. Which of these is a true statement?
    a. The complexity of an organism does not necessarily correlate with the number of coding genes.
    b. Genomes do not contain both coding and noncoding DNA.
    c. Bioinformatics is not used as a tool for studying genomes.
    d. Alternative splicing of existing genes is not possible.
29. If you knew the sequence of genes on the chromosomes,
    a. it would reveal which genes are active in which cells.
    b. it would reveal how genes are regulated in a cell.
    c. more genes could be isolated and used for gene therapy.
    d. All of these are correct.

THINKING SCIENTIFICALLY

1. Design an experiment based on Figure 12.4B that would allow you to determine where a dominant gene for "tailless" is located on mouse chromosome 10.
2. When doing a gene therapy study, what is the advantage of utilizing an ex vivo instead of an in vivo procedure? See Section 12.5.

ONLINE RESOURCE

www.mhhe.com/maderconcepts2

Enhance your study with animations that bring concepts to life and practice tests to assess your understanding. Your instructor may also recommend the interactive eBook, individualized learning tools, and more.

CONNECTING THE CONCEPTS

This chapter is divided into the study of biotechnology and genomics. Biotechnology is the use of organisms for the benefit of human beings, reproductive cloning is an extension of artificial selection during which humans choose which animals and plants will reproduce. Therapeutic cloning uses a human embryo as a source of stem cells to produce tissues. The use of induced pluripotent skin cells (see p. 152) may do away with the need to use embryonic stem cells or adult stem cells for this purpose.

Recombinant DNA (rDNA) technology allows researchers to use bacteria to clone a human gene and produce GM products such as vaccines, hormones, and growth factors for use in humans. Being able to acquire a source of human genes has led to the production of GM plants and animals and gene therapy in humans. Today, plants and animals are also engineered to make a product or to possess desired characteristics. Gene therapy offers the promise of curing human genetic disorders, such as muscular dystrophy, cystic fibrosis, hemophilia, and many others.

We now know the sequence of the bases in the human genome, thanks to the use of automated PCR and DNA base sequencers. Our genome contains only about 20,000–25,000 protein-coding DNA

sequences, even though it is 3 billion base pairs long. Research indicates that 98% of our genome is noncoding and consists largely of introns and repetitive DNA, which includes transposons (see p. 205). Researchers are now scrambling to discover the usefulness of noncoding DNA, much of which is apparently transcribed into RNA. Could it be that a vast RNA regulatory network accounts for the complexity of humans?

The alteration of species as a result of genetic changes is one of the definitions of evolution, the topic of Part III. Charles Darwin, who knew nothing about genes, was the first to present significant evidence that evolution occurs.

PUT THE PIECES TOGETHER

1. Biotechnology is correctly named because it is applied biology. How so?
2. List at least three types of evidence for a vast RNA regulatory network that accounts for our complexity. (See pp. 218–219.)
3. Why might laypeople object to both biotechnology and genomics?

Part III

Enhance your understanding of evolution and diversity through media and applications!

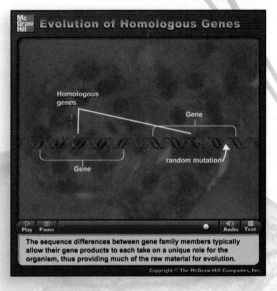

The image within shows a media player titled "Evolution of Homologous Genes" with labels: Homologous genes, Gene, random mutation, Gene. Caption: "The sequence differences between gene family members typically allow their gene products to each take on a unique role for the organism, thus providing much of the raw material for evolution." Copyright © The McGraw-Hill Companies, Inc.

Organisms Are Related and Adapted to Their Environment

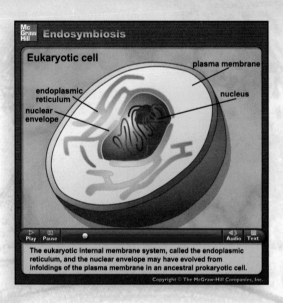

The eukaryotic internal membrane system, called the endoplasmic reticulum, and the nuclear envelope may have evolved from infoldings of the plasma membrane in an ancestral prokaryotic cell.

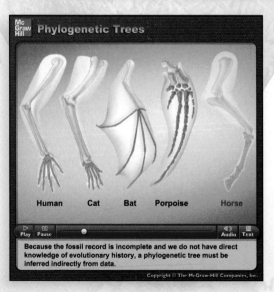

Because the fossil record is incomplete and we do not have direct knowledge of evolutionary history, a phylogenetic tree must be inferred indirectly from data.

Applications

13

Darwin and Evolution

CHAPTER OUTLINE

APPLICATIONS

The "Vice Versa" of Animals and Plants

Adaptations provide powerful evidence for evolution. Bacteria that are able to survive and reproduce in the presence of an antibiotic have become adapted to their environment. Penguins are birds adapted to swimming in the ocean, and bats are mammals that can fly due to wings made of skin stretched over long fingers.

Insects are adapted to taking nectar from particular plants. It might seem as if bees go to all flowers, but they don't. They prefer sweet-smelling flowers with ultraviolet shadings that lead them to where nectar, a surgery liquid that serves as food, can be found. The bee feeding apparatus is a long, specialized tongue, called a proboscis, that is just the right size to reach down into a narrow floral tube where the nectar is located. As the bee goes about the business of feeding, pollen clings to its hairy body, and then as the bee moves from flower to flower of the species to which it is adapted, the pollen is distributed. Why does a flower provide the bee with nectar? By providing bees with nectar, flowers are helping to ensure their reproduction.

The orchid *Ophrys apifera* has a unique appearance that causes a bumblebee to visit it. The center of the flower looks like a female bumblebee is resting there. Actually, this is due to a petal that resembles a bumblebee. Occasionally, a male bee tries to mate with the petal, and when it does, it gets dusted with pollen, which the male bee takes to the next flower of this species.

Butterflies tend to feed from colorful composite flowers that provide them with a flat landing platform. Each individual flower of the composite has a floral tube that allows

Honey bee pollinated flower

packet of pollen

petal resembles
a female bumblebee

Bumblebee-pollinated flower,
Ophrys elegans

flat landing
platform

Butterfly-
pollinated
flower

long thin beak

hummingbirds
hover

floral tube with
curved back margins

Hummingbird-pollinated flower

proboscis

hawk moth hovers

Hawk moth
pollinated flower

the long, thin butterfly proboscis to reach the nectar. Hummingbirds flap their wings rapidly—called hovering—in order to remain in one spot while they feed during the day from odorless, red flowers that curve backward. A hummingbird's long, thin beak can access the nectar through a slender floral tube.

Moth-pollinated flowers are white, pale yellow, or pink—colors that are visible at night, when moths are active. The flowers give off a strong, sweet perfume that attracts moths, which hover as they extend a long, thin proboscis to gather the nectar at the base of a floral tube. The Madagascar star orchid (*Angraecum sesquipedale*) has a very long floral tube that holds its nectar much like a long, thin goblet would hold a drink. When Darwin first saw a picture of this orchid, he exclaimed, "What insect could suck it?" Later, he said in his book on orchids, "In Madagascar there must be moths with proboscises capable of an extension to ten and eleven inches [25.4 cm–27.7 cm]!" Many were skeptical, but Darwin was vindicated when in 1903, the zoologists Lionel Walter Rothschild and Karl Jordan discovered a large hawk moth living in Madagascar that has a proboscis 25–30 cm in length. As the hawk moth approaches the flower, it unrolls its proboscis and inserts it into the floral tube in order to feed.

We begin our study of evolution in this chapter by examining the work of Charles Darwin, who provided evidence that evolution consists of descent from a common ancestor and adaptation to the environment. Further, Darwin offered a mechanism for evolution he called natural selection. He called it natural selection because the environment, in a sense, chooses which members of a population reproduce, and in that way, adaptation to the environment is eventually achieved.

Darwin Developed a Natural Selection Hypothesis

Learning Outcomes

▶ Name two early biologists who attempted to explain evolution but lacked a suitable mechanism. (13.1)

▶ Describe Darwin's trip aboard the HMS Beagle and some of the observations he made. (13.1)

▶ Give examples of artificial selection carried out by human beings. (13.2)

▶ Explain Darwin's hypothesis for natural selection. (13.3)

▶ Tell how Wallace's contribution paralleled that of Darwin's. (13.4)

Other scientists before Darwin hypothesized that evolution occurs, but developed no mechanism. Darwin concluded that evolution occurs after taking a trip around the world as a naturalist aboard the HMS *Beagle*. After studying artificial selection and the work of Thomas Malthus, Darwin—and later Alfred Wallace—suggested natural selection as a mechanism for evolution.

13.1 Darwin made a trip around the world

Biologists before Darwin had suggested that evolution occurs. Georges Cuvier, who founded the science of **paleontology,** the study of fossils, knew that fossils showed a succession of different life-forms through time (**Fig. 13.1A**). He hypothesized that a series of past catastrophes (local extinctions) had occurred and that after each one, a region was repopulated by species from surrounding areas. The result of all these catastrophes was change appearing over time.

In contrast to Cuvier, Jean-Baptiste de Lamarck, an invertebrate biologist, concluded on the basis of fossil evidence that more complex organisms are descended from less complex organisms. To explain the process of adaptation to the environment, Lamarck offered the idea of *inheritance of acquired characteristics,* which proposes that use and disuse of a structure can bring about inherited change. One example Lamarck gave—and the one for which he is most famous—is that the long neck of a giraffe developed over time because animals stretched their necks to reach food high in trees and then passed on a longer neck to their offspring (**Fig. 13.1B**).

Neither Cuvier nor Lamarck arrived at a satisfactory explanation for the evolutionary process. The inheritance of acquired characteristics has never been substantiated by experimentation. For example, if acquired characteristics were inherited, people who use tanning machines would have tan children, and people who have LASIK surgery to correct their vision would have children with perfect vision.

However, in December 1831, a new chapter in the history of biology began. A 22-year-old naturalist, Charles Darwin (1809–1882), set sail on the journey of a lifetime aboard the British naval vessel HMS *Beagle* (**Fig. 13.1C**). Darwin's primary mission on this journey around the world was to expand the navy's knowledge of natural resources in foreign lands. The captain of the *Beagle*, Robert Fitzroy, also hoped that Darwin would find evidence to support the biblical account of creation. Contrary to Fitzroy's wishes, Darwin amassed observations that would eventually support another way of thinking and change the history of science and biology forever.

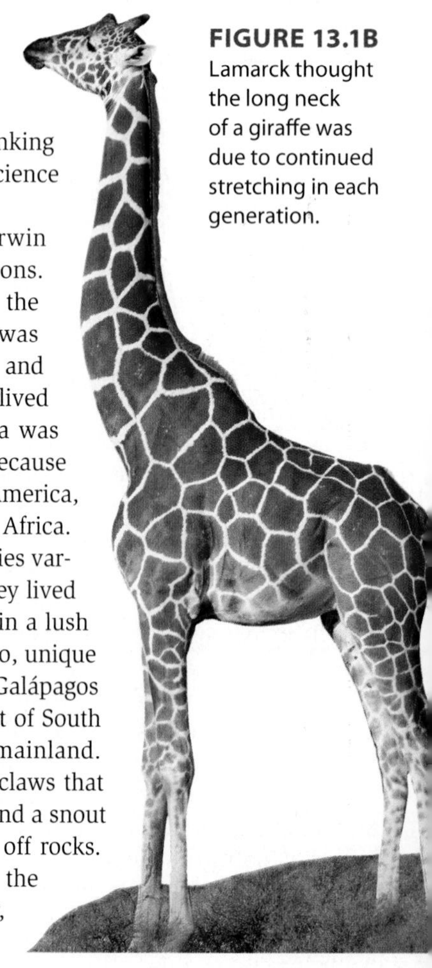

During the trip, Darwin made numerous observations. For example, he noted that the rhea of South America was suited to living on a plain and looked like the ostrich that lived in Africa. However, the rhea was not an ostrich. Why not? Because the rhea evolved in South America, while the ostrich evolved in Africa. Darwin also found that species varied according to whether they lived in the Patagonian desert or in a lush tropical rain forest. Then, too, unique animals lived only on the Galápagos Islands, located off the coast of South America, not on the mainland. A marine iguana had large claws that allowed it to cling to rocks and a snout that enabled it to eat algae off rocks. One type of finch, lacking the long bill of a woodpecker, used a cactus spine to

FIGURE 13.1B Lamarck thought the long neck of a giraffe was due to continued stretching in each generation.

FIGURE 13.1A One of the animals that Cuvier reconstructed from fossils was the mastodon.

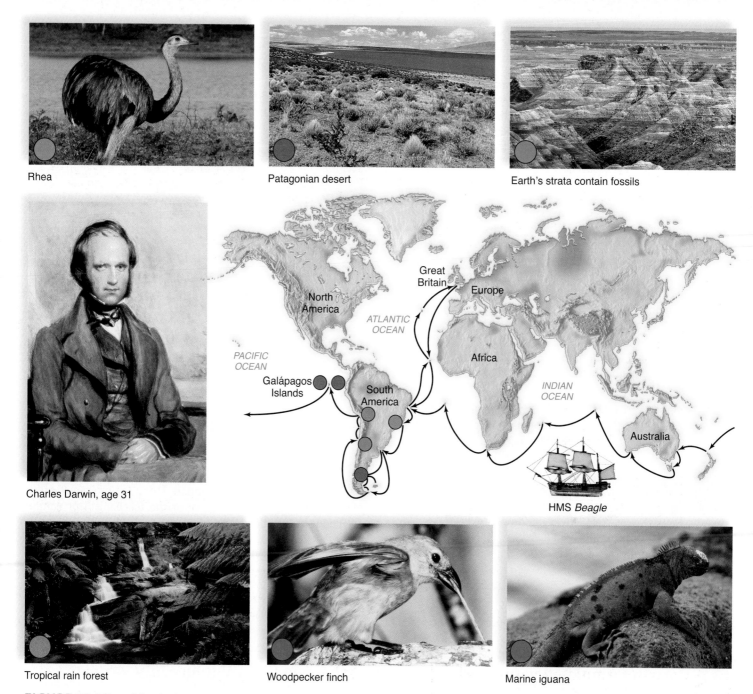

Rhea

Patagonian desert

Earth's strata contain fossils

Charles Darwin, age 31

Great Britain

Europe

North America

ATLANTIC OCEAN

PACIFIC OCEAN

Galápagos Islands

South America

Africa

INDIAN OCEAN

Australia

HMS *Beagle*

Tropical rain forest

Woodpecker finch

Marine iguana

FIGURE 13.1C *Middle:* Charles Darwin and the route of the HMS *Beagle*. Circles pinpoint highlights of Darwin's trip.

probe for insects. Why were these animals found only in the Galápagos Islands? Had they evolved there?

When Darwin explored the region that is now Argentina, he saw raised beaches for great distances along the coast. He thought it would have taken a long time for such massive movements of the Earth's crust to occur. While Darwin was making geologic observations, he also collected fossils that showed today's plants and animals resemble, but are not exactly like, their forebears. Darwin had brought Charles Lyell's *Principles of Geology* on the *Beagle* voyage. This book said that weathering causes erosion and that, thereafter, dirt and rock debris are washed into the rivers and transported to oceans. When these loose sediments are deposited, layers of soil called **strata** (sing., stratum) result. The strata, which

often contain fossils, are uplifted from below sea level to form land. Lyell's book went on to support a **uniformitarianism** hypothesis, which states that geologic changes occur at a uniform rate. This idea of slow geologic change is still accepted today, although modern geologists have concluded that rates of change have not always been uniform. Darwin was convinced that the Earth's massive geologic changes are the result of slow processes and that, therefore, in contrast to thought at that time, the Earth was old enough to have allowed *evolution* to occur.

▶ **13.1 Check Your Progress** Look again at Figure 1.1B, a diagram that illustrates the scientific method. Which part of the diagram applies to Darwin's approach so far?

13.2 Artificial selection mimics natural selection

Darwin made a study of **artificial selection,** a process by which humans choose, on the basis of certain traits, the animals and plants that will reproduce. For example, foxes are very shy and normally shun the company of people, but in 40 years time, Russian scientists have produced silver foxes that now allow themselves to be petted and even seek attention (**Fig. 13.2A**). They did this by selecting the most docile animals to reproduce. The scientists noted that some physical characteristics changed as well. The legs and tails became shorter, the ears became floppier, and the coat color patterns changed. Artificial selection is only possible because the original population exhibits a range of characteristics, allowing humans to select which traits they prefer to perpetuate.

To take another example, several varieties of vegetables can be traced to a single ancestor that exhibits various characteristics. Chinese cabbage, brussels sprouts, and kohlrabi are all derived from one species of wild mustard (**Fig. 13.2B**). Cabbage was produced by selecting for reproduction only plants that had overlapping leaves; brussels sprouts came from crossing only plants with certain types of buds; and kohlrabi was produced by crossing only the plants that had enlarged stems.

Chinese cabbage   Brussels sprouts   Kohlrabi

Wild mustard

FIGURE 13.2B These three vegetables came from the wild mustard plant through artificial selection.

FIGURE 13.2A Artificial selection has produced domesticated foxes.

Darwin thought that a process of selection might occur in nature without human intervention. Using the process of artificial selection helped him arrive at the mechanism of natural selection, which allows evolution to occur.

In Section 13.3, we see that Darwin was also influenced by Thomas Malthus when he formulated natural selection as a mechanism for evolution.

> **13.2 Check Your Progress** If you wanted to use artificial selection to achieve a particular type of flower, would you allow the flower to pollinate naturally?

13.3 Darwin formulated natural selection as a mechanism for evolution

Darwin was very much impressed by an essay written by Thomas Malthus about the reproductive potential of human beings. Malthus had proposed that death and famine are inevitable because the human population tends to increase faster than the supply of food. Darwin applied this concept to all organisms and saw that available resources were insufficient for all members of a population to survive. For example, he calculated the reproductive potential of elephants. Assuming a life span of about 100 years and a breeding span of 30–90 years, a single female probably bears no fewer than six young. If all these young survive and continue to reproduce at the same rate, after only 750 years, the descendants of a single pair of elephants would number about 19 million! Each generation has the same reproductive potential as the previous generation. Therefore, Darwin hypothesized, there is a constant struggle for existence, and only certain members of a population survive and reproduce in each generation.

What members might those be? The members that have some advantage and are best able to compete successfully for limited resources.

Applying Darwin's thinking to giraffes, we can see that long-necked giraffes would be better able to feed off leaves in trees than short-necked giraffes. The longer neck gives giraffes an advantage that, in the end, would allow them to produce more offspring than short-necked giraffes. So, eventually, all the members of a giraffe population (individuals of a species in one locale) would have long necks. Or, what about bacteria living in an environment of antibiotics? The few bacteria that can survive in this environment have a tremendous advantage, and therefore their offspring will make up the next generation of bacteria, and this strain of bacteria will be resistant to the antibiotic.

Darwin called the process by which organisms with an advantage reproduce more than others of their kind **natural** selection because some aspect of the environment acts as a **selective agent** and chooses the members of the population with the advantageous phenotype to reproduce more than the other members.

Natural selection has these essential components:

- *The members of a population have inheritable variations.* For example, a wide range of differences exists among the members of a population. Many of these variations are inheritable. Inheritance of variations is absolutely essential to Darwin's hypothesis, even though he did not know the means by which inheritance occurs.
- *A population is able to produce more offspring than the environment can support.* The environment contains only so much food and water, places to live, potential mates, and so forth. The environment can't support all the offspring that a population can produce, and each generation is apt to be too large for the environment to support.
- *Only certain members of the population survive and reproduce.* Certain members have an advantage suited to the environment that allows them to capture more resources than other members, as when long-necked giraffes are better able to browse on tree leaves. This advantage allows these members of the population to survive and produce more offspring. This is called differential reproduction because the members of a population differ as to how many surviving offspring they will have.
- *Natural selection results in a population adapted to the local environment.* In each succeeding generation, an increasing proportion of individuals will have the adaptive characteristics—the characteristics suited to surviving and reproducing in that environment (**Fig. 13.3**).

FIGURE 13.3 The brightly colored tree frog can hide among tropical plants where the large red eyes confuse predators. The frog climbs trees and other plants assisted by toes with suction cups.

Now it is possible to form a definition of evolution. **Evolution** consists of changes in a population over time due to the accumulation of inherited differences. Evolution explains the unity and diversity of organisms. "Unity" means organisms share the same characteristics of life because they share a common ancestry, traceable even to the first cell or cells. "Diversity" comes about because each type of organism (each species) is adapted to one of the many different environments in the biosphere (e.g., oceans, deserts, mountains, etc.).

Independently, Alfred Wallace also arrived at natural selection as a mechanism for evolution, as explained next.

▶ **13.3 Check Your Progress** Why is it advantageous for a plant to have a flower structure suited to a particular pollinator?

13.4 Wallace independently formulated a natural selection hypothesis

Like Darwin, Alfred Russel Wallace (1823–1913) was a naturalist. While he was a schoolteacher at Leicester in 1844–1845, he met Henry Walter Bates, a biologist who interested him in insects. Together, they went on a collecting trip to the Amazon that lasted several years. Wallace's knowledge of the world's flora and fauna was further expanded by a tour he made of the Malay Archipelago from 1854 to 1862. Later, he divided the islands into a western group and an eastern group on the basis of their different plants and animals. The dividing line between these islands is a narrow but deep strait now known as the Wallace Line.

Just as Darwin had done, Wallace wrote articles and books that clearly showed his belief that species change over time and it was possible for new species to evolve. Later, he said he had pondered for many years about a mechanism to explain the origin of a species. He, too, had read Malthus's essay on human population increases, and in 1858, while suffering an attack of malaria, the idea of "survival of the fittest" came upon him. He quickly completed an essay outlining a natural selection process, which he chose to send to Darwin for comment. Darwin was stunned upon its receipt. Here before him was the hypothesis he had formulated as early as 1844, but never published.

Darwin told his friend and colleague Charles Lyell that Wallace's ideas were so similar to his own that even Wallace's "terms now stand as heads of my chapters" in the book he had begun in 1856.

Darwin suggested that Wallace's paper be published immediately, even though he himself had nothing in print yet. Lyell and others who knew of Darwin's detailed work substantiating the process of natural selection suggested that a joint paper be read to the Linnean Society. The title of Wallace's section was "On the Tendency of Varieties to Depart Indefinitely from the Original Type." Darwin allowed the abstract of a paper he had written in 1844 and an abstract of his book *On the Origin of Species* to be read. This book was published in 1859.

By now, evolution by natural selection has been supported by so many observations and experiments that it is considered a theory rather than a hypothesis. Modern investigators have shown that it is possible to observe the process of natural selection, as described in the How Science Progresses on the next page.

▶ **13.4 Check Your Progress** Did the work of Wallace lend support to the natural selection hypothesis? Explain.

13A Natural Selection Can Be Witnessed

Darwin formed his natural selection hypothesis, in part, by observing the adaptations of tortoises and finches on the Galápagos Islands. Tortoises with domed shells and short necks live on well-watered islands, where grass is available. Those with shells that flare up in front have long necks and are able to feed on tall cacti. They live on arid islands, where treelike prickly-pear cactus is the main food source. Similarly, the islands are home to many different types of finches (**Fig. 13A.1**). The heavy beak of the large, ground-dwelling finch is suited to a diet of seeds. The beak of the warbler-finch is suited to feeding on insects found among ground vegetation or caught in the air. The longer, somewhat more pointed beak and split tongue of the cactus-finch are suited for probing cactus flowers for nectar.

Beak Size and Natural Selection

Today, investigators, such as Peter and Rosemary Grant of Princeton University, are actually watching natural selection as it occurs. In 1973, the Grants began a study of the various finches on Daphne Major, near the center of the Galápagos Islands. The weather swung widely back and forth from wet years to dry years, and they found that the beak size of the medium ground finch, *Geospiza fortis,* adapted to each weather swing, generation after generation (**Fig. 13A.2**). These finches like to eat small, tender seeds that require a smaller beak, but when the weather turns dry, they have to eat larger, drier seeds, which are harder to crush. Then, the birds that have a larger beak depth have an advantage and produce more offspring. Dry weather acts as a selective agent for a *G. fortis* beak size that has more depth than in the previous generation.

Silent Crickets and Natural Selection

A research team led by Marlene Zuk, a professor of biology, reported that prior to 2001 the Hawaiian field cricket population (*Teleogryllus oceanicus*) on the island of Kauai contained very few silent males. Chirping males have a wing structure that produces the chirping sound that attracts females. By 2006, over 90% of male crickets were silent because their wings were flat and unable to produce the chirping sound. In just 20 generations, the population had undergone this dramatic evolutionary change due to a particular selective agent that caused the silent phenotype to be advantageous. A deadly parasitic fly (*Ormia ochracea*) uses the male crickets' chirping as a way to locate them. The fly deposits her eggs on a male cricket's back, and they develop into maggots. Over a week's time, the maggots eat the cricket's internal organs and then emerge from its dead body to undergo metamorphosis into adult flies. The silent males were not parasitized and increased in number because many of them mated with females and passed on their genes. How did they do it? The silent males wait near any remaining chirping males and intercept incoming females. Normally, female crickets will not accept a male until he completes a final mating song, but even that is beginning to change and females will now accept silent males, thereby allowing them to increase in number.

A ground-dwelling finch feeds on seeds.

A cactus-finch probes flowers for nectar.

FIGURE 13A.1 Finches on the Galápagos Islands.

A warbler-finch feeds on insects.

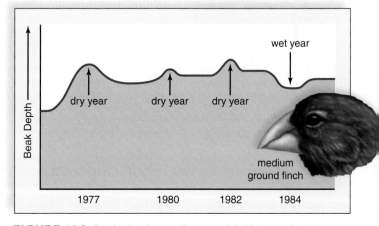

FIGURE 13A.2 The beak size of a ground finch varies from generation to generation, according to the weather.

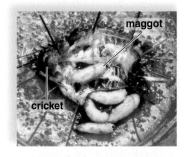

FIGURE 13A.3 Maggots feeding on a cricket.

FORM YOUR OPINION

1. Cite some examples of natural selection that involve resistance to drugs or pesticides. Now that we know how powerful natural selection can be, how can we keep resistance from happening?

2. Today's drug designers biochemically create drugs for a particular purpose, and then they keep testing and selecting which ones to improve. Is this natural selection at work?

Population Genetics Tells Us When Microevolution Occurs

Learning Outcomes

▶ Tell how the human population has microvariations. (13.10)

▶ Use the Hardy-Weinberg principle to explain when microevolution occurs. (13.11)

▶ Explain how mutations, nonrandom mating, gene flow, genetic drift, and natural selection contribute to the process of microevolution. (13.12–13.15)

▶ Name three kinds of natural selection, and discuss the effect of each on a population. (13.15)

▶ Give an example to show that stabilizing selection can maintain heterozygotes in a population. (13.16)

Microevolution is evolution beneath the species level. The Hardy-Weinberg principle states that allele frequencies in a population, calculated by using the equation $p^2 + 2pq + q^2$, will stay constant generation after generation, unless evolution occurs. Usually evolution, defined as an allele frequency change, does occur.

13.10 The human population is diverse

Darwin stressed that diversity exists among the members of a population. A **population** is all the members of a single species occupying a particular area at the same time; even the human population has local populations (**Fig. 13.10**). All humans are the same species, as can be witnessed by the fact that any two ethnicities can reproduce and produce healthy offspring. Genomic studies have allowed investigators to discover that much of the genomic diversity of humans is due to microvariations such as **single nucleotide polymorphisms** (differences), or **SNPs** (pronounced "snips"). These are DNA sequences that differ by a single nucleotide. For example, compare ACGTACGTA to ACGTACCTA and notice that there is only a single base difference between the two sequences. Investigators would say that the SNP has two alleles—in this case, G and C. SNPs generally have two alleles.

SNPs that occur within a protein-coding DNA sequence may or may not result in a changed sequence of amino acids, due to the redundancy of the genetic code (see Fig. 10.4B). SNPs that do not result in a changed amino acid sequence may still cause regulatory differences. Therefore, SNPs are now thought to be an important source of genetic diversity among humans. Another interesting finding is that humans inherit patterns of base sequence differences now called haplotypes (from the terms haploid and genotype). To take an example, if a chromatid has a G rather than a C at a particular location, this change is most likely accompanied by other base differences near the G. Researchers are in the process of discovering the most common haplotypes among African, Asian, and European populations. They want to link haplotypes to the risk of specific illnesses, hoping this will lead to new methods of preventing, diagnosing, and treating disease. Also, certain haplotypes may respond better than others to particular medicines, vaccines, and other treatment strategies.

▶ **13.10 Check Your Progress** Why is it important for the members of a population to be both genetically similar but also different?

FIGURE 13.10 The HapMap project compares DNA sequences among African, Asian, and European populations to discover unique base sequence differences.

13.11 A Hardy-Weinberg equilibrium is not expected

Not until the 1930s were population geneticists able to apply the principles of genetics to populations and thereafter develop a way to recognize when microevolution has occurred. The **gene pool** of a population is composed of all the alleles in all the individuals making up the population. When the allele frequencies for a population change, microevolution has occurred. Microevolution does not necessarily result in a visible change but let's take an example that does.

A peppered moth can be light-colored or dark-colored. Suppose you research the literature and find that the color of peppered moths is controlled by a single set of alleles, and you decide to use the following key: D = dark color and d = light color. Furthermore, you find that in one Great Britain population, only 4% (0.04) of the moths are homozygous dominant (DD), 32% (0.32) are heterozygous (Dd), and 64% (0.64) are homozygous recessive (dd). From these genotype frequencies, you can calculate the allele frequencies, in the population:

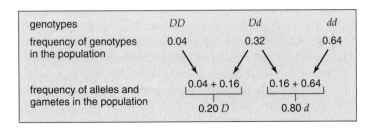

The frequency of the gametes (sperm and egg) produced by this population will necessarily be the same as the allele frequencies. Assuming random mating (all possible gametes have an equal chance to combine with any other), we can use these gamete frequencies to calculate the ratio of genotypes in the next generation by using a Punnett square (**Fig. 13.11**).

There is an important difference between a Punnett square that represents a cross between individuals and the one shown in Figure 13.11. In Figure 13.11, we are using the gamete frequencies in the population to determine the genotype frequencies in the next generation. As you can see, the results show that the genotype frequencies (and therefore the allele frequencies) in the next generation are the same as they were in the previous generation. In other words, the homozygous dominant moths are still 0.04; the heterozygous moths are still 0.32; and the homozygous recessive moths are still 0.64 of the population. This remarkable finding tells us that *sexual reproduction alone cannot bring about a change in genotype and allele frequencies.* Also, the dominant allele need not increase from one generation to the next. Dominance does not cause an allele to become a common allele.

The potential constancy, or equilibrium state, of gene pool frequencies was independently recognized in 1908 by G. H. Hardy, an English mathematician, and W. Weinberg, a German physician. They used the binomial equation ($p^2 + 2pq + q^2 = 1$) to calculate the genotype and allele frequencies of a population, as illustrated in Figure 13.11. From their findings, they formulated the **Hardy-Weinberg principle,** which states that an equilibrium of allele frequencies in a gene pool will remain in effect in each

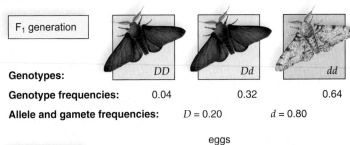

F_1 generation			
Genotypes:	DD	Dd	dd
Genotype frequencies:	0.04	0.32	0.64
Allele and gamete frequencies:	$D = 0.20$	$d = 0.80$	

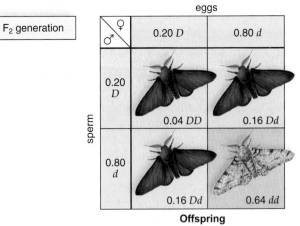

Genotype frequencies: $0.04\ DD + 0.32\ Dd + 0.64\ dd = 1$

$p^2 + 2pq + q^2 = 1$

p^2 = frequency of DD genotype (dark-colored) = $(0.20)^2$ = 0.04

$2pq$ = frequency of Dd genotype (dark-colored) = $2(0.20)(0.80)$ = 0.32

q^2 = frequency of dd genotype (light-colored) = $(0.80)^2$ = 0.64

1.00

FIGURE 13.11 Calculating gene pool frequencies for F_1 and F_2.

succeeding generation of a sexually reproducing population as long as five conditions are met:

1. No mutations: Allele changes do not occur, or changes in one direction are balanced by changes in the opposite direction.
2. No gene flow: Migration of alleles into or out of the population does not occur.
3. Random mating: Individuals pair by chance, not according to their genotypes or phenotypes.
4. No genetic drift: The population is very large, and changes in allele frequencies due to chance alone are insignificant.
5. No natural selection: No selective agent favors one genotype over another.

In real life, these conditions are rarely met, if ever, and allele frequencies in the gene pool of a population do change from one generation to the next. For example, when the trees darken due to industrial pollution, gene pool frequencies change because predatory birds (the selective agent) can find and therefore eat light-colored moths. The dark melanic color becomes common among moth populations. This is called **industrial melanism.**

▶ **13.11 Check Your Progress** How do you know when microevolution has occurred?

13.12 Both mutations and sexual recombination produce variations

The Hardy-Weinberg principle recognizes mutation as a force that can cause allele frequencies to change in a gene pool and cause microevolution to occur. **Mutations,** which are permanent genetic changes, are the raw material for evolutionary change because, without mutations, there could be no inheritable phenotypic variations among members of a population. The rate of mutations is generally very low—on the order of one per 100,000 cell divisions. Also, it is important to realize that evolution is not goal-oriented, meaning that no mutation arises because the organism "needs" one. For example, the mutation that causes bacteria to be resistant was already present before antibiotics appeared in the environment.

Mutations are the primary source of genetic differences among prokaryotes that reproduce asexually. Generation time is so short that many mutations can occur quickly, even though the rate is low, and since these organisms are haploid, any mutation that results in a phenotypic change is immediately tested by the environment. In diploid organisms, a recessive mutation can remain hidden and become significant only when a homozygous recessive genotype arises. The importance of recessive alleles increases if the environment is changing; it's possible that the homozygous recessive genotype could be helpful in a new environment, if not the present one. It's even possible that natural selection will maintain a recessive allele if the heterozygote has advantages (see Section 13.16).

In sexually reproducing organisms, sexual recombination is just as important as mutation in generating phenotypic differences, because sexual recombination can bring together a new and different combination of alleles. This new combination might produce a more successful phenotype. Success, of course, is judged by the environment and counted by the relative number of healthy offspring an organism produces.

Nonrandom mating and gene flow are possible causes of microevolution, as discussed in Section 13.13.

▶ **13.12 Check Your Progress** Would you expect mutations to have helped flowers become adapted to a particular pollinator? Explain.

13.13 Nonrandom mating and gene flow can contribute to microevolution

Random mating occurs when individuals pair by chance. You make sure random mating occurs when you do a genetic cross on paper or in the lab, and cross all possible types of sperm with all possible types of eggs. **Nonrandom mating** occurs when only certain genotypes or phenotypes mate with one another. **Assortative mating** is a type of nonrandom mating that occurs when individuals mate with those having the *same* phenotype with respect to a certain characteristic. For example, flowers such as the garden pea usually self-pollinate—therefore, the same phenotype has mated with the same phenotype (**Fig. 13.13A**). Assortative mating can also be observed in human society. Men and women tend to marry individuals with characteristics such as intelligence and height that are similar to their own. Assortative mating causes homozygotes for certain gene loci to increase in frequency and heterozygotes for these loci to decrease in frequency.

Gene flow, also called gene migration, is the movement of alleles between populations. When animals move between populations or when pollen is distributed between species (**Fig. 13.13B**), gene flow has occurred. When gene flow brings a new or rare allele into the population, the allele frequency in the next generation changes. When gene flow between adjacent populations is constant, allele frequencies continue to change until an equilibrium is reached. Therefore, continued gene flow tends to make the gene pools similar and reduce the possibility of allele frequency differences between populations.

Genetic drift is another possible cause of microevolution, as discussed in Section 13.14.

▶ **13.13 Check Your Progress** Create a scenario in which assortative mating causes flowers to become adapted to their pollinators.

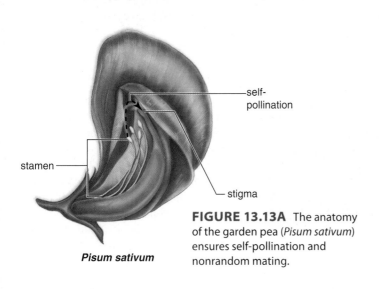

FIGURE 13.13A The anatomy of the garden pea (*Pisum sativum*) ensures self-pollination and nonrandom mating.

Pisum sativum

self-pollination

stamen

stigma

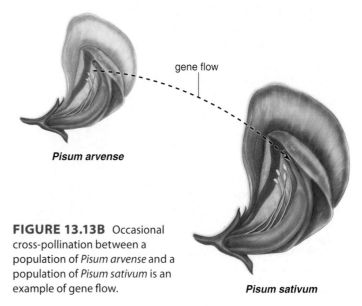

Pisum arvense

gene flow

Pisum sativum

FIGURE 13.13B Occasional cross-pollination between a population of *Pisum arvense* and a population of *Pisum sativum* is an example of gene flow.

13B Sometimes Mutations Are Beneficial

Imagine trying to redesign a vital mechanical part of an airplane, while still keeping that plane in flight. Sounds nearly impossible, doesn't it? This was one of the puzzles facing early evolutionary biologists. After all, mutations are the main way in which new traits and features arise during evolution, and yet most mutations cause damage. If a feature is important, how can it be altered while still allowing an organism and its offspring to survive?

Geneticists have shown one possible way mutations can accumulate without impairing present function: gene duplication (**Fig. 13B.1**). An extra (and possibly unused) copy of a gene may result from errors during cell division, efforts to repair breakage to DNA, or other mechanisms. The surprising idea here is that these seeming accidents actually can provide raw material for natural selection. Particularly in plants, many examples of gene duplication have been found—for example, the wild mustard plant has undergone at least two duplications of *all* its chromosomes in the past, as well as duplication of several individual genes at various times in history.

An intriguing example of gene duplication involves the sweet-tasting proteins. Of the thousands of proteins studied so far, most have no noticeable flavor—but about half a dozen have an intensely sweet taste. These rare, sweet-tasting proteins are found in plants and plant products from several different continents: The protein "curculin" is found in the fruit of a Malaysian herb (**Fig. 13B.2**); "mabinlin" can be extracted from a traditional Chinese herb; "thaumatin" is found in the fruit of a West African rain forest shrub; and "brazzein" comes from a fruit that grows wild in Gabon, Cameroon, and Zaire. Each of these proteins tastes sweet only to humans and certain monkeys. From the plant's point of view, the proteins likely provided an advantage: Sweeter fruits would be eaten more often and their seeds distributed more widely, ensuring the growth of more plants with genes for making sweet proteins. A question still remains: How did these unusual proteins come about?

No one yet knows exactly how these proteins originated, but gene duplication is a likely answer. The proteins look nothing alike, are found in unrelated plants, and clearly did not come from some ancient shared plant gene. Each protein, however, does resemble other proteins normally found in healthy plants. Brazzein and mabinlin, for example, closely resemble "proteinase inhibitors," proteins that can help prevent further damage when a plant is injured. Interestingly, however, neither sweet protein has that function. Similar stories are true of most sweet-tasting proteins: They closely resemble other plant proteins with ordinary functions, but the sequences necessary for those other functions seem to be missing or mutated. It's as though pre-existing genes were recycled to become genes for sweet proteins. Presumably a gene duplication in the distant past resulted in an "extra" gene that could mutate freely, while still leaving a "good" copy of the gene to support the plant's functions. In time, the extra copy of the gene acquired mutations that happened to provide a sweet taste, and plants with that mutation gained a special appeal for local diners.

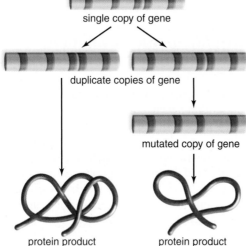

FIGURE 13B.1 Duplication of a gene followed by a mutation in one of the genes is a way for complexity to arise: The new protein might function differently than the original one.

A *Curculigo* plant   The fruits develop at base of leaves.

FIGURE 13B.2 The sweet protein curculin is present in the fruit of a *Curculigo* plant.

FORM YOUR OPINION

1. Humans and perhaps apes and monkeys like sweet foods. How does this benefit plants containing sweet proteins?
2. Are humans influencing the evolution of plants when they propagate them? When they genetically modify them and then propagate them?
3. In what way is artificial selection harmful to the plants and animals selected to reproduce?

above waterfall

below waterfall

a. Experimental site

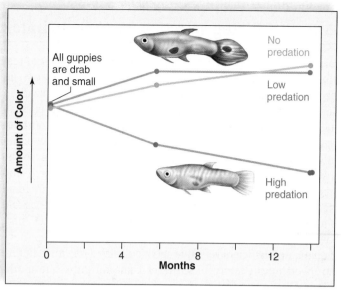

No predation

All guppies are drab and small

Low predation

High predation

Amount of Color

Months

0   4   8   12

b. Result

FIGURE 13.15C Directional selection in guppies.

much less or much greater than usual). When a baby is small, its systems may not be fully functional, and when a baby is large, it may have experienced a difficult delivery. Stabilizing selection reduces the variability in birth weight in human populations (**Fig. 13.15B**).

Directional selection occurs when an extreme phenotype is favored, and the distribution curve shifts in that direction. Such a shift can occur when a population is adapting to a changing environment (Fig. 13.15A*b*).

Two investigators, John Endler and David Reznick, both at the University of California, conducted a study of guppies, which are known for their bright colors and reproductive potential. These investigators noted that on the island of Trinidad, when male guppies are subjected to high predation by other fish, they tend to be drab in color and to mature early and at a smaller size. The drab color and small size are most likely protective against being found and eaten. On the other hand, when male guppies are exposed to minimal or no predation, they tend to be colorful, to mature later, and to attain a larger size.

Endler and Reznick performed many experiments, and one set is of particular interest. They took a supply of guppies from a high-predation area (below a waterfall) and placed them in a low-predation area (above a waterfall) (**Fig. 13.15C***a*). The waterfall prevented the predator fish (pike) from entering the low-predation area. They monitored the guppy population for 12 months, and during that year, the guppy population above the waterfall underwent directional selection (Fig. 13.15C*b*). The male members of the population became colorful and large in size. The members of the guppy population below the waterfall (the control population) remained drab and small.

In **disruptive selection,** two or more extreme phenotypes are favored over any intermediate phenotype (Fig. 13.15A*c, right*). For example, British land snails (*Cepaea nemoralis*) have a wide habitat range that includes low-vegetation areas (grass fields and hedgerows) and forests. In forested areas, thrushes feed mainly on light-banded snails, and the snails with dark shells become more prevalent. In low-vegetation areas, thrushes feed mainly on snails with dark shells, and light-banded snails become more prevalent. Therefore, these two distinctly different phenotypes are found in the population (**Fig. 13.15D**).

Stabilizing selection, discussed in Section 13.16, maintains the heterozygote, especially if it has an advantage over the homozygote, as seen in sickle-cell disease.

▶ **13.15 Check Your Progress** If the flowers of a species are presently only one color and the pollinator prefers this color, is stabilizing selection occurring? Explain.

FIGURE 13.15D Disruptive selection in snails.

Forested areas

Low-lying vegetation

13.16 Stabilizing selection can help maintain the heterozygote

Variations are maintained in a population for any number of reasons. Mutation still creates new alleles, and recombination still recombines these alleles during gametogenesis and fertilization. Gene flow might still occur. If the receiving population is small and mostly homozygous, gene flow can be a significant source of new alleles. Genetic drift also occurs, particularly in small populations, and the end result may be contrary to adaptation to the environment. Natural selection never starts from scratch and therefore the result is often a compromise. An erect posture freed the hands of humans but subjected the spine to injury because it is imperfectly adapted. But the benefit of freeing the hands must have been worth the risk of spinal injuries or it would not have evolved. An inefficient selective agent can play a role in maintaining diversity; predatory birds never catch all the white moths when pollutants darken the vegetation. A changing environment retains the ability of the medium ground finch on the Galapagos island to change its beak size as appropriate to the food supply. Clearly, the maintenance of variation among a population has survival value for the species. Here, we consider that heterozygote superiority in a particular environment can assist the maintenance of genetic, and therefore phenotypic, variations in future generations.

Sickle-cell Disease Sickle-cell disease can be a devastating condition. Patients may have severe anemia, physical weakness, poor circulation, impaired mental function, pain and high fever, rheumatism, paralysis, spleen damage, low resistance to disease, and kidney and heart failure. In these individuals, the red blood cells are sickle-shaped and tend to pile up and block flow through tiny capillaries. The condition is due to an abnormal form of hemoglobin (Hb), the molecule that carries oxygen in red blood cells. People with sickle-cell disease (Hb^SHb^S) tend to die early and leave few offspring, due to hemorrhaging and organ destruction. Interestingly, however, geneticists studying the distribution of sickle-cell disease in Africa have found that the recessive allele (Hb^S) has a higher frequency in regions (purple color) where the disease malaria is also prevalent (**Fig. 13.16**). Malaria is caused by a protozoan parasite that lives in and destroys the red blood cells of the normal homozygote (Hb^AHb^A). Individuals with this genotype have fewer offspring, due to an early death or to debilitation caused by malaria.

People who are heterozygous (Hb^AHb^S) have an advantage over both homozygous genotypes because they don't die from sickle-cell disease and they don't die from malaria. The parasite causes any red blood cell it infects in these individuals to become sickle-shaped. Sickle-shaped red blood cells lose potassium, and this causes the parasite to die. **Heterozygote advantage** causes all three alleles to be maintained in the population. It's as if natural selection were a store owner balancing the advantages and disadvantages of maintaining the recessive allele Hb^S in the warehouse. As long as the protozoan that causes malaria is present in the environment, it is advantageous to maintain the recessive allele, as shown in the following table:

Genotype	Phenotype	Result
Hb^AHb^A	Normal	Dies due to malarial infection
Hb^AHb^S	Sickle-cell trait	Lives due to protection from both
Hb^SHb^S	Sickle-cell disease	Dies due to sickle-cell disease

Heterozygote advantage is also an example of stabilizing selection because the genotype Hb^AHb^S is favored over the two extreme genotypes, Hb^AHb^A and Hb^SHb^S. In the parts of Africa where malaria is common, one in five individuals is heterozygous (has sickle-cell trait) and survives malaria, while only 1 in 100 is homozygous, Hb^SHb^S, and dies of sickle-cell disease.

What happens in the United States where malaria is not prevalent? As you would expect, the frequency of the Hb^S allele is declining among African Americans because the heterozygote has no particular advantage in this country.

Cystic Fibrosis Stabilizing selection is also thought to have influenced the frequency of other alleles. Cystic fibrosis is a debilitating condition that leads to lung infections and digestive difficulties. In this instance, the recessive allele, common among individuals of northwestern European descent, causes the person to have a defective plasma membrane protein. The agent that causes typhoid fever can use the normal version of this protein, but not the defective one, to enter cells. Here again, heterozygote superiority caused the recessive allele to be maintained in the population.

▶ **13.16 Check Your Progress** Could heterozygote advantage be used to show that natural selection does not always favor the dominant genotype?

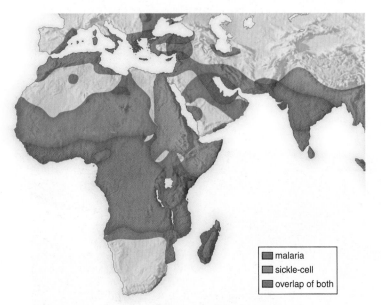

FIGURE 13.16 Sickle-cell disease is more prevalent in areas of Africa where malaria is more common.

Legend:
- malaria
- sickle-cell
- overlap of both

SUMMARY

Darwin Developed a Natural Selection Hypothesis

13.1 Darwin made a trip around the world

- Cuvier founded the science of **paleontology** and said that catastrophes cause evolution to occur.
- Lamarck proposed the inheritance of acquired characteristics as a mechanism of evolution.
- On his trip around the world, Darwin observed that species change from place to place and through time.
- In his book Lyell explained how fossils come to be in **strata** and suggested the idea of **uniformitarianism** (geologic changes occur at a uniform rate). The book and his observations of fossils convinced Darwin that the Earth had existed long enough for evolution to have occurred.

13.2 Artificial selection mimics natural selection

- In **artificial selection,** humans (not the environment) select certain characteristics to perpetuate.

13.3 Darwin formulated natural selection as a mechanism for evolution

- During **natural selection,** an environmental **selective agent** selects which organisms will reproduce.
- Natural selection has several components:
  - The members of a population have inheritable variations.
  - A population is able to produce more offspring than the environment can support.
  - Certain members of a population survive and reproduce more than other members because they have an advantage suited to the environment.
  - Natural selection results in a population adapted to its environment.
- **Evolution** can be defined as changes in a population over time due to an accumulation of inherited differences.

13.4 Wallace independently formulated a natural selection hypothesis

- Wallace was a naturalist who had also read Malthus and arrived at conclusions similar to those of Darwin.

The Evidence for Evolution Is Strong

13.5 Fossils provide a record of the past

- **Fossils** are hard parts of organisms or other traces of life found in sedimentary rock.
- **Paleontologists** find and study fossils.
- The **fossil record** indicates that life has progressed from simple to complex.

13.6 Fossils are evidence for common descent

- During evolution, organisms share **common ancestors** just as you and your cousins share grandparents.
- **Transitional fossils** have the characteristics of two different groups and thus provide clues to the evolutionary relationships between organisms.

13.7 Anatomic evidence supports common descent

- **Homologous structures** are anatomical similarities due to common ancestry.

- **Analogous structures** have the same functions in different organisms but are not anatomically similar.

bat   bird

- Only homologous structures (not analogous structures) indicate that organisms have a *recent* common ancestor.
- Organisms have **vestigial structures** despite their being reduced and nonfunctional because they were once functional in an ancestor.
- All vertebrates share the same embryonic features but they are later modified for different purposes.

13.8 Biogeographic evidence supports common descent

- **Biogeography** is the study of the distribution of organisms around the globe.
- Plants and animals evolved in particular locations, and therefore widely separated similar environments contain different but similarly adapted organisms.

13.9 Molecular evidence supports common descent

- The degree of similarity of DNA base sequences or amino acid sequences shows a pattern of relatedness consistent with fossil record data.

Population Genetics Tells Us When Microevolution Occurs

13.10 The human population is diverse

- **Microevolution** refers to genetic changes below the species level.
- A **population** is composed of all the members of a species in a particular locale at the same time.
- The existence of **SNPs (single nucleotide polymorphisms)** reveals the genetic diversity of humans.

13.11 A Hardy-Weinberg equilibrium is not expected

- Microevolution is evidenced by changes in **gene pool** allele frequencies.
- Hardy and Weinberg showed that it was possible to calculate the genotype and allele frequencies of a population by using the following equation:

$$p^2 + 2\,pq + q^2 = 1$$

- This equation predicts a Hardy-Weinberg equilibrium. The **Hardy-Weinberg principle** states that microevolution does not occur as long as mutations, gene flow, nonrandom matings, genetic drift, and natural selection do not occur.
- Generally, allele frequencies do change between generations, and microevolution does occur. For example, dark moths become prevalent in moth populations when trees become dark due to pollution. This is called **industrial melanism.**

13.12 Both mutations and sexual recombination produce variations

- **Mutations** are the primary source of genetic differences in prokaryotes.
- Sexual recombination and mutations are equally important in eukaryotes.

13.13 Nonrandom mating and gene flow can contribute to microevolution

- **Nonrandom mating** occurs when only certain genotypes or phenotypes mate with one another.
- **Assortative mating** is a type of nonrandom mating in which individuals mate with those that have the same phenotype for a particular characteristic.
- **Gene flow** results when alleles move between populations due to migration.

13.14 The effects of genetic drift are unpredictable

- **Genetic drift** refers to changes in allele frequency in a gene pool due to chance.
- The **bottleneck effect** prevents the majority of genotypes from participating in production of the next generation.
- The **founder effect** occurs when rare alleles contributed by the founders of a population occur at a higher frequency in isolated populations.

13.15 Natural selection can be stabilizing, directional, or disruptive

- In **stabilizing selection,** extreme phenotypes are selected against while intermediate phenotypes are favored.
- In **directional selection,** an extreme phenotype is favored.
- In **disruptive selection,** two or more extreme phenotypes are favored over the intermediate phenotype.

13.16 Stabilizing selection can help maintain the heterozygote

- **Heterozygote advantage** causes the sickle-cell allele to be maintained in Africa, even though the homozygous recessive is lethal because the heterozygote is protective against malaria.
- The recessive allele for cystic fibrosis is believed to have been maintained because a faulty membrane protein doesn't allow the typhoid bacterium to enter cells.

TESTING YOURSELF

Darwin Developed a Natural Selection Hypothesis

1. Why was it helpful to Darwin to learn that Lyell had concluded the Earth was very old?
   a. An old Earth has more fossils than a new Earth.
   b. It meant there was enough time for evolution to have occurred slowly.
   c. It meant there was enough time for the same species to spread into all continents.
   d. Darwin said artificial selection occurs slowly.
   e. All of these are correct.
2. Which of these pairs is mismatched?
   a. Charles Darwin—natural selection
   b. Cuvier—series of catastrophes explains the fossil record
   c. Lamarck—uniformitarianism
   d. All of these are correct.
3. Which is most likely to be favored during natural selection, but not artificial selection?
   a. fast seed germination rate

b. short generation time
c. efficient seed dispersal
d. lean pork meat production

4. Which of these is/are necessary to natural selection?
   a. variations
   b. differential reproduction
   c. inheritance of differences
   d. All of these are correct.
5. Natural selection is the only process that results in
   a. genetic variation.
   b. adaptation to the environment.
   c. phenotypic change.
   d. competition among individuals in a population.
6. **THINKING CONCEPTUALLY** The adaptive results of natural selection cannot be determined ahead of time. Explain.

The Evidence for Evolution Is Strong

7. The fossil record offers direct evidence for common descent because you can
   a. see that the types of fossils change over time.
   b. sometimes find common ancestors.
   c. trace the ancestry of a particular group.
   d. trace the biological history of living things.
   e. All of these are correct.
8. Which of the following is not an example of a vestigial structure?
   a. human tailbone   c. pelvic girdle in snakes
   b. ostrich wings   d. dog kidney
9. If evolution occurs, we would expect different biogeographic regions with similar environments to
   a. all contain the same mix of plants and animals.
   b. each have its own specific mix of plants and animals.
   c. have plants and animals with similar adaptations.
   d. have plants and animals with different adaptations.
   e. Both b and c are correct.
10. DNA nucleotide differences between organisms
    a. indicate how closely related organisms are.
    b. indicate that evolution occurs.
    c. explain why there are phenotypic differences.
    d. are to be expected.
    e. All of these are correct.

For questions 11–14, match the evolutionary evidence in the key to the description. Choose more than one answer if correct.

KEY:

   a. biogeographic evidence   c. molecular evidence
   b. fossil evidence   d. anatomic evidence

11. Islands have many unique species not found elsewhere.
12. All vertebrate embryos have pharyngeal pouches.
13. Distantly related species have more amino acid differences in cytochrome *c*.
14. Transitional links have been found between major groups of animals.
15. **THINKING CONCEPTUALLY** Why can researchers make decisions about who is related to whom using only DNA base sequence data? (See Section 13.9.)

Population Genetics Tells Us When Microevolution Occurs

For questions 16 and 17, consider that about 75% of white North Americans can taste the chemical phenylthiocarbamide. The ability to taste is due to the dominant allele *T*. Nontasters are *tt*. Assume this population is in Hardy-Weinberg equilibrium.

16. What is the frequency of *t*?
    a. 0.25   d. 0.09
    b. 0.70   e. 0.60
    c. 0.55
17. What is the frequency of heterozygous tasters?
    a. 0.50   c. 0.2475
    b. 0.21   d. 0.45
18. The offspring of better-adapted individuals are expected to make up a larger proportion of the next generation. The most likely explanation is
    a. mutations and nonrandom mating.
    b. gene flow and genetic drift.
    c. mutations and natural selection.
    d. mutations and genetic drift.
19. The Northern elephant seal went through a severe population decline as a result of hunting in the late 1800s. The population has rebounded but is now homozygous for nearly every gene studied. This is an example of
    a. negative assortative mating.   d. a bottleneck.
    b. migration.   e. disruptive selection.
    c. mutation.
20. When a population is small, there is a greater chance of
    a. gene flow.   d. mutations occurring.
    b. genetic drift.   e. sexual selection.
    c. natural selection.

THINKING SCIENTIFICALLY

1. You decide to repeat the guppy experiment described in Section 13.15 because you want to determine what genotype changes account for the results. What might you do to detect such changes?
2. A cotton farmer applied a new pesticide against the boll weevil for several years. At first, the treatment was successful, but then the insecticide became ineffective and the boll weevil rebounded. Did evolution occur? Explain.

ONLINE RESOURCE

www.mhhe.com/maderconcepts2

Enhance your study with animations that bring concepts to life and practice tests to assess your understanding. Your instructor may also recommend the interactive eBook, individualized learning tools, and more.

CONNECTING THE CONCEPTS

Darwin took a trip around the world as the naturalist aboard the HMS *Beagle*. During his trip, he collected fossils and made several observations that made him think evolution occurs. Darwin was aware of artificial selection, and he had read an essay by Malthus suggesting that the members of a population compete with one another for resources. Darwin began to see that a competitive edge would allow certain members of a population to survive and reproduce more than other members of the population. Assuming that advantageous traits are inheritable, future generations would eventually acquire adaptations to the local environment. Darwin called this process, by which a population adapts to its environment, natural selection because nature selects which members of a population will reproduce to a greater extent. Natural selection is like artificial selection except the environment instead of a breeder selects which plants or animals will reproduce.

Evolution explains the unity and diversity of life. Life is unified because of common descent, and it is diverse because of adaptations to particular environments. Darwin used the expression "descent with modification" to explain evolution. Support for common descent includes transitional fossils, anatomic features (homologous structures, vestigial structures, and embryologic similarities), biogeographic data, and molecular evidence.

In the 1930s, biologists developed a way to apply the principles of genetics to evolution. Populations would be in a Hardy-Weinberg equilibrium (allele frequencies stay the same) if mutation, gene flow, nonrandom mating, genetic drift, and natural selection did not occur. However, these events do occur, and they are the agents of evolutionary change that lead to microevolution, recognizable by allele frequency changes. Mutations provide the raw material for evolution. Genetic drift results in allele frequency changes due to a chance event, as when only a few members of a population are able to reproduce because of a natural disaster or because they have founded a colony. Natural selection is the only agent of evolution that results in adaptation to the environment.

Chapter 14 concerns macroevolution, the manner in which new species arise. The origin of new species is essential to the history of life on Earth, which we consider in Chapter 15.

PUT THE PIECES TOGETHER

1. We now know that evolution by natural selection can be observed over a short period of time (years, months). Give examples.
2. Why would you expect evolution to have a genetic basis? Use industrial melanism to support the genetic basis of evolution.
3. Why would it be *incorrect* to say that bacteria became resistant in order to escape being killed by antibiotics?

14

Speciation and Evolution

Hybrid Animals Do Exist

The immense liger, an offspring of a lion father and a tiger mother, really impressed Brian. Upon returning from the show, he immediately began researching more information. To his surprise, he found that ligers are one of many hybridized species that have been recorded. His search led him to common hybrid websites that discussed mules, zorses, zonkeys, and beefalos. He also discovered several strange hybrids, such as the wolphin, a cross between a false killer whale and a dolphin; a grolar, a cross between a grizzly bear and a polar bear; and a cama, a cross between a camel and a llama. Usually, in naming hybrids, the name of the male parent is used first. Thus, a zorse has a zebra father and a horse mother.

A hybrid results from breeding two closely related, but distinct, species. Lions and tigers meet this criterion, but a hybrid between a cat and a rabbit would not exist because these animals are not closely related. Hybrids are usually the result of human activities, either by direct intervention or by placing related species in the same setting. For example, humans have mated female donkeys and male horses to develop mules for centuries. The vast majority of hybrids have been born in zoos as a

Liger

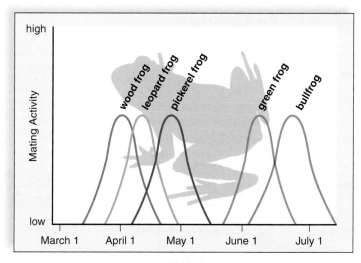

FIGURE 14.2B Mating activity peaks at different times of the year for these species of frogs.

FIGURE 14.2C Male blue-footed boobie doing a courtship dance for a female.

sperm of one species may not be able to survive in the reproductive tract of another species, or the egg may have receptors only for sperm of its species. In plants, pollen grains are species-specific and will not form a pollen tube for another species. Without a pollen tube, the sperm cannot successfully reach the egg.

Postzygotic (after the formation of a zygote) **isolating mechanisms** prevent hybrid offspring from developing or breeding, even if reproduction attempts have been successful.

Zygote mortality A hybrid zygote may not be viable, and so it dies. A zygote with two different chromosome sets may fail to go through mitosis properly, or the developing embryo may receive incompatible instructions from the maternal and paternal genes so that it cannot continue to exist.

Hybrid sterility The hybrid zygote may develop into a sterile adult. As is well known, a cross between a male horse and a female donkey produces a mule, which is usually sterile—it cannot reproduce (**Fig. 14.2D**). Sterility of hybrids generally results from complications in meiosis that lead to an inability to produce viable gametes. A cross between a cabbage and a radish produces offspring that cannot form gametes, most likely because the cabbage chromosomes and the radish chromosomes cannot align during meiosis (see Section 14.5).

F_2 fitness Even if hybrids can reproduce, their offspring may be unable to reproduce. In some cases, mules are fertile, but their offspring (the F_2 generation) are not fertile.

Having discussed how to define a species and what keeps them separate, we will discuss in Section 14.3 how species generally arise.

▶ **14.2 Check Your Progress** *a.* Which of the prezygotic isolating mechanisms apparently keeps lions and tigers from mating in the wild? Explain. *b.* Which of the postzygotic isolating mechanisms is still working to a degree to keep lions and tigers separate species? Explain.

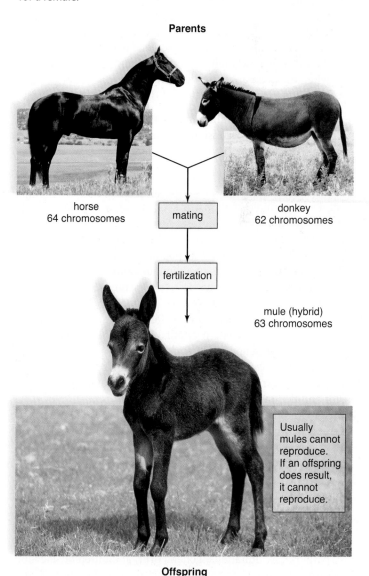

Parents

horse
64 chromosomes

mating

donkey
62 chromosomes

fertilization

mule (hybrid)
63 chromosomes

Usually mules cannot reproduce. If an offspring does result, it cannot reproduce.

Offspring

FIGURE 14.2D Mules cannot reproduce due to chromosome incompatibility.

Origin of Species Usually Requires Geographic Separation

Learning Outcomes

▶ Describe and give examples of allopatric speciation. (14.3)
▶ Describe and give examples of adaptive radiation. (14.4)

Geographic isolation fosters the genetic changes that result in allopatric speciation. Modern-day examples of allopatric speciation include the evolution of distinct forms of *Ensatina* salamanders in California. Adaptive radiation occurs when an ancestral species evolves into several new and different species, each adapted to a different environment. The evolution of a wide variety of honeycreepers on the Hawaiian Islands is an example of adaptive radiation.

14.3 Allopatric speciation utilizes a geographic barrier

In 1942, Ernst Mayr, an evolutionary biologist, published the book *Systematics and the Origin of Species,* in which he proposed the biological species concept and this process by which speciation could occur:

- Two subpopulations of a species are experiencing gene flow and therefore have a single gene pool.
- A geographic barrier appears and prevents any further gene flow between the two populations.
- Genetic drift and different selection pressures cause divergence between the isolated gene pools.
- Reproductive isolation has occurred and continues even when the geographic barrier is removed.
- Speciation is now complete and two separate species exist.

This process is termed **allopatric speciation** (allopatric means "different country") because it requires that the subpopulations be separated by a geographic barrier.

***Ensatina* Salamanders** Much data in support of allopatric speciation have since been discovered. **Figure 14.3A** features an example of allopatric speciation that has been extensively studied in California. An ancestral population of *Ensatina* salamanders lives in the Pacific Northwest. **1** Members of this ancestral population migrated southward, establishing a series of subpopulations. Each subpopulation was exposed to its own selective pressures along the coastal mountains and the Sierra Nevada mountains. **2** Due to the presence of the Central Valley of California, gene flow rarely occurs between the eastern populations and the western populations. **3** Genetic differences increased from north to south, resulting in distinct forms of *Ensatina* salamanders in southern California that differ dramatically in color and no longer interbreed.

Geographic isolation is even more obvious in other examples. The green iguana of South America is believed to be the common ancestor for both the marine iguana on the Galápagos Islands (to the west) and the rhinoceros iguana on Hispaniola, an island to the north. If so, how could it happen? Green iguanas are strong swimmers, so by chance, a few could have migrated to these islands, where they formed populations separate from each other and from the parent population back in South America. Each population continued on its own evolutionary path as new mutations, genetic drift, and different selection pressures occurred. Eventually, reproductive isolation developed, and the result was three species of iguanas that are reproductively isolated from each other.

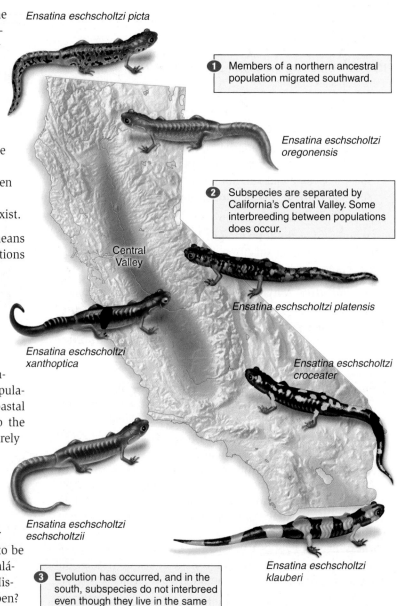

Ensatina eschscholtzi picta

1 Members of a northern ancestral population migrated southward.

Ensatina eschscholtzi oregonensis

2 Subspecies are separated by California's Central Valley. Some interbreeding between populations does occur.

Central Valley

Ensatina eschscholtzi platensis

Ensatina eschscholtzi xanthoptica

Ensatina eschscholtzi croceater

Ensatina eschscholtzi eschscholtzii

3 Evolution has occurred, and in the south, subspecies do not interbreed even though they live in the same environment.

Ensatina eschscholtzi klauberi

FIGURE 14.3A Allopatric speciation among *Ensatina* salamanders.

Sockeye Salmon and *Anolis* Lizards A more detailed example of allopatric speciation involves sockeye salmon in Washington state. In the 1930s and 1940s, hundreds of thousands of sockeye salmon were introduced into Lake Washington.

FIGURE 14.3B Sockeye salmon at Pleasure Point Beach, Lake Washington.

FIGURE 14.3C Sockeye salmon in Cedar River. The river connects with Lake Washington.

Some colonized an area of the lake near Pleasure Point Beach (**Fig. 14.3B**). Others migrated into the Cedar River (**Fig. 14.3C**). Andrew Hendry, a biologist at McGill University, is able to tell Pleasure Point Beach salmon from Cedar River salmon because they differ in shape and size due to the demands of reproducing in the river. In the river, males tend to be more slender than those along the beach. A slender body is better able to turn sideways in a strong current, and the courtship ritual of a sockeye salmon requires this maneuver. On the other hand, the females tend to be larger than those along the beach. This larger body helps them dig slightly deeper nests in the gravel beds on the river bottom. Their deeper nests are not disturbed by river currents and will remain warm enough for egg viability.

Hendry has another way to tell beach salmon from river salmon. Ear stones called otoliths reflect variations in water temperature while a fish embryo is developing. Water temperatures at Pleasure Point Beach are relatively constant compared to Cedar River temperatures. By checking otoliths in adults, Hendry found that a third of the sockeye males at Pleasure Point Beach had grown up in the river. Yet the distinction between male and female shape and size according to the two locations remains. Therefore, these males are not successful breeders along the beach. In other words, reproductive isolation has occurred.

This example shows that a side effect to adaptive changes can be reproductive isolation. Another example is seen among *Anolis* lizards, which court females by extending a colorful flap of skin, called a "dewlap." The dewlap must be seen in order to attract mates. Therefore, populations of *Anolis* in a dim forest tend to evolve light-colored dewlaps that reflect light, while populations in open habitats evolve dark-colored dewlaps. This change in dewlap color causes the populations to be reproductively isolated, because females distinguish males of their species by the color of the dewlap.

Ficedula **Flycatchers** As populations become reproductively isolated, postzygotic isolating mechanisms may arise before prezygotic isolating mechanisms. Postzygotic isolating mechanisms can keep species separate but they represent a large investment of energy to no avail. For example, the production of a hybrid requires an investment of energy that does not result in the passage of genes to future generations. Therefore, natural selection would favor the evolution of prezygotic isolating mechanisms over postzygotic isolating mechanisms. The term *reinforcement* is given to the process of natural selection favoring variations that lead to prezygotic reproductive isolation. An example of reinforcement has been seen in *Ficedula* flycatchers of the Czech Republic and Slovakia. When the pied and collared flycatchers occur in close proximity, the pied flycatchers have evolved a different coat color from that of the collared flycatchers. The difference in color helps the two species recognize and mate with their own species.

Adaptation to new environments can result in multiple species from a single ancestral species, as discussed in Section 14.4.

▶ **14.3 Check Your Progress** Knowing that the coat colors of lions and tigers is adaptive to their habitats, construct a hypothetical scenario by which they evolved from an ancestral species.

14.4 Adaptive radiation produces many related species

Adaptive radiation occurs when a single ancestral species gives rise to a variety of species, each adapted to a specific environment. An *ecological niche* is where a species lives and how it interacts with other species. When an ancestral finch arrived on the Galápagos Islands, its descendants spread out to occupy various niches. Geographic isolation of the various finch populations caused their gene pools to become isolated. Because of natural selection, each population adapted to a particular habitat on its island. In time, the many populations became so genotypically different that now, when by chance they reside on the same island, they do not interbreed, and are therefore separate species. The finches use beak shape to recognize members of the same species during courtship. Rejection of suitors with the wrong type of beak is a behavioral type of prezygotic isolating mechanism.

Similarly, on the Hawaiian Islands, a wide variety of honeycreepers are descended from a common goldfinch-like ancestor that arrived from Asia or North America about 5 million years ago. Today, honeycreepers have a range of beak sizes and shapes for feeding on various food sources, including seeds, fruits, flowers, and insects (**Fig. 14.4**).

Adaptive radiation has occurred in both plants and animals throughout the history of life on Earth when a group of organisms exploits a new environment. For

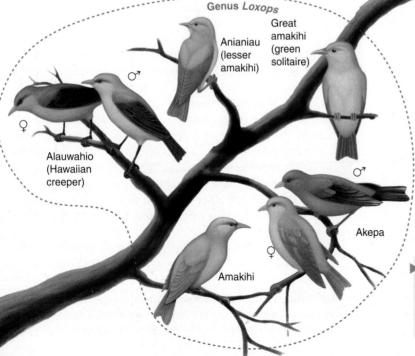

FIGURE 14.4 Adaptive radiation in Hawaiian honeycreepers.

example, with the demise of the dinosaurs about 66 million years ago, mammals underwent adaptive radiation as they exploited niches previously occupied by the dinosaurs.

This completes our discussion of allopatric speciation. The next part of the chapter discusses speciation when there is no geographic barrier.

▶ **14.4 Check Your Progress** Five species of big cats are classified in a single genus: *Panthera leo* (lion), *P. tigris* (tiger), *P. pardus* (leopard), *P. onca* (jaguar), and *P. uncia* (snow leopard). What evidence would you need to show that this is a case of adaptive radiation?

Origin of Species Can Occur in One Place

Learning Outcomes

▶ Relate sympatric speciation in plants to polyploidy. (14.5)
▶ Distinguish between autoploidy and alloploidy. (14.5)

Speciation without the presence of a geographic barrier does occur, and the best examples are due to chromosome number changes in plants. Hybridization, followed by doubling of the chromosome number, can occur naturally or as a result of artificial selection. Such events must have occurred during the artificial selection of corn over the years.

14.5 Speciation occasionally occurs without a geographic barrier

Speciation without the presence of a geographic barrier is termed **sympatric speciation.** Sympatric speciation has been difficult to substantiate in animals. For example, two populations of the Meadow Brown butterfly, *Maniola jurtina*, have different distributions of wing spots. The two populations are both in Cornwall, England, and they maintain the difference in wing spots, even though there is no geographic boundary between them. But, as yet, no reproductive isolating mechanism has been found. In contrast, we know of instances in plants by which a postzygotic isolating mechanism has given rise to a new species within the range and habitat of the parent species. In other words, no geographic barrier was required. All instances in plants involve **polyploidy,** additional sets of chromosomes beyond the diploid (2n) number. Sympatric speciation is more common in flowering plants than in animals due to self-pollination. A polyploid plant can reproduce only with itself, and cannot reproduce with the parent (2n) population because not all the chromosomes would be able to pair during meiosis. Two types of polyploidy are known: autoploidy and alloploidy.

Speciation through **autoploidy** is seen in diploid plants when nondisjunction occurs during meiosis and the diploid species produces diploid gametes. If this diploid gamete fuses with a haploid gamete, a triploid plant results. A triploid (3n) plant is sterile and cannot produce offspring because the chromosomes cannot pair during meiosis. Humans have found a use for sterile plants because they produce fruits without seeds. **Figure 14.5A** contrasts a diploid banana with seeds to today's polyploid banana that produces no seeds. If two of the diploid gametes fuse, the plant is a tetraploid (4n) and the plant is fertile, as long as it reproduces with another of its own kind. The fruits of polyploid plants are much larger than those of diploid plants. The huge strawberries of today are produced by octaploid (8n) plants.

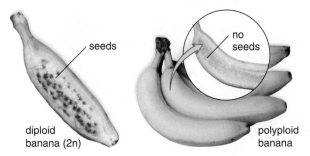

FIGURE 14.5A Autoploidy: The small, diploid-seeded banana is contrasted with the large, polyploid banana that produces no seeds.

diploid banana (2n) — seeds

no seeds — polyploid banana

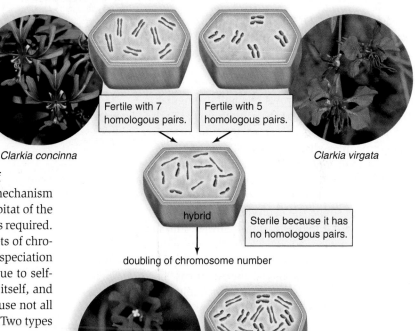

Clarkia concinna — Fertile with 7 homologous pairs.

Clarkia virgata — Fertile with 5 homologous pairs.

hybrid — Sterile because it has no homologous pairs.

doubling of chromosome number

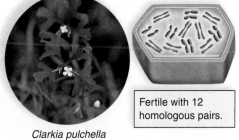

Clarkia pulchella — Fertile with 12 homologous pairs.

FIGURE 14.5B Alloploidy results in a fertile third *Clarkia* species.

Speciation through **alloploidy** requires two steps. The prefix *allo-*, which means "different," is appropriate because the process begins when two different but related species of plants hybridize. First, when two different but related species of plants hybridize, the hybrid is sterile because it has no homologous pairs of chromosomes. Second, if and when a doubling of the chromosome number occurs a new fertile plant results. **Figure 14.5B** gives an example of alloploidy. The Western wildflower, *Clarkia concinna*, has seven (7) pairs of homologous chromosomes; a related species, *C. virgata*, has five (5) pairs of chromosomes. The hybrid has twelve chromosomes but is sterile because it has no homologous pairs and therefore meiosis of gametogenesis cannot occur. However, researchers have located a plant now called *C. pulchella* that is fertile due to doubling of the chromosome number, which allows the twelve (12) chromosomes to pair during meiosis. Alloploidy also occurred during the evolution of the wheat plant, which is commonly used today to produce bread.

▶ **14.5 Check Your Progress** What fossil evidence might support the hypothesis that the different species of cats arose sympatrically?

14A The Many Uses of Corn, an Allotetraploid

When the world record for eating corn on the cob was set at 33½ ears in 12 minutes, the last thing on anyone's mind was the evolution of corn. Corn, also known as maize (*Zea mays*), represents one of the most remarkable plant-breeding achievements in the history of agriculture. Today, modern society literally reaps the benefits of corn as a domestic product.

Modern corn bears little resemblance to its ancient ancestor, an inconspicuous wild grass called teosinte from southern Mexico. Teosinte is a drought-tolerant grass that produces reproductive spikes fairly close to the ground. Each spike is filled with two rows of small, triangular kernels (seeds) enclosed in a tough husk. Each seed is encased and protected by a hard shell. Ancient peoples discovered that teosinte was a source of food and began selecting spikes to plant near their homes, close to irrigation systems. Thus, between 4000 and 3000 B.C., the hand of artificial selection began to shape the evolution of corn.

Experimental hybridization followed, and many varieties of corn were developed. By A.D. 1070, corn had reached North America and was being grown by the Iroquois in New York. By the time Columbus visited the Americas, corn was being grown in a number of environments. Columbus even commented on the fields of corn and its great taste. We now know

Teosinte
(Zea mexicana)

that corn is an allotetraploid, meaning it is 4n. Hybridization between two related species must have been followed by doubling of the chromosomes, accounting for why ears of corn are now so large (**Fig. 14A**).

Today corn is America's number-one field crop, yielding approximately 9.5 billion bushels yearly. It is an important food source for both humans and livestock. Corn is a component of over 3,000 grocery products, including cereals, corn syrup, cornstarch, ice cream, soft drinks, chips, snack foods, and even peanut butter. It is also used in making glue, shoe polish, ink, soaps, and synthetic rubber. Now, corn is also a source for the production of ethanol to fuel our vehicles. The uses of corn seem to be limited only by our imaginations (Fig. 14A).

FORM YOUR OPINION

1. Using corn to produce ethanol raises the cost of corn because it makes less available for food and feed in the United States and abroad. Should we continue to convert corn to ethanol? Why or why not?
2. Much corn is grown as feed for animals. The sewage produced by animals can be a threat to our health and eating beef can lead to circulatory problems. Should we stop eating beef?

FIGURE 14A Among the many of its uses today, corn is a fuel source, a component of many products that absorb water, a feed for animals, and a delicious food for people.

The fossils tell us that the ancient seas were teeming with weird-looking, invertebrate animals. All of today's groups of animals can trace their ancestry to one of these strange-looking forms, which include sponges, arthropods, worms, and tribolites, as well as spiked creatures and oversized predators. The animals featured in Figure 14B have been assigned to these genera and because they are believed to be the type of animal mentioned:

Opabinia, a crustacean
Thaumaptilon, a sea pen
Vauxia, a sponge
Wiwaxia, a segmented worm

The vertebrates, including humans, are descended from *Pikaia,* the only one of the fossils that has a supporting rod called a notochord. (In vertebrates, the notochord is replaced by the vertebral column during development.)

Unicellular organisms have also been preserved at the Burgess Shale site. They appear to be bacteria, cyanobacteria, dinoflagellates, and other protists. Fragments of algae are preserved in thin, shiny carbon films. A technique has been perfected that allows the films to be peeled off the rocks.

Anyone can travel to Yoho National Park, look at the fossils, and get an idea of the types of animals that dominated the world's oceans for nearly 300 million years. Some of the animals had external skeletons, but many were soft-bodied. Interpretations of the fossils vary. Some authorities hypothesize that the great variety of animals in the Burgess Shale evolved within 20–50 million years, and therefore the site supports the hypothesis of punctuated equilibrium. Others believe that the animals started evolving much earlier and that we are looking at the end result of an adaptive radiation requiring many more millions of years to accomplish. Some investigators present evidence that all the animals are related to today's animals and should be classified as such. Others believe that several of them are unique creatures unrelated to the animals of today. Regardless of the controversies, the fossils tell us that speciation, diversification, and eventual extinction are part of the history of life.

FORM YOUR OPINION

1. What should the scientific community do when confronted with a phenomenon like the Burgess Shale?
2. Should students be exposed to phenomena that cannot as yet be fully explained? Why or why not?

Thaumaptilon

Vauxia

Wiwaxia

14.7 Development plays a role in speciation

Whether slow or fast, how could evolution have produced the myriad of animals in the Burgess Shale and, indeed, in the history of life? Or, to ask the question in a genetic context, how can genetic changes bring about such major differences in form? It has been suggested since the time of Darwin that the answer must involve developmental processes. In 1917, D'Arcy Thompson asked us to imagine an ancestor in which all parts are developing at a particular rate. A change in regulatory gene expression could stop a developmental process or continue it beyond its normal time. For instance, if the growth of limb bones were stopped early, the result would be shorter limbs, and if it were extended, the result would be longer limbs compared to those of an ancestor. Or, if the whole period of growth were extended, a larger animal would result, accounting for why some species of horses are so large today.

Using new kinds of microscopes and the modern techniques of cloning and manipulating genes, investigators have indeed discovered genes whose *differential expression* can bring about changes in body shapes (**Fig. 14.7A**). More surprisingly, these same regulatory genes occur in all organisms. This finding suggests that these genes must date back to a common ancestor that lived more than 600 MYA (before the Burgess Shale animals), and that despite millions of years of divergent evolution, all animals share the same regulatory switches for development. Previously in Section 11.4, p. 216, we pointed out how the same regulatory gene, *Pax6,* turns on eye development even though the animal kingdom contains many different types of eyes, and it was long thought that each type would require its own set of genes. Flies, crabs, and other arthropods have compound eyes composed of hundreds of individual visual units. Humans and all other vertebrates have a camera-type eye with a single lens. So do squids and octopuses. Humans are not closely related to either flies

> Despite millions of years of divergent evolution, all animals share the same regulatory genes for development.

or squids, so wouldn't it seem likely that all three types of animals evolved "eye" genes separately? Not so. In 1994, Walter Gehring and his colleagues at the University of Basel, Switzerland, discovered that *Pax6* is required for eye formation in all animals tested (see Fig. 11.4B). Mutations in the *Pax6* gene lead to failure of eye development in both people and mice, and remarkably, the mouse *Pax6* gene can cause an eye to develop on the leg of a fruit fly.

Eye on fruit fly leg.

Increase in Complexity The developmental regulatory genes called *Hox* genes have been much studied, and investigators tell us that the number of these genes increased twice during the evolution of animals. Both expansions are associated with an increase in complexity, defined by the appearance of different cell types. One expansion occurred during the evolution of vertebrates. Invertebrates have 13 *Hox* genes, while vertebrates, including humans, have four copies of the 13 *Hox* gene set.

It appears that the set underwent a series of duplications, and some of the duplicate genes may have taken on new functions, a process mentioned in How Life Changes, p. 262. Similarly, some other sets of regulatory genes that operate in development were duplicated when vertebrates evolved. This increase in the number of regulatory gene numbers may have contributed to the evolution of vertebrates and to their complexity.

The limbs of these terrestrial mammals are shaped for running (or walking).

The limbs of birds are shaped for flight.

FIGURE 14.7A Differential expression of the same regulatory genes during development can account for differences in vertebrate limbs.

Development of Limbs Wings and arms are very different, but both humans and birds express the *Tbx5* regulatory gene in developing limb buds. *Tbx5* codes for a transcription factor that turns on the genes needed to make a limb. What seems to have changed as birds and mammals evolved are the genes that *Tbx5* turns on. Perhaps in an ancestral tetrapod, the Tbx5 protein triggered the transcription of only one gene. In mammals and birds, a few genes are expressed in response to Tbx5 protein, but the particular genes are different.

Hindlimb reduction has occurred during the evolution of other mammals. For example, as whales and manatees evolved from land-dwelling ancestors into fully aquatic forms, the hindlimbs became greatly reduced in size. Similarly, legless lizards have evolved many times. A stickleback study has shown how natural selection can lead to major skeletal changes in a relatively short time. The three-spined stickleback fish occurs in two forms in North American lakes. In the open waters of a lake, long pelvic spines help protect the stickleback from being eaten by large predators. But on the lake bottom, long pelvic spines are a disadvantage because dragonfly larvae seize and feed on young sticklebacks by grabbing them by their spines. The presence of short spines in bottom-dwelling stickleback fish can be traced to a reduction in the development of the pelvic-fin bud in the embryo, and this reduction is due to the altered expression of a regulatory gene.

> Animal diversity is due in large part to variations in the expression of ancient regulatory genes during development.

Development of Overall Shape Vertebrates have repeating segments, as exemplified by the vertebral column. In general, *Hox* genes control the development of repeated structures along the main body axes of vertebrates. Shifts in how long *Hox* genes are expressed per segment in embryos are responsible for why the snake has hundreds of rib-bearing vertebrae and essentially no neck in contrast to other vertebrates, such as a chick (**Fig. 14.7B**). Changes in the timing of *Hox* gene expression can also account for the evolution of four legs rather than a fin. In vertebrates with legs, the *Hox* genes are turned on again in a later phase of development. This phase is associated with the further growth outwards of the limb bones to form the limb and digits where a fin formerly existed. On the other hand, the inability of a *Hox* gene to turn on other regulatory genes in certain segments can explain why insects have just six legs, and other arthropods, such as crayfish, have ten legs. In general, the study of *Hox* genes has shown how animal diversity is due to variations in the expression of ancient genes rather than to wholly new and different genes.

Human Evolution The sequencing of genomes has shown us that our DNA base sequence is very similar to that of chimpanzees, mice, and, indeed, all vertebrates. Based on this knowledge and the work just described, investigators no longer expect to find new genes to account for the evolution of humans. Instead, they predict that differential gene expression and/or new functions for "old" genes will explain how humans evolved.

We have to keep in mind that developmental changes result in a phenotype that is subject to natural selection. We would expect that during the history of life many changes in phenotype were not advantageous and therefore did not become prevalent in future generations.

▶ **14.7 Check Your Progress** a. Why does it seem that differential regulatory gene expression must occur during the development of ligers? Why might their numbers increase? b. Assume ligers live in the wild and they can reproduce. Create a scenario by which their numbers increase while those of lions and tigers decrease.

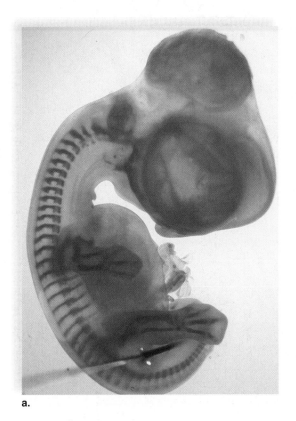

a.

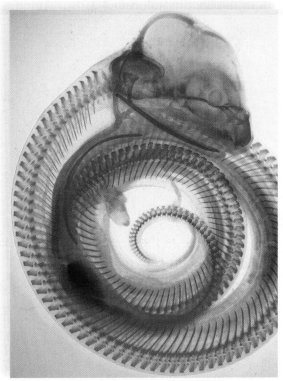

b.

FIGURE 14.7B

Differential expression of a *Hox* gene causes **(a)** a chick to have fewer vertebrae than **(b)** a snake in a particular region (colored pink) of the spine.

Burke, A. C. 2000. *Hox* genes and the global patterning of the somitic mesoderm. In Somitogenesis. C. Ordahl (ed.) *Current Topics in Developmental Biology*, Vol. 47. Academic Press.

14.8 Speciation is not goal-oriented

The evolution of the horse, *Equus*, has been studied since the 1870s, and at first the ancestry of this genus seemed to represent a model for gradual, straight-line evolution until its goal, the modern horse, had been achieved. Three trends were particularly evident during the evolution of the horse: increase in overall size, toe reduction, and change in tooth size and shape.

By now, however, many more fossils have been found, making it easier to tell that the lineage of a horse is complicated by the presence of many ancestors with varied traits. The family tree in **Figure 14.8** is an oversimplification because each of the names is a genus that contains several species, and not all past genera in the horse family are included. It is apparent, then, that the ancestors of *Equus* form a thick bush of many equine species and that straight-line evolution did not occur. Because *Equus* alone remains and the other genera have died out, it might seem as if evolution was directed toward producing *Equus*, but this is not the case. Instead, each of these ancestral species was adapted to its environment. Adaptation occurs only because the members of a population with an advantage are able to have more offspring than other members. Natural selection is opportunistic, not goal-oriented.

Fossils named *Hyracotherium* have been designated as the first probable members of the horse family, living about 57 MYA. These animals had a wooded habitat, ate leaves and fruit, and were about the size of a dog. Their short legs and broad feet

with several toes would have allowed them to scamper from thicket to thicket to avoid predators. *Hyracotherium* was obviously well adapted to its environment because this genus survived for 20 million years.

The family tree of *Equus* tells us once more that speciation, diversification, and extinction are common occurrences in the fossil record. The first adaptive radiation of horses occurred about 35 MYA. The weather was becoming drier, and grasses were evolving. Eating grass requires tougher teeth, and an increase in size and longer legs would have permitted greater speed to escape enemies. The second adaptive radiation of horses occurred about 15 MYA and included *Merychippus* as a representative of these groups of speedy grazers that lived on the open plain. By 10 MYA, the horse family had become quite diversified. Some species were large forest browsers, some were small forest browsers, and others were large plains grazers. Many species had three toes, but some had one strong toe. (The hoof of the modern horse includes only one toe.)

Modern horses evolved about 4 MYA from ancestors who had features adaptive for living on an open plain, such as large size, long legs, hoofed feet, and strong teeth. The other groups of horses prevalent at the time became extinct, no doubt for complex reasons.

> **14.8 Check Your Progress** There are only five species of cats in the genus *Panthera*. Does this represent a goal of evolution?

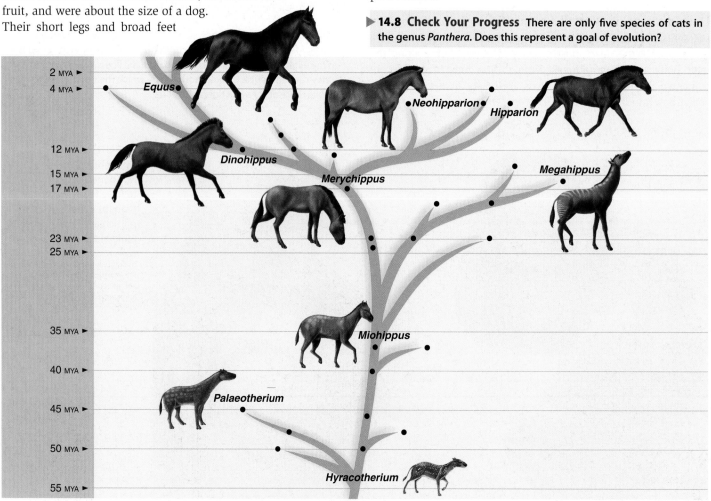

FIGURE 14.8 Simplified family tree of *Equus*. Every dot represents a genus.

SUMMARY

Evolution of Diversity Requires Speciation

14.1 Species have been defined in more than one way

- **Macroevolution** depends on speciation.
- **Speciation** occurs when one species splits into two or more species or when one species becomes a new species over time.
- According to the **evolutionary species concept,** every species has its own evolutionary history, and a species can be recognized by diagnostic traits.
- According to the **biological species concept,** members of a species are reproductively isolated from members of other species. They can only reproduce with members of their own species.

14.2 Reproductive barriers maintain genetic differences between species

- **Prezygotic isolating mechanisms** prevent reproductive attempts.
- **Postzygotic isolating mechanisms** prevent zygote development or F_1 and F_2 hybrid offspring from breeding.

Prezygotic Isolating Mechanisms		Postzygotic Isolating Mechanisms
Premating →	Mating →	Fertilization
Habitat isolation	Mechanical isolation	Zygote mortality
Temporal isolation		Hybrid sterility
Behavioral isolation	Gamete isolation	F_2 fitness

Origin of Species Usually Requires Geographic Separation

14.3 Allopatric speciation utilizes a geographic barrier

- **Allopatric speciation** begins when populations derived from a larger one are separated by a barrier and they start to differ genetically and phenotypically.
- Following separation, postzygotic mechanisms followed by prezygotic mechanisms can develop over time.

14.4 Adaptive radiation produces many related species

- When **adaptative radiation** occurs, several new species evolve from an ancestral species, and they adapt to fill different niches separated by geographic barriers.
- The many types of Hawaiian honeycreepers are a result of adaptive radiation.

Origin of Species Can Occur in One Place

14.5 Speciation occasionally occurs without a geographic barrier

- **Sympatric speciation** occurs without a geographic barrier.
- **Polyploidy** is present when plants have additional sets of chromosomes beyond the diploid (2n) number. The sudden occurrence of polyploidy is speciation because a polyploid cannot reproduce with parental 2n plants.
- Speciation through **autoploidy** occurs when a diploid gamete fuses with a haploid gamete, resulting in a triploid plant, which is sterile.
- Speciation through **alloploidy** occurs when two different but related species of plants hybridize, and then the chromosome number doubles making the hybrid fertile.

Macroevolution Involves Changes at the Species Level and Beyond

14.6 Speciation occurs at different tempos

- According to the gradualistic model, speciation occurs gradually, perhaps due to a gradually changing environment.
- According to the punctuated equilibrium model, periods of equilibrium are interrupted by rapid speciation. Perhaps, if the environment changes rapidly, new species may suddenly arise.
- On occasion, fossil record data may fit one model of speciation, and on another occasion, it may fit the other model.
- Speciation, diversification, and eventual extinction are part of the history of life.

14.7 Development plays a role in speciation

- Despite millions of years of divergent evolution, all animals share the same regulatory genes for development.
- *Hox* gene duplications could have brought about increased complexity in animals.
- Eye development, limb development, and shape determination are controlled by the same regulatory genes in different animals. But differential expression can account for differences in outcome.
- Investigators hypothesize that differential gene expression during development coupled with natural selection can account for the process of evolution, including human evolution.

14.8 Speciation is not goal-oriented

- In horses, each ancestral species adapted to its environment, but due to a changing environment, only *Equus* survived.
- The family record of *Equus* shows speciation, diversification, and extinction. At least two major adaptive radiations occurred in the past.
- Natural selection is opportunistic, not goal-oriented; adaptation occurs because members with an advantage can have more offspring.

Evolution of Diversity Requires Speciation

1. A biological species
   a. always looks different from other species.
   b. always has a different chromosome number from that of other species.
   c. is reproductively isolated from other species.
   d. never occupies the same niche in different environments.

For questions 2–7, indicate the type of isolating mechanism described in each scenario.

KEY:

   a. habitat isolation   e. gamete isolation
   b. temporal isolation   f. zygote mortality
   c. behavioral isolation   g. hybrid sterility
   d. mechanical isolation   h. low F_2 fitness

2. Males of one species do not recognize the courtship behaviors of females of another species.
3. One species reproduces at a different time than another species.
4. A cross between two species produces a zygote that always dies.
5. Two species do not interbreed because they occupy different areas.
6. The sperm of one species cannot survive in the reproductive tract of another species.
7. The offspring of two hybrid individuals exhibit poor vigor.
8. Which of these is a prezygotic isolating mechanism?
   a. habitat isolation   d. zygote mortality
   b. temporal isolation   e. Both a and b are correct.
   c. hybrid sterility
9. Male moths recognize females of their species by sensing chemical signals called pheromones. This is an example of
   a. gamete isolation.   d. mechanical isolation.
   b. habitat isolation.   e. temporal isolation.
   c. behavioral isolation.
10. Which of these is mechanical isolation?
    a. Sperm cannot reach or fertilize an egg.
    b. Courtship patterns differ.
    c. The organisms live in different locales.
    d. The organisms reproduce at different times of the year.
    e. Genitalia are unsuited to each other.
11. **THINKING CONCEPTUALLY** Regardless of how speciation occurs or how species are defined, what is required for separate species to be present?

Origin of Species Usually Requires Geographic Separation

12. Complete the following diagram illustrating allopatric speciation by using these phrases: genetic changes (used twice), geographic barrier, species 1, species 2, species 3.

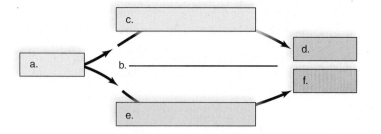

13. The creation of new species without the need of a geographic barrier is called
    a. isolation speciation.   d. sympatric speciation.
    b. allopatric speciation.   e. symbiotic speciation.
    c. allelomorphic speciation.
14. The many species of Galápagos finches are each adapted to eating different foods. This is the result of
    a. gene flow.   d. genetic drift.
    b. adaptive radiation.   e. All of these are correct.
    c. sympatric speciation.
15. **THINKING CONCEPTUALLY** The Hawaiian Islands are some distance from any mainland, and the plants and animals on each island are unique. Only short distances separate the Florida Keys from each other and the mainland. The mainland and the Keys all contain the same species. Explain.

Origin of Species Can Occur in One Place

16. Allopatric, but not sympatric, speciation requires
    a. reproductive isolation.
    b. geographic isolation.
    c. spontaneous differences in males and females.
    d. prior hybridization.
    e. rapid rate of mutation.
17. Which of the following is not a characteristic of plant alloploidy?
    a. hybridization
    b. chromosome doubling
    c. self-fertilization
    d. All of these are characteristics of plant alloploidy.
18. Corn is an allotetraploid, which means that its
    a. chromosome number is 4n.
    b. development resulted from hybridization.
    c. development required a geographic barrier.
    d. Both a and b are correct.

Macroevolution Involves Changes at the Species Level and Beyond

19. Transitional links are least likely to be found if evolution proceeds according to the
    a. gradualistic model.
    b. punctuated equilibrium model.
    c. Both a and b are correct.
    d. None of these are correct.
20. Adaptive radiation is only possible if evolution is punctuated.
    a. true
    b. false
21. Why are there no fish fossils in the Burgess Shale?
    a. The habitat was not aquatic.
    b. Fish do not fossilize easily because they do not have shells.
    c. The fossils of the Burgess Shale predate vertebrate animals.
    d. There are fish fossils in the Burgess Shale.
22. Which of the following can influence the rapid development of new species of animals?
    a. the influence of molecular clocks
    b. a change in the expression of regulating genes
    c. the sequential expression of genes
    d. All of these are correct.
23. Which of the following does not seem to influence speciation?
    a. the evolution of different types of *Hox* genes

b. the evolution of new types of genes that control development
c. Only the environment and not genes influence speciation.
d. Both a and b are correct.

24. Which gene is incorrectly matched to its function?
    a. *Hox*—body shape
    b. *Pax6*—body segmentation
    c. *Tbx5*—limb development
    d. All of these choices are correctly matched.

25. **THINKING CONCEPTUALLY** Explain the statement that "*Hox* genes are ancient genes."

26. In the evolution of the modern horse, which was the goal of the evolutionary process?
    a. large size
    b. single toe
    c. Both a and b are correct.
    d. Neither a nor b is correct.

27. Which of the following does not pertain to *Hyracotherium*, an ancestral horse genus?
    a. small size
    b. single toe
    c. wooded habitat
    d. All of these are characteristics of *Hyracotherium*.

THINKING SCIENTIFICALLY

1. You want to decide what definition of a species to use in your study. What are the advantages and disadvantages of the evolutionary and biological species concepts?

2. You decide to create a hybrid by crossing two species of plants. If the hybrid is a fertile plant that produces normal-sized fruit, what conclusion is possible?

ONLINE RESOURCE

www.mhhe.com/maderconcepts2  |BIOLOGY

Enhance your study with animations that bring concepts to life and practice tests to assess your understanding. Your instructor may also recommend the interactive eBook, individualized learning tools, and more.

CONNECTING THE CONCEPTS

Macroevolution, the study of the origin and history of the species on Earth, is the subject of this chapter and the next. The biological species concept states that the members of a species have an isolated gene pool and can only reproduce with one another.

The origin of species is called speciation. Speciation usually occurs after two populations derived from a larger one are separated geographically. If the members of a salamander population are suddenly divided by a barrier, each new population becomes adapted to its particular environment over time. Eventually, the two populations may become so genetically different that even if members of each population come into contact, they will not be able to produce fertile offspring. Because gene flow between the two populations is no longer possible, the salamanders are considered separate species. Aided by geographic separation, multiple species can repeatedly arise from an ancestral species, as when a common ancestor from the mainland led to many species of Hawaiian honeycreepers, each adapted to its own particular environment.

Does speciation occur gradually, as Darwin supposed, or rapidly (in geologic time), as described by the punctuated equilibrium model? The fossils of the Burgess Shale support the punctuated equilibrium model. How can genetic changes bring about such major changes in form, whether fast or slow? Investigators have now discovered ancient regulatory genes (e.g., *Hox* genes), whose differential expression can bring about changes in body shapes and organs.

Evolution is not directed toward any particular end, and the traits of the species alive today arose through common descent with adaptations to a local environment. The subject of Chapter 15 is the evolutionary history and classification of living organisms today.

PUT THE PIECES TOGETHER

1. Scientists make observations and then formulate testable hypotheses to explain the observations. What testable hypotheses have biologists made about speciation? (*Hint:* How might species arise? What might cause them to arise?)

2. Paleontologists suggested the punctuated equilibrium model. What data did they use?

3. Is the study of evolution a scientific endeavor? Explain your reasoning.

Part VI

Enhance your understanding of ecology through media and applications!

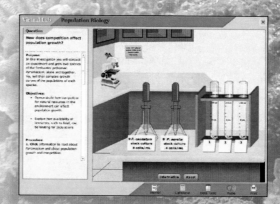

Organisms Live in Ecosystems

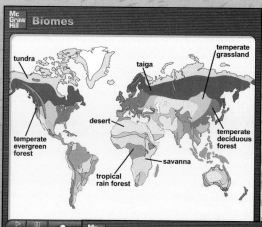

Biomes

tundra
taiga
temperate grassland
desert
temperate evergreen forest
temperate deciduous forest
savanna
tropical rain forest

Play Pause

Biomes are major c...
characteristic appea...
defined largely by v...

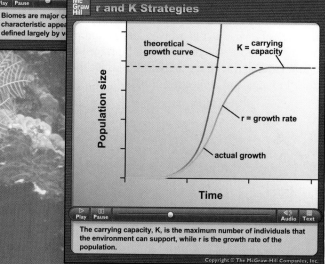

r and K Strategies

theoretical growth curve
K = carrying capacity
r = growth rate
actual growth

Population size

Time

Play Pause
Audio Text

The carrying capacity, K, is the maximum number of individuals that the environment can support, while r is the growth rate of the population.

Copyright © The McGraw-Hill Companies, Inc.

World Hunger

World Hunger

Use the buttons below to view specific sections of this animation or press play.

About the World Hunger Problem

What is being done?

The Hunger Project

Play Pause
Audio Text

Press play or press the buttons above to play that section of the animation.

Copyright © The McGraw-Hill Companies, Inc.

Applications

McGraw Hill connect™
|BIOLOGY

36

Population Ecology

When a Population Grows Too Large

White-tailed deer, which live from southern Canada to below the equator in South America, are prolific breeders. In one study, investigators found that two male and four female deer produced 160 offspring in six years. Theoretically, the number could have been 300 because a large proportion of does (female deer) breed their first year, and once they start breeding, produce about two young each year of life.

A century ago, the white-tailed deer population across the eastern United States was less than half a million. Today, it is well over 200 million deer—even more than existed when Europeans first arrived to colonize America. This dramatic increase in population size can probably be attributed to a lack of predators. For one thing, hunting is tightly controlled by government agencies, and in some areas, it is banned altogether because of the danger it poses to the general public. Similarly, the natural predators of deer, such as wolves and mountain lions, are now absent from most regions. This can be traced to a large human population that fears large predators because they could possibly attack humans and domestic animals.

Buck

We like to see a mother with her fawns by the side of the road or scampering off into the woods with tails raised to show off the white underside. And we find it thrilling to see a large buck (male deer) with majestic antlers partially hidden in the woods. But the sad reality is that, in those areas where deer populations have become too large, the deer suffer from starvation as they deplete their own food supply. For example, after deer hunting was banned on Long Island, New York, the deer population quickly outgrew available food resources. The animals became sickly and weak and weighed so little that their ribs, vertebrae, and pelvic bones were visible through their skin.

Then, too, a very large deer population causes humans many problems. A homeowner is dismayed to see new plants decimated and evergreen trees damaged by munching deer. The economic damage that large deer populations cause to agriculture, landscaping, and forestry exceeds a billion dollars per year. Even more alarming, a million deer-vehicle collisions take place in the United State each year, resulting in over a billion dollars in insurance claims, thousands of human injuries, and hundreds of human deaths. Lyme disease, transmitted by deer ticks to humans, infects over 3,000 people annually. Untreated Lyme disease can lead to debilitating arthritic symptoms.

Deer overpopulation hurts not only deer and humans, but other species as well. The forested areas that are overpopulated by deer have fewer understory plants. Furthermore, the deer selectively eat certain species of plants, while leaving others alone. This can cause long-lasting changes in the number and diversity of trees in forests, leading to a negative economic impact on logging and forestry. The number of songbirds, insects, squirrels, mice, and other animals declines with an increasing deer population. It behooves us, therefore, to learn to manage deer populations. And the good news is that in some states, such as Texas, large landowners now set aside a portion of their property for a deer herd. They improve the nutrition of the herd and restrict the harvesting of young bucks, but allow the harvesting of does. The result is a self-sustaining herd that brings economic benefits—the landowners charge others for the privilege of hunting on their land.

In this chapter, we examine the general characteristics of populations. You will learn how the size, distribution, and age structure of a population can change over time and what factors influence populations. You will see that, like the deer in eastern North America, human populations too may suffer the consequences of overpopulation.

Doe running

Doe and fawn

Ecology Studies Where and How Organisms Live in the Biosphere

Learning Outcome

▶ Name and compare the ecological levels of study. (36.1)

As previously shown in Figure 1.3A, the levels of biological organization extend beyond the organism to include the population, community, ecosystem, and biosphere. Ecology studies these higher levels of organization.

36.1 Ecology is studied at various levels

In 1866, the German zoologist Ernst Haeckel coined the word ecology from two Greek roots (*oikos*, home, and *-logy*, study of). He said that **ecology** is the study of the interactions of organisms with other organisms and with the physical environment. Haeckel also pointed out that ecology and evolution are intertwined because ecological interactions are selection pressures that result in evolutionary change, which in turn affects ecological interactions.

Ecology, like so many biological disciplines, is wide-ranging. An ecologist can study how the individual organism is adapted to its environment. For example, they might study how a fish is adapted to and survives in its **habitat** (the place where the organism lives) (**Fig. 36.1**). Most organisms do not exist singly; rather, they are part of a **population,** defined as all the organisms within an area belonging to the same species and interacting with the environment. At this level of study, ecologists are interested in factors that affect the growth and regulation of population size.

A **community** consists of all the various populations interacting at a locale. In a coral reef, there are numerous populations of algae, corals, crustaceans, fishes, and so forth. At this level, ecologists want to know how interactions such as predation and competition affect the organization of the community.

An **ecosystem** encompasses a community of populations as well as the abiotic environment (e.g., the availability of sunlight for plants). Ecosystems rarely have distinct boundaries and are not totally self-sustaining. Usually, a transition zone called an *ecotone*, composed of a mixture of organisms from adjacent ecosystems, exists between ecosystems.

The **biosphere** encompasses the zones of the Earth's land, water, and air where living organisms are found. Taking the global view, the entire biosphere is an ecosystem, a place where organisms interact among themselves and with the physical and chemical environments. These interactions help maintain ecosystems and, in turn, the biosphere.

▶ **36.1 Check Your Progress** What ecological levels are affected by deer overpopulation?

FIGURE 36.1
Ecological levels.

Organism → Population → Community → Ecosystem

Coral reef ecosystem

Populations Are Not Static—They Change Over Time

Learning Outcomes

▶ Define density, and contrast three patterns of population distribution. (36.2)

▶ Understand the relationship between growth rate and biotic potential. (36.3)

▶ Describe three types of survivorship curves and contrast three age structure diagrams. (36.3)

▶ Compare exponential growth to logistic growth with reference to the carrying capacity of the environment. (36.4)

A population is defined as all the members of a species living in the same locale at the same time. A population's **demographics** such as its density, distribution, and other characteristics discussed in this chapter shift over time. Researchers have identified three common survivorship curves that influence a population's life history pattern.

36.2 Density and distribution are aspects of population structure

Density Once population size has been estimated, it is possible to calculate the **population density,** which is the number of individuals per unit area. For example, the population density of the United States is estimated at 76 persons per square mile. Population density figures make it seem as if individuals are uniformly distributed, but this is often not the case. For example, we know full well that most people in the United States live in cities, where the number of people per unit area is dramatically higher than in the country. And even within a city, more people live in particular neighborhoods than others. Furthermore, such distributions can change over time. Therefore, basing ecological models solely on population density can lead to misleading results.

Distribution **Population distribution** is the pattern of dispersal of individuals across an area of interest. The availability of resources can affect where populations of a species are found. **Resources** are nonliving (abiotic) and living (biotic) components of an environment that support living organisms. Light, water, space, mates, and food are some important resources for populations. **Limiting factors** are those environmental aspects that particularly determine where an organism lives. For example, trout live only in cool mountain streams, where the oxygen content is high, but carp and catfish are found in rivers near the coast because they can tolerate warm waters, which have a low concentration of oxygen. The timberline is the limit of tree growth in mountainous regions or in high latitudes because of low temperatures. The distribution of organisms can also be due to biotic factors. In Australia, the red kangaroo does not live outside arid inland areas because it is adapted to feeding on the grasses that grow there.

Three descriptions—*clumped, random,* and *uniform*—are often used to characterize observed patterns of distribution. Suppose you were to consider the distribution of a species across its full **range,** that portion of the globe where the species can be found. For example, red kangaroos live in Australia. On that scale, you would expect to find a clumped distribution because organisms are located in areas suitable to their adaptations. That is why red kangaroos live in grasslands, and catfish live in warm river water near the coast.

Within a smaller area, such as a single body of water or a single forest, the availability of resources again influences which distribution pattern is common for a particular population. A study of the creosote bush, a desert shrub (**Fig. 36.2A**), revealed that the distribution changed from clumped to random to uniform as the plants matured. As time passed, competition for

belowground resources caused the distribution pattern to become uniform. In another example, Cape gannet populations are clumped over their range, but in a nesting colony, the birds are uniformly distributed (**Fig. 36.2B**).

▶ **36.2 Check Your Progress** There are over 30 deer per square mile in Pennsylvania. This is an estimate of deer population _____.

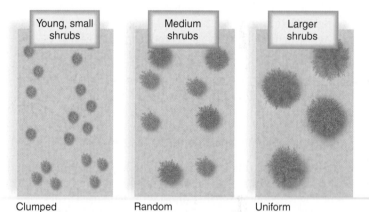

| Young, small shrubs | Medium shrubs | Larger shrubs |
| Clumped | Random | Uniform |

Mature desert shrubs

FIGURE 36.2A Distribution patterns of the creosote bush.

FIGURE 36.2B Nesting colony of Cape gannets off the coast of New Zealand.

36.3 The growth rate results in population size changes

A population's annual growth rate is dependent upon the number of individuals born each year, the number of individuals that die each year, and annual immigration and emigration. Usually, it is possible to assume that immigration and emigration are equal and need not be considered in the calculation. Therefore, in a simple example, if the number of births is 30 per year, and the number of deaths is 10 per year per 1,000 individuals, the growth rate is 2.0%:

$$(30 - 10)/1,000 = 0.02 = 2.0\%$$

This population will grow because the number of births exceeds the number of deaths. On the other hand, if the number of deaths exceeds the number of births, the value of the growth rate is negative, and the population will shrink.

The **biotic potential** of a population is its highest possible growth rate when resources are unlimited. Whether the biotic potential is high or low depends primarily on the following factors:

1. Usual number of offspring per reproduction
2. Chances of survival until age of reproduction and until reproduction ceases
3. Age structure diagram; age reproduction begins
4. Length of time and how often an individual reproduces

For example, a pig population in which pig females produce many offspring that quickly mature to produce more offspring, has a much higher biotic potential than a rhinoceros population in which rhinoceros females produce only one or two offspring per infrequent reproductive event (**Fig. 36.3A**).

Survivorship Curves
The population growth rate does not take into account that the individuals of a population are in different stages of their life span. **Cohort** is the term used to describe population members that are the same age and have the same chances of surviving. Some investigators study population dynamics and construct life tables that show how many members of a cohort are still alive after certain intervals of time. For example, **Figure 36.3B** *left* is a life table for Dall sheep. The cohort contains 1,000 individuals. The table tells us that after one year, 199 individuals have died. Another way to express this same statistic, however, is to consider that 801 individuals are still alive—have survived—after one year. **Survivorship** is the probability of cohort members surviving to particular ages.

If we plot the number surviving at each age, a survivorship curve is produced (Fig. 36.3B *right*). The results of such investigations show that each species has a particular survivorship curve. Three typical survivorship curves, numbered I, II, and III, are seen (Fig. 36.3B*b*). Mammals, represented here by the Dall sheep, usually have a type I survivorship curve; they survive well past the midpoint of the life span, and they do not die until near the end of the life span. On the other hand, the type III curve is typical of a population, such as oysters, in which most individuals will probably die very young. This type of survivorship curve occurs in many invertebrates, fishes, and humans in less-developed countries. In the type II curve, survivorship decreases at a constant rate throughout the life span;

FIGURE 36.3A Biotic potential is dependent on many factors, among them the number of offspring per reproductive event. Pigs, which produce many offspring that quickly mature to produce more offspring, have a much higher biotic potential than rhinoceroses, which produce only one or two offspring per infrequent reproductive event.

this pattern is typical of hydras, many songbirds, small mammals, and some invertebrates, for which death is usually unrelated to age.

Much can be learned about the life history of a species by studying its life table and the survivorship curve constructed from this table. For example, a type III survivorship curve indicates that since death probably comes early for most members, only a few live long enough to reproduce. How do you think the other two types of survivorship curves affect reproduction?

Other types of information are also derived from studying life tables. In the life table for a plant called blue grass, per capita seed production increases as plants mature, and then seed production drops off. The survivorship curve for blue grass shows that most individuals survive six to nine months, and then the chances of survivorship diminish at an increasing rate.

Age Structure Diagrams
When the individuals in a population reproduce repeatedly, several generations may be alive at any given time. From the perspective of population growth, a population contains three major age groups: prereproductive, reproductive, and postreproductive. Populations differ according to what proportion of the population falls in each age group.

Age (years)	Number of survivors at beginning of year	Number of deaths during year
0–1	1,000 1,000 − 199 =	199
1–2	801	12
2–3	789	13
3–4	776	12
4–5	764	30
5–6	734	46
6–7	688	48
7–8	640	69
8–9	571	132
9–10	439	187
10–11	252	156
11–12	96	90
12–13	6	3
13–14	3	3
14–15	0	

a.

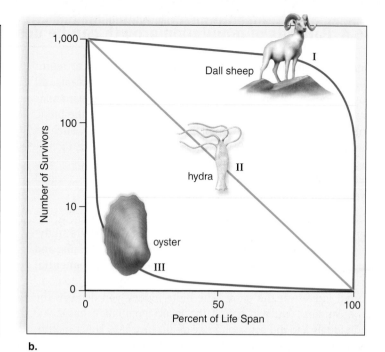

b.

FIGURE 36.3B (*Left*) **a.** A life table for Dall sheep based on data collected as the population aged. (*Right*) **b.** Three typical survivorship curves. The curves are based on life history tables, such as the one for Dall sheep.

At least three patterns are possible, as shown in the **age structure diagrams** in **Figure 36.3C.**

When the prereproductive group is the largest of the three groups, the birthrate is higher than the death rate, and a *pyramid-shaped* diagram is expected. Under such conditions, even if the growth for that year were matched by the deaths for that year, the population would continue to grow in subsequent years. Why? Because there are more individuals entering than leaving the reproductive years. Eventually, as the size of the reproductive group equals the size of the prereproductive group, a *bell-shaped* diagram results. The postreproductive group is still the smallest, however, because of mortality. If the birthrate falls below the death rate, the prereproductive group becomes smaller than the reproductive group. The age structure diagram is then *urn-shaped,* because the postreproductive group is the largest.

Age distribution reflects the past and future history of a population. Because a postwar baby boom occurred in the United States between 1946 and 1964, the postreproductive group will soon be the largest group in this country.

Typically, the pattern of population growth results in one of two growth curves described in Section 36.4.

▶ **36.3 Check Your Progress** Which age group in an increasing population (Figure 36.3C) should be hunted and killed in order to quickly alter the survivorship curve and reduce the biotic potential of a deer population that has expanded beyond the ability of the environment to sustain it?

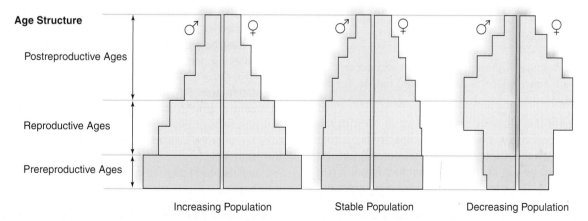

FIGURE 36.3C Typical age structure diagrams for hypothetical populations that are increasing, stable, or decreasing. Different numbers of individuals in each age class create these distinctive shapes. In each diagram, the left half represents males while the right half represents females.

36.4 Patterns of population growth can be described graphically

One of the characteristics of life is organisms' ability to reproduce. When the rate of reproduction exceeds the death rate, all populations have an enormous ability to grow. The particular pattern of a population's growth is dependent on (1) the biotic potential of a population combined with other factors, such as their age structure, and (2) the availability of resources, including environmental factors such as nesting sites and food. The two fundamental patterns of population growth are termed exponential growth and logistic growth.

Exponential Growth The capacity for population growth can be quite dramatic, as witnessed by ecologists who are studying the growth of a population of insects capable of infesting and taking over an area. Under these circumstances, **exponential growth** is expected. This growth pattern can be likened to compound interest at the bank: The more money you deposit, the more interest you will get. If the insect population has 2,000 individuals and the per capita rate of increase is 20% per month, there will be 2,400 insects after one month, 2,880 after two months, 3,456 after three months, and so forth. An exponential pattern of population growth results in a J-shaped curve (**Fig. 36.4A**). Notice that a J-shaped curve has these phases:

Lag phase Growth is slow because the number of individuals in the population is small.
Exponential growth phase Growth is accelerating due to biotic potential (see Section 36.3).

Usually, exponential growth can only continue as long as resources in the environment are unlimited. When the number of individuals in the population approaches the number that can be supported by available resources, competition among individuals for these resources increases.

Logistic Growth As resources decrease, population growth levels off, and a pattern of population growth called **logistic growth** is expected. Logistic growth results in an S-shaped growth curve (**Fig. 36.4B**). Notice that an S-shaped curve has these phases:

Lag phase Growth is slow because the number of individuals in the population is small.
Exponential growth phase Growth is accelerating due to biotic potential.
Deceleration phase The rate of population growth slows because of increased competition among individuals for available resources.
Stable equilibrium phase Although fluctuations can occur, little if any growth takes place because births and deaths are about equal.

The stable equilibrium phase is said to occur at the carrying capacity of the environment. The **carrying capacity** is the total number of individuals the resources of the environment can support for an extended period of time. This number is not a constant and varies with the circumstances and the environment. For example, a large island can support a larger population of penguins than a small island, because the smaller island has a limited amount of space for nesting sites. When the number of nesting sites is inadequate, some birds do not reproduce.

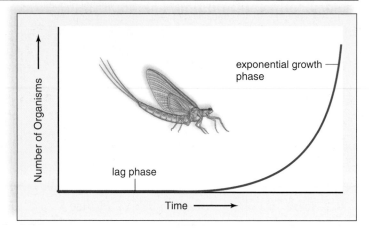

FIGURE 36.4A Exponential growth.

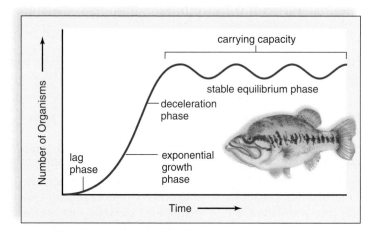

FIGURE 36.4B Logistic growth.

Applications Our knowledge of logistic growth has practical applications. The model predicts that exponential growth will occur only when population size is much lower than the carrying capacity. So, if humans are using a fish population as a continuous food source, it would be best to maintain that population size in the exponential phase of growth when biotic potential is having its full effect and the birthrate is the highest. If people overfish, the fish population will sink into the lag phase, and it may be years before exponential growth recurs. On the other hand, if people are trying to limit the growth of a pest, it is best to reduce the carrying capacity rather than to reduce the population size. Reducing the population size only encourages exponential growth to begin once again. For example, farmers can reduce the carrying capacity for a pest by alternating rows of different crops instead of growing one type of crop throughout the entire field.

Regulation of population size is discussed in the next part of the chapter.

▶ **36.4 Check Your Progress** If there were abundant but limited food resources for the deer living in a region where hunting was no longer allowed, what population growth pattern would likely occur?

Environmental Interactions Influence Population Size

Learning Outcome

▶ Give examples of density-independent factors and density-dependent factors, telling how they relate to population size. (36.5; 36.6)

Regulation of population size cannot be achieved by density-independent factors (e.g., natural disasters) but can be achieved by density-dependent factors (e.g., predators). The former only sporadically reduce population size.

36.5 Density-independent factors affect population size

So far, we have observed that a population's particular density and growth pattern determine the population size. In addition, ecologists have long recognized that environmental interactions play an important role in population size. Abiotic environmental factors include droughts (lack of rain), freezes, hurricanes, floods, and forest fires. Any one of these natural disasters can cause individuals to die and lead to a sudden and catastrophic reduction in population size. However, such an event does not necessarily kill a larger percentage of a dense population compared to a less dense population. Therefore, an abiotic factor is usually a **density-independent factor,** meaning that the percentage of individuals killed remains the same regardless of the population size. In other words, the intensity of the effect does not increase with increased population size. The red line in **Figure 36.5A** shows that mortality percentage (percentage killed) remains the same, regardless of the density of the population.

An example of a density-independent factor is a drought on the Galápagos Islands that caused the population size of one of Darwin's finches (*Geospiza fortis*) to decline from 1,400 to 200 individuals. (The drought caused reduced availability of seeds this species ate.) This is a reduction of 86% of the original population size. Assuming no competition between members of the population, drought, in this instance, is acting as a density-independent factor. We can assume, then, that if the population began with 2,800 individuals, the population would reduce to 400 members, which is the same percentage reduction.

Natural disasters such as hurricanes and floods can have a drastic effect on a population and cause sudden and catastrophic reductions in population size. However, a flash flood does not necessarily kill a larger percentage of a dense population than a less dense population. Therefore, such a flood cannot be counted on to regulate population size, keeping it within the carrying capacity of the environment. Nevertheless, as with our first example, the larger the population, the greater the

Death rate = 60%

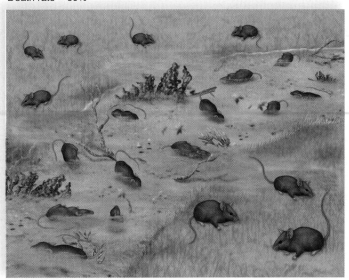

Death rate = 64%

FIGURE 36.5B A flood has a density-independent effect. At the top, a low-density population has a death rate of 3/5, or 60% while at the bottom a high-density population has a similar death rate of 12/20, or 64%.

number of individuals probably affected. In the impact of a flash flood on a low-density population of mice living in a field (mortality rate of 3/5, or 60%) **Fig. 36.5B** *top* is similar to the impact on a high-density population (mortality rate of 12/20, or 64%) (**Fig. 36.5B** *bottom*).

▶ **36.5 Check Your Progress** What are some examples of density-independent factors in a region overpopulated by deer?

FIGURE 36.5A
Percentage that die per density of population.

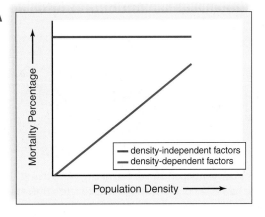

Biotic factors tend to be **density-dependent factors.** The percentage of the population affected by these factors does increase as the density of the population increases (see the blue line in Figure 36.5A). Competition, predation, and parasitism are all biotic factors that increase in intensity as the density increases. We will discuss these interactions between populations again in Chapter 38 because they influence community composition and diversity.

Competition occurs when members of the same species attempt to use needed resources (such as light, food, or space) that are in limited supply. As a result, not all members of the population have access to the resource to the degree necessary to ensure survival or reproduction. As a theoretical example of a density-dependent effect, let's consider a woodpecker population in which members have to compete for nesting sites. Each pair of birds requires a tree hole to raise offspring. In **Figure 36.6A** (*left*), if there are more holes than breeding pairs, each pair can have a hole in which to lay eggs and rear young birds. But if there are fewer holes than breeding pairs, each pair must compete to acquire a nesting site (Fig. 36.6A, *right*). Pairs that fail to gain access to holes will be unable to contribute new members to the population.

As an actual example of competition, four male and 21 female reindeer (*Rangifer*) were released on St. Paul Island in the Bering Sea off Alaska in 1911. St. Paul Island was a completely undisturbed environment, with little hunting pressure and no predators. By 1939, the herd had grown exponentially to about 2,000 reindeer, which overgrazed the habitat and then abruptly declined to about eight animals by 1950.

Predation occurs when one living organism, the predator, eats another, the prey. In the broadest sense, predation can include not only animals such as lions, which kill zebras, but also filter-feeding blue whales, which strain krill from the ocean waters; parasitic ticks, which suck blood from their hosts; and even herbivorous deer, which browse on trees and bushes. The effect of predation on a prey population generally increases as the population grows more dense, because prey are easier to find when hiding places are limited. Consider a field inhabited by a population of mice. Each mouse must have a hole in which to hide

to avoid being eaten by a hawk. If there are 100 mice, but only 98 holes, two mice will be left out in the open (**Fig. 36.6B,** *left*). It might be hard for the hawk to find only two mice in the field. If neither mouse is caught, then the predation rate is 0/2 = 0%. However, if there are 200 mice and only 100 holes, there is a greater chance that hawks will be able to find some of these 100 mice without holes (Fig. 36.6B, *right*). If half of the *exposed* mice are caught, the predation rate is 50/100 = 50%. Therefore, increasing the density of the available prey has increased the proportion of the population preyed upon.

In the next part of the chapter, we consider life history patterns.

▶ **36.6 Check Your Progress** What are some examples of density-dependent factors in a region overpopulated by deer?

FIGURE 36.6A Competition has a density-dependent effect. At left, when density is low, every woodpecker has a tree hole for raising young, but at right, when density is high, some birds will not have a hole.

FIGURE 36.6B Predation has a density-dependent effect. At left, when density is low, only two mice cannot find a place to hide and the hawk cannot find them (predation rate = 0%). At right, when density is high, 100 mice are unable to hide, and the hawk captures say ½ of them (predation rate = 50%).

The Life History Pattern Can Predict Extinction

Learning Outcomes

▶ Contrast the characteristics of an opportunistic population with those of an equilibrium population. (36.7)

▶ List factors that help determine whether a population will become extinct. (36.7)

The life history of a species is based on the population demographics we have just studied as well as on the attributes that result in these demographics. The life history pattern can be used to predict the possibility of extinction.

36.7 Life history patterns consider several population characteristics

Populations vary in terms of the number of births per reproductive event, the age at reproduction, the life span, and the probability of living the entire life span. Such particulars are part of a species' **life history,** and life histories often involve trade-offs. For example, each population is able to capture only so much of the available energy, and how this energy is distributed between its life span (short versus long), reproductive events (few versus many), care of offspring (little versus much), and so forth has evolved over the years. Natural selection shapes the final life history of individual species, and therefore it is not surprising that even related species, such as frogs and toads, may have different life history patterns if they occupy different types of environments.

Analysis of exponential and logistic population growth patterns suggests that some populations follow an opportunistic pattern and others follow an equilibrium pattern. An **opportunistic population** tends to live in a fluctuating and/or unpredictable environment. The population remains small until favorable conditions promote exponential growth. The members of the population are small in size, mature early, have a short life span, and provide limited parental care for a great number of offspring. Density-independent effects dramatically affect population size, which is large enough to survive an event that threatens to annihilate it. The population has a high dispersal capacity. Various types of insects and weeds are the best examples of opportunistic species (**Fig. 36.7A**), but there are others. A cod is a rather large fish, weighing up to 12 kg and measuring nearly 2 m in length—but the cod releases gametes in vast numbers, the zygotes form in the sea, and the parents make no further investment in developing offspring. Of the 6–7 million eggs released by a single female cod, only a few will become adult fish.

In contrast, some environments are relatively stable and predictable, allowing population size to remain fairly stable. **Equilibrium populations** exhibit logistic population growth, and the size of the population remains close to, or at, the carrying capacity. Resources are relatively scarce, and the individuals best able to compete—those with phenotypes best suited to the environment—have the largest number of offspring. Members allocate energy to their own growth and survival, and to the growth and survival of their few offspring. Therefore, they are fairly large, slow to mature, and have a relatively long life span (**Fig. 36.7B**). The size of equilibrium populations tends to be regulated by density-dependent effects. The best possible examples include long-lived plants (saguaro cacti, oaks, cypress, and pine), birds of prey (hawks and eagles), and large mammals (whales, elephants, bears, and gorillas).

Extinction is the total disappearance of a species or higher group. Which species, the dandelion or the mountain gorilla, is apt to become extinct? Because the dandelion matures quickly,

Opportunistic Pattern

- Small individuals
- Short life span
- Fast to mature
- Many offspring
- Little or no care of offspring

FIGURE 36.7A Dandelions are opportunistic species.

produces many offspring at one time, and has seeds that are dispersed widely by wind, it can more easily withstand a local decimation than can the mountain gorilla.

▶ **36.7 Check Your Progress** Which type of species best describes a deer: opportunistic or equilibrium? Explain why the deer population is exploding while other mammals are (e.g. gorilla) on the brink of extinction.

FIGURE 36.7B Bears are equilibrium species.

Equilibrium Pattern

- Large individuals
- Long life span
- Slow to mature
- Few and large offspring
- Much care of offspring

36A Adaptability of Small Populations

Small populations are typically very vulnerable and may often be considered threatened or endangered with extinction. Florida panthers, black-footed ferrets, California condors, whooping cranes, and leatherback turtles are examples of small populations (**Fig. 36A**). We usually find small populations in areas where there is a considerable amount of habitat destruction, overharvest of species, or a high level of introduced or invasive species. A considerable amount of time and money is spent each year trying to save or manage these populations. Therefore, it is important to consider if they have enough genetic diversity to adapt to future changes in the environment.

One major problem of small populations is inbreeding, or the mating of closely related individuals who may be heterozygous for the same disorder. In humans, hereditary conditions such as cystic fibrosis, hemophilia, and some forms of muscular dystrophy are passed on relatively rarely because the human population is large and the chances of both parents carrying the same recessive alleles are fairly low. But in a small population, matings between individuals with the same recessive alleles are more likely. Cheetahs, for example, are known to have limited genetic diversity, and today zoos take all possible steps to prevent inbreeding between closely related animals. Among other conditions, this should help prevent Cheetahs from succumbing to the same infectious disease as has happened in the past.

FIGURE 36A Leatherback turtles are sea turtles that once numbered about 115,000. The population size is now estimated to be as low as 26,000 because human activities have killed off many turtles or prevented them from reproducing.

How did the cheetah population—or how does any population—lose its genetic diversity? A review of population genetics and the Hardy-Weinberg principle illustrates how many endangered populations have lost their genetic diversity. The Hardy-Weinberg principle states that genetic diversity will remain the same from generation to generation unless, for example, genetic drift occurs. Genetic drift is a change in a population's usual allele frequencies due to chance alone. For example, the leatherback turtle population has now crashed due to overharvesting, accidental capture by fishermen, and destruction of nesting sites. Many members of the population have died, thus losing the opportunity to reproduce. Under these circumstances, gene pool allele frequencies have changed, and some alleles may have been lost. The loss of alleles can affect a population's ability to adapt to future changes, as the following example shows.

Let's refer to the peppered moth and industrial melanism to illustrate how the loss of genetic diversity can affect a population's ability to adapt to new environmental circumstances. Researchers have shown that a peppered moth population ordinarily contains mostly light-colored moths and a few dark-colored moths. When the natural vegetation becomes dark due to industrial pollutants, the dark-colored moths become more prevalent due to the ability of birds to find and eat mainly the light-colored moths. Suppose a natural disaster occurs and wipes out the few remaining light-colored moths, along with their alleles that code for light coloring. Will the population be able to adapt if pollution control measures are introduced and the vegetation returns to its natural color? Under these circumstances, birds will be able to see and eat dark-colored moths, but the population will be unable to return to its original coloration.

Because we now know that genetic diversity is important to the future adaptability of small populations, it is essential that biologists not only restore the habitat of endangered organisms, but also take steps to restore their genetic diversity. Only in this way can we increase the likelihood that a small population will be able to adapt to future changes in the environment.

FORM YOUR OPINION

1. Some locations around the globe are called "hotspots" because they contain more diverse organisms than most other locations. Should we put our efforts into preserving hotspots rather than individual species?
2. Cheetahs are not faring well in their natural habitat, but they have been preserved in zoos. Is this okay, or should organisms only be preserved in their original natural environment?
3. Humans need to preserve the natural environments that provide us with food, absorb our wastes, and keep ecological cycles functioning. This being the case, should we preserve only enough species to keep natural environments in good health and forget about unique endangered species? Why or why not?

Many Human Populations Continue to Increase in Size

Learning Outcomes

▶ Explain how the world population is still undergoing exponential growth. (36.8)
▶ Contrast the population growth and age distributions of the more-developed and the less-developed countries. (36.8)

The human population continues to increase, but demographics differ for the more-developed and the less-developed countries.

36.8 World population growth is exponential

The world's population has risen steadily to a present size of about 6.9 billion people (**Fig. 36.8**). Prior to 1750, the growth of the human population was relatively slow, but as more reproducing individuals were added, growth increased, until the curve began to slope steeply upward, indicating that the population was undergoing exponential growth. The number of people added annually to the world population peaked at about 87 million around 1990, and currently it is a little over 75 million per year. This is roughly equal to the current populations of Argentina, Ecuador, and Peru combined.

The potential for future population growth can be appreciated by considering the **doubling time,** the length of time it takes for the population size to double. Currently, the doubling time is estimated to be 51 years. This means that in 51 years, the world would need double the amount of food, jobs, water, energy, and so on just to maintain the present standard of living.

Many people are gravely concerned that the amount of time needed to add each additional billion persons to the world population has become shorter and shorter. The first billion didn't occur until 1800; the second billion was attained in 1930; the third billion in 1960; and thereafter, a billion has been added every 12–15 years. Only when the number of young women entering the reproductive years is the same as those leaving those years can there be zero population growth, meaning that the birthrate equals the death rate, and population size remains steady. The world's population may level off at 7.5, 9, or 14 billion, depending on the speed at which the growth rate declines.

More-Developed and Less-Developed Countries The countries of the world can be divided into two groups. In the **more-developed countries (MDCs),** typified by countries in North America, Europe, Japan, and Australia, population growth is low, and most people enjoy a good standard of living. In the **less-developed countries (LDCs),** such as countries in Latin America, Africa, and Asia, population growth is expanding rapidly, and the majority of people live in poverty.

The MDCs doubled their populations between 1850 and 1950. This was largely due to a decline in the death rate, the development of modern medicine, and improved socioeconomic conditions. The decline in the death rate was followed shortly thereafter by a decline in the birthrate, so that populations in the MDCs experienced only modest growth between 1950 and 1975. This sequence of events (i.e., decreased death rate followed by decreased birthrate) is termed a **demographic transition.** Yearly growth of the MDCs as a whole has now stabilized at 0.2%.

Although the death rate in the LDCs began to decline steeply following World War II with the importation of modern medicine from the MDCs, the birthrate remained high. The yearly growth of the LDCs peaked at 2.5% between 1960 and 1965. Since that time, a demographic transition has occurred: The decline in the death rate slowed, and the birthrate fell. The yearly growth rate is now 1.2% and the LDCs are in the deceleration phase of exponential growth (see Fig. 36.4). Still, they may explode from 5.6 billion today to 8 billion in 2050. The LDCs continue to experience a population momentum because they have more women entering the reproductive years than older women leaving them. Today, 88% of the world's population lives in Asia (India and China), Africa, and Latin America.

▶ **36.8 Check Your Progress** How would using injectable birth control on a wild deer population affect the doubling time of the population?

FIGURE 36.8 World population growth over time.

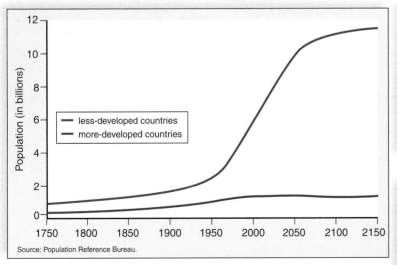

Source: Population Reference Bureau.

Living conditions in more-developed countries

Living conditions in less-developed countries

36B Sustainability of the U.S. Population

Is the United States population sustainable? *Sustainability* occurs when future generations are able to enjoy the same quality of life as the present generation. How can we judge when a population is sustainable? One way applies the following formula proposed by scientists Paul Ehrlich and John Holdren:

$$I = PAT$$

Impact = Population × Affluence × Technology

I = impact of the population on the environment
P = population size
A = affluence, the amount of consumption of goods and services per capita
T = technology, the degree to which inefficient and environmentally unsafe methods are used to produce goods and services

The less impact a population has on the environment, the more likely it will be sustainable. The United States could reduce its impact on the environment—for example, by having a zero population growth, reducing consumption, and improving the efficiency and cleanliness of technology. What is the possibility of stabilizing the U.S. population size? The United States is a more-developed country (MDC) with a growth rate of just under 1%, which is higher than many other MDCs. Its growth rate is due to a young age structure, which results in more births than deaths. The U.S. 2009 population of 308 million will continue to increase because it has a young age structure and also because the fertility rate is on the increase (**Fig. 36B,** *top*). Teen births have increased 3%, and third births per couple have increased since 1990. Immigration is another factor that causes the U.S. population to increase. Even a modest immigration of 1.1 million to 1.6 million per year would lead to a population increase if 399 million by 2050, even if fertility were not on the increase.

The total impact of the U.S. population on the environment is also due to high consumption of energy and minerals. The term consumption includes not only resource use but also waste production (Fig. 36B, *bottom*). Consumption in and of itself is not necessarily a problem, but it becomes one when a resource is consumed in a negligent way. For example, fishing becomes undesirable when fisheries are overharvested and future yield is in jeopardy. The surface mining of coal creates environmental problems when whole mountains are reduced to rubble and toxic run-offs contaminate water supplies. Technology can come to the rescue, as when automobile engines are designed to reduce emissions or when we can use renewable energy sources,

such as solar and wind which create less pollution than do fossil fuels. The aim is to manage our consumption of energy and minerals so that the natural environment can continue to provide for our needs without creating much waste. However, population growth drives up consumption of resources. For example, between 1980 and 1993, per capita energy consumption in the United States fell slightly, but the total energy consumption rose by 10%. What happened? The population increased, and total consumption went up despite the decline in per capita use.

Several countries, such as India and China, are now moving from being less-developed to more-developed. Previously, their very large populations had minimal impact on the biosphere because of low consumption of resources, but this is no longer the case, because their level of consumption is increasing rapidly.

FORM YOUR OPINION

1. Are families in the United States acting selfishly when they have more than two children? Why or why not?
2. What benefits might arise if the U.S. population were to achieve sustainability? How might this affect the economy?
3. The United States has a high environmental impact, and yet we don't want other countries to have similar impacts. Should we reduce our environmental impact and expect other countries to do the same? Why or why not?

FIGURE 36B (*Above*) The U.S. fertility rate is on the increase, and now it is apparently in vogue for a couple to have three children instead of two. (*Below*) Technology allows us to consume resources and it leads to pollution unless it is well managed.

SUMMARY

Ecology Studies Where and How Organisms Live in the Biosphere

36.1 Ecology is studied at various levels

- **Ecology** is the study of the interactions of organisms with other organisms and with the physical environment.
- The levels of ecological study are: **organism, population, community, ecosystem,** and **biosphere.**

Populations Are Not Static—They Change Over Time

36.2 Density and distribution are aspects of population structure

- **Population density** refers to the number of individuals per unit area.
- **Population distribution** (whether clumped, random, or uniform) is the pattern of dispersal of individuals across a **range.**
- **Resources** are the components of the environment that support living organisms.
- **Limiting factors** are aspects of the environment, such as nutrient availability, that determine where an organism lives.

36.3 The growth rate results in population size changes

- Yearly birth and death rates mainly determine a population's growth rate.
- A population's **biotic potential** is its highest possible growth rate when resources are unlimited. Biotic potential is:
  - Affected by **survivorship,** the probability of **cohort** members surviving to a particular age as shown in a **life table.**
  - Dependent on the age structure as shown in an **age structure diagram,** which includes prereproductive, reproductive, and postreproductive age groups. A pyramid shape means the population will expand rapidly; a bell shape indicates the population is stabilized; and an urn shape means the population will decline in size.

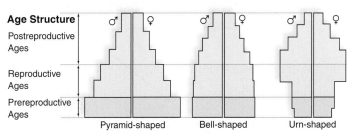

Age Structure		
Postreproductive Ages		
Reproductive Ages		
Prereproductive Ages		
Pyramid-shaped	Bell-shaped	Urn-shaped

36.4 Patterns of population growth can be described graphically

- **Exponential growth,** which has a lag phase and an exponential growth phase, accelerates over time and results in a J-shaped curve.

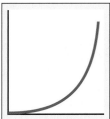

J-shaped curve

- **Logistic growth,** which has an exponential growth phase, a deceleration phase, and a stable equilibrium phase, stabilizes when the **carrying capacity** has been reached, resulting in an S-shaped curve.

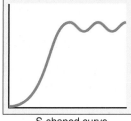

S-shaped curve

Environmental Interactions Influence Population Size

36.5 Density-independent factors affect population size

- **Density-independent factors** are abiotic factors that affect population size, such as droughts, freezes, hurricanes, floods, and forest fires.
- Density-independent means that mortality (% killed) remains the same, regardless of density.

36.6 Density-dependent factors affect large populations more

- **Density-dependent factors** are biotic factors that affect population size, such as competition, predation, and parasitism.
- Density-dependent means that mortality increases as the density of the population increases.

The Life History Pattern Can Predict Extinction

36.7 Life history patterns consider several population characteristics

- Population characteristics (life span, biotic potential, etc.) shape the population's **life history.**
- **Opportunistic populations** exhibit exponential growth; small individuals have a short life span and may die before reproducing.
- **Equilibrium populations** exhibit logistic growth; large individuals have a long life span, and most of their offspring survive to reproductive age.
- Opportunistic populations are adapted to a fluctuating environment, and equilibrium species are adapted to a relatively stable environment and more likely to experience **extinction.**

Opportunistic Pattern	Equilibrium Pattern
• Small individuals • Short life span • Fast to mature • Many offspring • Little or no care of offspring	• Large individuals • Long life span • Slow to mature • Few and large offspring • Much care of offspring
Example: dandelions	Example: mountain gorillas

Human Populations Continue to Increase in Size

36.8 World population growth is exponential

- The current world population is 6.8 billion people.
- Based on the predicted **doubling time,** the world population will require double the amount of current resources in 51 years.
- **More-developed countries (MDCs)** are characterized by low population growth and generally a good standard of living.

- **Less-developed countries (LDCs)** are known for rapidly expanding populations and generally poor living conditions.
- **Once the LDCs have** passed through the **demographic transition** and deaths equal births, growth will stabilize.

Ecology Studies Where and How Organisms Live in the Biosphere

1. Which of the following levels of ecological study involves both abiotic and biotic components?
   a. organism
   b. population
   c. community
   d. ecosystem
   e. All of these are correct.
2. Place the following levels of organization in order, from lowest to highest.
   a. community, ecosystem, population, organism
   b. organism, community, population, ecosystem
   c. population, ecosystem, organism, community
   d. organism, population, community, ecosystem

Populations Are Not Static—They Change Over Time

3. The distribution of the human population is
   a. variable.
   b. clumped.
   c. random.
   d. uniform.
4. If the human birthrate were reduced to 15 per 1,000 per year and the death rate remained the same (9 per thousand), what would be the growth rate?
   a. 9%
   b. 6%
   c. 10%
   d. 0.6%
   e. 15%
5. A population's maximum growth rate is also called its
   a. carrying capacity.
   b. biotic potential.
   c. growth curve.
   d. replacement rate.
6. Which of the following statements about a plant species is not relevant for determining its biotic potential?
   a. It produces 10 kg of mass per year.
   b. It produces its first flowers at five years of age.
   c. 50% of seedlings grow into mature plants.
   d. On average, 100 seedlings are produced by each plant every year.
7. If a population has a type I survivorship curve (most of its members live the entire life span), which of the following events would you also expect?
   a. a single reproductive event per adult
   b. most individuals reproduce
   c. sporadic reproductive events
   d. reproduction occurring near the end of the life span
   e. None of these are correct.
8. Exponential growth is best described by
   a. steep, unrestricted growth.
   b. an S-shaped growth curve.
   c. a constant rate of growth.
   d. growth that levels off after rapid growth.
   e. Both b and d are correct.
9. When the carrying capacity of the environment is exceeded, the population typically
   a. increases, but at a slower rate.
   b. stabilizes at the highest level reached.
   c. decreases.
   d. dies off entirely.

10. **THINKING CONCEPTUALLY** The range of a plant that reproduces asexually by runners would be smaller from one that reproduces by windblown seeds. Explain.
11. Label this diagram.

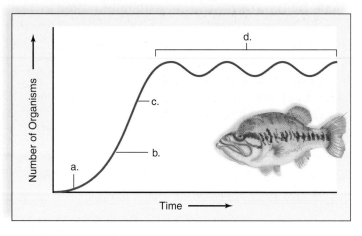

Environmental Interactions Influence Population Size

12. Which of these is a density-independent factor?
    a. competition
    b. predation
    c. weather
    d. resource availability

For statements 13–15, indicate the factor in the key exemplified by the scenario.

KEY:
   a. density-independent factor
   b. competition
   c. predation

13. A severe drought destroys the entire food supply of a herd of gazelle.
14. Only the swiftest coyotes are able to catch the limited supply of rabbits available as a food source. The remaining animals are not strong enough to reproduce.
15. Deer in a forest damage a dense thicket of oak saplings more severely than a few young oak trees.
16. Label each line on the following as representing density-independent factors or density-dependent factors.

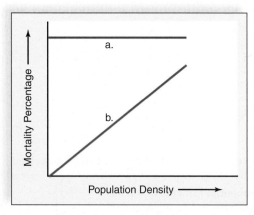

The Life History Pattern Can Predict Extinction

17. Which of the following is not a feature of an opportunistic life history pattern?
    a. many offspring
    b. little or no care of offspring
    c. long life span
    d. small individuals
    e. fast to mature

18. An equilibrium life history pattern does not include
    a. large individuals.   c. few offspring.
    b. long life span.   d. little or no care of offspring.
19. **THINKING CONCEPTUALLY** Under what conditions is it advantageous for a population to produce a large number of small, uncared-for offspring rather than large, well-cared-for offspring?

Many Human Populations Continue to Increase in Size

20. The human population
    a. is undergoing exponential growth.
    b. is not subject to environmental resistance.
    c. fluctuates from year to year.
    d. grows only if emigration occurs.
    e. All of these are correct.
21. The current doubling time for the world's population is 54 years. Therefore, if the population is 6.9 billion people today, what will it be in 108 years if the doubling rate does not change?
    a. 13.8 billion   c. 40.4 billion
    b. 27.6 billion   d. 108 billion
22. Decreased death rate followed by decreased birthrate has occurred in
    a. MDCs.   c. MDCs and LDCs.
    b. LDCs.   d. neither MDCs nor LDCs.
23. The overall reason the LDCs population is still expected to explode in the near future is that
    a. annual growth rates are higher than ever.
    b. death rates are near zero.
    c. families are getting larger.
    d. the population is in the deceleration phase of exponential growth stage.

24. A pyramid-shaped age distribution means that
    a. the prereproductive group is the largest group.
    b. the population will grow for some time in the future.
    c. the country is more likely an LDC than an MDC.
    d. fewer women are leaving the reproductive years than entering them.
    e. All of these are correct

THINKING SCIENTIFICALLY

1. The right whale population remains dangerously small, despite many decades of complete protection. Formulate a hypothesis based on the four factors listed in Section 36.3 to explain this observation. How would you test your hypothesis?
2. You are a river manager charged with maintaining the water flow through the use of dams so that trees, which have equilibrium life histories, can continue to grow along the river. What would you do?

ONLINE RESOURCE

www.mhhe.com/maderconcepts2

Enhance your study with animations that bring concepts to life and practice tests to assess your understanding. Your instructor may also recommend the interactive eBook, individualized learning tools, and more.

CONNECTING THE CONCEPTS

Modern ecology began with descriptive studies by nineteenth-century naturalists. In fact, an early definition of the field was "scientific natural history." However, modern ecology has now grown from a simple descriptive field to an experimental, predictive science.

Much of the success in the development of ecology as a predictive science has come from studies of populations and the creation of models that examine how populations change over time. The simplest models are based on population growth when resources are unlimited. This results in exponential population growth, a type only rarely seen in nature. Pest species may exhibit exponential growth until they run out of resources. Because so few natural populations exhibit exponential growth, population ecologists realized they must incorporate resource limitation into their models. The simplest models that account for limited resources result in logistic growth. Populations that exhibit logistic growth stop growing when they reach the environmental carrying capacity.

Many modern ecological studies are concerned with identifying the factors that limit population growth and set the environmental carrying capacity. A combination of careful descriptive studies,

experiments done in nature, and sophisticated models has allowed ecologists to accurately predict which factors have the greatest influence on biotic potential, population growth, and life history patterns.

We continue this study in Chapter 37 as we see how the behavior of an organism is adapted to the environment. Adaptations to the environment, as you know, result in reproductive success, leading possibly to an increase in population size, or at least maintenance of population size, in that environment.

PUT THE PIECES TOGETHER

1. Discuss why a moderate population size is desirable and either a very large or a very small population size could be undesirable.
2. The U.S. population continues to increase, unlike those of other more-developed countries. Should we be concerned about how this affects consumption and possibly the sustainability of the population?
3. With reference to Figure 36.3C, discuss the statement that a population will continue to grow in size as long as more woman are entering than leaving their reproductive years.

38

Community and Ecosystem Ecology

CHAPTER OUTLINE

APPLICATIONS

Ridding the Land of Waste

If it weren't for scavengers and decomposers, dead organic matter would accumulate in deep piles so that you wouldn't even be able to step outside your door! But thanks to decomposition, that doesn't happen. As soon as an animal dies, all of the microorganisms in its gut set to work, and decomposition begins. The faint smell of decay very quickly attracts scavengers, which seek out dead animals and eat them.

One well-known scavenger is the vulture, a bird equipped with an excellent sense of smell that helps it locate an animal carcass from miles away. Vultures attract a lot of attention because they are rather large, usually black birds with bald heads devoid of feathers. In some rural mountainous areas of the world, humans rely on vultures for assistance with "sky burials," in which a human corpse is cut into small pieces and left for the scavenging birds to eat. In Tibet, this practice is necessary because the frozen ground is too hard to bury the dead, and wood is too scarce for cremation. This ritual is also based on an appreciation for nutrient recycling; the deceased is providing nutrients that ultimately sustain all living beings.

Besides vultures, other scavengers include beetles, earthworms, and some insects. We can't include carrion beetles and flies because they are attracted to decomposing animals not as a source of food but as a nutrient-rich place to lay their eggs. Dung beetles are not scavengers either, but they are of interest because they eat and raise their young in animal feces. They have no need to

Vulture

Vultures assist in a sky burial.

eat other foods or drink water, because feces provide them with complete nutrition. By helping recycle fecal nutrients back into the land and by improving the hygiene of livestock pastures, dung beetles provide $380 million worth of services to farmers in the United States every year.

Decomposers are not scavengers either because they do not take into their bodies pieces of dead animals or plants, as scavengers do. Instead, they are saprotrophs that secrete their digestive juices into the environment and then absorb the nutrients. The most abundant and widespread saprotrophs in the world are microbes, predominantly bacteria and fungi. In order to compete with scavengers for the nutrients in decaying matter, microbes often secrete chemicals that are foul-smelling, distasteful, and/or toxic. According to biologist Dan Janzen, this is why fruits rot, seeds mold, and meat spoils. If you have ever avoided eating a moldy strawberry or drinking curdled milk, the microbes have won.

Decomposers perform a service for the entire biosphere when they recycle nutrients to plants, which produce food for themselves directly and for all living things indirectly. Of increasing interest is the use of microbial decomposers to obtain high energy biogas from leftover organic matter. For example, microbes anaerobically convert wood chips, animal (e.g., cow) feces, and all kinds of organic matter into biogas, which can be captured and used for heating, cooking, and generating electricity. In Rwanda, there are "poop-powered" prisons in which prisoners' feces are digested into biogas, and in San Francisco, biogas may soon be made from the huge quantity of pet feces produced within the city.

Also, microbial decomposers can clean up oil spills. A few days after an oil rig in the Gulf of Mexico suffered an explosion in 2010, a massive oil slick was seen approaching land. As scientists grappled with how best to clean up the oil, containment devices were placed along the coast and airplanes were used to apply chemical dispersants. Bioremediation scientists have shown that often the best results can be achieved by letting microbes living in the water decompose the oil. In the long run, microbes do the best job in the shortest length of time.

In this chapter, we will look at how the populations in a community interact. Then we will consider how populations interact not only among themselves, but also with the physical environment in ecosystems. Our society can also tap into the leftover high-energy compounds produced by decomposers. Someday, your house may be heated, your food may be cooked, or your electronics may be powered using methane (biogas) obtained from decomposing matter!

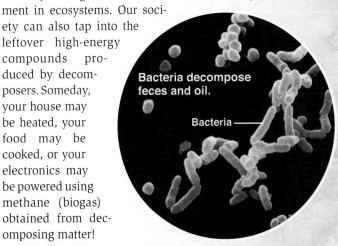
Bacteria decompose feces and oil.

Bacteria

Dung beetles rolling dung

Dung beetles assist in dung cleanup.

Biogas plants

Bacteria decompose feces and produce biogas.

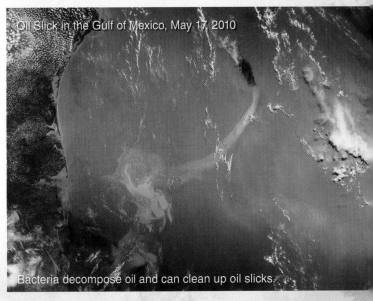
Oil Slick in the Gulf of Mexico, May 17, 2010

Bacteria decompose oil and can clean up oil slicks.

A Community Contains Several Interacting Populations in the Same Locale

Learning Outcomes

▶ Show that competition leads to resource partitioning. (38.1)
▶ Define predation, and discuss predator-prey population size dynamics. (38.2)
▶ Discuss various types of prey defenses, and give examples of two types of mimicry. (38.2)
▶ Contrast parasitism, commensalism, and mutualism, giving examples of each. (38.3–38.5)

Step into a forest and look around. Most likely, you will notice populations of animals interacting with plants and other animals. Insects will be feeding on the leaves of trees, or visiting flowers or even grasses. If you are lucky, you might see a hawk dart from a tree on the edge of the forest and grab a rodent running through an adjoining meadow. All the populations interacting in the forest form a **community.** The populations interact particularly through competition, predation, and various symbiotic relationships (parasitism, commensalism, and mutualism).

38.1 Competition can lead to resource partitioning

Competition is rivalry between populations for the same resources, such as light, space, nutrients, or mates. In the 1930s, G. F. Gause grew two species of *Paramecium* in one test tube containing a fixed amount of bacterial food. Although populations of each species survived when grown in separate test tubes, only one species, *Paramecium aurelia,* survived when the two species were grown together (**Fig. 38.1A**). *P. aurelia* acquired more of the food resource and had a higher population growth rate than did *P. caudatum.* Eventually, as the *P. aurelia* population grew and obtained an increasingly greater proportion of the food, the number of *P. caudatum* individuals decreased, and the population died out. This experiment and others helped ecologists formulate the **competitive exclusion principle,** which states that no two species can occupy the same niche at the same time. The **ecological niche** of an organism is the role it plays in its community, including its **habitat** (where the organism lives) and its interactions with other organisms and the environment. See Figure 38.7 for a more complete description of niche.

Competition for resources does not always lead to localized extinction of a species. Multiple species can coexist in communities by partitioning resources. In another laboratory experiment using other species of *Paramecium,* Gause found that two species could survive in the same test tube if one species consumed bacteria at the bottom of the tube and the other ate bacteria suspended in solution. This **resource partitioning** decreased competition between the two species. What could have been one niche became two more-specialized niches due to species differences in feeding behavior.

When small and medium ground finches live on the same island of the Galápagos, their beak sizes differ because they feed on different-sized seed (**Fig. 38.1B**). When these ground finches live on different islands, the beak size does not differ and they feed on the same preferred range of seeds. Such so-called **character displacement** is often viewed as evidence that competition and resource partitioning do take place when closely related species share the same resource, such as seeds.

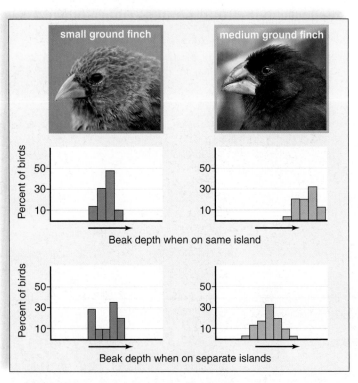

FIGURE 38.1B Character displacement occurs in finches when they coexist. Notice the similarity in beak depth when they are on separate islands.

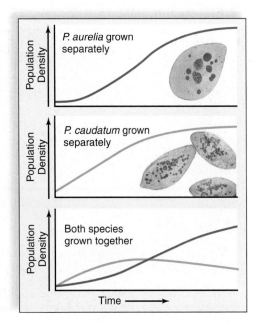

FIGURE 38.1A Competition only occurs between two species of *Paramecium* when they are grown together.

The niche specialization that permits coexistence of multiple species can be very subtle. Species of warblers that live in North American forests are all about the same size, and all feed on bud-worms, a type of caterpillar found on spruce trees. Robert MacArthur recorded the length of time each warbler species spent in different regions of spruce canopies to determine where each species did most of its feeding. He discovered that each species primarily used different parts of the tree canopy and, in that way, had a more specialized niche (**Fig. 38.1C**). As another example, consider that three types of birds—swallows, swifts, and martins—all eat flying insects and parachuting spiders. These birds even frequently fly in mixed flocks. But each type of bird has a different nesting site and migrates at a slightly different time of year.

In all these cases of niche specialization, we have merely assumed that what we observe today is due to competition in the past. Some ecologists are fond of saying that in doing so we have invoked the "ghosts of competition past." Are there any instances in which competition has actually been observed? Joseph Connell has studied the distribution of barnacles on the Scottish coast, where a small barnacle (*Chthamalus stellatus*) lives on the high part of the intertidal zone, and a large barnacle (*Balanus balanoides*) lives on the lower part (**Fig. 38.1D**). Why should that be, when their free-swimming larvae attach themselves to rocks at any point in the intertidal zone? The answer is that the faster-growing *Balanus* crowds out *Chthamalus* in the lower tidal zone, but cannot do so in the upper tidal zone because it is more susceptible to drying out than *Chthamalus*.

In Section 38.2, we consider predation, which is another common type of interaction between populations in a community.

▶ **38.1 Check Your Progress** The activities of decomposers illustrate that competitors are not always passive toward another competitor. Explain.

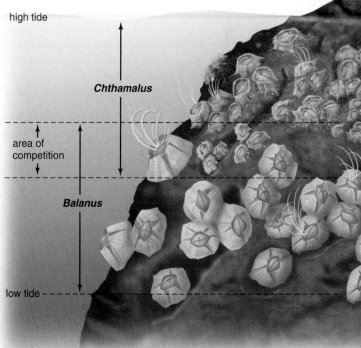

FIGURE 38.1C Niche specialization occurs among five species of coexisting warblers.

FIGURE 38.1D Competition occurs between two species of barnacles.

Predation occurs when one living organism, called the predator, feeds on another, called the prey. In its broadest sense, predaceous consumers include not only animals such as lions, which kill zebras, but also filter-feeding blue whales, which strain krill from ocean waters; herbivorous deer, which browse on trees and shrubs; parasitic ticks, which suck blood from their victims; and *parasitoids,* which are wasps that lay their eggs inside the body of a host. The resulting larvae feed on the host, sometimes causing death. Parasitism can be considered a type of predation because one individual obtains nutrients from another (see Section 38.3). Predation and parasitism are expected to increase the abundance of the predator and parasite at the expense of the abundance of the prey or host.

Predator-Prey Population Dynamics

Do predators reduce the population density of prey? In another classic experiment, G. F. Gause reared the ciliated protozoans *Paramecium caudatum* (prey) and *Didinium nasutum* (predator) together in a culture medium. He observed that *Didinium* ate all the *Paramecium* and then died of starvation. In nature, we can find a similar example. When a gardener brought prickly-pear cactus to Australia from South America, the cactus spread out of control until millions of acres were covered with nothing but cactus. The cactuses were brought under control when a moth from South America, whose caterpillar feeds only on the cactus, was introduced. The caterpillar was a voracious predator on the cactus, efficiently reducing the cactus population. Now both cactus and moth are found at greatly reduced densities in Australia.

This raises an interesting point: The population density of the predator can be affected by the prevalence of the prey. In other words, the predator-prey relationship is actually a two-way street. In that context, consider that at first the biotic potential (maximum reproductive rate) of the prickly-pear cactus was maximized, but factors that oppose biotic potential came into play after the moth was introduced. And the biotic potential of the moth was maximized when it was first introduced, but the carrying capacity decreased after its food supply was diminished.

Sometimes, instead of remaining in a steady state, predator and prey populations first increase in size and then decrease. We can appreciate that an increase in predator population size is dependent on an increase in prey population size. But what causes a decrease in population size instead of the establishment of a steady population size? At least two possibilities account for the reduction: (1) Perhaps the biotic potential (reproductive rate) of the predator is so great that its increased numbers overconsume the prey, and then as the prey population declines, so does the predator population; or (2) perhaps the biotic potential of the predator is unable to keep pace with the prey, and the prey population overshoots the carrying capacity and suffers a crash. Now the predator population follows suit because of a lack of food. In either case, the result will be a series of peaks and valleys, with the predator population size lagging slightly behind that of the prey population.

A famous example of predator-prey cycles occurs between the snowshoe hare and the Canadian lynx, a type of small predatory cat (**Fig. 38.2A**). The snowshoe hare is a common herbivore in the coniferous forests of North America, where it feeds on terminal twigs of various shrubs and small trees. The Canadian lynx feeds on snowshoe hares but also on ruffed grouse and spruce grouse, two types of birds. Studies have revealed that the hare and lynx populations cycle regularly, as graphed in Figure 38.2A. Investigators at first assumed that the lynx brings about a decline in the hare population and that this accounts for the cycling. But others have noted that the decline in snowshoe hare abundance was accompanied by low growth and reproductive rates, which could be signs of a food shortage. Experiments were done to test whether factor (1), predation, or factor (2), lack of food, caused the decline in the hare population. The results suggest that both factors combined to produce a low hare population and the cycling effect.

Prey Defenses

Prey defenses are mechanisms that thwart the possibility of being eaten by a predator. Prey species have evolved a variety of mechanisms that enable them to avoid predators, including heightened senses, speed, protective armor, protective

FIGURE 38.2A
Predator-prey interaction between a snowshoe hare and a lynx.

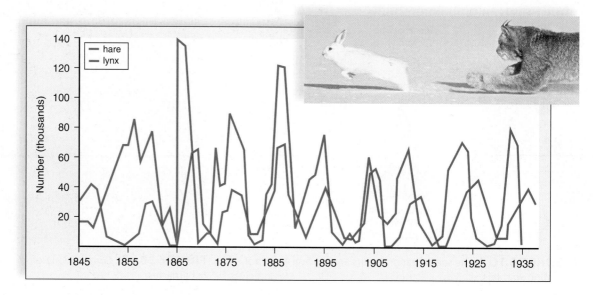

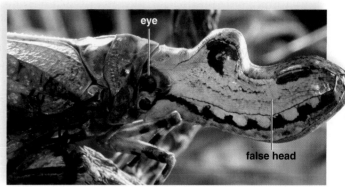

eye

false head

Camouflage   Warning coloration   Fright

FIGURE 38.2B Antipredator defenses.

spines or thorns, tails and appendages that break off, and chemical defenses. Consider, for the moment, only animals. There are a number of ways that a predator deceives its prey and that prey avoids capture by predators. One common strategy is **camouflage,** or the ability to blend into the background. Some animals have cryptic coloration that allows them to blend into their surroundings. For example, flounders can take on the same coloration as their background (**Fig. 38.2B,** *left*). Many examples of protective camouflage are known: Walking sticks look like twigs; katydids look like sprouting green leaves; some caterpillars resemble bird droppings; and some insects and moths blend into the bark of trees.

Another common antipredator defense among animals is *warning coloration,* which tells the predator that the prey is potentially dangerous. As a warning to possible predators, poison-dart frogs are brightly colored (Fig. 38.2B, *middle*). Also, many animals, including caterpillars, moths, and fishes, possess false eyespots that confuse or startle another animal. Other animals have elaborate anatomic structures that cause *fright.* The South American lantern fly has a large false head with false eyes, making it resemble the head of an alligator (Fig. 38.2B, *right*). However, warning coloration and a fright defense are not always false. A porcupine certainly looks formidable, and for good reason. Its arrowlike quills have barbs that dig into the predator's flesh and penetrate even deeper as the enemy struggles after being impaled. In the meantime, the porcupine runs away.

Association with other prey is another common strategy that may help avoid capture. Flocks of birds, schools of fish, and herds of mammals stick together as protection against predators. Baboons that detect predators visually, and antelopes that detect predators by smell, sometimes forage together, gaining double protection against stealthy predators. The gazellelike springboks of southern Africa jump stiff-legged 2–4 m into the air when alarmed. Such a jumble of shapes and motions might confuse an attacking lion, allowing the herd to escape.

Mimicry **Mimicry** occurs when one species resembles another that possesses an overt antipredator defense. A mimic that lacks the defense of the organism it resembles is called a Batesian mimic (named for Henry Bates, who discovered the phenomenon). Once an animal experiences the defense of the model, it remembers the coloration and avoids all animals that look similar. **Figure 38.2C** (*top row*) shows two insects (flower fly and longhorn beetle) that resemble a yellow jacket wasp but lack the wasp's ability to sting.

Classic examples of Batesian mimicry include the scarlet kingsnake mimicking the venomous coral snake and the viceroy butterfly mimicking the foul-tasting monarch butterfly.

There are also examples of species that have the same defense and resemble each other. Many stinging insects—bees, wasps, hornets, and bumblebees—have the familiar black and yellow bands. Once a predator has been stung by a black and yellow insect, it is wary of that color pattern in the future. Mimics that share the same protective defense are called Müllerian mimics, after Fritz Müller, who suggested that this, too, is a form of mimicry. In Figure 38.2C (*bottom row*), the bumblebee is a Müllerian mimic of the yellow jacket wasp because both of them can sting.

The last three relationships we will explore—parasitism, commensalism, and mutualism—are symbiotic relationships in which two species are intimately related. Let's begin with parasitism in Section 38.3.

▶ **38.2 Check Your Progress** Could scavengers be considered predators when they eat decomposing meat? How so?

flower fly   longhorn beetle

bumblebee   yellow jacket

FIGURE 38.2C Mimicry: All of these insects have the same coloration.

38.3 Parasitism benefits one population at another's expense

Parasitism is similar to predation in that an organism, called the **parasite,** derives nourishment from another, called the **host.** Parasitism is one type of **symbiosis,** an association in which at least one of the species is dependent on the other **(Table 38.3).**

Viruses, such as HIV, that reproduce inside human lymphocytes are always parasitic, and parasites occur in all of the kingdoms of life as well. Bacteria (e.g., strep infection), protists (e.g., malaria), fungi (e.g., rusts and smuts), plants (e.g., mistletoe), and animals (e.g., tapeworms and fleas) all have parasitic members. While small parasites can be endoparasites (pinworms), larger ones are more likely to be ectoparasites (leeches), which remain attached to the exterior of the body by means of special-ized organs and appendages. The effects of parasites on the health of the host can range from slightly weakening them to actually killing them over time. When host populations are at a high density, parasites readily spread from one host to the next, causing intense infestations and a subsequent decline in host density. Parasites that do not kill their host can still play a role in reducing the host's population density because an infected host is less fertile and becomes more susceptible to another cause of death.

In addition to nourishment, host organisms also provide their parasites with a place to live and reproduce, as well as a mechanism for dispersing offspring to new hosts. Many parasites have both a primary and a secondary host. The secondary host may be a vector that transmits the parasite to the next primary host. Usually both hosts are required in order to complete the life cycle. The association between parasite and host is so intimate that parasites are often specific and even require certain species as hosts.

We take a look at commensalism in Section 38.4 and mutualism in Section 38.5.

TABLE 38.3	Symbiotic Relationships
Interaction	**Expected Outcome**
Parasitism	Abundance of parasite increases, and abundance of host decreases.
Commensalism	Abundance of one species increases, and the other is not affected.
Mutualism	Abundance of both species increases.

▶ **38.3 Check Your Progress** Explain why decomposers are not parasites.

38.4 Commensalism benefits only one population

Commensalism is a symbiotic relationship between two species in which one species is benefited and the other is neither benefited nor harmed.

Instances are known in which one species provides a home and/or transportation for the other species. For example, barnacles that attach themselves to the backs of whales and the shells of horseshoe crabs get both a home and transportation. It is possible, though, that the movement of the host is impeded by the presence of the attached animals, and therefore some scientists are reluctant to call these examples of commensalism.

Epiphytes, such as Spanish moss and some species of orchids and ferns, grow in the branches of trees, where they receive light, but they take no nourishment from the trees. Instead, their roots obtain nutrients and water from the air. Clownfishes live within the waving tentacles of sea anemones **(Fig. 38.4).** Because most fishes avoid the anemones' poisonous tentacles, clownfishes are protected from predators. Perhaps this relationship borders on mutualism, because the clownfishes may actually attract other fishes on which the anemone can feed.

Commensalism often turns out, on closer examination, to be an instance of either mutualism or parasitism. Cattle egrets are so named because these birds stay near cattle, which flush out their prey—insects and other animals—from vegetation. The relationship becomes mutualistic when egrets remove ectoparasites from the cattle. Remoras are fishes that attach themselves to the bellies of sharks by means of a modified dorsal fin acting as a suction cup. Remoras benefit by getting a free ride, and they also feed on a shark's leftovers. However, the shark benefits when remoras remove its ectoparasites. To some, it seems like wasted effort to try to classify symbiotic relationships into the three categories of parasitism, commensalism, and mutualism. Often, the amount of harm or good two species seem to do to one another depends on what the investigator chooses to measure.

We will take a break and discuss coevolution, a hallmark of symbiotic relationships, in How Life Changes on the next page.

FIGURE 38.4 A clownfish living among a sea anemone's tentacles.

▶ **38.4 Check Your Progress** How would you determine that remoras are commensalistic, not parasitic, on a shark?

Coevolution is present when two species adapt in response to selective pressure imposed by the other. In other words, an evolutionary change in one species results in an evolutionary change in the other. Organisms in symbiotic associations, which include parasitism, commensalism, and mutualism (see Table 38.3), are especially prone to the process of coevolution. As an example of coevolution, flowers pollinated by animals have features that attract them. Therefore, a butterfly-pollinated flower is often a composite, containing many individual flowers; the broad expanse provides room for the butterfly to land, and the butterfly has a proboscis that it inserts into each flower in turn. In this case, coevolution is highly beneficial to the flower because the insect will carry pollen to other flowers of the same type.

Coevolution also occurs between predators and prey. For example, a cheetah sprints forward to catch its prey, and this behavior might be selective for those gazelles that are able to run away or jump high in the air (such as a springbok) to avoid capture. The adaptation of the prey may very well put selective pressure on the predator to adapt to the prey's defense mechanism. Hence, an "arms race" can develop.

The process of coevolution has been studied in the cuckoo, a social parasite that reproduces at the expense of other birds. A cuckoo lays its eggs in another bird species' nest, and when the cuckoo egg hatches, that species ends up caring for the cuckoo. It is odd to see a small bird feeding a cuckoo nestling several times its size. How did this strange behavior develop? Investigators discovered that in order to "trick" a host bird, the adult cuckoo must (1) lay an egg that mimics the host's egg, (2) lay its egg very rapidly (only 10 seconds are required) in the afternoon while the host is away from the nest, and (3) leave most of the eggs in the nest because hosts will desert a nest that has only one egg in it. (The cuckoo chick hatches first and is adapted to removing any other eggs in the nest [**Fig. 38A**].) It seems that the host birds may very well next evolve a way to distinguish the cuckoo from their own young.

Coevolution can take many forms. In the case of *Plasmodium*, a cause of malaria, the sexual portion of the life cycle occurs within mosquitoes (the vector), and the asexual portion occurs in humans. The human immune system uses surface proteins to detect pathogens, and *Plasmodium* has numerous genes for surface proteins. But it is capable of changing its surface proteins repeatedly, and in this way it stays one step ahead of the host's immune system. HIV has a similar capability, which has added to the difficulty of producing an AIDS vaccine.

The relationship between parasite and host can include the ability of parasites to seemingly manipulate the behavior of their hosts in self-serving ways. Ants infected with the lance fluke (but not those uninfected) mysteriously cling to blades of grass with their mouthparts. There, the infested ants are eaten by grazing sheep, and the flukes are transmitted to the next host in their life cycle. Similarly, snails of the genus *Succinea* are parasitized by worms of the genus *Leucochloridium*. As the worms mature, they invade the snail's eyestalks, making them resemble edible caterpillars. Birds eat the snails, and now the parasites release

their eggs, and the embryos complete development inside the urinary tracts of the birds.

It used to be thought that as host and parasite coevolved, each would become more tolerant of the other since, if the opposite occurred, the parasite would soon run out of hosts. Parasites could first become commensal, or harmless to the host. Then, given enough time, the parasite and host might even become mutualists. In fact, the evolution of the eukaryotic cell by endosymbiosis is predicated on the supposition that bacteria took up residence inside a larger cell, and then the parasite and cell became mutualists.

However, this argument is too complex for some; after all, no organism is capable of "looking ahead" at its evolutionary fate. Rather, if an aggressive parasite could transmit more of itself in less time than a benign one, aggressiveness would be favored by natural selection. But other factors, such as the life cycle of the host, can determine whether aggressiveness is beneficial or not. For example, a benign parasite of newts will do better than an aggressive one. Why? Because newts take up solitary residence outside ponds in the forest for six years, and parasites have to wait that long before they are likely to meet up with another possible host.

FORM YOUR OPINION

1. How is a predator-prey relationship similar to and different from a parasite-host relationship?
2. Compare the HIV virus to the H1N1 virus in order to show that the HIV virus is a highly successful parasite.
3. Coevolution between a pollinator and a flower and between a parasite and its host differs widely. How so?

FIGURE 38A Social parasitism in the cuckoo.

Cuckoo pushes out host's eggs after hatching first

38.5 Mutualism benefits both populations

Mutualism is a symbiotic relationship in which both members benefit. As with other symbiotic relationships, it is possible to find numerous examples among all organisms. Bacteria that reside in the human intestinal tract acquire food, but they also provide us with vitamins, molecules we are unable to synthesize for ourselves. Termites would not be able to digest wood if not for the protozoans that inhabit their intestinal tracts and digest cellulose. Mycorrhizae are mutualistic associations between the roots of plants and fungal hyphae. The hyphae improve the uptake of nutrients for the plant, protect the plant's roots against pathogens, and produce plant growth hormones. In return, the plant provides the fungus with carbohydrates. Some sea anemones make their home on the backs of crabs. The crab uses the stinging tentacles of the sea anemone to gather food and to protect itself; the sea anemone gets a free ride that allows it greater access to food than other anemones. Lichens can grow on rocks because their fungal member conserves water and leaches minerals that are provided to the algal partner, which photosynthesizes and provides organic food for both populations. However, it's been suggested that the fungus is parasitic, at least to a degree, on the algae.

In tropical America, the bullhorn acacia tree is adapted to provide a home for ants of the species *Pseudomyrmex ferruginea* (see section 23.12, page 483). Unlike other acacias, this species has swollen thorns with a hollow interior, where ant larvae can grow and develop. In addition to housing the ants, acacias provide them with food. The ants feed from nectaries at the base of the leaves and eat fat- and protein-containing nodules called Beltian bodies, found at the tips of the leaves. The ants constantly protect the plant from herbivores and other plants that might shade it because, unlike other ants, they are active 24 hours a day.

The relationship between plants and their pollinators, mentioned previously, is a good example of mutualism. Perhaps the relationship began when herbivores feasted on pollen. The provision of nectar by the plant may have spared the pollen and, at the same time, allowed the animal to become an agent of pollination. By now, pollinator mouthparts are adapted to gathering the nectar of a particular plant species, and this species is dependent on the pollinator for dispersing pollen. The mutualistic relationships between flowers and their pollinators are examples of coevolution (see How Life Changes, p. 493). A striking example is the flower of the orchid *Ophrys apitera*. This flower resembles the body of a bumblebee, and its odor mimics the pheromones of a female bee. Therefore, male bees are attracted to the flower, and when they attempt to mate with it, they become covered with pollen, which they transfer to the next orchid flower (see page 248). The orchid is dependent upon bees for pollination because neither wind nor other insects pollinate these flowers.

The outcome of mutualism is an intricate web of species interdependencies critical to the community. For example, in areas of the western United States, the branches and cones of whitebark pine are turned upward, meaning that the seeds do not fall to the ground when the cones open. Birds called Clark's nutcrackers eat the seeds of whitebark pine trees and store them in the ground **(Fig. 38.5A)**. Therefore, Clark's nutcrackers are critical seed dispersers for the trees. Also, grizzly bears find the stored seeds and consume them. Whitebark pine seeds do not germinate unless

FIGURE 38.5A Clark's nutcrackers store and disperse the seeds of whitebark pine trees.

their seed coats are exposed to fire. When natural forest fires in the area are suppressed, whitebark pine trees decline in number, and so do Clark's nutcrackers and grizzly bears. When lightning-ignited fires are allowed to burn, or prescribed burning is used in the area, the whitebark pine populations increase, as do the populations of Clark's nutcrackers and grizzly bears.

Cleaning symbiosis is a symbiotic relationship in which crustaceans, fish, and birds act as cleaners for a variety of vertebrate clients. Large fish in coral reefs line up at cleaning stations and wait their turn to be cleaned by small fish that even enter the mouths of the large fish **(Fig. 38.5B)**. Whether cleaning symbiosis is an example of mutualism has been questioned because of the lack of experimental data. If clients respond to tactile stimuli by remaining immobile while cleaners pick at them, then cleaners may be exploiting this response by feeding on host tissues, as well as on ectoparasites.

This completes our study of interactions between populations in a community, including symbiotic relationships. In the next part of the chapter, we consider community composition and diversity and how these attributes can change over time.

▶ **38.5 Check Your Progress** What is the benefit for protozoans living in the gut of a termite?

FIGURE 38.5B
Cleaning symbiosis occurs when small fish clean large fish.

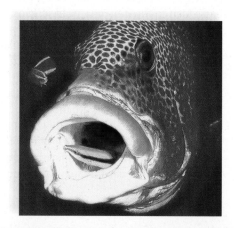

A Community Develops and Changes Over Time

Learning Outcomes

▶ Discuss several models for the process of succession. (38.6)

▶ Compare and contrast the stages of primary and secondary succession. (38.6)

The composition and diversity of a community can change over time, a fact that is dramatically illustrated by ecological succession. Various models have been proposed to explain the changes that take place during succession. As we discuss in Chapter 40, climate dictates to a degree what type of community will develop, but other factors also influence the exact composition.

38.6 During ecological succession, community composition and diversity change

A series of species replacements in a community following a disturbance is called ecological succession. Consider for example, the eruption of Mount St. Helens volcano on May 18, 1980 that cleared an area of 350 kilometers. A few plants managed to survive the blast either by being covered with snow or by regrowing from underground roots. Plants such as fireweed (Chamerion) and prairie lupine (Lupinus) that specialized in colonizing disturbed areas joined these survivors. But only two types of trees, the lodgepole pine and the red alder have been able to take hold so far and it may take 500 years for the blast zone to become the rich forest it was before.

Scientists speak of *primary succession* which occurs in areas where no soil is present, such as following a volcanic eruption or a glacial retreat and *secondary succession* which begins in areas where soil is present. **Figure 38.6A** shows the stages of succession to a large coniferous forest in central New York State. Succession in the Mount St. Helens area is expected in general to follow this model.

Models of Succession In 1916, F. E. Clements proposed the *climax-pattern model* of succession, which suggests that succession in a particular area will always lead to the same type of community, called a **climax community.** Clements believed that climate, in particular, determines whether a desert, a type of grassland, or a particular type of forest results. This is the reason, he

said, that coniferous forests occur in northern latitudes, deciduous forests in temperate zones, and tropical rain forests in the tropics. Secondarily, he believed that soil conditions might also affect the results. Shallow, dry soil might produce a grassland where a forest would otherwise be expected, or the rich soil of a riverbank might produce a woodland where a prairie would be expected.

Further, Clements believed that each stage facilitated the invasion and replacement by organisms of the next stage. As in the examples given, shrubs can't arrive until grasses have made the soil suitable for them. Each successive community prepares the way for the next, so that grass-shrub-forest development occurs sequentially. This is known as the *facilitation model* of succession.

Aside from the facilitation model, there is also an *inhibition model.* That model predicts that colonists hold onto their space and inhibit the growth of other plants until the colonists die or are damaged. Still another model, called the *tolerance model,* predicts that different types of plants can colonize an area at the same time. Sheer chance determines which seeds arrive first, and successional stages may simply reflect the length of time it takes species to mature. This alone could account for the grass-shrub-forest sequence that is often seen. The length of time it takes for trees to develop might give the impression that plant communities develop in a recognizable series, from the simple to the complex. But in reality, the models we have mentioned are

FIGURE 38.6A Primary succession begins on areas of bare rock. Secondary succession begins at the grass stage.

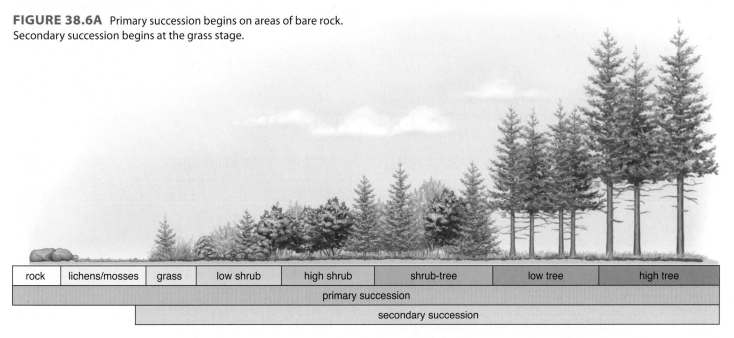

rock	lichens/mosses	grass	low shrub	high shrub	shrub-tree	low tree	high tree
primary succession								
secondary succession								

not mutually exclusive, and succession is probably a complex process of these models at one time or another.

The Stages of Succession Whereas primary succession begins on bare rock, secondary succession begins on disturbed soil. We can imagine that following a forest fire the first event during recovery would be a grass stage followed by the other stages depicted in Figure 38.6A. Secondary succession can also begin after an agricultural field has been abandoned and we have photo evidence of these stages in **Figure 38.6B:**

❶ During the first year, only the remains of corn plants are seen.

❷ During the second year, wild grasses have invaded the area.

❸ By the fifth year, the grasses look more mature, and sedges have joined them.

❹ During the tenth year, there are goldenrod plants, shrubs (blackberry), and juniper trees.

❺ After 20 years, the juniper trees are mature, and birch and maple trees are present, in addition to the blackberry shrubs.

Although it may not have been apparent to early ecologists, we now recognize that the most outstanding characteristic of natural communities is their dynamic nature. Also, complex communities most likely consist of habitat patches that are at various stages of succession. Each successional stage has its own mix of plants and animals, and if various stages are present at the same time, community diversity is greatest. Ecologists have concluded that we don't know if succession continues to a certain end point, because the process may not be complete anywhere on the face of the Earth.

Composition and Diversity When comparing successive communities, two fundamental characteristics that are examined are composition and diversity. The *composition* of a community is a thorough listing of the various species in a particular community. For example, pictorially, it is evident that broadleaved trees are numerous in a temperate deciduous forest (see Fig. 39.7), while succulent cacti and nonsucculent shrubs are numerous in some deserts (see Fig. 39.10). The animal inhabitants are also different.

The *diversity* of a community goes beyond composition because it includes not only a listing of species but also the abundance of each species. To take an extreme example: A forest in West Virginia has, among other species, 76 yellow poplar trees but only one American elm. If we were simply walking through this forest, we might miss seeing the American elm. If, instead, the forest had 36 poplar trees and 41 American elms, the forest would be more diverse. The greater the diversity, the greater the number—and the more even the distribution—of species.

The composition and diversity of a community can change over time due to succession and also due to various human activities that reduce the size of the community as described in How Science Progresses on the next page.

▶ **38.6 Check Your Progress** If decomposers were in short supply, could succession occur? Why or why not?

FIGURE 38.6B Secondary succession in a cultivated cornfield.

38B Preservation of Community Composition and Diversity

Would you expect larger coral reefs to have a greater number of species, called **species richness,** than smaller coral reefs? The area (space) occupied by a community can have a profound effect on its biodiversity. American ecologists Robert MacArthur and E. O. Wilson developed a general **model of island biogeography** to explain and predict how (1) distance from the mainland and (2) size of an island affect community diversity.

Imagine two new islands that, as yet, contain no species at all. One of these islands is near the mainland, and one is far from the mainland. Which island will receive more immigrants from the mainland? Most likely, the near one because it's easier for immigrants to get there (**Fig. 38B.1**). Similarly, imagine two islands that differ in size. Which island will be able to support a greater number of species? The large one, because its greater amount of resources can support more populations, while species on the smaller island may eventually face extinction due to scarce resources (**Fig. 38B.2**). MacArthur and Wilson studied the biodiversity on many island chains, including the West Indies, and discovered that species richness does correlate positively with island distance from mainland and island size. They developed a model of island biogeography that takes into account both factors. An equilibrium is reached when the rate of species immigration matches the rate of species extinction due to limited space. Notice in **Figure 38B.3** that the equilibrium point results in higher species richness for an island near the mainland (high immigration) having a large size (low extinction). The equilibrium could be dynamic (new species keep arriving, and new extinctions keep occurring), or the composition of the community could remain steady unless disturbed.

Biodiversity

Conservationists note that the trends graphed in Figure 38B.3 in particular apply to their work because humans often create pre-

served areas surrounded by farms, towns, and cities, or even water. For example, in Panama, Barro Colorado Island (BCI) was created in the 1910s when a river was dammed to form a lake. As predicted by the model of island biogeography, BCI lost species because it was a small island that had been cut off from the mainland. Among the species that became extinct were the top predators on the island, namely the jaguar, puma, and ocelot. Thereafter, medium-sized terrestrial mammals, such as the coatimundi, increased in number. Because the coatimundi is an avid predator of bird eggs and nestlings, soon there were fewer bird species on BCI, even though the island is large enough to support them.

The model of island biogeography suggests that the larger the conserved area, the better the chance of preserving more species. Is it possible to increase the amount of space without using more area? Two possibilities come to mind. If the environment has patches, it has a greater number of habitats—and thus greater diversity. As gardeners, we are urged to create patches in our yards if we wish to attract more butterflies and birds! One way to introduce patchiness is through stratification, the use of layers. Just as a high-rise apartment building allows more human families to live in an area, so can stratification within a community provide more and different types of living space for different species.

FORM YOUR OPINION

1. Humans are apt to kill off large predators and introduce alien species to an area. What will happen to the normal composition and diversity of an area following such activities?
2. You are a member of a town board charged with deciding whether a subdivision can be built. The subdivision will separate one large natural area into two smaller areas. How might the information given here influence your decision?

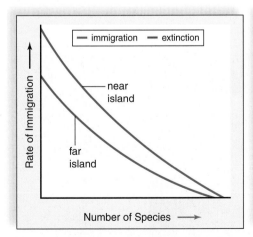

FIGURE 38B.1 More species migrate from the mainland to a near island than to a far island due to travel distance.

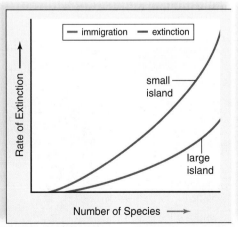

FIGURE 38B.2 More species become extinct on a small island than on a large island due to a shortage of resources.

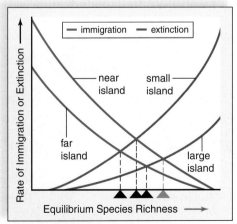

FIGURE 38B.3 Equilibrium model of species richness. Higher species richness occurs on a near, large island compared to the other possible combinations.

An Ecosystem Is a Community Interacting with the Physical Environment

Learning Outcomes

▶ Characterize the biotic components of a community according to their food source. (38.7)
▶ Compare and contrast energy flow through an ecosystem with chemical cycling within an ecosystem. (38.8)
▶ Contrast a food web with a food chain. (38.9)
▶ Explain the shape of an ecological pyramid, whether considering biomass or energy. (38.10)
▶ State the major steps of the phosphorus, nitrogen, and carbon cycles. (38.11–14)

When we study an ecosystem, we are concerned with the living community along with its physical environment. **Ecology** is the study of the interactions of populations with each other and with the physical environment. An ecosystem is characterized by energy flow and chemical cycling, as we first discussed in Section 1.6, p. 12.

38.7 Ecosystems have biotic and abiotic components

An ecosystem possesses both living (biotic) and nonliving (abiotic) components. The abiotic components include resources, such as sunlight and inorganic nutrients, and conditions, such as type of soil, water availability, prevailing temperature, and amount of wind. The biotic components of an ecosystem are influenced by the abiotic components, as when the force of the wind has affected the growth of a tree in **Figure 38.7** (*left*). Each biotic component has an *ecological niche* whose aspects are listed in Figure 38.7 for both plants and animals.

Biotic Components of an Ecosystem Among the biotic components of an ecosystem, **autotrophs** require only inorganic nutrients and an outside energy source to produce organic nutrients for their own use and indirectly for all the other members of a community. Photosynthetic organisms produce most of the organic nutrients for the biosphere. They are called **producers** because they produce food. Algae of all types contain chlorophyll and carry on photosynthesis in freshwater and marine habitats. Algae make up the phytoplankton, which are photosynthesizing organisms suspended in water. Green plants, such as trees in forests and corn plants in fields, are the dominant photosynthesizers on land.

Heterotrophs need a preformed source of organic nutrients. They are called **consumers** because they consume food. **Herbivores** are animals that graze directly on plants or algae. In terrestrial habitats, insects are small herbivores, and antelopes

and bison are large herbivores. In aquatic habitats, zooplankton, which is composed of protozoans and tiny invertebrates, are small herbivores while some fishes, as well as manatees, are large herbivores. **Carnivores** feed on other animals; for example, birds that feed on insects are carnivores, and so are hawks that feed on birds. **Omnivores** are animals that feed on both plants and animals. Chickens, raccoons, and humans are omnivores.

Scavengers, such as jackals and vultures (see chapter introduction), feed on the dead remains of animals and also on plants that have recently begun to decompose. **Detritus** refers to organic remains in the water and soil that are in the final stages of decomposition. Marine fan worms take detritus from the water, while clams take it from the substrate. Earthworms, some beetles, and termites feed on detritus in the soil. Bacteria and fungi, including mushrooms, are the **decomposers.** They use their digestive secretions to chemically break down dead organic matter, including animal wastes, in the external environment. Notice that decomposers are heterotrophs that produce detritus. Without decomposers, plants would be completely dependent only on physical processes, such as the release of minerals from rocks, to supply them with inorganic nutrients.

▶ **38.7 Check Your Progress** Why is it correct to say that autotrophs support all the biotic components (including decomposers) of an ecosystem?

Aspects of Niche for Plants

- Season of year for growth and reproduction
- Sunlight, water, and soil requirements
- Relationships with other organisms
- Effect on abiotic environment

Aspects of Niche for Animals

- Time of day for feeding and season of year for reproduction
- Habitat and food requirements
- Relationships with other organisms
- Effect on abiotic environment

FIGURE 38.7 Niche specifications of plants compared to animals.

38.8 Energy flow and chemical cycling characterize ecosystems

The diagram in **Figure 38.8A** illustrates that every ecosystem is characterized by two fundamental phenomena: energy flow and chemical cycling. Energy is lost from the biosphere, but inorganic nutrients are not. They recycle within and between ecosystems. Decomposers return inorganic nutrients directly to autotrophs, or they are imported or exported between ecosystems in global cycles.

Energy flow begins when producers absorb solar energy, and chemical cycling begins when producers take in inorganic nutrients from the physical environment. Thereafter, via photosynthesis, producers make organic nutrients (food) directly for themselves and indirectly for the other populations of the ecosystem. Energy flows through an ecosystem via photosynthesis because, as organic nutrients pass from one component of the ecosystem to another, as when an herbivore eats a plant or a carnivore eats an herbivore, a portion of those nutrients is used as an energy source. The rest of the energy dissipates into the environment as heat. Therefore, the vast majority of ecosystems cannot exist without a continual supply of solar energy.

Only a portion of the organic nutrients made by producers is passed on to consumers because plants use organic molecules to fuel their own cellular respiration. Similarly, only a small percentage of nutrients consumed by lower-level consumers, such as herbivores, is available to higher-level consumers, or carnivores. As **Figure 38.8B** demonstrates, a certain amount of the food eaten by an herbivore is never digested and is eliminated as feces. Metabolic wastes are excreted as urine. Of the assimilated energy, a large portion is used during cellular respiration for the production of ATP, and thereafter it becomes heat. Only the remaining energy, which is converted into increased body weight or additional offspring, becomes available to carnivores.

The elimination of feces and urine by a heterotroph, and indeed the death of all organisms, does not mean that organic nutrients are lost to the ecosystem; instead, they are made available to scavengers and decomposers. Decomposers convert the organic nutrients, such as glucose, back into inorganic chemicals, such as carbon dioxide and water, and release them to the soil or the atmosphere. Chemicals complete their cycle within an ecosystem when inorganic chemicals are absorbed by the producers from the atmosphere or from the soil.

The first law of thermodynamics states that energy cannot be created (or destroyed). This explains why ecosystems are dependent on a continual outside source of energy. The second law of thermodynamics states that, with every transformation, some energy is degraded into a less available form, such as heat. For example, because plants carry on cellular respiration, only 55% of the original energy absorbed by plants is available to an ecosystem.

In Section 38.9, we apply the principles of energy flow and chemical cycling to an actual ecosystem.

▶ **38.8 Check Your Progress** Once decomposers have broken down glucose, what happens to its inorganic components, such as carbon dioxide and water?

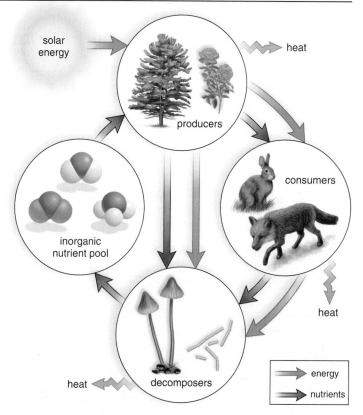

FIGURE 38.8A Energy flow and chemical cycling in an ecosystem.

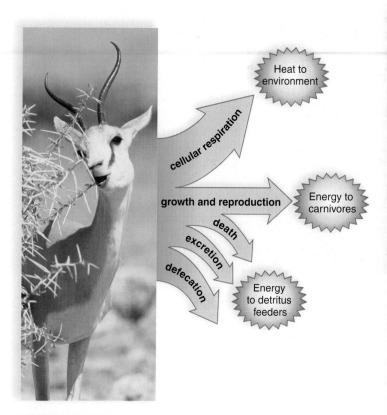

FIGURE 38.8B Energy balances for an herbivore.

38.9 Energy flow involves food webs and food chains

The principles discussed in the previous section can now be applied to an actual ecosystem—a forest of 132,000 m² in New Hampshire. The various interconnecting paths of energy flow may be represented by a **food web,** a diagram that describes trophic (feeding) relationships. **Figure 38.9** (*top*) is a **grazing** food web because it begins with producers, specifically ❶ the oak tree, herbs, and grass. ❷ Insects, in the form of caterpillars, feed on leaves, while ❸ mice, rabbits, and deer feed on plant material at or near the ground. Mice also feed on nuts, while ❹ birds, collectively, are omnivorous, feeding on both nuts and

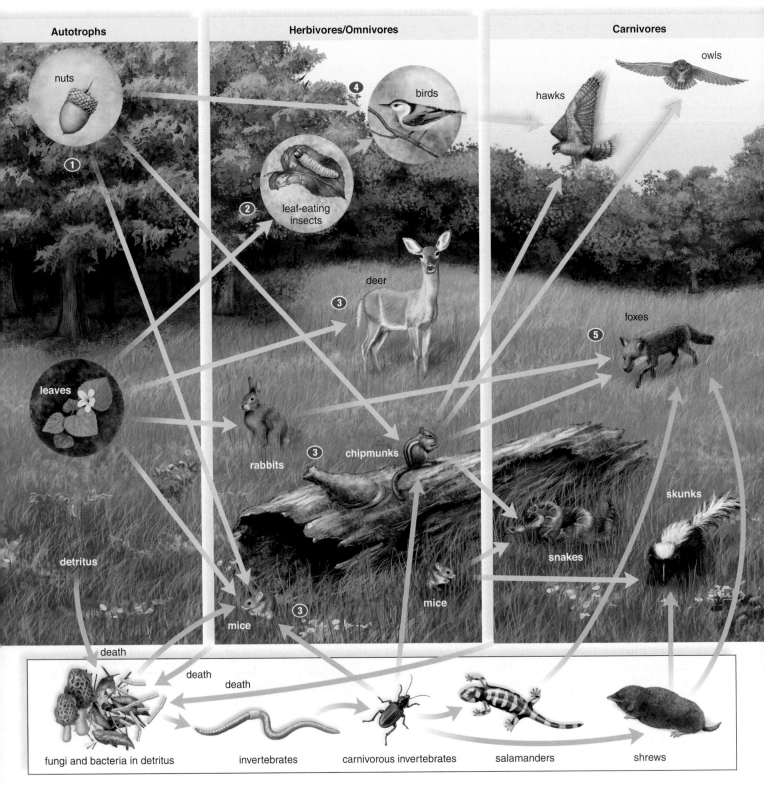

FIGURE 38.9 Grazing food web (*top*) and detrital food web (*bottom*).

caterpillars. Herbivores and omnivores all provide food for ⑤ a number of different carnivores.

Figure 38.9 (*bottom*) is a **detrital food web,** which begins with detritus. Detritus is food for soil organisms such as earthworms. Earthworms are, in turn, eaten by carnivorous invertebrates, and these may be consumed by salamanders or shrews. Because the members of a detrital food web may become food for aboveground carnivores, the detrital and grazing food webs are connected.

We naturally tend to think that aboveground plants such as trees are the largest storage form of organic matter and energy, but this is not necessarily the case. In this particular forest, the organic matter lying on the forest floor and mixed into the soil contains over twice as much energy as the leaf matter of living trees. Therefore, more energy in a forest may be funneling through the detrital food web than through the grazing food web.

Trophic Levels The arrangement of the species in Figure 38.9 suggests that organisms are linked to one another in a straight line, according to feeding relationships, or who eats whom. Diagrams that show a single path of energy flow in an ecosystem are called **food chains.** For example, in the grazing food web, we could find this food chain:

$$\text{leaves} \longrightarrow \text{caterpillars} \longrightarrow \text{birds} \longrightarrow \text{hawks}$$

And in the detrital food web, we could find this food chain:

$$\text{detritus} \longrightarrow \text{earthworms} \longrightarrow \text{carnivore}$$

A **trophic level** (feeding level) is composed of organisms that occupy the same position within a food web or chain. In the grazing food web in Figure 38.9 (*top*), going from left to right, the trees are producers (first trophic level), the first series of animals are primary consumers (second trophic level), and the next group of animals are secondary consumers (third trophic level). Energy moves from trophic level to level, but some is lost between the various levels because energy has been used to do biological work. As Section 38.10 shows, if we successively diagram the relative energy content of each trophic level of a food web, a pyramid results.

▶ **38.9 Check Your Progress** What type of organisms are found in detritus at the start of a detrital food chain?

38.10 Ecological pyramids are based on trophic levels

An **ecological pyramid** is a graphic representation of the number of organisms, the biomass, or the relative energy content of the various trophic levels in an ecosystem. For example, **Figure 38.10** shows the biomass content of each trophic level of a bog in Silver Springs, Florida. Data regarding the biomass or energy content of trophic levels place the producer trophic level at the base of the pyramid, and each succeeding trophic level, which has less biomass and energy, follows thereafter. In general, only about 10% of the energy of one trophic level is available to the next trophic level because of energy losses between trophic levels. Therefore, if an herbivore population consumes 1,000 kg of plant material, only about 100 kg is converted to herbivore tissue, 10 kg to first-level carnivores, and 1 kg to second-level carnivores. The so-called 10% rule of thumb explains why ecosystems have only a few trophic levels and why a food web can support only a few carnivores.

Ecological pyramids are helpful for explaining energy loss in an ecosystem, but they oversimplify energy flow. Most likely, a pyramid based on the number of organisms in each trophic level wouldn't work. For example, in Figure 38.9, each tree would contain numerous caterpillars, so there would be more herbivores than autotrophs! Similarly, in aquatic ecosystems, such as some lakes and open seas where algae are the only producers, the herbivores may have a greater biomass than the producers when they are measured, because the algae are consumed at a high rate. In any case, ecological pyramids based on grazing food webs don't account for energy that passes to decomposers. The energy content between the autotroph level and the herbivore level is disproportionate in Figure 38.10 because much of the energy in a bog flows through the detrital food web, not the grazing food web.

This completes our discussion of energy flow in an ecosystem. In Section 38.11, we examine in more detail how chemicals cycle through ecosystems.

FIGURE 38.10 This ecological pyramid based on the biomass content of bog populations could also be used to represent an energy pyramid.

▶ **38.10 Check Your Progress** In an ecological pyramid, what trophic level (if any) accounts for decomposers?

38.11 Chemical cycling includes reservoirs, exchange pools, and the biotic community

The pathways by which chemicals circulate through ecosystems involve both living (biotic) and nonliving (geologic) components; therefore, they are known as **biogeochemical cycles.** In the next sections of this chapter, we describe three of the biogeochemical cycles: the phosphorus, nitrogen, and carbon cycles. A biogeochemical cycle may be sedimentary or gaseous. The phosphorus cycle is a sedimentary cycle; the chemical is absorbed from the soil by plant roots, passed to heterotrophs, and eventually returned to the soil by decomposers. The carbon and nitrogen cycles are gaseous, meaning that the chemical returns to and is withdrawn from the atmosphere as a gas.

Chemical cycling involves the components of ecosystems shown in **Figure 38.11.** A *reservoir* is a source normally unavailable to producers, such as the carbon present in calcium carbonate shells on ocean bottoms. An *exchange pool* is a source from which organisms do generally take chemicals, such as the atmosphere or soil. Chemicals move along food chains in a *biotic community,* perhaps never entering an exchange pool.

Human activities (purple arrow) remove chemicals from reservoirs (or exchange pools) and make them available to the

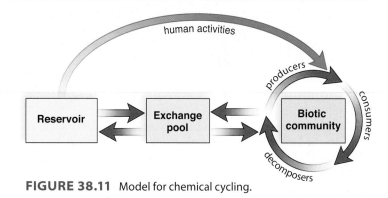

FIGURE 38.11 Model for chemical cycling.

biotic community. In this way, human activities result in pollution because they upset the normal balance of nutrients for producers in the environment.

▶ **38.11 Check Your Progress** Which portion of Figure 38.11 represents the abiotic environment?

38.12 The phosphorus cycle is sedimentary

Figure 38.12 depicts the phosphorus cycle. ❶ Phosphorus, trapped in oceanic sediments, moves onto land after a geologic upheaval. ❷ On land, the very slow weathering of rocks places ❸ phosphate ions (PO_3^- and HPO_4^2) in the soil. ❹ Some of these become available to plants, which use phosphate in a variety of molecules, including phospholipids, ATP, and the nucleotides that become a part of DNA and RNA. ❺ Animals eat producers and incorporate some of the phosphate into their teeth, bones, and shells, which take many years to decompose. ❻ However, eventually the death and decay of all organisms and also the decomposition of animal wastes make phosphate ions available to producers once again. Because the available amount of phosphate is already being used within food chains, phosphate is usually a limiting inorganic nutrient for plants—that is, the lack of it limits the size of populations in ecosystems.

❼ Some phosphate naturally runs off into aquatic ecosystems, where algae acquire phosphate from the water before it becomes trapped in sediments. Phosphate in marine sediments does not become available to produc-

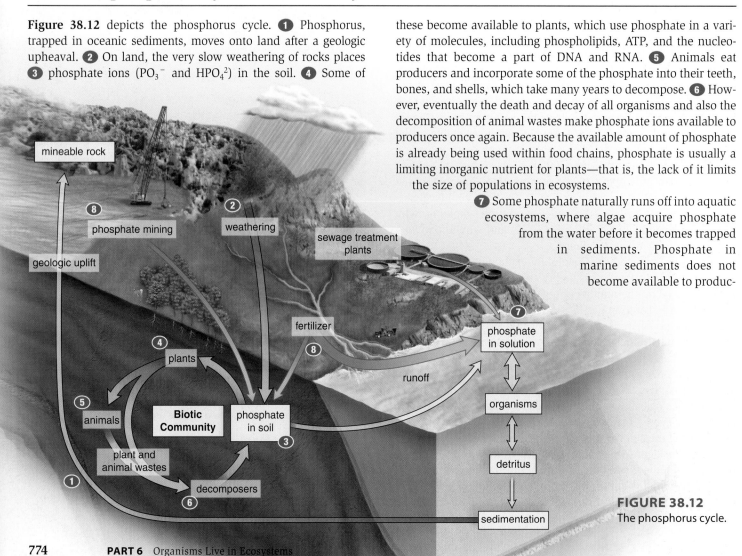

FIGURE 38.12
The phosphorus cycle.

ers on land again until a geologic upheaval exposes sedimentary rocks on land. Now, the cycle begins again.

Human Activities and the Phosphorus Cycle ⑧

Humans boost the supply of phosphate by mining phosphate ores for producing fertilizer and detergents. Runoff of phosphate and nitrogen due to fertilizer use, animal wastes from livestock feedlots, and discharge from sewage treatment plants results in **eutrophication** (overenrichment) of waterways.

▶ **38.12 Check Your Progress** How do the phosphate ions in animal bones become available to producers?

38.13 The nitrogen cycle is gaseous

Nitrogen gas (N_2) makes up about 78% of the atmosphere, but plants cannot use nitrogen in its gaseous form. Therefore, nitrogen can be a nutrient that limits the amount of growth in an ecosystem.

Ammonium (NH_4^+) Formation and Use In the nitrogen cycle, N_2 **(nitrogen) fixation** occurs when nitrogen gas (N_2) is converted to ammonium (NH_4^+), a form plants can use (**Fig. 38.13**). ① Some cyanobacteria in aquatic ecosystems and some free-living bacteria in soil are able to fix atmospheric nitrogen in this way. Other nitrogen-fixing bacteria live in nodules on the roots of legumes, such as beans, peas, and clover. They make organic compounds containing nitrogen available to the host plants so that the plant can form proteins and nucleic acids.

Nitrate (NO_3^-) Formation and Use Plants can also use nitrates (NO_3^-) as a source of nitrogen. The production of nitrates during the nitrogen cycle is called **nitrification**. ② Nitrification can occur in two ways: (1) Nitrogen gas (N_2) is converted to NO_3^- in the atmosphere when cosmic radiation, meteor trails, and lightning provide the high energy needed for nitrogen to react with oxygen. (2) Ammonium (NH_4^+) in the soil from various sources, including decomposition of organisms and animal wastes, is converted to NO_3^- by nitrifying bacteria in soil. Specifically, NH_4^+ (ammonium) is converted to NO_2^- (nitrite), and then NO_2^- is converted to NO_3^- (nitrate). ③ During the process of assimilation, plants take up NH_4^+ and NO_3^- from the soil and use these ions to produce proteins and nucleic acids.

Notice in Figure 38.13 that the subcycle involving the biotic community, which occurs on land and in the ocean, need not depend on the presence of nitrogen gas at all.

Formation of Nitrogen Gas

④ **Denitrification** is the conversion of nitrate back to nitrogen gas, which then enters the atmosphere. Denitrifying bacteria living in the anaerobic mud of lakes, bogs, and estuaries carry out this process as a part of their own metabolism. In the nitrogen cycle, denitrification would counterbalance nitrogen fixation if not for human activities.

Human Activities and the Nitrogen Cycle ⑤ Humans sig-

nificantly alter the transfer rates in the nitrogen cycle by producing fertilizers from N_2—in fact, they nearly double the fixation rate. Fertilizer, which also contains phosphate, runs off into lakes and rivers and results in an overgrowth of algae and rooted aquatic plants. When the algae die off, enlarged populations of decomposers use up all the oxygen in the water, and the result is a massive fish kill.

Acid deposition occurs because nitrogen oxides (NO_x) and sulfur dioxide (SO_2) enter the atmosphere from the burning of fossil fuels. Both these gases combine with water vapor to form acids that eventually return to the Earth. Acid deposition has drastically affected forests and lakes in northern Europe, Canada, and the northeastern United States because their soils are naturally acidic and their surface waters are only mildly alkaline (basic). Acid deposition reduces agricultural yields and corrodes marble, metal, and stonework (see also p. 38).

▶ **38.13 Check Your Progress** Nitrate production by soil microbes is called _____.

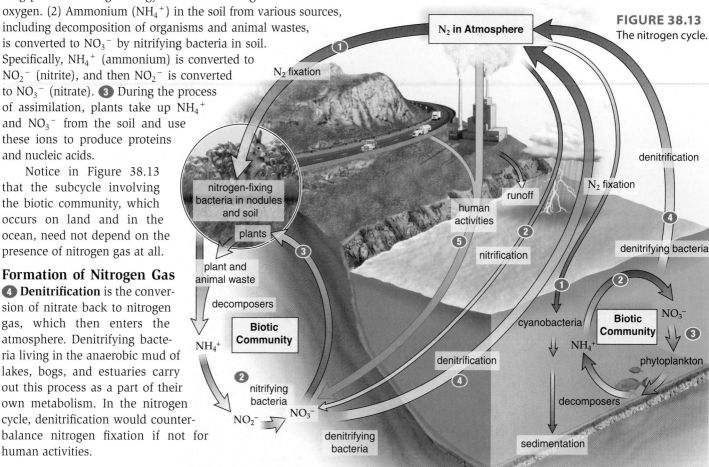

FIGURE 38.13
The nitrogen cycle.

38.14 The carbon cycle is gaseous

In the carbon cycle, organisms in both terrestrial and aquatic ecosystems exchange carbon dioxide (CO_2) with the atmosphere (**Fig. 38.14**). Therefore, the CO_2 in the atmosphere is the exchange pool for the carbon cycle. On land, plants take up CO_2 from the air, and through photosynthesis, they incorporate carbon into nutrients that are used by autotrophs and heterotrophs alike. ❶ When organisms, including plants, respire, carbon is returned to the atmosphere as CO_2. ❷ CO_2 then recycles to plants by way of the atmosphere.

In aquatic ecosystems, the exchange of CO_2 with the atmosphere is indirect. ❸ Carbon dioxide from the air combines with water to produce bicarbonate ion (HCO_3^-), a source of carbon for algae that produce food for themselves and for heterotrophs. Similarly, when aquatic organisms respire, the CO_2 they give off becomes HCO_3^-. ❹ The amount of bicarbonate in the water is in equilibrium with the amount of CO_2 in the air.

Reservoirs Hold Carbon Living and dead organisms contain organic carbon and serve as one of the reservoirs for the carbon cycle. ❺ The world's biotic components, particularly trees, contain 800 billion tons of organic carbon, and an additional 1,000–3,000 billion metric tons are estimated to be held in the remains of plants and animals in the soil. ❻ Ordinarily, decomposition of animals returns CO_2 to the atmosphere.

Some 300 MYA, plant and animal remains were transformed into coal, oil, and natural gas, the materials we call fossil fuels. Another reservoir for carbon is the inorganic carbonate that accumulates in limestone and in calcium carbonate shells. Many marine organisms have calcium carbonate shells that remain in bottom sediments long after the organisms have died. Geologic forces change these sediments into limestone.

Human Activities and the Carbon Cycle ❼ More CO_2 is being deposited in the atmosphere than is being removed, largely due to the burning of fossil fuels and the destruction of forests to make way for farmland and pasture. When we humans do away with forests, we reduce a reservoir and also the very organisms that take up excess carbon dioxide. Today, the amount of CO_2 released into the atmosphere is about twice the amount that remains in the atmosphere. Scientists hypothesize that much of this has been dissolving into the ocean.

Carbon dioxide, and other gases as well, are being emitted due to human activities. The other gases include nitrous oxide (N_2O) from fertilizers and animal wastes and methane (CH_4) from bacterial decomposition that takes place particularly in the guts of animals, in sediments, and in flooded rice paddies. These gases are known as **greenhouse gases** because, just like the panes of a greenhouse, they allow solar radiation to pass through but hinder the escape of infrared rays (heat) back into space. The greenhouse gases are contributing to an overall rise in the Earth's ambient temperature, a trend called **global climate change.** The global climate has already warmed about 0.6°C since the Industrial Revolution.

Scientists predict that, as the oceans warm, temperatures in the polar regions will rise to a greater degree than in other regions. If so, glaciers will melt, and sea level will rise, not only due to this melting but also because water expands as it warms. Increased rainfall is likely along the coasts, while dryer conditions are expected inland. Coastal agricultural lands, such as the deltas of Bangladesh and China, will be inundated with sea water, and billions of dollars will have to be spent to keep coastal cities such as New Orleans, New York, Boston, Miami, and Galveston from disappearing into the sea.

▶ **38.14 Check Your Progress** If humans used biogas as an energy source instead of fossil fuels, how would global temperature be affected?

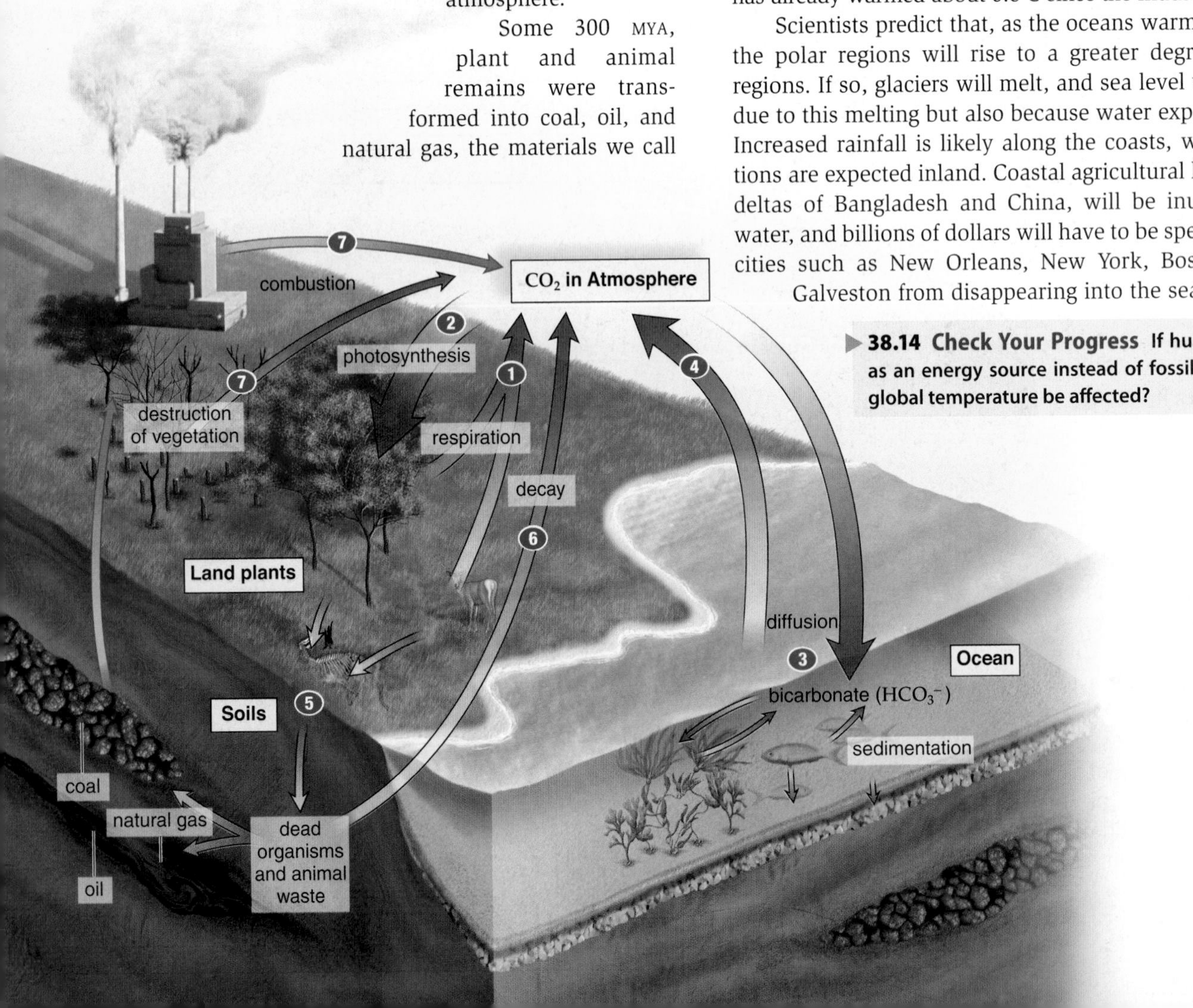

combustion
photosynthesis
CO_2 in Atmosphere
respiration
destruction of vegetation
decay
Land plants
diffusion
Ocean
Soils
bicarbonate (HCO_3^-)
sedimentation
coal
natural gas
dead organisms and animal waste
oil

FIGURE 38.14
The carbon cycle.

SUMMARY

A Community Contains Several Interacting Populations in the Same Locale

38.1 Competition can lead to resource partitioning

- **Competition** is rivalry for the same resources (e.g., nesting sites, food).
- The **competitive exclusion principle** states that no two species can occupy the same niche at the same time.
- An **ecological niche** is the role an organism plays in its community, including both **habitat** and interactions.
- **Resource partitioning** decreases competition for resources between two species.
- Characteristics tend to diverge when similar species belong to the same community, a phenomenon known as **character displacement.**

38.2 Predator-prey interactions affect both populations

- **Predation** occurs when one organism feeds on another population.
- Predator-prey populations cycle: More predators/fewer prey result in fewer predators/more prey.
- Prey defenses include senses, speed, protective body parts, and chemicals.
- Ways to deceive predators include **camouflage,** cryptic coloration, and **mimicry.**

38.3 Parasitism benefits one population at another's expense

- **Parasitism** occurs when a **parasite** derives nourishment from a host.
- Parasitism is a type of **symbiosis;** other types are commensalism and mutualism.

38.4 Commensalism benefits only one population

- Although **commensalism** benefits only one species, closer examination sometimes reveals more of a mutualistic or parasitic relationship.

38.5 Mutualism benefits both populations

- **Mutualism** results in an intricate web of species interdependencies critical to the community.

A Community Develops and Changes Over Time

38.6 During ecological succession, community composition and diversity change

- **Ecological succession** involves a series of species replacements in a community:
  - Primary succession occurs where there is no soil present.
  - Secondary succession occurs where soil is present and certain plant species can begin to grow.
- Various models for succession have been proposed; one model suggests that it results in a **climax community** typical of that area.

An Ecosystem Is a Community Interacting with the Physical Environment

38.7 Ecosystems have biotic and abiotic components

- Biotic components are living components:
  - **Autotrophs** are **producers.**
  - **Heterotrophs** are **consumers;** types of consumers include **herbivores, carnivores,** and **omnivores.**
  - **Scavengers** feed on dead remains of animals and plants.
  - **Detritus** is composed of the organic remains of decomposition found in water and soil.
  - **Decomposers** include heterotrophic bacteria and fungi.
- Abiotic components are resources (e.g., sunlight, inorganic nutrients) and conditions (e.g., soil, water, temperature, wind).

decomposers

38.8 Energy flow and chemical cycling characterize ecosystems

- Energy flows through ecosystems because as food passes from producers through consumers, each population makes energy conversions that result in a loss of usable energy in the form of heat.

producers

consumers

- Chemicals cycle because they pass from one population to the next until decomposers return them once more to the environment where producers can take them up again.

38.9 Energy flow involves food webs and food chains

- A **food web** is an interconnecting path of energy flow that describes trophic (feeding) relationships:
  - A **grazing food web** begins with a producer, such as an oak tree.
  - A **detrital food web** begins with detritus.
  - Grazing and detrital food webs are joined.
- A **food chain** is a single path of energy flow.
- A **trophic level** is composed of organisms that occupy the same feeding position within a food web.

38.10 Ecological pyramids are based on trophic levels

- An **ecological pyramid** is a graphic representation of the number of organisms, biomass, or energy content of trophic levels.

38.11 Chemical cycling includes reservoirs, exchange pools, and the biotic community

- **Biogeochemical cycles** may be sedimentary (phosphorus cycle) or gaseous (carbon and nitrogen cycles).

- Chemical cycling involves a reservoir, an exchange pool for an inorganic nutrient, and a biotic community.

38.12 The phosphorus cycle is sedimentary

- Geologic upheavals move phosphorus from the ocean to land.
- Slow weathering of rocks returns phosphorus to the soil.
- Most phosphorus is recycled within a community, and phosphorus is a limiting nutrient except when humans add phosphate to fertilizers.

38.13 The nitrogen cycle is gaseous

- Plants cannot use nitrogen gas (N_2) from the atmosphere.
- During **nitrogen fixation,** N_2 converts to ammonium, making nitrogen available to plants.
- **Nitrification** is the production of nitrates, while **denitrification** is the conversion of nitrate back to N_2, which enters the atmosphere.
- Human activities increase transfer rates in biogeochemical cycles.
- Due to fossil fuel combustion, oxides (and sulfur dioxide) enter the atmosphere. There they combine with water vapor, and then return to Earth as **acid deposition.**

38.14 The carbon cycle is gaseous

- CO_2 in the atmosphere is an exchange pool for the carbon cycle; terrestrial and aquatic plants and animals exchange CO_2 with the atmosphere.
- Living and dead organisms serve as reservoirs for the carbon cycle because they contain organic carbon.
- Due to fossil fuel combustion, the levels of CO_2 and other **greenhouse gases** have risen in the atmosphere. Greenhouse gases contribute to **global climate change.**

TESTING YOURSELF

A Community Contains Several Interacting Populations in the Same Locale

1. According to the competitive exclusion principle,
   a. one species is always more competitive than another for a particular food source.
   b. competition excludes multiple species from using the same food source.
   c. no two species can occupy the same niche at the same time.
   d. competition limits the reproductive capacity of species.
2. Resource partitioning pertains to
   a. niche specialization.
   b. character displacement.
   c. increased species diversity.
   d. the development of mutualism.
   e. All but d are correct.

For statements 3–7, indicate the type of interaction in the key that is described in each scenario.

KEY:

a. competition	d. commensalism
b. predation	e. mutualism
c. parasitism	

3. An alfalfa plant gains fixed nitrogen from the bacterial species *Rhizobium* in its root system, while *Rhizobium* gains carbohydrates from the plant.

4. Both foxes and coyotes in an area feed primarily on a limited supply of rabbits.
5. Roundworms establish a colony inside a cat's digestive tract.
6. A fungus captures nematodes as a food source.
7. An orchid plant lives in the treetops, gaining access to sun and pollinators, but not harming the trees.
8. **THINKING CONCEPTUALLY** You want to reintroduce a predator into an area. What concern might you have?

A Community Develops and Changes Over Time

9. The model of island biogeography is pertinent to
   a. only islands surrounded by water.
   b. explaining decreases in community composition and diversity.
   c. explaining the intermediate disturbance hypothesis.
   d. why exotics are such a problem today.
   e. All of these are correct.
10. Mosses growing on bare rock will eventually help create soil. These mosses are involved in _____ succession.
    a. primary   c. tertiary
    b. secondary
11. Assume that a farm field is allowed to return to its natural state. By chance, the field is first colonized by native grasses, which begin the succession process. This is an example of which model of succession?
    a. climax pattern   c. facilitation
    b. tolerance   d. inhibition

An Ecosystem Is a Community Interacting with the Physical Environment

12. The ecological niche of an organism
    a. is the same as its habitat.
    b. includes how it competes and acquires food.
    c. is specific to the organism.
    d. is usually occupied by another species.
    e. Both b and c are correct.
13. Label this diagram.

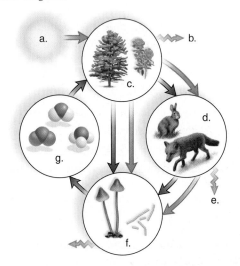

14. In what way are decomposers like producers?
    a. Either may be the first member of a grazing or a detrital food chain.
    b. Both produce oxygen for other forms of life.
    c. Both require nutrient molecules and energy.
    d. Both are present only on land.
    e. Both produce organic nutrients for other members of ecosystems.

15. When a heterotroph takes in food, only a small percentage of the energy in that food is used for growth. The remainder is
    a. not digested and eliminated as feces.
    b. excreted as urine.
    c. given off as heat.
    d. All of these are correct.
    e. None of these are correct.
16. During chemical cycling, inorganic nutrients are typically returned to the soil by
    a. autotrophs.   c. decomposers.
    b. detritivores.   d. tertiary consumers.
17. In a grazing food web, carnivores that eat herbivores are
    a. producers.   c. secondary consumers.
    b. primary consumers. d. tertiary consumers.
18. Choose the statement that is true concerning this food chain:
    grass ⟶ rabbits ⟶ snakes ⟶ hawks
    a. Each predator population has a greater biomass than its prey population.
    b. Each prey population has a greater biomass than its predator population.
    c. Each population is omnivorous.
    d. Each population returns inorganic nutrients and energy to the producer.
    e. Both a and c are correct.
    f. Both a and b are correct.
19. Which of the following is a sedimentary biogeochemical cycle?
    a. carbon
    b. nitrogen
    c. phosphorus
20. Which of the following is not a component of the nitrogen cycle?
    a. proteins   d. photosynthesis
    b. ammonium   e. bacteria in root nodules
    c. decomposers

21. How do plants contribute to the carbon cycle?
    a. When plants respire, they release CO_2 into the atmosphere.
    b. When plants photosynthesize, they consume CO_2 from the atmosphere.
    c. When plants photosynthesize, they provide oxygen to heterotrophs.
    d. Both a and b are correct.
22. **THINKING CONCEPTUALLY** Could several different photosynthetic and nonphotosynthetic aquatic species living in the same pond occupy the same trophic level? Explain.

THINKING SCIENTIFICALLY

1. As per Figure 14.1B, you observe three species of *Empidonax* flycatchers in the same general area, and you hypothesize that they occupy different niches. How could you substantiate your hypothesis?
2. In order to improve species richness, you decide to add phosphate to a pond. How might you determine how much phosphate to add in order to avoid eutrophication?

ONLINE RESOURCE

www.mhhe.com/maderconcepts2

Enhance your study with animations that bring concepts to life and practice tests to assess your understanding. Your instructor may also recommend the interactive eBook, individualized learning tools, and more.

CONNECTING THE CONCEPTS

Community ecology is concerned with how populations of different species interact with each other. Population size is influenced by negative interactions such as competition, predation, and parasitism. But positive interactions such as mutualism are also fairly common in nature (especially for plants) and are presumed to increase or maintain population sizes. Perhaps one of the most important recent discoveries about communities is that they are highly dynamic, meaning that the number of species, kinds of species, and sizes of populations within most communities are constantly changing. This dynamic quality is well demonstrated by the process of ecological succession.

Instead of studying the composition of diversity of communities, some ecologists concentrate on the movement of energy and nutrients through communities. The physical environment has a large influence on energy flow and chemical cycling within a community. Therefore, our study of communities must include the abiotic environment. Human activities also influence the operation of ecosystems. For example, burning fossil fuels and trees adds carbon dioxide to the atmosphere. Carbon dioxide and other greenhouse gases allow the sun's rays to pass through, but they absorb and reradiate heat back to

the Earth. Therefore fossil fuel combustion may be leading to global warming. Transfer rates in both the phosphorus and nitrogen cycles are affected when we produce fertilizers and detergents. Nitrogen and phosphorus runoff causes eutrophication in aquatic ecosystems. Many human activities negatively impact the functioning of the biosphere, the largest ecosystem of all and threatens the existence of all species, including our own. In Chapter 39, we take a look at the specific types of ecosystems that make up the biosphere.

PUT THE PIECES TOGETHER

1. If comparing a community to your college, what would be the populations? Give examples to show that (1) the populations interact, (2) it would be best if the populations were balanced one to the other, and (3) the composition and diversity of the community change over time.
2. What evidence shows that the human population is part of an ecosystem in the biosphere? (See the introduction to Chapter 5, p. 84.) If the natural environment is "home" for the human population, should people work to preserve it? Why do many of our actions fail to preserve the natural environment?

39

Major Ecosystems of the Biosphere

Life Under Glass

Just a 20-minute drive north of Tucson, in the desert of Arizona, a futuristic glass structure emerges from the surrounding landscape. Called Biosphere 2, the structure was built to help establish a new field called ecological engineering and to investigate the interaction and evolution of ecosystems enclosed within a heavily subsidized environment. Pumps kept the hydrologic cycle going, blowers provided atmospheric movement, and huge "lungs" relieved the pressure that builds up in a glass-enclosed system.

The name, Biosphere 2, means that the structure was modeled after the Earth's biosphere, which is sometimes called Biosphere 1. Biosphere 2 contained representative living organisms, as well as nonliving components of five major natural biomes (a tropical rain forest, a savanna, a coastal fog desert, a mangrove wetland, and an ocean) plus two human habitats where eight biospherians lived for two years. Their contact with Biosphere 1 where we live was extremely limited.

The cost of more than $200 million to build Biosphere 2 was funded by billionaire Edward P. Bass. The structure, when sealed, was not entirely airtight, but it was 30 times less leaky than the space shuttle, and thousands of times less leaky than a typical skyscraper. Ecosystems did not flourish as had been planned, but this gave information and insight into the workings of their analogs in nature. CO_2 concentrations soared, and O_2 concentrations dipped to below normal during the first years, indicating the importance of the world's oceans in absorbing CO_2 and the world's forests in producing O_2. Soil microbes and the building's concrete components also played a role in creating the imbalance of these gases in Biosphere 2. Some of the crops did not bear fruit because of pests, diseases,

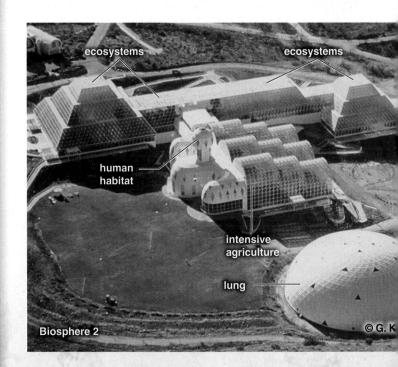

Biosphere 2

Biosphere agriculture

Biosphere harvest © A. Alling

and the lack of pollinators. Oxygen was piped in, but many vertebrates died off. When cockroaches proliferated, toads and geckoes were introduced from the outside to eat them. The biospherians were stressed by living within a confined structure.

Still, the success of the Biosphere 2 project can be measured by the quality of the observations and extensive data now available to the scientific community. Biosphere 2, it turns out, was immensely valuable to many scientific disciplines, and it inspired quite a few scientific publications. Some papers presented computer models to describe the hydrologic balance and the heat versus humidity within the system. Other papers told of the changes that occurred in the rain forest, mangrove, ocean, and agronomic ecosystems in this CO_2-rich environment.

The overall ecological message is clear—we should appreciate and try to better understand the workings of the ecosystems within Biosphere 1. While Biosphere 2 was a start, more experimentation is needed before a self-sustaining habitat can be established on the Moon or on Mars. Biosphere 2 was only the first step toward achieving such a system.

Biosphere feast © A. Alling

Climate Is Dictated by Temperature and Rainfall

Learning Outcome

▶ Discuss the factors that determine and affect the climate of a region. (39.1)

Weather consists of short-term changes in the atmosphere that affect temperature and rainfall whereas **climate** is the prevailing temperature and rainfall over a long period of time. The temperature and rainfall of a region are determined by (1) variations in solar radiation due to the curvature and tilt of the Earth as it orbits the sun and also by (2) the topography of an area and (3) the nearness and currents of the oceans.

39.1 Solar radiation and winds determine climate

The sun's rays have a direct affect on temperature. Because the Earth is a sphere, the sun's rays are more direct at the equator and more spread out at the polar regions (**Fig. 39.1A,** *left*). Therefore, the tropics are warmer than the temperate regions and the poles. However, the tilt of the Earth as it orbits the sun causes one pole or the other to be closer to the sun (except at the spring and fall equinoxes, when the sun aims directly at the equator), and this accounts for the seasons that occur in all parts of the Earth, but not at the equator (Fig. 39.1A, *right*). When the Northern Hemisphere is having winter, the Southern Hemisphere is having summer, and vice versa.

Air currents have a direct affect on rainfall. Because the Earth rotates on its axis daily and its surface consists of continents and oceans, an overall flow of warm and cold air currents are modified into three large circulation cells in each hemisphere (**Fig. 39.1B,** *large arrows*). At the equator, the sun heats the air and evaporates water. The warm, moist air rises, cools, and loses most of its moisture as rain. The greatest amounts of rainfall on Earth are near the equator. The rising air flows toward the poles, but at about 30° north and south latitude, it sinks toward the Earth's surface and reheats. As the air descends and warms, it is very dry, creating zones of low rainfall. The great deserts of Africa, Australia, and the Americas occur at these latitudes. At about 60° north and south latitude, the air rises and cools, producing additional zones of high rainfall. This moisture supports the great forests of the temperate zone. Part of this rising air flows equatorward, and part continues poleward, descending near the poles, which are zones of low precipitation.

The spinning of the Earth causes a curving pattern of the winds and ocean currents (Fig. 39.1B). Periods of calm called the *doldrums* occur at the equator. At about 30° latitude (below and above the equator), the winds blow from the east-southeast in the Southern Hemisphere and from the east-northeast in the

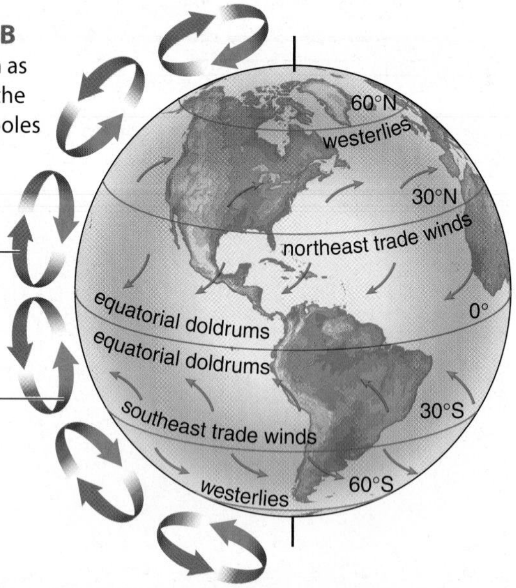

FIGURE 39.1B
Wind circulation as air moves from the equator to the poles and back again.

Ascending moist air cools and loses moisture.

Descending dry air warms and retains moisture.

Northern Hemisphere (the east coasts of continents at these latitudes are wet). These are called trade winds because sailors depended on them to fill the sails of their trading ships. Between 30° and 60° north and south latitudes, strong winds, called the prevailing westerlies, blow from west to east.

▶ **39.1 Check Your Progress** What two prevailing atmospheric conditions determine the climate of an area?

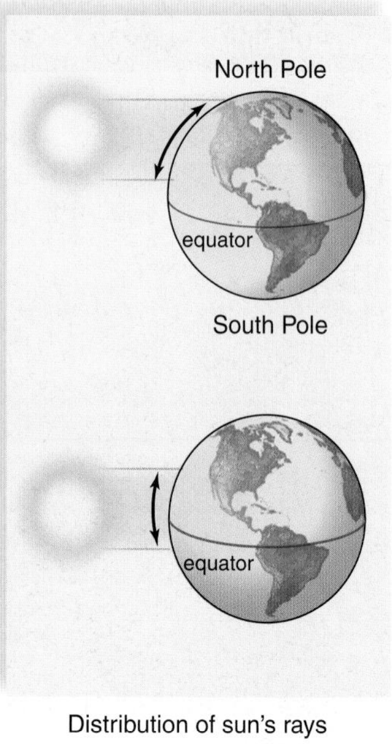

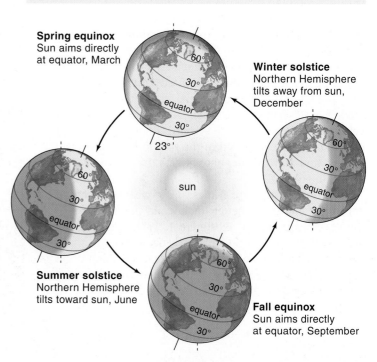

FIGURE 39.1A (*left*)
Distribution of the sun's rays striking the Earth. (*right*) Distribution of solar energy as the Earth orbits the sun.

Distribution of sun's rays

Spring equinox
Sun aims directly at equator, March

Winter solstice
Northern Hemisphere tilts away from sun, December

Summer solstice
Northern Hemisphere tilts toward sun, June

Fall equinox
Sun aims directly at equator, September

39.2 Topography and other effects also influence climate

Topography refers to the surface features of the land. Mountains are topographic features that affect climate, and therefore the distribution of ecosystems. For example, traveling from the equator to the North Pole, you might see first a tropical rain forest, followed by a temperate deciduous forest, a coniferous forest, and tundra in that order because of the change in temperature. This same sequence is seen when ascending a mountain (**Fig. 39.2A**). The coniferous forest of a mountain is called a montane coniferous forest, and the tundra near the peak of a mountain is called an alpine tundra.

Mountains also affect precipitation. As air blows up and over a coastal mountain range, it rises and releases its moisture as it cools. One side of the mountain, called the windward side, receives more rainfall than the other side, called the leeward side. On the leeward side, the air descends, picks up moisture, and produces clear weather (**Fig. 39.2B**). The difference between the windward side and the leeward side can be quite dramatic. In the Hawaiian Islands, for example, the windward side of a mountain receives more than 750 cm of rain a year, while the leeward side, which is in a **rain shadow,** gets on the average only 50 cm of rain and is generally sunny. In the United States, the western side of the Sierra Nevada Mountains is lush, while the eastern side is a semidesert.

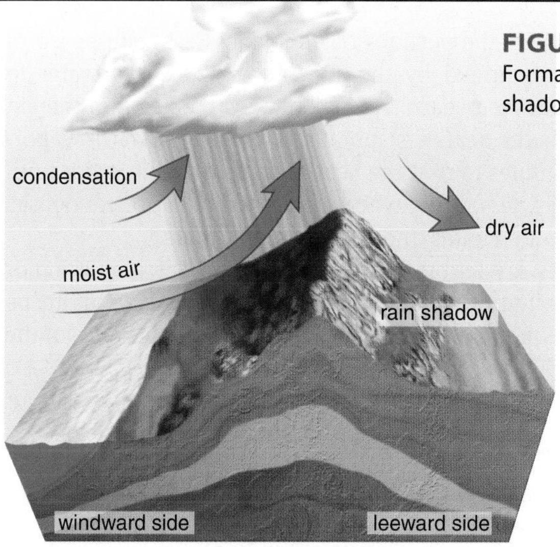

Nearby Bodies of Water The temperature of the oceans is more stable than that of the landmasses. Ocean water gains or loses heat more slowly than terrestrial environments do. This gives coasts a unique weather pattern that is not observed inland. During the day, the land warms more quickly than the ocean, and the air above the land rises. Then a cool sea breeze

FIGURE 39.2B Formation of a rain shadow.

blows in from the ocean. At night, the reverse happens; the breeze blows from the land toward the sea.

India and some other countries in southern Asia have a **monsoon** climate, in which wet ocean winds blow onshore for almost half the year. During spring, the land heats more rapidly than the waters of the Indian Ocean, resulting in a temperature differential between the land and the ocean and a gigantic circulation of air: Warm air rises over the land, and cooler air comes in off the ocean to replace it. As the warm air rises, it loses its moisture, and the monsoon season begins. As just discussed, rainfall is particularly heavy on the windward side of hills. The town of Cherrapunji in northern India receives an average of 1,090 cm of rain per year because of its high altitude. By November, the weather pattern has reversed. The land is now cooler than the ocean; therefore, dry winds blow from the Asian continent across the Indian Ocean. In the winter, the air over the land is dry, the skies cloudless, and temperatures pleasant. The chief crop of India is rice, which starts to grow when the monsoon rains begin.

In the United States, people often speak of the "lake effect," meaning that in the winter, arctic winds blowing over the Great Lakes become warm and moisture-laden. As these winds rise and lose their moisture, snow begins to fall. Places such as Buffalo, New York, get heavy snowfalls due to the lake effect and have snow on the ground for an average of 90–140 days every year.

> **39.2 Check Your Progress** When going from the equator to the South Pole, you would not reach a region that corresponds to the coniferous forest and tundra of the Northern Hemisphere. Explain.

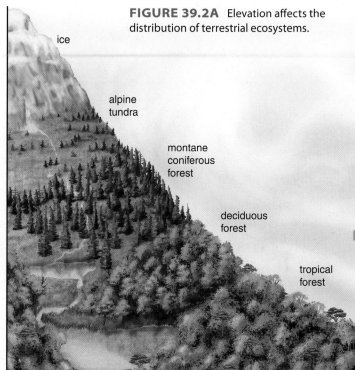

FIGURE 39.2A Elevation affects the distribution of terrestrial ecosystems.

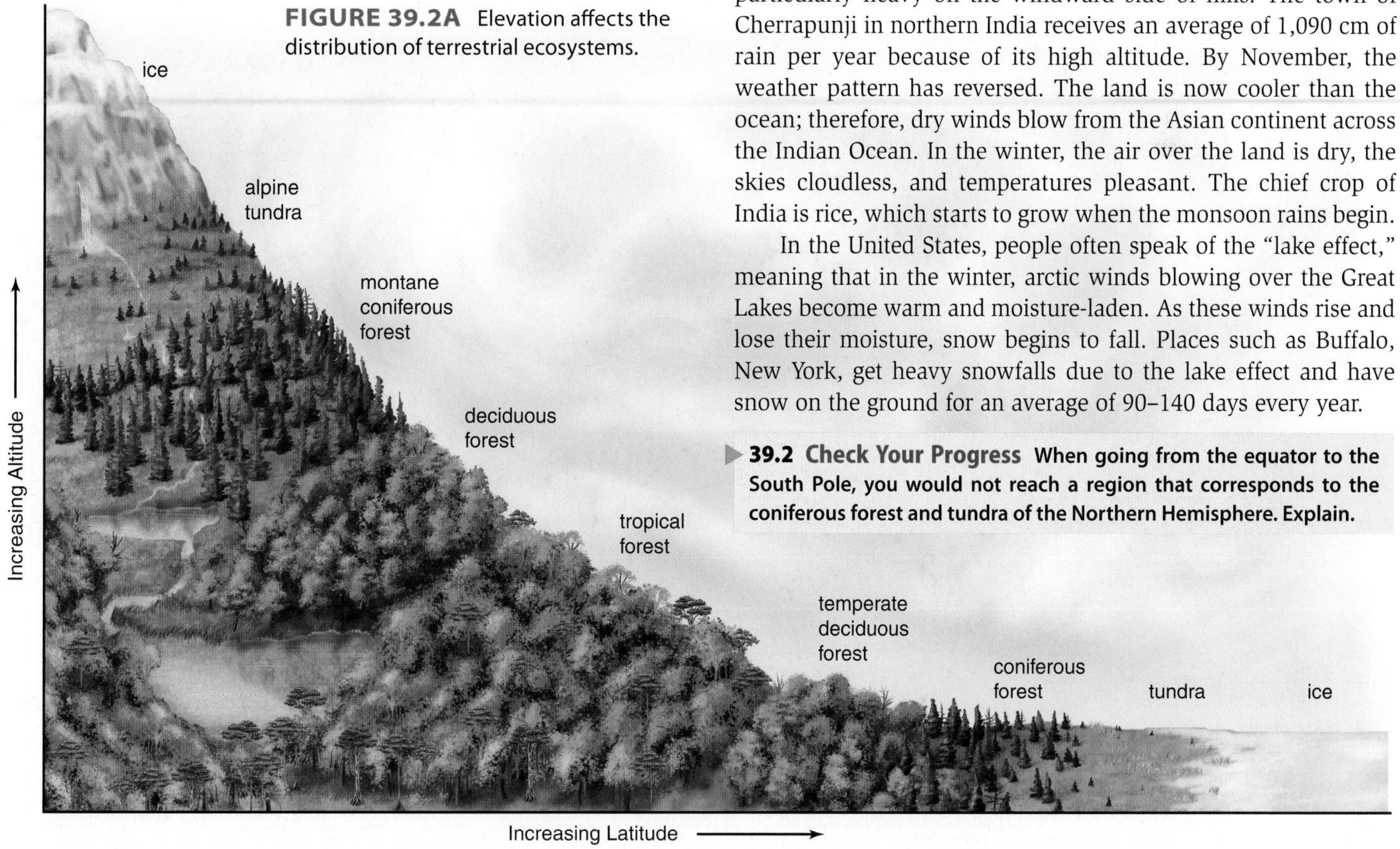

ice

alpine tundra

montane coniferous forest

deciduous forest

tropical forest

temperate deciduous forest

coniferous forest · tundra · ice

Increasing Altitude

Increasing Latitude

39.3 Ocean currents affect climate

The hydrosphere, the portions of the planet Earth composed of water, is also warmed by the sun, and that causes water to evaporate from the oceans. As moisture evaporates into the air, it carries along the heat of evaporation. When such warm, vapor-laden air continues to rise, the heat remains with the vapor until the air reaches an altitude where cooler temperature condenses the moisture into clouds and precipitation occurs.

Climate is driven by the sun, but the oceans play a major role in redistributing heat in the biosphere. Water tends to be warm at the equator and much cooler at the poles because of the distribution of the sun's rays, discussed earlier (see Fig. 39.1A). Air takes on the temperature of the water below, and warm air moves from the equator to the poles. In other words, the oceans make the winds blow. (Landmasses also play a role, but the oceans hold heat longer and remain cool longer during periods of changing temperature than do continents.)

When the wind blows strongly and steadily across a great expanse of ocean for a long time, friction from the moving air begins to drag the water along with it. Once the water has been set in motion, its momentum, aided by the wind, keeps it moving in a steady flow called a current. Because the ocean currents eventually strike land, they move in a circular path—clockwise in the Northern Hemisphere and counterclockwise in the Southern Hemisphere (**Fig. 39.3**). As the currents flow, they take warm water from the equator to the poles. One such current, called the Gulf Stream, brings tropical Caribbean water to the east coast of North America and the higher latitudes of western Europe. Without the Gulf Stream, Great Britain, which has a relatively warm temperature, would be as cold as Greenland. In the Southern Hemisphere, another major ocean current warms the eastern coast of South America.

Also in the Southern Hemisphere, a current called the Humboldt Current flows toward the equator. The Humboldt Current carries phosphorus-rich cold water northward along the west coast of South America. During a process called **upwelling,** cold offshore winds cause cold, nutrient-rich waters to rise and take the place of warm, nutrient-poor waters. In South America, the enriched waters cause an abundance of marine life that supports the fisheries of Peru and northern Chile. Birds feeding on these organisms deposit their droppings on land, where they are mined as guano, a commercial source of phosphorus.

When the Humboldt Current is not as cool as usual, upwelling of nutrients does not occur, stagnation results, the fisheries decline, and climate patterns change globally. This phenomenon, called an **El Niño–Southern Oscillation,** has a profound effect on weather; a severe El Niño affects the weather over three-quarters of the globe. This phenomenon is discussed in How Science Progresses on page 794.

▶ **39.3 Check Your Progress** Ordinarily, strong winds help move the waters away from the coast so that cold, nutrient-rich water rises to the surface. Do you predict these winds would be as strong as usual during an El Niño?

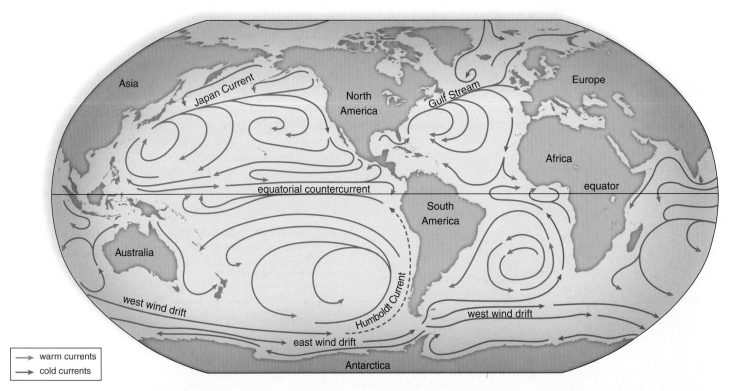

FIGURE 39.3 The arrows on this map indicate the locations and directions of the major ocean currents set in motion by the global wind circulation. By carrying warm water to cool latitudes (e.g., the Gulf Stream) and cool water to warm latitudes (e.g., the Humboldt Current), these currents have a major effect on the world's climates.

On Land, the Biosphere Is Organized into Terrestrial Ecosystems

Learning Outcome

▶ List the major ecosystems of the biosphere, relate their climate to their location, and describe the major groups of organisms that live in each one. (39.4–39.11)

Each major terrestrial ecosystem (sometimes called a **biome**) has a particular mix of plants and animals that are adapted to living under the prevailing environmental conditions.

39.4 Major terrestrial ecosystems are characterized by particular climates

As we have seen, climate consists of the prevailing temperature and rainfall of a region. When terrestrial ecosystems are plotted according to their climate, a particular distribution pattern results. The distribution of a number of terrestrial ecosystems is shown in **Figure 39.4**. However, we are going to concentrate on the selected ecosystems listed in **Table 39.4.** The table tells you about the climate but not about the organisms that are adapted to living in the ecosystem. The descriptions in the next few sections describe some of the major populations in each biome.

Be sure to note where the ecosystems listed in Table 39.4 are distributed. Even though Figure 39.4 shows definite demarcations, keep in mind that ecosystems gradually change from one type to the other. Also, although we will be discussing different ecosystems separately, we should remember that each one has inputs from and outputs to all the other terrestrial and aquatic ecosystems of the biosphere.

▶**39.4 Check Your Progress** Why would you expect greater biodiversity in a rain forest than in a desert?

TABLE 39.4	Selected Terrestrial Ecosystems
Name	**Characteristic**
Tundra	Around North Pole; very cold (−12°C to −6°C); little rainfall (less than 25 cm/year); permafrost (permanent ice) year-round within a meter of surface.
Taiga (coniferous forest)	Large northern biome just below the Arctic Circle; temperature is below freezing for half the year; moderate precipitation (30–85 cm/year); long nights in winter and long days in summer.
Temperate deciduous forest	Eastern half of United States, Canada, Europe, and parts of Russia; four seasons of the year with hot summers and cold winters; ample precipitation (75–150 cm/year).
Grasslands	Savanna in Africa and temperate grassland elsewhere; hot in summer and cold in winter (U.S.); moderate precipitation; good soil for agriculture.
Tropical rain forest	Located near the equator in Latin America, Southeast Asia, and West Africa; warm (20–25°C) and heavy precipitation (190 cm/year).
Desert	Northern and Southern Hemispheres at 30° latitude; hot (38°C) days and cold (7°C) nights; low precipitation (less than 25 cm/year).

FIGURE 39.4 Pattern of ecosystem distribution on land.

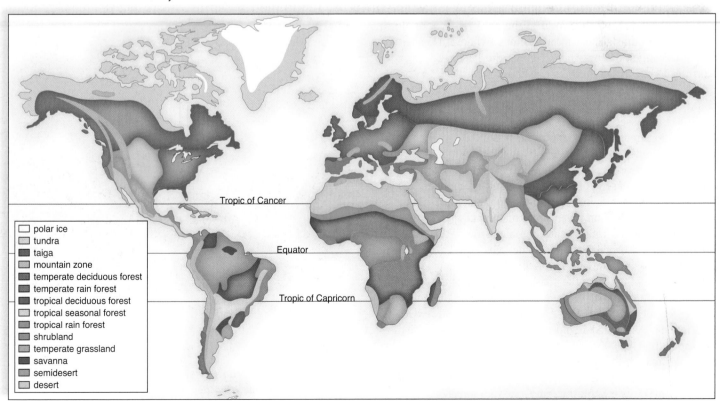

- polar ice
- tundra
- taiga
- mountain zone
- temperate deciduous forest
- temperate rain forest
- tropical deciduous forest
- tropical seasonal forest
- tropical rain forest
- shrubland
- temperate grassland
- savanna
- semidesert
- desert

Tropic of Cancer

Equator

Tropic of Capricorn

39.5 The tundra is cold and dark much of the year

The **Arctic tundra** ecosystem, which encircles the Earth just south of the ice-covered polar seas in the Northern Hemisphere, covers about 20% of the Earth's land surface (**Fig. 39.5**). (A similar ecosystem, called the alpine tundra, occurs above the timberline on mountain ranges.) The Arctic tundra is cold and dark much of the year. Its winters are extremely long, cold, and harsh, and its summers are short (6–8 weeks). Because rainfall amounts to only about 20 cm a year, the tundra could possibly be considered a desert, except that melting snow creates a landscape of pools and mires in the summer, especially because so little evaporates. Only the topmost layer of soil thaws; the **permafrost** beneath this layer is always frozen, and therefore drainage is minimal. The available soil in the tundra is nutrient-poor.

Trees are not found in the tundra because the growing season is too short, their roots cannot penetrate the permafrost, and they cannot become anchored in the boggy soil of summer. In the summer, the ground is covered with short grasses and sedges, as well as numerous patches of lichens and mosses. Flowers and dwarf woody shrubs, such as dwarf birch, seed quickly while there is plentiful sun for photosynthesis.

A few animals live in the tundra year-round. For example, the mouselike lemming stays beneath the snow; the ptarmigan, a grouse, burrows in the snow during storms; and the musk ox conserves heat because of its thick coat and short, squat body. Other animals that live in the tundra include snowy owls, lynx, voles, Arctic foxes, and snowshoe hares. In the summer, the tundra is alive with numerous insects and birds, particularly

FIGURE 39.5 Tundra, the northern-most ecosystem.

shorebirds and waterfowl that migrate inland. Caribou in North America and reindeer in Asia and Europe also migrate to and from the tundra, as do the wolves that prey upon them. Polar bears are common near the coastal regions.

The next section discusses the plants and animals of a coniferous forest.

▶ **39.5 Check Your Progress** Give reasons why Biosphere 2 didn't have an Arctic tundra.

39.6 Coniferous forests are dominated by gymnosperms

Coniferous forests are found in three locations: in the **taiga**, which extends around the world in the northern part of North America and Eurasia; near mountaintops (where it is called a montane coniferous forest); and along the Pacific coast of North America, as far south as northern California.

The taiga, also called boreal (northern) forest, exists south of the tundra and covers approximately 11% of the Earth's landmasses (**Fig. 39.6**). The needlelike leaves of its cone-bearing trees can withstand the weight of heavy snow. There is a limited understory of plants, but the floor is covered with low-lying mosses and lichens beneath a layer of needles. Birds harvest the seeds of the conifers, and bears, deer, moose, beavers, and muskrats live around the cool lakes and along the streams. Wolves prey on these larger mammals.

The coniferous forest that runs along the west coasts of Canada and the United States is sometimes called a **temperate rain forest.** Winds moving in off the Pacific Ocean lose their moisture when they meet the coastal mountain range. The plentiful rainfall and rich soil have produced some of the tallest conifer trees ever in existence, including the coastal redwoods. This forest is also called an old-growth forest because some trees are more than 1,000 years old. It truly is an evergreen forest because mosses, ferns, and other plants grow on all the tree trunks. Squirrels, lynx, and numerous species of amphibians, reptiles, and birds inhabit the temperate rain forest.

FIGURE 39.6 Taiga, a northern coniferous forest.

Section 39.7 describes what a temperate deciduous forest is like.

▶ **39.6 Check Your Progress** What types of trees would be needed to simulate the taiga in Biosphere 2?

39A Land of Beringia

The different, distinct communities in various locations on Earth result from interactions among various biotic and abiotic factors in the environment. Ecologists have demonstrated that locations with similar combinations of environmental conditions support similar biological communities. This understanding of how climatic and other factors shape community composition allows paleoecologists to use the rich fossil record to reconstruct ecological communities of the past. One example of a reconstructed terrestrial community that exists no more is an area called Beringia.

Beringia was located between present-day Siberia in northeastern Russia and Alaska in extreme northwestern North America. These two areas are now separated by the Bering Strait, an 80-km-wide body of water that connects the Arctic and Pacific Oceans. Over the long history of Earth, temperatures have fluctuated and sea levels have risen and fallen as part of natural processes. During the cold periods, large volumes of water were held in ice and snow. Consequently, there was less water in the oceans and sea levels dropped. Ecologists believe that during the last Ice Age 12,000–20,000 years ago, sea levels were 100–150 m lower than at present. The lower sea level exposed Beringia, a

large stretch of land that formed a land bridge approximately 1,000 miles wide from north to south linking the two continents (**Fig. 39A,** *top*).

Paleoecologists have determined that Beringia was a cold, dry, open plain. There was likely little snowfall due to a "rain shadow"

effect caused by the Siberian mountain ranges (see Fig. 39.2B). Fossils found on either side of the Bering Strait indicate that Beringia supported a steppe community with a flora dominated by grasses and numerous shrubs. Fossils have also shown that the fauna of Beringia included the large mammals of the Ice Age such as mammoths, steppe bison, and the scimitar cat (Fig. 39A, *bottom*). Beringia served as an important link between Asia and North America and provided a route for the exchange of plants, animals, fungi, and other life-forms that migrated between continents. For example, the alders (*Alnus* spp.) are shrubs and small trees that originated in Asia. They migrated through Beringia and spread throughout North America. Now, members of this genus are important components of many North American wetlands and stream-side communities. Many other genera show a similar history of migration from Asia into new areas where they became established and diversified. Possibly one of the most significant migrations through Beringia was that of humans. Ecologists believe that human populations from Asia migrated into Beringia and then into North America as the glaciers melted and made passage south possible. When the glaciers melted, sea levels rose, and the biologically important communities inhabiting this link between Asia and North America disappeared under the sea.

FORM YOUR OPINION

1. Revisit Figure 15.2 and explain why all continents have the major groups of organisms, but particular types can vary between continents. If organisms such as the Alders occur only on two continents what does it tell you?

2. Recently, the sequencing of DNA from a 4,000 year-old human found in Greenland showed that he came from Siberia. Siberia is west and Greenland is east of North America. Speculate on how the man got to Greenland. Could he have migrated by way of Beringia or did he travel between land masses by sea?

FIGURE 39A (*Top*) Beringia (purple) included a land bridge that is now under water. (*Bottom*) Beringia existed when humans hunted big game such as mammoths.

39.7 Temperate deciduous forests have abundant life

Temperate deciduous forests are found south of the taiga in eastern North America, eastern Asia, and much of Europe (**Fig. 39.7**). The climate in these areas is moderate, with relatively high rainfall (75–150 cm per year). The seasons are well defined, and the growing season ranges between 140 and 300 days. The trees, which include oak, beech, sycamore, and maple, have broad leaves and are termed deciduous trees; they lose their leaves in the fall and grow them in the spring. In southern temperate deciduous forests, evergreen magnolia trees can be found.

The tallest trees form a canopy, an upper layer of leaves that are the first to receive sunlight. Even so, enough sunlight penetrates to provide energy for another layer of trees, called understory trees. Beneath these trees are shrubs that may flower in the spring before the trees have put forth their leaves. Still another layer of plant growth—mosses, lichens, and ferns—resides beneath the shrub layer. This *stratification* provides a variety of habitats for insects and birds. Ground life is also plentiful. Squirrels, cottontail rabbits, shrews, skunks, woodchucks, and chipmunks are small herbivores. These and ground birds, such as turkeys, pheasants, and grouse, are preyed on by red foxes. White-tailed deer and black bears have increased in number in recent years. In contrast to the taiga, amphibians and reptiles live in this ecosystem because the winters are not as cold. Frogs and turtles prefer an aquatic existence, as do the beavers and muskrats, which are mammals.

Autumn fruits, nuts, and berries serve as food for the winter. The leaves, after turning brilliant colors and falling to the ground, contribute to a rich layer of humus. The minerals within the rich soil are washed far into the ground by spring rains, but the deep tree roots capture these minerals and bring them back up into the forest system again.

FIGURE 39.7 Temperate deciduous forest in the fall.

▶**39.7 Check Your Progress** To simulate a temperate forest for Biosphere 2, would it be enough to simply bring in many types of deciduous trees? Explain.

39.8 Temperate grasslands have extreme seasons

The **temperate grasslands** include the Russian steppes, the South American pampas, and the North American prairies (**Fig. 39.8**). In these grasslands, winters are bitterly cold, and summers are hot and dry. When traveling across the United States from east to west, temperate deciduous forest transitions into *tall-grass prairie* roughly along the border between Illinois and Indiana. The tall-grass prairie requires more rainfall than does the *short-grass prairie,* which occurs near deserts. Large herds of bison—estimated at hundreds of thousands—once roamed the prairies, as did herds of pronghorn antelope. Now, small mammals, such as mice, prairie dogs, and rabbits, typically live belowground, but usually feed aboveground. Hawks, snakes, badgers, coyotes, and foxes feed on these mammals. However, virtually all of these grasslands have been converted to agricultural lands because of their fertile soils.

▶**39.8 Check Your Progress** If you put a simulated prairie in Biosphere 2, would you give it the same amount of rainfall as the deciduous forest? See Table 39.4.

FIGURE 39.8 Temperate grassland in the summer.

39.9 Savannas have wet-dry seasons

Savannas occur in regions where a relatively cool dry season is followed by a hot rainy season. The largest savannas are in central and southern Africa; other savannas exist in Australia, Southeast Asia, and South America (**Fig. 39.9**). The savanna is characterized by large expanses of grasses with sparse populations of trees. The plants of the savanna have extensive and deep root systems that enable them to survive drought and fire. One tree that can survive the severe dry season is the thorny flat-topped acacia, which sheds its leaves during a drought. The African savanna supports the greatest variety and number of large herbivores of all the biomes (Fig. 39.9). Elephants and giraffes are browsers that feed on tree vegetation. Antelopes, zebras, wildebeests, water buffalo, and some rhinoceroses are grazers that feed on grasses. Any plant litter that is not consumed by grazers is attacked by a variety of small organisms, among them termites. Termites build towering nests in which they tend fungal gardens, their source of food. The herbivores support a large population of carnivores. Lions and hyenas sometimes hunt in packs, cheetahs hunt singly by day, and leopards hunt singly by night.

▶ **39.9 Check Your Progress** If Biosphere 2 housed a simulated savanna ecosystem suitable for giraffes, elephants, and zebras, what type of plants would be needed?

FIGURE 39.9 The African savanna.

39.10 Deserts have very low annual rainfall

Deserts are usually found at latitudes of about 30° in both the Northern and Southern Hemispheres (**Fig. 39.10**). The winds that descend in these regions lack moisture, and the annual rainfall is less than 25 cm. Days are hot because lack of cloud cover allows the sun's rays to penetrate easily, but nights are cold because heat escapes easily into the atmosphere.

The Sahara Desert, which stretches all the way from the Atlantic coast of Africa to the Arabian peninsula, and a few other deserts have little or no vegetation. But most have a variety of plants. Desert plants are highly adapted to survive long droughts, extreme heat, and extreme cold. Adaptations to these conditions include thick epidermal layers, water-storing stems and leaves, and the ability to set seeds quickly in the spring. The best-known desert perennials in North America are the succulent, spiny-leafed cactuses, which have stems that store water and carry on photosynthesis.

Some animals are adapted to the desert environment. To conserve water, many desert animals are nocturnal or burrowing and have a protective outer body covering. A desert has numerous insects, which pass through the stages of development when there is rain. Reptiles, especially lizards and snakes, are perhaps the most characteristic group of vertebrates found in deserts, but running birds (e.g., the roadrunner) and rodents (e.g., the kangaroo rat) are also well known. Larger mammals, such as the kit fox, prey on the rodents, as do hawks.

Section 39.11 discusses tropical rain forests.

FIGURE 39.10 Desert with some vegetation.

▶ **39.10 Check Your Progress** Are the nights in the desert outside the Biosphere 2 structure hot or cold?

39.11 Tropical rain forests are warm with abundant rainfall

In the **tropical rain forests** of South America, Africa, and the Indo-Malayan region near the equator, the temperature is always warm (between 20° and 25°C), and rainfall is plentiful (a minimum of 190 cm per year). This may be the richest ecosystem, in terms of both number of different kinds of species and their abundance. The diversity of species is enormous—a 10-km² area of tropical rain forest may contain 1,500 species of flowering plants, including the trees.

A tropical rain forest has a complex structure, housing many levels of life, including the forest floor, the understory, and the canopy. The canopy filters out sunlight, and the plants of the forest floor, such as ferns, can tolerate minimal light. The understory consists of shorter trees that receive some light and bear epiphytes. **Epiphytes** are plants that grow on other plants but usually have roots of their own to absorb moisture and minerals leached from their hosts; others catch rain and debris in hollows produced by overlapping leaf bases. The most common epiphytes are related to pineapples, orchids, and ferns. The canopy, topped by the crowns of tall trees, is the most productive level of the tropical rain forest (**Fig. 39.11A**). Some of the broadleaf evergreen trees grow to 15–50 m or more. These tall trees often have trunks buttressed at ground level to prevent them from toppling over. Lianas, or woody vines, which encircle the tree as it grows, also help strengthen the trunk.

Although some animals live on the forest floor (e.g., pacas, agoutis, peccaries, and armadillos), most live in the trees (**Fig. 39.11B**). Insect life is so abundant that the majority of species have not been identified yet. Termites play a vital role in decomposing woody plant material, and ants are everywhere, particularly in the trees. The various birds, such as hummingbirds, parakeets, parrots, and toucans, are often beautifully colored. Amphibians and reptiles are well represented by many

FIGURE 39.11A Levels of life in a tropical rain forest.

types of frogs, snakes, and lizards. Lemurs, sloths, and monkeys are well-known primates that feed on the fruits of the trees. The largest carnivores are the big cats—the jaguars in South America and the leopards in Africa and Asia.

This completes our discussion of terrestrial ecosystems. The next section discusses aquatic ecosystems.

▶ **39.11 Check Your Progress** In the tropical rain forest ecosystem of Biosphere 2, the plants growing on other plants high up in the canopy are called _____.

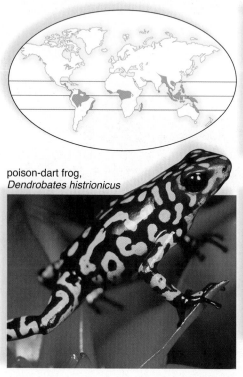

poison-dart frog,
Dendrobates histrionicus

blue and gold macaw,
Ara ararauna

cone-headed katydid,
Panacanthus cuspidatus

ocelot,
Felis pardalis

brush-footed butterfly,
Anartia amalthea linnaeus

lemur,
Lemur catta

arboreal lizard,
Calotes calotes

FIGURE 39.11B Representative animals of the tropical rain forests of the world.

Akohekohe

Akiapolaau

grass, are alien organisms that have caused much destruction in Hawaii.

The damage caused by feral pigs has gained a lot of attention in particular, and these animals are a good example of the problems created by alien species. The pigs voraciously eat all kinds of plants and animals, and create disturbed areas, allowing other aliens to come in. Kahili ginger, banana poke, and strawberry guava are examples of alien plants that thrive in pig-damaged areas. Furthermore, the water held in pig wallows allows mosquitoes to breed and spread avian malaria. Both the mosquitoes and the parasite that causes avian malaria have wreaked havoc on Hawaii's native bird populations.

Feral-pig

Nonnative species are just part of the reason for the biodiversity crisis in Hawaii. Humans have depleted natural resources, created pollution, and overpopulated fragile coastal areas. Hawaii has some of the fastest-growing cities in the United States; the demand for fresh water is so high that frequent water-use restrictions exist in some areas; and almost a third of the landfills are at, or will soon reach, capacity. Hawaii is fast becoming a lost paradise with degraded and damaged vistas.

As you will see in this chapter, the first step toward a sustainable society in which resources, such as those of Hawaii, are protected for the present and future generations, is to recognize the damage that has been done. Then we must put our energies into correcting the activities that endanger the environment and enacting measures that will preserve it.

Waikiki, Hawaii

Conservation Biology Wants to Understand and Protect Biodiversity

Learning Outcomes

▶ Define and characterize the field of conservation biology. (40.1)

▶ Distinguish between an endangered and a threatened species. (40.1)

▶ Explain how biodiversity is classified into four levels. (40.2)

▶ State the significance of biodiversity "hotspots" when conserving species. (40.2)

Conservation biology is an important part of achieving a **sustainable society,** one that conserves all resources for this generation and future generations. We should pay attention to preserving species, particularly in areas where biodiversity is the most complex.

40.1 Conservation biology is a practical science

Conservation biology is a new discipline that focuses on conserving natural resources for this generation and all future generations. Conservation biology is unique in that it is concerned with both developing scientific concepts and applying those concepts to the everyday world. A primary goal is the management of biodiversity for sustainable use by humans. To achieve this goal, conservation biologists are interested in, and come from, many subfields of biology that only now have been brought together into a cohesive whole:

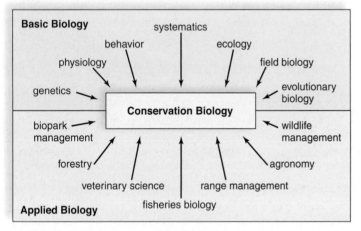

Like a physician, a conservation biologist must be aware of the latest findings, both theoretical and practical, and be able to use this knowledge to diagnose the source of trouble and suggest a suitable treatment. Often, it is necessary for conservation biologists to work with government officials at both the local and federal levels. Public education is another important duty of conservation biologists.

Conservation biology is unique among the life sciences because it supports the following ethical principles: (1) Biodiversity is desirable for the biosphere and, therefore, for humans; (2) extinctions due to human actions are therefore undesirable; (3) the complex interactions in ecosystems support biodiversity and are desirable; and (4) biodiversity brought about by evolutionary change has value in and of itself, regardless of any practical benefit.

Conservation biology is often called a crisis discipline—never before in the history of the Earth are so many extinctions expected in such a short period of time. Estimates vary, but at least 10–20% of all species now living most likely will become extinct in the next 20–50 years, unless immediate action is taken. It is urgently important, then, that all citizens understand the concept of biodiversity, the value of biodiversity, the likely causes of present-day extinctions, and the potential consequences of reduced biodiversity.

To protect biodiversity, bioinformatics, the science of collecting and analyzing biological information, is applied. Throughout the world, molecular, descriptive, and biogeographical information about organisms is being collected. Eventually, this information will be used to help us understand and protect biodiversity.

▶ **40.1 Check Your Progress** What are the main goals of conservation biology?

40.2 Biodiversity has levels of complexity

At its simplest level, **biodiversity** is the variety of life on Earth. Scientists have estimated that between 10 and 50 million species may exist in all. If this is the case, many species are still to be found and described. Of the described species, nearly 1,200 in the United States and 40,000 worldwide are in danger of **extinction,** the total disappearance of a species or higher group. An **endangered species** is in peril of immediate extinction throughout all or most of its range. Examples of endangered species include the black lace cactus, armored snail, hawksbill sea turtle, California condor, West Indian manatee, and the snow leopard. **Threatened species** are organisms that are likely to become endangered in the foreseeable future. Examples of threatened species include the Navaho sedge, puritan tiger beetle, gopher tortoise, bald eagle, gray wolf, and Louisiana black bear.

To develop a meaningful understanding of life on Earth, we need to know more about species than their total number. Ecologists also study biodiversity as an attribute of three other levels of biological organization: genetic diversity, ecosystem diversity, and landscape diversity.

Genetic diversity includes the variations that occur among the members of a population. Populations with high genetic diversity are more likely to have some individuals that can survive a change in the structure of their ecosystem. For example, the 1846 potato blight in Ireland, the 1922 wheat failure in the Soviet Union, and the 1984 outbreak of citrus canker in Florida were all made worse by limited genetic variation among these crops. If a species' populations are quite small and isolated, that species is more likely to eventually become extinct because of a loss of genetic diversity. As organisms become endangered and threatened, they lose their genetic diversity.

Ecosystem diversity is dependent on the interactions of species at a particular locale. Although past conservation efforts frequently concentrated on saving particular charismatic species, such as the California condor, the black-footed ferret, or the spotted owl, this is a shortsighted approach. A better approach is to conserve species that play a critical role in an ecosystem. Saving an entire ecosystem can save many species, and the contrary is also true—disrupting an ecosystem threatens the existence of more than one species. For example, opossum shrimp, *Mysis relicta,* were introduced into Flat-head Lake in Montana and its tributaries as food for salmon. But the shrimp ate so much zooplankton that there was, in the end, far less food for the salmon and ultimately for the grizzly bears and bald eagles as well (**Fig. 40.2**).

Landscape diversity involves a group of interacting ecosystems; within one landscape, for example, there may be plains, mountains, and rivers. Any of these ecosystems can be so fragmented that they are connected by only patches (remnants) or strips of land that allow organisms to move from one ecosystem to the other. Fragmentation of the landscape reduces reproductive capacity and food availability and can disrupt seasonal behaviors.

Distribution of Biodiversity Biodiversity is not evenly distributed throughout the biosphere; therefore, protecting particular areas will help save more species. Biodiversity is highest at the tropics, and it declines toward the poles whether considering terrestrial, freshwater, or marine ecosystems. Also, for example, more species are present in the coral reefs of the Indonesian archipelago than in coral reefs west of this archipelago.

Some regions of the world are called **biodiversity hotspots** because they contain unusually large concentrations of species. Although hotspots harbor about 44% of all known higher plant species and 35% of all terrestrial vertebrate species, they are present in only about half of the Earth's landmass. The island of Madagascar, the Cape region of South Africa, Indonesia, the coast of California, and the Great Barrier Reef of Australia are all biodiversity hotspots.

One surprise of late has been the discovery that rain forest canopies and the deep-sea benthos have many more species than formerly thought. Some conservationists refer to these two areas as biodiversity frontiers.

The direct and indirect value of biodiversity is explained in the next part of the chapter.

▶ **40.2 Check Your Progress** Why might ecosystem-level conservation be more important than species-level conservation?

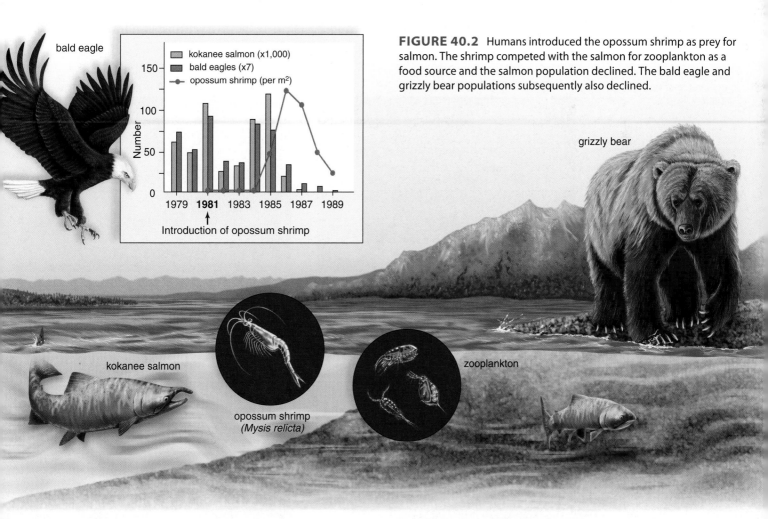

FIGURE 40.2 Humans introduced the opossum shrimp as prey for salmon. The shrimp competed with the salmon for zooplankton as a food source and the salmon population declined. The bald eagle and grizzly bear populations subsequently also declined.

Biodiversity Has Direct Value and Indirect Value for Humans

Learning Outcomes

▶ Explain the direct value of biodiversity with reference to (1) medicinal, (2) agricultural, and (3) consumptive use values. (40.3)

▶ Explain the indirect value of biodiversity with reference to (1) the disposal of wastes within biogeochemical cycles; (2) the provision of fresh water, prevention of soil erosion, and regulation of climate by natural areas; and (3) ecotourism. (40.4)

The direct value of biodiversity is observable in the services of individual wild species. The indirect value is evidenced by the many services provided by ecosystems.

40.3 The direct value of biodiversity is becoming better recognized

Conservation biology strives to reverse the trend toward the possible extinction of tens of thousands of living things. To bring this about, it is necessary to make all people aware of the various ways that biodiversity has direct value and indirect value. Following are some of the ways that wildlife has direct value.

Wildlife Has Medicinal Value Most of the prescription drugs used in the United States, valued at over $200 billion, were originally derived from living organisms. The rosy periwinkle from Madagascar is an excellent example of a tropical plant that has provided us with useful medicines (**Fig. 40.3a**). Potent chemicals from this plant are now used to treat two forms of cancer: leukemia and Hodgkin disease. Researchers tell us that, judging from the success rate in the past, an additional 328 types of drugs are yet to be found in tropical rain forests, and the value of this resource to society is probably $147 billion.

You may already know that the antibiotic penicillin is derived from a fungus and that certain species of bacteria produce the antibiotics tetracycline and streptomycin. These drugs have been indispensable in the treatment of diseases, including sexually transmitted diseases such as gonorrhea and syphilis.

Leprosy is among the diseases for which there is, as yet, no cure. The bacterium that causes leprosy will not grow in the laboratory, but scientists have discovered that it grows naturally in the nine-banded armadillo (Fig. 40.3b). Having a source for the bacterium may make it possible to find a cure for leprosy. The blood of horseshoe crabs contains a substance called limulus amoebocyte lysate, which is used to ensure that medical devices such as pacemakers, surgical implants, and prosthetic devices are free of bacteria. Blood is taken from 250,000 crabs a year for extraction of this chemical, and then the crabs are returned to the sea unharmed.

Wildlife Has Agricultural Value Crops such as wheat, corn, and rice are derived from wild plants that have been modified to be high producers. The same high-yield, genetically

FIGURE 40.3
Direct value of diverse wildlife.

a. Wild species, such as the rosy periwinkle, *Catharanthus roseus,* are sources of many medicines.

c. Wild species, including ladybugs, *Coccinella,* play a role in the biological control of agricultural pests.

b. Wild species, such as the nine-banded armadillo, *Dasypus novemcinctus,* play a role in medical research.

d. Wild species, such as certain bats (e.g., *Leptonycteris curasoae)*, are pollinators of agricultural and other plants.

similar strains tend to be grown worldwide. When rice crops in Africa were being devastated by a virus, researchers grew wild rice plants from thousands of seed samples until they found one that contained a gene for resistance to the virus. They then used these wild plants in a breeding program to transfer the gene into high-yield rice plants. If this variety of wild rice had become extinct before it was discovered, rice cultivation in Africa might have collapsed.

Biological pest controls—natural predators and parasites—are often preferable to chemical pesticides. When a rice pest called the brown planthopper became resistant to pesticides, farmers began to use natural brown planthopper enemies instead. The economic savings were calculated at well over $1 billion. Similarly, cotton growers in Cañete Valley, Peru, found that pesticides were no longer working against the cotton aphid because of resistance. Research identified natural predators, such as the ladybug, that cotton farmers are now using to an ever greater degree (Fig. 40.3c).

Most flowering plants are pollinated by animals, such as bees, wasps, butterflies, beetles, birds, and bats (Fig. 40.3d). The honeybee, *Apis mellifera*, has been domesticated, and it pollinates almost $10 billion worth of food crops annually in the United States. However, the danger of this dependency on a single species is exemplified by mites, which have now wiped out more than 23% of the commercial honeybee population in the United States. Where can we get resistant bees? From the wild, of course. The value of wild pollinators to the U.S. agricultural economy has been calculated at $4.1–$6.7 billion a year.

Wildlife Has Consumptive Use Value

Humans have had much success cultivating crops, keeping domesticated animals, growing trees in plantations, and so forth. But so far, aquaculture, the growing of fish and shellfish for human consumption, has contributed only minimally to human welfare. Instead, most freshwater and marine harvests depend on the catching of wild animals, such as crustaceans (e.g., lobsters, shrimps, and crabs), mammals (e.g., whales), and fishes (e.g., trout, cod, tuna, and flounder) (Fig. 40.3e).

The environment provides a variety of other products that are sold in the marketplace worldwide, including wild fruits and vegetables, skins, fibers, beeswax, and seaweed. Also, by hunting and fishing, some people obtain their meat directly from the environment. In one study, researchers calculated that the economic value of the wild pig in the diet of native hunters in Sarawak, East Malaysia, was approximately $40 million per year.

Similarly, many trees in the natural environment are still felled for their wood. Researchers have calculated that a species-rich forest in the Peruvian Amazon is worth far more if the forest is used for fruit and rubber production than for timber production (Fig. 40.3f). Fruit and the latex needed to produce rubber can be brought to market for an unlimited number of years, whereas once the trees are gone, no more products can be harvested.

▶ **40.3 Check Your Progress** From a "consumptive" perspective, why is it important to preserve aquatic biodiversity?

e. Wild species, including many marine species, provide us with food.

f. Wild species, such as rubber trees, *Hevea*, can provide a product indefinitely if the forest is not destroyed.

40.4 The indirect value of biodiversity is immense

Ecosystems perform many services for modern humans, who increasingly live in cities. The services discussed in this section are said to be indirect because they are pervasive and not easily discernible.

Biogeochemical Cycles Help Dispose of Waste The biodiversity within ecosystems contributes to the workings of the water, carbon, phosphorus, and nitrogen cycles. We are dependent on these cycles for fresh water, removal of carbon dioxide from the atmosphere, uptake of excess soil nitrogen, and provision of phosphate. When human activities upset the usual workings of biogeochemical cycles, the dire environmental consequences include the release of excess pollutants that are harmful to us. Technology is unable to artificially contribute to or create any of the biogeochemical cycles.

As discussed in the introduction to Chapter 38, if not for decomposition, waste would soon cover the entire surface of our planet. We can build sewage treatment plants, but they are expensive, and few of them break down solid wastes completely to inorganic nutrients. It is less expensive and more efficient to water plants and trees with partially treated wastewater and let soil bacteria cleanse it completely. Biological communities are also capable of breaking down and immobilizing pollutants, such as heavy metals and pesticides, that humans release into the environment. A review of wetland functions in Canada assigned a value of $50,000 per hectare (25 acres, or 10,000 m²) per year to the ability of natural areas to purify water and take up pollutants.

Natural Areas Provide Fresh Water, Prevent Soil Erosion, and Regulate Climate Few terrestrial organisms are adapted to living in a salty environment—they need fresh water. We can remove salt from sea water to obtain fresh water, but the cost of desalination is about four to eight times the average cost of fresh water acquired via the water cycle. Humans use fresh water in innumerable ways, including for drinking and for irrigating their crops. Freshwater ecosystems such as rivers and lakes also provide us with fish and other types of organisms for food.

Forests and other natural ecosystems exert a "sponge effect" (**Fig. 40.4**). The leaves of trees acquire water from the roots and then release it at a regular rate. The water-holding capacity of forests and wetlands reduces the possibility of flooding. The value of a marsh outside Boston, Massachusetts, has been estimated at $72,000 per hectare per year based solely on its ability to reduce floods. Forests release water slowly for days or weeks after the rains have ceased. Rivers flowing through forests in West Africa release twice as much water halfway through the dry season, and between three and five times as much at the end of the dry season, as do rivers bordered by coffee plantations.

Due to deforestation ecosystems naturally retain soil and prevent erosion. Due to deforestation the Tarbela Dam in Pakistan is losing its storage capacity of 13.5 billion cubic meters many years sooner than expected because silt is building up behind the dam. At one time, the Philippines were exporting $240.8 million worth of oysters, mussels, clams, and cockles each year. Now, silt carried down rivers following deforestation is smothering the mangrove ecosystem that serves as a nursery for the sea.

Globally, forests ameliorate the climate because they take up carbon dioxide. The leaves of trees use carbon dioxide when they photosynthesize, and the bodies of the trees store carbon. When trees are cut and burned, carbon dioxide is released into the atmosphere. Carbon dioxide makes a significant contribution to global warming, which is expected to be stressful for many plants and animals. If temperatures become warmer, only a small percentage of wildlife will be able to move northward to find weather suitable for them.

Ecotourism Is Enjoyed by Many In the United States, nearly 100 million people enjoy vacationing in a natural setting. To do so, they spend $4 billion each year on fees, travel, lodging, and food. Many tourists want to go sport fishing, whale watching, boat riding, hiking, birdwatching, and the like (Fig. 40.4). Others merely want to immerse themselves in the beauty and serenity of a natural environment.

The next part of the chapter discusses the causes of extinction.

FIGURE 40.4 Tourists (*inset*) love to visit natural ecosystems, such as this forest, which has indirect value because of its water-holding capacity and its ability to take up carbon dioxide.

▶ **40.4 Check Your Progress** What are ecotourists in Hawaii interested in seeing?

The Causes of Today's Extinctions Are Known

Learning Outcome

▶ Describe the five major reasons for the loss of biodiversity. (40.5–40.8)

Researchers have identified the major causes of extinction. They are, in order of significance, habitat loss, introduction of alien species, pollution, overexploitation, and disease. These causes can work together to reduce biodiversity.

40.5 Habitat loss is a major cause of wildlife extinctions

To stem the tide of extinction due to human activities, it is first necessary to identify the causes. Based on the records of 1,880 threatened and endangered wild species in the United States, habitat loss was involved in 85% of the cases (**Fig. 40.5A**). Other significant causes of extinction are introduction of alien species, pollution, overexploitation, and disease. In Figure 40.5A, the percentages add up to more than 100% because most species are imperiled for more than one reason. Macaws are a good example of a species in decline due to a combination of factors.

Habitat loss has occurred in all ecosystems, but concern has now centered on tropical rain forests and coral reefs because they are particularly rich in species. A sequence of events in Brazil offers a fairly typical example of how rain forest is converted to land uninhabitable for wildlife. The construction of a major highway first provided a way to reach the interior of the forest. Small towns and industries sprang up along the highway, and roads branching off the main highway gave rise to even more roads. The result was fragmentation of the once immense

Distant view

Close-up view

FIGURE 40.5B Destruction of a rain forest in Brazil.

forest. The government offered subsidies to anyone willing to take up residence in the forest, and people began to cut and burn trees in patches (**Fig. 40.5B**). Tropical soils contain limited nutrients, but when the trees are burned, nutrients are released that support a lush growth so that cattle can be grazed for about three years. Once the land has been degraded, farmers move on to another portion of the forest and start over again.

Loss of habitat also affects freshwater and marine biodiversity. Coastal degradation is mainly due to the large concentration of people living on or near the coast. Already, 60% of coral reefs have been destroyed or are on the verge of destruction; it is possible that all coral reefs may disappear during the next 40 years. Mangrove forest destruction is also a problem; Indonesia, with the most mangrove acreage, has lost 45% of its mangroves, and the percentage is even higher for other tropical countries. Wetland areas, estuaries, and seagrass beds are also being rapidly destroyed by the actions of humans.

▶ **40.5 Check Your Progress** What is the main cause of coastal degradation in places such as Hawaii?

FIGURE 40.5A Macaws, *Ara macao*, and other species are endangered for the reasons graphed here.

40.6 Introduction of alien species contributes to extinctions

Ecosystems around the globe are characterized by unique assemblages of organisms that have evolved together in one location. Migrating to a new location is not usually possible because of barriers such as oceans, deserts, mountains, and rivers. Humans, however, have introduced **alien species**, nonnative members, into new ecosystems through the following means:

Colonization Europeans, in particular, brought various familiar species with them when they colonized new places. For example, the pilgrims brought the dandelion to the United States as a familiar salad green. In addition, they introduced pigs that have become feral, reverting to their wild state. In some parts of the continental United States, feral pigs are very destructive, just as they are in Hawaii.

Horticulture and agriculture Some aliens now taking over vast tracts of land have escaped from cultivated areas. Kudzu is a vine from Japan that the U.S. Department of Agriculture thought would help prevent soil erosion. The plant now covers much of the landscape in the South, including even walnut, magnolia, and sweet gum trees (**Fig. 40.6A**). The water hyacinth was introduced to the United States from South America because of its beautiful flowers. Today, it clogs waterways and diminishes natural diversity.

Accidental transport Global trade and travel accidentally bring many new species from one country to another. Researchers found that the ballast water released from ships into Coos Bay, Oregon, contained 367 marine species from Japan. The zebra mussel from the Caspian Sea was accidentally introduced into the Great Lakes in 1988. It now forms dense beds that squeeze out native mussels. Other organisms accidentally introduced into the United States include the Formosan termite, the Argentinian fire ant, and the nutria, a type of rodent.

Alien species can disrupt food webs. As mentioned earlier, opossum shrimp introduced into a lake in Montana added a trophic level that in the end meant less food for bald eagles and grizzly bears (see Fig. 40.2). Introduction of alien species, sometimes called exotic species, plays a role in nearly 50% of extinctions (see Fig. 40.5A).

Aliens on Islands Islands are particularly susceptible to environmental discord caused by the introduction of alien species. Islands have unique assemblages of native species that are closely adapted to one another and cannot compete well against aliens. Myrtle trees, *Myrica faya*, introduced into the Hawaiian Islands from the Canary Islands, are symbiotic with a type of bacterium that is capable of nitrogen fixation. This feature allows the species to establish itself on nutrient-poor volcanic soil, a distinct advantage in Hawaii. Once established, myrtle trees halt the normal succession of native plants on volcanic soil.

The brown tree snake has been inadvertently introduced onto a number of islands in the Pacific Ocean. The snake eats eggs, nestlings, and adult birds. On Guam, it has reduced ten native bird species to the point of extinction. On the Galápagos Islands, black rats have reduced populations of giant tortoises,

FIGURE 40.6A Kudzu, a vine from Japan, has displaced many native plants in the southern United States.

FIGURE 40.6B Mongooses, introduced into Hawaii, prey on the native birds.

while goats and feral pigs have changed the vegetation from highland forest to pampaslike grasslands and destroyed stands of cactus. In Australia, mice and rabbits have stressed native marsupial populations. In Hawaii, mongooses introduced to control rats also prey on native birds (**Fig. 40.6B**) and feral pigs continue to devastate forests. The pigs especially seem to prefer eating native species and their wallows allow other alien species to spread. Exterminating the pigs would be helpful but native peoples are opposed because they use them as a source of food. Fencing is being used to keep them out of national parks, however.

Section 40.7 shows that pollution also contributes to extinctions.

▶ **40.6 Check Your Progress** What effect do alien species have on biodiversity?

40.7 Pollution contributes to extinctions

So far, we have discussed habitat loss and alien species as causes of extinction. Now, we will discuss pollution, which is a factor in 24% of extinctions (see Fig. 40.5A). In the present context, **pollution** can be defined as any environmental change that adversely affects the lives and health of living things. Biodiversity is particularly threatened by the following types of environmental pollution:

Acid Deposition Both sulfur dioxide from power plants and nitrogen oxides in automobile exhaust are converted to acids when they combine with water vapor in the atmosphere. These acids return to Earth as either wet deposition (acid rain or snow) or dry deposition (sulfate and nitrate salts). Acid deposition causes trees to weaken and increases their susceptibility to disease and insects. Many lakes in the northern United States are now lifeless because of the effects of acid deposition.

Ozone Depletion The ozone shield is a layer of ozone (O_3) in the stratosphere, some 50 k above the Earth. The ozone shield absorbs most of the wavelengths of harmful ultraviolet (UV) radiation so that they do not strike the Earth. The cause of ozone depletion can be traced to chlorine atoms (Cl^-) that come from the breakdown of chlorofluorocarbons (CFCs). Severe ozone shield depletion can impair crop and tree growth and also kill plankton (microscopic plant and animal life) that sustain oceanic life. Due to an international agreement, manufacture of CFCs ceased in the United States in 1996, but the chemicals linger because they are chemically stable. The amount of depletion over Antarctica varies with weather conditions; the amount of depletion in 2008 was greater than that in 2007 but less than in 2006.

Organic Chemicals Our modern society uses organic chemicals in all sorts of ways. Organic chemicals called nonylphenols are in products ranging from pesticides to dishwashing detergents, cosmetics, plastics, and spermicides. These chemicals mimic the effects of hormones and, in that way, most likely harm wildlife. Salmon are born in fresh water but mature in salt water. After investigators exposed young fish to nonylphenol, they found that 20–30% were unable to make the transition between fresh and salt water. Nonylphenols cause the pituitary to produce prolactin, a hormone that may prevent saltwater adaptation.

Global Climate Change Recall that certain gases, such as carbon dioxide and methane, are known as greenhouse gases because, just like the panes of a greenhouse, they allow solar radiation to pass through but hinder the escape of its heat back into space. Data collected around the world show a steady rise in the concentration of the various greenhouse gases due to the burning of fossil fuels and forests. A rise in greenhouse gases parallels a rise in global temperatures. The response of organisms to global climate change will be dramatic, as discussed in How Life Changes on page 808. For example, the growth of corals is very dependent on mutualistic algae living in their walls.

FIGURE 40.7 (*Top*) Normal coral reef. (*Bottom*) Bleaching of a coral reef. A temperature rise of only a few degrees causes coral reefs to "bleach" and become lifeless. As the oceans warm and land recedes, coral reefs could move northward.

When the temperature rises by 4°, corals expel their algae and are said to be "bleached" (**Fig. 40.7**).

Solid Waste Disposal Due to high consumption, the United States is one of the largest global generators of municipal wastes per capita. Between 1990 and 2005, Japan maintained its municipal waste generation at 405 kg per capita, but waste generation in the United States rose from 600 to 770 kg per capita. According to the Solid Waste Disposal Act of 1976, states are to maximize recycling and minimize waste, but many states have not yet complied. Plastic, which accounts for 90% of the solid waste now floating in the oceans, is a danger to wildlife. An estimated 1 million seabirds and 100,000 sea turtles die annually by choking on floating plastic objects or becoming entangled in them.

Eutrophication Lakes are also under stress due to over-enrichment. When lakes receive excess nutrients due to runoff from agricultural fields and wastewater from sewage treatment, algae begin to grow in abundance. An algal bloom is apparent as a green scum or excessive mats of filamentous algae. Upon death, the decomposers break down the algae, but in so doing, they use up oxygen. Thus a decreased amount of oxygen is available to fish, sometimes leading to a massive fish kill.

▶ **40.7 Check Your Progress** Which form of pollution could have the most dramatic effect on wildlife?

40A Response of Organisms to Global Climate Change

Even though January 2010 was unusually cold in much of the United States, globally it was the second hottest January since ambient temperatures were first measured some 130 years ago. Warmer global temperatures increased the rate of evaporation from the oceans and the increased moisture in the atmosphere caused the Northeast to receive heavy snow falls. Climate change is occurring globally and all ecosystems on Earth are affected. In general the growing season is extending as the number of frost-free days increases; however, the preferred environmental conditions for certain species are shifting northward.

Biologists want to know how species are coping with the temperature and rainfall changes they are experiencing. Some species are able to shift their distributions poleward. For example, Edith's checkerspot butterfly (**Fig. 40A.1**), a North American species, has become rare in southern locations and is now found with greater frequency at northern locations. Similar range shifts are noted in European butterflies as well. A recent study of forest ecosystems in Europe found that several species are moving to higher elevations at a rate of approximately 29 meters per decade. A new study of Sierra Nevada birds showed that 48 of 53 bird species adjusted to climate change over the last century by moving to where their favored temperature and/or rainfall conditions now exist. The Clark's nutcracker has moved upward to secure its favored temperature, while the Bullock's oriole is following its favored rainfall (**Fig. 40A.2**). The western bluebird shifted its range to achieve both suitable temperature and rainfall.

In addition to distribution changes, evolutionary effects are also expected. North American tree swallows (**Fig. 40A.3**) normally lay eggs in May, which indicates that the signal to start laying eggs is determined by temperature and day length. Over the past 40 years, researchers have documented that some members of this species are now laying their eggs nine days earlier than usual. This behavior increases fitness and will be favored by natural selection. To the degree that it is genetically determined, more tree swallows will exhibit this behavior in the future. Similarly, wild female Soay sheep on the island of Hirta (**Fig. 40A.4**) have gotten smaller by 5% during the past two decades. Size is partly inherited, and up to now cold winters have favored large-sized sheep, which have better survival power during times of food scarcity. The population's phenotypic ratio is now changing, however, because milder winters do not select for large size, and small, weak youngsters have been able to survive.

The topic of species responses to climate change is not only interesting to ecologists and evolutionary biologists but also has serious implications for public health. For example, consider a common and often unpopular insect, the mosquito. The life cycle of blood-sucking mosquitoes is strongly influenced by day length. During the long days of summer, they seek a blood meal to support their reproduction, but as the days shorten and temperatures cool, they hibernate. A study of the pitcher plant mosquito in North America found that most individuals also follow this day length–sensitive cycle, but a genetically distinct group continues to reproduce as the days shorten. As temperatures warm, this genetically distinct group is breeding longer and shifting its distribution northward, two adjustments that will spread its genes and increase its fitness. Pitcher plant mosquitoes feed on nectar, not blood, but many of their relatives do feed on blood. If these relatives also experience shifts in distribution and duration of reproduction, any diseases they carry could increase. Other diseases may also increase. For example, it's been determined that higher temperatures have favored the spread of the fungal infection that is causing the Harlequin toad, shown in Figure 40.9, to become extinct.

FORM YOUR OPINION

1. Climate change is a powerful new consideration for all people who wish to preserve species. How might scientists use artificial selection to help species survive?
2. If a milder winter causes a population shift toward small, weak members, extinction could occur even when plenty of food is available. Explain.
3. Suppose a species is adapted to living in a particular ecosystem. Even if it could follow its favored temperature, why might it not survive in its new surroundings?

FIGURE 40A.1 Edith's checkerspot butterfly, *Euphydryas editha.*

FIGURE 40A.2 Bullock's oriole, *Icterus bullockii.*

FIGURE 40A.3 Tree swallow, *Tachycineta ssp.*

FIGURE 40A.4 Soay sheep *Ovis aries.*

40.8 Overexploitation contributes to extinctions

Overexploitation occurs when the number of individuals taken from a wild population is so great that the population becomes severely reduced in number. Overexploitation accounts for 17% of extinctions (see Fig. 40.5A). A positive feedback cycle ensues when the members of a small population are particularly prized. Poachers and members of criminal organizations collect and sell endangered and threatened species because it has become so lucrative. The overall international value of trading wildlife species is $20 billion, of which $8 billion is attributed to the illegal sale of rare species.

Declining species of mammals, such as the Siberian tiger, are still hunted for their hides, tusks, horns, or bones. Because of its rarity, a single Siberian tiger is now worth more than $500,000—its bones are pulverized and used as a medicinal powder. The horns of rhinoceroses become ornate carved daggers, and their bones are ground up to sell as a medicine. The ivory of an elephant's tusk is used to make art objects, jewelry, or piano keys. The fur of a Bengal tiger sells for as much as $100,000 in Tokyo.

The U.N. Food and Agricultural Organization tells us that humans have now overexploited 11 of 15 major oceanic fishing areas. Larger and more efficient fishing fleets are now decimating fishing stocks. Pelagic species such as tuna are captured by purse-seine fishing, in which a very large net surrounds a school of fish and is then closed like a drawstring purse. Up to thousands of dolphins that swim above schools of tuna are often captured and then killed in this type of net. Other fishing boats drag huge trawling nets, large enough to accommodate 12 jumbo jets, along the seafloor to capture bottom-dwelling fish (**Fig. 40.8**). Only large fish are kept; undesirable small fish and sea turtles are discarded, dying, back into the ocean. Other reptiles are sought for consumption. Collection and trade of terrestrial tortoises and freshwater turtles for food and other uses has surged in Asia over the past two decades and is now spreading around the globe. These practices have wiped out populations in Asia and have brought others to the brink of extinction in a matter of years.

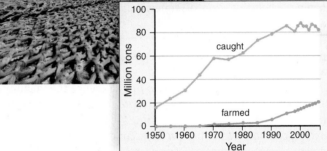

FIGURE 40.8 Huge nets catch massive numbers of fish. The graph below shows that the number of fish caught increased until 1995 and since then has remained fairly the same.

A marine ecosystem can be disrupted by overfishing, as exemplified on the U.S. West Coast. When sea otters began to decline in numbers, investigators found that they were being eaten by orcas (killer whales). Usually orcas prefer seals and sea lions to sea otters, but they began eating sea otters when few seals and sea lions could be found. What caused a decline in seals and sea lions? Their preferred food sources—perch and herring—were no longer plentiful due to overfishing. Ordinarily, sea otters keep the population of sea urchins, which feed on kelp, under control. But with fewer sea otters around, the sea urchin population exploded and decimated the kelp beds.

▶ **40.8 Check Your Progress** Reducing the numbers of certain species of Hawaiian fish due to overfishing is an example of _____.

40.9 Disease contributes to extinctions

Scientists tell us the number of pathogens that cause diseases is on the rise, threatening human health as well as that of wildlife. Due to the encroachment of humans on their habitat and other

FIGURE 40.9 The Harlequin toad is near extinction due to a fungal pathogen.

general interventions, wildlife have been exposed to emerging diseases. For example, canine distemper was spread from domesticated dogs to lions in the African Serengeti, causing population declines. Avian influenza likely emerged from domesticated fowl (e.g., chicken) populations and could lead to the deaths of many wild birds.

Pollution can weaken organisms so that they are more susceptible to disease. Almost half of sea otter deaths along the coast of California are now due to infectious diseases. Pollution, most likely, plays a role in the worldwide decline of amphibians due to disease (**Fig. 40.9**).

The next part of the chapter discusses habitat preservation and restoration.

▶ **40.9 Check Your Progress** The rapid decline of amphibians worldwide is at least partially due to _____.

Habitat Preservation and Restoration Require Much Effort and Expertise

Learning Outcomes

▶ Explain the basis for deciding which species to preserve and what methodology to use. (40.10)
▶ Explain the purpose and the methodology for restoring an ecosystem that has been seriously damaged. (40.11)

To preserve species, it is necessary to preserve their habitat, or possibly restore a habitat. Conservation aims for sustainable development, which allows multiple uses of the land.

40.10 Habitat preservation is of primary importance

Preserving a species' habitat is a major concern, but first we must decide which species to preserve. As mentioned previously, the biosphere contains biodiversity hotspots, relatively small areas having a concentration of endemic (native) species not found anyplace else. In the tropical rain forests of Madagascar, 93% of the primate species, 99% of the frog species, and over 80% of the plant species are endemic to Madagascar. Preserving these forests and other hotspots will save a wide variety of organisms.

Keystone species are species that influence the viability of a community, although their numbers may not be excessively high. The extinction of a keystone species can lead to other extinctions and loss of biodiversity. For example, bats are designated a keystone species in tropical forests of the Old World. They are pollinators that also disperse the seeds of trees. When bats are killed off and their roosts destroyed, the trees fail to reproduce. The grizzly bear is a keystone species in the northwestern United States and Canada (**Fig. 40.10A**). Bears disperse the seeds of berries; as many as 7,000 seeds may be in one dung pile. Grizzlies also kill the young of many hoofed animals and thereby keep their populations under control. In addition, grizzlies are a principal mover of soil when they dig up roots and prey upon hibernating ground squirrels and marmots. Other keystone species are beavers in wetlands, bison in grasslands, alligators in swamps, and elephants in grasslands and forests.

The grizzly bear population is actually a **metapopulation**, a population inadvertently fragmented by humans into several small, isolated populations. Originally, there were probably 50,000–100,000 grizzlies south of Canada, but this number has been reduced because communities have encroached on their home range and bears have been killed by frightened homeowners. Now there are six virtually isolated subpopulations, totaling about 1,000 individuals. The Yellowstone National Park population numbers 200, but the others are even smaller.

Saving metapopulations sometimes requires determining which of the populations is the source and which are sinks. A **source population** is one that lives in a favorable area, and its birthrate is most likely higher than its death rate. Individuals from source populations move into **sink populations**, where the environment is not as favorable and where the birthrate equals the death rate at best. When trying to save the northern spotted owl, conservationists decided to prevent owls from leaving old-growth rain forests of the Pacific Northwest where they successfully reproduce (**Fig. 40.10B**). This decision proved beneficial in maintaining the populations.

Landscape Preservation May Be Necessary Grizzly bears inhabit a number of different types of ecosystems, including plains, mountains, and rivers. Saving any one of these types of ecosystems alone would not be sufficient to preserve grizzly bears. Instead, it is necessary to save diverse ecosystems that are at least connected by corridors. You will recall that a landscape encompasses different types of ecosystems. An area called the Greater Yellowstone Ecosystem, where bears are free to roam, has now been defined. It contains millions of acres in Yellowstone National Park; state lands in Montana, Idaho, and Wyoming; five different national forests; various wildlife refuges; and even private lands.

Landscape protection for one species is often beneficial for other wildlife that share the same space. The last of the contiguous 48 states' harlequin ducks, bull trout, westslope cutthroat trout, lynx, pine martens, wolverines, mountain caribou, and great gray owls are found in areas occupied by grizzlies. The recent return of gray wolves has occurred in this territory also. Then, too, the grizzly range overlaps with 40% of Montana's vascular plants of special conservation concern.

▶ **40.10 Check Your Progress** A population of native plants subdivided by towns built by humans is a _____.

FIGURE 40.10B Old-growth forest, home of the northern spotted owl, *Strix occidentalis caurina.*

FIGURE 40.10A Landscape preservation will help grizzly bears, *Ursus arctos horribilis,* survive.

40.11 Habitat restoration is sometimes necessary

Restoration ecology is a new subdiscipline of conservation biology that seeks scientific ways to return ecosystems to their former state. Three principles have so far emerged: First, it is best to begin as soon as possible before remaining fragments of the original habitat are lost. These fragments are sources of wildlife and seeds from which to restock the restored habitat. Second, once the natural history of the habitat is understood, it is best to use biological techniques that mimic natural processes to bring about restoration. This might take the form of using controlled burns to bring back grassland habitats, biological pest controls to rid the area of alien species, or bioremediation techniques to clean up pollutants. Third, the goal is **sustainable development,** the ability of an ecosystem to maintain itself while providing services to humans. We will use the Everglades ecosystem to illustrate these principles.

The Everglades The Everglades, located in southern Florida, is a vast sawgrass prairie, interrupted occasionally by hardwood tree islands. Within these islands, both temperate and tropical evergreen trees grow amongst dense and tangled vegetation. Mangroves are found along sloughs (creeks) and at the shoreline. The prop roots of red mangroves protect over 40 different types of juvenile fishes as they grow to maturity. During the wet season, from May to November, animals disperse throughout the region, but in the dry season, from December to April, they congregate wherever pools of water are found. Alligators are famous for making "gator holes," where water collects and fish, shrimp, crabs, birds, and a host of living things survive until the rains come again. The Everglades once supported millions of large and beautiful birds, including herons, egrets, the white ibis, and the roseate spoonbill. **Figure 40.11** shows various animals that live in the Everglades.

At the turn of the twentieth century, settlers began to drain land in central Florida to grow crops in the newly established Everglades Agricultural Area (EAA). A large dike was used to keep water in a large lake called Lake Okeechobee. The dike prevents water from overflowing its banks and moving slowly southward. Water is contained not only in the lake but also in three so-called conservation areas established to the south of the lake. Water must be conserved to irrigate the farmland and to recharge the Biscayne aquifer (underground river), which supplies drinking water for the cities on the east coast of Florida. The Everglades National Park receives only water that is discharged artificially from a conservation area, and the discharge is scheduled according to the convenience of humans rather than the natural wet/dry season of southern Florida. Largely because of this, the Everglades is now dying, as witnessed by declining bird populations. The birds, which formerly numbered in the millions, now exist in only thousands.

A restoration plan has been developed that will sustain the Everglades ecosystem while maintaining the services society requires. The Everglades is to receive a more natural flow of water from Lake Okeechobee. This will require flooding the EAA and growing only crops such as sugarcane and rice that can tolerate these conditions. This has the benefit of stopping the loss of topsoil and preventing possible residential development in the area. There will also be an extended buffer zone between an expanded Everglades and the urban areas on Florida's east coast. The buffer zone will contain a contiguous system of interconnected marsh areas, detention reservoirs, seepage barriers, and water treatment areas. This plan is expected to stop the decline of the Everglades, while still allowing agriculture to continue and providing water and flood control to the eastern coast. Sustainable development will maintain the ecosystem indefinitely and still meet human needs.

Florida panther, *Puma concolor coryi*

American alligator, *Alligator mississippiensis*

White ibis, *Eudocimus albus*

Roseate spoonbill, *Ajaia ajaja*

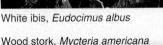

Wood stork, *Mycteria americana*

FIGURE 40.11 A variety of animals make their home in the Everglades.

▶ **40.11 Check Your Progress** What is the goal of restoration ecologists in preserved areas of the Hawaiian Islands that have been heavily damaged?

40B Captive Breeding Programs

Captive breeding provides a means for conserving species and perhaps releasing them back into the wild. Through captive breeding, zoos have reintroduced various animals into their native habitats—for example, a monkey, the golden lion tamarin; a bird, the Guam rail; and a mammal, the black-footed ferret. Reintroduction is not possible unless a captive population has a suitable age structure and is able to reproduce successfully and to withstand disease. In order to accomplish this, the gene pool must be as varied as possible. Since zoos typically have space for only a few animals of each species, the "population" is actually spread out between several zoos that cooperate in breeding the animals. In order to maintain genetic variations, zoos keep a pedigree or "family tree" for each animal in their care. A coordinator uses these to determine which animals should breed and with whom. Animals are shipped between zoos in order to ensure the best pairings. Zoos have veterinarians that care for the animals and treat any problems in order to maintain their good health. They often advertise new arrivals, as the Perth Zoo did when a Nepalese red panda cub was born.

Hatcheries, on the other hand, raise massive numbers of fish that are then released them to maintain stocks for sport fishing (**Fig. 40B**). Alaska hatcheries, for example, stock millions of salmon, char, and trout into hundreds of lakes and streams throughout the state. The hatchery programs contribute significantly to sport fishing and to conservation by protecting wild fish stocks from overharvesting. Further south, other hatcheries restock populations of salmon in the Pacific Northwest of the United States and Canada and bolster endangered fishes of the Rio Grande and Colorado river drainage basins.

Hatchery managers are always careful to maintain genetic variation of each type of fish by using as parents many different individuals and by obtaining new or wild individuals for breeding purposes whenever possible. If genetic variation is reduced, it becomes difficult for a wild population to adapt to environmental changes. Without the ability to evolve, a population may become extinct. Therefore, hatcheries, like zoos, work at maintaining genetic variation.

Hatcheries also preserve unique species. The Pacific Northwest contains five species of salmon: chinook, chum, coho, pink, and sockeye. Each species lays its eggs in a particular freshwater stream. After they hatch, the young migrate to the Pacific Ocean where they grow to adulthood. Adults then migrate back to the stream where they were born to lay their eggs. The adults that return to each stream are genetically distinct from individuals of other streams. Hatchery managers want to maintain the reproductive isolation of these species because local economies rely on a salmon stock that is adapted to living in a nearby stream. If a hatchery manager were to mix parents from different streams, genetic variation might increase but unique species would be lost, and the single fish stock might not live successfully in all stream ecosystems.

An example shows how a hatchery can contribute to conservation of a unique species: The Leon Springs pupfish (*Cyprinodon bovinus*) is an endangered fish species native to only a small

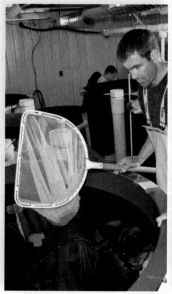

FIGURE 40B Fish hatcheries and zoos breed animals. Fish hatcheries routinely release fishes into the wild. Occasionally zoos also release animals they have raised in captivity.

spring in southwest Texas. The Leon Springs pupfish is closely related to another fish, the sheepshead minnow (*Cyprinodon variegatus*), which is often used as bait by fishermen in Texas. The two fish species do not occur together in nature, but because they are closely related, they form hybrids easily when put together. In the 1990s, scientists discovered that the Leon Springs pupfish had hybridized with the sheepshead minnow in its native spring, probably because sheepshead minnows had been dumped there from a bait bucket.

This situation greatly concerned conservationists because the hybridization possibility meant that the uniqueness of the Leon Springs pupfish was in danger of being lost forever. Fortunately, however, a hatchery had been maintaining a population of Leon Springs. Therefore, all the hybrid individuals were removed from the spring and replaced with genetically pure individuals from the hatchery. By removing the hybrid individuals, scientists were able to prevent the extinction of a species and preserve the uniqueness of this particular ecosystem in Texas.

FORM YOUR OPINION

1. Sometimes zoos hybridize animals if they have no other way to bring about reproduction of a nearly extinct species. Why is hybridization an unfortunate alternative to maintaining reproductive isolation?
2. Why is it sometimes necessary for a zoo or hatchery to maintain a species? What does this signify about the particular species and/or the natural habitat?
3. Does your answer to question 2 suggest that it is better to maintain ecosystems than individual species? Explain.

A Sustainable Society Is Achievable

Learning Outcomes

▶ State the characteristics of a sustainable society. (40.12)

▶ Describe the current and future renewable sources of energy. (40.13)

▶ Tell how water can be conserved and agriculture can be improved to protect the environment. (40.14–40.15)

A **sustainable society** will protect biodiversity and at the same time will be able to provide the same amount of goods and services for future generations as it does at present. In a sustainable society, energy sources will be renewable, water will be conserved, and agriculture will not harm the environment.

40.12 A sustainable society will preserve resources

To achieve a sustainable society, resources such as clean air, water, an adequate amount of food, and living space for humans and wildlife will have to be preserved. This goal is not possible unless we carefully regulate our consumption of these resources today, taking into consideration that the human population is ever increasing.

A natural ecosystem can offer clues about how to make today's society sustainable. A natural ecosystem uses renewable solar energy, and its materials cycle through the various populations back to the producer once again. For example, coral reefs have been sustaining themselves for millions of years. At the same time, the reefs have provided sustenance to humans. The value of coral reefs has been assessed at over $300 billion a year. Their aesthetic value is immeasurable.

It is clear that if we want to develop a sustainable society, we too should use renewable energy sources and recycle materials. We should protect natural ecosystems such as coral reefs that help sustain our modern society. At least a quarter of the coral reefs exist close to the shores of an MDC (more-developed country), and the chances are good that these coral reefs are at least somewhat protected. Unfortunately, other coral reefs are threatened by unsustainable practices. The good news is that reefs are remarkably regenerative and will return to their former condition if left alone. The message of today's environmentalists is about what can be done to improve matters and make the environment sustainable (**Fig. 40.12**). There is still time to make changes and improvements.

Sustainability should be practiced in all areas of human endeavor, from agriculture to business. Efficiency is the key to sustainability. For example, an efficient car would be ultralight and gas thrifty. Efficient cars could be just as durable and speedy as the inefficient ones of today. Only through efficiency can we meet the challenges of limited resources and finances in the future.

▶ **40.12 Check Your Progress** In what ways would a sustainable society preserve biodiversity?

multi-use farming

integrated pest management

wetland, delta preservation and restoration

conservation of water

recycling and composting

mass transit and energy-efficient transportation

FIGURE 40.12 These activities are characteristic of a sustainable society. Arrows point inward to signify that these activities increase the carrying capacity of the Earth.

40.13 Energy sources should be renewable

The goal of a sustainable society is to primarily use renewable resources and to increase the efficiency with which they are used. **Renewable resources** are capable of being naturally replenished; for example, solar energy is a renewable source of energy because the sun shines on the Earth every day without fail. In contrast, **nonrenewable resources** are in limited supply. Consider that the present supply of fossil fuels (oil, natural gas, and coal), which were formed many millions of years ago from the compressed remains of plants and animals, can run out. Much needs to be done to increase our reliance on renewable energy sources because in 2008, about 84% of the world's energy came from fossil fuels and 6% came from nuclear power, which is also a nonrenewable source. Fossil fuels cause air pollution, and nuclear power plants give off radioactive solid wastes that threaten our health.

Traditional Renewable Energy Sources Renewable energy sources, such as hydropower, geothermal energy, wind power, and solar energy, have been under development for some time (**Fig. 40.13A**).

Hydroelectric plants convert the energy of falling water into electricity. Worldwide, hydropower presently generates 3% of all the electricity utilized. Most of the presently available hydropower comes from enormous dams. Unfortunately, constructing these dams involved the destruction of ecosystems, and large dams are impractical for the reasons discussed in Section 40.14. Small-scale dams that generate less power per dam, but do not have the same environmental impact, are believed to be the more environmentally responsible choice.

Geothermal energy occurs because the Earth has an internal source of heat. Elements such as uranium, thorium, radium, and plutonium undergo radioactive decay underground and then heat the surrounding rocks to hundreds of degrees Celsius. When the rocks are in contact with underground streams or lakes, huge amounts of steam and hot water are produced. This steam can be piped up to the surface to supply hot water for home heating or to run steam-driven turbogenerators. The California Geysers Project, for example, is one of the world's largest geothermal electricity–generating complexes.

Wind power is expected to account for a significant percentage of our energy needs in the future. Despite the common belief that a huge amount of land is required for "wind farms" that produce commercial electricity, the actual amount of space for a wind farm compares favorably to the amount of land required by a coal-fired power plant or a solar thermal energy system. A community that generates its own electricity by using wind power can solve the problem of uneven energy production by selling electricity to a local public utility when an excess is available and buying electricity from the same facility when wind power is in short supply.

Solar energy is diffuse energy that must be (1) collected, (2) converted to another form, and (3) stored if it is to compete with other available forms of energy. Solar energy plants use massive mirrors to track the sun and reflect the heat toward storage tanks that drive a steam turbine. Passive solar heating of a house is successful when the windows of the house face the sun, the

Hydropower dams

Wind power

Solar panels on roof-top

Sun-tracking mirrors of a solar energy plant

FIGURE 40.13A Traditional sources of renewable energy

building is well insulated, and heat can be stored in water tanks, rocks, bricks, or some other suitable material. The use of photovoltaic (solar) cells is another way to tap the energy of the sun. In photovoltaic cells, one metal wafer absorbs solar energy and emits electrons that are collected by another wafer and passed on to appropriate wiring. Spurred by the oil shortages of the 1970s and most recently of 2008, the U.S. government has been supporting the development of photovoltaic cells, and their cost has dropped dramatically.

Biofuels and Electric Cars In the future, biofuels which are derived from organic matter may run power plants or your car (**Fig. 40.13B** *left*). Biofuels such as ethanol, methanol, diesel gas, and methane are derived from plant material including agricultural crops (e.g., corn) or grasses (e.g., switchgrass) or algae. Biofuels can also be made from wastes such as wood chips or animal sewage. The use of animal sewage to produce biofuels is an excellent example of how recyling can avoid polluting the environment. Such a solution to the environmental problem of animal sewage disposal also shows how technology can help our society become more sustainable. Biofuels are derived from renewable sources of energy because crops and trees regrow and animals constantly produce sewage.

Traditional cars have internal combustion engines that run on gasoline, but hybrid cars that are increasing in popularity due to rising fuel costs run on both gasoline and electricity. The electricity is produced by a battery that is charged when the car is idle.

FIGURE 40.13B Cars of the future may be powered by a biofuel or by electricity that recharges a battery.

Hybrid cars have improved mileage per gallon, and purely electric cars may be capable of 200 miles per gallon. The battery of an electric car can be charged much as your cell phone is charged—by plugging it into a home electrical outlet (**Fig. 40.13B** *right*). Ideally, the power plants will be using a renewable source of energy such as those we have been discussing. Also, cars of the future may run on hydrogen. The car either burns hydrogen in an internal combustion engine, or a fuel cell produces electricity by combining hydrogen with oxygen. In either case, a car that burns hydrogen releases water and not carbon dioxide. Biofueled cars and hydrogen cars are now being produced and are available for sale.

▶ **40.13 Check Your Progress** What are the benefits for a society that makes use of renewable energy supplies?

40.14 Water sources should be conserved

While people and wildlife need a constant supply of fresh water, at present most fresh water is utilized by industry and agriculture. Worldwide, 70% of all fresh water is used to irrigate crops! Although the needs of the human population overall do not exceed the renewable supply of water, this is not the case in certain regions of the United States and the world. When needed, humans increase the supply of fresh water by damming rivers and withdrawing water from aquifers. Dams have drawbacks: (1) Reservoirs behind the dam lose water due to evaporation and seepage into underlying rock beds. The amount of water lost sometimes equals the amount dams make available! (2) The salt left behind by evaporation and agricultural runoff increases salinity and can make a river's water unusable farther downstream. (3) Over time, dams hold back less water because of sediment buildup. Sometimes a reservoir becomes so full of silt that it is no longer useful for storing water. (4) The reduced water below the dam has a negative impact on the native wildlife.

Another mistaken practice is to meet freshwater needs by pumping vast amounts of water from aquifers, which are reservoirs just below, or as much as 1 km below, the ground's surface. Aquifers hold about 1,000 times the amount of water that falls on land as precipitation each year. In the past 50 years, groundwater depletion has become a problem in many areas of the world. Removal of water is causing land subsidence—that is, settling of the soil as it dries out. In California's San Joaquin valley, an area of more than 13,000 square kilometers has subsided at least 30 cm due to groundwater depletion, and in the worst spot, the surface of the ground has dropped more than 9 m! Subsidence damages canals, buildings, and underground pipes.

Conservation of Water By 2025, two-thirds of the world's population may be facing serious water shortages. Agriculture could cut down on its use of water by planting drought- and salt-tolerant crops (**Fig. 40.14a**). Development of salt-tolerant traditional crops is already under way due to genetic engineering, as discussed in Section 12.3. Using drip irrigation delivers more water to crops and saves about 50% over traditional methods while increasing crop yields as well (**Fig. 40.14b**). Although the first drip systems were developed in 1960, they are currently used on less than 1% of irrigated land. At fault are government subsidies to farmers who irrigate in the usual manner. Industries could also cut their water needs by as much as one-half by reusing water and adopting other conservation measures. Power plants could use air rather than water for cooling purposes. The point is that we do have some leeway to conserve water in the future.

Much can also be done on the homefront. Domestically in MDCs, more water is usually used for bathing, flushing toilets, and watering lawns than for drinking and cooking. But houses could be equipped to recycle washing machine water and bath and sink water for reuse before it is discarded. Home yard irrigation should occur during dusk and dawn hours, as opposed to in the middle of the day when evaporation is at its highest. Purchasing and using water-saving toilets can save millions of gallons of water per year. Instead of running tap water to cool it, place a bottle of water in the refrigerator so that your drinking water is sure to be cool right away. You can go online to find many more ways to conserve water.

FIGURE 40.14 Drip irrigation saves water.

▶ **40.14 Check Your Progress** How might farmers and industry conserve water instead of wasting it?

40.15 Agriculture can be more diverse

Farmers today need to put greater emphasis on procedures that will make farming consistent with the goals of a sustainable society. Presently some farmers plant only a few genetic varieties. Because each crop is a monoculture (a genetically identical crop), a single destructive parasite or pathogen could cause huge crop losses. Instead, farmers need to practice polyculture, or the planting of several varieties of a crop, which will reduce the susceptibility of crops to pests or diseases (**Fig. 40.15a**). Polyculture also reduces the amount of herbicides necessary to kill weeds and can be used to replenish nutrients to topsoil.

Some farmers still rely on the heavy use of herbicides and pesticides, although biotechnology has produced plants that require lesser application of these products. Pesticides reduce soil fertility because they kill off beneficial soil organisms as well as pests. Pesticides also select for resistant insects, causing farmers to increase the amount of pesticide they use. Organic farms are increasing in number, and as mandated by the U.S. Department of Agriculture, they do not use synthetic herbicides or pesticides. Organic farming has become increasingly profitable in recent years because people are more willing to purchase organic produce, despite its higher cost compared to nonorganic produce. Health concerns surrounding pesticide use, as well as the desire for better-tasting food, have encouraged this trend. One way that organic and nonorganic farmers can eliminate the need for pesticides is by using integrated pest management, which advocate the growth of competitive beneficial insects and uses biological pest control methods (also called "biocontrol"). As discussed in Section 40.3, biocontrol includes using natural predators, such as the ladybug beetles in Figure 40.15b.

Crop rotation can help reduce the use of nitrogen-containing fertilizers by farmers. When crop rotation is practiced, a nitrogen-fixing crop, notably a legume, which replenishes soil nutrition, is alternated with a crop such as corn that takes nitrogen from the soil. Multiuse farming techniques generally help increase the amount of organic matter and nutrients in the soil, as was confirmed by the experiment described in Section 1.2.

In Section 40.14, we discussed how farmers could reduce the amount of fresh water they use by planting drought-resistant plants and using drip irrigation. Once biofuels are readily available, farmers could use these renewable sources of energy to run heavy equipment including irrigation pumps and large machines to harvest crops. Another long-term goal might be to reduce the amount of animal husbandry because much of the grain produced in MDCs is used to feed livestock rather than humans. Eating grain instead of meat would feed more people one-sixth of the world's population (over 1 billion people) is currently considered malnourished due to lack of food.

Techniques such as contour farming (Fig. 40.15c) are available to reduce erosion and help minimize topsoil loss. Avoiding farming on steep slopes helps reduce erosion. Terrace farming involves converting steep slopes into steplike hills to minimize erosion. Farmers can plant "natural fences," such as rows of trees, around crops to prevent topsoil loss due to wind or other factors. These trees can also supply a useful product; some trees produce nuts and others are a good source of a particular chemical. Also, cover crops, which are often a mixture of legumes and grasses, help stabilize soil between rows of cash crops. Soil nutrients can be increased through composting, organic farming techniques, or other self-renewable methods. Finally, farmers should consider using precision farming (PF) techniques that help them micromanage the planting and harvesting of crops, while saving water and improving crop yields.

▶ **40.15 Check Your Progress** Name and explain three improvements that can make farming more sustainable.

a. Polyculture

b. Biological pest control

c. Contour farming

FIGURE 40.15 A variety of methods can make farming more sustainable. **a.** Polyculture reduces the ability of one parasite to wipe out an entire crop and reduces the need to use an herbicide to kill weeds. This farmer has planted alfalfa between strips of corn, which also replenishes the nitrogen content of the soil (instead of adding fertilizers). Alfalfa, a legume, has root nodules that contain nitrogen-fixing bacteria. **b.** Instead of pesticides, it is possible to use a natural predator. Here, ladybugs are feeding on cottony-cushion scale insects on citrus trees. **c.** Contour farming with no-till conserves topsoil because water has less tendency to run off.

Conservation Biology Attempts to Understand and Protect Biodiversity

40.1 Conservation biology is a practical science

- **Conservation biology** studies biodiversity with the goal of conserving natural resources and preserving biodiversity.

40.2 Biodiversity has levels of complexity

- **Biodiversity** refers to the variety of life on Earth.
- **Extinction** is the total disappearance of a species or higher group.
- **Endangered species** are at immediate risk of extinction.
- **Threatened species** are likely to soon become endangered.
- Biologists study biodiversity in terms of **genetic diversity, ecosystem diversity,** and **landscape diversity.**
- Diversity is highest at the tropics and declines toward the poles; **biodiversity hotspots** contain large concentrations of species.

Biodiversity Has Direct Value and Indirect Value for Humans

40.3 The direct value of biodiversity is becoming better recognized

- Many prescription drugs were originally derived from living organisms, and still more drugs may be derived from rain forest species.
- Biodiversity can help protect crops against disease and save billions of dollars for a nation's agricultural economy.
- The environment produces wild fruits, vegetables, meats, and fish, and also sustainable products such as rubber.

40.4 The indirect value of biodiversity is immense

- Biodiversity contributes to the successful workings of the water, carbon, phosphorus, and nitrogen cycles.
- Freshwater ecosystems provide fresh water and fish; forests soak up and release water at a regular rate and take up carbon dioxide; and intact ecosystems retain soil.
- Ecotourists enjoy vacations in natural settings.

The Causes of Today's Extinctions Are Known

40.5 Habitat loss is a major cause of wildlife extinctions

- Habitat loss is the cause of 85% of threatened/ endangered cases.
- Coastal degradation destroys freshwater and marine biodiversity.

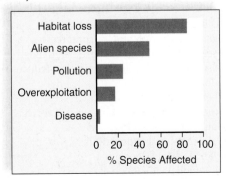

40.6 Introduction of alien species contributes to extinctions

- **Alien species** are nonnative species introduced through colonization, horticulture and agriculture, and accidental transport.
- Islands are particularly susceptible to disturbances by introduced aliens.

40.7 Pollution contributes to extinctions

- **Pollution** is any change in the environment that adversely impacts living things.
- Forms of environmental pollution include acid deposition, eutrophication, ozone depletion, organic chemicals, climate change, and solid waste disposal.

40.8 Overexploitation contributes to extinctions

- **Overexploitation** is the removal of a number of individuals so that the population is severely reduced.
- The market for exotic plants and pets supports the legal and illegal trade of wild species.
- Declining species are still being hunted, and fisheries are being overfished.

40.9 Disease contributes to extinctions

- Pathogens are on the rise, subjecting wildlife to emerging diseases.

Habitat Preservation and Restoration Require Much Effort and Expertise

40.10 Habitat preservation is of primary importance

- Biodiversity hotspots must be preserved.
- **Keystone species** influence the viability of a community; their extinction can lead to other extinctions and loss of biodiversity.
- A **metapopulation** is subdivided into small, isolated populations, sometimes due to habitat fragmentation.
- A **source population** reproduces well most likely due to a favorable environment; a **sink population** has more deaths than births most likely due to an unfavorable environment.
- Preserving keystone species requires landscape preservation, which will lead to preservation of other species as well.

40.11 Habitat restoration is sometimes necessary

- **Restoration ecology** seeks scientific ways to return ecosystems to their former state through the use of natural processes and with the goal of **sustainable development.**

A Sustainable Society Is Achievable

40.12 A sustainable society will preserve resources

- Like an ecosystem, a **sustainable society** preserves resources for use by the generations to come.

40.13 Energy sources should be renewable

- **Nonrenewable resources** are finite, and the supply can run out. **Renewable resources** are in constant supply because they are automatically replenished.
- A sustainable society will primarily use renewable energy sources such as hydroelectric plants, geothermal energy, wind power, solar energy, and in the future biofuels and cars that run on electricity alone.

40.14 Water sources should be conserved

- Most water is used by agriculture and industry, and both should reduce their use, as should domestic users.

40.15 Agriculture can be more diverse

- Agriculture should also use polyculture, biological pest control, and contour farming to be sustainable.

TESTING YOURSELF

Conservation Biology Attempts to Understand and Protect Biodiversity

1. Which of these tasks would not be within the realm of conservation biology?
   a. helping to manage a national park
   b. a government board charged with restoring an ecosystem
   c. writing textbooks and/or popular books about the value of biodiversity
   d. introducing endangered species back into the wild
   e. All of these are concerns of conservation biology.

2. Most likely, ecosystem performance improves
   a. the more diverse the ecosystem.
   b. as long as selected species are maintained.
   c. as long as species have both direct and indirect value.
   d. if extinctions are diverse.
   e. Both b and c are correct.

3. Biodiversity hotspots
   a. have few populations because the temperature is too hot.
   b. contain a large proportion of the Earth's species even though their area is small.
   c. are always found in tropical rain forests and coral reefs.
   d. are sources of species for the ecosystems of the world.
   e. All except a are correct.

4. Which of these associations does not show a contrast in the number of species?
   a. temperate zone—tropical zone
   b. hotspots—cold spots
   c. rain forest canopy—rain forest floor
   d. pelagic zone—deep-sea benthos

5. **THINKING CONCEPTUALLY** Draw an energy pyramid (see Section 38.10) to show that if salmon only ate shrimp in Figure 40.2 the salmon population would get less energy than if they ate zooplankton.

Biodiversity Has Direct Value and Indirect Value for Humans

6. The value of wild pollinators to the U.S. agricultural economy has been calculated to be $4.1–$6.7 billion a year. What is the implication?
   a. Society could easily replace wild pollinators by domesticating various types of pollinators.
   b. Pollinators may be valuable, but that doesn't mean any other species won't provide us with valuable services also.
   c. If we did away with all natural ecosystems, we wouldn't be dependent on wild pollinators.
   d. Society doesn't always appreciate the services that wild species provide naturally and without any fanfare.
   e. All of these statements are correct.

7. Consumptive use value
   a. means we should think of conservation in terms of the long run.
   b. means we are placing too much emphasis on living things that are useful to us.
   c. means some organisms, other than crops and farm animals, are valuable as products.
   d. is a type of direct value.
   e. Both c and d are correct.

8. The services provided to us by ecosystems are unseen. This means
   a. they are not valuable.
   b. they are noticed particularly when the service is disrupted.
   c. biodiversity is not needed in order for ecosystems to keep functioning as before.
   d. we should be knowledgeable about ecosystems and protect them.
   e. Both b and d are correct.

9. Which of the following is not a function that ecosystems can perform for humans?
   a. purification of water
   b. immobilization of pollutants
   c. reduction of soil erosion
   d. removal of excess soil nitrogen
   e. breakdown of heavy metals such as lead

10. Which of these is not an indirect value of a species?
    a. participates in biogeochemical cycles
    b. participates in waste disposal
    c. helps provide fresh water
    d. prevents soil erosion
    e. All of these are indirect values.

The Causes of Today's Extinctions Are Known

11. The most significant cause of the loss of biodiversity is
    a. habitat loss.   d. disease.
    b. pollution.   e. overexploitation.
    c. alien species.

12. Eagles and bears feed on spawning salmon. If shrimp are introduced that compete with salmon for food,
    a. the salmon population will decline.
    b. the eagle and bear populations will decline.
    c. only the shrimp population will decline.
    d. all populations will increase in size.
    e. Both a and b are correct.

13. Global climate change has nothing to do with
    a. habitat loss.
    b. introduction of alien species into new environments.
    c. pollution.
    d. overexploitation.
    e. Global climate change pertains to all of these.

14. Which of these is not expected because of global climate change?
    a. changes in the composition of ecosystems
    b. the bleaching and drowning of coral reefs
    c. rise in sea levels and loss of coastal wetlands
    d. pest preservation because cold weather reduces their population size
    e. All of these are expected.

15. Which of the following associations is not correct?
    a. excess nutrients—eutrophication
    b. carbon dioxide—ozone depletion
    c. sulfur dioxide—acid deposition
    d. methane—global climate change

16. **THINKING CONCEPTUALLY** Considering the food web diagram in Figure 38.9, why would you expect a predator, such as a mongoose, to prey on more than one type of organism?

Habitat Preservation and Restoration Require Much Effort and Expertise

17. Why is a grizzly bear a keystone species existing as a metapopulation?
    a. Grizzly bears require many thousands of miles of preserved land because they are large animals.
    b. Grizzly bears have functions that increase biodiversity, but presently the population is subdivided into isolated subpopulations.
    c. When grizzly bears are preserved, so are many other types of species within a diverse landscape.
    d. Grizzly bears are a source population for many other types of organisms across several population types.
    e. All of these statements are correct.
18. A population in an unfavorable area with a high infant mortality rate would be a
    a. metapopulation.   c. sink population.
    b. source population.   d. new population.
19. The goal of restoration ecology is
    a. to return damaged ecosystems to their former states.
    b. to maximize direct values of ecosystems.
    c. sustainable development.
    d. Both a and c are correct choices.
    e. a, b, and c are all correct choices.

A Sustainable Society Is Achievable

20. A sustainable society would as much as possible
    a. use renewable energy sources.
    b. recycle materials.
    c. conserve water.
    d. All of these are correct.
21. Biofuels are made from
    a. both renewable and nonrenewable sources.
    b. any organic matter, including crops and waste materials.
    c. any pollutant in the environment.
    d. All of these are correct.
22. A sustainable agriculture will
    a. liberally irrigate crops.
    b. use limited amounts of pesticides, herbicides, and fertilizer.
    c. make sure a field contains only one species at a time.
    d. All of these are correct.

THINKING SCIENTIFICALLY

1. Hypothesize the effect of overharvesting on genetic diversity (see Section 13.14), even if the population is protected for a while and allowed to return to its normal level. How would you test your hypothesis?
2. A conservationist wants to rescue a species of songbirds from extinction by gathering a few eggs and raising a population that s/he can reintroduce into the wild. Criticize the plan.

ONLINE RESOURCE

www.mhhe.com/maderconcepts2

Enhance your study with animations that bring concepts to life and practice tests to assess your understanding. Your instructor may also recommend the interactive eBook, individualized learning tools, and more.

CONNECTING THE CONCEPTS

Our industrial societies are overusing the environment to the point of exhaustion. It is time to turn matters around and develop a sustainable society in which resources are preserved for the present and future generations. At the same time, biodiversity will be preserved. One goal of conservation biology is to protect, restore, and use biodiversity wisely because we now realize it is a resource of enormous economic value. If properly managed, sustainable yields of food and fiber can be obtained from many natural lands and waters. Modern genetic engineering technologies make the genes of millions of wild species available for breeding improved crops and domestic animals and for use as biological control agents. Enjoyment of nature can also enrich human life enormously.

As natural forests, grasslands, streams, lakes, and seas are degraded, human society must expend greater amounts of energy and materials to substitute for the benefits that biodiversity provides at no cost. Lost species, and ultimately lost ecosystems, cannot be replaced. To that end, the vision of conservation biology is a world where:

1. Leaders are committed to long-term environmental protection and to international leadership and cooperation in addressing the world's environmental problems, including the loss of biodiversity.
2. An environmentally literate citizenry has the knowledge, skills, and ethical values needed to protect biodiversity and achieve sustainable development.
3. Market prices and economic indicators reflect the full environmental and social costs of human activities.
4. A new generation of technologies contributes to the conservation of resources and the protection of the environment.
5. The landscape sustains natural systems, maximizes biological diversity, and uplifts the human spirit.
6. Human numbers are stabilized, all people enjoy a decent standard of living through sustainable development, and the global environment is protected for future generations. Modified from the *Report of the National Commission on the Environment*, 1993.

PUT THE PIECES TOGETHER

1. Biotechnology has been offered as a way to improve crop yields to feed an ever-increasing world population. Do you agree with this solution? Offer and discuss an alternative one.
2. Why is it necessary to emphasize renewable energy sources in order to achieve a sustainable society? Do you agree with this emphasis? Why or why not?
3. Are you willing to pay extra for organic foods as a way to encourage farmers to reduce pesticide and herbicide use? Why would this be beneficial to society?
4. Do you agree that the size of the human population should be stabilized in order to achieve a sustainable society? What would that mean in terms of the number of children each couple can have?

Appendix | Answer Key

CHAPTER 1

Check Your Progress

1.1 Observation data; observing that a worker ant produces eggs. **1.2** Test group: colonies exposed to the parasite; control group: colonies not exposed to the parasite. **1.3** a. Levels of organization from cells to organism illustrate order; (b) unicellular organisms divide, multicellular ones produce sperm and egg (c) metabolizes nutrients. **1.4** When organisms reproduce they pass on a copy of their genes. **1.5** Only by responding to stimuli can organisms remain homeostatic. **1.6** Natural ecosystems absorb pollutants. **1.7** The first suggests that humans are apes; the second means that apes and humans are on their own evolutionary pathway. **1.8** a. Domain Eukarya and kingdom Animals b. Fossil and molecular data **1.9** Better adapted members have the opportunity through natural selection to reproduce more, and in that way a species becomes adapted to its environment. **1.10** The hawk has levels of organization; catches food for herself and offspring; remains homeostatic because she can respond to stimuli, lives in a semidesert ecosystem; and is adapted to flying.

Form Your Opinion

Page 6: 1. No answer: The United States should not continue to export its current farming technology. Exporting technology that is known to be detrimental to ground water and top soil will eventually reduce agricultural yields, resulting in a food shortage. The United States would be better served to encourage sustainable farming practices like crop rotation to foster long-term success in agriculture. Yes answer: The United States should continue to export farming technology to other countries in order to support the global food market. As solutions to the long-term problems of these technologies arise, the U.S. should make these available to other countries as well. 2. Circumstances such as labor costs, profits, and marketing challenges might discourage a farmer from growing organically. These obstacles might be overcome through government subsidies for sustainable farming practices, sharing best practices through networking with successful organic farmers, and a world-wide movement towards eating primarily locally grown and seasonal produce.
Page 17: 1. Practical problems in agriculture, medicine, and conservation can be solved with a knowledge of evolution. Because we know that natural selection drives the evolution of pesticide resistant insects, changes to farming practices and pesticide use are possible. In medicine, awareness of the evolution of antibiotic resistant bacteria allows patients and doctors alike to make changes to the way antibiotics are prescribed and used. In conservation efforts, knowledge of evolution can be used to make informed decisions regarding endangered species; directed evolution can also be used to select for organisms to clean up the environment. 2. By naturally allowing for the growth of nonresistant insect populations, farmers

can reduce the influence of pesticide resistant insects on their fields and farming practices. 3. The salmon must be successfully raised in an environment that mimics nature as closely as possible, with exposure to pressures such as normal predation and pathogens, for example, if they are to succeed in the wild. For instance, if the salmon have no exposure to pathogens that they might encounter in the wild, these salmon are at high risk of infection upon introduction without the benefit of building immune defenses from previous exposure.

Testing Yourself

1. a; 2. d; 3. c; 4. Scientific theories arise due to innumerable observations and experimentation. 5.b; 6. c; 7. b; 8. c; 9. c; 10. d; 11. Each type organism has its own sequence of bases in its genes. 12. e; 13. b; 14. d; 15. a; 16. d; 17. d; 18. A college campus has a location, as does an ecosystem. The populations of students, faculty, and administrators communicate with each other and the physical environment (the buildings). 19. c; 20. e; 21. d; 22. d; 23. c; 24. a; 25. c; 26. c; 27. Evolution is related to all the other theories; for example, all organisms are cellular because their common ancestor was cellular. 28. e; 29. f; 30. c; 31. g

Thinking Scientifically

1. a. Bacteria don't die in sunlight when dye is present. b. Dye is protective against UV radiation. c. Experiment consists of exposing control and test groups to UV light. d. Hypothesis is not supported. 2. Plant the same species of tomato plants in three large plots. All plots receive the same treatment, except plot 1, your control, receives no fertilizer; plot 2 receives the name brand fertilizer in the same quantity as plot 3 which receives the generic brand. Measure the tomatoes from each plot and calculate the average size to determine which plot results in the largest tomatoes.

Put the Pieces Together

Page 21: 1. One example, that shows the relationship between two theories, is the link between ecosystems and evolution. Different species of organisms are the result of evolution over time from a common ancestor. The evolution of new species creates new populations that interact to form communities, which in turn interact to form ecosystems. Ecosystems also evolve over time as new species evolve and change the populations and communities within the ecosystem. 2. The evolution of antibiotic resistant bacteria results from natural selection. Mutations in bacterial DNA created resistant individuals. These bacteria survive to reproduce in the presence of antibiotics, whereas non-resistant individuals die off. This process creates a population of antibiotic resistant bacteria.

CHAPTER 2

Check Your Progress

2.1 Carbon, nitrogen, phosphorus, sulfur. **2.2** See Figure 2.3B, page 29, in text. **2.3** a. One. Hydrogen

has one shell, which is complete with two electrons; b. Two. Oxygen has two shells with six valence electrons in the outer shell. Therefore, oxygen requires two more electrons for a completed outer shell. **2.4** H^+, OH^-. **2.5** a. See Figure 2.6, page 32, in text; b. This is the formula that gives each atom a completed outer shell. **2.6** One end of the molecule is negative and the other end is positive because oxygen attacts electron more than hydrogen does. **2.7** Yes, because electropositive hydrogens are attracted to either electronegative oxygen or nitrogen. **2.8** Hydrogen bonding causes water molecules to stick together and to other polar molecules. **2.9** The air loses heat as it causes water in the pad to evaporate. **2.10** Polarity makes the emulsifiers hydrophilic. **2.11** The blocks of ice trap heat inside and prevent it from escaping to the environment. **2.12** a. H^+; b. OH^-. **2.13** a. Acidic; b. More H^+. **2.14** a. Down; b. Carbonic acid froms and releases H; therefore the pH decreases.

Form Your Opinion

Page 28: 1. Though controversy will undoubtedly arise over moral, monetary and other issues, science must be free to ask and answer questions about the world in which we live. However, scientists should conduct research with minimal risks to their own safety and that of others. As technology advances, the restrictions placed upon research should be reevaluated to ensure their relevance. With careful and balanced monitoring, scientific endeavors should be supported and encouraged. 2. Safety should be paramount in experimentation. The best way to proceed is to aware of advisements regarding safety and to learn from experience about how to modify procedures to make them safe. 3. Yes answer: Depending on the benefits that an experiment might have, I would consider being a guinea pig. However, research using people should be entirely voluntary and provide an explanation of the potential risks. I would be particularly willing to be an experimental subject in the field of medical research, especially if the results of experimentation had the potential to prove widely useful. No answer: I would not be willing to serve as a guinea pig in experiments that may prove harmful to me. Because of known risks, and the fact that the risks associated with experimentation on humans and animals cannot always be predicted, I would be unwilling to subject myself to the potentially hazardous side effects of being a human subject in experiments.
Page 38: 1. The changes in lakes due to acid rain kill fish and other wildlife and sometimes eliminate it altogether. Trees suffer as a result of acid rain's effects, becoming diseased or dying. If this continues, not only will the atmosphere's oxygen be affected, but the lumber industry will suffer. The food supply is at risk if plants as well as fish are negatively affected by acid rain. 2. Human beings must take some responsibility for what they do to the planet and make attempts to control their negative impact. Driving less could help to preserve lakes and the wildlife in them, forests, buildings made of limestone and marble, and

the respiratory health of humans. Because of these factors, I would certainly be willing to drive less to help prevent acid rain. 3. Despite other stresses, environmental degradation should concern people at all times. If we do not preserve our planet and its ecosystems, our current way of life will become unsustainable and economic development will cease.

Testing Yourself

1. c; 2. b; 3. e; 4. d; 5. a; 6. c; 7. c; 8. d; 9. a; 10. c; 11. b; 12. a; 13. b; 14. d; 15. d; 16. Nitrogen needs three more electrons in the outer shell to be stable and each hydrogen shares one electron. 17. Gaining six electrons by sharing is not as likely as losing two electrons to become an ion. 18. a; 19. b; 20. c; 21. e; 22. Blood is transported in a tube (blood vessel) and water fills a tube due to its cohesive and adhesive properties. 23. a; 24. a; 25. a; 26. b; 27. c; 28. A bicarbonate buffer combines immediately with H^+ or OH^-, normalizing the blood pH. Respiration, by removing carbon dioxide from the blood, provides a slower response that decreases H_2CO_3 concentration. The kidneys excrete H^+ and provide the slowest of the three responses, but the kidenys also have the ability to cause the greatest overall change in the pH level.

Thinking Scientifically

1. Na^+Cl^- interrupts hydrogen bonding enough to prevent the formation of the ice lattice that forms during freezing. 2. Chemical behavior is dependent on the number of electrons in the outer shell, not the number of neutrons in the nucleus.

Put the Pieces Together

Page 41: 1. Methane gas is formed when a carbon atom binds four hydrogen atoms. The bonds of methane are nonpolar covalent bonds in which electrons are shared equally between the atoms. Each bond in methane points to a corner of a tetrahedron. Water is formed when two hydrogen atoms bind one oxygen atom. The sharing of electrons is not entirely equal in this bent molecule. Oxygen, being more electronegative attracts the electrons more than hydrogen does and the result is a polar molecule. 2. The properties of water which result from its structure are critical to life. Cohesion, adhesion, high surface tension, high heat capacity and high heat of vaporization all result from hydrogen bonding. These properties of water allow it to be a transport medium that also maintains the internal temperature of organisms. The difference in the density of frozen water compared to liquid water means that life is preserved under a layer of ice. Water being a polar molecule acts as a universal solvent that allows metabolism to occur.

CHAPTER 3

Check Your Progress

3.1 All living things contain biomolecules 3.2 Hydrophilic functional groups, which would make them water soluble. 3.3 It uses the water for hydrolysis reactions. 3.4 Fructose is an isomer of glucose. 3.5 Both store glucose as a complex carbohydrate, but plants store it as starch, and animals store it as glycogen. 3.6 Plants produce glucose through photosynthesis, but animals do not photosynthesize. 3.7 Cholesterol contains rings and both phospholipids and waxes contain long hydrocarbon chains. 3.8 Plant cells carry out more varied reactions (e.g., photosynthesis) than an animal cell does. 3.9 Proteins are made from the same amino acids in all organisms. 3.10 Globular proteins are enzymes present in all organisms, fibrous proteins are structural proteins, and plants do not use proteins as structural compounds. 3.11 The

complementary DNA sequence would be CTAGGT. 3.12 The sugar in RNA is ribose not deoxyribose as in DNA; uracil in RNA replaced thymine in DNA; RNA is single stranded not a double stranded helix. 3.13 Yes, that's the only way a mutation can lead to an altered protein. 3.14 Plant cells absorb solar energy and produce glucose. Glucose in food leads to ATP buildup in cells. In muscle cells, ATP breakdown leads to muscle contraction and movement.

Form Your Opinion

Page 51: 1. Yes. Because of the increased instances of obesity, especially in children, it would be responsible for restaurants to decrease portion sizes. This change in the food service industry could help to reduce obesity and create a healthier overall population. No. People should be able to eat responsibly on their own. Restaurants should not have to manage the diets of their customers. 2. Due to the implication of cornstarch-based sweeteners and other ingredients in manufactured foods, manufacturers should be required to limit the use of such ingredients in their foods. Also, as required by the Food and Drug Administration, nutrition information should continue to be clearly printed on the labels of manufactured foods. Manufacturers could also monetarily support research into alternative sweeteners and healthier ingredients to create healthier products. It is also the responsibility of the consumer, however, to intake cornstarch-based sweeteners and saturated fats in moderation.

Page 55: 1. Scientists are not called upon to judge whether a study is worthwhile; rather they are only concerned with its accuracy. Often, even studies with negative results precede a breakthrough. Studies should be encouraged as much as possible and considered worthwhile until evidence suggests otherwise. 2. Presently, we assume that evolution has a genetic basis and scientists will not be satisfied until they can point to the genetic cause of each evolutionary event. Studying whole organisms always leaves the genetic basis unknown. 3. Yes answer: By inserting a gene that allows tomato plants to thrive when watered with salty water, a genetic change has occurred within the organism. If the plants reproduce other genetically altered individuals, and a new population results, then evolution has occurred. No answer: This is an example of artificial evolution, and more appropriately, genetic engineering. Because the change was not the result of natural selection, it should not be termed evolution.

Testing Yourself

1. c; 2. c; 3. b; 4. b; 5. Like carbon, silicon has four outer electrons and can form four covalent bonds, as in SiO_2, the main component of sand. Carbon has two, but silicon has three, shells of electrons. Because of its larger size, silicon rarely forms chains, nor does it bond to four different types of atoms. 6. b; 7. a; 8. d; 9. c; 10. d; 11. c; 12. c; 13. Cellulose chains can form fibers because they lie side-by-side and hydrogen bonds form between them. The branching observed in starch makes fiber formation more unlikely. 14. a; 15. b; 16. d; 17. d; 18. c; 19. The hydrophilic heads interact with fluids, allowing the hydrophobic tails to orient toward each other. 20. c; 21. c; 22. d; 23. c; 24. d; 25. e; 26. a; 27. c; 28. Nucleic acid is a sequence of nucleotides and proteins are a sequence of amino acids.

Thinking Scientifically

1. a. Subject the seeds of temperate and tropical plants, for which you know the amount and kind of oil content, to a range of temperatures from above freezing to below freezing for an extended length of time. Plant the seeds and compare the percentage

of survivals per type of plant. b. The presence of unsaturated oils in temperate plant seeds may be an adaptation to the environment. 2. Possible hypothesis: (1) The abnormal enzyme will not produce as much product per unit time as the normal enzyme. (2) The abnormal enzyme will have a different shape from the normal enzyme due to changes in organization.

Put the Pieces Together

Page 61: 1. Energy storage and use: lipids, which contain many energy-storing bonds; carbohydrates, which are a source of quick energy in the form of glycogen and starches. Genetic information storage: nucleic acids, like RNA and DNA which store genetic information in a sequence of nucleotides. Ongoing activities of the cell: proteins, which provide structure and support in the cell, speed chemical reactions, transport molecules (i.e., oxygen), and which are used in defense and regulation; lipids, which make up membranes, serve as hormones, and protect plants and animals in the form of waxes. 2. Just as the alphabet has only 26 letters and yet can produce many different words, DNA contains only 4 bases but the particular order of these bases in each gene can vary. This means that each gene specifies a different sequence of amino acids in each type protein. 3. I would expect each cell types to have its own particular combination of proteins.

CHAPTER 4

Check Your Progress

4.1 The parts individually cannot perform all the functions of a living cell. 4.2 Small cells have a larger surface-area-to-volume ratio and are better able to exchange materials. 4.3 Prokaryotic cells do not have a nucleus. 4.4 The electron microscope, not the light microscope, allows us to "see" this amount of detail, and the electron microscope was not available until the 20th century. 4.5 The eukaryotes: Nerve cells, onion root cells, and Euglena (a protist). Only eukaryotes, not prokaryotes (bacteria and archaea), have a nucleus. 4.6 First the ribosomal subunits, and then mRNA, pass from the nucleus to the cytoplasm, by way of the nuclear pores. They combine when protein synthesis begins. 4.7 Yes. Polyribosomes are in the cytoplasm. Other ribosomes are temporarily attached to the ER, and only the synthesized polypeptides enter the interior of the ER. 4.8 Synthesized polypeptides enter the interior of the RER, and some are incorporated into its membrane. The RER sends vesicles to the Golgi apparatus and the vesicles that leave the Golgi become incorporated into the plasma membrane. 4.9 Lysosomes combine with and digest microorganisms brought into the cell by vesicle formation. 4.10 Peroxisomes pass fatty acid breakdown products to mitochondria for further metabolism. 4.11 Lysosomes only digest; the plant cell central vacuole has storage and structural functions, as well as digestive functions. 4.12 Genes located in the nucleus code for the polypeptides that are produced by rough ER. The endomembrane system exports them from the cell. 4.13 Both are membranous organelles involved in energy transformations. They differ in that chloroplasts carry out photosynthesis and mitochondria carry out cellular respiration. 4.14 Interaction of actin filaments and microtubules with motor molecules. 4.15 The only anatomical difference is length; cilia are short and flagella are long. Cilia move like an oar, and flagella move in an undulating, snakelike fashion.

Form Your Opinion

Page 66: 1. I would give a friend the opportunity to see for his/herself by taking him/her into a biological laboratory and allowing them to examine a cell, for example, microscopically. 2. Color enhancement of TEMs does not border on misrepresentation because it is often necessary to enhance images to view and analyze them more clearly. However, I would encourage a side-by-side comparison of colored and non-colored TEMs images to show what a cell actually looks like. **Page 73:** 1. Carbon is present in all organic molecules but sulfur is unique to amino acids. 2. Palade may have also found the labeled amino acids on free ribosomes in the cytoplasm. **Page 77:** 1. The first cells to contain mitochondria and also chloroplast had an evolutionary advantage because they were more efficient energy users; therefore they could produce more offspring than other members of the population. 2. I would expect to find that both have membrane bound pigments capable of absorbing light energy. I would also expect to find that both have centrally located DNA. The cyanobacterium would be surrounded by a single membrane but the chloroplast is surrounded by a double membrane. The outer membrane is derived from the host plasma membrane.

Testing Yourself

1. c; 2. a; 3. c; 4. e; 5. d; 6. c; 7. d; 8. microscopically examine swab of skin; 9. b; 10. b; 11. c; 12. a; 13. The nuclear envelope has pores; transport vesicles; 14. d; 15. c; 16. c; 17. b; 18. anatomical and experimental data; 19. a; 20. a; 21. d; 22. Chloroplasts capture solar energy and form the carbohydrate broken down by mitochondria to produce ATP; 23. d; 24. b; 25. b; 26. c; 27. b; 28. a; 29. e; 30. d

Thinking Scientifically

1. Labeling RNA. You expect to find RNA in the nucleus, passing through a nuclear pore, and on RER. 2. Mitochondria have their own DNA and make their own proteins; therefore, they have RNA. The mitochondrial double membrane does not have any pores.

Put the Pieces Together

Page 83: 1. Prokaryotes are smaller than eukaryotic cells but they have DNA and ribosomes. Therefore, after being engulfed by a eukaryotic cell, they became what we call mitochondria and chloroplasts which are bounded by a double membrane and are capable of protein synthesis. 2. The folding of the endoplasmic reticulum creates a large area for the attachment of ribosomes outside and presence of enzymes for lipid synthesis inside. Rough ER, studded with ribosomes, is structurally equipped for protein synthesis while smooth ER, void of ribosomes, synthesizes lipids. The membranous nature of the membrane allows it to form transport vesicles. 3. The cytoskeleton assists in cell movement and serves to move items within the cell. These are functions consistent with the presence of microtubules in the cilia and flagella, structures used for locomotion and attachment.

CHAPTER 5

Check Your Progress

5.1 a. ATP represents potential energy; the energy is present in chemical bonds; b. Muscle movement is kinetic energy because motion is occurring. **5.2** Yes; any motion or cellular reaction that requires the breakdown of ATP increases entropy. **5.3** As long as cellular respiration is possible, ATP is constantly replenished by joining ADP with (P). **5.4** Because ATP breakdown is coupled to the energy-requiring reaction of muscle contraction, the overall reaction increases entropy. **5.5** Each enzyme's active site allows only its substrate to bind. **5.6** The optimum pH gives the active site the correct shape to bind the substrate;

body temperature increases the number of encounters between the substrate and the enzyme. **5.7** Inhibition of enzyme requires an abundance of a product and is easily reversed if the amount of product decreases. **5.8** Like the colored tiles, the proteins in a plasma membrane are different. But unlike the tiles, which are cemented in place, the proteins are free to move from side to side in the fluid phospholipid layer. **5.9** Channel proteins and carrier proteins. **5.10** Without water, organisms dry out and die. **5.11** A turnstile provides a way for only paying customers to pass through and the carrier protein provides a way for a molecule to pass through the plasma membrane if it can bind to the carrier. **5.12** Cholesterol accumulates in blood vessels where it can cause health problems. **5.13** Both plants and animals secrete substances that lie between the cells.

Form Your Opinion

Page 92: 1. Even though poisons can be ingested accidentally they should not be banned. Poisons are used to preserve foods, control pests, eliminate weeds, and to preserve buildings. Proper storage and use is important when using poisons, as well as posting notice when dangerous substances such as rat poison are present. It might prove useful for countries to have poison detectors to provide warning in the event of a biological attack. Though the warning system may not be able to detect all poisons, it could save many lives if a system were in place to alert the public or a country's government of an impending attack. **Page 95:** 1. People could be convinced of the benefits of nutrition and exercise in the prevention of type 2 diabetes if shown case studies or other documentation of individuals with type 2 diabetes who have eliminated their disease through proper diet and fitness. Also, statistics correlating the poor eating and exercise habits of people with type 2 diabetes support the fact that this type of diabetes is the result of lifestyle and is preventable. 2. Versions of the text can be created for students with color blindness and other visual impairments (i.e., poor eyesight) for those individuals who would benefit from them. **Page 100:** 1. It seems reasonable that human and bacterial plasma membranes are the same when we consider that all organisms are descended from an original ancestor. All cells need a surface separating them from the outside world that is selectively permeable and capable of sending and receiving signals in order to support homeostasis. 2. The lack of a cell wall in animal cells is disadvantageous in that animal cells do not have the added protection and support provided by a cell wall surrounding the plasma membrane. Animal cells do have an extracellular matrix that can be quite hard as in compact bone. An extracellular matrix that can vary instead of a cell wall may have alowed animals to develop a greater diversity of cell types, tissues, and organs. Because of the development of nerves and muscles, animals gained mobility that is not found in plants and other organisms composed of cells with cell walls.

Testing Yourself

1. c; 2. a; 3. e; 4. d; 5. a; 6. Food in bulk is stored food in your pantry; glycogen is stored energy in the liver and muscles; meals provide only enough energy till you eat again; ATP is just enough energy for a reaction. 7. a; 8. e; 9. c; 10. b; 11. c; 12. b; 13. b; 14. b; 15. c; 16. d; 17. c; 18. Through osmosis solutes retain the liquid portion of blood in the vessels, allowing the blood to flow. 19. a, b, c; 20. b, c, d; 21. d; 22. b, d; 23. d; 24. e

Thinking Scientifically

1. Ecosystems need a source of energy because energy cannot be created. They need a continous supply

because with each energy transformation, heat is lost; eventually, all the energy taken in is lost to the system as heat. 2. You need to decide the proper enzyme versus substrate concentrations, type of glassware, amount of time needed for the reaction, how to vary the temperature and the pH, and how to test for the product.

Put the Pieces Together

Page 103: 1. An enzyme serves to lower activation barriers by bringing reactants together within its active site. This is only possible due to the specific structure, or shape, of enzymes. The enzyme shape complements the shape(s) of the reactant(s), allowing them to interact chemically. 2. Polypeptide synthesis will not occur unless amino acids, enzymes, and the proper nucleic acids are present. Environmental pH and temperature must be appropriate. For any endergonic reaction to occur, ATP must be present to supply the necessary chemical energy. 3. Cell recognition glycoproteins, receptor proteins, and junction proteins found in the plasma membrane are all are involved in cell-to-cell communication.

CHAPTER 6

Check Your Progress

6.1 Plants can use the carbon dioxide and water from cellular respiration to carry on photosynthesis and produce food. **6.2** Thylakoids absorb solar energy because they contain chlorophyll; carbohydrates form in the stroma, because it contains enzymes. **6.3** NADH and ATP; NADP$^+$ and ADP + (P) **6.4** Warm weather allows enzymes to constantly remake chlorophyl. **6.5** Antenna molecules absorb energy and pass it to a reaction center. **6.6** The energy of motion, i.e., kinetic energy. **6.7** Water supplies electrons. NADPH is the final acceptor of electrons. **6.8** "Get ready": NADP reductase has received electrons, and a H$^+$ gradient is present. "Payoff": NADPH and ATP. **6.9** The Calvin cycle can take place in the light or in the dark. The Calvin cycle requires NADPH and ATP from the light reactions. **6.10** Glucose phosphate can react to produce sucrose, starch, or cellulose. **6.11** C$_3$ photosynthesis takes its name from first detectable molecule following carbon dioxide fixation in a plant cell. **6.12** Bundle sheath cells (the location of the Calvin cycle) are not exposed to the open spaces of a leaf where O$_2$ is located. **6.13** CO$_2$ is fixed at night but does not enter the Calvin cycle until the next day.

Form Your Opinion

Page 112: 1. The evolution of oxygen-releasing photosynthesis is an example of the concept of "adding on" rather than starting over in that photosystem II (PSII), which is necessary for the splitting of water to release oxygen, evolved after photosystem I (PSI) but did not replace it. 2. Cyanobacteria can revert to a cyclic electron pathway, using hydrogen sulfide (H$_2$S) as a hydrogen source to reduce carbon dioxide like other autotrophic bacteria. Chloroplasts cannot revert to using H$_2$S in place of water. **Page 118:** 1. Preserving tropical rain forests is advantageous because it protects and preserves the habitats of many of the plants and animals that can only be found in these forests while contributing to stable global temperatures. 2. Countries without tropical rain forests can assist in preservation through contributing money to conservation efforts, publicly supporting the protection of these dynamic ecosystems, and refusing to consume or use products that result from deforestation.

Testing Yourself

1. c; 2. d; 3. d; 4. c; 5. a. granum; b. thylakoid; c. O$_2$; d. Calvin cycle; e. stroma; 6. Only plants produce

organic food, and if animals only ate animals, food would run out. 7. a; 8. a; 9. a; 10 e; 11. d; 11. a; 12. a; 13. e; 14. b; 15. Solar energy is unable to participate directly in the chemical reactions that reduce carbon dioxide to carbohydrate, but ATP can do so. 16. d; 17. c; 18. a

Thinking Scientifically

1. Conditions have to be kept constant otherwise the result may not be due to a difference in the light provided. For a control, do the same experiment without elodea. 2. Photosynthesis takes place in leaf cells, showing that cells, and not organs, are the basic units of a plant.

Put the Pieces Together

Page 121: 1.Cyanobacteria gave rise to chloroplasts once they were taken up by a pre-eukaryotic cell, making them significant in the history of life as an integral part in the evolution of photosynthetic eukaryotes. These organisms are also credited with introducing oxygen into the atmosphere. 2. Using only words and arrows, the diagram based on Figure 6.7 should include all 11 steps; the diagram for Figure 6.9 should include the molecules listed in the upper box and all 5 steps. Eliminate the box in Figure 6.7 that represents the Calvin cycle reactions. Instead, stack your diagrams so that you can show how steps #8 and #11 in Figure 6.7 connect to steps # 3, 4, 5 in Figure 6.9. 3. C_4 photosynthesis is more advantageous to organisms (rather than C_3 photosynthesis) when the atmosphere contains significant amounts of O_2. C_3 photosynthesis was advantageous to the first photosynthesizers because the atmosphere didn't yet contain significant amounts of O_2.

CHAPTER 7

Check Your Progress

7.1 The oxygen we breathe in is necessary to cellular respiration which produces ATP. **7.2** It is a mechanism that allows oxidation to occur slowly so that more ATP are produced per glucose molecules. **7.3** Due to glycolysis 2 NADH and a net grain of 2 ATP have been produced. Some energy was lost as heat, and this heat can help warm bodies. **7.4** The reaction is getting ready for the Krebs cycle.The end product of the prep reaction (an acetyl group) enters the Kerbs cycle. **7.5** Per glucose molecule Krebs cycle accounts for 2 ATP directly and much indirectly because it produces 6 NADH and 2 FADH. **7.6** 22 ATP **7.7** "Get ready": H^+ gradient is established. "Pay off": ATP is produced. **7.8** Only glycolysis, because the other metabolic pathways occur in mitochondria. **7.9** Grapes are sometimes coated with yeasts that can start fermenting sugars (and producing alcohol) if the weather is conducive. **7.10** a. Hydrolytic reactions are catabolic. Dehydration reactions are anabolic; b. A hydrolytic reaction occurs when ATP breaks down to ADP + (P) (catabolic).

Form Your Opinion

Page 134: 1. The discovery that bacteria in addition to yeast ferment may have seemed irrelevant at first but it lead to the production of many products such as yogurt, pickles, and certain types of beer. 2. The products of this page do not negate that food is ultimately derived from plants. Fermentation is a process through which sugar is broken down in the absence of oxygen. Since sugar is produced by autotrophic organisms, namely plants, they play a large role in producing these products.
Page 136: 1. Statistical information on the correlation between illness and exercise would substantiate the claim that exercise can help to prevent a wide range of ailments. Evidence from studies on diabetics and cancer patients, for example, that showed higher

instances of these diseases in individuals that do not exercise regularly, would support this claim. Since aerobic exercise burns fat, statistics that show higher rates of diabetes and cancer in patients with excess body fat would also support this claim. 2. Yes, evidence linking exercise to disease prevention would cause me to exercise more. Some diseases are genetic or result from exposure; however, if evidence shows that exercise is useful in warding off diabetes, heart disease, or some forms of cancer, I would find it beneficial to prevent those ailments that are avoidable.

Testing Yourself

1. a; 2. c; 3. b; 4. Glucose breakdown begins with glycolysis; oxygen becomes water at the end of the ETC; carbon dioxide is produced by the prep reaction and Krebs cycle. ATPs are produced by glycolysis (2 ATP), Krebs cycle (2 ATP per two turns), and 32-34 ATP by the ETC. 5. a; 6. e; 7. d; 8. b; 9. b; 10. c; 11. d; 12. d; 13. b; 14. Inner membrane space serves as an area where hydrogen ions collect before passing through an ATP synthase complex; b. Matrix is location of preparatory reaction and Krebs cycle; c. Cristae contain electron transport chain and ATP synthase complex. 15. Only 39% of available energy becomes ATP and the rest becomes heat. 16. c; 17. d; 18. c; 19. b; 20. b; 21. c; 22. Chloroplasts and mitochondria were originally independent prokaryotes. Prokaryotes evolved from a common ancestor, which must have used an ETC.

Thinking Scientifically

1. Acid, because for ATP to be produced, H^+ must flow through the ATP synthase complex.
2. The acetyl group that enters the Kreb cycle is oxidized to CO_2.

Put the Pieces Together

Page 139: 1. The pre-eukaryotic cell must have been a fermenter living off abiotically produced organic molecules. Cellular respiration couldn't have evolved until oxygen entered the atmosphere due to the evolution of photosynthesis. The eukaryotic cell became capable of cellular respiration after it engulfed a prokaryote that could carry out cellular respiration. 2. Structural similarities often point to evolutionary ties. Both the chloroplasts and mitochondria have an internal membrane system where various complexes are located. They both have a semiliquid interior where enzymes carry out carbohydrate metabolism. They both have an outer boundary that allows substances to pass into or out of the organelle.

CHAPTER 8

Check Your Progress

8.1 Abnormal because mutations can affect the normal structure of a chromosome. **8.2** Interphase because cancer cells spend all their time dividing. **8.3** Duplicated chromosomes contain sister chromatids and each one becomes a daughter chromosome. **8.4** Prophase-chromosomes are scattered; metaphase-chromosomes are aligned at equator; anaphase- daughter chromosomes are between equator and poles, telophase- daughter nuclei have formed. **8.5** A new cell wall in addition to a plasma membrane is needed for each daughter cell. **8.6** a. Loss of cell cycle control: lack of differentiation; abnormal nuclei; form tumors. b. Beyond loss of control: angiogenesis and metastasis. **8.7** Haploid, because each daughter cell receives one member from each homologous pair of chromosomes. **8.8** Sister chromatids have the same genetic information. Nonsister chromatids have genetic information for the same traits, but the

specifics are different. For example, one sister chromatid could call for freckles, and the other could call for no freckles. **8.9** The chromosomes of relatives are more likely to carry some of the same genetic information. Therefore, fertilization may bring together like homologues. **8.10** Plant cells do not have centrioles or asters during both mitosis and meiosis. You can recognize meiosis by the pairing and separation of homologues during meiosis I. **8.11** In the haploid and alternation of generation cycles meiosis produces haploid spores that undergo mitosis to produce a haploid individual. **8.12** Meiosis I has the same phases as mitosis, but homologous chromosomes separate during prophase I. Meiosis II has the same phases as mitosis, but the cells are haploid. **8.13** An excess of genetic material would cause protein and metabolic abnormalities. **8.14** Meiosis II because the only way for YY to occur is through the nonseparation of chromatids during meiosis II. **8.15** No. For example, if the child inherited both chromosomes that participated in the translocation, one chromosome would be too short and the other would be too long, therefore the homologues for these chromosomes would look different in a karyotype.

Form Your Opinion

Page 147: 1. If bacteria make a protein similar to tubulin it does strengthen the hypothesis that bacteria contributed to the evolution of the spindle apparatus. 2. Evolution must necessarily make use of the structures and molecules currently available. For example the jaw evolved from the first two gill arches of jawless fishes; humans walk erect by standing on the hind legs of quadrupeds that preceded them.
Page 151: 1. Yes answer: If I had lived 75 years and was facing a diminished quality of life including memory loss, the inability to maintain personal hygiene, or eat and drink, I would be willing to risk cancer in order to correct Alzheimer disease. Even though cancer has its own problems, I would not want to lose the memory of my family, friends, and myself as I lived my final years. No answer: Though the possibility of cancer is not absolute, I would not be willing to risk spending the last years of my life being treated for, or dying from, cancer in order to cure Alzheimer disease. I would seek other treatments to slow the progression of Alzheimer disease and attempt to maintain my quality of life for as long as it may last. 2. Yes answer: A scientist should be able to patent independent work because our society now recognizes that a person has a right to his or her intellectual work. No answer: A scientist should not be allowed to patent intellectual endeavors because it is the custom for scientists to work together and share knowledge for the benefit of society.
Page 154: People who sunbathe, or drink or smoke cigarettes might be prone to follow the popular trend. They might feel that being one of a group engaged in these activities is worth it to them even though they may eventually die from them. You could give them examples of people who are popular even though they do not engage in these practices. 2. Because cancer does not occur immediately, the risk of cancer may seem unrealistic or too far into the future to be immediately relevant. However, having a friend or family member who has cancer, might make the illness more real to them.

Testing Yourself

1. a; 2. a; 3. a; 4. c; 5. a; 6. d; 7. c; 8. b; 9. c. 10. a. chromatid of chromsome; b. centriole; c. spindle fiber or aster; d. nuclear envelope (fragment). 11. c; 12. a; 13. e; 14. b; 15. d; 16. Due to crossing-over and independent alignment, that occurs during each meiotic event, the chromosomes in the egg and

sperm carry different genetic information. 17. a; 18. d; 19. a; 20. e; 21. b

Thinking Scientifically

1. Both parents because the egg had to be missing this chromosome and the sperm had to have two of this chromosome. 2. While theoretically possible, it would be practically impossible to find two gametes with the exact same genetic information that produced this indiviudal.

Put the Pieces Together

Page 167: 1. The proximity of the homologous chromosomes during synapsis allows for the exchange of genetic information that occurs through crossing-over. Synapsis also allows for the alignment of homologous chromosomes during independent assortment. 2. In addition to crossing-over and independent assortment of chromosomes, the random fertilization that occurs through sexual reproduction results in increased variation among offspring. 3. As discussed in previous chapters, evolution is sometimes considered a process of "adding on" as opposed to starting over. Mitosis and meiosis being very similar events in which DNA is copied and passed on to a new cell, it is possible that a mitotic cell division gone awry was the first meiosis. For instance, a genetic defect occurred that allowed homologous chromosomes to pair by mistake during mitosis. Then, crossing over occurs between chromosomes, resulting in a new allele combination that benefits an organism. This "modified" mitosis which we call meiosis was passed on the next reproductive generation.

CHAPTER 9

Check Your Progress

9.1 The artificial selection of certain traits (controlled by genes) brings about recognizable breed changes. 9.2 Compared to dogs, pea plants are smaller, have a shorter maturation time, have traits that are easier to distinguish, can both self- and cross-pollinate, and produce many more offspring. 9.3 Hip dysplasia only occurs when offspring inherit two recessive alleles for hip dysplasia. 9.4 (1) a. RR b. Rr (2) a. all W; b. ½ R, ½ r; c. ½ T, ½ t; d. all T;(3) bb (4) 3 black rabbits: 1 white rabbit; 30 rabbits/120 are white. 9.5 TtGg, TTGG, TtGG, TTGg. 9.6 (1)RRPP, round seeds, purple flowers; (2) 75%; (3) 9:3:3:1, $^1/_{16}$; 9.7 (1) ¼; (2) Ss; (3) Tt x tt, tt. 9.8 Without careful records, the breeder may not know that all the individuals in row III are cousins who could carry the same recessive allele for, say, hip dysplasia. 9.9 Each parent is heterozygous. 9.10 Yes, if each were heterozygous. 9.11 The phenotypes of the potential offspring are: ¼ are normal; ½ may suffer a heart attack as young adults; and ¼ may suffer a heart attack in childhood. 9.12 Child: ii, mother: I^{A}i; father: I^{A}i, ii, I^{B}i; 9.13 (1) see Figure 9.13, page 183, in text. (2) Resistance is a polygenic trait with alleles on the X chromosome and chromosomes 2 and 3. (3) Diet is an environmental influence. 9.14 In CF, faulty chloride channels occur throughout the body and lead to problems in several organs, including the skin, lungs, and pancreas. 9.15 The Y chromosome is quite small. 9.16 (1) mother X^{B}X^b, father X^{b}Y, daughter X^{b}X^b; (2) X^{R}X^R, X^{R}Y; (3) (b); 1:1.

Form Your Opinion

Page 177: 1. The bulleted statements in the application show that the theory of evolution and the gene theory are compatible. When two theories are compatible it means that experimentation in one field supports the findings of another field as when two structures are supported by a wall they have in common. 2. Artificial selection allows us to

reason that human beings are playing the role of the environment when natural selection occurs. 3. It worked because the phenotype is dependent upon the genotype. Darwin observed that the phenotype changes over time but Mendel deduced that the an organism has two factors (now called alleles) for each phenotypic trait. Page 181: 1. Testing either the 8-celled embryo or the egg prior to implantation is more acceptable than testing a child in utero and then terminating the pregnancy if the child tests positive for a genetic disorder. 2. IVF is acceptable to me, especially when used by people who struggle getting pregnant on their own. I do prefer testing the egg to testing the embryo because an egg will not produce a life without fertilization. Therefore, testing the egg and choosing not to use it cannot be considered termination of a life. However testing and disgarding an embryo that tests positive for a genetic disorder can be considered a termination of life.

Testing Yourself

1. c; 2. The blending model of inheritance results in no variations, whereas Mendel's model does result in variations among the offspring. Evolution requires variations. 3. d; 4. c; 5. d; 6. a; 7. a; 8. b; 9. It shows that a chromosome(and a chromatid) has a sequence of alleles; 10.a; 11 b; 12. c; 13. c; 14. b; 15. Egg testing because only eggs free of the faulty allele are fertilized. 16. e; 17.b; 18. a; 19. c; 20. e; 21. a; 22 d; 23.a; 24. X^{A}X^a.

Thinking Scientifically

1. Cross it now with a fly that lacks the characteristic. Most likely, the fly is heterozygous and only a single autosomal mutation has occurred. Therefore, the cross will be Aa x aa with 1:1 results. If the characteristic disappears in males, cross F$_1$ flies to see if it reappears; it could be X-linked (see Fig. 9.16). 2. Give plants with a particular leaf pattern different amounts of fertilizer from none (your control) to over-enriched, and observe the results. Keep other conditions, such as amount of water, the same for all.

Put the Pieces Together

Page 189: 1. Just as flipping a coin many times is more likely to give 50% heads and 50% tails so counting many F$_2$ is more likely to give a 3:1 ratio when the parent plants are heterozygous because the particular gametes that join with each fertilization is by chance. 2. Meiosis explains Mendels laws. Mendel's law of segregation holds because the homologous pairs separate during meiosis I. Mendel's law of independent assortment holds because either homologous chromosome of each pair of homologues can face either pole during metaphase I of meiosis. 3. Mendelian genetics laid the groundwork to eventually understand how genes function. Because of its many applications to human beings, Mendel's work allows us to understand the inheritance patterns of genetic disorders, including autosomal recessive and dominant disorders. Today, we can determine if parents are carriers for numerous genetic disorders and advise them of the chances they will pass on a particular disorder because of Mendel's laws.

CHAPTER 10

Check Your Progress

10.1 a. DNA contains deoxyribose, and the base T; RNA contains ribose and the base U instead of T. b. The particular sequence of the nucleotide bases. 10.2 DNA is a double helix in all organisms. 10.3 Complementary base pairing between the template strand and the new strand. 10.4 Transcription produces an mRNA molecule that is the same as

the gene strand in DNA except that U occurs instead of T. mRNA splicing removes introns from mRNA and the introns removed can vary due to alternative mRNA splicing. 10.5 proline, tyrosine, arginine; 10.6 a. TAC in DNA = start codon in mRNA. b. ATT, ATC, or ACT in DNA = stop condons in mRNA; 10.7 The cell makes a protein by the process of transcription complementary base pairing with template strand and translation (tRNAs pair with mRNA codons)at a ribosome (rRNA). 10.8 A greater number of codons in mRNA and a greater number of amino acids would be incorrect.

Form Your Opinion

Page 197: 1. PCR should be used. Collection procedures should be standardized to eliminate the possibility of stray DNA entering the sample. Perhaps more than one lab technician could independently collect a sample and one of these technicians could be from an independent lab rather than a police lab. 2. Yes answer: Once a person has been convicted of a felony, it would make sense for their DNA fingerprints to remain on file in the event that another crime was committed. It would save time and money to already have this information readily available. No answer: Despite the fact that one crime was committed and a conviction made, there should be some degree of privacy with DNA fingerprinting, even for convicted felons. DNA fingerprinting can always be redone in the event of future crimes. 3. Yes answer: In the interest of science, public health and safety, PCR should be readily available. No answer: Government agencies like the Department of Health and Human Services could potentially regulate the use of PCR in instances where PCR would interfere with the privacy rights of an individual.

Page 205: 1. Transposons replicate within the DNA without regard to the consequences. DNA can be considered selfish because just as the most successful members of a population have the most offspring, the most successful DNA passes itself to the most members of the next generation without regard to consequences. 2. It is possible that P elements produced some evolutionary advantage in *Drosophila melanogaster* which was passed on via natural selection to spread into all populations of the species.

Page 206: 1. Yes answer: Health insurance should be fairly priced and affordable for all people. It is not guaranteed that sunbathers and smokers will get cancer and require extended medical care. No answer: Health insurance prices should take into account the likelihood that smokers and sunbathers will be sick and require long-term medical care for the treatment of diseases like cancer. Because there is a proven correlation between sunbathing, smoking, and cancer, it would make sense for insurance rates to be higher for people who choose these activities. 2. Yes answer: Bacterial response to mutagens can be relied upon as at least a predictor of human cell responses to these same substances. Though prokaryotes and eukaryotes differ, the Ames test can be used to indicate potential hazards and further testing could be conducted. No answer: Testing the effect of a mutagen on a prokaryote is not a completely reliable predictor of the response of a eukaryotic human cell to the same substance.

Testing Yourself

1. c; 2. e; 3. b; 4. a; 5. d; 6. c; 7. b; 8. DNA analogues prevent the formation of new DNA molecules, and each new virus requires a DNA molecule. 9. b; 10. b; 11. e; 12. a; 13. c; 14. b. 15. d; 16. d; 17. c; 18. b; 19. a. polypeptide b. amino acid c. tRNA d. anticodon e. codon f. ribosome; 20. c; 21. a. ACU CCU GAA UGC AAA; b. UGA GGA CUU ACG

UUU c. threonine—proline—glutamate—cysteine—lysine; 22. genetic information, in the sequence of its bases; 23. b; 24. b; 25. A change from ATG to ATA has no effect because both of the resulting codons code for tyrosine. 26. Without mutations, new adaptations cannot occur and new life forms cannot evolve.

Thinking Scientifically

1. Determine if any transposon base sequence occurs in the sequence for the neurofibromatosis gene.
2. Place the isolated gene in *Arabidopsis* cells and look for the mutation in cloned adult plants.

Put the Pieces Together

Page 209: 1. The criteria for a genetic material: (1) it must be variable, accounting for the differences between species. DNA is variable. Differences in the base pairing combinations found in DNA molecules produce differences in proteins, which account for the variation between species; (2) it must be able to replicate, as DNA does, in a semi conservative process by which it duplicates itself; (3) it must be able to undergo mutations. DNA undergoes mutations, another factor which accounts for variability in organisms. DNA can undergo mutations during the replication process, due to contact with external factors like radiation, or due to random events like jumping genes, or transposons, which in turn alter gene expression and cause many changes in organisms. 2. This suggests that protein-coding genes in specialized cells may be activate or inactive at different points in the cell's life. 3. Futuristic drugs might affect the early synthesis procedure, changing or eliminating the proteins to be produced by making changes in mRNA before it reaches the ribosomes.

CHAPTER 11

Check Your Progress

11.1 Regulatory genes code for DNA-binding proteins. **11.2** Transcription factors and transcription activators. **11.3** Inactive means that the DNA is not being transcribed; heterochromatin means that the chromatin is tightly packed. **11.4** Because *Pax6* could not be present in so many different animals unless they are related through evolution **11.5** Introns are removed during processing. **11.6** miRNAs lead to limited amount of mRNA translation while siRNA lead to no translation of mRNA **11.7** Translation repressor proteins can prevent translation of mRNA; enzymes may have to cleave a protein to activate it; tagging of a protein makes it vulnerable to digesion inside a proteasome. **11.8** a. transcription factor b. euchromatin c. introns removed d. RISC e. proteasome **11.9** a. Cell cycle keeps going when it should stop. b. The gene is now coding for a faulty protein in an inhibitory transduction pathway. **11.10** Cancer is caused by a series of mutations and all these mutations may or may not occur.

Form Your Opinion

Page 217: 1. Yes answer: The brain is a fascinating organ about which scientists, doctors, and everyday people have many questions. The more avenues we explore to help answer these questions, the more headway we might be able to make in matters involving the brain, such as Alzheimer disease or human intelligence. Evolutionary changes in the brain and its development might serve to teach us much more than we could ever imagine. No answer: Research should focus on the human brain alone and how it works. There is no guarantee that looking into the differences between human and ape brains will give us any relevant or useful information. 2. This reading tells us that our brain continues to develop after

we are born and this accounts for its large size. It suggests that coordination between brain parts and the functioning of limbs was sacrificed to this enlargement. 3. Yes, it does make sense. Initially, cells divide to make exact copies of themselves which serves to produce a larger organism. As the cell number grows, regulatory genes bring about differentiation of cell types so that they perform different functions. Without this specialization, cell division would simply create copy after copy of the original cell and development of an organism would not occur. A human-sized clump of cells and a human being differ greatly due to specialization through regulatory genes.

Page 224: 1. Yes answer: By making a young person aware that they could carry a cancer gene, they can make informed decisions about life, including screening to detect cancer early and often to potentially treat it as soon as it appears. A young person might lead a healthier life to help ward off illness with exercise and a proper diet. An informed person may also decide, based upon knowing the probability, whether or not to have children and potentially pass the gene along. No answer: Making a young person aware that they could carry a cancer gene could potentially make the person's life miserable with paranoia and trips to the doctor for every ache and pain. A person may decide against having a family, participating in activities that expose them to sun or other carcinogens, and lead a depressing and anxious life. I think the choice to find out if you could carry a cancer gene should be made by each person individually. 2. Yes answer: Especially when there is a family history of cancer, the testing can help doctors catch and treat the cancer earlier, and advise the patient on the healthiest life possible to avoid the cancer. Decisions can also be made regarding reproduction and passing the alleles to children. However, just because the testing for cancer-causing alleles should be advised, it should be voluntary. All people are different and some individuals may not want to know every last detail about their future health.

Testing Yourself

1. a. DNA; b. regulator gene; c. promoter; d; operator; e. active repressor; 2. b; 3. b; 4. b; 5. d; 6. b; 7. b; 8. b; 9. b; 10. c; 11. e; 12. e; 13. d; 14. a; 15. c; 16. b; 17. Benefit is refinement of control; drawback is more chances of losing control; 18. b,c; 19. a,c; 20. a,d; 21. a,d; 22. c,d,a,b

Thinking Scientifically

1. You should also show that the genes having homeoboxes result in similar developmental stages.
2. Culture normal cells in the presence of the pollutant and observe the results. Culture the same types of cells in the same manner but without the pollutant and observe the results.

Put the Pieces Together

Page 227: 1. Many of the anatomical differences between apes and humans pertain to differences that might have arisen due to a change in gene regulation. For example differences in brain development and infant strength could be due to particular protein activities during development. 2. A knowledge of regulation can be used to understand the onset and progression of diseases, particularly those that result from genetic mutations that effect protein production. With an understanding of how regulation turns protein production "on" and "off" we might discover methods to artificially "flip the switch" to head off potentially detrimental changes in protein levels. 3. Genetic regulation is to cells as a teacher is to a class room. The students (cells) need clear

instructions on what tasks to perform (when protein production is needed) or chaos (disease) will result.

CHAPTER 12

Check Your Progress

12.1 The nucleus contains the genes that determine the phenotype. **12.2** The GFP gene only causes living organisms to glow in dark. **12.3** Genes function the same in all organisms. **12.4** By cloning you're assured of producing only females that produce milk. **12.5** A virus **12.6** How the pieces should be sequenced. **12.7** a. introns, unique and repetitive b. repetitive DNA is the largest portion and investigators are determining if it has a regulatory function. **12.8** a. You would know what proteins are made by specialized cells and why some cells malfunction. b. Bioinformatics can find similarities and differences between proteomes, for example.

Form Your Opinion

Page 231: 1. Reproductive cloning can help to preserve rare animals that might otherwise become extinct. It can also provide a large number of agricultural plants for farmers. Once an animal has been genetically modified for a particular purpose, it can produce other animals with the same genotype and phenotype. Reproductive cloning also helps the scientific community increase its knowledge of gene interactions and embryonic development. 2. Yes answer: Reproductive cloning has many potential side effects that are less than desirable. Because we do not completely understand and cannot predict the possible hazards of cloning animals and human beings, I find the process to be risky and potentially dangerous. Animals and people can be created that suffer from premature aging and disease, or worse, a person with uncontrolled aggression or mental imbalance. If this occurs, we have created a life that will cost money to diagnose and treat or poses a danger to itself or others. There are also religious and moral issues regarding the production of life. No answer: When used to preserve endangered species I find the cloning of animals to be a useful procedure. Also it can help populate the world with humans, animals, and plants that have a beneficial genotype and phenotype. 3. Because the harvesting of stem cells from embryos creates controversy over moral issue, I think that we should explore therapeutic cloning using adult stem cells and treated skin cells since this method is already in the works and is less controversial for the general public.

Page 235: 1. Based on the ability of scientists to perform simulated digestion of GM crops using enzymes to test for the characteristics of allergens, as well as feeding the GM crops to test animals like rats, it seems that scientists have the ability to decide pre-market if a GM crop is potentially harmful. 2. Yes answers: Because of the unpredictable risks and the newness of the technology, I am in favor of banning GM crops until long-term studies have informed scientists on the long-term effects of consuming these foods. And I do approve of ecoterrorists burning crops and destroying labs that could potentially be harmful to the public. Getting rid of the crops and the labs they are genetically engineered in slows the spread of GM crops to the market and protects the public from what might create health problems in the long-term. No answer: I do not favor a ban of GM crops. GM crops have increased yields, decreased losses due to herbicides and pests, and have been tested before hitting the shelf. I do favor the proper labeling of such crops and the decision to consume these or other crops being left up to the consumer. And I do not approve of ecoterrorism or the burning of crops and labs that could be useful in scientific research. Boycotting GM

products or informing the public in peaceful displays would be desirable alternatives to destroying crops and property. 3. If a genetically modified food can provide an otherwise lacking vitamin, it should be used where it will benefit the people and prevent childhood blindness. Data on any side effects of the GM rice and whether or not they outweigh its benefits would help in decisively banning or allowing the public consumption of GM rice enhanced with vitamin A.
Page 242: 1. Yes, I would have expected gene regulation to account for major evolutionary differences because the control of protein production results in the different characteristics we see between species. The types and amount of proteins being produced by an organism determine important attributes like appearance and development. It makes sense then, that control of protein production accounts for differences among the species. 2. Yes answer: If a study of my genome and the diseases prone to others with similar genetic make-up might lead to beneficial findings for other human beings, I would be willing to participate in a comparative human study. No answer: I think that genome studies should rely on testing plants and approved animals. The privacy of human subjects is at risk in comparative studies and I would prefer to preserve my privacy rather than participate in a study that exposes my genetic weaknesses. 3. Since we are not identical twins, I would expect my genome to differ slightly from my siblings. Though we have a great deal in common, there must be differences in our DNA because we are all different people.

Testing Yourself

1. b; 2. a; 3. a; 4. d; 5. e; 6. c,a,b,d; 7. c; 8.e; 9. begins: AATT; ends: TTAA; 10. a; 11. a; 12. e; 13 Plants and animals can trace their ancestry to a common source, and therefore plants are able to express a human gene. 14. a; 15. c; 16. d; 17. e; 18. Genetically modified stem cells pass on their modification to their offspring (more white blood cells) indefinitely. 19. b; 20. c; 21. a; 22. Each gene performs only one function, so despite increased number of genes, only 30 gene functions would be available. 23. a; 24. d; 25. d; 26. c; 27. d; 28. a; 29. c

Thinking Scientifically

1. Use restriction enzymes to fragment the DNA of chromosome 10. Inject these fragments, one at a time, into groups of one-celled mouse embryos. Following development, see which mice have no tails. 2. An ex vivo study allows you to perfect your procedure in the lab and possibly avoid harm to the patient.

Put the Pieces Together

Page 245: 1. Biotechnology takes what we know about nature and utilizes developments in technology to artificially produce desired results for human beings. Because of the blending of science and technology, biotechnology is aptly named. 2. (1) Our cells contain many more proteins that there are genes that code for proteins. (2) Introns may help regulate the number and kind of exons in each type protein. (3) Repetitive DNA is translated into RNA and it appears that several types of small RNAs are involved in both transcription and translation. 3. To the layperson, biotechnology and genomics may appear to be tampering with nature and playing "God." Many of the procedures and technologies associated with biotechnology might seem extreme to the layperson, or difficult to understand. If portrayals in movies are the only source of information regarding cloning and other biotechnology, the layperson may believe that scientists are "evil" and science itself as unregulated and self-serving.

CHAPTER 13
Check Your Progress

13.1 Darwin made observations that would help him formulate a hypothesis. **13.2** No, you would pollinate it by hand with the pollen of your choice. **13.3** Any plant that provided food (nectar) to a particular pollinator had an advantage that resulted in more offspring than other members of the population because its pollen was being distributed. **13.4** Yes. Whenever independent sources come to the same conclusion based on the data they have collected, the hypothesis is supported. **13.5** Flowers are delicate and decompose quickly, not allowing time for them to become fossils. **13.6** The flowers would have shorter and thicker floral tubes. **13.7** The flowers probably had a common ancestor. **13.8** These species of finches evolved on the Galápagos Islands. **13.9** All organisms are related through common descent from the first cell or cells. **13.10** Genetic similarity maintains the characteristics of the species; genetic variation allows evolution (adaptation) to occur. **13.11** Microevolution has occurred when allele frequency changes are observed due to mutations, gene flow, nonrandom mating, genetic drift, and natural selection. **13.12** Yes; any flower mutation that increases the chances of being pollinated and any mutation in the pollinator that increases the chances of getting food results in more offspring with the same adaptation. **13.13** Imagine a pollinator that only pollinates a particular species and can only see flowers of a certain color. Only flowers of that color would produce seeds, and soon all flowers of that species would be that color. **13.14** Yes, because genetic drift causes a change in allele frequencies, but does not necessarily contribute to adaptation. **13.15** Yes, because a flower of any other color has little chance of being pollinated. **13.16** Yes, because, in this instance, natural selection favors the heterozygote. Natural selection favors whichever genotype/phenotype is most advantageous in a particular environment.

Form Your Opinion

Page 254: 1. The now common occurrence of MRSA (methicillin-resistant Staphylococcus aureus) is an example of antibiotic resistance that many people now know about. Many patients think of antibiotics as a universal cure for all ailments and pressure doctors into prescribing them. However, physicians should stop overprescribing antibiotics and patients should be sure to take all doses that were prescribed. Also instead of increasing pesticide use or changing pesticides, farmers should set aside farmland that encourages the reproduction of non-resistant insects. If a farmer can increase the number of non-resistant insects on their land, lower levels of pesticides will continue to eliminate these insects. Current practices call for the increased use of pesticides and development of new ones as resistant insects rise in population. 2. Due to extent of human involvement, drug development, design, and improvement is artificial selection for the best drugs, but not natural selection at work.
Page 262: 1. A taste for sweet foods in humans, apes and monkeys benefits plants containing sweet proteins because the more these plants are ingested, the more widely the distribution of their seeds in the waste of humans and animals. The spreading of these seeds over larger areas and at high rates gives the plants a reproductive advantage over plants that are not eaten as much. 2. Humans are influencing the evolution of plants when they propagate them. When humans step in to produce more of one plant than another, for food or other purposes, they are artificially selecting for some plants to have more reproductive success than others.

When humans genetically modify and breed plants, they certainly influence the plants' evolution. Changing something about the plant, which would only occur over time due to mutations and natural selection in nature, at least speeds the evolutionary process—that is, if the genetic modification made by humans would occur in nature at all. Any human involvement in plant reproduction or genetic composition influences evolution. The engineered plants humans create may evolve entirely differently than non-engineered plants would have. 3. Artificial selection can be harmful to plants and animals because it (1) reduces variation and (2) can make organisms prone to disease and (3) can select for traits that do not help the animal survive in the wild.

Testing Yourself

1. b; 2. c; 3. c; 4. d; 5. b; 6. Neither the occurrence of mutations nor the changing of environmental conditions are known ahead of time. 7. e; 8. d; 9. e; 10. e; 11. a; 12. d; 13. c; 14. b; 15. Their DNA base sequences were inherited from a common ancestor. 16. a; 17. a; 18. c; 19. d; 20. b

Thinking Scientifically

1. If you know the genotype of the various colors, you could use the Hardy-Weinberg equation to calculate changes in gene pool frequencies. Otherwise, you could base sequence before and after the experiment to determine a change in the genome. 2. Yes; due to natural selection of boll weevils resistant to the insecticide.

Put the Pieces Together

Page 269: 1. Evolution via natural selection can be witnessed, particularly in organisms that have short life cycles and thus reproduce multiple generations over short periods of time. For example, over 5 years silent male field crickets increased from 10% to 90% of the population in a study conducted in Hawaii. The silent cricket had an advantage over the chirping cricket in its inability to be detected by a predator. This selective pressure caused silent crickets to survive to reproduce while chirping crickets were preyed upon. Other examples can be seen in the evolution of pesticide-resistant insects as a result of the increased use of pesticides and antibiotic-resistant bacteria due to the selective pressure of increased antibiotic use. 2. We expect evolution to have a genetic basis because genes control the phenotype of an individual including structural, metabolic, and behaviorial traits. Thus genetic changes had to precede the observation of phenotypic changes. 3. Because evolution is not directional, it would be incorrect to say that bacteria became resistant in order to escape being killed by antibiotics. The mutations that allow bacteria to become resistant had to have occurred before they were exposed to the antibiotic. Nature selected *for* resistant individuals and *against* the non-resistant.

CHAPTER 14
Check Your Progress

14.1 No, because ligers share the ancestry of both lions and tigers, and they do not ordinarily occur in the wild. **14.2** a. Habitat isolation; lions live on the plains, and tigers live in forests; b. F_2 fitness; ligers are usually sterile (due to mispairing of chromosomes during meiosis). **14.3** Members of the ancestral species separated into those that lived on the plains and those that lived in the forest. Over time, each became adapted to its habitat, including a change in coat color. Now, lions and tigers do not mate because they rarely come into contact, and also because the coat color allows them to recognize members of their own species. **14.4** You need evidence that each of the cats is adapted to fill a different niche. **14.5** The fossil record would have to show fossils of the different types of cats existing in the same location at the same time—before they begin to appear in various locations. **14.6** A gradualistic model if the ligers are transitional links. **14.7** a. Ligers are larger than either parent. b. The large size of ligers is an advantage that is selected for. **14.8** No, evolution is not goal oriented.

Form Your Opinion

Page 280: 1. Yes answer: We should continue to convert corn to ethanol. Despite increased cost of corn, we must produce alternative energy sources in order to reduce our reliance on non-renewable resources. Since eventually we will have no choice but to use alternative methods, it is best that we explore those we have already developed, including the conversion of corn to ethanol. It is possible that the increased cost of corn could be offset by the decreased need for expensive petroleum-based fuels. No answer: We should not continue to convert corn to ethanol if it raises the cost of corn needed to feed humans and animals around the world. We should explore other alternative fuel methods and temporarily maintain our reliance on petroleum while we still have it. We must develop alternative methods for energy, particularly those that are more efficient and less disruptive than converting corn to ethanol. 2. Yes answer: We should grow more corn for energy production through conversion to ethanol and use less in the process of creating waste and feeding beef. This might lead to limited beef in human diets and less waste to dispose of, solving problems associated with pollution of ground water, circulatory problems in humans, and even obesity in our fast-food fed nation. If corn was primarily grown to produce energy, we might explore alternative foods for animals and humans alike. No answer: We should not grow more corn for ethanol conversion and decrease its use as food for humans and animals. We should develop better waste management practices and moderate our consumption of beef while continuing to use corn for food. If we can grow more corn, this is not an either/or situation and we can have enough corn for ethanol production and food uses.

Page 283: 1. Since science seeks to answer questions about the natural world, the scientific community should use phenomenon like the Burgess Shale to help answer these questions. Since fossil evidence can help to fill in blanks in evolutionary history, the fossils should be examined and evaluated in an attempt to figure out how they fit into the story of our planet. The scientific community should do its best to preserve such phenomenon while objectively examining the history hidden inside. Potentially detrimental "shots in the dark" should be avoided and in some cases, samples should be preserved until technology can be developed to meet the demands of dissecting fragile fossil evidence. 2. Students should be presented objective information about the unexplained. This can encourage students to understand the progressive nature of science, along with how much we do not know about the world in which we live. Exposure to phenomena that is yet to be fully explained can help students understand the scientific process. These students may someday be scientists themselves, developing techniques or technology that will help us learn more about these phenomena.

Testing Yourself

1. c; 2. c; 3. b; 4. f; 5. a; 6. e; 7. h; 8. e; 9. c; 10. e; 11. Genetic differences; 12. a. species 1; b. geographic barrier; c. genetic changes; d. species 2; e. genetic changes; f. species 3. 13. d; 14. b; 15. Allopatric

speciation was possible on the Hawaiian Islands, but not on the Florida Keys. 16. b; 17. c; 18. d; 19. b; 20. b; 21. c; 22. b; 23. d; 24. b; 24. d; 25. Hox genes evolved early in the history of life. 26. d; 27. b

Thinking Scientifically

1. The evolutionary species concept allows you to trace the history of an organism in the fossil record, and the biological species concept provides a way to identify species without the need to examine them anatomically. 2. Their chromosomes are compatible, and the two species are very closely related. It's doubtful they should be considered different species.

Put the Pieces Together

Page 289: 1. Biologists have made testable hypotheses about (1) the activity of *Hox* genes in many different species; (2) the effects of regulatory genes on developmental processes; (3) the need for geographic and reproductive isolation in order for a new species to arise; (4) the role of polyploidy in the origination of new plant species and (5) the role of gradualist and punctuated equilibrium models in speciation. 2. Paleontologists suggested the punctuated equilibrium model using data from the fossil record that supports the sudden appearance of new species. These species then undergo little morphologoical change until becoming extinct. 3. Yes, the study of evolution is a scientific endeavor. In order to understand the process of evolution, scientists have formulated hypotheses and tested these hypothesis in the natural world. This has resulted in the collection of data and a conclusion that evolution does occur. Natural selection can be used to explain observations in other fields of biology from genetics to behavior.

CHAPTER 15

Check Your Progress

15.1 When tracing the evolution of life, you need to start with the past and move toward the present. The dates are in MYA; therefore, the larger numbers in the timescale are more distant from the present than are the smaller numbers. **15.2** Yes, because dinosaurs evolved at the start of the Mesozoic era, when the continents were all still joined. **15.3** Humans didn't evolve until the Holocene epoch, long after the last mass extinction. The possibility exists that humans could become extinct due to their own activities. **15.4** Only plants that resemble virgina creeper are in the same genus. Domain Eukarya contains the plants, animals, fungi, and protists. **15.5** Animals share the same way of life; they are all motile and ingest their food. **15.6** Monkeys and gorillas share a more recent common ancestor than do reindeer and gorillas. **15.7** epidermal scales **15.8** Yes, dinosaurs being vertebrates share the homologous structures of vertebrates.

Form Your Opinion

Page 299: 1. In some instances the ability to readily identify any species of organism could be beneficial to society. In fields such as farming, education, and medicine this technology would prove particularly useful for identifying organisms that propose a threat to plants and/or human beings. For example, a farmer, doctor, or student could differentiate poisonous or otherwise harmful insects or plant species that differ only subtly in appearance from non-harmful species. This could assist in medical diagnostics for rashes, insect or snake bites if some portion of the organism were available for identification. Because of the need to scan either the organism or a portion of it, the ability to identify a species may not always be possible, however. 2. The conversion of the CBOL methods to a criminal identification process would most likely require

the isolation of definitive nucleotide sequences that differ between individuals or would otherwise require the sequencing of a person's entire genome. It could potentially work through inserting a sample of hair, blood, semen, or skin into a scanning device. Individuals could be required to have their DNA sequenced upon birth, arrest, or medical care such that a catalog of DNA could be used as a reference for comparison of the scanned genetic material, much like the catalog that exists for organisms that have been sequenced by scientists. 3. Yes answer: I would try to make money from human bar-coding, as should individuals involved in developing this procedure. If the technology was developed to bar-code to the level of identifying individual people, it should be marketed for a profit. Scientists and inventors alike should be able to earn a living from the procedures and technology that they spend time developing, testing, and improving. No answer: I would not try to make money from human bar-coding technology and the individuals involved should not try to sell their procedure for a profit. It would make sense for individuals involved to be compensated for their work but not to profit. Selling procedures to the highest bidder puts science beyond the reach of everyday people, who should have just as much access to scientific development as more affluent individuals. **Page 302:** 1. Cladistics is considered more objective than evolutionary systematic because it presents its data for all to see and no conclusions are subjective. This is why cladistics has most likely been welcomed and will continue to be well received by the scientific community. 2. Science should be willing to change while still retaining traditional methods that are also useful. We should particularly keep any traditional methods have been well tested. Innovation, however, propels science forward and is only natural in a field driven by hypotheses and experimentation.

Testing Yourself

1. b; 2. d; 3. a; 4. c; 5. e; 6. e; 7. a; 8. d; 9. d; 10. a; Ferns; b. produce seeds; c. naked seeds; d. needle-like leaves, Conifers; e. fan-shaped leaves, Gingkos; f. enclosed seeds; g. one embryonic leaf, Monocots; h. two embryonic leaves, Eudicots. 11. b; 12. d; 13. e; 14. b; 15. e; 16. b; 17. New and different stuctures arise due to DNA differences. 18. b; 19. a, b, c; 20. d, e; 21. b; 22. The three-domain system is based on differences/similarities in the sequencing of rRNA. This is backed up by differences in structure.

Thinking Scientifically

1. The tree shows that all life forms have a common source and how they are related, despite the occurrence of divergence, which gives rise to different groups of organisms. 2. The specialized environmental niche of these organisms is the same as it was when they first evolved.

Put the Pieces Together

Page 307: 1. Yes answer: Putting the biosphere and all of its organisms into a tree of life would put the vast nature of the world in perspective and would make me want to preserve all species now alive. No answer: The overwhelming nature of a complete tree of life might decrease my interest in the preservation of species by sheer over-stimulation. Seeing that so many species exist, some being very similar to one another might detract from the value of each species individually. 2. Yes answer: I do look forward this because determining the ancestry of humans all the way to the first living source is an exciting concept that seems to fit naturally into the human desire to understand who we are and where we came from. No answer: I do not look forward to tracing the ancestry of humans to the very first living source and do not trust the data that traces the ancestry of humans to the first living source. 3. It does not surprise me that humans are related to all other organisms on the planet. An understanding of genetics and evolution helps explain why connections exist between all living organisms. Also, the shared characteristics of all living things (see page 18) help to support the undeniable interrelatedness of every organism, past and present.

CHAPTER 16

Check Your Progress

16.1 The genes become incorporated into the virus's nucleic acid core. **16.2** The virus should be lysogenic and should never undergo the lytic cycle. **16.3** Only plant cells have receptors for plant viruses. **16.4** To avoid unintentionally infecting the researcher. **16.5** DNA animal viruses do not carry out reverse transcription and integration. **16.6** As yet, there were no enzymes to allow reactions at mild temperatures to occur. **16.7** a. RNA can store, replicate, and transmit genetic information; b. RNA can perform enzymatic functions, including those for replicating itself. **16.8** a. Proteins (enzymes) allow a cell to acquire energy and grow; b. Genetic information (either in the form of RNA or DNA) is needed for reproduction. **16.9** The capsule protects bacteria from the host defenses, and the pili help bacteria adhere to parts of the human body. **16.10** Binary fission will quickly produce a large number of bacteria, which will all have an ability to feed on oil. **16.11** During sexual reproduction, each parent passes a complete copy of its genome to an offspring. During transformation, conjugation, and transduction, a fully formed bacterium receives a few genes from another fully formed bacterium. **16.12** a. All humans require oxygen and bacteria differ in their need for oxygen; b. All humans are heterotrophs and bacteria can be photosynthetic, chemosynthetic, or heterotrophic. **16.13** Cyanobacteria are believed to be the first organisms to release oxygen into the atmosphere. Cyanobacteria still release oxygen, just as algae and plants do. **16.14** Bacteria and archaea arose from a common ancestor; eukaryotes arose from archaea. **16.15** Bacteria are saprotrophs whose digestive enzymes break down materials in the environment.

Form Your Opinion

Page 313: 1. The special concerns associated with catching a newly discovered emergent disease include the potential of catching a new strain that cannot be treated or cured in the same manner as previous strains. A new disease may not be diagnosed and treated properly. 2. It is both a service and disservice for the media to publicize emergent diseases to the level that they do. It serves the public to be informed and take precautions to avoid infection. It does not serve the public to be worked into frenzy over worst-case scenarios that suggest the world may be coming to an end. 3. We are probably unnecessarily accusatory. A country cannot be exclusively blamed for being the origin of a disease due to factors that are largely out of the control of that country's people. It would benefit the entire world if we helped developing countries by campaigning for and helping to implement programs for clean water, good hygiene, and medical care in order to prevent the spread of disease.

Page 316: 1. Hypothetical evolutionary stages between the first viruses and bacteria might include intermediate stages. 1) It would be necessary for the virus to independently carry out protein synthesis Since a virus already has either RNA and DNA, they would only need to acquire both at the same time. In fact some RNA viruses even now carry out reverse transcription in order to form DNA. A virus could also take for itself some of the DNA from

a host cell. With the ability to produce enzymes, cellular respiration would be a possibility. Now the virus could live independently. 2) The virus would need to gain a plasma membrane and this may have happened by keeping a portion of the plasma membrane of the host cell. 2. If the viruses of today are degenerate forms of viruses that gave rise to cells, their parasitic life style may have caused them to lose certain abilities out of disuse. In their degeneration, viruses of the past would have lost the ability to replicate independently, carry on metabolic activity independently, and thus to live outside of a host cell. 3. A parasite needs to produce a sufficient number of offspring so that some will go on to parasitize other hosts. Many offspring are expected to never find another host; the greater the number of offspring the more likely a new host will be infected.

Page 327: 1. I would explain the symptoms of gonorrhea, including pain with urination, bloody or milky discharge, pelvic inflammatory disease (PID), reduced fertility, tubal pregnancy, blindness in infants who pass through an infected birth canal, and possible spread to internal organs leading to heart disease or painful arthritis. I would also stress the many ways in which gonorrhea can be contracted and parts of the body it can infect, including the eyes, mouth, throat, and tonsils. The two most important points I would raise are that the risk of contracting HIV is increased when a person has gonorrhea, and that it is possible that some strains of gonorrhea will be incurable with antibiotics if this bacteria continues to evolve new strains, increasing the risk of permanent side effects when major organs are infected. 2. Children should be instructed about gonorrhea early, in late elementary to early middle school years. Just like other diseases, it is important to inform children about the risk of and precautions against sexually transmitted infection. The earlier the instruction takes place, the greater the chances that infection can be avoided instead of having to be treated. Teaching children to be responsible, even in matters that might make parents and other adults uncomfortable, provides them with the information they need to be safe and healthy.

Page 328: 1. No answer: If we discontinue flyovers, bioterrorists would certainly just find another method to attack with. We should take precaution to control air traffic during sports events and not discontinue activities in fear of possible attack. Yes answer: Bioterrorists might take advantage of the gathering of a large crowd and the fact that a flyover is not an abnormal event during a sporting event. Discontinuing flyovers may prevent a catastrophic attack using biological weapons. 2. Yes answer: Though the Unites States should not retaliate with biological weapons, it has a responsibility to retaliate and defend its people in the event of a bioterrorism attack. No answer: The United States should not retaliate and perpetuate a cycle of destruction using biological weapons, which pose a threat to all living things and has potentially unknown and far-reaching side effects.

Testing Yourself

1. c; 2. e; 3. c; 4. d; 5. b; 6. a. Lytic cycle: the virus is immediately produced and can go on to infect other cells. In life cycle b. Lysogenic cycle: the virus is being replicated along with the host cells and is protected from exposure to host defenses. 7. c; 8. c; 9. c; 10. a; 11. e; 12. b; 13. c; 14. c; 15. a; 16. c; 17. b; 18. e; 19. a; 20. b; 21. a; 22. d; 23. b

Thinking Scientifically

1. Viruses replicate inside human cells, and therefore, medications aimed at a virus can interfere with the workings of human cells. 2. The bacterium *E. coli* has the same genetic machinery as all other

cells, including eukaryotic cells. They reproduce quickly and a large number can be kept in a small container. Since bacteria are haploid, mutations can be immediately observed.

Put the Pieces Together

Page 331: 1. Not all bacteria cause disease. There are bacteria present in a healthy digestive system, in foods including yogurt and cheeses, and in food and beverage production processes like fermentation in bread and alcohol. 2. The first stages of the scenario described in figure 16.7 can be explained using the iron-sulfur world hypothesis through which thermal vents in the ocean could have heated water containing iron and nickel sulfides which then served as catalysts in the conversion of N_2 into NH_3. This conversion could have produced nutrient molecules capable of supporting life. Under the conditions of the thermal vents, inorganic molecules could have given rise to organic monomers, which could combine to form polymers like amino acids which form peptides in the presence of iron and nickel sulfides. Once this chemical evolution was complete, the raw materials for biological evolution were readily available for the formation of membranes, proteins, and genetic materials that are the building blocks of the cell. 3. Cyanobacteria first carried on photosynthesis. The endosymbiotic theory explains the evolution of photosynthetic eukaryotes by taking up cyanobacteria, organisms believed to be responsible for introducing oxygen into the early atmosphere and thus allowing the evolution of animals. Without the introduction of oxygen to the atmosphere, the world as we know it would not exist.

CHAPTER 17

Check Your Progress

17.1 Yes, all protists are eukaryotes and have a nucleus. **17.2** Protists are a variable group and differ in size from microscopic to macroscopic; exhibit all possible life cycles, and ingest, absorb, or make their own food. **17.3** Contaminated water is a common source of Giardia infections. **17.4** A structural role. Silica is found in the tests of radiolarians. (It is also found in the cell walls of some plants and in the spicules of some sponges.) **17.5** Cilia give an organism the ability to move through the water and to direct water and food particles into a gullet for digestion. **17.6** A negative test for the spores merozoites. **17.7** As a result of the Irish potato famine, a large number of people emigrated from Ireland to the United States. **17.8** They are bound by protective cellulose plates that are impregnated by silicates. They also, typically, have two flagella. **17.9** A gelatinous product derived from some species of red algae. It is used as a solidifying agent for bacterial cultures. **17.10** Nucleic acid sequencing data.

Form Your Opinion

Page 337: 1. The theory of evolution has been supported by experimental evidence (see page 254) and by observation of fossil record, comparative anatomy, development, and chemistry of organisms. There are those who might point to gaps in the fossil record to cast doubt about the theory but the fossils record is becoming more complete as time passes. Science always seeks to broaden the scope of the theory of evolution. 2. The most reliable method for determining evolutionary lineages is a combination of both types of data. Using similarities and differences alone will not suffice because evolution is a variable process that can proceed "backwards" at times, reverting organisms back to their former state under some conditions. To bolster the data taken from simply comparing protist groups structurally, we can use genetic comparison as well. The combination of both types of data creates a more reliable case for evolutionary lineages than either type of data alone. 3. In order to avoid mistaken conclusions based on observational data, scientists should record results precisely and avoid bias as much as possible. They should check their conclusions with other scientists and observations should be conducted repeatedly to confirm findings.

Testing Yourself

1. d; 2. c; 3. a; 4. e; 5. Mitochondria were at one time free-living heterotrophic bacteria. 6. c; 7. b; 8. b; 9. c; 10. Flagella; trypanosomes cause disease, euglenoids contain chloroplasts. Pseudopods; amoeboids sometimes cause disease, foraminiferans and radiolarians form tests. Cilia; ciliates are complex and have trichocysts and undergo conjugation. None; apicomplexans cause diseases. 11. b; 12. c; 13. b; 14. b; 15. d; 16. b; ; 17. a; 18. b; 19. a; 20. b, c; 21. a, d; 22. b; 23. b; 24. b; 25. a; 26. b; 27. c; 28. d; 29. c; 30. a; 31. e; 32. Diatoms have a two valve shell of silica and become diatomaceous earth. Dinoflagellates have two flagella and cellulose plates and are responsible for "red tides." Red algae are variously structured seaweeds and are sources of agar and carrageean. Brown algae are seaweeds harvested for food and are a source of alginate (algin). 33. Brown algae, diatoms, and water molds are traditionally separate groups based on mode of nutrition and/or structure, but they are grouped together in the Stramenopila. This means that their DNA shows they are closely related.

Thinking Scientifically

1. If single cells do not separate, and if each cell divides in a way that allows the cells to join end on end, the end result could be a filament. 2. Merozoites enter red blood cells, and if you knew by what process they enter red blood cells, you might be able to develop a way to stop them from doing so.

Put the Pieces Together

Page 349: 1. Studying the first eukaryotes, the protists, with regard to their diversity of nutrition, reproduction, movement, and organization contributes to the study of biology in many ways. Protists can be used as models in the study of photosynthesis, examined for the role they play in the food chain, and studied for their medical impacts including malaria, dysentery, giardiasis, and Chagas disease. Through understanding the disease-causing ability of some protists, the large role others play in the food chain, or even the discrepancy in size between single-celled and multicellular protists, we gain an understanding of the diversity of life on our planet. 2. An evolutionary approach to relating the protists is a good one because it explores molecular data that can be analyzed more objectively than observational data. By analyzing the genome of protists and comparing it to that of other organisms, we can determine the relationship between the first eukaryotes and organisms like plants and animals. 3. The term kingdom Protista is longer used because of molecular evidence and suggestions that many more kingdoms exist within the diverse group of protists and that protists are not closely related to one another. Some protists are more closely related to plants or animals than to each other. To place them into a kingdom together, then, is inaccurate. The term protist remains because it refers to an organism that is not a plant, animal, or fungi.

CHAPTER 18

Check Your Progress

18.1 Cellulose cell walls, apical cells, plasmodesmata, and alternation of generations that includes protection of the zygote. 18.2 As in all plants the gametophyte produces gametes. 18.3 The sporophyte has vascular tissue and is protected from drying out by a cuticle interrupted by stomata. 18.4 Advantages: The sporophyte embryo is protected from drying out, and the sporophyte produces windblown spores that are resistant to drying out. Disadvantage: The sperm are flagellated and need an outside source of moisture in order to swim to the egg. 18.5 The sporophyte is dominant and lycophytes have vascular tissue. 18.6 The independent gametophyte generation lacks vascular tissue, and it produces flagellated sperm. 18.7 (1) Water is not required for fertilization because pollen grains (male gametophytes) are windblown, and (2) ovules protect female gametophytes and become seeds that disperse the sporophyte, the generation that has vascular tissue. 18.8 Yes, insects do pollinate carnivorous plants, and seeds are produced and enclosed by fruit. The fruit is a dry capsule that contains seeds. 18.9 Fungi have the haploid life cycle in which only the zygote is diploid and the zygote undergoes meiosis to produce haploid spores. Plants have the alternation of generation life cycle in where are are two generations: the sporophyte produces spores by meiosis and the gametophyte produces gametes by mitosis. 18.10 Both are a mutualistic relationship between a fungus and a photosynthesizer and in both the fungus acquires food. 18.11 zyygospore fungi, black bread mold; sac fungi, truffles;club fungi, mushrooms.

Form Your Opinion

Page 364: 1. The plants present in an ancient swamp forest are the evolutionary predecessors of today's plants as well as the source of much of the energy that human beings use in the form of coal. Because we depend on plants for oxygen, food, and the energy produced by decomposed plants from millions of years ago, we are dependent on the plants that gave rise to present day plants. 2. Because the great swamp forest existed in what is now northern Europe, the Ukraine and the Appalachian mountains of the United States, I would predict that they occurred when the continents drifted and coalesced near the equator. Because the forest spanned what are now separate continents, they must have been present at a point when theses continents came together and these regions were near one another in a warm and humid environment not found in all of these locations today. The equator was the perfect setting for the tall seedless vascular plants to thrive before falling into the rising swamp waters.
Page 369: 1. Because it is possible that an infection could wipe out any or all of these three flowering grains, it is unfortunate that humans are so dependent upon only wheat, corn, and rice. To get people to eat more varied grains there would have to be an effort made to market alternative options at affordable prices. 2. In addition to the food they provide us, we are also dependent on plants because they are a source of oxygen, provide us with building materials, medicine, and fuel. We rely on plants for many things and thus could not live without them.
Page 374: 1. Decomposition, nutrient cycling, fermentation (yeast), food (mushrooms), antibiotic production, pest control. 2. No. Many organisms, including fungi and bacteria can be considered "bad" or "good" depending on the specific organism in question. While some fungi cause disease that can harm humans, others are a source of food, nutrient cycling, antibiotics, or pest control. For instance, fungi used for pest control also cause disease, but they do so in pests that might harm crops that humans use as food sources. Thus, all disease causing fungi are not "bad" since some are used to human advantage. 3. Plants can make their own

food and need not live off of another organism for nourishment. A parasite like the fungus that causes athlete's foot can be likened to a predator, such as a lion, because they are heterotrophic and must find and consume food. Predators cannot make their own food either, and must hunt for and consume food.

Testing Yourself

1. a; 2. a; 3.a; 4. e; 5. Tall plants have better access to sunlight. 6. b; 7. a; 8. a; 9. e; 10. c; 11. b; 12. a. stigma; b. style; c. carpel; d. ovary; e. ovule; f. receptacle; g. sepal; h. petal; i. stamen; j. filament; k. anther. 13. a; 14. c; 15. e; 16. Pollen is less likely to be moved from the pollen cone to the seed cone of the same tree. 17. e; 18. e; 19. e; 20. e; 21. a; 22. e; 23. Mycorrhiza fungi are more likely to go along with the seedling in the native soil.

Thinking Scientifically

1. Only group (b) because mosses require a film of moisture in order for flagellated sperm to swim to an egg. 2. Because male moths attempt to mate with these flowers, they carry pollen only between flowers of this type.

Put the Pieces Together

Page 377: 1. It is not a good strategy to have a separate and water dependent gametophyte on land. It is a better strategy for the gametophyte to be protected by the sporophyrw which has vascular tissue. It is also better to have the sperm transported to the egg in a way that does not require external water. 2. DNA is a selfish molecule, copying itself without regard for any other processes taking place in a cell or an organism. The energy expended by plants for reproduction is merely a means to perpetuate the plant's DNA; reproduction, after all, is meant to pass on the genetic information of an organism to later generations so that the species may live on. 3. Yes answer: Reproduction of land plants and animals can be compared, because the adaptations of animals and plants are alike as they moved from aqueous environments to dry land. Both flowering plants and humans are able to protect all stages of their life cycle from drying our internal fertilization are all good adaptations required for reproduction on land. No answer: I do not approve of comparing reproduction in plants to reproduction in humans. Plants often require intervention from other organisms or abiotic factors like wind or water in order to reproduce successfully, while the reproductive process in humans involves direct contact between a male and female.

CHAPTER 19

Check Your Progress

19.1 Bats acquire nutrients from an outside source, ingest food and digest it internally, and have muscles and nerves. 19.2 Yes, because all animals can trace their ancestry to the same protistan ancestor. 19.3 Multicellular; tissue layers; bilateral symmetry, three tissue layers; body cavity; deuterostome development. 19.4 a. Sponges have the cellular level of organization, and bats have the organ-system level of organization; b. No, vampire bats simply have a liquid food, namely blood. 19.5 a. Microscopically, compare the development of cnidarians to that of bats; b. Cnidarians are predators that feed on live protists and small animals. Vampire bats are external parasites that feed on the blood of a host. 19.6 a. Yes; a longitudinal cut would divide the body in two equal halves; b. Bats are not hermaphrodites; the sexes are separate. 19.7 Vampire bats are external parasites; tapeworms and flukes are internal parasites that feed on nutrients meant for their host 19.8 Deuterostomes, as are all vertebrates. 19.9 Both bats and molluscs are multicellular, have three germ layers, have bilateral symmetry, and are coelomates with internal organs. However, molluscs are photostomes and bats are deuterostomes. **19.10** The sequential vertebrae of the spinal column. **19.11** This is not a feature that is used to distinguish relatedness because it appears in both protostomes and deuterostomes. **19.12** a. Bats have jointed appendages, are segmented, and have a well-developed nervous system; b. Bats have an endoskeleton, not an exoskeleton; they all breathe by lungs; and they have reduced competition by diversifying. Some are fruit eaters, some are insect eaters, and some, such as vampire bats, are parasites. **19.13** Spiders, scorpions, millipedes, and centipedes. **19.14** Analogous, because insects and bats do not have a recent common ancestor. **19.15** a. Symmetry. Bats are bilaterally symmetrical and echinoderms are radially symmetrical; b. Both types of animals are deuterostomes. **19.16** As embryos. **19.17** Vertebrae, jaws, bony skeleton, lungs, limbs, amniotic egg, mammary glands. **19.18** Predaceous; actively ingesting chunks of food. **19.19** Yes; they have four limbs. **19.20** It provided a means for reptiles including birds, and mammals to reproduce on land in the absence of external water. **19.21** They are the only mammal that can fly (as opposed to glide) and the only mammal to hang by their feet alone.

Form Your Opinion

Page 389: 1. Before molecular analysis, biologists had to use observational comparison of organisms to decide who was related to whom. By comparing structure, nutrition and developmental information, among other characteristics, biologists did their best to determine relationships between organisms. 2. As seen in the example of the nemertine worm, anatomic data might lead scientists to believe that these organisms are closely related to flat worms; however, DNA data shows a closer relationship to the annelids and mollusks. Because of the complex evolutionary relationship between organisms, it is best if anatomic and DNA data support the same conclusion. 3. Biologists should certainly go into the field to study organisms. Observation of an organism within its natural environment is extremely important in understanding behavioral characteristics, reproduction and nutrition, for example. Therefore, the study of organisms should take place in the field as well as in the lab.
Page 406: 1. Scientists think that it is unlikely that viruses will cross the species barrier; however, this has occurred in the past and may likely occur again due to the suppressed immune system of the human recipient along with the novelty of the animal disease(s) that may or may not be known human pathogens. Other unseen health consequences could result from the rapid and violent rejection of organs belonging to animal species that might lead to the death of the human recipient. There is also some concern over the genetic programming of humans versus animals: pigs, for example, age at a different rate than humans, presenting challenges in making any permanent transplants. 2. Yes answer: it is ethical to change the genetic makeup of vertebrates for use in drug or organ "manufacturing" so long as the animal is not harmed or killed in the process. No answer: It is not ethical to alter the vertebrate, use it as a factory or incubator, and then kill it in the process of harvesting the desired product. 3. It is possible that we are altering the relationship between humans and other vertebrates in a mutually detrimental way. The relationship between humans and the rest of the natural world should not be one of human expoitation and should avoid using vertebrates solely for our own purposes. If we slowly begin to alter every aspect of the planet for our own benefit, we may be forced to face consequences we never imagined possible.

Testing Yourself

1. d; 2. e; 3. e; 4. a; 5. b; 6. a; 7. e; 8. d; 9. d; 10. b; 11. a; 12. Flatworms are small, have a large absorptive surface, and are hermaphroditic. 13. e; 14. c; 15. e.; 16. a; 17. e; 18. b; 19. e; 20. Traditional fossils show how evolution occurred.

Thinking Scientifically

1. As per Section 19.1, study whole sponges and determine how they acquire food, whether they move, how they reproduce, and what developmental stages they have. Microscopically, determine the structure and function of their cells. 2. a. DNA/RNA sequencing; b. The data mentioned in Section 15.7: Fossil record and homologies in anatomy and development.

Put the Pieces Together

Page 409: 1. Ancestral protist, multicellularity, tissue layers, bilateral symmetry and 3 tissue layers and body cavity, deuterstome development, anestral chordates, vertebrae, jaws, bony skeleton, lungs, limbs, amniotic egg, mammary glands, mammals, humans (16 steps). 2. The advantages of the parasitic way of life include the reliance of a parasite on its host for food, shelter, and a place to disperse offspring with little to no energy expelnded by the parasite. Parasites, specialized for their way of life, can also reproduce at higher rates (more quickly and in greater numbers) than their host. The disadvantages of the parasitic way of life include dealing with any harm done to the host from the parasite leeching nutrients and invading the host organism. Parasites reduce the "fitness" of their host organism while increasing their "fitness" via exploitation of the host. 3. The relationship or sharing of a common descent, between humans and echinoderms can teach us that over time, changes in organisms including specialization, adaptation, and mutation create new organisms that may appear to have little in common though they originate from some common place in evolutionary history.

CHAPTER 20

Check Your Progress

20.1 Yes, because Ardi was a primate. **20.2** Mammalian ancestor to a common ancestor with prosimians; anthropoids, hominoids, and finally hominins in that order. **20.3** Ardi's features, including bipedalism, means that she is a hominin, even though her brain is small. **20.4** Southern African specimens were bipedal, but the arms were longer than the legs. Lucy, an East African species, was bipedal, and the arms were shorter than the legs. **20.5** This migration accounts for how the first Homo species arrived in Asia and Europe out of Africa. **20.6** An incomplete fossil record and the sudden appearance of Cro Magnon in Africa. **20.7** Their tool-making ability and other cultural attributes such as their artisitc talents. **20.8** a. People from any two ethnic groups produce fertile offspring. b. within ethnic groups.

Form Your Opinion

Page 420: 1. Culture is evident in almost all aspects of my daily life. Culture exists in traditions of cooking, eating, making a home, and using tools for cleaning, cooking, hanging a picture, creating written documents or drawing. 2. Aspects of my life that are influenced solely by biological inheritance have nothing to do with culture. For instance, I breathe, I eat, and I sleep because of the biology of being human. 3. Though our sources of food may be different than the hunter-gatherers, we still function in a similar manner, bringing nourishment back to a central location from a grocery store, farm, restaurant, etc. Also, it is still more customary for

women to stay home to take care of the young and for men to go out and be aggressive in order to maintain the home base.
Page 423: 1. Many U.S. citizens can trace their ancestry to forbearers in the various other continents. This means they are descended from immigrants. This does not involve a migration pattern. 2. Yes, as humans migrated from continent to continent, genetic drift (founder effect) would have occurred and may have contributed to the similarity between members of a common ethnicity, but natural selection would have also occurred to favor advantageous phenotypes for the new environment. For instance, close to the equator and exposed to hot sun, darker pigments in the skin would have been beneficial and thus evolutionarily favorable. 3. I think that migration patterns show that all humans are related to one another. Studies that examine mtDNA show relatedness of populations on separate continents. The founder effect helps explain how differences in appearance might result from decreased genetic variation in a region inhabited by a small population. Natural selection helps to explain evolution of groups with different skin color, hair color or texture, and eye color.

Testing Yourself

1.a; 2. c; 3. common ancestor for prosimians, anthropoids, hominoids, hominins; 4. e; 5. Ardi evolved before Lucy and yet it has fewer chimp-like features than Lucy has; 6. d; 7. b; 8. b; 9. b; 10. d; 11. e; 12. b; 13. d; 14. e; 15 b; 16. Darwinian evolution is dependent on genetic differences, and biocultural evolution is dependent on advances that cannot be inherited. The ability to learn is inherited and learning is necessary to biocultural evolution. 17. c; 18. a; 19. c; 20. d; 21. d; 22. a. modern humans; b. archaic humans; c. Homo erectus; d. Homo erectus; e. Homo ergaster. 23. d; 24. There is more variation within ethnic groups. This tells us that all humans are one species.

Thinking Scientifically

1. The benefits of bipedalism must have outweighed the cost or else bipedalism wouldn't have evolved. 2. Sequence the Neandertal genome using DNA from Neandertal bones, and compare the sequence to the human genome of today. Look for sequences present in both genomes.

Put the Pieces Together

Page 427: 1. See page 382 figure 19.3A, and page 414 figure 20.2A. 2. I would suggest that biocultural evolution, "in which natural selection is influenced by cultural achievements rather than by anatomic phenotype," is more influential today than human biological evolution because of modern inventions like technology and medicine. Humans now have the ability to adapt to the environment through man-made methods including treating illness, and moving from one climate to another. Populations in regions without technology to keep water clean and treat illness are less successful than groups with clean water and medical care. 3. Through education we can explain the necessity of preserving habitats of organisms other than ourselves, and explain how biodiversity is necessary to the preservation of our planet and all its inhabitants including humans. Education could be used to demonstrate what happens when small or large changes are made to an ecosystem.

CHAPTER 21

Check Your Progress

21.1 When water is plentiful, leaves grow larger, maximizing solar absorption. When water is not available, narrow leaves help conserve water.

21.2 Eudicot. **21.3** Collenchyma cells have areas of thicker primary cell walls, without having an entirely rigid secondary cell wall. **21.4** Xylem is located in the vascular cylinder of a root, the vascular bundles of a stem, and in the leaf veins of a leaf. **21.5** Shoot apical meristem produces more stem (including vascular bundles), axillary buds, leaves, and sometimes flowers. **21.6** It would signify a consistent amount of rainfall rather than a wet followed by a dry spell. **21.7** Epidermis protects, allows gas exchange, and regulates water loss. Closely packed epidermal cells covered by a waxy cuticle prevent water loss; however the stomata particularly on the lower surface allow gas exchange. The stomata close when water is scarce. Trichomes particularly on the upper suface help protect a plant from parasites. **21.8** Fungus roots help supply a plant with the water needed for photosynthesis; defense mechanisms prevent hungry insects from eating leaves; the organization of a plant is geared to carrying on photosynthesis.

Form Your Opinion

Page 435: 1. No answer: I do not find the consumption of an embryo, in the form of a grain, disturbing. Eating any plant is eating a living organism, and eating a steak, or chicken, or pork, is eating what used to be a living organism. Because nearly everything I consume used to be alive, eating grains, the embryos of plants, does not disturb me. Yes answer: I find it disturbing because of the word "embryo" and my tendency to equate that word with something immature that needs my help to become mature. 2. No answer: I would not mind eating only grains so that more people could be fed. Since grains provide more energy and cattle are polluting the environment, I would be happy to eat grains and not cattle. Grain can continue to be planted and harvested while cattle must be taken care of until old enough to be used as food. Yes answer: I would mind eating only grains so that more people could be fed. I like eating beef and want to continue to do so. People have been consuming cattle and other animals for some time and need to consider that our rapidly growing population needs all sorts of foods. **Page 443:** 1. Trees take in carbon dioxide, the byproduct of breathing in humans and animals, give off oxygen needed by most forms of life. Autotrophic plants produce sugar, the ultimate source of energy for animals and humans. Trees also create habitats above the ground for birds and many other animals. Because trees put oxygen into the atmosphere while removing carbon dioxide, provide energy for animals and humans in the form of sugar produced through photosynthesis, and create above ground habitats, they have and will continue to play a necessary role in the life of humans.

Testing Yourself

1. c; 2. c; 3. b; 4. c; 5. a; 6. Terminal bud is at the shoot tip and produces cells that add to the length of the stem and become new leaves and new axillary buds. Axillary bud activity produces new branches (and flowers). 7. A cereal grain is a dry fruit that contains a seed. 8. b; 9. c; 10. c; 11. b; 12. a; 13. d; 14. e; 15. c; 16. d; 17. a; 18. d; 19. b; 20. b; 21. b; 22. They all consists of parenchyma cells that fill the interior of an organ. 23. e; 24. c; 25. b; 26. b; 27. e; 28. c; 29. b; 30. Apical meristem (shoot tip and root tip meristem) is responsible for primary growth and the result is increase in the length of stem and root. Vascular cambium is responsible for secondary growth and the result is increase in girth. Girth increases because secondary xylem builds up as annual rings (wood). 31. c; 32. a. Broader expanse to collect sunlight; b. Prevents loss of water; c. Collects sunlight; d. Allows gas exchange; e. Allows carbon

dioxide to enter and water to exit. 33. Photosynthesis allows a plant to produce the building blocks and ATP it needs to maintain metabolism and its structure. 34. e; 35. d; 36. b; 37. a; 38. c; 39. e

Thinking Scientifically

1. Confirm that plamodesmata do run between companion cells and sieve-tube members. Same as Palade, use labeled amino acids to show that proteins pass by way of plasmodesmata from companion cells to sieve-tube members. 2. Zone of cell division slides should show small cells dividing; zone of elongation slides should show cells that are longer than the previous zone—no cell division is occurring; zone of maturation should show mature tissues and epidermal cells with root hairs.

Put the Pieces Together

Page 449: 1. The presence of an epidermis and cuticle, stomata that open and close based upon the surrounding conditions, a root system, and a stem to carry water from the roots to leaves and flowers is evidence enough to convince me that the vegetative organs of plants have adapted to living on land. 2. A bush has more stems leading to its increased number of leaves, providing more vascular tissue for them. 3. Rhizomes provide an efficient way for plants to asexually multiply because each shoot represents an offspring of the parent plant.

CHAPTER 22

Check Your Progress

22.1 We will see that transport of sugar requires a functional plasma membrane. **22.2** Transpiration provides a means of transport for water and minerals and helps maintain internal leaf temperatures by providing evaporative cooling. **22.3** Cellular respiration, which requires oxygen, takes place in plant cells, even in the dark. **22.4** The roots are the source, and the flowers are the sink. **22.5** a. Nitrogen and sulfur are needed to form protein, and all plant roots take up nitrate (NO_3^-) and sulfate (SO_4^{2-}) from the soil; b. Nitrogen and phosphate (HPO_4^{2-}) are needed to make nucleic acids, and plant roots also take up phosphate from the soil. **22.6** The nonpolar tails of phospholipid molecules make the center of the plasma membrane nonpolar. **22.7** Plants develop root nodules when the amount of nitrate in the soil is not sufficient to support growth.

Form Your Opinion

Page 453: 1. Because of their remarkably long lives and great size, I would expect that redwoods are good competitors. Their shallow roots, capture water as it seeps into the ground from rainfall. Their thick fire-resistant bark allows them to survive a fire when other plants would burn. 2. Plant native grasses, trees, and shrubs along ditches or other unusable parts of land to prevent runoff and erosion, and promote insects that are natural pollinators and predators. Use pesticides sparingly and with deliberate attempts to avoid spraying during risky times for local insects, fish, or other wildlife. Plant various crops including those useful for ground cover. 3. I am certainly willing to eat new grains in order for farmers to increase biodiversity. Maintaining biodiversity is good for the planet as a whole. If simple changes like eating habits can assist in keeping our planet a suitable home for many organisms, I'd be happy to do so. **Page 457:** 1. Plants are a source of food, make oxygen, take in carbon dioxide, provide shelter, serve as building materials, clean up nitrate pollution, grow materials used for clothing like cotton, produce or aid in production of medicines, and serve to preserve soil. 2. Find some way to prevent pets and other animals from having access

to these plants; actully it would be best to stop polluting the biosphere; then, we would not have to use plants to rid an area of the pollutant. 3. Society has to be willing to pay the cost of cleaning up the environment or else people and other living things may perish. I personally would be willing to pay a price for the rare and beneficial service of a plant that could filter pollutants from soil or water to benefit the environment.

Testing Yourself

1. a; 2. Leaves must receive water for photosynthesis, and they produce sugar as a result of photosynthesis. 3. c; 4. d; 5 Atmospheric pressure cannot account for the ability of water to rise above 76 cm in a plant. However, transpiration does allow water to rise above 76 cm. 6. c; 7. d; 8. e; 9. c; 10. d; 11. b; 12. a; 13. e; 14. Water enters the first bulb by osmosis and this creates a pressure flow that moves the solute to the second bulb and beyond. 15. c; 16. d; 17. b; 18. d; 19. a; 20. b; 21. e; 22. c; 23. e; 24. c

Thinking Scientifically

1. Due to diversity, some species may not be susceptible to the assault. Also, the susceptible plants may be protected by the unsusceptible. For example, insects may not find all the susceptible plants, or most of the available water will go to those plants that need it. 2. Divide a large number of identical plants into control and experimental groups. Both groups are to receive the same treatment, including all necessary nutrients, but the experimental group will not be given any calcium. It is expected that only the experimental group will suffer any ill effects. If only the control or if both groups do poorly, some unknown variable is affecting the results.

Put the Pieces Together

Page 467: 1. Plants require inorganic nutrients from the environment in order to build organic molecules necessary for life. Carbohydrates are used to form their cell walls and to respire. Cellular respiration provides the plant's cells with energy. 2. Plant cells absorb water and minerals through their root systems. The minerals are taken into the cells in their charged or ionic forms. The movement of ions across the plant cell plasma membrane requires active transport but it allows plants to concentrate minerals in their cells. When animals consume plants, they take in these concentrated minerals. 3. It is beneficial to have xylem and phloem in the same vascular bundle because in this way they are supported by the same sclerenchyma cells (in stems) and are surrounded by the same bundle sheath cells (in leaves).

CHAPTER 23

Check Your Progress

23.1 Different second messengers can bring about various cellular activities in the same or different types of plant cells. **23.2** Yes, because if the hormone remained, it would continue to trigger a response long after the response was no longer needed. For example, it would bring about bending after the light source was no longer present. **23.3** The plant in (a) most likely doesn't produce gibberellin, and the receptor in (b) is more likely defective. **23.4** You could apply cytokinins to increase the number of cells and gibberellins to increase the size of the cells. **23.5** a. Abscisic acid maintains dormancy and closes stomata; b. Gibberellins have the opposite effect. **23.6** To be an effective hormone, a molecule needs only to combine with its receptor. **23.7** It is adaptive for roots to grow toward water because it enhances their ability to extract water and dissolve minerals from the soil for plant tissues. **23.8** Rotation will prevent the statoliths from settling and triggering differential growth. Therefore, neither the root nor the shoot is expected to curve up or down. **23.9** These animals are nocturnal, so it would be a waste of energy to produce scent during the day. **23.10** Red light converts P_r to P_{fr}; P_{fr} binds to a transcription factor; and the complex moves to the nucleus, where it binds to DNA so that genes are turned on or off. **23.11** The plant is responding to a short night, not to the length of the day. **23.12** Most likely not. Many activities of organisms are simply adaptations to the environment that occur automatically.

Form Your Opinion

Page 484: 1. Humans rely upon plants as a source of food and oxygen as well as filters to remove carbon dioxide from the air. Plants provide human beings with the raw materials for shelter, a means to clean up nitrate pollution, grow materials used for clothing like cotton, produce or aid in production of medicines, and tools in soil preservation. 2. Some secondary metabolites produced by plants for defense, can inhibit cellular respiration and block DNA or RNA synthesis, making them useful in the fight against cancer.

Testing Yourself

1. c; 2. a; 3. d; 4. a; 5. c; 6. c; 7. d; 8. e; 9. d; 10. d; 11. b; 12. e; 13. a; 14. c; 15. Place the banana in a closed container with a ripened fruit. 16. d; 17. c; 18. d; 19. e; 20. a. active form of phytochrome, b. biological response, c. far-red light; d. red light 21. c; 22. b; 23. e; 24. a; 25. e; 26. b; 27. d

Thinking Scientifically

1. Use a plant that tracks the sun as your experimental material. Make tissue slides to confirm the presence of a pulvinus, as in Figure 23.9. Apply ABA to live pulvinus tissue under the microscope to test for the results described in Figure 23.9. 2. Shine a light underneath a plant growing on its side (see Fig. 23.8A, upper left). If the stem now curves down, the phototropic response is greater than the gravitropic response and your hypothesis is not supported.

Put the Pieces Together

Page 487: 1. Population: Members of a plant population that opened and closed their stomata morning and night had an advantage over plants that did not do this. Organism: Sunlight acts as a stimulus that causes stomata to open during the day; the absence of sunlight causes stomata to close. Cellular: When K^+ enters guard cells, water follows, and stomata open. When K^+ exits guard cells water follows, and stomata close. Abscisic acid brings about closure of stomata in a plant that is water stressed. 2. (1) Reception of the stimulus: red light, in day light, activates phytochrome. (2) Transduction of the stimulus: activated phytochrome moves into the nucleus, binding specific proteins, and activating specific genes. (3) Response to the stimulus: Flowering occurs. 3. Auxins: suppress lateral growth; Gibberellins: result in stem (internode) growth; Cytokinins: stimulate cell division; Abscisic acid: promotes dormancy; Ethylene: causes abscission of leaves; therefore reduces growth.

CHAPTER 24

Check Your Progress

24.1 Pollen grains (the male gametophytes) are visible when the anther releases them. To find the female gametophyte, you would have to microscopically examine the contents of an ovule just before fertilization takes place. **24.2** One sperm unites with the egg to form an embryo and the other combines with two polar nuclei forming a triploid (3n)

endosperm cell. **24.3** The ovule is a sporophyte structure produced by the female parent. Therefore, the ovule wall (becomes seed coat) is 2n. The embryo inside the ovule is the product of fertilization and is, therefore, 2n. **24.4** Showy, colorful flowers attract pollinators; colorful fruit that is a good food source attracts animals which transport seeds away from the parent plant. **24.5** The sheaths protect the shoot and root apical meristems from damage as they push through the soil. **24.6** Advantages to asexual reproduction include: (1) By passes the requirements for sexual reproduction: gamete production, pollination, seed production and dispersal. (2) if the parent is ideally suited for the environment of a given area, the offspring will be as well. **24.7** a. Either somatic embryogenesis or meristem tissue culture. b. Cell suspension culture would allow you to collect chemicals produced by a plant.

Form Your Opinion

Page 492: 1. A series of mutations are needed for a non-seed life cycle to evolved into the seed life cycle: (1) Sporophyte produces heterospores that develop into microscopic male and female gametophytes. (2) Female gametophyte is retained by sporophyte (3) Male gametophyte becomes pollen grain. (4) Following fertilization, the embryo sac becomes a seed. (5) Seed contains sporophyte embryo, food, and seed coat. 2. Humans are reproductively adapted to protect all stages of reproduction in a dry environment, much like seed plants. Human gametes are housed in the ovaries and testes and fertilization occurs internally. A fertilized egg implants in the uterus and is protected and nourished here until it is mature enough for birth and development outside the body of the mother. 3. Flowers and seed cones both bear ovules that develop into seeds. Ovules first contain a megaspore and then a female gametophyte. Following fertilization, both flowers and seed cones produce seeds. Only the seeds of angiosperm are protected by fruit. A seed cone plays no part in the development of pollen as most flowers do.

Page 493: 1. Observe several different flower types and and see if they are visited by only one type or several types of pollinators. 2. The efficiency of wind pollination is most likely low since gymnosperms produce a large amount of pollen.

Testing Yourself

1. b; 2. b; 3. a; 4. e; 5. a. anther; b. filament; c. stamen; d. stigma; e. style; f. ovary; g. ovule; h. carpel. 6. d; 7. c; 8. b; 9. a; 10. e; 11. c; 12. d; 13. b; 14. d; 15. a; 16. A wind pollinated plant produces more pollen because the method of pollen transfer is less efficient. 17. b; 18. a; 19. e; 20. c; 21. b; 22. d; 23. e; 24. The need for a period of cold weather helps ensure that the seeds germinate when the weather will be favorable to continued growth. 25. c; 26. e; 27. a; 28. When the environment is not changing or when male and female plants are not in close proximity.

Thinking Scientifically

1. Study (a) the anatomy of the wasp and flower, trying to determine if the mouth parts of the wasp are suitable for collecting nectar from this flower; (b) Study the appearance of the flower in sunlight/ ultraviolet light to determine suitability to the vision of the wasp; and (c) Study the behavior of the wasp to see if it is compatible to that of the flower (i.e. flower is open when wasp is active). 2. Protoplasts can be made from leaf cells and then cultured to grow entire plants. These plants are expected to produce seeds that you can use to propagate the plant.

Put the Pieces Together

Page 503: 1. Within the seeds of angiosperms, the endosperm provides nutrients. 2. (1) Flowers have

benefited from the use of animals in pollination. This has made flowers successful reproducers on land, producing more seeds. Animals have benefited from this relationship because they received food in the form of sugary nectar from plants. (2) Fruit produced by plants, eaten by animals, has aided flowering plants in seed dispersal. In this relationship, the animal also benefits from the nutrition received from the fruit of the flowering plant. 3. Flowering plants (but not ferns) produce (1) two types of spores, microspores and megaspores and (2) two types of gametophytes: male and female gametophytes.

CHAPTER 25

Check Your Progress

25.1 Fur traps heat and does not release it. **25.2** Evaporative cooling; water in sweat absorbs heat energy to become vapor. **25.3** Polar bear; adipose tissue helps keep the polar bear warm and is a source of nutrients when food is scarce. **25.4** Blood vessels taking blood to the surface constrict in order to reduce heat loss through the skin. **25.5** Dendrites are numerous and gather input from other neurons; the long axon is appropriate for conveying nervous impulses some distance. **25.6** The thick skin of a gila monster helps prevent the loss of water, rather than helping to regulate body temperature. However, a thick skin would help lessen the gain of heat in a warm environment. **25.7** Sensory receptors respond to a change in body temperature and communicate this information to the brain, which then commands motor activity to perform the behavior that will warm or cool the body, as needed. **25.8** Enzymatic reactions are necessary to the life of a cell, and enzymes function best at a moderate body temperature. **25.9** An early morning cool body temperature causes the lizard to move into the sun, where it stays until the body temperature is too hot, causing the lizard to seek shade. Thus, its behavior alternates back and forth.

Form Your Opinion

Page 514: 1. Yes, I am willing to contribute to stem cell research if my involvement could give someone the ability to regain function in their limbs, to walk again, for example. We all engage in voluntary activities that can cause injury. No, I am not willing to contribute to stem cell research because stem cell research is a controversial field of science and medicine. 2. I believe it is unfair to limit new and innovative therapies to the well-known or wealthy and it should be available to any one. 3. Yes, celebrities, like Christopher Reeve, should be used to increase interest in nervous system regeneration research. Putting a recognizable name and face on science and its potential advancements can be advantageous to everyone involved. No, celebrities should not be used to endorse or publicize causes like nervous system regeneration research. By involving celebrities the treatment might become political.

Page 520: 1. For instance, the brain must communicate with the heart and lungs in order for heart to pump blood and the lungs exchange gases in a coordinated manner. 2. A terrestrial animal but not an aquatic one has the added burden of water conservation. 3. Our skin prevents water loss, our large intestine absorbs water and our kidneys can excrete a hypertonic urine if we do not drink enough that day. Blood volume is maintained so that tissue fluid can provide an aquatic environment for our cells.

Testing Yourself

1. c; 2. a; 3. a; 4. d; 5. e; 6. d; 7. b; 8. d; 9. The dendrites offer wide surface area for the reception of stimuli and the long axon is suitable for the transmission of stimuli. 10. a, c, g; 11. b, d, e;

12. b, c, f; 13. a; 14. b; 15. c; 16. Epithelial cells are exposed to mutagens (agents that cause mutations) in the environment. Also, high rate of cell division means that spontaneous mutations may occur that lead to cancer. 17. e; 18. c; 19. The epidermis is composed of stratified epithelium, which provides an impenetrable barrier to invasion by microorganisms. 20. a; 21. b; 22. e; 23. d; 24. e; 25. c; 26. a; 27. a; 28. e; 29. Shivering is due to muscle contraction which gives off heat. 30. You would expect the cardiovascular system to have a pump (the heart) to move a liquid (blood) through tubular vessels.

Thinking Scientifically

1. Examine the tissue visually, trying to determine the particular organ before preparing microscope slides so that you can compare the slides you have made to known tissue slides. 2. Test two groups: (1) People who visit tanning salons, say two or more times a week. (2) People who never vistit tanning salons. Find out how many people in each group have been treated for skin cancer. Compare the percentages and determine if the difference is significant.

Put the Pieces Together

Page 523: 1. When the human body is cold, signals are sent to the bones and muscles to initiate movement which results in shivering. Shivering increases blood flow and body temperature. As soon as possible humans move to a more suitable environment to achieve homeostasis. 2. People who travel to the South Pole wear special clothing and take shelters that help maintain body temperature and prevent water loss. People who walk in space have a space suit that maintains their normal environment and provides them with the support systems they need (e.g., availability of oxygen). 3. No, because blood and tissue fluid are external to cells. Yes, because blood and tissue fluid are inside the body.

CHAPTER 26

Check Your Progress

26.1 a. neurons and neuroglia; interneurons; b. sensory neurons and motor neurons **26.2** a. It distributes the ions appropriately because Na$^+$ is pumped to the outside of an axon, and K$^+$ is pumped to the inside. b. Na$^+$ moves to the inside of the axon and then K$^+$ moves to the outside of an axon. **26.3** Saltatory conduction. **26.4** Neurotransmitters that cross the synaptic cleft. **26.5** Inhibition of AChE would cause ACh to remain in a synapse. A drug that interferes with neurotransmitter breakdown enhances its action. **26.6** The neurons of the brain receive signals via the spinal cord from all the rest of the nervous system. **26.7** A chimpanzee's brain would be very similar to ours but smaller. **26.8** When sleeping occurs, the sleep center is active and the RAS is inactive. **26.9** The amygdala adds emotional overtones to experiences. **26.10** Without the PNS, the CNS would neither receive stimuli nor be able to direct a response to the stimuli. **26.11** a. spinal cord; b. brain **26.12** Sensing danger because of input from sensory receptors, the brain sends nerve impulses via the spinal cord to the skeletal musces and to nerve fibers of the sympathetic division of the autonomic system. The sympathetic division shuts down unnecessary functions and enhances those that can help manage the crises.

Form Your Opinion

Page 533: 1. Both animals have a central and peripheral nervous system. Planarians have a ladder-like nervous system with two nerve chords connected to the cerebral ganglia and extend to the posterior end of the body. Transverse nerves connect the nerve chords and the ganglia to the eye spots. The human nervous system is composed of a brain, and spinal cord from which branches a network of nerves throughout the body. 2. The arthropod nerve cord is ventrally placed while the vertebrate nerve cord is dorsally placed. 3. No, the structure and function of the nervous system in all mammals is about the same.

Testing Yourself

1. d; 2. c; 3. b; 4. a; 5. b; 6. New characters often arise by modifications of previously evolved characters. 7. c; 8. b; 9. Myelination enables signals to travel quickly down an axon, which helps motor skills. 10. a; 11. c; 12. d; 13. e; 14. Learning requires the formation fo new associations and this is mirrored in the brain by the formation of new synapses. 15. a central canal; b. gray matter; c. white matter; d. interneuron; e. dorsal root ganglion; f. cell body of motor neuron; 16. a; 17. d; 18. d; 19. d; 20. They affect the limbic system and either promote or decrease the action of a particular neurotransmitter.

Thinking Scientifically

1. Administer a medication that interferes with the reception of norepinephrine at a synapse. The patient may not respond properly to a real danger. 2. Severed sensory neurons are still releasing neurotransmitters in the spinal cord, resulting in messages to the brain that are interpreted as pain in the limb.

Put the Pieces Together

Page 547: 1. The nervous system is composed of two parts, the brain and spinal cord (central nervous system) and the nerves and ganglia (peripheral nervous system). The central nervous system receives information from the body, integrates it , and sends instructions to the body's muscles and glands via the nerves of the peripheral nervous system. They respond. 2. Neurons are the functional units of both the CNS and the PNS; therefore, every thought, feeling, and emotion we have and action we take is dependent on the nerve impulse and transmission across a synapse. 3. The limbic system influences motor output by its communication with the forebrain.

CHAPTER 27

Check Your Progress

27.1 Eyes are sensitive to visible light rays and sometimes to ultraviolet rays, both of which are part of the electromagnetic spectrum. **27.2** Eyes receive stimuli and initiate nerve impulses; the optic nerve sends impulses to the brain; and the visual cortex of the brain interprets the stimuli, resulting in formation of an image. **27.3** a. Pheromones combine with a chemoreceptor that initiates a nerve impulse; b. Pheromones are signals sent by one member of a species to affect the behavior of another member. **27.4** No, photoreceptors contain pigments that absorb light. **27.5** The color we see is dependent upon which combination of cones is stimulated. **27.6** The compound eye has many independent visual units, but the retina of the camera-type eye is one large visual unit. **27.7** A lens can accommodate—change shape as needed. **27.8** a. Ganglion cell layer, bipolar cell layer, rod and cone cell layer; b. Rod and cone cell layer, bipolar cell layer, ganglion cell layer (whose axons form the optic nerve). **27.9** Maintain muscle tone and help maintain the body's balance and posture. **27.10** outer: gather sound waves; middle:amplify sound waves; inner: hearing **27.11** Bending of hair cells is a mechanical event. **27.12** a. When the head rotates cupulas are displaced and this causes stereocilia in the ampullae of the semicircular canals to bend. b. When the head bends, otoliths are displaced causing a membrane in the utricle and saccule to sag and stereocilia to bend.

Form Your Opinion

Page 555: 1. Damage to the retina will cause loss of vision; other damages may be repaired. For example, inflammation of the conjunctivae, may cause some blurring of vision but if treated , vision will improve. 2. Yes answer: My vision is important to me for my safety as well as enjoyment of the world around me. No answer: I would rather enjoy life as I like and be willing to take the consequences.

Page 556: 1. This is reasonable because of cultural influences that make a person seem disabled if they wear glasses or that make them they are "nerds". However, I think it is wise to disregard any stigmatism and do what is best for oneself. 2. Everyone should weigh the consequences of their actions and after being well informed, do what is best for them.

Page 561: 1. I would rather participate in rock concerts and exercise classes with the aid of earplugs to preserve my hearing. 2. We should not be annoyed because it could be too that they did protect their hearing and their hearing loss is due to no fault of their own.

Page 564: 1. It shows that evolution makes use of the structures available to it rather than inventing something new. 2. The inner ear of mammals evolved from our predecessors, water dwelling animals. As such, it would make evolutionary sense that the inner ear of mammals makes use of fluid pressure waves, as our aquatic ancestors would have. 3. Mammals evolved on land and use vision as well as sound to detect the presence of other organisms. Sound waves are amplified by the presence of three ossicles surrounded by air in the middle ear.

Testing Yourself

1. e; 2. c; 3. The brain requires input from sensory receptors in order to produce sensations about the world at large. 4. a; 5. See Fig. 27.6; 6. near object; 7. d; 8. c; 9. c; 10. c; 11. b; 12. e; 13. d; 14. c; 15. Both procedures can correct an inability to focus properly; The first with an artificial lens and the second by changing the shape of the cornea. 16. Rather than visual information, a blind person uses information from proprioceptors in joints and tendons and touch receptors for example in the buttocks to know they are sitting in a chair. 17. See Fig. 27.10; 18. a; 19. a; 20. c; 21. c; 22. c; 23. c; 24. b; 25. a; 26. b

Thinking Scientifically

1. One possible answer: The size of the auditory cortex is larger in those who have perfect pitch. Test the pitch ability of subjects, and then stimulate the brain directly to determine the size of the auditory cortex.
2. LASIK surgery only corrects the shape of the cornea in order to achieve 20/20 vision.

Put the Pieces Together

Page 567: 1. Human beings' keenest senses are probably hearing and vision, which would have been adaptive for a primate dwelling on land and seeking food and shelter and protection in trees. 2. Parents use touch, vision and sound to bond with their children. Birds use the same senses. 3. I would give up taste as a weight control mechanism.

CHAPTER 28

Check Your Progress

28.1 Exoskeletons and endoskeletons are likely to be a part of the fossil record because they do not decompose, as do the soft hydrostatic skeletons of animals. **28.2** The bones provide a frame for the body after death. Even disconnected bones can help a forensics expert determine what the person looked like. **28.3** skull: zygomatic and parietal bone; rib cage: sternum; vertebral column: sacrum. **28.4** Gender of the individual and the condition of the pubic symphysis, which gives an indication of age. **28.5** A long bone in the appendicular skeleton, such as the humerus or the femur, would be suitable for calculating height. **28.6** As we age, the joints deteriorate, so their condition can be used to roughly indicate age. **28.7** During shivering, the skeletal muscles contract quite rapidly, generating heat, which can help maintain normal body temperature. **28.8** More motor units are recruited to lift three books. **28.9** A myofibril is a long, cylindrical structure in a muscle cell. A sarcomere is a section of a myofibril. **28.10** The events shown in Figure 28.10B #1–3. **28.11** A neuromuscular junction occurs between an axon terminal and a muscle cell; a synapse occurs between an axon terminal of one neuron and either the dendrite or cell body of the next neuron. **28.12** The CP pathway uses creatine phosphate. **28.13** To a degree—for example, a weight lifter would have larger bones with larger protuberances. If the musculature could be observed, it would be well developed.

Form Your Opinion

Page 575: 1. A larger human brain and upright posture might be evolutionarily connected because as walking upright evolved, increased brain size was also needed to ensure the coordination and balance required for upright posture. 2. Arthritis, tendonitis, ligament tears and other injuries suggest that the knee is not fully adapted to bearing weight. Also, the knees are subject to injury when playing sports.
Page 578: 1. We should give people the benefit of the doubt because knowledge about osteoporosis is relatively new some people are more prone to the disease than others. 2. Screening for osteoporosis should be part of any type of physical exam. 3. Payment for health insurance should be on a sliding scale dependent on the health habits of the individual. Smoking can be detected by chronic bronchitis; lack of exercise can be detected by their musculature.
Page 581: 1. People say they are too busy, do not belong to a gym, and don't know how to work it into their daily lives. However, many alternative methods for exercising can be done even at home. 2. It is not helpful and it would be more accurate to say that results do not come without work.

Testing Yourself

1. a; 2. c; 3. e; 4. b; 5. c; 6. b; 7. c; 8. b; 9. f; 10. c; 11. e; 12. c; 13. d; 14. a; 15. c; 16. a; 17. e; 18. b; 19. Pelvic girdle is too small for a normal delivery. 20. a; 21. b; 22. c; 23. b; 24. d; 25. a; 26. e; 27. Unless they were attached, myosin couldn't cause the actin filaments to move thereby shortening sarcomeres. 28. b; 29. a; 30. a

Thinking Scientifically

1. Remove muscle tissue from a corpse in rigor mortis, slice it thin. While watching under the microscope, flood your slide with ATP and necessary ions to see if muscle relaxes and then contracts. 2. Acquire two test groups: aerobic instructors and confirmed couch potatoes. Oxygen tanks supply their only air, while they are running on a tread mill. Those who routinely exercise have more mitochondria than those who do not exercise, accounting for why the first group uses less oxygen and has less lactate (lactic acid) in their blood.

Put the Pieces Together

Page 587: 1. Animals are heterotrophs and have to seek their food. Nerves and muscles assist animals in pursuing their way of life, whether being a predator or escaping predation. 2. To take an example, the pelvis and femur meet in a ball and socket, a synovial joint that allows for the rotational mobility of the hip, while the fibrous joints of the skull are immovable. These immovable joints have an important function since the bones of the skull must remain intact in order to protect the brain. There are three types of muscles: (1) Skeletal muscles are striated for strength and voluntary contraction when needed to move bones. (2) Cardiac muscle is striated for strength, but involuntary, ensuring that the heart continues to beat. (3) Smooth muscle is nonstriated and involuntary, ensuring that the muscles of the digestive tract always perform peristalsis. 3. Jointed appendages allow arthropods and vertebrates to perform flexible movements needed for walking, running, jumping on land.

CHAPTER 29

Check Your Progress

29.1 Open systems utilize hemolymph; run freely into a hemocoel; heart has ostia. Closed systems utilize blood; always contained in vessels; heart has no ostia. **29.2** The right side of the heart contains more O_2-poor blood and the left side of the heart contains more O_2-rich blood. **29.3** a. SA node activity is responsible for atrial systole; b. AV node activity is responsible for ventricular systole. **29.4** a. Blood pressure moves blood in arteries; b. Mechanical pressure exerted by skeletal muscle contraction helps move blood in veins. **29.5** No, try as you will in Figure 29.8. This ensures that all blood passes through the lungs. **29.6** No, it is highest close to the heart and falls off dramatically after moving through the capillaries. **29.7** Blood is composed of blood cells (plus platelets) in a liquid matrix called plasma. **29.8** Tissue fluid is derived from plasma at cardiovascular capillaries. Excess tissue fluid is absorbed by lymphatic vessels and becomes lymph. **29.9** The steps prevent clotting from occurring unnecessarily. **29.10** A type B recipient has anti-A antibodies in the plasma, and they will react with the donor's red blood cells, causing agglutination.

Form Your Opinion

Page 593: 1. Most likely reptiles (bird and crocodiles) and mammals express this gene because their heart has a septum, which completely separates the ventricles.
Page 596: 1. I believe that open heart surgery should be paid for by insurance, especially in cases where the need for the surgery is a genetic condition or birth defect. I believe the operation should be paid for by the patient based on ability to pay to help offset the cost of insurance premiums, especially in cases where cardiac health has suffered due to poor diet, lack of exercise, or drug abuse. 2. Ideally, people would follow the guidelines for staying fit and would not need to rely on the medical profession to make them healthy after they've abused their bodies.
Page 597: 1. Recommendations not to smoke or abuse drugs would be easier for me to follow than recommendations for diet and exercise. Food and laziness are easier for me to buy into than cigarettes and drugs. 2. I think education including the opportunity to see the effects of poor diet, lack of exercise and/or effects of drug use is the best method to make for making young people realize that they should take care of their bodies.
Page 601: 1. Because our culture emphasizes success, athletes are inclined to use performance-enhancing procedures or drugs in order to win competitions. Athletes found to be using illegal drugs and procedures should be banned from competition in their respective sport and any medical personnel or trainer that assists the athlete should be prosecuted and face loss of medical license, because the drugs and procedures can cause death.
Page 603: 1. I would be willing to let leaches feed on my blood for a few minutes if it would improve my chances of recovery from an injury, especially since this treatment is FDA approved. No, I would not be willing to let leaches feast on my blood because it would make me uncomfortable. 2. The idea that diseases could be transported throughout the body by the circulatory system might have given physicians the idea that by removing blood the illness might also be lessened.

Testing Yourself

1. d; 2. c; 3. b; 4. Efficient delivery of oxygen to the muscles allows birds and mammals to have an active lifestyle and generate heat to maintain a warm body temperature. 5. a; 6. See Fig. 29.2; 7. d; 8. c; 9. c; 10. b; 11. d; 12. c; 13. b; 14. a. blood pressure b. osmotic pressure c. blood pressure d. osmotic pressure; 15. a; 16. d; 17. e; 18. b; 19 Erthropoietin increases the number of red blood cells, and Rita's problem is lack of iron in her diet.

Thinking Scientifically

1. (1) By dissecting animals, you will see three different types of blood vessels; the valves in the heart directed toward the arteries and in the veins valves directed toward the heart. (2) A deep cut to a vertebrate limb draws bright, red arterial blood under pressure; pressing on a vein causes it to expand on the far side. This could only be if the blood circulates. 2. The amount of amino acids, sugar, and oxygen is higher in arterial blood and the amount of bicarbonate ion is higher in venous blood. Nutrients and oxygen leave a capillary and carbon dioxide enters a capillary midway along it's length. When carbon dioxide enters the capillary, the main portion becomes the bicarbonate ion.

Put the Pieces Together

Page 607: 1. Circulatory systems always have exchange surfaces with the external environment so they can keep the internal environment constant. For example, aquatic animals have gills and terrestrial animals have lungs where gas exchange occurs.They also exchange materials with the cells because their ultimate function is to serve the needs of cells. 2. When the blood is returning to the heart, it lacks the blood pressure provided by the pumping of the heart and venous blood may be traveling against gravity to move from the extremities back to the heart. 3. Blood pressure and therefore blood flow would be reduced due to the movement of water into tissue fluid.

CHAPTER 30

Check Your Progress

30.1 They return excess tissue fluid to cardiovascular veins. Without the return of this fluid, the tissues would become water-logged, blood pressure would drop dramatically, and blood circulation would falter. **30.2** The red bone marrow can produce thousands of T cells every day to stay ahead of those being killed by the virus. As long as the red bone marrow can produce more helper T cells than are being destroyed by an HIV infection, the person can fight off infections. **30.3** All three categories are helpful. The lining of the vagina is protective; interferons, macrophages, and natural killer cells should be helpful as well. **30.4** Macrophages and dendritic cells, because they activate T cells. **30.5** Yes, because it is specific to the virus and foreign to humans. **30.6** As long as active antibodies are present in the body, the person remains immun to a disease. **30.7** HIV attacks and lives inside helper T cells. Destruction of helper T cells occurs when the viruses bud from the cell. Therefore, as the infection progresses, fewer T cells are available to perform their usual functions, and the immune system fails. **30.8** No; each antibody is effective only against one specific antigen. **30.9** HIV destroys helper

T cells, and the number of cytokine-secreting helper T cells declines. Eventually, the immune system is ineffective, and the person, if untreated, dies. **30.10** The compromised immune system would make rejection less of an issue, but the patient would be susceptible to all sorts of possible pathogen infections due to the surgery. **30.11** If the disease is untreated, the quality of life suffers. If the disease is treated with immunosuppressive drugs, patients may be more susceptible to pathogenic infections.

Form Your Opinion

Page 613: 1. Fever seems beneficial when it makes us slow down but harmful because it makes us realize we are sick. 2. Most people cannot resist treating a fever because a fever makes them feel uncomfortable and just doing away with the fever makes them feel better.

Page 620: 1. Cancer is caused by an agent that can affect our genes. Monoclonal antibodies do not activate transduction pathways nor activate genes. 2. Yes, the patient should have been asked for her consent and should have been compensated. Even now her heirs could be compensated.

Page 622: 1. Contact with an allergen over a period of time can lead to an allergic response. 2. The presence of IgG antibodies can prevent an allergic response. Good hygiene in developed countries has resulted in fewer types of antibodies in people's blood and tissues.

Testing Yourself

1.a; 2. b; 3. d; 4. b; 5. It collects excess tissue fluid at the blood capillaries and returns it to the subclavian veins of the cardiovascular system. 6. b; 7. e; 8. d; 9. a; 10. Fever creates an unfavorable environment for an invader and may stimulate the immune system. 11. See Fig. 30.7; 12. c; 13. d; 14. a; 15. a; 16. a; 17. b; 18. e; 19. e; 20. B and T cells are specific to the agent that has harmed the body. 21. c

Thinking Scientifically

1. Hypothesis: each type of antibody is coded for by a different sequence of exons from the same gene or genes. 2. Control group is vaccinated against a specific disease and then the pathogen is administered. They are expected to remain well. The test group is vaccinated against a specific disease and then is administered the drug plus the pathogen. If the drug suppresses antibody mediated defense, the test group will become ill. Repeat the procedure for other diseases.

Put the Pieces Together

Page 625: 1. An antibody-mediated response is needed to identify and destroy the virus once it is in the blood. If the viral DNA has integrated itself into the infected cell's genome, then cell-mediated immunity is also needed. During cell-mediated immunity, cytotoxic T cells destroy a cell infected with a virus. 2. The clonal selection process results in the production of a specific antibody. Therefore, the antibodies produced after exposure to HIV would not be present if exposure had not taken place. 3. Following a viral infection a body cell might mistakenly display a viral antigen. Natural killer cells (innate immunity) attack these body cells. Also, an APC cell detects the antigen and presents it to a T cell. (adaptive immunity). The T cell attacks the body cell even though it is no longer infected.

CHAPTER 31
Check Your Progress

31.1 Carnivores are predators that attack and kill other animals. Digestion (both mechanical and chemical) of meat is more easily accomplished than the digestion of

carbohydrates. **31.2** a. Mouth: chew food; esophagus: conduct food bolus to the stomach; b. Salivary glands contain salivary amylase, an enzyme for carbohydrate digestion. **31.3** Carbohydrates: mouth and small intestine; proteins: stomach and small intestine **31.4** Our intestines are very long. The long small intestine gives time for digestion (particularly carbohydrate digestion) to be completed and also absorption to occur. **31.5** The liver breaks down the medicine prior to its excretion, so it is necessary to keep taking it in order to maintain a certain level in the body. **31.6** Low-fiber, refined carbohydrates lead to poor health; high-fiber, whole-grain carbohydrates lead to good health. **31.7** Oils containing unsaturated fatty acids lead to good health. Fats containing saturated fatty acids and/or trans fatty acids, in particular, lead to poor health. **31.8** Vegetables supply nutrients and do not overtax the body's metabolism the way protein does. **31.9** Salts increase the osmolarity of blood and cause more water to be absorbed by the kidneys, leading to hypertension. **31.10** Whole grains, fruits, and vegetables, in general, supply vitamins in the diet.

Form Your Opinion

Page 631: 1. Birds are adapted for flight and a beak is light because it does not have teeth. The food a bird eats whether a seed or a fish does not need to be chewed. Cows are large animals that have few predators; they can take their time eating grass which requires much chewing and digestion. 2. I would rather be an herbivore so that I would not have to hunt and kill in order to eat. I could spend all my time eating and digesting my food. A carnivorous lifestyle does have its benefits as well: I could eat large meals high in protein and spend less time digesting my food. 3. When humans first evolved, they were not tool makers and didn't have the means to hunt and kill animals. As the brain increased in size, humans made tools and learned to use fire. When they migrated to Europe the weather turned cold, and because of their spears and greater intelligence, men could cooperate to hunt and kill large animal and use their skins for clothing.

Page 635: 1. To do a controlled experiment, Dr. Marshall needed two groups of volunteers; the test group would ingest a sample of *Heliobacter pylori* and the control group would ingest a sample that does not contain *Heliobacter pylori*. Each group is later tested for the presence of ulcers. 2. The absence of ulcer in the control group supports the hypothesis that *Heliobacter pylori* is the cause of ulcer in the test group.

Page 637: 1. Antibiotic therapy might kill off the bacteria that can help you digest lactose. 2. Pro-pill answer: I would prefer to take a pill that supplies enzymes because I love milk and other dairy products. If the intolerance could be managed with a simple pill I would take it over excluding some of my favorite foods from my diet. Pro-watch diet answer: I would prefer to manage my diet for lactose intolerance because I don't think a pill should be the answer to every ailment, and the pill may have side effects.

Page 643: 1. A person might have an unhealthy diet due to family dietary habits, lack of money, or a poor knowledge of a balanced diet. Schools could provide healthy foods in the dining room and should teach students the essentials of good nutrition. 2. Yes answer: Warning labels should be used because the government should protect us so we do not make poor food choices. No answer: Warning labels should not be used because education is a better protective measure than warning labels. The government should not be involved in every choice we make during our lifetimes.

Page 644: 1. Our society admires thinness and to avoid being seen as overweight, a person

might develop an eating disorder. Advertisements encourage children to eat high-calorie foods and that could start them on the road to obesity. 2. You could offer emotional support for any underlying issue that may contribute to the disorder.

Testing Yourself

1. d; 2. a; 3. Life is sustained by a source of energy, and the digestive system provides the nutrients that provide energy to animals. 4. a; 5. d; 6. b; 7. b; 8. a. salivary glands b. esophagus c. stomach d. duodenum e. large intestine f. small intestine g. colon; 9. d because it contains the right enzyme, the right pH, and the right substrate; 10. e; 11. c; 12. d; 13. b; 14. b; 15. c; 16. b; 17. a. bile canals, b. hepatic artery, c. hepatic portal vein, d. bile duct e. central vein; 18. a; 19. e; 20. c; 21. b; 22. d; 23. The source of amino acids is of no consequence because the DNA of each cell specifies the types of proteins for that cell.

Thinking Scientifically

1. Pepsin, HCL, substrate (e.g., piece of cooked egg white), water. Omit the pepsin. If digestion still occurs, pepsin may not be the cause of digestion. 2. The use of a control group and a large number of participants makes the correlation more certain.

Put the Pieces Together

Page 647: 1. The digestive system provides the nutrients that allow all the systems of the body to acquire ATP and synthesize the molecules needed to maintain structure. 2. The placement of the liver between the digestive system and the circulatory system stresses that the liver monitors the quantity and purity of the molecules received from our food; it breaks down poisonous molecules and stores excess glucose. 3. Reducing the size of the stomach can reduce food intake by making us feel full sooner. Malnutrition can arise due to limited food intake or imbalance of the diet.

CHAPTER 32
Check Your Progress

32.1 Ventilation does not occur. **32.2** A counter flow mechanism ensures that blood is always exposed to a higher O_2 concentration; therefore, O_2 is continually taken up by blood. **32.3** Larger insects have a means of ventilating the tracheae, but external respiration (exchange of gases with incoming air), and internal respiration (exchange of gases in the tissues) comprise a single event in insects. **32.4** nasal cavity, pharynx, glottis, larynx, trachea, bronchus, bronchiole and alveoli of lungs. The path of air does not change when a person dives. However, note that air does not enter the body when a person dives but exchange continues in the lungs as long as possible. **32.5** Penguins can store air in the posterior air sacs. **32.6** When the spleen contracts, more red blood cells (more hemoglobin) enter the blood. This not only raises the amount of available oxygen, but the hemoglobin also helps control pH (see Section 32.7). **32.7** Oxyhemoglobin transports oxygen from the lungs to the tisssues. Most CO_2 is transported as the bicarbonate ion but some combines with hemoglobin forming carboaminohemoglobin. The globin portion of hemoglobin combines with H^+ forming HBH^+. Therefore hemoglobin plays a role in maintaining normal blood pH. Hemolgobin's essential function is transport of oxygen.

Form Your Opinion

Page 651: 1. (1) A hydra lives in an aquatic environment, which ensures a moist exchange surface. (2) Earthworms keep themselves moist by living in moist soil. (3) Fish live in aquatic environments and thus have moist exchange surfaces. (4) Insects have fluid filled tracheoles, which aid in exchange. (5) Mammals use the internal environment to keep exchange surfaces moist. 2. Fishes must use the motion of their mouths to power water over the gills in order receive oxygen from water. Humans can breathe through their noses; insects, earthworms and hydra also do not use their mouths to breathe. 3. Cellular respiration requires O_2 and gives off CO_2.

Page 655: 1. Yes answer: Smokers have a right to smoke, but should confine their smoking to non-public places since second hand smoke is a serious threat to anyone near a smoker. No answer: Smokers do not have a right to smoke and smoking should be outlawed because nonsmokers should not have to pay for the health costs of smoking. 2. Smokers suffer from bronchitis and often lung cancer and other types of cancer. 3. Cigarette manufacturers should be held responsible for providing cigarettes to the world, while friends and family members of smokers might bear some blame if they do not do their best to prevent smoking in their families.

Page 660: 1. Both activities bring pollutant irritants into the lungs and can cause conditions like chronic bronchitis and lung cancer. 2. An organic chemical could stimulate or inhibit a transduction pathway that ends with a transcription factor or activator that regulates gene activity. The end result of this altered gene regulation could be cancer. 3. Walking, household chores, climbing or descending a stairway, and heavy lifting would be troublesome for a person with emphysema.

Testing Yourself

1. c; 2. e; 3. a; 4. b; 5. b; 6. d; 7. b; 8. c; 9. c; 10. See Fig. 32.4; 11. b; 12. d; 13. f; 14. d; 15. a; 16. b; 17. e; 18. d; 19. left: a. rib cage up and out; b. diaphragm moves down; right: a. rib cage down and in; b. diaphragm moves up. 20. b; 21. b; 22. b; 23. d; 24. a; 25. e; 26. The shape of hemoglobin changes when the pH changes from near neutral in the lungs to slightly acidic in the tissues, and this causes it to unload its oxygen. 27. d; 28. b; 29. e; 30. The body has a limited capacity to store oxygen and has a better ability to store energy.

Thinking Scientifically

1. Fat metabolism results in acids that enter the bloodstream; a lower pH stimulates the respiratory center and causes increased breathing, which lowers the CO_2, but raises the O_2 blood level. Test the blood of a diabetic group and a normal group for these blood levels and compare the results of the tests. 2. A severed spinal cord prevents the medulla oblongata from communicating with the rib cage and diaphragm via the phrenic nerve and intercostal nerves.

Put the Pieces Together

Page 663: 1. The lungs have external exchange surfaces because air from the external environment enters the lungs. 2. The respiratory system excretes CO_2 which arises due to cellular metabolism. The digestive system rids the body of nondigestible remains which have never been a part of the body. 3. Hemoglobin (1) transports O_2 to the cells, (2) helps transport CO_2 to the lungs, (3) combines with H^+ and thereby helps buffer the blood.

CHAPTER 33

Check Your Progress

33.1 a. Urea is not as toxic as ammonia, and it does not require as much water to excrete;

b. It takes less energy to prepare urea than uric acid. **33.2** No, the workings of the nephridia stay the same, regardless of respiration. The worm might gain less water from the environment because of its thicker skin and produce less urine as a result. **33.3** glomerular capsule, proximal convoluted tubule, loop of nephron, distal convoluted tubule, collecting duct, renal pelvis. **33.4** All small molecules enter the filtrate, and the tubule reabsorbs nutrients and salts into the blood as required to maintain normal blood concentrations. **33.5** It fine-tunes the reabsorption of sodium ions. **33.6** Fig. 33.6 shows how the kidneys regulate the pH of the blood: If the blood is basic, bicarbonate ions are excreted and not reabsorbed and H^+ is not excreted. If the blood is acidic, bicarbonate ions are reabsorbed and H^+ is excreted. Ammonia combines with H^+ to buffer it.

Form Your Opinion

Page 669: 1. Evolution would have followed this pathway: fresh-water fishes; to lobe-finned fishes in small bodies of freshwater on land; to amphibians that could locomote on land but had to return to fresh water to reproduce. 2. Excretion of ammonia is consistent with the early life of amphibians in the water; excretion of urea is consistent with their later life on land. You would predict that amphibians osmoregulate as their ancestors (freshwater fishes) did. 3. Humans osmoregulate by regulating the amount of salt and water in their blood as do freshwater fishes in that both have no way other than the kidneys to rid the body of salt.

Page 673: 1. I think that it is a person's own business if they want to take drugs, but that they must consider the consequences of doing so and be held responsible for any harm they might cause others.; therefore, I believe they should be tested by employers if other people would be harmed by their habit. 2. Jail might scare some people to give up drugs, however, addictions should be treated as illnesses and treated safely with medical supervision and with the support of drug/alcohol counselors. 3. Yes answer: Because of the risks associated with child drug use, including overdose, long term addictions, and death, I am a proponent of physicians testing children who raise suspicion of drug use. No answer: Children should not be tested for drug use. Children should be well-educated on the risks of drug use and monitored by parents and guardians to an extent that would prevent them from using drugs.

Page 676: 1. I might treat a dialysis patient that has to spend hours of the week in the hospital for hemodialysis like a "sick" person who needs special care. People have so many organ replacements today that I probably would not treat a person with a replaced bladder differently. 2. Except in cases of neglect or malpractice, I do not think that doctors, nurses, or technicians should be held responsible for unsuccessful hemodialysis. 3. If a person is able to perform the duties associated with a job and needs time off for medical treatment, some provisions should be made so they can be hired.

Testing Yourself

1. a; 2. d; 3. b; 4. b; 5. c; 6. See Fig. 33.3C; 7. c; 8. c; 9. a; 10. d; 11. These cells reabsorb most of the contents of the nephron and need increased surface area and energy to better pump molecules back into the blood. 12. e; 13.a,b,d; 14. a, b, d; 15. a, b; 16 c, b; 17. b; 18. a; 19. c,d; 20. a,b; 21. d 22. b; 23. d; 24 c; 25. a; 26. a; 27. The presence of salt in the blood causes more water to be passively reabsorbed, and the resulting increase in blood volume contributes to high blood pressure.

1. A microscopic study of their kidneys should reveal that they have a reduced glomerulus and a very long loop of the nephron. 2. Use the pump to increase the pressure of the blood passing through the tubing, increase the length of the tubing, and increase the rapidity with which the dialysis fluid passes through the apparatus.

Put the Pieces Together

Page 679: 1. Hormonal control of kidneys: (1) ADH regulates water reabsorption from collecting duct. (2) aldosterone promotes reabsorption of Na^+ at distal convoluted tubule, (3) ANH inhibits aldosterone secretion by adrenal cortex. 2. Blood pH is regulated through the carbonate buffer system in the blood and by the excretory and respiratory systems. The carbonate buffer system combines with acid or base to keep the pH constant; to raise pH the respiratory system excretes carbon dioxide and the kidneys excrete H^+ and reabsorb bicarbonate. The kidneys can also do the opposite to lower the pH when necessary. 3. The kidneys regulate the composition of the blood by excreting metabolites, and they regulate the salt-water balance so that the tonicity and volume of blood stays constant.

CHAPTER 34

Check Your Progress

34.1 They all send a chemical message that is received by a receptor and reception brings about a change in the cell's/organism's metabolism. **34.2** Whereas pheromones result in nerve messages to the brain; hormones are transmitted by the bloodstream and act on body cells directly; peptide hormones stimulate an enzyme cascade; and steroid hormones stimulate protein synthesis. **34.3** All of them represent passage of hormone by the bloodstream. All organs have receptors; otherwise, stimulation and negative feedback would not occur. **34.4** A child that is short in stature can receive growth hormone; increased bone length and muscle mass are expected as metabolism increases. Too much growth hormone can result in a giant with diabetes mellitus. **34.5** Pheromone to VNO to hypothalamus to anterior pituitary to thyroid gland and release of hormones. **34.6** Calcitonin causes the blood calcium to fall, and PTH causes it to rise. **34.7** Epinephrine and norepinephrine by the adrenal medulla. **34.8** Diabetes type 2 which occurs when the cells are not responsive to insulin can be due to a diet rich in sugar and fat. The diet leads to inactivity and obesity which is associated with diabetes type 2. **34.9** Winter; melatonin secretion starts earlier in the PM and discontinues later in the AM because the nights are longer.

Form Your Opinion

Page 691: 1. It is a prescribing physician's responsibility to explain any and all risks associated with treatment including hormone therapy. It is then a patient's choice whether or not to receive such therapies, having been made aware of the side effects. 2. Yes, it does make me uncomfortable because one can never know for sure if the "possible" negative effects will occur.

Page 694: 1. Sleeping in a room without a window seemed to bring on a degree of seasonal affective disorder for me. Without morning light to rouse me from sleep, I found myself sleeping later and later into the day. Though I attributed the change to a shift in melatonin, it could have been psychological also. 2. Night owl: I am a night person that likes to sleep in and go to bed in the early morning hours. This could be attributed to secretion of melatonin in the morning. Early bird: I am a morning person that likes to get up with the sunrise and get to bed early. This could be attributed to secretion of melatonin in the afternoon. 3. I would be hesitant to take a supplement such as growth hormone due to the associated risks and reported cases of diabetes and other problems. I would employ conventional methods of eating a healthy diet, exercising, and getting plenty of rest in order to improve my overall health.

Testing Yourself

1. d; 2. b; 3. a; 4. d; 5. d; 6. f; 7. b; 8. c; 9. a; 10. e; 11. Caffeine would increase the stress effect of epinephrine because cAMP, which drives the effect, would be slower to breakdown. 12. c; 13. c; 14. a; inhibits, b. inhibits, c. releasiing hormone, d. tropic hormone, e. target gland hormone; 15. d; 16. e; 17. c; 18. d; 19. c; 20. e; 21. d; 22. b; 23. a; 24. d; 25. b; 26. b; 27. High blood calcium causes the thyroid to secrete calcitonin, which leads to the uptake of calcium by bone. Calcium level drops and thyroid is no longer stimulated to release calcitonin.

Thinking Scientifically

1. Calcitonin, being a peptide hormone, stimulates the metabolism of osteoblasts to form bone utilizing calcium. 2. Use two groups of volunteers; one group consists of the "night owls" and the other group are "early birds." Collect blood samples from all volunteers when they are typically sleepy and when they typically wake up. If all goes well, the melatonin level rises earlier at night and lowers earlier in the day for the early birds.

Put the Pieces Together

Page 697: 1. Stress is a stimulus that causes the hypothalamus to send nerve impulses (nervous system involvement) to the adrenal gland which then releases epinephrine (endocrine system involvement). 2. Example: Low blood calcium is a stimulus that causes the parathyroid glands to secrete parathyroid hormone and this hormone brings about a rise in blood calcium level. The increase in blood calcium does away with the original stimulus and the parathyroid glands no longer release parathyroid hormone. 3. Biologists originally called the anterior pituitary gland the master gland because the anterior pituitary gland secretes many different hormones and some of these control the secretion of other endocrine glands. Later, biologists discovered that the hypothalamus secretes hormones that control the secretion of the pituitary gland and therefore it is the master gland.

CHAPTER 35

Check Your Progress

35.1 This asexual phenotype is the one that is already successful in the environment; the sexual production of various phenotypes is sure to produce at least one new phenotype that will be successful should the environment change the next season. 35.2 Sperm must be kept moist to survive. 35.3 They travel through the epididymis, the vas deferens, the ejaculatory duct, and, finally, the urethra. 35.4 The vagina receives the penis, which delivers the sperm; therefore, the sperm do not dry out. The egg is fertilized in the oviduct, where body fluids provide moisture. The embryo develops in the uterus, where it cannot dry out. 35.5 To produce the female sex hormones (estrogen and progesterone) and to produce an oocyte. 35.6 Birth control pills and any various other hormone delivery methods (patch, injections, implant). 35.7 Lancelets develop quickly into a free-living aquatic larva; birds develop inside a shelled egg and need a food source (the yolk); human embryos develop in the uterus and get nutrients from

the mother. 35.8 establishment of the germ layers during gastrulation 35.9 The notochord is formed from mesoderm and is a supportive structure that lies underneath the neural tube, which is formed from ectoderm. In vertebrates, the notochord is replaced by the vertebral column, and the neural tube becomes the nervous system. 35.10 Chemical signals tell cells how they are to behave and how they will become specialized. 35.11 Induction causes cells to move and form a particular structure. 35.12 To make internal development possible; the chorion is a part of the placenta, for example. 35.13 Sponges have the cellular level of organization; cnidarias (e.g., hydras) have the tissue level of organization; flatworms (e.g., planarian) have the organ level of organization; and all animals thereafter have the systems level of organization. 35.14 The systems are just about fully formed during embryonic development, even though the embryo is tiny and weighs little. During fetal development there is weight gain and refinement of structures. 35.15 Before birth, the placenta supplied the needs of the fetus.

Form Your Opinion

Page 701: 1. When the relationship is monogamous, males are fairly assured that the offspring is theirs. Females exercise choice by selecting as mates, males that appear to evolutionarily fit. When the relationship is not monogamous, males become sexually aggressive and females become defensive and only let down their defenses when they choose to. 2. Each sex wants their particular alleles to be passed on to the next generation. 3. Traditionally, before marriage males chase females and females withhold sexual favors. This might cause males to become deceptive and make the female believe they are interested in marriage when they are not interested. It might make the female be the first to break off a relationship that does not seem to be headed toward marriage. To test the hypothesis, I would take a survey of females to determine how many broke off a relationship because marriage did not seem in the offing.

Page 708: 1. It is evolutionary beneficial for sex to be a powerful motivator in order to perpetuate a species. It is personally disadvantageous because of the risk of sexually transmitted infections such as those discussed in this passage. Women who reproduce earlier than planned may have to give up plans for a career or will find it more difficult to pursue a career while caring for children. 2. Social consequences that might result from having a non-treatable sexually transmitted disease (STD) range from economical to interpersonal. Treatment for STDs and lost work time represent an economic consequence. Socially, infertility and the risk of transmission to a partner could make a person less desirable as a long-term mate. 3. Yes answer: I do approve of allowing young girls to receive the HPV vaccine. I think the benefits of decreasing the risk of cervical cancer are enormous and it is no different than a vaccine to protect a child from any other disease. No answer: I do not approve of allowing girls as young as 9 to receive the HPV vaccine. I think that a girl should be presented with this option at an age deemed appropriate by a parent or physician in the early teen years.

Page 709: 1. sperm donor- because the donor is the genetic parent of the child. egg donor—because the donor is the genetic parent of the child. surrogate mother—because she carries a child and is ultimately responsible for its being born a healthy, viable child. contracting mother—because of legal agreement to care for the child produced from the pregnancy of the surrogate mother. contracting father—because of legal agreement to care for the child produced from the pregnancy of the surrogate mother. 2. Pros: successful pregnancy, overcoming reproductive challenges.

Cons: Multiple failed attempts at pregnancy, cost of procedures, pain surrounding hormone injection, legal issues surrounding surrogates or sperm/ egg donations, emotional wear and tear. For couples who have struggled with reproducing and are forced to utilize these technologies to produce an offspring, the benefits outweigh the drawbacks. 3. Legislation should regulate which of the "5 potential parents" listed above actually does have the best claim to the child. Decisions should be made beforehand, like in an adoption, whether or not to make a sperm or egg donor available to a child later in life. In addition, the use of reproductive technology should be limited in cases like the "Octo-mom" where a large single parent family exists; thus creating the risk that the children will be neglected or the single parent will be unable to support all of the children.

Testing Yourself

1. e; 2. c; 3. Sexual reproduction produces variations among the offspring and one of these may be phenotypes that can deal with the new conditions. 4. b; 5. See Fig. 35.2; 2 6. a; 7. c; 8. b; 9. A high blood testosterone level shuts down the anterior pituitary production of gonadotropic hormones, reducing sperm production. 10. c; 11. b; 12. b; 13. c; 14. d; 15. zygote, cleavage, morula, blastula, gastrula, neurula.16. a. chorion (gas exchange), b. amnion (protection), c. embryo, d. alllanois (umbilical blood vessels), e. yolk sac (blood cell formation) f. and g. (placenta is area of exchange with mother); 17. c; 18. d

Thinking Scientifically

1. Testosterone causes increased cell division in the prostate. Microscopically, observe the effect of testosterone on cells taken from the prostate. 2. Progesterone maintains the uterine lining, and if the placenta doesn't begin producing it when it should, a woman could lose the embryo embedded in the lining.

Put the Pieces Together

Page 723: 1. The human male reproductive organs are adapted to the production and storage of sperm in the temperature-regulated scrotum, secretion of protective fluids for the safe transfer of mature sperm, as well as direct deposit of seminal fluids into the female reproductive organs. Internal development of a fetus in amniotic fluid shows that human development is still tied to an aquatic environment. 2. Animals go through the same developmental stages and this would not develop similarly if they were not related and descended from a common ancestor. 3. Many genes are active only during development and they get turned off as the organism matures.

CHAPTER 36

Check Your Progress

36.1 The population, habitat, community, and ecosystem levels are all affected. 36.2 Density. 36.3 Reproductive because the age structure diagram would resemble a stable population. 36.4 Exponential growth would occur until competition for resources slowed the population growth to meet the carrying capacity. 36.5 Severe natural disasters (such as hurricanes) and weather-related food shortages are two examples. 36.6 Competition for food and habitat resources are two examples. 36.7 Equilibrium species, because of their large body size, relatively long life span, and the few offspring produced per deer each year. Deer are exploding because they have no predators and are able to live in the vacinity of people. Gorillas prefer a restricted environment that is shrinking and they form small populations. 36.8 It would lengthen the doubling time, because the deer would add fewer offspring to the population.

Form Your Opinion

Page 736: 1. In efforts to protect individual species, we pay special attention to preserving their habitats. As such, protecting "hotspots" would essentially be a means to protect many organisms and their homes. However, if "hotspots" are not home to any endangered species, we should still preserve individual species that inhabit other locations. 2. Yes answer: Though it is a controversial issue, I support the preservation of cheetahs in zoos if it can help increase the population. Continued monitoring of genetic diversity is essential. Perhaps cheetahs can be bred in zoos for a period of time and later strategically released onto protected lands, I see the use of zoos as beneficial. No answer: I think that efforts should be made to preserve cheetahs in their natural environment and not in the captivity of a zoo where they are unable to run freely and hunt food, skills that are characteristic of cheetahs in the wild. 3. Although it is important for our own needs to preserve specific species and natural environments, we should not neglect unique endangered species. Minor changes in ecosystems can have widespread and unpredictable effects. The loss of unique endangered species might alter our planet in ways we did not anticipate. Because we are the cause of much of the loss of habitat, pollution, and introduction of non-native plants or animals that causes endangering of species, we should make every effort to preserve as much of the natural environment as possible. **Page 738:** 1. Yes answer: Considering that our current way of living and reproducing is not sustainable, families in the US are acting selfishly when they have more than two children. This is selfish behavior because it has little regard for the future and the impact we are making on our planet that will be detrimental, and possibly preventative, of generations of human beings to come. No answer: I believe families in the US that have more than two children are not acting selfishly if they make efforts to have minimal impact on the environment. It is more important, no matter the size of families, that people in the US pay attention to energy use and exploitation of resources in order to have less negative impact on the planet. 2. Sustainability would provide a quality of life for future generations that is equal to the current conditions. This would help the economy by providing a steady source of materials for production, thus stabilizing prices in the long run. 3. The United States should hold itself, along with other countries, to the same standards with regard to environmental impact. More developed countries tend to have a greater impact on the environment and should be keenly aware of the predicament this puts the planet in for the future. The U.S. should certainly reduce its environmental impact while expecting other countries to do the same. The benefits for the planet and the future of humanity depend upon our responsible management of resources and preservation of the planet we inhabit today.

Testing Yourself

1. d; 2. d; 3. b; 4. d; 5. b; 6. a; 7. b; 8. a; 9. c; 10. The offspring of a plant that reproduces by runners would remain near the parent. The offspring of a plant that reproduces by windblown seeds could be taken far away from the parent. 11. See Fig. 36.4B; 12. c; 13. a; 14. b; 15. c; 16. a. density independent factor, b. density dependent factor; 17. c; 18. d; 19. When the environment is unstable due to density-independent and density-dependent factors, a few of the many small, uncared for offspring might have a better chance of dispersal to a favorable environment. 20. a; 21. a; 22. c; 23. d; 24. e.

Thinking Scientifically

1. You might hypothesize that the right whale has only one offspring per reproduction and chances of death before maturity are good. The right whale begins reproducing well after maturity, and reproduces infrequently. To test your hypothesis, you would have to observe a captive population or tag individuals in the wild and observe them from a distance. 2. Determine the original normal flow of the river and maintain the flow as close to normal as possible.

Put the Pieces Together

Page 741: 1. A moderate population size in desirable because it strikes a balance between the negative aspects of very large and very small populations. Very large populations over-exploit the resources of their environment, and might become extinct due to lack of resources. Very small populations lose genetic variability and run the risk of extinction from disease associated with inbreeding, infectious diseases, or extreme environmental changes (flood, drought, etc). 2. We should definitely be concerned about how the growing U.S. population affects consumption and sustainability of our population. Eventually, our non-renewable resources will run out and renewable resources will not be able to keep up with our consumption. If we persist in a trend of increased population without regard to the environmental impact we are making, we run the risk of not only running out of natural resources, but also destroying ecosystems due to pollution and overdevelopment. 3. As demonstrated in Figure 36.3C, more women entering than leaving their reproductive years means that births will continue to increase population over time. A population that consists of more young members than old lends itself to growth that is not balanced out by deaths. In populations with a balance between older and younger members, stabilization occurs.

CHAPTER 37

Check Your Progress

37.1 Because all members of the colony have the same mother, they would all inherit the gene, and the colony would die out as tunnel excavating ceased. **37.2** Observe a mole rat in its colony from the time of birth and see if efficiency in building tunnels improves over time. **37.3** Operant conditioning because the younger workers would be rewarded for tunnel work. **37.4** One reason animals are territorial is to forage for foood. **37.5** No, because all mole rats are close relatives. **37.6** Raise birds that are unable to perform this behavior and then compare the fitness of birds that sing to mark their territory with those that do not.

Form Your Opinion

Page 749: 1. Yes answer: Evolutionary principles should be applied to human reproductive behavior. Like other animals, humans demonstrate sexual selection and the mating behavior of both males and females indicates a preference towards selecting the partner with the optimal fitness. No answer: I believe evolutionary principles should not be applied to human reproductive behavior, since our complex culture influences reproduction in ways that are not possible in other animals. For example, selection of males based on financial security is unique to humans. In addition, our technological advances can help "less fit" individuals survive and reproduce. 2. I have observed many examples that support male competition for females and female choice based on financial stability. On average, men marry and have children with younger women. Traditional dating behavior follows a trend of a man impressing a woman in order to "earn the privilege" of mating and reproduction. **Page 754:** 1. My experience with dogs leads me to suggest that dogs do feel affection for their owners, anger demonstrated through aggression, excitement for food and play, shame when admonished for undesirable behavior, and mourning at the permanent loss of a playmate (another animal) or human companion. 2. With regard to pets, I would take care not to provoke aggression, and reward them and praise them for desirable behaviors. In nature, I would also refrain from provoking aggressive or territorial behavior in an animal, bearing in mind that the emotions of wild animals are tied closely to instincts. 3. Yes answer: The conclusion that animals do have emotions makes them seem closer to human beings, thus making eating an animal nearly cannibalistic in nature. Though I tend to associate emotions more with pets than animals raised for food, I would reconsider eating meat with evidence that all animals display emotions. No answer: I would continue to be an omnivore even with conclusions that animals have emotions. I think that animal emotions differ from human emotions and are tied largely to instinctual response to stimuli.

Testing Yourself

1. c; 2. b; 3. e; 4. c; 5. c; 6. b; 7. See Fig. 37.3; 8. a; 9. d; 10. c; 11. c; 12. a; 13. Because females produce few gametes and have few offspring during their lifetime, they place an emphasis on quality of offspring. Because males produce many gametes all the time, they place an emphasis on quantity of offspring. 14. d; 15. e; 16. a; 17. They would be increasing their inclusive fitness when they help their parents at a time they cannot be reproducing themselves. Reciprocal altruism would ensure that they will successfully reproduce when the time comes. 18. a; 19. c; 20. b; 21. d

Thinking Scientifically

1. Mate the two types of rats and test how the offspring react to limburger cheese. If they show an intermediate response, such as being willing to approach the cheese but still not eating it, then the behavior may be genetically controlled. 2. Observe sentry behavior more cloesly. Recent observations have shown that sentries are the first ones to reach safety when a predator is spotted, and meerkats only serve as sentries after they have eaten.

Put the Pieces Together

Page 757: 1. Natural selection favors the successful competitor for territory while the losing animal(s) may not survive to reproduce without having a territory. 2. The idea that behavior is largely response to stimulus, and that some responses yield increased fitness might be offensive to people who prefer to think of behavior as learned and correlated with cognitive choice. 3. Crickets make calls to attract mates. This behavior is risky, and can lead to predation. However, the benefits of attracting a mate have overcome the risk evolutionarily, since natural selection has perpetuated populations of crickets that make calls for mates.

CHAPTER 38

Check Your Progress

38.1 Decomposers release chemicals that make dead material smell and taste unpleasant to many other animals. Some animals, such as scavengers, are not repulsed, however. **38.2** When scavengers eat decomposing meat, they are also eating the decomposers that are devouring the food source before them. **38.3** Parasites but not decomposers use nutrients meant for the host organism. If the host dies, the parasite is also threatened with death. **38.4** Study the feeding behavior of a remora when not attached to a shark. If it can survive independently, it is more likely commensalistic with the shark. **38.5** The protozoans are provided with food and habitat. **38.6** Succession would essentially stop. Most chemical nutrients would be tied up in dead organisms making new growth very limited. **38.7** Only autotrophs can use an outside energy source to produce organic food required by all the biotic components of an ecosystem. **38.8** The inorganic chemicals are taken up by plants and the recycling of chemicals in an ecosystem begins again. **38.9** Bacteria and fungi of decay. **38.10** None; ecological pyramids do not include decomposers. This is one of their shortcomings. **38.11** The reservoir and the exchange pool are abiotic. **38.12** Decomposers gradually break down the bones making phosphate ions and other chemicals available. **38.13** Nitrification. **38.14** It would decrease greenhouse emissions and reduce the threat of a rise in global temperature.

Form Your Opinion

Page 765: 1. In both the predator-prey and parasite-host relationships, one of the individuals (predator and parasite) benefits more than the other (prey and host). The difference is that in a predator-prey relationship, the death of prey is guaranteed, while the death of a host is not always the case in parasitism. 2. HIV cannot currently be effectively vaccinated against, and even if caught early, remains incurable. H1N1 can be vaccinated against and is also treatable in certain stages of illness. HIV is a retrovirus capable of producing DNA from its RNA within a host cell, thus taking over the host entirely over time. 3. A pollinator coevolves with a flower such that the flower evolves to attract the pollinator and the pollinator adapts to feed from the flower (i.e. long proboscis when the flower is deep). This coevolution takes place in the same "direction" the flower to be pollinated and the pollinator in order to feed. Coevolution between parasite and host differs in that hosts evolve under selective pressure to avoid being infected by parasites, while parasites evolve under pressures to evade host defenses. The parasite and host are evolving in different "directions"- the host to avoid the parasite and the parasite to overcome attempts to be avoided. **Page 769:** 1. Food chains will be altered; killing off large predators or the introduction of alien species will create new predator-prey relationships, potentially exterminating some prey. Each minor change to the area has trickle down effects that touch not only the animals, but plants as well as abiotic resources. 2. Small areas, cut off from former connections lose species, altering predator-prey relationships and causing other potentially disruptive changes throughout an environmental system.

Testing Yourself

1. c; 2. e; 3. e; 4. a; 5. c; 6. b; 7. d; 8. Will the area be able to meet the niche requirements of this predator? (see Fig. 38.7); 9. b; 10. a; 11. b; 12. e; 13. See Fig. 38.8A; 14. c; 15. d; 16. c; 17. c; 18. b; 19. c; 20. d; 21. d; 22. No; Photosynthetic species are always at the first trophic level and nonphotosynthetic species are always at a higher level.

Thinking Scientifically

1. Observe the birds carefully to see if they differ in ways suggested by Figure 38.7. 2. Measure and fill a large container with water from the pond. Add measured amounts of phosphate slowly over several days or months, and when you see growth, calculate the amount of phosphate you need for the pond.

Put the Pieces Together

Page 779: 1. Three populations would be students, faculty, professors: (1) Students interact with professors for the exchange of information, mostly professor to student. Professors interact with faculty for record keeping, financial exchanges etc. (2) Faculty must not be too small to meet the needs of students and professors, but also not too large to be sustainable financially. (3) With a small student body, fewer faculty and staff are needed and able to be sustained. A larger student body bears the necessity of a larger faculty and staff of professors who are then financially sustainable through more incoming tuition from students. 2. The human population is dependent on natural resources and people should definitely work to preserve the natural environment in order to maintain the resources needed for life. Many of our actions fail to preserve the natural environment because we exploit natural resources, alter the habitats of many organisms, and create large amounts of waste at a rate unmatched by our efforts to replenish and repair the damage we do.

CHAPTER 39

Check Your Progress

39.1 temperature and rainfall **39.2** Look at the distribution of landmasses in this chapters various maps. They are shifted toward the northern latitudes. **39.3** No, the winds are weaker than usual. **39.4** Rain forests receive much rainfall and solar energy; therefore, they produce enough food for many organisms. The various plants in a tropical rain forest provide many different types of niches for many different organisms. These two factors help account for why tropical rain forests exhibit species richness. **39.5** It would be difficult to simulate the winter of a tundra and to stock it with animals as large as caribou. **39.6** Coniferous trees are soft wood. **39.7** No, you need the rich soil, the understory plants, and the many animals. **39.8** No, prairies receive less rainfall than do forests. **39.9** Grasses and scattered trees. **39.10** Cold. **39.11** Epiphytes. **39.12** Wetlands. **39.13** Euphotic.

Form Your Opinion

Page 787: 1. The major groups of organisms can be found on all continents because the present-day land masses used to be a supercontinent. Types of organisms can vary between continents depending upon when the animals evolved relative to the separation of the continents. 2. Because of the age of the man, he most likely traveled across sea or ice but did not make his way to Greenland from Siberia via Beringia since this land bridge is believed to have been exposed during the last ice age 12,000 to 20,000 years ago.
Page 794: 1. (1) The effect of the barometric pressure over the Southeast Pacific and the Indian Ocean upon weather on the coasts of the United States is an example of this connection. (2) Everything is truly connected to everything else if we trace carbon through its cycle: essentially all of the carbon present even in the bodies of human has been present in many other molecules since carbon first appeared in the atmosphere. Carbon makes its way from the atmosphere into soil, plants, animals, and water (etc). 2. Prior to the completion of a dam in 1970, the annual flooding of the Nile River left behind fertile silt capable of sustaining agriculture in Egypt. A small flood or no flood at all would result in famine for this area. The annual flood was a dangerous event, but without it, Egypt's farming would have been impossible.

Testing Yourself

1. b; 2. e; 3. See Fig. 39.2B; 4. c; 5. b; 6. a; 7. Hot air from the equator moves toward the poles. 8. d; 9. d; 10. a; 11. a; 12. a; 13. d; 14. e; 15. d ; 16. b; 17. Decomposers use up any available oxygen, leaving none for the fish. 18. b; 19. c; 20 c; 21 c; 22. d; 23. e; 24. Sea level would be too deep for previous estuaries to exist, and new ones may not develop further inland due to development of coastal regions.

Thinking Scientifically

1. You will be able to see if a rising global temperature affects the distribution of biomes in the biosphere. 2. Coral houses microscopic algae and if the dirty water blots out the sun, the algae will die.

Put the Pieces Together

Page 797: 1. (a) Squirrels: small herbivorous animals which are behaviorally adapted to collect and store foods (like nuts) in order to have nourishment through the winter. The thick fur coats of squirrels are also adaptations to colder winters in the temperate deciduous forest. (b) Sloths: slow-moving within the trees, these animals are adapted to expend very little energy which coincides with the slow digestion of fruit and leaves carried out by their specially adapted digestive system. Since sloths use very little energy, they do not need to eat much. (c) Squid: have a very large eye for hunting in the extremely low light levels of the deep sea as well as the ability to maneuver through water via jet propulsion, making them mostly fast-moving creatures. 2. Due to the protection offered by the mangrove swamp, it would certainly benefit a human population to restore a mangrove swamp over a housing development that would likely see damage or devastation shortly after it was rebuilt. Hurricane damage can be avoided if we resist the urge to build homes as close to the shore as possible, and instead guard our shores with protective barriers such as mangrove forests. 3. Five negative effects of the human population on the oceans: Pollution from developed areas including sewage, toxic chemicals, insecticides, and detergents invades the ocean and is carried by the tides throughout the ocean where they can invade the habits of animals, or even be consumed by them. Burning of fossil fuels has increased acidity of rain and lakes to the detriment of forests and freshwater inhabitants. Litter and improperly disposed trash is trapping and being eaten by animals, killing them. Dredging the ocean floor with heavy nets and chains as a method of fishing disturbs the ocean floor habitat and kills many non-target fish/animals in the process (by-catch). Drilling for oil sometimes results in oil spills and causes long-term damage to the oceans, killing animals and destroying shoreline habitats.

CHAPTER 40

Check Your Progress

40.1 To preserve natural resources/biodiversity. **40.2** Ecosystem-level conservation has the potential to save a large number of species instead of just one. **40.3** Reduced aquatic biodiversity would limit the amount and types of seafood we consume. **40.4** Native animals and plants in their natural environment. **40.5** A large number of people living and building structures a long the coast. **40.6** They reduce biodiversity by causing other species to become extinct. **40.7** Global climate change because it will affect so many species. **40.8** Overexploitation. **40.9** Disease. **40.10** Metapopulation. **40.11** To return the area to its former state (i.e., a thriving ecosystem). **40.12** Primarily by preserving ecosystems and areas of species richness. **40.13** Preservation of natural resources and less pollution of the enviironment. **40.14** Famers can grow salt tolerant plants and otherwise use drip irrigation; industry can use air instead of water for cooling purposes **14.15.** Use other means of controlling pests rather than pesticides such as polyculture and biological pest control; use drip irrigation to water plants, saving water; use legumes to fertilize land insted of artificial fertilizers.

Form Your Opinion

Page 808: 1. Scientists could use artificial selection to breed members of species that display adaptive traits or behaviors that make them tolerable of climate change in order to help these species survive, essentially fast forwarding what might occur via natural selection over a longer period of time. 2. Extinction could occur even when plenty of food is available to small, weak members of a population due to the ease with which predators can feed on the smaller, weaker members of a population. 3. Though the temperature might be suitable for survival, the new surroundings could be home to predators not previously encountered by a species and may not contain an adequate food supply. The ecosystem in which the species is adapted to living is suitable due to many factors, not temperature alone.

Page 812: 1. Hybridizing essentially creates an animal that is not technically an original member of the nearly extinct species. Mixing in a new animal creates a new species, creating a risk of extinction among the pure species, an unfortunate method of preservation that can contribute to the loss of characteristics unique to the nearly extinct species. 2. Zoos and hatcheries must sometimes maintain a species because its numbers are too low for it to sustain itself naturally. The habitat is unable to meet the needs of the species and the species is unable to adapt to changes occurring in the habitat. 3. Yes. If the habitat was maintained to begin with, rather than in need of restoration, the species would be able to sustain itself naturally. The ecosystem likely supports a range of species of plants and animals that would benefit from efforts to maintain it rather than efforts to maintain individual species outside the natural environment for reintroduction to nature.

Testing Yourself

1. e; 2. a; 3. b; 4. b; 5. The added shrimp pushes the salmon to a higher place in the food pyramid, indicating that less energy is now available to them. 6. d; 7. e; 8. e; 9. e; 10. e; 11. a; 12. e; 13. d; 14. e; 15. b; 16. Food webs show many connections between different populations. 17. b; 18. c; 19. e; 20. d; 21. b; 22. b

Thinking Scientifically

1. Overharvesting reduces genetic diversity due to the bottleneck effect. As with the cheetah, determine how many loci are now homozygous. 2. Besides having produced a population with limited genetic diversity, none of the problems that brought the species to near extinction (see Sections 40.5–40.9) have been solved.

Put the Pieces Together

Page 819: 1. Instead of increasing the manipulation of plants and animals via biotechnology, I would rather see the needs of the growing population met with an alternative method. For example, if the human population was to shift to growing and consuming locally, fostering crops suitable to the environment in which they are grown rather than the most popular crops that yield the best profits, we could use nature to our advantage to feed the growing population. 2. Emphasis on renewable energy is necessary in order to achieve sustainability because nonrenewable energy sources are quickly being depleted and cannot ever be replaced. I agree with this emphasis. It is important for people to understand that the sources of energy we are accustomed to using cannot feasibly be utilized long term and will, sooner than later, run out.
3. Yes, I am willing to pay extra for organic foods. The societal benefits of reduced pesticide and herbicide use include reduction of pollution of water and air and decreased side effects on non-target populations of animals/insects. 4. Yes answer: I agree that the human population should stabilize and that each couple should only replace itself because resources are finite. No answer: I do not agree that human population should stabilize and believe technology will always find a way to increase the availability of resources.

Glossary

A

abscisic acid (ABA) Plant hormone that causes stomata to close and initiates and maintains dormancy. 474

abscission Dropping of leaves, fruits, or flowers from a plant. 441, 474

acceptor end In tRNA, the end that binds to the amino acid. 200

accessory fruit Fruit, or an assemblage of fruits, whose fleshy parts are derived from tissues other than the ovary (e.g., strawberry). 497

acetylcholine (ACh) (uh-seet-ul-koh-leen) Neurotransmitter active in both the peripheral and central nervous systems. 530

acetylcholinesterase (AChE) (uh-seet-ul-koh-luh-nes-tuh-rays) Enzyme that breaks down acetylcholine bound to postsynaptic receptors within a synapse. 531

acid Molecules tending to raise the hydrogen ion concentration in a solution and to lower its pH numerically. 36

acoelomate Animal that has no body cavity (i.e., tapeworm). 387

actin (ak-tin) One of two major proteins of muscle; makes up thin filaments in myofibrils of muscle fibers. (See myosin.) 582

actin filament Cytoskeletal filaments of eukaryotic cells composed of the protein actin; also refers to the thin filaments of muscle cells. 78

action potential Electrochemical changes that take place across the axomembrane; the nerve impulse. 528

active site Region on the surface of an enzyme where the substrate binds and where the reaction occurs. 90

active transport Use of a plasma membrane carrier protein and energy to move a substance into or out of a cell from lower to higher concentration. 98

adaptation An organism's modification in structure, function, or behavior suitable to the environment. 16

adaptive radiation Evolution of several species from a common ancestor into new ecological or geographical zones. 278

addiction Physiological and psychological need for a habit-forming drug. 542

adenosine Portion of ATP and ADP that is composed of the base adenine and the sugar ribose. 58

adenosine diphosphate (ADP) (ah-den-ah-seen dy-fahs-fayt) Nucleotide with two phosphate groups that can accept another phosphate group and become ATP. 58

adenosine triphosphate (ATP) (ah-den-ah-seen try-fahs-fayt) Nucleotide with three phosphate groups. The breakdown of ATP into ADP + P makes energy available for energy-requiring processes in cells. 58

adhesion Attachment of cells, as when water adheres to the vessel walls of plants. 33

adipose tissue Connective tissue in which fat is stored. 511

adrenal cortex (uh-dree-nul kor-teks) Outer portion of the adrenal gland; secretes mineralocorticoids, such as aldosterone, and glucocorticoids, such as cortisol. 690

adrenal gland (uh-dree-nul) An endocrine gland that lies atop a kidney, consisting of the inner adrenal medulla and the outer adrenal cortex. 690

adrenal medulla (uh-dree-nul muh-dul-uh) Inner portion of the adrenal gland; secretes the hormones epinephrine and norepinephrine. 690

adrenocorticotropic hormone (ACTH) (uh-dree-noh-kawrt-ih-koh-troh-pik) Hormone secreted by the anterior lobe of the pituitary gland that stimulates activity in the adrenal cortex. 686

adult stem cells Cells in a mature body that have the ability to divide; found in red bone marrow. 145

aerobic Phase of cellular respiration that requires oxygen. 125, 323

afterbirth Placenta and the extraembryonic membranes, which are delivered (expelled) during the third stage of birth. 720

age structure diagram In demographics, a display of the age groups of a population; a growing population has a pyramid-shaped diagram. 731

aggregate fruit Fruit developed from several separate carpels of a single flower. 497

aldosterone (al-dahs-tuh-rohn) Hormone secreted by the adrenal cortex that decreases sodium and increases potassium excretion; raises blood volume and pressure. 675, 691

alga Type of protist that carries on photosynthesis; unicellular forms are a part of phytoplankton, and multicellular forms are called seaweed. 335

alien species Nonnative species that migrate or are introduced by humans into a new ecosystem; also called exotics. 806

alkaloids Bitter-tasting nitrogenous compounds that are basic (e.g., caffeine). 482

allantois (uh-lan-toh-is) Extraembryonic membrane that contributes to the formation of umbilical blood vessels in humans. 715

allele (uh-leel) Alternative form of a gene; alleles occur at the same locus on homologous chromosomes. 173

allergy Immune response to substances that usually are not recognized as foreign. 622

allopatric speciation Origin of new species between populations that are separated geographically. 276

alloploidy Polyploid organism that contains the genomes of two or more different species. 279

alternation of generations Life cycle, typical of plants, in which a diploid sporophyte alternates with a haploid gametophyte. 160, 354

alternative mRNA splicing Variation in pre-mRNA processing resulting in different mRNAs and different protein products. 199

altruism Social interaction that has the potential to decrease the lifetime reproductive success of the member exhibiting the behavior. 750

alveolus (pl., alveoli) Air sac of a lung. 654

Alzheimer disease (AD) Brain disorder characterized by a general loss of mental abilities. 538

amino acid Organic molecule having an amino group and an acid group, which covalently bonds to produce peptide molecules. 53

ammonia Colorless gas that has a penetrating odor and is soluble in water. 666

amniocentesis Procedure in which a sample of amniotic fluid is removed through the abdominal wall of a pregnant woman. Fetal cells in it are cultured before doing a karyotype of the chromosomes. 181

amnion (am-nee-ahn) Extraembryonic membrane that forms an enclosing, fluid-filled sac. 715

amniotic egg Egg that has an amnion, as seen during the development of reptiles, birds, and mammals. 402

amoeboid Cell that moves and engulfs debris with pseudopods. 339

amphibian Member of a class of vertebrates that includes frogs, toads, and salamanders; they are still tied to a watery environment for reproduction. 401

ampulla Expansion at the end of each semicircular canal that houses the receptors for rotational balance. 562

amygdala (uh-mig-duh-luh) Portion of the limbic system that functions to add emotional overtones to memories. 538

anabolism Metabolic process by which larger molecules are synthesized from smaller ones; anabolic metabolism. 135

anaerobic Growing or metabolizing in the absence of oxygen. 125

analogous structure Structure that has a similar function in separate lineages but differs in anatomy and ancestry. 257, 303

anaphylactic shock Severe systemic form of allergic reaction involving bronchiolar constriction, impaired breathing, vasodilation, and rapid drop in blood pressure with a threat of circulatory failure. 622

anchoring junction Junction between animal cells that attaches the cells to each other. 99

ancestral character Structural, physiological, or behavioral trait that is present in a common ancestor and all members of a group. 298

anemia (uh-nee-mee-uh) Inefficiency in the oxygen-carrying ability of blood due to a shortage of hemoglobin. 600

aneuploid Individual whose chromosome number is not an exact multiple of the haploid number for the species. 162

angiogenesis (an-jee-oh-jen-uh-sis) Formation of new blood vessels, an event that occurs to promote the enlargement of a tumor. 153, 223

angiosperm Flowering plant that produces seeds within an ovary, which develops into a fruit; therefore, the seeds are covered. 365

angiotensin II Hormone produced from angiotensinogen (a plasma protein) by the kidneys and lungs; raises blood pressure. 675

animal Multicellular, heterotrophic organism belonging to the animal kingdom. 15

annelid Member of a phylum of invertebrates that contains segmented worms, such as the earthworm and the clam worm. 392

annual ring Layer of wood (secondary xylem) usually produced during one growing season. 442

anorexia nervosa (a-nuh-rek-see-uh nur-vohsuh) Eating disorder characterized by a morbid fear of gaining weight. 644

anterior pituitary (pih-too-ih-tair-ee) Portion of the pituitary gland that is controlled by the hypothalamus and produces six types of hormones, some of which control other endocrine glands. 686

anther In flowering plants, pollen-bearing portion of stamen. 491

anthropoid ancestor Group of primates that includes monkeys, apes, and humans. 415

antibody (an-tih-bahd-ee) Protein produced in response to the presence of an antigen; each antibody combines with a specific antigen. 601

antibody-mediated defense Specific mechanism of defense in which plasma cells derived from B cells produce antibodies that combine with antigens. 600

anticodon (an-tih-koh-dahn) Three-base sequence in a transfer RNA molecule base that pairs with a complementary codon in mRNA. 200

anticodon end In tRNA, the end that binds to mRNA. 200

antidiuretic hormone (ADH) (an-tih-dy-uh-ret-ik) Hormone secreted by the posterior pituitary that increases the permeability of the collecting ducts in a kidney. 674, 686

antigen (an-tih-jun) Foreign substance, usually a protein or a polysaccharide, that stimulates the immune system to produce antibodies. 601, 615

antigen-presenting cell (APC) Cell that displays the antigen to the cells of the immune system so they can defend the body against that particular antigen. 616

antigen receptor Receptor proteins in the plasma membrane of immune system cells whose shape allows them to combine with a specific antigen. 616

antioxidant Substances, such as vitamins C, E, and A, which defend the body against free radicals. 642

aorta (ay-or-tuh) Major systemic artery that receives blood from the left ventricle. 592

aortic body Sensory receptor in the aortic arch sensitive to the O_2, CO_2, and H^+ content of the blood. 657

apical dominance Influence of a terminal bud in suppressing the growth of axillary buds. 470

apical meristem In vascular plants, masses of cells in the root and shoot that reproduce and elongate as primary growth occurs. 436

apoptosis (ap-uh-toh-sis, ahp-) Programmed cell death involving a cascade of specific cellular events leading to death and destruction of the cell. 152

appendicular skeleton (ap-un-dik-yuh-lur) Portion of the skeleton forming the pectoral girdles and upper extremities and the pelvic girdle and lower extremities. 572

appendix In humans, small, tubular appendage that extends outward from the cecum of the large intestine. 611

aquaporin Protein membrane channel through which water can diffuse. 97, 463, 674

arachnid Group of arthropods that contains spiders and scorpions. 395

arboreal Living in trees. 412

Archaea One of the three domains of life; contains prokaryotic cells that often live in extreme habitats and have unique genetic, biochemical, and physiological characteristics; its members are sometimes referred to as archaea. 14, 67, 297, 325

archaic human Regionally diverse descendants of *H. erectus* that lived in Africa, Asia, and Europe; considered by some to be a separate species. 421

archegonium Egg-producing structure, as in the moss life cycle. 355

Arctic tundra Biome that encircles the Earth just south of ice-covered polar seas in the Northern Hemisphere. 786

Ardi Fossilized remains of *Ardipithecus ramidus,* a hominin that lived 4.4 MYA. 416

ardipithecine One of several species of *Ardipithecus*, a genus that contains humanlike hominins and lived some 4–5 MYA. 416

arteriole (ar-teer-ee-ohl) Vessel that takes blood from an artery to capillaries. 595

artery Vessel that takes blood away from the heart to arterioles; characteristically possesses thick, elastic, muscular walls. 592

arthropod Member of a phylum of invertebrates that contains, among other groups, crustaceans and insects that have an exoskeleton and jointed appendages. 394

articular cartilage (ar-tik-yuh-lur) Hyaline cartilaginous covering over the articulating surface of the bones of synovial joints. 576

artificial selection Change in the genetic structure of populations due to selective breeding by humans. 17, 252

ascus Fingerlike sac where ascospores are produced during sexual reproduction of sac fungi. 372

asexual reproduction Reproduction that requires only one parent and does not involve gametes. 160, 700

A site In a ribosome, the place where a tRNA carrying an amino acid is bound to mRNA. 200

associative learning Acquired ability to associate two stimuli or a stimulus and a response. 747

assortative mating Individuals tend to mate with those that have the same phenotype as themselves with respect to certain characteristics. 261

aster Short, radiating fibers about the centrioles at the poles of a spindle. 148

asthma (az-muh, as-) Condition in which bronchioles constrict and cause difficulty in breathing. 622, 660

atom Smallest particle of an element that displays the properties of the element. 9, 26

atomic mass Mass of an atom equal to the number of protons plus the number of neutrons within the nucleus. 27

atomic number Number of protons within the nucleus of an atom. 27

atomic symbol One or two letters that represent the name of an element—e.g., H stands for a hydrogen atom. 26

ATP synthase complex Complex formed of enzymes and their carrier proteins; functions in the production of ATP in chloroplasts and mitochondria. 110, 131

atrial natriuretic hormone (ANH) (ay-tree-ul nay-tree-yoo-ret-ik) Hormone secreted by the heart that increases sodium excretion and, therefore, lowers blood volume and pressure. 675

atrioventricular valve Valve located between the atrium and the ventricle. 592

atrium (ay-tree-um) One of the upper chambers of the heart, either the left atrium or the right atrium, that receives blood. 592

australopithecine One of several species of *Australopithecus*, a genus that contains the first generally recognized hominids. 418

Australopithecus africanus Hominid that lived between 3.6 and 3 MYA; e.g., Lucy, discovered at Hadar, Ethiopia, in 1974. 418

autoimmune disorder Disorder that results when the immune system mistakenly attacks the body's own tissues. 621

autonomic system (aw-tuh-nahm-ik) Branch of the peripheral nervous system that has control over the internal organs; consists of the sympathetic and parasympathetic divisions. 541

autoploidy Polyploid organism that contains a duplicated genome of the same species. 279

autosomal chromosome Any chromosome of a type that is the same in males and females of a species. 178

autosome (aw-tuh-sohm) Any chromosome other than the sex chromosomes. 144

autotroph Organism that can capture energy and synthesize organic nutrients from inorganic nutrients. 106, 770

auxins A group of plant hormones regulating growth, particularly cell elongation; most often indoleacetic acid (IAA). 470

avian influenza Flu caused by a virus that is able to spread from birds to humans. 313

axial skeleton (ak-see-ul) Portion of the skeleton that supports and protects the organs of the head, the neck, and the trunk. 572

axillary bud Bud located in the axil of a leaf. 432

axon (ak-sahn) Elongated portion of a neuron that conducts nerve impulses, typically from the cell body to the synapse. 527

B

Bacteria One of the three domains of life; contains prokaryotic cells that differ from archaea because they have their own unique genetic, biochemical, and physiological characteristics. 14, 67, 304

bacteriophage Virus that infects bacteria. 311

ball-and-socket joint The most freely movable type of joint (e.g., the shoulder or hip joint). 577

bark External part of a tree, containing cork, cork cambium, and phloem. 442

Barr body Dark-staining body (discovered by M. Barr) in the nuclei of female mammals that contains a condensed, inactive X chromosome. 214

basal body Cytoplasmic structure that is located at the base of and may organize cilia or flagella. 79

basal nuclei (bay-sul) Subcortical nuclei deep within the white matter that serve as relay stations for motor impulses and produce dopamine to help control skeletal muscle activities. 535

base Molecules tending to lower the hydrogen ion concentration in a solution and raise the pH numerically. 36

basement membrane Layer of nonliving material that anchors epithelial tissue to underlying connective tissue. 509

basidium Clublike structure in which nuclear fusion, meiosis, and basidiospore production occur during sexual reproduction of club fungi. 373

B cell Lymphocyte that matures in the bone marrow and, when stimulated by the presence of a specific antigen, gives rise to antibody-producing plasma cells. 601, 611

B cell receptor (BCR) Molecule on the surface of a B cell that binds to a specific antigen. 616

beneficial nutrient In plants, element that is either required or enhances the growth and production of a plant. 460

behavior Observable, coordinated responses to environmental stimuli. 744

bicarbonate ion Ion that participates in buffering the blood; the form in which carbon dioxide is transported in the bloodstream. 658

bilateral symmetry Body plan having two corresponding or complementary halves. 381

bile Secretion of the liver that is temporarily stored and concentrated in the gallbladder before being released into the small intestine, where it emulsifies fat. 634

binary fission Bacterial reproduction into two daughter cells without utilizing a mitotic spindle. 321

binge-eating disorder Condition characterized by overeating episodes that are not followed by purging. 644

biocultural evolution Phase of human evolution in which cultural events affect natural selection. 420

biodiversity Variety of life within an ecosystem, biome, or biosphere. 800

biodiversity hotspot Region of the world that contains unusually large concentrations of species. 801

biogeochemical cycle (by-oh-jee-oh-kem-ih-kul) Circulating pathway of elements such as carbon and nitrogen involving exchange pools, storage areas, and biotic communities. 774

biogeography Study of the geographical distribution of organisms. 258

bioinformatics Computer technologies used to study the genome. 240

biological clock Internal mechanism that maintains a biological rhythm in the absence of environmental stimuli. 479

biological species concept The concept that defines species as groups of populations that have the potential to interbreed and are reproductively isolated from other groups. 272

biome One of the biosphere's major terrestrial communities, characterized by certain climatic conditions and particular types of plants. 785

biomolecules Organic molecules common to organisms: carbohydrates, proteins, fats, and nucleic acids. 44

biosphere (by-oh-sfeer) Zone of air, land, and water at the surface of the Earth in which living organisms are found. 12, 728

biotechnology Use of a natural biological system to produce a product or achieve an end desired by humans; may involve using recombinant DNA technology. 230

biotechnology product Product created by using biotechnology techniques. 233

biotic potential Maximum reproductive rate of an organism, given unlimited resources and ideal environmental conditions. 730

bipedalism Walking erect on two feet. 416

bird Endothermic vertebrate that has feathers and wings, is often adapted for flight, and lays hard-shelled eggs. 402

bivalve Type of mollusc with a shell composed of two valves; includes clams, oysters, and scallops. 391

blade Broad, expanded portion of a plant leaf that may be single or compound. 433

blastocoel Fluid-filled cavity of a blastula. 710

blastocyst (blas-tuh-sist) Early stage of human embryonic development that consists of a hollow, fluid-filled ball of cells. 716

blastopore Opening into the primitive gut formed at gastrulation. 711

blastula Hollow, fluid-filled ball of cells occurring during animal development prior to gastrula formation. 710

blind spot Region of the retina lacking rods or cones where the optic nerve leaves the eye. 554

blood pressure Force of blood pushing against the inside wall of an artery. 599

bone Connective tissue having protein fibers and a hard matrix of inorganic salts, notably calcium salts. 511

bottleneck effect Cause of genetic drift; occurs when a majority of genotypes are prevented from participating in the production of the next generation as a result of a natural disaster or human interference. 263

brain stem Portion of the brain consisting of the medulla oblongata, pons, and midbrain. 536

bronchi (sing., bronchus) Two major divisions of the trachea leading to the lungs. 654

bronchioles (brahng-kee-ohlz) Smaller air passages in the lungs that begin at the bronchi and terminate in alveoli. 654

brown algae Marine photosynthetic protists with a notable abundance of xanthophyll pigments; this group includes well-known seaweeds of northern rocky shores. 344

bryophyte Member of one of three phyla of nonvascular plants—the mosses, liverworts, and hornworts. 356

buffer Substance or group of substances that tends to resist pH changes of a solution, thus stabilizing its relative acidity and basicity. 37

bulbourethral gland (bul-boh-yoo-ree-thrul) Either of two small structures located below the prostate gland in males; each adds secretions to semen. 702

bulimia nervosa (byoo-lee-mee-uh, -lim-ee-, nur-voh-suh) Eating disorder characterized by binge eating followed by purging via self-induced vomiting or use of a laxative. 644

bulk feeder Animal that eats relatively large pieces of food. 628

bulk transport Movement of elements in an organism in large amounts. 98

bundle sheath Sheath located around the veins of a leaf; formed from tightly packed cells. 444

bursa (bur-suh) Saclike, fluid-filled structure, lined with synovial membrane, that occurs near a joint. 577

C

C₃ photosynthesis Type of photosynthesis in which the first stable product following carbon dioxide fixation is a 3-carbon compound produced by the Calvin cycle. 116

C₄ photosynthesis Type of photosynthesis in which the first stable product is a 4-carbon molecule that releases carbon dioxide to the Calvin cycle. 116

calcitonin (kal-sih-toh-nin) Hormone secreted by the thyroid gland that increases the blood calcium level. 689

Calorie (kcal) Amount of heat energy required to raise the temperature of 1 g of water 1°C. 34

Cambrian explosion Sudden appearance in the fossil record of most major groups of complex animals around 530 MYA. 381

camouflage Method of hiding from predators in which the organism's behavior, form, and pattern of coloration allow it to blend into the background and prevent detection. 763

CAM photosynthesis Crassulacean-acid metabolism; plant fixes carbon dioxide at night to produce a C₄ molecule that releases carbon dioxide to the Calvin cycle during the day. 117

capillary (kap-uh-lair-ee) Microscopic vessel connecting arterioles to venules; exchange of substances between blood and tissue fluid occurs across its thin walls. 595

capsid Protein coat or shell that surrounds a virion's nucleic acid. 310

capsule Gelatinous layer surrounding the cells of blue-green algae and certain bacteria. 67

carbaminohemoglobin Hemoglobin carrying carbon dioxide. 658

carbohydrate Class of organic compounds that includes monosaccharides, disaccharides, and polysaccharides. 639

carbonic anhydrase (kar-bahn-ik an-hy-drays, -drayz) Enzyme in red blood cells that speeds the formation of carbonic acid from the reactants water and carbon dioxide. 658

carcinogenesis (kar-suh-nuh-jen-uh-sis) Development of cancer. 153, 223

cardiac conduction system System of specialized cardiac muscle fibers that conduct impulses from the SA node to the chambers of the heart, causing them to contract. 594

cardiac cycle One complete cycle of systole and diastole for all heart chambers. 594

cardiac muscle Striated, involuntary muscle found only in the heart. 512

cardiac pacemaker Mass of specialized cardiac muscle tissue that controls the rhythm of the heartbeat; the SA node. 594

cardiovascular system Organ system in which blood vessels distribute blood under the pumping action of the heart. 517, 592

carnivore (kar-nuh-vor) Consumer in a food chain that eats other animals. 770

carotenoid Yellow or orange pigment that serves as an accessory to chlorophyll in photosynthesis. 109

carotid body (kuh-raht-id) Structure located at the branching of the carotid arteries; contains chemoreceptors sensitive to the O_2, CO_2, and H^+ content in blood. 657

carpel Ovule-bearing unit that is a part of a pistil. 365, 491

carrier Heterozygous individual who has no apparent abnormality but can pass on an allele for a recessively inherited genetic disorder. 178

carrying capacity Maximum number of individuals of any species that can be supported by a particular ecosystem on a long-term basis. 732

cartilage Connective tissue in which the cells lie within lacunae separated by a flexible proteinaceous matrix. 511

Casparian strip Layer of impermeable lignin and suberin bordering four sides of root endodermal cells; prevents water and solute transport between adjacent cells. 463

catabolism Metabolic process that breaks down large molecules into smaller ones; catabolic metabolism. 135

cecum (see-kum) Small pouch that lies below the entrance of the small intestine and is the blind end of the large intestine. 630

cell Smallest unit that displays the properties of life; always contains cytoplasm surrounded by a plasma membrane. 9

cell body Portion of a neuron that contains a nucleus and from which dendrites and an axon extend. 527

cell cycle Repeating sequence of cellular events that consists of interphase, mitosis, and cytokinesis. 145

cell-mediated defense Specific mechanism of defense in which T cells destroy antigen-bearing cells. 616

cell plate Structure across a dividing plant cell that signals the location of new plasma membranes and cell walls. 150

cell suspension culture Plant tissue extraction of chemicals performed in a laboratory without needing to disturb plants in their natural environments. 500

cell theory One of the major theories of biology; states that all organisms are made up of cells and that cells come only from preexisting cells. 9, 64

cellular respiration Metabolic reactions that use the energy primarily from carbohydrates but also from fatty acid or amino acid breakdown to produce ATP molecules. 123

cellular slime mold Free-living amoeboid cells that feed on bacteria and yeasts by phagocytosis and aggregate to form a plasmodium that produces spores. 342

cellulose (sel-yuh-lohs, -lohz) Polysaccharide that is the major complex carbohydrate in plant cell walls. 48

cell wall Structure that surrounds a plant, protistan, fungal, or bacterial cell and maintains the cell's shape and rigidity. 67

central nervous system (CNS) Portion of the nervous system consisting of the brain and spinal cord. 526, 533

central vacuole In a plant cell, a large, fluid-filled sac that stores metabolites. During growth, it enlarges, forcing the primary cell wall to expand and the cell surface-area-to-volume ratio to increase. 74

centriole (sen-tree-ohl) Cellular structure, existing in pairs, that possibly organizes the mitotic spindle for chromosomal movement during mitosis and meiosis. 79

centromere (sen-truh-meer) Constriction where sister chromatids of a chromosome are held together. 144

centrosome Central microtubule organizing center of cells. In animal cells, it contains two centrioles. 78, 146

cephalization Having a well-recognized anterior head with a brain and sensory receptors. 382, 532

cephalopod Type of mollusc in which a modified foot develops into the head region; includes squid, cuttlefish, octopus, and nautilus. 391

cerebellum (ser-uh-bel-um) Part of the brain located posterior to the medulla oblongata and pons that coordinates skeletal muscles to produce smooth, graceful motions. 536

cerebral cortex (suh-ree-brul, ser-uh-brul kor-teks) Outer layer of cerebral hemispheres; receives sensory information and controls motor activities. 535

cerebral hemisphere One of the large, paired structures that together constitute the cerebrum of the brain. 535

cerebrospinal fluid Fluid found in the ventricles of the brain, in the central canal of the spinal cord, and in association with the meninges. 513, 534

cerebrum (sair-uh-brum, suh-ree-brum) Main part of the brain consisting of two large masses, or cerebral hemispheres; the largest part of the brain in mammals. 535

cervix (sur-viks) Narrow end of the uterus, which projects into the vagina. 704

cesarean section Birth by surgical incision of the abdomen and uterus. 719

character Any structural, chromosomal, or molecular feature that distinguishes one group from another. 296

character displacement Tendency for characteristics to be more divergent when similar species belong to the same community than when they are isolated from one another. 760

chemiosmosis Ability of certain membranes to use a hydrogen ion gradient to drive ATP formation. 113, 131

chemoreceptor (kee-moh-rih-sep-tur) Sensory receptor that is sensitive to chemical stimuli—for example, receptors for taste and smell. 550

chemosynthetic Organism able to synthesize organic molecules by using carbon dioxide as the carbon source and the oxidation of an inorganic substance (such as hydrogen sulfide) as the energy source. 323

chitin Strong but flexible nitrogenous polysaccharide found in the exoskeleton of arthropods. 48, 394

chlamydia infection (kluh-mid-ee-uh) Sexually transmitted disease, caused by the bacterium *Chlamydia trachomatis*; can lead to pelvic inflammatory disease. 708

chlorophyll, chlorophyll *a*, chlorophyll *b* Green pigment that absorbs solar energy and is important in algal and plant photosynthesis; occurs as chlorophyll *a* and chlorophyll *b*. 107, 109

chloroplast Membrane-bounded organelle in algae and plants with chlorophyll-containing membranous thylakoids; where photosynthesis takes place. 76, 107

cholesterol One of the major lipids found in animal plasma membranes; makes the membrane impermeable to many molecules. 93, 640

chordate Member of the phylum Chordata, which includes lancelets, tunicates, fishes, amphibians, reptiles, birds, and mammals; characterized by a notochord, dorsal tubular nerve cord, pharyngeal gill pouches, and a postanal tail at some point in the life cycle. 398

chorion (kor-ee-ahn) Extraembryonic membrane that contributes to placenta formation. 715

chorionic villi (kor-ee-ahn-ik vil-eye) Treelike extensions of the chorion that project into the maternal tissues at the placenta. 717

chorionic villi sampling (CVS) Removal of cells from the chorionic villi portion of the placenta. Karyotyping is done to determine if the fetus has a chromosomal abnormality. 181

choroid (kor-oyd) Vascular, pigmented middle layer of the eyeball. 554

chromatin (kroh-muh-tin) Network of fine threads in the nucleus that are composed of DNA and proteins. 70, 214

chromatin remodeling complex During transcription, a protein complex that moves aside nucleosomes so that mRNA polymerase and transcription factors have access to and can start transcription of a gene. 215

chromosome (kroh-muh-som) Chromatin condensed into a compact structure. 70

chronic bronchitis Obstructive pulmonary disorder that tends to recur; marked by inflamed airways filled with mucus and degenerative changes in the bronchi, including loss of cilia. 660

chyme Thick, semiliquid food material that passes from the stomach to the small intestine. 634

ciliary body (sil-ee-air-ee) Structure associated with the choroid layer that contains ciliary muscle and controls the shape of the lens of the eye. 554

ciliary muscle Within the ciliary body of the vertebrate eye, the ciliary muscle controls the shape of the lens. 555

ciliate Complex unicellular protist that moves by means of cilia and digests food in food vacuoles. 340

cilium (pl., cilia) (sil-ee-um) Short, hairlike projection from the plasma membrane, occurring usually in large numbers. 79

circadian rhythm Regular physiological or behavioral event that occurs on an approximately 24-hour cycle. 479, 693

clade Taxon or other group consisting of an ancestral species and all of its descendants, forming a distinct branch on a phylogenetic tree. 300

cladistics Method of systematics that uses shared derived characters to place organisms in clades and construct cladograms. 300

cladogram In cladistics, a branching diagram that shows the relationship among species in regard to their shared derived characters. 300

class One of the categories, or taxa, used by taxonomists to group species; class is the taxon above the order level. 14, 296

classical conditioning Type of learning whereby an unconditioned stimulus that elicits a specific response is paired with a neutral stimulus so that the response becomes conditioned. 747

cleavage Cell division without cytoplasmic addition or enlargement; occurs during the first stage of animal development. 710

cleavage furrow In animal cells, an indentation that encircles the cell to divide the cytoplasm during cytokinesis. 150

climate Weather condition of an area, including especially prevailing temperature and average/yearly rainfall. 782

climax community In ecology, community that results when succession has come to an end. 767

clitoris Small, erectile, female organ located in the vulva; homologous to the penis. 704

cloaca Posterior portion of the digestive tract in certain vertebrates that receives feces and urogenital products. 630

clonal selection model Concept that an antigen selects which lymphocyte will undergo clonal expansion and produce more lymphocytes bearing the same type of antigen receptor. 617

closed circulatory system Blood is confined to vessels and is kept separate from the interstitial fluid. 590

cnidarian Invertebrate in the phylum Cnidaria existing as either a polyp or a medusa with two tissue layers and radial symmetry. 386

coal Fossil fuel formed millions of years ago from plant material that did not decay. 364

cochlea (kohk-lee-uh, koh-klee-uh) Portion of the inner ear that resembles a snail's shell and contains the spiral organ, the sense organ for hearing. 559

codominance Inheritance pattern in which both alleles of a gene are equally expressed. 182

codon Three-base sequence in messenger RNA that causes the insertion of a particular amino acid into a protein or termination of translation. 198

coelom (see-lum) Embryonic body cavity lying between the digestive tract and body wall that becomes the thoracic and abdominal cavities. 383

coelomate Animal having a coelom. 390

coenzyme (koh-en-zym) Nonprotein organic molecule that aids the action of the enzyme to which it is loosely bound. 91

coevolve (coevolution) Interaction of two species such that each influences the evolution of the other. 495

cofactor Nonprotein adjunct required by an enzyme in order to function; many cofactors are metal ions, others are coenzymes. 91

cohesion Clinging together of water molecules. 33

cohesion-tension model Explanation for upward transport of water in xylem, based upon transpiration-created tension and the cohesive properties of water molecules. 454

cohort Group of individuals having a statistical factor in common, such as year of birth, in a population study. 730

coleoptile Protective sheath that covers the young leaves of a seedling. 471

collecting duct Duct within the kidney that receives fluid from several nephrons; the reabsorption of water occurs here. 671

collenchyma cell Plant tissue composed of cells with unevenly thickened walls; supports growth of stems and petioles. 436

colon (koh-lun) The major portion of the large intestine, consisting of the ascending colon, the transverse colon, and the descending colon. 636

colonial flagellate hypthesis The proposal first put forth by Haeckel that protozoans descended from colonial protists; supported by the similarity of sponges to flagellated protists. 381

colony Loose association of cells that remain independent for most functions. 346

columnar epithelium Type of epithelial tissue with cylindrical cells. 509

commensalism Symbiotic relationship in which one species is benefited, and the other is neither harmed nor benefited. 764

common ancestor Ancestor held in common by at least two lines of descent. 13, 256, 298

communication Signal by a sender that influences the behavior of a receiver. 752

community Assemblage of populations interacting with one another within the same environment. 12, 728, 760

compact bone Type of bone that contains osteons consisting of concentric layers of matrix and osteocytes in lacunae. 511, 576

companion cell Cell associated with sieve-tube members in the phloem of vascular plants. 437, 452

comparative genomics Study of genomes through a comparison of their coding and noncoding DNA sequences. 221

competition Interaction between two organisms in which both require the same limited resource, which results in harm to both. 760

competitive exclusion principle Theory that no two species can occupy the same niche. 760

competitive inhibition Form of enzyme inhibition whereby the substrate and inhibitor are both able to bind to the enzyme's active site; each complexes with the enzyme. Only when the substrate is at the active site will product form. 92

complement Collective name for a series of enzymes and activators in the blood, some of which may bind to antibody and may lead to rupture of a foreign cell. 612

complementary base pairing Hydrogen bonding between particular bases. In DNA, thymine (T) pairs with adenine (A), and guanine (G) pairs with cytosine (C); in RNA, uracil (U) pairs with A, and G pairs with C. 57, 194

complex carbohydrates Mixture of carbohydrates that must be digested to release sugars; preferably also contain cellulose that acts as roughage in the diet. 48

compound Substance having two or more different elements, united chemically in fixed ratio. 29

compound light microscope Consists of a two-lens system, one above the other, to magnify an object. 66

concentration gradient Amount that changes from high to low or vice versa. 96

conclusion Statement following an experiment as to whether the results support the hypothesis. 5

conifer Member of a group of cone-bearing gymnosperm plants that includes pine, cedar, and spruce trees. 362

conjugation Transfer of genetic materials from one cell to another. 322, 345

conjunctiva Delicate membrane that lines the eyelid protecting the sclera. 554

connective tissue Type of tissue characterized by cells separated by a matrix that often contains fibers. 510

conservation biology Scientific discipline that seeks to understand the effects of human activities on species, communities, and ecosystems and to develop practical approaches to preventing the extinction of species and the destruction of ecosystems. 800

consumer Organism that feeds on another organism in a food chain; primary consumers eat plants, and secondary consumers eat animals. 770

control group Sample that goes through all the steps of an experiment but lacks the factor or is not exposed to the factor being tested; used as a standard against which experimental results are checked. 5

copulation Sexual union between a male and a female. 700

coral reef Area of biological abundance in warm, shallow tropical waters on and around coral formations. 793

cork cambium Lateral meristem that produces cork. 442

corm Underground, upright plant stem where food is stored, usually in the form of starch. 499

cornea (kor-nee-uh) Transparent, anterior portion of the outer layer of the eyeball. 554

corpus luteum (kor-pus loot-ee-um) Yellow body that forms in the ovary from a follicle that has discharged its secondary oocyte; secretes progesterone and some estrogen. 705

cortex In plants, ground tissue bounded by the epidermis and vascular tissue in stems and roots; in animals, outer layer of an organ such as the cortex of the kidney or the adrenal gland. 438

cortisol (kor-tuh-sawl) Glucocorticoid secreted by the adrenal cortex that responds to stress on a long-term basis; reduces inflammation and promotes protein and fat metabolism. 690

cotyledon Seed leaf for the embryo of a flowering plant; provides nutrient molecules for the developing plant before photosynthesis begins. 365, 496

countercurrent flow mechanism Fluids flow side-by-side in opposite directions, as in the exchange of fluids in the kidneys. 473, 652

coupled reaction Reaction that occurs simultaneously; one is an exergonic reaction that releases energy, and the other is an endergonic reaction that requires energy in order to occur. 89

covalent bond (coh-vay-lent) Chemical bond in which atoms share one pair of electrons. 31

cranial nerve Nerve that arises from the brain. 539

cristae Short, fingerlike projections formed by the folding of the inner membrane of mitochondria. 128

Cro-Magnon Common name for the first fossils to be designated *Homo sapiens*. 422

crop Part of the digestive tract in birds and some invertebrates that stores or digests food. 630

crossing-over Exchange of segments between nonsister chromatids of a tetrad during meiosis. 156

crustacean Member of a group of marine arthropods that contains, among others, shrimps, crabs, crayfish, and lobsters 395

cuboidal epithelium Type of epithelial tissue with cube-shaped cells. 509

culture Total pattern of human behavior; includes technology and the arts and is dependent upon the capacity to speak and transmit knowledge. 420

Cushing syndrome (koosh-ing) Condition resulting from hypersecretion of glucocorticoids; characterized by thin arms and legs and a "moon face," and accompanied by high blood glucose and sodium levels. 691

cuticle Waxy layer covering the epidermis of a plant that protects the plant against water loss and disease-causing organisms. 355, 436

cyanobacteria Photosynthetic bacteria that contain chlorophyll and release oxygen; formerly called blue-green algae. 324

cyanogenic glycoside Plant compound that contains sugar; produces cyanide. 482

cycad Type of gymnosperm with palmate leaves and massive cones; cycads are most often found in the tropics and subtropics. 362

cyclic adenosine monophosphate (cAMP) (sy-klik, sih-klik) ATP-related compound that acts as the second messenger in peptide hormone transduction; it initiates activity of the metabolic machinery. 684

cytochrome Any of several iron-containing protein molecules that serve as electron carriers in photosynthesis and cellular respiration. 130

cytokine (sy-tuh-kyn) Type of protein secreted by a T lymphocyte that stimulates cells of the immune system to perform their various functions. 473, 613

cytokinesis (sy-tuh-kyn-ee-sus) Division of the cytoplasm following mitosis and meiosis. 145

cytokinin Plant hormone that promotes cell division; often works in combination with auxin during organ development in plant embryos. 473

cytoplasm (sy-tuh-plaz-um) Contents of a cell between the nucleus and the plasma membrane that contains the organelles. 67

cytoskeleton Internal framework of the cell, consisting of microtubules, actin filaments, and intermediate filaments. 78

cytotoxic T cell (sy-tuh-tahk-sik) T lymphocyte that attacks and kills antigen-bearing cells. 616

D

data Facts or pieces of information collected through observation and/or experimentation. 5

daughter cell Cell that arises from a parental cell by mitosis or meiosis. 146

day-neutral plant Plant whose flowering is not dependent on day length, e.g., tomato and cucumber. 481

deamination Removal of an amino group ($-NH_2$) from an amino acid or other organic compound. 135

deciduous Plant that sheds its leaves annually. 433

decomposer Organism, usually a bacterium or fungus, that breaks down organic matter into inorganic nutrients that can be recycled in the environment. 770

dehiscent Anther, fruit, or other plant structure that opens to permit the release of reproductive bodies inside. 497

dehydration reaction Chemical reaction resulting in a covalent bond and the loss of a water molecule. 46

delayed allergic response Allergic response initiated at the site of the allergen by sensitized T cells, involving macrophages and regulated by cytokines. 622

deletion Change in chromosome structure in which the end of a chromosome breaks off or two simultaneous breaks lead to the loss of an internal segment; often causes abnormalities (e.g., cri du chat syndrome). 164

demographic transition Due to industrialization, a decline in the birthrate following a reduction in the death rate so that the population growth rate is lowered. 737

denatured (denaturation) Loss of an enzyme's normal shape so that it no longer functions; caused by a less than optimal pH or temperature. 91

dendrite (den-dryt) Branched ending of a neuron that conducts signals toward the cell body. 527

dendritic cell Antigen-presenting cell of the epidermis and mucous membranes. 613

denitrification Conversion of nitrate or nitrite to nitrogen gas by bacteria in soil. 775

dense fibrous connective tissue Type of connective tissue containing many collagen fibers packed together and found in tendons and ligaments, for example. 511

density-dependent factor Biotic factor, such as disease or competition, that affects population size according to the population's density. 734

density-independent factor Abiotic factor, such as fire or flood, that affects population size independent of the population's density. 733

dental caries (kar-eez) Tooth decay that occurs when bacteria within the mouth metabolize sugar and give off acids that erode teeth; a cavity. 633

deoxyribose Pentose sugar found in DNA that has one less hydroxyl group than ribose. 47

depolarization Loss in polarization, as when a nerve impulse occurs. 528

derived character Structural, physiological, or behavioral trait that is present in a specific lineage and is not present in the common ancestor for several lineages. 298

dermis Region of skin that lies beneath the epidermis. 515

desert Ecological biome characterized by a limited amount of rainfall; deserts have hot days and cool nights. 789

detrital food web (dih-tryt-ul) Complex pattern of interlocking and crisscrossing food chains that begins with detritus. 773

detritus Partially decomposed organic matter derived from tissues and animal wastes. 770

deuterostomes Group of coelomate animals in which the second embryonic opening is associated with the mouth; the first embryonic opening, the blastopore, is associated with the anus. 383

diaphragm (dy-uh-fram) Dome-shaped horizontal sheet of muscle and connective tissue that divides the thoracic cavity from the abdominal cavity. 707

diastole (dy-as-tuh-lee) Relaxation period of a heart chamber during the cardiac cycle. 594

diastolic pressure (dy-uh-stahl-ik) Arterial blood pressure during the diastolic phase of the cardiac cycle. 599

diatom Golden-brown alga with a cell wall having two parts, or valves; significant part of phytoplankton. 343

diencephalon (dy-en-sef-uh-lahn) Portion of the brain in the region of the third ventricle that includes the thalamus and hypothalamus. 536

differentially permeable Ability of plasma membranes to regulate the passage of substances into and out of the cell, allowing some to pass through and preventing the passage of others. 96

digestive system Organ system that includes the mouth, esophagus, stomach, small intestine, and large intestine (colon), which receives food and digests it into nutrient molecules. Also has associated organs: teeth, tongue, salivary glands, liver, gallbladder, and pancreas. 517

dihybrid cross Single genetic cross involving two different traits, such as flower color and plant height. 174

dinoflagellate Photosynthetic unicellular protist with two flagella, one whiplash and the other located within a groove between protective cellulose plates; a significant part of phytoplankton. 343

diploid life cycle Presence of two of each type of chromosome at interphase of the cell cycle. 160

diploid (2n) number Cell condition in which two of each type of chromosome are present in the nucleus. 146

directional selection Outcome of natural selection in which an extreme phenotype is favored, usually in a changing environment. 265

disaccharide (dy-sak-uh-ryd) Sugar that contains two units of a monosaccharide (e.g., maltose). 47

disruptive selection Outcome of natural selection in which the two extreme phenotypes are favored over the average phenotype, leading to more than one distinct form. 265

distal convoluted tubule Final portion of a nephron that joins with a collecting duct; associated with tubular secretion. 671

DNA (deoxyribonucleic acid) Nucleic acid polymer produced from covalent bonding of nucleotide monomers that contain the sugar deoxyribose; the genetic material of nearly all organisms. 10, 56, 192

DNA fingerprinting The use of DNA fragment lengths resulting from restriction enzyme cleavage to identify particular individuals. 197

DNA ligase (ly-gays) Enzyme that links DNA fragments; used during production of recombinant DNA to join foreign DNA to vector DNA. 232

DNA microarrays Thousands of different DNA fragments (probes) arranged in an array (grid); used to detect and measure gene expression. 240

DNA polymerase During replication, an enzyme that joins the nucleotides complementary to a DNA template. 196

DNA replication Synthesis of a new DNA double helix prior to mitosis and meiosis in eukaryotic cells and during prokaryotic fission in prokaryotic cells. 196

domain The primary taxonomic group above the kingdom level; all living organisms may be placed in one of three domains. 14, 296

dominant allele (uh-leel) Allele that exerts its phenotypic effect in the heterozygote; it masks the expression of the recessive allele. 173

dormancy In plants, a cessation of growth under conditions that seem appropriate for growth. 472

dorsal root ganglion (gang-glee-un) Mass of sensory neuron cell bodies located in the dorsal root of a spinal nerve. 539, 540

double fertilization In flowering plants, one sperm joins with polar nuclei within the embryo sac to produce a 3n endosperm nucleus, and another sperm joins with an egg to produce a zygote. 367, 495

double helix Double spiral; describes the three-dimensional shape of DNA. 194

doubling time Number of years it takes for a population to double in size. 737

drug abuse Compulsive and self-damaging use of a drug that primarily affects the nervous system. 542

dryopithecine Tree dweller; ancestral to apes. 415

duodenum (doo-uh-dee-num) First part of the small intestine where chyme enters from the stomach. 634

duplication Change in chromosome structure in which a particular segment is present more than once in the same chromosome. 164

E

Ebola One of a number of different viruses; causes a deadly hemorrhagic fever. 313

ecdysozoa Protostome characterized by periodic molting of the exoskeleton. Includes the roundworms and the arthropods. 383

echinoderm Phylum of marine animals that includes sea stars, sea urchins, and sand dollars; characterized by radial symmetry and a water vascular system. 397

ecological niche Role an organism plays in its community, including its habitat and its interactions with other organisms. 760

ecological pyramid Pictorial graph based on the biomass, number of organisms, or energy content of various trophic levels in a food web—from the producer to the final consumer populations. 773

ecology Study of the interactions of organisms with other organisms and with the physical and chemical environment. 728, 770

ecosystem (ek-oh-sis-tum, ee-koh-) Biological community together with the associated abiotic environment; characterized by energy flow and chemical cycling. 12, 728

ecosystem diversity Variety of species in a particular locale, dependent on the species interactions. 801

ectoderm Outermost primary tissue layer of an animal embryo; gives rise to the nervous system and the outer layer of the integument. 711

ectotherm Organism having a body temperature that varies according to the environmental temperature. 402

electrocardiogram (ECG) (ih-lek-troh-kar-dee-uh-gram) Recording of the electrical activity associated with the heartbeat. 594

electromagnetic receptor Sensory receptor that detects energy of different

wavelengths, such as electricity, magnetism, and light. 550

electron Negative subatomic particle, moving in an energy level around the nucleus of an atom. 27

electronegativity Ability of an atom to attract electrons toward itself in a chemical bond. 32

electron shell Concentric energy levels in which electrons orbit. 27

electron transport chain (ETC) Passage of electrons along a series of membrane-bounded carrier molecules from a higher to lower energy level; the energy released is used for the synthesis of ATP. 110, 125, 130

element Substance that cannot be broken down into substances with different properties; composed of only one type of atom. 26

El Nino—Southern Oscillation Warming of water in the Eastern Pacific equatorial region such that the Humboldt Current is displaced with possible negative results, including reduction in marine life. 784

elongation During DNA replication or the formation of mRNA during transcription, elongation is the step whereby the bases are added to the new or "daughter" strands of DNA or the mRNA transcript strand is lengthened, respectively. 202

embryonic development Period of development from the second through eighth weeks. 715

embryonic disk Stage of embryonic development following the blastocyst stage that has two layers; one layer will be endoderm, and the other will be ectoderm. 717

embryophyta Land plants that produce embryos protected from drying out. 353

embryo sac Female gametophyte of flowering plants that produces an egg cell. 366, 490

emphysema (em-fih-see-muh) Degenerative lung disorder in which the bursting of alveolar walls reduces the total surface area for gas exchange. 660

endangered species A species that is in peril of immediate extinction throughout all or most of its range (e.g., California condor, snow leopard). 800

endergonic reaction Chemical reaction that requires an input of energy; opposite of exergonic reaction. 88

endocrine system Organ system involved in the coordination of body activities; uses hormones as chemical signals secreted into the bloodstream. 516, 682

endocytosis Process by which substances are moved into the cell from the

environment by phagocytosis (cellular eating) or pinocytosis (cellular drinking); includes receptor-mediated endocytosis. 98

endoderm Innermost primary tissue layer of an animal embryo that gives rise to the linings of the digestive tract and associated structures. 711

endodermis Plant root tissue that forms a boundary between the cortex and the vascular cylinder. 438

endomembrane system A collection of membranous structures involved in transport within the cell. 75

endometrium Mucous membrane lining the interior surface of the uterus. 704

endoplasmic reticulum (ER) (en-duh-plaz-mik reh-tik-yuh-lum) System of membranous saccules and channels in the cytoplasm, often with attached ribosomes. 71

endoskeleton Protective internal skeleton, as in vertebrates. 571

endosperm In angiosperms, the 3n tissue that nourishes the embryo and seedling and is formed as a result of a sperm joining with two polar nuclei. 495

endospore Spore formed within a cell; certain bacteria form endospores. 321

endosymbiotic theory Possible explanation of the evolution of eukaryotic organelles by phagocytosis of prokaryotes. 334

endotherm Animal that maintains a constant body temperature independent of the environmental temperature. 403

energy Capacity to do work and bring about change; occurs in a variety of forms. 9, 86

energy of activation Energy that must be added in order for molecules to react with one another. 90

enhancer DNA sequence that increases the level of transcription when a transcription activator binds to it. 213

entropy Measure of disorder or randomness. 87

enzyme (en-zym) Organic catalyst, usually a protein, that speeds a reaction in cells due to its particular shape. 46, 90

eosinophil (ee-oh-sin-oh-fill) White blood cell containing cytoplasmic granules that stain with acidic dye. 613

epidermal tissue Exterior tissue, usually one cell thick, of leaves, young stems, roots, and other parts of plants. 436

epidermis In plants, tissue that covers roots, leaves, and stems of a nonwoody organism; in animals, the outer protective region of the skin. 436, 515

epididymis (ep-uh-did-uh-mus) Coiled tubule next to the testes where sperm mature and may be stored for a short time. 702

epiglottis (ep-uh-glaht-us) Structure that covers the glottis during the process of swallowing. 633, 654

epinephrine (ep-uh-nef-rin) Hormone secreted by the adrenal medulla in times of stress; adrenaline. 690

epiphyte Plant that takes its nourishment from the air because its placement among other plants gives it an aerial position. 790

episiotomy (ih-pee-zee-aht-uh-mee) Surgical procedure performed during childbirth in which the opening of the vagina is enlarged to avoid tearing. 720

epithelial tissue Type of tissue that lines hollow organs and covers surfaces; epithelium. 508

equilibrium population Population whose members exhibit logistic population growth and whose size remains at or near the carrying capacity. Its members are large in size, slow to mature, have a long life span, have few offspring, and provide much care to offspring (e.g., bears, lions). 735

erection Increase in blood flow to the penis during sexual arousal, causing the penis to stiffen and become erect. 702

E site In a ribosome, the place where a spent tRNA exits the ribosome. 200

esophagus (ih-sahf-uh-gus) Muscular tube for moving swallowed food from the pharynx to the stomach. 633

essential nutrient In plants, substance required for normal growth, development, or reproduction. 460

estrogen (es-truh-jun) Female sex hormone that helps maintain sex organs and secondary sex characteristics. 705

estuary Portion of the ocean located where a river enters and fresh water mixes with salt water. 792

ethylene Plant hormone that causes ripening of fruit and is also involved in abscission. 475

euchromatin Chromatin that is extended and accessible for transcription. 214

eudicot Abbreviation of eudicotyledon. Flowering plant group; members have two embryonic leaves (cotyledons), net-veined leaves, vascular bundles in a ring, flower parts in fours or fives and their multiples, and other characteristics. 365, 434

Eudicotyledones Class of flowering plants, characterized by two embryonic leaves (cotyledons), net-veined leaves, vascular bundles in a ring, flower parts in fours or fives and their multiples, and other characteristics. 365

euglenoid Flagellated and flexible freshwater unicellular protist that usually contains chloroplasts and has a semirigid cell wall. 338

Eukarya One of the three domains of life, consisting of organisms with eukaryotic cells and further classified into the kingdoms Protista, Fungi, Plantae, and Animalia. 14, 68

eukaryotic cell (eukaryote) Type of cell that has a membrane-bounded nucleus and membranous organelles. 14, 68, 304

eutrophication Enrichment of water by inorganic nutrients used by phytoplankton. Often, overenrichment caused by human activities leads to excessive bacterial growth and oxygen depletion. 775, 791

eutrophic lake Lake containing many nutrients and decaying organisms, often tinted green with algae. 791

evolution Descent of organisms from common ancestors with the development of genetic and phenotypic changes over time that make them more suited to the environment. 253

evolutionary tree Diagram that shows how groups of organisms are related by way of common ancestors. 13, 298

evolutionary species concept Every species has its own evolutionary history, which is partly documented in the fossil record. 272

excretion Elimination of metabolic wastes by an organism at exchange boundaries such as the plasma membrane of unicellular organisms and excretory tubules of multicellular animals. 666

exergonic reaction Chemical reaction that releases energy; opposite of endergonic reaction. 88

exocytosis Process in which an intracellular vesicle fuses with the plasma membrane so that the vesicle's contents are released outside the cell. 98

exon A segment of a gene that codes for a protein. 199

exophthalmic goiter (ex-op-thowl-mick goi-tur) Enlargement of the thyroid gland accompanied by an abnormal protrusion of the eyes. 689

exoskeleton Protective external skeleton, as in arthropods. 570

experiment Test of an experimental variable for the purpose of collecting data. 5

experimental variable A value that is expected to change as a result of an experiment; represents the factor being tested by the experiment. 5

expiration (ek-spuh-ray-shun) Act of expelling air from the lungs; also called exhalation. 656

exponential growth Growth at a constant rate of increase per unit of time; can be expressed as a constant fraction or exponent. 732

external respiration Exchange of oxygen and carbon dioxide between alveoli and blood. 650

extinction Total disappearance of a species or higher group. 292, 735, 800

extracellular matrix (ECM) Materials secreted by animal cells that form a complex network which supports the cells and allows them to communicate. 99

extraembryonic membrane (ek-struh-em-bree-ahn-ik) Membrane that is not a part of the embryo but is necessary to the continued existence and health of the embryo. 700, 715

F

F$_1$ generation In genetics, the first (filial) generation of offspring. 172

F$_2$ generation In genetics, the second (filial) generation of offspring. 172

facilitated diffusion Passive transfer of a substance into or out of a cell along a concentration gradient by a process that requires a carrier. 96

facultative anaerobe Prokaryote that is able to grow in either the presence or the absence of gaseous oxygen. 323

FAD Flavin adenine dinucleotide; a coenzyme of oxidation-reduction that becomes FADH$_2$ as oxidation of substrates occurs, and then delivers electrons to the electron transport chain in mitochondria during cellular respiration. 124

family One of the categories, or taxa, used by taxonomists to group species; the taxon above the genus level. 14, 296

fat Organic molecule that contains glycerol and fatty acids and is found in adipose tissue. 49, 640

fatty acid Molecule that contains a hydrocarbon chain and ends with an acid group. 49

female gametophyte In seed plants, the gametophyte that produces an egg; in flowering plants, an embryo sac. 363, 490

fermentation Anaerobic breakdown of glucose that results in a gain of two ATP and end products such as alcohol and lactate. 125, 133

fern Member of a group of plants that have large fronds; in the sexual life cycle, the independent gametophyte produces flagellated sperm, and the vascular sporophyte produces windblown spores. 360

fertilization Union of a sperm nucleus and an egg nucleus, which creates a zygote. 155, 705

fetal development Period of development from the ninth week through birth. 718

fiber Structure resembling a thread; also, plant material that is undigestible. 639

fibrin Insoluble protein threads formed from fibrinogen during blood clotting. 603

fibroblast Cell in connective tissues that produces fibers and other substances. 510

filament End-to-end chains of cells that form as cell division occurs in only one plane; in plants, the elongated stalk of a stamen. 345

filter feeder Method of obtaining nourishment by certain animals that strain minute organic particles from the water in a way that deposits them in the digestive tract. 385, 628

fimbria (pl., fimbriae) (fim-bree-uh) Fingerlike extension from the oviduct near the ovary. 704

first messenger Chemical signal such as a peptide hormone that binds to a plasma membrane receptor protein and alters a cell's metabolism because a second messenger is activated. 684

fitness Ability of an organism to reproduce and pass its genes to the next fertile generation; measured against the ability of other organisms to reproduce in the same environment. 748

fixed action pattern (FAP) Innate behavior pattern that is stereotyped, spontaneous, independent of immediate control, genetically encoded, and independent of individual learning. 746

flagellum (pl., flagella) (fluh-jel-um) Slender long extension that propels a cell through a fluid medium. 79, 383

flame cell Found along excretory tubules of planarians; functions in propelling fluid through the excretory canals and out of the body. 387, 667

flatworm Unsegmented worm lacking a body cavity; phylum Platyhelminthes. 387

fluid feeder Animal that gains needed nutrients by sucking nutrient-rich fluids from another living organism. 628

fluid-mosaic model Model for the plasma membrane based on the changing location and pattern of protein molecules in a fluid phospholipid bilayer. 93

follicle (fahl-ih-kul) Structure in the ovary that produces a secondary oocyte and the hormones estrogen and progesterone. 705

follicle-stimulating hormone (FSH) Hormone secreted by the anterior pituitary gland that stimulates the development of an ovarian follicle in a female or the production of sperm in a male. 703

follicular phase First half of the ovarian cycle, during which the follicle matures and much estrogen (and some progesterone) is produced. 706

fontanel (fahn-tun-el) Membranous region located between certain cranial bones in the skull of a fetus or infant. 572, 718

food chain The order in which one population feeds on another in an ecosystem, from detritus (detrital food chain) or producer (grazing food chain) to final consumer. 773

food web In ecosystems, complex pattern of interlocking and crisscrossing food chains. 772

foraging behavior Manner in which an animal finds and eats food. 748

foramen magnum (fuh-ray-mun mag-num) Opening in the occipital bone of the vertebrate skull through which the spinal cord passes. 572

foraminiferan Member of the phylum Foraminifera bearing a calcium carbonate test with many openings through which pseudopods extend. 339

foreign antigen Organism does not produce this type of antigen. 615

foreskin Skin covering the glans penis in uncircumcised males. 702

formed element Constituent of blood that is either cellular (red blood cells and white blood cells) or at least cellular in origin (platelets). 600

fossil Evidence of usually an extinct species that has been preserved in the Earth's crust. 255

fossil record History of life recorded from remains from the past. 255

founder effect Cause of genetic drift due to colonization by a limited number of individuals who, by chance, have different gene frequencies than the parent population. 263

fovea centralis Region of the retina consisting of densely packed cones; responsible for the greatest visual acuity. 554

frameshift mutation Alteration in a gene due to deletion of a base, so that the reading "frame" is shifted; can result in a nonfunctional protein. 204

frond Leaf of a fern. 360

fruit Flowering plant structure consisting of one or more ripened ovaries that usually contain seeds. 367, 490, 497

functional genomics Study of DNA function at the genomic level; involves the study of many genes simultaneously and the use of microarrays. 240

functional group Specific cluster of atoms attached to the carbon skeleton of organic molecules that enters into reactions and behaves in a predictable way. 45

fungus (pl., fungi) Saprotrophic decomposer; the body is made up of filaments called hyphae that form a mass called a mycelium. 370

G

G$_0$ stage In the cell cycle, a period of time that occurs should a cell leave the cycle during the G$_1$ stage before committing to the complete cycle. 145

G$_1$ stage In the cell cycle, a period of time during which the cell grows in size; includes the G$_1$ checkpoint when cells commit to completing the cycle. 145

G$_2$ stage In the cell cycle, a period of time after the S stage and before the M stage during which growth includes organelle duplication. 145

G3P In photosynthesis, a Krebs cycle molecule that is the starting point for many types of organic molecules produced by plants, including glucose and starch. In cellular respiration, the molecule that occurs after glucose is split during glycolysis. 114, 126

gallbladder Organ attached to the liver that stores and concentrates bile. 638

gamete (ga-meet, guh-meet) Haploid sex cell; the egg or a sperm, which join in fertilization to form a zygote. 155, 709

gametophyte Haploid generation of the alternation of generations life cycle of a plant; produces gametes that unite to form a diploid zygote. 354

ganglion Collection or bundle of neuron cell bodies usually outside the central nervous system. 532, 540

gap junction Junction between animal cells that provides a passageway for intercellular transport. 99

gastropod Mollusc with a broad flat foot for crawling (e.g., snails and slugs). 391

gastrovascular cavity In animals with an incomplete digestive tract, a cavity that serves for digestion of food and transport of oxygen and nutrients to body cells. 386

gastrulation Stage of animal development during which germ layers form, at least in part, by invagination. 711

gene Unit of heredity existing as alleles on the chromosomes; in diploid organisms, typically two alleles are inherited—one from each parent. 10, 57, 199

gene cloning Production of one or more copies of the same gene. 232

gene flow Sharing of genes between two populations through interbreeding. 261

gene locus Specific location of a particular gene on homologous chromosomes. 173

gene pharming Use of a transgenic organism to produce a commercial medical product. 236

gene pool Total of all the genes of all the individuals in a population. 200, 260

gene theory Concept that organisms contain coded information dictating their form, function, and behavior. 10

gene therapy Correction of a detrimental mutation by the addition of normal DNA and its insertion into a genome. 237

genetically engineered Alteration of genomes for medical or industrial purposes. 232

genetically modified organism (GMO) Organism that carries the genes of another organism as a result of DNA technology. 232

genetic code Universal code that has existed for eons; specifies protein synthesis in the cells of all living things. Each codon consists of three letters standing for the DNA nucleotides that make up one of the 20 amino acids found in proteins. 198

genetic diversity Variety among members of a population. 800

genetic drift Mechanism of evolution due to random changes in the allelic frequencies of a population; more likely to occur in small populations or when only a few individuals of a large population reproduce. 263

genetic mutation Alteration in chromosome structure or number and also an alteration in a gene due to a change in DNA composition. 58, 204

genetic profile Gene expression in an individual or a cell as detected by the use of a microarray. 240

genome Full set of genetic information for a species or a virus. 57, 238

genotype (jee-nuh-typ) Genes of an individual for a particular trait or traits; often designated by letters, for example, *BB* or *Aa*. 173

genus One of the categories, or taxa, used by taxonomists to group species; contains those species that are most closely related through evolution. 14, 296

germinate Beginning of growth of a seed, spore, or zygote, especially after a period of dormancy. 498

germ layer Primary tissue layer of a vertebrate embryo—namely, ectoderm, mesoderm, or endoderm. 383, 711

geologic timescale History of the Earth since the beginning time divided into eras, periods, and epochs based in part on the fossil record. 292

gibberellin Plant hormone promoting increased stem growth; also involved in flowering and seed germination. 472

gills Respiratory organ in most aquatic animals; in fish, an outward extension of the pharynx. 593, 651

ginkgo Member of phylum Ginkgophyta; maidenhair tree. 362

gizzard Muscular part of the digestive tract that grinds food in some animals. 630

gland Epithelial cell or group of epithelial cells that are specialized to secrete a substance. 509

global climate change Predicted increase in the Earth's temperature due to human activities that promote the reradiation of solar heat toward the Earth. 770

globular stage Stage of development of a sporophyte embryo; root-shoot axis is established and dermal tissue is formed. 496

glomerular capsule (gluh-mair-yuh-lur) Double-walled cup that surrounds the glomerulus at the beginning of the nephron. 671

glomerular filtrate Filtered portion of blood contained within the glomerular capsule. 672

glomerular filtration Movement of small molecules from the glomerulus into the glomerular capsule due to the action of blood pressure. 672

glomerulus (gluh-mair-uh-lus, gloh-mair-yuh-lus) Cluster; for example, the cluster of capillaries surrounded by the glomerular capsule in a nephron, where glomerular filtration takes place. 671

glottis (glaht-us) Opening for airflow in the larynx. 633, 654

glucagon (gloo-kuh-gahn) Hormone secreted by the pancreas that causes the liver to break down glycogen and raises the blood glucose level. 692

glucocorticoid (gloo-koh-kor-tih-koyd) Type of hormone secreted by the adrenal cortex that influences carbohydrate, fat, and protein metabolism; see cortisol. 690

glucose (gloo-kohs) Six-carbon sugar that organisms degrade as a source of energy during cellular respiration. 47

glycerol Three-carbon carbohydrate with three hydroxyl groups attached; a component of fats and oils. 49

glycogen (gly-koh-jun) Storage polysaccharide that is composed of glucose molecules joined in a linear fashion but having numerous branches. 48

glycolipid Lipid in plasma membranes that bears a carbohydrate chain attached to a hydrophobic tail. 93

glycolysis Anaerobic breakdown of glucose that results in a gain of two ATP. 125, 126

glycoprotein Protein in plasma membranes that bears a carbohydrate chain. 93

gnetophyte Member of one of the four phyla of gymnosperms; Gnetophyta has only three living genera, which differ greatly from one another—e.g., *Welwitschia* and *Ephedra*. 362

Golgi apparatus (gohl-jee) Organelle, consisting of saccules and vesicles, that processes, packages, and distributes molecules about or from the cell. 73

gonad (goh-nad) Organ that produces gametes; the ovary produces eggs, and the testis produces sperm. 700

gonadotropic hormone (goh-nad-uh-trahp-ic, -troh-pic) Chemical signal secreted by the anterior pituitary that regulates the activity of the ovaries and testes; principally, follicle-stimulating hormone (FSH) and luteinizing hormone (LH). 686

gonorrhea (gahn-nuh-ree-uh) Sexually transmitted disease caused by the bacterium *Neisseria gonorrhoeae* that can lead to pelvic inflammatory disease. 708

granum (pl., grana) Stack of chlorophyll-containing thylakoids in a chloroplast. 107

gravitational balance Maintenance of balance when the head and body are motionless. 562

gravitropism Growth response of roots and stems of plants to the Earth's gravity; roots demonstrate positive gravitropism, and stems demonstrate negative gravitropism. 476

gray crescent Gray area that appears in an amphibian egg after being fertilized by the sperm; thought to contain chemical signals that turn on the genes that control development. 713

gray matter Nonmyelinated axons and cell bodies in the central nervous system. 534

grazing food web Complex pattern of interlocking and crisscrossing food chains that begins with populations of autotrophs serving as producers. 772

green algae Members of a diverse group of photosynthetic protists; contain chlorophylls *a* and *b* and have other biochemical characteristics like those of plants. 345

greenhouse gases Gases involved in the reradiation of solar heat toward the Earth, sometimes called the greenhouse effect. 776

ground tissue Tissue that constitutes most of the body of a plant; consists of parenchyma, collenchyma, and sclerenchyma cells that function in storage, basic metabolism, and support. 436

growth hormone (GH) Substance secreted by the anterior pituitary; controls the size of an individual by promoting cell division, protein synthesis, and bone growth. 687

guard cell One of two cells that surround a leaf stoma; changes in the turgor pressure of these cells cause the stoma to open or close. 456

guttation Liberation of water droplets from the edges and tips of leaves. 454

gymnosperm Type of woody seed plant in which the seeds are not enclosed by fruit and are usually borne in cones, such as those of the conifers. 362

H

H1N1 virus Emerging virus that causes a flu commonly called swine flu. 313

habitat Place where an organism lives and is able to survive and reproduce. 728, 760

habituation Simplest form of learning, in which an animal learns not to respond to irrelevant stimuli. 747

halophile Type of archaean that lives in extremely salty habitats. 325

haploid life cycle Presence of one of each type of chromosome during meiosis of the cell cycle. 160, 345

haploid (n) number (hap-loyd) The n number of chromosomesomes—half the diploid number; the number characteristic of gametes, which contain only one set of chromosomes. 146

hard palate (pal-it) Bony, anterior portion of the roof of the mouth. 632

Hardy-Weinberg principle Law stating that the gene frequencies in a population remain stable if evolution does not occur due to nonrandom mating, selection, migration, and genetic drift. 260

hay fever Seasonal variety of allergic reaction to a specific allergen. Characterized by sudden attacks of sneezing, swelling of nasal mucosa, and often asthmatic symptoms. 622

heart murmur Clicking or swishy sounds, often due to leaky valves. 592

heart stage Stage of development of a sporophyte embryo; cotyledons appear. 496

heat Type of kinetic energy; captured solar energy eventually dissipates as heat in the environment. 86

helper T cell T lymphocyte that secretes cytokines that stimulate all kinds of immune system cells. 616

heme Iron-containing portion of a hemoglobin molecule. 658

hemocoel Residual coelom found in molluscs and arthropods that is filled with hemolymph. 590

hemodialysis (he-moh-dy-al-uh-sus) Cleansing of blood by using an artificial membrane that causes substances to diffuse from blood into a dialysis fluid. 676

hemoglobin (Hb) (hee-muh-gloh-bun) Iron-containing pigment in red blood cells that combines with and transports oxygen. 600, 658

hemolymph Circulatory fluid that is a mixture of blood and tissue fluid; seen in animals that have an open circulatory system, such as molluscs and arthropods. 590

hemophilia Most common of the severe clotting disorders caused by the absence of a blood clotting factor. 603

hepatic portal system Pathway of blood flow between intestinal capillaries and liver capillaries. 598

herbaceous Nonwoody stem. 438

herbivore (ur-buh-vor) Primary consumer in a grazing food chain; a plant eater. 770

hermaphrodite Animal having both male and female sex organs. 387

herpes simplex virus (HSV) Virus that causes genital herpes, a sexually transmitted disease. 708

heterochromatin Highly compacted chromatin that is not accessible for transcription. 214

heterocyst Cyanobacterial cell that synthesizes a nitrogen-fixing enzyme when nitrogen supplies dwindle. 324

heterotroph Organism that cannot synthesize organic molecules from inorganic nutrients and therefore must take in organic nutrients (food). 106, 770

heterozygote advantage Situation in which individuals heterozygous for a trait have a selective advantage over those who are homozygous; an example is sickle-cell anemia. 266

heterozygous Possessing unlike alleles for a particular trait. 173

hinge joint Type of joint that allows movement as a hinge does, such as the movement of the knee. 577

hippocampus (hip-uh-kam-pus) Portion of the limbic system where memories are stored. 538

histamine (his-tuh-meen, -mun) Substance, produced by basophils in blood and mast cells in connective tissue, that causes capillaries to dilate. 614

histone Protein molecule responsible for packing chromatin. 214

HIV provirus Viral DNA that has been integrated into host cell DNA. 315

homeobox 180-nucleotide sequence located in all homeotic genes. 216

homeostasis (hoh-mee-oh-stay-sis) Maintenance of normal internal conditions in a cell or an organism by means of self-regulating mechanisms. 445, 516

hominid Classification category that includes the great apes, humans, and species very closely related to humans. 410

hominin Classification category that includes chimpanzees, humans, and species very closely related to humans. 415

hominoid Classification category that includes all apes, humans, and species very closely related to humans. 414

homologous chromosome (hoh-mahl-uh-gus, huh-mahl-uh-gus) Member of a pair of chromosomes that are alike and come together in synapsis during prophase of the first meiotic division. 155

homologous pair Chromosomes that are the same length, with the centromere occurring in the same position and having genetic information for the same traits. Each member of the pair is a homologue to the other member. 144

homologous structure Structure that is similar in two or more species because of common ancestry. 257, 303

homozygote advantage Situation in which individuals homozygous for a trait have a selective advantage over those who are heterozygous. 266

homozygous Possessing two identical alleles for a particular trait. 173

horizon Major layer of soil visible in vertical profile; for example, topsoil is the A horizon. 462

hormone Chemical signal produced in one part of an organism that controls the activity of other parts. 446, 682

horsetail Division of seedless vascular plants having only one genus (*Equisetum*) in existence today; characterized by rhizomes, scalelike leaves, strobili, and tough, rigid stems. 359

Hox gene Gene that controls the overall body plan by controlling the fate of groups of cells during development. 216

human chorionic gonadotropin (HCG) (kor-ee-ahn-ik goh-nad-uh-trahp-in, -troh-pin) Hormone produced by the chorion that functions to maintain the uterine lining. 716

Human Genome Project (HGP) Initiative to determine the complete sequence of the human genome and to analyze this information. 238

human papillomavirus (HPV) Virus that causes genital warts, a common sexually transmitted disease; also linked to cervical cancer. 708

humus Decomposing organic matter in the soil. 462

Huntington disease Genetic disease marked by progressive deterioration of the nervous system due to deficiency of a neurotransmitter. 535

hyaline cartilage Cartilage whose cells lie in lacunae separated by a white translucent matrix containing very fine collagen fibers. 511

hydrogen bond Weak bond that arises between a slightly positive hydrogen atom of one molecule and a slightly negative atom of another or between parts of the same molecule. 32

hydrogen ion (H⁺) Hydrogen atom that has lost its electron and therefore bears a positive charge. 36

hydrolysis reaction (hy-drahl-ih-sis re-ak-shun) Splitting of a compound by the addition of water, with the H^+ being incorporated in one fragment and the OH^- in the other. 46

hydrophilic (hy-druh-fil-ik) Type of molecule that interacts with water by dissolving in water and/or forming hydrogen bonds with water molecules. 34, 45

hydrophobic (hy-druh-foh-bik) Type of molecule that does not interact with water because it is nonpolar. 34, 45

hydroponics Technique for growing plants by suspending them with their roots in a nutrient solution. 460

hydrostatic skeleton Fluid-filled body compartment that provides support for muscle contraction resulting in movement; seen in cnidarians, flatworms, roundworms, and segmented worms. 570

hydrothermal vent Hot springs in the seafloor along ocean ridges where heated sea water and sulfate react to produce hydrogen sulfide; here, chromosynthetic bacteria support a community of varied organisms. 793

hydroxide ion (OH⁻) One of two ions that results when a water molecule dissociates; it has gained an electron, and therefore bears a negative charge. 36

hypersensitive response (HR) Plants respond to pathogens by selectively killing plant cells to block the spread of the pathogen. 483

hypertension Elevated blood pressure, particularly the diastolic pressure. 596

hypertonic solution Higher solute concentration (less water) than the cytoplasm of a cell; causes cell to lose water by osmosis. 97

hypha (pl., hyphae) Filament of the vegetative body of a fungus. 370

hypothalamic-releasing hormone One of several hormones produced by the hypothalamus that stimulates the secretion of an anterior pituitary hormone. 686

hypothalamus (hy-poh-thal-uh-mus) Part of the brain located below the thalamus that helps regulate the internal environment of the body and produces releasing factors that control the anterior pituitary. 536

hypothesis (hy-pahth-ih-sis) Supposition that is formulated after making an observation; it can be tested by obtaining more data, often by experimentation. 4

hypotonic solution Lower solute (more water) concentration than the cytoplasm of a cell; causes cell to gain water by osmosis. 97

I

immediate allergic response Allergic response that occurs within seconds of contact with an allergen; caused by the attachment of the allergen to IgE antibodies. 622

immune system All the cells in the body that protect the body against foreign organisms and substances and also cancerous cells. 517

immunity Ability of the body to protect itself from foreign substances and cells, including disease-causing agents. 612

immunization (im-yuh-nuh-zay-shun) Use of a vaccine to protect the body against specific disease-causing agents. 617

immunoglobulin (Ig) (im-yuh-noh-glahb-yuh-lin, -yoo-lin) Globular plasma protein that functions as an antibody. 617

implantation Attachment and penetration of the embryo into the lining of the uterus (endometrium). 715

imprinting Learning to make a particular response to only one type of animal or object. 746

inclusive fitness Fitness that results from personal reproduction and from helping nondescendant relatives reproduce. 750

incomplete dominance Inheritance pattern in which the offspring has an intermediate phenotype, as when a red-flowered plant and a white-flowered plant produce pink-flowered offspring. 182

indehiscent Remaining closed at maturity, as are many fruits. 497

independent assortment Alleles of unlinked genes segregate independently of each other during meiosis so that the gametes contain all possible combinations of alleles. 156

induced fit model Change in the shape of an enzyme's active site that enhances the fit between the active site and its substrate(s). 90

induction Ability of a chemical or a tissue to influence the development of another tissue. 714

industrial melanism Increased frequency of a darkly pigmented (melanic) form in a population when predators more easily see and capture the lightly pigmented form because it is more visible against vegetation that has turned dark due to industrial pollution. 260

inflammatory response Tissue response to injury that is characterized by redness, swelling, pain, and heat. 614

ingroup In cladistics, the organisms whose relationships will be determined by shared derived characteristics. 300

initiation During DNA replication or transcription, initiation is the step whereby DNA replication begins or transcription begins; this step is catalyzed by specific enzymes such that the DNA "unravels" and forms a bubble. 202

inner ear Portion of the ear consisting of a vestibule, semicircular canals, and the cochlea where equilibrium is maintained and sound is transmitted. 559

insect Member of a group of arthropods in which the head has antennae, compound eyes, and simple eyes; the thorax has three pairs of legs and often wings; and the abdomen has internal organs. 396

insight learning Ability to apply prior learning to a new situation without trial-and-error activity. 747

inspiration (in-spuh-ray-shun) Act of taking air into the lungs; also called inhalation. 656

insulin (in-suh-lin) Hormone secreted by the pancreas that lowers the blood glucose level by promoting the uptake of glucose by cells and the conversion of glucose to glycogen by the liver and skeletal muscles. 692

integration Summing up of excitatory and inhibitory signals by a neuron or by some part of the brain. 531, 551

integumentary system Organ system consisting of skin and various organs, such as hair, that are found in skin. 516

intercalated disks Region that holds adjacent cardiac muscle cells together and appears as dense bands at right angles to the muscle striations. 512

interferon (in-tur-feer-ahn) Antiviral agent produced by an infected cell that blocks the infection of another cell. 613

interkinesis Period of time between meiosis I and meiosis II during which no DNA replication takes place. 155, 159

intermediate filaments Ropelike assemblies of fibrous polypeptides in the cytoskeleton that provide support and strength to cells; so called because they are intermediate in size between actin filaments and microtubules. 78

internal respiration Exchange of oxygen and carbon dioxide between blood and tissue fluid. 650

intermembrane space Space between the inner and outer membranes of a mitochondrion where hydrogen ions collect prior to passing through an ATP synthase complex. 128

interneuron Neuron located within the central nervous system that conveys messages between parts of the central nervous system. 527

internode In vascular plants, the region of a stem between two successive nodes. 432

interphase Portion of the cell cycle that includes the G_1, S, and G_2 stages but not the mitotic stage. 145

interspersed repeat Sequence of DNA nucleotides that is repeated in several different regions of the same chromosome or across multiple chromosomes. 240

intertidal zone Region along a coastline where the tide recedes and returns. 792

intervertebral disk (in-tur-vur-tuh-brul) Layer of cartilage located between adjacent vertebrae. 573

intron Segment of a gene that does not code for a protein. 199, 239

inversion Change in chromosome structure in which a segment of a chromosome is turned around 180 degrees; this reversed sequence of genes can lead to altered gene activity and abnormalities. 164

invertebrate An animal without a serial arrangement of vertebrae. 384

invertebrate chordate Chordate in which the notochord is never replaced by the vertebral column. 398

ion (eye-un, -ahn) Charged particle that carries a negative or positive charge. 30

ionic bond (eye-ahn-ik) Chemical bond in which ions are attracted to one another by opposite charges. 30

iris (eye-ris) Muscular ring that surrounds the pupil and regulates the passage of light through this opening. 554

isomers Molecules with the same molecular formula but a different structure, and therefore a different shape. 45

isotonic solution Solution that is equal in solute concentration to that of the cytoplasm of a cell; causes cell to neither lose nor gain water by osmosis. 97

isotope (eye-suh-tohp) One of two or more atoms with the same atomic number but a different atomic mass due to the number of neutrons. 27

J

jawless fish Type of fish that has no jaws; includes today's hagfishes and lampreys. 400

K

karyotype (kar-ee-uh-typ) Duplicated chromosomes arranged by pairs according to their size, shape, and general appearance. 144

keystone species Species whose activities significantly affect community structure. 810

kidneys Paired organs of the vertebrate urinary system that regulate the chemical composition of the blood and produce a waste product called urine. 670

kilocalorie Caloric value of food; 1,000 calories. 86

kinetic energy Energy associated with motion. 86

kinetochore Disk-shaped structure within the centromere of a chromosome to which spindle microtubules become attached during mitosis and meiosis. 147

kingdom One of the categories used to classify organisms; the category above phylum. 14, 296

kin selection Indirect selection; adaptation to the environment due to the reproductive success of an individual's relatives. 750

Klinefelter syndrome Condition caused by the inheritance of XXY chromosomes. 163

Krebs cycle Cycle of reactions in mitochondria that begins with citric acid; it breaks down an acetyl group as CO_2, ATP, NADH, and $FADH_2$ are given off; also called the citric acid cycle. 125, 129

L

lacteal (lak-tee-ul) Lymphatic vessel in an intestinal villus; it aids in the absorption of lipids. 610, 635

lacuna Small pit or hollow cavity, as in bone or cartilage, where a cell or cells are located. 511, 576

ladderlike nervous system In planarians, two lateral nerve cords joined by transverse nerves. 387, 532

lake Body of fresh water, often classified by nutrient status, such as oligotrophic (nutrient-poor) or eutrophic (nutrient-rich). 791

lancelet Invertebrate chordate with a body that resembles a lancet and has the

four chordate characteristics as an adult. 398

land fungi Fungi (zygospore, sac, and club) that live on land and reproduce by producing windblown spores. 370

landscape diversity Variety of habitat elements within an ecosystem (e.g., plains, mountains, and rivers). 801

large intestine Last major portion of the digestive tract, extending from the small intestine to the anus and consisting of the cecum, the colon, the rectum, and the anal canal. 636

larva Immature form in the life cycle of some animals; it sometimes undergoes metamorphosis to become the adult form. 387, 700

larynx (lar-ingks) Cartilaginous organ located between the pharynx and the trachea that contains the vocal cords; also called the voice box. 654

law of independent assortment During gametogenesis, each pair of alleles assorts (separates) independently of other pairs, and therefore all possible combinations of alleles can occur in the gametes. 174

leaf Lateral appendage of a stem, highly variable in structure, often containing cells that carry out photosynthesis. 432

learning Relatively permanent change in behavior that results from practice and experience. 746

legume Plant with root nodules containing bacteria able to fix atmospheric nitrogen. 6

lens Clear, membranelike structure found in the eye behind the iris; brings objects into focus. 554

lenticel Frond of usually numerous, slightly raised, somewhat spongy groups of cells in the bark of woody plants. Permits gas exchange between the interior of a plant and the external atmosphere. 442

less-developed country (LDC) Country that is becoming industrialized; typically, population growth is expanding rapidly, and the majority of people live in poverty. 737

lichen Symbiotic relationship between certain fungi and algae, in which the fungi possibly provide inorganic food or water and the algae provide organic food. 324, 371

life history Adaptations in characteristics that influence an organism's biology, such as how many offspring it produces, its survival, and factors such as age and size that determine its reproductive maturity. 735

ligament Tough cord or band of dense fibrous connective tissue that joins bone to bone at a joint. 511

limbic system Association of various brain centers, including the amygdala and hippocampus; governs learning and memory and various emotions, such as pleasure, fear, and happiness. 538

limiting factor Resource or environmental condition that restricts the abundance and distribution of an organism. 729

linkage group Alleles of different genes that are located on the same chromosome and tend to be inherited together. 173

Linnaean classification Use of traditional categories (domain, kingdom, phylum, class order, family, and genus) to group organisms according to anatomical and genetic homologies. 296

lipase Fat-digesting enzyme secreted by the pancreas. 634

lipid (lip-id, ly-pid) Class of organic compounds that tends to be soluble only in nonpolar solvents such as alcohol; includes fats and oils. 49

liposome Droplet of phospholipid molecules formed in a liquid environment. 319

liver Large, dark red internal organ that produces urea and bile, detoxifies the blood, stores glycogen, and produces the plasma proteins, among other functions. 638

lobe-finned fish Type of fish with limblike fins. 401

logistic growth Population increase that results in an S-shaped curve; growth is slow at first, steepens, and then levels off due to environmental resistance. 732

long-day plant Plant that flowers when day length is longer than a critical length (e.g., wheat, barley, clover, spinach). 481

loop of the nephron (nef-rahn) Portion of the nephron lying between the proximal convoluted tubule and the distal convoluted tubule that functions in water reabsorption. 671

loose fibrous connective tissue Tissue composed mainly of fibroblasts widely separated by a matrix containing collagen and elastic fibers. 510

lumen Cavity inside any tubular structure, such as the lumen of the digestive tract. 509

lungs Paired, cone-shaped organs within the thoracic cavity; function in internal respiration and contain moist surfaces for gas exchange. 651

luteal phase Second half of the ovarian cycle, during which the corpus luteum develops and much progesterone (and some estrogen) is produced. 706

luteinizing hormone (LH) Hormone produced by the anterior pituitary gland that stimulates the development of the corpus luteum in females and the production of testosterone in males. 703

lymph (limf) Fluid, derived from tissue fluid, that is carried in lymphatic vessels. 511, 602, 610

lymphatic (lymphoid) organ Organ other than a lymphatic vessel that is part of the lymphatic system; includes lymph nodes, tonsils, spleen, thymus gland, and bone marrow. 611

lymphatic system Organ system consisting of lymphatic vessels and lymphatic organs that transports lymph and lipids and aids the immune system. 517, 610

lymphatic vessel Vessel that carries lymph. 610

lymph node Mass of lymphatic tissue located along the course of a lymphatic vessel. 611

lymphocyte (lim-fuh-syt) Specialized white blood cell that functions in specific defense; occurs in two forms— T lymphocyte and B lymphocyte. 601

lysogenic cycle Bacteriophage life cycle in which the virus incorporates its DNA into that of a bacterium; occurs preliminary to the lytic cycle. 311

lysosome (ly-suh-sohm) Membrane-bounded vesicle that contains hydrolytic enzymes for digesting macromolecules. 74

lytic cycle Bacteriophage life cycle in which the virus takes over the operation of the bacterium immediately upon entering it and subsequently destroys the bacterium. 311

M

macroevolution Large-scale evolutionary change, such as the formation of new species. 272

macronutrient Essential element needed in large amounts for plant growth, such as nitrogen, calcium, or sulfur. 460

macrophage (mak-ruh-fayj) Large phagocytic cell derived from a monocyte that ingests microbes and debris. 613

malaria Serious infectious illness caused by the parasitic protozoan *Plasmodium*. Malaria is characterized by bouts of chills and high fever that occur at regular intervals. 341

male gametophyte In seed plants, the gametophyte that produces sperm; a pollen grain. 363, 490

Malpighian tubule Blind, threadlike excretory tubule near the anterior end of an insect's hindgut. 667

mammal Homeothermic vertebrate characterized especially by the presence of hair and mammary glands. 404

marsupial Member of a group of mammals bearing immature young nursed in a marsupium, or pouch (e.g., kangaroo and opossum). 404

mass extinction Episode of large-scale extinction in which large numbers of species disappear in a few million years or less. 292

mast cell Cell to which antibodies attach, causing it to release histamine, thus producing allergic symptoms. 612

master developmental regulatory genes Genes that regulate the transcription of other genes so that development can proceed normally. 216

maternal inheritance Type of inheritance in which all offspring have the genotype and phenotype of only the female parent; exemplified by mitochondrial genes because mitochondria are passed to offspring only from the mother, not the father. 423

matrix (may-triks) Unstructured semifluid substance that fills the space between cells in connective tissues or inside organelles. 128, 510

matter Anything that takes up space and has mass. 26

mature embryo Sporophyte embryo after all the stages of development. 496

mechanoreceptor (mek-uh-noh-rih-sep-tur) Sensory receptor that responds to mechanical stimuli, such as that from pressure, sound waves, or gravity. 550

medulla oblongata (muh-dul-uh ahb-lawng-gah-tuh) Part of the brain stem that is continuous with the spinal cord; controls heartbeat, blood pressure, breathing, and other vital functions. 536

megaspore One of the two types of spores produced by seed plants; develops into a female gametophyte (embryo sac). 366

meiosis, meiosis I, meiosis II (my-oh-sis) Type of nuclear division that occurs as part of sexual reproduction, in which the daughter cells receive the haploid number of chromosomes in varied combinations. 155

melanocyte-stimulating hormone (MSH) Substance that causes melanocytes to secrete melanin in lower vertebrates. 687

melatonin (mel-uh-toh-nun) Hormone, secreted by the pineal gland, that is involved in biorhythms. 693

membrane attack complex Group of complement proteins that form channels in a microbe's surface, thereby destroying it. 612

memory Capacity of the brain to store and retrieve information about past sensations and perceptions; essential to learning. 538

memory B cell Forms during a primary immune response but enters a resting phase until a secondary immune response occurs. 617

memory T cell T cell that differentiates during an initial infection and responds rapidly during subsequent exposure to the same antigen. 618

meninges (sing., meninx) (muh-nin-jeez) Protective membranous coverings about the central nervous system. 534

meningitis Condition that refers to inflammation of meninges that cover the brain and spinal cord. 534

meniscus (pl., menisci) (muh-nis-kus,-kee, -sy) Cartilaginous wedges that separate the surfaces of bones in synovial joints. 577

menstruation (men-stroo-ay-shun) Loss of blood and tissue from the uterus at the end of a uterine cycle. 706

meristem tissue Undifferentiated, embryonic tissue in the active growth regions of plants. 353, 440

mesoderm Middle primary tissue layer of an animal embryo that gives rise to muscle, several internal organs, and connective tissue layers. 711

mesoglea In animals with only two tissue layers, a transparent, jellylike packing material that occurs between the ectoderm and the endoderm. 386

mesophyll Inner, thickest layer of a leaf consisting of palisade and spongy mesophyll; the site of most photosynthesis. 438

messenger RNA (mRNA) Type of RNA formed from a DNA template that bears coded information for the amino acid sequence of a polypeptide. 57, 199

metabolic pathway Series of linked reactions, beginning with a particular reactant and terminating with an end product. 92

metabolic pool Metabolites that are the products of and/or substrates for key reactions in cells, allowing one type of molecule to be changed into another type, such as carbohydrates converted to fats. 135

metabolism All of the chemical reactions that occur in a cell. 9

metapopulation Population subdivided into several small, isolated populations due to habitat fragmentation. 810

metastasis (muh-tas-tuh-sis) Spread of cancer from the place of origin throughout the body; caused by the ability of cancer cells to migrate and invade tissues. 153, 223

methanogen Type of archaean that lives in oxygen-free habitats, such as swamps, and releases methane gas. 325

MHC (major histocompatibility complex) protein Protein marker that is a part of cell-surface markers anchored in the plasma membrane, which the immune system uses to identify "self." 618

microevolution Change in gene frequencies between populations of a species over time. 259

micronutrient Essential element needed in small amounts for plant growth, such as boron, copper, and zinc. 460

microRNAs (miRNA) Type of small RNA that may bind to mRNA and thereby regulate its activity following transcription. 219

microspores One of two types of spores produced by seed plants; develops into a male gametophyte (pollen grain). 366

microtubule (my-kro-too-byool) Small, cylindrical structure that contains 13 rows of the protein tubulin surrounding an empty central core; present in the cytoplasm, centrioles, cilia, and flagella. 78

microvillus Cylindrical process that extends from an epithelial cell of a villus of the intestinal wall and serves to increase the surface area of the cell. 635

midbrain Part of the brain located below the thalamus and above the pons; contains reflex centers and tracts. 536

middle ear Portion of the ear consisting of the tympanic membrane, the oval and round windows, and the ossicles; where sound is amplified. 559

mimicry Superficial resemblance of two or more species; a mechanism that avoids predation by appearing to be noxious. 763

mineral Naturally occurring inorganic substance containing two or more elements; certain minerals are needed in the diet. 460, 641

mineralocorticoid (min-ur-uh-loh-kor-tih-koyd) Type of hormone secreted by the adrenal cortex that regulates salt and water balance, leading to increases in blood volume and blood pressure. 690

mitochondrion (mite-oh-KAHN-dree-uhn) Membrane-bounded organelle in which ATP molecules are produced during the process of cellular respiration. 76

mitosis (my-toh-sis) Type of cell division in which daughter cells receive the exact chromosomal and genetic makeup of the parent cell; occurs during growth and repair. 145

model Stand-in for an experimental subject that is not available for experimentation. 5

model of island biogeography Model developed by ecologists Robert MacArthur and E. O. Wilson to explain the effects of distance from the mainland and size of an island on its diversity. 769

molecular clock Mutational changes that accumulate at a presumed constant rate in regions of DNA not involved in adaptation to the environment. 304

molecule Union of two or more atoms of the same element; also, the smallest part of a compound that retains the properties of the compound. 9, 29

molting Periodic shedding of the exoskeleton in arthropods. 393

monoclonal antibody One of many antibodies produced by a clone of hybridoma cells that all bind to the same antigen. 620

monocot Abbreviation of monocotyledon. Flowering plant group; among other characteristics, members have one embryonic leaf, parallel-veined leaves, and scattered vascular bundles. 365, 434

monocotyledones Class of flowering plants characterized by one embryonic leaf, parallel-veined leaves, and scattered vascular bundles. 365

monocyte (mahn-uh-syt) Type of agranular white blood cell that functions as a phagocyte and an antigen-presenting cell. 601

monohybrid cross Single genetic cross involving only one trait, such as flower color. 172

monomer Small molecule that is a subunit of a polymer—e.g., glucose is a monomer of starch. 46

monosaccharide (mahn-uh-sak-uh-ryd) Simple sugar; a carbohydrate that cannot be decomposed by hydrolysis (e.g., glucose). 47

monosomy One less chromosome than usual. 162

monotreme Egg-laying mammal (e.g., duckbill platypus and spiny anteater). 404

monsoon Climate in India and southern Asia caused by wet ocean winds that blow onshore for almost half the year. 783

more-developed country (MDC) Country that is industrialized; typically, population growth is low, and the people enjoy a good standard of living. 737

morphogenesis Emergence of shape in tissues, organs, or entire embryo during development. 713

morula Spherical mass of cells resulting from cleavage during animal development prior to the blastula stage. 710

moss Type of bryophyte. 356

motor neuron Nerve cell that conducts nerve impulses away from the central nervous system and innervates effectors (muscles and glands). 527

motor unit Motor neuron and all the muscle fibers it innervates. 580

M stage In the cell cycle, the period of time during which mitosis occurs to produce daughter cells. 145

multifactorial trait Trait or illness determined by several genes and the environment. 183

multiple alleles (uh-leelz) Inheritance pattern in which there are more than two alleles for a particular trait; each individual has only two of all possible alleles. 182

multiple fruit Cluster of mature ovaries produced by a cluster of flowers, as in a pineapple. 497

muscle dysmorphia Mental state in which a person thinks his or her body is underdeveloped, and becomes preoccupied with body building and diet; affects more men than women. 644

muscular system System of muscles that produces movement within the body and movement of its limbs; principal components are skeletal muscle, smooth muscle, and cardiac muscle. 516

muscular tissue Type of tissue composed of fibers that can shorten and thicken. 512

mutate To undergo a permanent genetic change. 10

mutation Alteration in chromosome structure or number; also, alteration in a gene due to a change in DNA composition. 152, 261

mutualism Symbiotic relationship in which both species benefit in terms of growth and reproduction. 766

mycelium Mass of hyphal filaments composing the vegetative body of a fungus. 370

mycorrhizae Mutually beneficial symbiotic relationship between a fungus and the roots of vascular plants. 371, 464

myelin sheath (my-uh-lin) White, fatty material, derived from the membrane of Schwann cells, that forms a covering for nerve fibers. 527

myofibril (my-uh-fy-brul) Contractile portion of muscle cells that contains a linear arrangement of sarcomeres and shortens to produce muscle contraction. 582

myosin (my-uh-sin) One of two major proteins of muscle; makes up thick filaments in myofibrils of muscle fibers. (See actin.) 582

myxedema (mik-sih-dee-muh) Condition resulting from a deficiency of thyroid hormone in an adult. 689

N

N₂ (nitrogen) fixation Process whereby free atmospheric nitrogen is converted into compounds, such as ammonium and nitrates, usually by bacteria. 775

NAD⁺ Nicotinamide adenine dinucleotide; coenzyme of oxidation-reduction that accepts electrons and hydrogen ions to become NADH + H⁺ as oxidation of substrates occurs. During cellular respiration, NADH carries electrons to the electron transport chain in mitochondria. 124

nasopharynx (nay-zoh-far-ingks) Region of the pharynx associated with the nasal cavity. 633

natural killer (NK) cell Lymphocyte that causes an infected or cancerous cell to burst. 613

natural selection Mechanism resulting in adaptation to the environment. 16, 252

negative feedback Mechanism of homeostatic response by which the output of a system suppresses or inhibits activity of the system. 519, 682

nematocyst In cnidarians, a capsule that contains a threadlike fiber whose release aids in the capture of prey. 386

nephridia Segmentally arranged, paired excretory tubules of many invertebrates, as in the earthworm. 392, 667

nephron (nef-rahn) Microscopic kidney unit that regulates blood composition by glomerular filtration, tubular reabsorption, and tubular secretion. 670

nerve Bundle of nerve fibers outside the central nervous system. 513, 539

nerve fiber Axon; conducts nerve impulses away from the cell. Nerve fibers are classified as either myelinated or unmyelinated, based on the presence or absence of a myelin sheath. 526

nerve net Diffuse, noncentralized arrangement of nerve cells in cnidarians. 532

nervous system Organ system consisting of the brain, spinal cord, and associated nerves that coordinates the other organ systems of the body. 516

nervous tissue Tissue that contains nerve cells (neurons), which conduct impulses, and neuroglia, cells that support, protect, and provide nutrients to neurons. 513

neural plate Region of the dorsal surface of the chordate embryo that marks the future location of the neural tube. 712

neural tube Tube formed by closure of the neural groove during development. In vertebrates, the neural tube develops into the spinal cord and the brain. 712

neuroglia Nonconducting nerve cells that are intimately associated with neurons and function in a supportive capacity. 513, 527

neuron Nerve cell that characteristically has three parts: dendrites, cell body, and axon. 513, 527

neurotransmitter Chemical stored at the ends of axons that is responsible for transmission across a synapse. 530

neurula The early embryo during the development of the neural tube from the neural plate, marking the first appearance of the nervous system; the next stage after the gastrula. 712

neutron (noo-trahn) Neutral subatomic particle, located in the nucleus and having a weight of approximately one atomic mass unit. 27

neutrophil (noo-truh-fill) Granular leukocyte that is the most abundant of the white blood cells; first to respond to infection. 601, 613

nitrification Process by which nitrogen in ammonia and organic molecules is oxidized to nitrites and nitrates by soil bacteria. 775

node In plants, the place where one or more leaves attach to a stem. 432, 527

node of Ranvier (rahn-vee-ay) Gap in the myelin sheath around a nerve fiber. 527

noncompetitive inhibition Form of enzyme inhibition by which the inhibitor binds to an enzyme at a location other than the active site; while at this site, the enzyme shape changes, the inhibitor is unable to bind to its substrate, and no product forms. 92

nondisjunction Failure of homologous chromosomes or daughter chromosomes to separate during meiosis I and meiosis II, respectively. 162

nonpolar covalent bond Bond in which the sharing of electrons between atoms is fairly equal. 32

nonrandom mating Mating among individuals on the basis of their phenotypic similarities or differences, rather than randomly. 261

nonrenewable resource Resource that is finite and cannot be replenished by a natural means at the same rate it is being consumed. 814

nonvascular plants Land plants (i.e., bryophytes) that have no vascular tissue and therefore are low-lying and generally found in moist locations. 356

norepinephrine (NE) (nor-ep-uh-nef-rin) Neurotransmitter of the postganglionic fibers in the sympathetic division of the autonomic nervous system; also, a hormone produced by the adrenal medulla. 530, 690

notochord Cartilaginous-like supportive dorsal rod in all chordates sometime in their life cycle; replaced by vertebrae in vertebrates. 398

nuclear envelope Double membrane that surrounds the nucleus and is connected to the endoplasmic reticulum; has pores that allow substances to pass between the nucleus and the cytoplasm. 70

nuclear pore Opening in the nuclear envelope that permits the passage of proteins into the nucleus and ribosomal subunits out of the nucleus. 70

nucleic acid Polymer of nucleotides; both DNA and RNA are nucleic acids. 57, 192

nucleoid An irregularly shaped region in the prokaryotic cell that contains its genetic material. 67

nucleolus (noo-klee-uh-lus, nyoo-) Dark-staining, spherical body in the cell nucleus that produces ribosomal subunits. 70

nucleosome In the nucleus of a eukaryotic cell, a unit composed of DNA wound around a core of eight histone proteins, giving the appearance of a string of beads. 214

nucleotide Monomer of DNA and RNA consisting of a 5-carbon sugar bonded to a nitrogen-containing base and a phosphate group. 56, 192

nucleus (noo-klee-us, nyoo-) Membrane-bounded organelle that contains chromosomes and controls the structure and function of the cell. 68

O

obligate anaerobe Prokaryote unable to grow in the presence of free oxygen. 323

observation Step in the scientific method by which data are collected before a conclusion is drawn. 4

obstructive pulmonary disorder Characterized by airflow restriction in the airways; includes chronic bronchitis, emphysema, and asthma. 660

octet rule States that an atom other than hydrogen tends to form bonds until it has eight electrons in its outer shell; an atom that already has eight electrons in its outer shell does not react and is inert. 29

oil Substance, usually of plant origin and liquid at room temperature, formed when a glycerol molecule reacts with three fatty acid molecules. 49

olfactory cell (ahl-fak-tuh-ree, -tree, ohl-) Modified neuron that is a sensory receptor for the sense of smell. 553

oligotrophic lake Lake with few nutrients, usually very blue. 791

omnivore (ahm-nuh-vor) Organism in a food chain that feeds on both plants and animals. 770

oncogene (ahng-koh-jeen) Cancer-causing gene. 222

oocyte Immature egg that is undergoing meiosis; upon completion of meiosis, the oocyte becomes an egg. 704

oogenesis (oh-uh-jen-uh-sis) Production of an egg in females by the process of meiosis and maturation. 705

open circulatory system Arrangement of internal transport in which blood bathes the organs directly, and there is no distinction between blood and interstitial fluid. 590

operant conditioning Learning that results from rewarding or reinforcing a particular behavior. 747

operator In an operon, the sequence of DNA that binds tightly to a repressor, and thereby regulates the expression of structural genes. 212

operon Group of structural and regulating genes that function as a single unit. 212

opportunistic population Population demonstrating a life history pattern in which members exhibit exponential population growth. Its members are small in size, mature early, have a short life span, produce many offspring, and provide little or no care to offspring (e.g., dandelions). 735

opposable thumb Fingers arranged in such a way that the thumb can touch the fingertips of all four fingers. 412

order One of the categories, or taxa, used by taxonomists to group species; the taxon above the family level. 14, 296

organ Combination of two or more different tissues performing a common function. 9, 508

organelle (or-guh-nel) Small membranous structure in the cytoplasm having a specific structure and function. 68

organic chemistry The study of carbon compounds; chemistry of the living world. 44

organism Individual living thing. 9, 508

organ of Corti Structure in the vertebrate inner ear that contains auditory receptors; also called the spiral organ. 560

organ system Group of related organs working together. 9, 508

orgasm Physiological and psychological sensations that occur at the climax of sexual stimulation. 702

osmosis (ahz-moh-sis, ahs-) Diffusion of water through a selectively permeable membrane. 97

ossicle (ahs-ih-kul) One of the small bones of the middle ear—malleus, incus, and stapes. 559

osteocyte (ahs-tee-uh-syt) Mature bone cell located within the lacunae of bone. 576

otolith One of several calcium carbonate granules associated with receptors for gravitational balance; in vertebrates, located in the utricle and saccule. 563

outer ear Portion of the ear consisting of the pinna and the auditory canal. 559

outgroup In cladistics, a group of organisms that possess at least one characteristic that is judged to be ancestral, because while it lacks the ingroup's other characteristics, it shares this one with all the members of the ingroup. 300

ovarian cycle (oh-vair-ee-un) Monthly follicle changes occurring in the ovary that control the level of sex hormones in the blood and the uterine cycle. 706

ovary In animals, the female gonad, the organ that produces eggs, estrogen, and progesterone; in flowering plants, the base of the pistil that protects ovules and, along with associated tissues, becomes a fruit. 365, 490, 700, 704

overexploitation Occurs when the number of individuals taken from a wild population is so great that the population becomes severely reduced in numbers. 809

oviduct Tube that transports oocytes to the uterus; also called a uterine tube. 704

ovulation (ahv-yuh-lay-shun, ohv-) Release of a secondary oocyte from the ovary; if fertilization occurs, the secondary oocyte becomes an egg. 705

ovule In seed plants, the structure in which the megaspore becomes an egg-producing female gametophyte; it develops into a seed following fertilization. 355

oxidation Loss of one or more electrons from an atom or molecule; in biological systems, generally the loss of hydrogen atoms. 108

oxygen debt Amount of oxygen needed to metabolize lactate, a compound that accumulates during vigorous exercise. 133, 584

oxyhemoglobin (ahk-see-hee-muh-gloh-bin) Compound formed when oxygen combines with hemoglobin. 658

oxytocin (ahk-sih-toh-sin) Hormone released by the posterior pituitary that causes contraction of the uterus and milk letdown. 686

P

p53 Protein coded for by the *p53* gene that halts the cell cycle when DNA mutates and is in need of repair. 152

pain receptor Sensory receptor that is sensitive to chemicals released by damaged tissues or excess heat or pressure stimuli. 550

paleontologist Individual who studies fossils and the history of life. 255

paleontology Study of fossils that results in knowledge about the history of life. 250

palisade mesophyll Layer of tissue in a plant leaf containing elongated cells with many chloroplasts. 438

pancreas (pang-kree-us, pan-) Internal organ that produces digestive enzymes and the hormones insulin and glucagon. 638, 692

pancreatic amylase Enzyme that digests starch to maltose. 634

pancreatic islets (islets of Langerhans) Masses of cells that constitute the endocrine portion of the pancreas. 692

parasite Species that is dependent on a host species for survival, usually to the detriment of the host species. 764

parasitism Symbiotic relationship in which one species (the *parasite*) benefits in terms of growth and reproduction to the detriment of the other species (the *host*). 764

parasympathetic division That part of the autonomic system that is active under normal conditions; uses acetylcholine as a neurotransmitter. 541

parathyroid gland (par-uh-thy-royd) Gland embedded in the posterior surface of the thyroid gland; it produces parathyroid hormone. 689

parenchyma cell Plant tissue composed of the least-specialized of all plant cells; found in all organs of a plant. 436

parent cell Cell that divides to form daughter cells. 146

Parkinson disease Progressive deterioration of the central nervous system due to a deficiency in the neurotransmitter dopamine. 535

parsimony In cladistics, the preference for a cladogram that has the least number of branches. 301

parthenogenesis Development of an egg cell into a whole organism without fertilization. 700

partial pressure Pressure exerted by each gas in a mixture of gases. 658

partitioning in space In C_4 photosynthesis, carbon dioxide is fixed in mesophyll cells but enters the Krebs cycle in bundle sheath cells. 117

partitioning in time In CAM photosynthesis, carbon dioxide is fixed during the night and enters the Krebs cycle during the day. 117

pattern formation Positioning of cells during development that determines the final shape of an organism. 713

pectoral girdle (pek-tur-ul) Portion of the skeleton that provides support and attachment for an arm; consists of a scapula and a clavicle. 574

pedigree Graphic representation of matings and offspring over multiple generations for a particular genetic trait. 178

pelagic zone Open portion of the sea. 793

pelvic girdle Portion of the skeleton to which the legs are attached; consists of the coxal bones. 574

penis External organ in males through which the urethra passes; also serves as the organ of sexual intercourse. 702

pepsin Enzyme secreted by gastric glands that digests proteins to peptides. 634

peptide Two or more amino acids joined together by covalent bonding. 53

peptide bond Type of covalent bond that joins two amino acids. 53

peptide hormone Type of hormone that is a protein, a peptide, or derived from an amino acid. 684

peptidoglycan Unique molecule found in bacterial cell walls. 48

pericarp Outer covering of a fruit that develops from the wall of an ovary. 497

pericycle Layer of cells surrounding the vascular tissue of roots; produces branch roots. 438

periderm Protective tissue that replaces epidermis; includes cork and cork cambium. 442

peripheral nervous system (PNS) (puh-rif-ur-ul) Nerves and ganglia that lie outside the central nervous system. 526

peristalsis (pair-ih-stawl-sis) Wavelike contractions that propel substances along a tubular structure, such as the esophagus. 633

peritubular capillary network (pair-ih-too-byuh-lur) Capillary network that surrounds a nephron and functions in reabsorption during urine formation. 671

permafrost Permanently frozen ground, usually occurring in the tundra, a biome of arctic regions. 786

peroxisome Enzyme-filled vesicle in which fatty acids and amino acids are metabolized to hydrogen peroxide that is broken down to harmless products. 74

petal A flower part that occurs just inside the sepals; often conspicuously colored to attract pollinators. 365, 491

petiole Part of a plant leaf that connects the blade to the stem. 433

Peyer patches Lymphatic organs located in the small intestine. 611

P generation In genetics, the parental generation. 172

phagocytize To ingest extracellular particles by engulfing them, as amoeboid cells do. 339

phagocytosis (fag-uh-sy-toh-sis) Process by which amoeboid-type cells engulf large substances, forming an intracellular vacuole. 98

pharynx (far-ingks) Portion of the digestive tract between the mouth and the esophagus that serves as a passageway for food and also for air on its way to the trachea. 633, 654

phenotype (fee-nuh-typ) Visible expression of a genotype—for example, brown eyes or attached earlobes. 173

pheromone Chemical signal released by an organism that affects the metabolism or influences the behavior of another individual of the same species. 552, 684, 752

phloem Vascular tissue that conducts organic solutes in plants; contains sieve-tube elements and companion cells. 358, 437, 452

phloem sap Solution of sugars, nutrients, and hormones found in the phloem tissue of a plant. 452

phospholipid (fahs-foh-lip-id) Molecule that forms the bilayer of the cell's membranes; has a polar, hydrophilic head bonded to two nonpolar hydrophobic tails. 50

phospholipid bilayer Comprises the plasma membrane; each polar, hydrophilic head is bonded to two nonpolar, hydrophobic tails; contains embedded proteins. 93

photoperiodism Relative lengths of daylight and darkness that affect the physiology and behavior of an organism. 480

photosynthesis Process occurring usually within chloroplasts whereby chlorophyll-containing organelles trap solar energy to reduce carbon dioxide to carbohydrate. 9, 106

photosystem I (PSI) and photosystem II (PSII) Photosynthetic unit where solar energy is absorbed and high-energy electrons are generated; contains a pigment complex and an electron acceptor. 110

phototropism Growth response of plant stems to light; stems demonstrate positive phototropism. 471, 476

pH scale Measurement scale for hydrogen ion concentration. 37

phylogenetic (evolutionary) tree Diagram that indicates common ancestors and lines of descent among a group of organisms. 296

phylogeny Evolutionary history of a group of organisms. 298

phylum One of the categories, or taxa, used by taxonomists to group species; the taxon above the class level. 14, 296

phytochrome Photoreversible plant pigment that is involved in photoperiodism and other responses of plants such as etiolation. 480

phytoplankton Part of plankton containing organisms that photosynthesize, releasing oxygen to the atmosphere and serving as food producers in aquatic ecosystems. 343, 793

phytoremediation The use of plants to restore a natural area to its original condition. 457

pili Threadlike appendages that allow bacteria to attach to surfaces and to each other. 67

pineal gland (pin-ee-ul, py-nee-ul) Endocrine gland located in the third ventricle of the brain; produces melatonin. 536, 693

pinocytosis Process by which vesicle formation brings macromolecules into the cell. 98

pioneer species First species to colonize an area devoid of life. 768

pith Parenchyma tissue in the center of some stems and roots. 438

pituitary gland Endocrine gland that lies just inferior to the hypothalamus; consists of the anterior pituitary and the posterior pituitary. 686

placenta Organ formed during the development of placental mammals from the chorion and the uterine wall; allows the embryo, and then the fetus, to acquire nutrients and rid itself of wastes; produces hormones that regulate pregnancy. 404, 700, 717

placental mammal Member of the mammalian subclass characterized by the presence of a placenta during the development of an offspring. 404

planarian Free-living flatworm with a ladderlike nervous system. 387

plant Multicellular, usually photosynthetic, organism belonging to the plant kingdom. 15

plant hormone Chemical signal that is produced by various plant tissues and coordinates the activities of plant cells. 470

plant tissue culture Process of growing plant cells in the laboratory. 473

plaque (plak) Accumulation of soft masses of fatty material, particularly cholesterol, beneath the inner linings of the arteries. 596

plasma (plaz-muh) Liquid portion of blood; contains nutrients, wastes, salts, and proteins. 600

plasma cell Cell derived from a B cell that is specialized to mass-produce antibodies. 616

plasma membrane Membrane surrounding the cytoplasm that consists of a phospholipid bilayer with embedded proteins; functions to regulate the entrance and exit of molecules from the cell. 67

plasmid (plaz-mid) Self-replicating ring of accessory DNA in the cytoplasm of bacteria. 232, 322

plasmodesmata (sing., plasmodesma) In plants, cytoplasmic strands that extend through pores in the cell wall and connect the cytoplasm of two adjacent cells. 99, 437

plasmodial slime mold Free-living mass of cytoplasm that moves by pseudopods on a forest floor or in a field, feeding on decaying plant material by phagocytosis; reproduces by spore formation. 342

plasmolysis Contraction of the cell contents due to the loss of water. 97

platelet Cell fragment that is necessary to blood clotting; also called a thrombocyte. 511

pleiotropy Inheritance pattern in which one gene affects many phenotypic characteristics of the individual. 184

point mutation Alteration in a gene due to a change in a single nucleotide; results of this mutation vary. 204

polar body In oogenesis, a nonfunctional product; two to three meiotic products are of this type. 181

polar covalent bond Bond in which the sharing of electrons between atoms is unequal. 32

pollen grain In seed plants, the sperm-producing male gametophyte. 355, 363, 490

pollen sacs In flowering plants, the portions of the anther where microspore mother cells undergo meiosis to produce microspores. 365

pollen tube In seed plants, a tube that forms when a pollen grain lands on the stigma and germinates. The tube grows, passing between the cells of the stigma and the style to reach the egg inside an ovule, where fertilization occurs. 367

pollination In seed plants, the delivery of pollen to the vicinity of the egg-producing female gametophyte. 363, 494

pollution Any environmental change that adversely affects the lives and health of living things. 807

polygenic inheritance Pattern of inheritance in which a trait is controlled by several allelic pairs; each dominant allele contributes to the phenotype in an additive and like manner. 183

polymer Macromolecule consisting of covalently bonded monomers; for example, a polypeptide is a polymer of monomers called amino acids. 46

polymerase chain reaction (PCR) (pahl-uh-muh-rays, -rayz) Technique that uses the enzyme DNA polymerase to produce millions of copies of a particular piece of DNA. 238

polyp (pahl-ip) Small, abnormal growth that arises from the epithelial lining. 636

polypeptide Polymer of many amino acids linked by peptide bonds. 53

polyploid Having a chromosome number that is a multiple greater than twice that of the monoploid number. 162

polyribosome (pahl-ih-ry-buh-sohm) String of ribosomes simultaneously translating regions of the same mRNA strand during protein synthesis. 201

polysaccharide (pahl-ee-sak-uh-ryd) Polymer made from sugar monomers; the polysaccharides starch and glycogen are polymers of glucose monomers. 48

pond Freshwater basin, smaller than a lake. 791

pons (pahnz) Portion of the brain stem above the medulla oblongata and below the midbrain; assists the medulla oblongata in regulating the breathing rate. 536

population Organisms of the same species occupying a certain area. 12, 259, 728

population density The number of individuals per unit area or volume living in a particular habitat. 729

population distribution The pattern of dispersal of individuals living within a certain area. 729

portal system Pathway of blood flow that begins and ends in capillaries, such as the portal system located between the small intestine and the liver. 598

positive feedback Mechanism in which the stimulus initiates reactions that lead to an increase in the stimulus. 686

posterior pituitary Portion of the pituitary gland that stores and secretes oxytocin and antidiuretic hormone produced by the hypothalamus. 686

postzygotic isolating mechanism Anatomical or physiological difference between two species that prevents successful reproduction after mating has taken place. 275

potential energy Stored energy as a result of location or spatial arrangement. 86

predation Interaction in which one organism (the *predator*) uses another (the *prey*) as a food source. 762

preparatory (prep) reaction Reaction that oxidizes pyruvate with the release of carbon dioxide; results in acetyl CoA and connects glycolysis to the Krebs cycle. 125, 128

prezygotic isolating mechanism Anatomical or behavioral difference between two species that prevents the possibility of mating. 274

primary growth In plants, growth that originates in the apical meristems of the shoot and root; causes the plant to increase in length. 440

primary motor area Area in the frontal lobe where voluntary commands begin; each section controls a part of the body. 535

primary somatosensory area (soh-mat-uh-sens-ree, -suh-ree) Area dorsal to the central sulcus where sensory information arrives from skin and skeletal muscles. 535

primate Member of the order Primate; includes prosimians, monkeys, apes, and hominids, all of whom have adaptations for living in trees. 412

prime mover Muscle most directly responsible for a particular movement. 580

prions Misfolded proteins that cause other proteins to also become misfolded; cause of mad cow disease and other rare diseases. 315

producer Photosynthetic organism at the start of a grazing food chain that makes its own food (e.g., green plants on land and algae in water). 770

proembryo Smaller portion of divided sporophyte embryo that, after dividing repeatedly, becomes the embryo of a plant. 496

progesterone (proh-jes-tuh-rohn) Female sex hormone that helps maintain sex organs and secondary sex characteristics. 705

prokaryotic cell (prokaryote) Organism that lacks the membrane-bounded nucleus and membranous organelles typical of eukaryotes. 14, 67

prolactin (PRL) (proh-lak-tin) Hormone secreted by the anterior pituitary that stimulates the production of milk from the mammary glands. 687

proliferative phase Phase of the uterine cycle in which there is increased production of estrogen, causing the endometrium to thicken. 706

promoter In an operon, a sequence of DNA where RNA polymerase binds prior to transcription. 212

proprioceptor Sensory receptor that responds to changes in muscle or tendon tension. 558

prosimian Group of primates that includes lemurs and tarsiers, and may resemble the first primates that evolved. 415

prostate gland (prahs-tayt) Gland located around the male urethra below the urinary bladder; adds secretions to semen. 702

protease Enzyme that digest proteins. 220

proteasome A large, cylindrical cellular structure that contains proteases and digests tagged proteins following translation. 220

protein Molecule consisting of one or more polypeptides. 10, 52, 640

proteome Collection of proteins resulting from the translation of genes into proteins. 240

proteomics The study of all proteins in an organism. 240

protist Member of the kingdom Protista. 15, 334

protocell In biological evolution, a possible cell forerunner that became a cell once it could reproduce. 318

proton Positive subatomic particle, located in the nucleus and having a weight of approximately one atomic mass unit. 27

proto-oncogene (proh-toh-ahng-koh-jeen) Normal gene that can become an oncogene through mutation. 222

protostome Group of coelomate animals in which the first embryonic opening (the blastopore) is associated with the mouth. 383

protozoan Heterotrophic, unicellular protist that moves by flagella, cilia, or pseudopodia, or is immobile. 335

proximal convoluted tubule Highly coiled region of a nephron near the glomerular capsule, where tubular reabsorption takes place. 671

pseudocoelom A body cavity lying between the digestive tract and the body wall that is incompletely lined by mesoderm. 390

pseudogene Gene copy that is nonfunctional due to a mutation. 239

pseudopod Cytoplasmic extension of amoeboid protists; used for locomotion and engulfing food. 339

pseudostratified ciliated columnar epithelium Appearance of layering in some epithelial cells when, actually, each cell touches a baseline and true layers do not exist. 509

puberty Period of life when secondary sex changes occur in humans; marked by the onset of menses in females and sperm production in males. 703

pulmonary artery (pool-muh-nair-ee, pul-) Blood vessel that takes blood away from the heart to the lungs. 592

pulmonary circuit Circulatory pathway that consists of the pulmonary trunk, the pulmonary arteries, and the pulmonary veins; takes O_2-poor blood from the heart to the lungs and O_2-rich blood from the lungs to the heart. 593, 598

pulmonary trunk Large blood vessel that divides into the pulmonary arteries; takes blood away from the heart to the lungs. 592

pulmonary vein Blood vessel that takes blood from the lungs to the heart. 592

pulse Vibration felt in arterial walls due to expansion of the aorta following ventricular contraction. 594

Punnett square Grid used to calculate the expected results of simple genetic crosses. 175

pupil (pyoo-pul) Opening in the center of the iris of the eye. 554

pyruvate End product of glycolysis; its further fate, involving fermentation or entry into a mitochondrion, depends on oxygen availability. 125

R

radial symmetry Body plan in which similar parts are arranged around a central axis, like spokes of a wheel. 381

radiolarian Member of the phylum Actinopoda bearing a glassy silicon test, usually with a radial arrangement of spines; pseudopods are external to the test. 339

rain shadow Leeward side (side sheltered from the wind) of a mountainous barrier, which receives much less precipitation than the windward side. 783

ray-finned fish Group of bony fishes with fins supported by parallel bony rays connected by webs of thin tissue. 400

receptacle Area where a flower attaches to a floral stalk. 365

receptor-mediated endocytosis Selective uptake of molecules into a cell by vacuole formation after they bind to specific receptor proteins in the plasma membrane. 98

recessive allele (uh-leel) Allele that exerts its phenotypic effect only in the homozygote; its expression is masked by a dominant allele. 173

reciprocal altruism The trading of helpful or cooperative acts, such as helping at the nest, by individuals—the animal that was helped will repay the debt at some later time. 751

recombinant DNA (rDNA) DNA that contains genes from more than one source. 232

recombinant DNA technology Use of DNA that contains genes from more than one source, often to produce transgenic organisms. 232

rectum (rek-tum) Terminal end of the digestive tube between the sigmoid colon and the anus. 636

red algae Marine photosynthetic protists with a notable abundance of phycobilin pigments; include coralline algae of coral reefs. 344

red blood cell (RBC) Formed element that contains hemoglobin and carries oxygen from the lungs to the tissues; erythrocyte. 511, 600

red bone marrow Blood-cell-forming tissue located in the spaces within spongy bone. 576, 611

red tide Occurs frequently in coastal areas and is often associated with population blooms of dinoflagellates. Dinoflagellate pigments are responsible for the red color of the water. Under these conditions, the dinoflagellates often produce saxitoxin, which can lead to paralytic shellfish poisoning. 343

redox reaction Oxidation-reduction reaction; one molecule loses electrons (oxidation) while another molecule simultaneously gains electrons (reduction). 108

reduced hemoglobin Hemoglobin molecule that is carrying hydrogen ions derived from carbonic acid. 658

reduction Chemical reaction that results in addition of one or more electrons to an atom, ion, or compound. Reduction of one substance occurs simultaneously with oxidation of another. 108

reflex Automatic, involuntary response of an organism to a stimulus. 540

reflex action An action performed automatically, without conscious thought (e.g., swallowing). 534, 633

refractory period (rih-frak-tuh-ree) Time following an action potential when a neuron is unable to conduct another nerve impulse. 529

regulatory gene In an operon, a gene that codes for a protein that regulates the expression of other genes. 212

renal cortex (ree-nul kor-teks) Outer portion of the kidney that appears granular. 670

renal medulla (ree-nul muh-dul-uh) Inner portion of the kidney that consists of renal pyramids. 670

renal pelvis Hollow chamber in the kidney that lies inside the renal medulla and receives freshly prepared urine from the collecting ducts. 670

renewable resource Resource that is replenished by a natural means at the same rate or faster than it is consumed. 814

renin (ren-in) Enzyme released by the kidneys that leads to the secretion of aldosterone and a rise in blood pressure. 675, 691

repolarization Recovery of a neuron's polarity to the resting potential after the neuron ceases transmitting impulses. 529

repetitive DNA Sequence of DNA nucleotides that is repeated several times in a genome. 239

repressor In an operon, protein molecule that binds to an operator, preventing transcription of structural genes. 212

reproduce To produce a new individual of the same kind. 9

reproductive cloning Production of an organism that is genetically identical to the original individual. 230

reproductive system Organ system that contains male or female organs and specializes in the production of offspring. 517

reptile Member of a class of terrestrial vertebrates characterized by internal fertilization, scaly skin, and an egg with a leathery shell; includes snakes, lizards, turtles, and crocodiles. 402

resource In economic terms, anything having potential use for creating wealth or giving satisfaction. 729

resource partitioning Mechanism that increases the number of niches by apportioning the supply of a resource such as food or living space between species. 760

respiration Sequence of events that results in gas exchange between the cells of the body and the environment. 650

respiratory center Group of nerve cells in the medulla oblongata that send out nerve impulses on a rhythmic basis, resulting in involuntary inspiration on an ongoing basis. 657

respiratory system Organ system consisting of the lungs and tubes that bring oxygen into the lungs and take carbon dioxide out. 517

resting potential Polarity across the plasma membrane of a resting neuron due to an unequal distribution of ions. 528

restoration ecology Subdiscipline of conservation biology that seeks ways to return ecosystems to their former state. 811

restriction enzyme Bacterial enzyme that stops viral reproduction by cleaving viral DNA; used to cut DNA at specific points during production of recombinant DNA. 232

retina (ret-n-uh, ret-nuh) Innermost layer of the eyeball that contains the rod cells and the cone cells. 554

retrovirus RNA virus containing the enzyme reverse transcriptase that carries out RNA-to-DNA transcription. 315

reverse transcriptase Enzyme that transcribes RNA into DNA. 315

rhizome Rootlike underground stem. 432, 499

rhodopsin (roh-dahp-sun) Light-absorbing molecule in rod cells and cone cells that contains a pigment and the protein opsin. 556

ribose Pentose sugar found in RNA. 47

ribosomal RNA (rRNA) (ry-buh-soh-mul) Type of RNA found in ribosomes where protein synthesis occurs. 200

ribosome (ry-buh-sohm) RNA and protein in two subunits; site of protein synthesis in the cytoplasm. 67

ribozyme Enzyme that carries out mRNA processing. 202, 318

rigor mortis Contraction of muscles at death due to lack of ATP. 583

river Freshwater channel that flows eventually to the oceans. 791

RNA interference Collective regulation of mRNA activity by miRNAs and siRNAs. 219

RNA (ribonucleic acid) (ry-boh-noo-klee-ik) Nucleic acid produced from covalent bonding of nucleotide monomers that contain the sugar ribose; occurs in three forms: messenger RNA, ribosomal RNA, and transfer RNA. 57, 192

root hair Extension of a root epidermal cell that increases the surface area for the absorption of water and minerals. 433, 463

root nodule Structure on a plant root that contains nitrogen-fixing bacteria. 464

root pressure Osmotic pressure caused by active movement of minerals into root cells; serves to elevate water in xylem for a short distance. 454

root system Includes the main root and any and all of its lateral (side) branches. 432

rotational balance Maintenance of balance when the head and body are suddenly moved or rotated. 562

rough ER (RER) Membranous system of tubules, vesicles, and sacs in cells; has attached ribosomes. 72

roundworm Member of the phylum Nematoda, having a cylindrical body with a complete digestive tract and a pseudocoelom; some forms are free-living in water and soil; many are parasitic. 393

RuBP carboxylase Enzyme that is required for carbon dioxide fixation (atmospheric CO_2 attaches to RuBP) in the Calvin cycle. 114

ruminant Cow and related mammals in which digestion of cellulose occurs in an extra stomach, or rumen, from which partially digested material can be ejected back into the mouth. 631

S

saccule (sak-yool) Saclike cavity in the vestibule of the inner ear; contains sensory receptors for gravitational equilibrium. 563

salivary amylase (sal-uh-vair-ee am-uh-lays, -layz) Secreted from the salivary glands; the first enzyme to act on starch. 632

salivary gland Gland associated with the mouth that secretes saliva. 632

salt Compound produced by a reaction between an acid and a base. 30

saltatory conduction Movement of nerve impulses from one neurolemmal node to another along a myelinated axon. 529

saprotroph Organism that secretes digestive enzymes and absorbs the resulting nutrients back across the plasma membrane. 323

sarcolemma (sar-kuh-lem-uh) Plasma membrane of a muscle fiber; also forms the tubules of the T system involved in muscular contraction. 582

sarcomere (sar-kuh-mir) One of many units, arranged linearly within a myofibril, whose contraction produces muscle contraction. 582

sarcoplasmic reticulum (sar-kuh-plaz-mik rihtik-yuh-lum) Smooth endoplasmic reticulum of skeletal muscle cells; surrounds the myofibrils and stores calcium ions. 582

SARS Severe acute respiratory syndrome caused by a virus that emerged in China and spread around the world. 313

saturated fatty acid Fatty acid molecule that lacks double bonds between the atoms of its carbon chain. 49

savanna Terrestrial biome that is a grassland in Africa, characterized by few trees and a severe dry season. 789

scanning electron microscope Beam of electrons scans over a specimen point by point and builds up an image on a fluorescent screen. 66

scavenger Animal that specializes in the consumption of dead animals. 770

Schwann cell Cell that surrounds a fiber of a peripheral nerve and forms the myelin sheath. 527

scientific theory Concept supported by a broad range of observations, experiments, and conclusions. 5

sclera (skleer-uh) White, fibrous, outer layer of the eyeball. 554

sclerenchyma cell Plant tissue composed of cells with heavily lignified cell walls; functions in support. 437

seaweed Multicellular forms of red, green, and brown algae found in marine habitats. 344

secondary growth In vascular plants, an increase in stem and root diameter made possible by cell division of the lateral meristems. 442

secondary metabolite Molecule not directly involved in growth, development, or reproduction of an organism; in plants, these molecules, which include nicotine, caffeine, tannins, and menthols, can discourage herbivores. 482

secondary sex characteristic Trait that is sometimes helpful but not absolutely necessary for reproduction and is maintained by the sex hormones in males and females. 703

second messenger Chemical signal such as cyclic AMP that causes the cell to respond to the first messenger—a hormone bound to a plasma membrane receptor. 684

secretory phase Phase of the uterine cycle in which increased production of progesterone causes the endometrium to double in thickness, producing a thick, mucoid secretion. 706

seed Mature ovule that contains an embryo with stored food enclosed in a protective coat. 362, 490

seedless vascular plant Land plants, such as lycophytes and ferns, which have vascular tissue but do not produce seeds. Reproduction involves flagellated sperm and production of windblown spores. 358

seed plant Land plant whose reproduction involves the production of seeds. Reproduction in seed plants is fully adapted to living on land because all reproductive structures are protected from drying out. Includes gymnosperms and angiosperms. 362

segmentation Repetition of body parts as segments along the length of the body; seen in annelids, arthropods, and chordates. 392

selective agent Environmental factor that affects the ability of an organism to survive and produce fertile offspring. 253

self-antigen Antigen that is produced by an organism. 615

semen (seminal fluid) (see-mun) Thick, whitish fluid consisting of sperm and secretions from several glands of the male reproductive tract. 702

semicircular canal (sem-ih-sur-kyuh-lur) One of three tubular structures within the inner ear that contain sensory receptors responsible for the sense of rotational equilibrium. 562

semiconservative replication Duplication of DNA resulting in two double helix molecules, each having one parental and one new strand. 196

semilunar valve (sem-ee-loo-nur) Valve resembling a half moon located between the ventricles and their attached vessels. 592

seminal vesicle (sem-uh-nul) Convoluted, saclike structure attached to the vas deferens near the base of the urinary bladder in males; adds secretions to semen. 702

seminiferous tubule (sem-uh-nif-ur-us) Long, coiled structure contained within chambers of the testis; where sperm are produced. 703

senescence Sum of the processes involving aging, decline, and eventual death of a plant or plant part. 473

sensation Conscious awareness of a stimulus due to a nerve impulse sent to the brain from a sensory receptor by way of sensory neurons. 551

sensory adaptation The phenomenon in which a sensation becomes less noticeable once it has been recognized by constant repeated stimulation. 551

sensory neuron Nerve cell that transmits nerve impulses to the central nervous system after a sensory receptor has been stimulated. 527

sensory receptor Structure that receives either external or internal environmental stimuli and is a part of a sensory neuron or transmits signals to a sensory neuron. 550

sepal Outermost, sterile, leaflike covering of the flower; usually green in color. 365, 491

Sertoli cell Type of cell in seminiferous tubules with FSH receptors; helps nourish and support developing sperm. 703

serum (seer-um) Light yellow liquid left after clotting of blood. 603

sessile Describes an animal that tends to stay in one place. 382

sex chromosome Chromosome that determines the sex of an individual; in humans, females have two

X chromosomes, and males have an X and a Y chromosome. 144

sexually transmitted disease (STD) Illness communicated primarily or exclusively through sexual contact. 708

sexual reproduction Reproduction involving meiosis, gamete formation, and fertilization; produces offspring with chromosomes inherited from each parent with a unique combination of genes. 160, 700

shared ancestral trait In cladistics, a characteristic shared by both the outgroup and the ingroup that is judged to have preceded those of all the ingroup clades. 300

shared derived trait In cladistics, a characteristic that evolved after the ancestral trait and is present in an ancestor and all the members of a clade. 300

shoot system Aboveground portion of a plant consisting of the stem, leaves, and flowers. 432

short-day plant Plant that flowers when day length is shorter than a critical length (e.g., cocklebur, poinsettia, and chrysanthemum). 481

sieve-tube member Member that joins with others in the phloem tissue of plants as a means of transport for nutrient sap. 437, 452

signaling molecule Molecule that stimulates or inhibits an event in the cell cycle. 100

simple diffusion Movement of molecules or ions from a region of higher to lower concentration; it requires no energy and tends to lead to an equal distribution. 96

simple goiter (goy-tur) Condition in which an enlarged thyroid produces low levels of thyroxine. 689

simple muscle twitch Contraction of a whole muscle in response to a single stimulus. 580

single nucleotide polymorphism (SNP) Site present in at least 1% of the population at which individuals differ by a single nucleotide. These can be used as genetic markers to map unknown genes or traits. 259

sink In the pressure-flow model of phloem transport, the location (roots) from which sugar is constantly being removed. Sugar will flow to the roots from the source. 459

sink population Population that is found in an unfavorable area where at best the birthrate equals the death rate; sink populations receive new members from source populations. 810

sister chromatid One of two genetically identical chromosomal units that are the result of DNA replication and are attached to each other at the centromere. 144

skeletal muscle Striated, voluntary muscle tissue that comprises skeletal muscles; also called striated muscle. 512

skeletal system System of bones, cartilage, and ligaments that works with the muscular system to protect the body and provide support for locomotion and movement. 516

skin Outer covering of the body; can be called the integumentary system because it contains organs such as sense organs. 515

skull Bony framework of the head, composed of cranial bones and the bones of the face. 572

sliding filament model An explanation for muscle contraction based on the movement of actin filaments in relation to myosin filaments. 582

slime mold Protists that decompose dead material and feed on bacteria by phagocytosis; vegetative state is mobile and amoeboid. 342

small interfering RNAs (siRNA) Type of small RNA that combines with a complex and thereafter silences (inactivates) a chosen mRNA. 219

small intestine In vertebrates, the portion of the digestive tract that precedes the large intestine; in humans, consists of the duodenum, jejunum, and ileum. 634

small RNAs (sRNA) RNAs of limited length that function in various ways within the nucleus to regulate gene expression following transcription. 218

smooth ER (SER) Membranous system of tubules, vesicles, and sacs in eukaryotic cells; lacks attached ribosomes. 72

smooth muscle Nonstriated, involuntary muscle tissue found in the walls of internal organs. 512

sociobiology Application of evolutionary principles to the study of social behavior of animals, including humans. 750

sodium-potassium pump Carrier protein in the plasma membrane that moves sodium ions out of and potassium ions into cells; important in nerve and muscle cells. 98

soft palate (pal-it) Entirely muscular posterior portion of the roof of the mouth. 632

soil Accumulation of inorganic rock material and organic matter that is capable of supporting the growth of vegetation. 462

soil profile Vertical section of soil from the ground surface to the unaltered rock below. 462

solute Substance that is dissolved in a solvent, forming a solution. 34, 97

solution Fluid (the solvent) that contains a dissolved solid (the solute). 34

solvent Liquid portion of a solution that serves to dissolve a solute. 34, 97

somatic system That portion of the peripheral nervous system containing motor neurons that control skeletal muscles. 540

sorus (pl., sori) Dark spot on the underside of fern fronds that is a collection of spore-producing structures. 361

source In the pressure-flow model of phloem transport, the location (leaves) of sugar production. Sugar will flow from the leaves to the sink. 459

source population Population that can provide members to other populations of the species because it lives in a favorable area, and the birthrate is most likely higher than the death rate. 810

speciation Origin of new species due to the evolutionary process of descent with modification. 272

species Group of similarly constructed organisms capable of interbreeding and producing fertile offspring; organisms that share a common gene pool; the taxon at the lowest level of classification. 14, 296

species richness Number of species in a community. 769

specific epithet In the binominal system of taxonomy, the second part of an organism's name; it may be descriptive. 15

spermatogenesis (spur-mat-uh-jen-ih-sis) Production of sperm in males by the process of meiosis and maturation. 703

sphincter (sfingk-tur) Muscle that surrounds a tube and closes or opens the tube by contracting and relaxing. 617, 633

spinal cord Part of the central nervous system; the nerve cord that is continuous with the base of the brain plus the vertebral column that protects the nerve cord. 534

spinal nerve Nerve that arises from the spinal cord. 539

spindle apparatus Microtubule structure that brings about chromosome movement during nuclear division. 146

spleen Large, glandular organ located in the upper left region of the abdomen; stores and purifies blood. 611

spongy bone Porous bone found at the ends of long bones where red bone marrow is sometimes located. 576

spongy mesophyll Layer of tissue in a plant leaf containing loosely packed

cells, increasing the amount of surface area for gas exchange. 438

sporangium (pl., sporangia) Structure that produces spores. 342, 357

spore Asexual reproductive or resting cell capable of developing into a new organism without fusion with another cell, in contrast to a gamete. 335, 354

sporophyte Diploid generation of the alternation of generations life cycle of a plant; produces haploid spores that develop into the haploid generation. 354, 490

squamous epithelium Type of epithelial tissue that contains flat cells. 509

S stage In the cell cycle, the period of time during which DNA replication occurs so that the chromosomes are duplicated. 145

stabilizing selection Outcome of natural selection in which extreme phenotypes are eliminated and the average phenotype is conserved. 264

stamen In flowering plants, the portion of the flower that consists of a filament and an anther containing pollen sacs where pollen is produced. 365, 491

starch Storage polysaccharide found in plants that is composed of glucose molecules joined in a linear fashion with few side chains. 48

statolith Sensors found in root cap cells that cause a plant to demonstrate gravitropism. 476

stem Usually the upright, vertical portion of a plant that transports substances to and from the leaves. 432

stereoscopic vision Vision characterized by depth perception and three-dimensionality. 413

steroid (steer-oyd) Type of lipid molecule having a complex of four carbon rings; examples are cholesterol, progesterone, and testosterone. 50

steroid hormone Type of hormone that has a complex of four carbon rings but different side chains from other steroid hormones. 684

stigma In flowering plants, portion of the pistil where pollen grains adhere and germinate before fertilization can occur. 365

stolon Stem that grows horizontally along the ground and may give rise to new plants where it contacts the soil—e.g., the runners of strawberry plants. 499

stoma (pl., stomata) Small opening between two guard cells on the underside of leaf epidermis through which gases pass. 107, 355, 436, 456

stratified As in the outer layer of skin, having several layers. 509

stratum (pl., strata) Ancient layer of sedimentary rock; results from slow deposition of silt, volcanic ash, and other materials. 251

stream Freshwater channel, smaller than a river. 791

striated Having bands; in cardiac and skeletal muscle, alternating light and dark crossbands produced by the distribution of contractile proteins. 512

strobilus Terminal cluster of specialized leaves that bear sporangia. 358

stroma Fluid within a chloroplast that contains enzymes involved in the synthesis of carbohydrates during photosynthesis. 107

structural gene Gene that codes for an enzyme in a metabolic pathway. 212

style Elongated, central portion of the pistil between the ovary and stigma. 365

subcutaneous layer A sheet that lies just beneath the skin and consists of loose connective and adipose tissue. 515

substrate Reactant in a reaction controlled by an enzyme. 90

substrate feeder Organism that lives in or on its food source. 628

substrate-level ATP synthesis Process in which ATP is formed by tranferring a phosphate from a metabolic substrate to ADP. 126

surface-area-to-volume ratio Ratio of a cell's outside area to its internal volume. 65

survivorship Probability of newborn individuals of a cohort surviving to particular ages. 730

sustainable development Management of an ecosystem so that it maintains itself while providing services to human beings. 811

sustainable society Interactive group of individuals who provide for their needs in a way that will allow future generations to enjoy the same standard of living. 800, 813

swallowing Muscular movement of the pharynx and esophagus to take the food bolus from the mouth to the stomach. 633

symbiosis Relationship that occurs when two different species live together in a unique way; it may be beneficial, neutral, or detrimental to one and/or the other species. 764

sympathetic division The part of the autonomic system that usually promotes activities associated with emergency (fight-or-flight) situations; uses norepinephrine as a neurotransmitter. 541

sympatric speciation Origin of new species in populations that overlap geographically. 279

synapse (sin-aps, si-naps) Junction between neurons consisting of the presynaptic (axon) membrane, the synaptic cleft, and the postsynaptic (usually dendrite) membrane. 530

synapsis (sih-nap-sis) Pairing of homologous chromosomes during prophase I of meiosis I. 155

synaptic cleft (sih-nap-tik) Small gap between presynaptic and postsynaptic membranes of a synapse. 530

syndrome Group of symptoms that appear together and tend to indicate the presence of a particular disorder. 163

synovial joint (sih-noh-vee-ul) Freely movable joint in which two bones are separated by a cavity. 577

syphilis (sif-uh-lis) Sexually transmitted disease caused by the bacterium *Treponema pallidum* that, if untreated, can lead to cardiac and central nervous system disorders. 708

systematics Study of the diversity of organisms to classify them and determine their evolutionary relationships. 296

systemic circuit Blood vessels that transport blood from the left ventricle and back to the right atrium of the heart. 593, 598

systemin In plants, an 18-amino-acid peptide that is produced by damaged or injured leaves and leads to the wound response. 483

systole (sis-tuh-lee) Contraction period of the heart during the cardiac cycle. 594

systolic pressure (sis-tahl-ik) Arterial blood pressure during the systolic phase of the cardiac cycle. 599

T

taiga Terrestrial biome that is a coniferous forest extending in a broad belt across northern Eurasia and North America. 786

tandem repeat Sequence of DNA nucleotides that is repeated many times in a row. 239

taste bud Sense organ containing the receptors associated with the sense of taste. 552

taxon Group of organisms that fills a particular classification category. 296

taxonomy Branch of biology concerned with identifying, describing, and naming organisms. 14, 296

T cell Lymphocyte that matures in the thymus. Cytotoxic T cells kill antigen-bearing cells outright; helper T cells release cytokines that stimulate other immune system cells. 601, 611

T cell receptor (TCR) Molecule on the surface of a T cell that can bind to a specific antigen fragment in combination with an MHC molecule. 616

temperate deciduous forest Forest found south of the taiga; characterized by deciduous trees such as oak, beech, and maple; moderate climate; relatively high rainfall; stratified plant growth; and plentiful ground life. 788

temperate grassland Grazing, fire, and drought restrict tree growth in this terrestrial biome. 788

temperate rain forest Coniferous forest— e.g., the forest running along the west coast of Canada and the United States—characterized by plentiful rainfall and rich soil. 786

template (tem-plit) Pattern or guide used to make copies; parental strand of DNA serves as a guide for the production of daughter DNA strands, and DNA also serves as a guide for the production of messenger RNA. 196

tendon Strap of fibrous connective tissue that connects skeletal muscle to bone. 511, 580

terminal bud Bud that develops at the apex of a shoot. 432

terminal bud scale scar Marking from the shedding of terminal bud scales; age of a stem can be determined by number of scars. 441

territoriality Marking and/or defending a particular area against invasion by another species member. 748

territory Area occupied and defended exclusively by an animal or group of animals; often used for the purpose of feeding, mating, and caring for young. 748

testcross Cross between an individual with the dominant phenotype and an individual with the recessive phenotype. The resulting phenotypic ratio indicates whether the dominant phenotype is homozygous or heterozygous. 176

test group Group that participates in an experiment and is exposed to the experimental variable. 5

testis (pl., testes) Male gonad that produces sperm and the male sex hormones. 700

testosterone (tes-tahs-tuh-rohn) Male sex hormone that helps maintain sexual organs and secondary sex characteristics. 703

tetrad Homologous chromosomes, each having sister chromatids that are joined during meiosis. 156

thalamus (thal-uh-mus) Part of the brain located in the lateral walls of the third ventricle that serves as the integrating center for sensory input; it plays a role in arousing the cerebral cortex. 536

theory of ecosystems Concept that organisms are members of populations that interact with each other and with the physical environment at a particular locale. 12

theory of evolution Concept that all living things have a common ancestor, but each is adapted to a particular way of life. 13

therapeutic cloning Used to create mature cells of various cell types. Also used to learn about specialization of cells and to provide cells and tissues for treating human illnesses. 230

thermoacidophile Type of archaean that lives in hot, acidic, aquatic habitats, such as hot springs or near hydrothermal vents. 325

thermoreceptor Sensory receptor that is sensitive to changes in temperature. 550

thigmotropism In plants, unequal growth due to contact with solid objects, as the coiling of tendrils around a pole. 476

threatened species Species that is likely to become endangered in the foreseeable future (e.g., bald eagle, gray wolf, Lousiana black bear). 800

threshold Electrical potential level (voltage) at which an action potential or nerve impulse is produced. 528

thrombin (thrahm-bin) Enzyme that converts fibrinogen to fibrin threads during blood clotting. 603

thylakoid Flattened sac within a granum whose membrane contains chlorophyll and where the light reactions of photosynthesis occur. 107, 324

thylakoid space Inner compartment of the thylakoid. 107

thymus gland Lymphatic organ, located along the trachea behind the sternum, involved in the maturation of T lymphocytes in the thymus gland. Secretes hormones called thymosins, which aid the maturation of T cells and perhaps stimulate immune cells in general. 611

thyroid gland Endocrine gland in the neck that produces several important hormones, including thyroxine, triiodothyronine, and calcitonin. 689

thyroid-stimulating hormone (TSH) Substance produced by the anterior pituitary that causes the thyroid to secrete thyroxine and triiodothyronine. 686

thyroxine (T_4) (thy-rahk-sin) Hormone secreted from the thyroid gland that promotes growth and development; in general, it increases the metabolic rate in cells. 689

tight junction Junction between animal cells that seals the cells to one another. 99

tissue Group of similar cells that perform a common function. 9, 508

tissue culture Process of growing tissue artificially, usually in a liquid medium in laboratory glassware. 500

tissue fluid Fluid that surrounds the body's cells; consists of dissolved substances that leave the blood capillaries by filtration and diffusion. 511, 602

tonsillitis Infection of the tonsils that causes inflammation and can spread to the middle ears. 632

tonsils Partially encapsulated lymph nodules located in the pharynx. 611

topography Surface features of the Earth. 783

torpedo stage Stage of development of a sporophyte embryo; embryo has a torpedo shape, and the root and shoot apical meristems are present. 496

totipotent Cell that has the full genetic potential of the organism, including the potential to develop into a complete organism. 500

touch receptor One of several cutaneous (skin) receptors that responds to light pressure. 558

toxin Substance produced by a bacterium that has a poisonous effect on the body and causes illness. 326

tracer Substance having an attached radioactive isotope that allows a researcher to track its whereabouts in a biological system. 28

trachea (tray-kee-uh) In birds and mammals, passageway that conveys air from the larynx to the bronchi; also called the windpipe. 654

tracheae In insects, air tubes located between the spiracles and the tracheoles. 591, 653

tracheid In flowering plants, type of cell in xylem that has tapered ends and pits through which water and minerals flow. 437, 452

tract Bundle of myelinated axons in the central nervous system. 534

transcription Process whereby a DNA strand serves as a template for the formation of mRNA. 198

transcription activator Protein that initiates transcription by RNA polymerase and thereby starts the process that results in gene expression. 213

transcription factor In eukaryotes, protein required for the initiation of transcription by RNA polymerase. 213

transduction Exchange of DNA between bacteria by means of a bacteriophage. 322

trans fats Fats known to cause cardiovascular disease because they contain partially hydrogenated fatty acids. 49

transfer RNA (tRNA) Type of RNA that transfers a particular amino acid to a ribosome during protein synthesis; at one end, it binds to the amino acid, and at the other end it has an anticodon that binds to an mRNA codon. 200

transformation Taking up of extraneous genetic material from the environment by bacteria. 322

transitional fossil A fossil that bears a resemblance to two groups that in the present day are classified separately. 256

translation Process whereby ribosomes use the sequence of codons in mRNA to produce a polypeptide with a particular sequence of amino acids. 198

translation repressor protein In the cytoplasm, one of a number of proteins that prevent the translation of an mRNA. 220

translocation Movement of a chromosomal segment from one chromosome to another nonhomologous chromosome, leading to abnormalities (e.g., Down syndrome). 164, 202

transmission electron microscope Similar to the scanning electron microscope, but the image is colored by a computer. 66

transpiration Plant's loss of water to the atmosphere, mainly through evaporation at leaf stomata. 455

transport vesicle Vesicle formed in the ER that carries proteins and lipids to the Golgi apparatus. 72

transposon DNA sequence capable of randomly moving from one site to another in the genome. 240

trichocyst Found in ciliates; contains long, barbed threads useful for defense and capturing prey. 340

trichomes Outgrowth of the epidermis, such as a hair or a thorn. 444

trichomoniasis Sexually transmitted disease caused by the parasitic protozoan *Trichomonas vaginalis*. 708

triglyceride (trih-glis-uh-ryd) Neutral fat composed of glycerol and three fatty acids. 49, 640

triplet code Each sequence of three nucleotide bases in the DNA of genes stands for a particular amino acid. 198

triploid endosperm In flowering plants, nutritive storage tissue that is derived from an egg uniting with polar nuclei during double fertilization. 367

trisomy One more chromosome than usual. 162

trochophore larva Independent motile feeding stage in the development of the trochozoa; recognized by two bands of cilia around its middle. 387

trochozoa Type of protostome that produces a trochophore larva, which has two bands of cilia around its middle. 383

trophic level Feeding level of one or more populations in a food web. 773

trophoblast Outer cells of a blastocyst that help form the placenta and other extraembryonic membranes. 716

tropical rain forest Biome near the equator in South America, Africa, and the Indo-Malay regions; characterized by warm weather, plentiful rainfall, a diversity of species, and mainly tree-living animal life. 790

tropism In plants, a growth response toward or away from a directional stimulus. 446, 476

trypsin Protein-digesting enzyme secreted by the pancreas. 634

tuber Enlarged, short, fleshy underground stem—e.g., potato. 499

tubular reabsorption Movement of primarily nutrient molecules and water from the contents of the nephron into blood at the proximal convoluted tubule. 672

tubular secretion Movement of certain molecules from blood into the distal convoluted tubule of a nephron so that they are added to urine. 673

tumor (too-mur) Cells derived from a single mutated cell that has repeatedly undergone cell division; benign tumors remain at the site of origin, and malignant tumors metastasize. 153

tumor suppressor gene Gene that codes for a protein that ordinarily suppresses cell division; inactivity can lead to a tumor. 222

tunicate Type of primitive invertebrate chordate. 398

turgor movement In plant cells, pressure of the cell contents against the cell wall when the central vacuole is full. 478

Turner syndrome Condition caused by the inheritance of a single X chromosome. 163

tympanic membrane (tim-pan-ik) Located between the outer and middle ear where it receives sound waves; also called the eardrum. 559

typhlosole Expanded dorsal surface of the long intestine of earthworms, allowing additional surface for absorption. 630

U

umbilical cord Cord connecting the fetus to the placenta through which blood vessels pass. 717

uniformitarianism Belief espoused by James Hutton that geological forces act at a continuous, uniform rate. 251

unique noncoding DNA DNA that does not code for a protein and whose unknown function may be different from that of other noncoding DNA. 240

unpacking Prior to transcription, the transformation of heterochromatin to euchromatin. 215

unsaturated fatty acid Fatty acid molecule that has one or more double bonds between the atoms of its carbon chain. 49

upwelling Upward movement of deep, nutrient-rich water along coasts; it replaces surface waters that move away from shore when the direction of prevailing winds shifts. 784

urea Main nitrogenous waste of terrestrial amphibians and most mammals. 666

uremia High level of urea nitrogen in the blood. 676

ureter (yoor-uh-tur) One of two tubes that take urine from the kidneys to the urinary bladder. 670

urethra (yoo-ree-thruh) Tubular structure that receives urine from the bladder and carries it to the outside of the body. 670

uric acid Main nitrogenous waste of insects, reptiles, and birds. 666

urinary bladder Organ where urine is stored before being discharged by way of the urethra. 670

urinary system Organ system consisting of the kidneys and urinary bladder; rids the body of nitrogenous wastes and helps regulate the water-salt balance of the blood. 517

urine Liquid waste product made by the nephrons of the vertebrate kidney through the processes of glomerular filtration, tubular reabsorption, and tubular secretion. 670

uterine cycle (yoo-tur-in, -tuh-ryn) Monthly occurring changes in the characteristics of the uterine lining (endometrium). 706

uterus (yoo-tur-us) Organ located in the female pelvis where the fetus develops; also called the womb. 704

utricle (yoo-trih-kul) Saclike cavity in the vestibule of the inner ear that contains sensory receptors for gravitational equilibrium. 563

V

vaccine Antigens prepared in such a way that they can promote active immunity without causing disease. 326, 615

vacuole Membrane-bounded sac, larger than a vesicle; usually functions in storage and can contain a variety of substances. In plants, the central vacuole fills much of the interior of the cell. 74

vagina Organ that leads from the uterus to the vestibule and serves as the birth canal and organ of sexual intercourse in females. 704

valence shell Outer shell of an atom. 28

valve Membranous extension of a vessel of the heart wall that opens and closes, ensuring one-way flow. 595

vascular cylinder In dicot roots, a core of tissues bounded by the endodermis, consisting of vascular tissues and pericycle. 438

vascular plants Land plants that have xylem and phloem. Xylem transports water and helps support an erect stem. 358

vascular tissue Transport tissue in plants consisting of xylem and phloem. 436

vas deferens (vas def-ur-unz, -uh-renz) Tube that leads from the epididymis to the urethra in males. 702

vegetative reproduction In seed plants, reproduction by means other than by seeds; in other organisms, reproduction by vegetative spores, fragmentation, or division of the somatic body. 499

vector (vek-tur) In genetic engineering, a means to transfer foreign genetic material into a cell (e.g., a plasmid). 232

vein Vessel that takes blood to the heart from venules; characteristically has nonelastic walls. 592

vena cava Large systemic vein that returns blood to the right atrium of the heart in tetrapods; either the superior or inferior vena cava. 598

ventilation Process of moving air into and out of the lungs; also called breathing. 650

ventricle (ven-trih-kul) Cavity in an organ, such as a lower chamber of the heart or the ventricles of the brain. 534, 592

venule (ven-yool, veen-) Vessel that takes blood from capillaries to a vein. 595

vermiform appendix Small, tubular appendage that extends outward from the cecum of the large intestine. 636

vertebrae Series of bones that enclose and protect the dorsal nerve cord. 399, 573

vertebral column (vur-tuh-brul) Series of joined vertebrae that extends from the skull to the pelvis. 573

vertebrate Chordate in which the notochord is replaced by a vertebral column. 384

vessel element Cell that joins with others to form a major conducting tube found in xylem. 437, 452

vestibule (ves-tuh-byool) Space or cavity at the entrance of a canal, such as the cavity that lies between the semicircular canals and the cochlea. 559

vestigial structure Remains of a structure that was functional in some ancestor but is no longer functional in the present-day organism. 257

villus (pl., villi) (vil-us) Small, fingerlike projection of the inner small intestinal wall. 635

viroids Naked strands of RNA that cause diseases in plants by directing the plant cell to produce more viroids. 315

visual accommodation Ability of the eye to focus at different distances by changing the curvature of the lens. 555

vitamin Essential requirement in the diet, needed in small amounts. Vitamins are often part of coenzymes. 91, 642

vocal cord Fold of tissue within the larynx; creates vocal sounds when it vibrates. 654

vulva External genitals of the female that surround the opening of the vagina. 704

W

waggle dance Figure-eight dance performed by honeybees to indicate locations of nectar sources. 753

water column In plants, water molecules joined together in xylem from the leaves to the roots. 454

water molds Filamentous organisms having cell walls made of cellulose; typically decomposers of dead freshwater organisms, but some are parasites of aquatic or terrestrial organisms. 342

water vascular system Series of canals that takes water to the tube feet of an echinoderm, allowing them to expand. 393

wax Sticky, solid, waterproof lipid consisting of many long-chain fatty acids usually linked to long-chain alcohols. 50

white blood cell (WBC) Leukocyte, of which there are several types, each having a specific function in protecting the body from invasion by foreign substances and organisms. 511, 601

white matter Myelinated axons in the central nervous system. 534

wood Secondary xylem that builds up year after year in woody plants and becomes the annual rings. 442

X

xenotransplantation Use of animal organs, instead of human organs, in human transplant patients. 236

xylem Vascular tissue that transports water and mineral solutes upward through the plant body; it contains vessel elements and tracheids. 358, 437, 452

xylem sap Solution of inorganic nutrients moved from a plant's roots to its shoots through xylem tissue. 452

Y

yeast Unicellular fungus that has a single nucleus and reproduces asexually by budding or fission, or sexually through spore formation. 372

yolk Dense nutrient material in the egg of a bird or reptile. 700

yolk sac Extraembryonic membrane that encloses the yolk of birds; in humans, it is the first site of blood cell formation. 715

Z

zone of cell division In plants, the part of the young root that includes the root apical meristem and the cells just posterior to it; cells in this zone divide every 12–36 hours. 440

zone of elongation In plants, the part of the young root that lies just posterior to the zone of cell division; cells in this zone elongate, causing the root to lengthen. 441

zone of maturation In plants, the part of the root that lies posterior to the zone of elongation; cells in this zone differentiate into specific cell types. 441

zooplankton Part of plankton containing protozoans and other types of microscopic animals. 339, 793

zoospore A motile spore. 342

zygospore Thick-walled resting cell formed during sexual reproduction of zygospore fungi; meiosis and spore formation occur upon germination. 372

zygote (zy-goht) Diploid cell formed by the union of sperm and egg; the product of fertilization. 155

Animals; (grasshopper): © Masterfile RF; (trout): © Tom & Pat Leeson/Photo Researchers, Inc.; (crab): © Michael Lustbader/Photo Researchers, Inc.; (student): © BananaStock/JupiterImages RF; 26.1B: © M.B. Bunge/Biological Photo Service; 26.1D: © Manfred Kage/Peter Arnold/Photolibrary; 26.5A: Courtesy Dr. E.R. Lewis, University of California Berkeley; 26B: © Evelyn Jo Johnson; 26.14A: © Vol. 94 PhotoDisc/Getty RF; 26.14B: © Reuters/Corbis.

Chapter 27

Openers(bee): © Steven P. Lynch; (flower mosaic): © James Gould; (squid): © Jeff Rotman/Photo Researchers, Inc.; (woman): © Roy Morsch; (zebra): © Ingrid Van Den Berg/Animals Animals; 27.1A: © Jeff Foott; 27.1B: © David M. Dennis/Animals Animals; 27.1C: © Dr. Merlin D. Tuttle/Bat Conservation International /Photo Researchers, Inc.; 27.4(all): © Omikron/SPL/Photo Researchers, Inc.; p. 553(ice cream): © Coneyl Jay/Photo Researchers, Inc.; Box 27A, p. 555: © Sue Ford/Photo Researchers, Inc.; 27.8: © Lennart Nilsson/SCANPIX; 27.11: © P. Motta/SPL/Photo Researchers, Inc.; 27C (both): Courtesy Dr. Yeohash Raphael, the University of Michigan, Ann Arbor; 27.12B: © Myrleen Ferguson Cate/PhotoEdit; 27.12C: © Dr. David Furness, Keele University/Photo Researchers, Inc.

Chapter 28

Openers(child, adult skulls): © 2007 Educational Images Ltd./Custom Medical Stock Photo; (fracture): © Scott Camazine/Phototake; (femur): © Dr. Fred Hossler/Visuals Unlimited; (pelvis): © L. Bassett/Visuals Unlimited; (skulls, male left, female right): © Ralph Hutchings/Visuals Unlimited; (forensics): © Fehim Demir/epa/Corbis; p. 570(exoskeleton): © Michael Fogden/OSF/Animals Animals; 28.1B: © Dynamic Graphics Group/PunchStock RF; 28.2: © Julie Lemberger/Corbis; 28.5(articular cartilage, bone): © Ed Reschke; 28.5(osteocyte): © Biophoto Associates/Photo Researchers, Inc.; 28.6(gymnast): © Gerard Vandystadt/Photo Researchers, Inc.; 28Ba(tennis player): © Susan Mullane/NewSport/Corbis; 28Ba(bone, both): © Michael Klein/Peter Arnold/Photolibrary; 28Bb: © Bill Aaron/PhotoEdit; p. 580(motor unit): © Victor B. Eichler, Ph.D.; 28.8A(girl): © David Young-Wolff/PhotoEdit; 28.10A: © Biology Media/Photo Researchers, Inc.; 28.13(left): © Lawrence Manning/Corbis; 28.13(center): © G. W. Willis/Visuals Unlimited; 28.13(right): © Corbis RF.

Chapter 29

Openers(panda): © Digital Vision RF; (lionfish): © Brand X Pictures/PunchStock RF; (tube worms): © Diane R. Nelson; (lobster): Ken Lucas/Visuals Unlimited; (wasps): © Carson Baldwin, Jr./Animals Animals; 29.1A(hydra): © CABISCO/Visuals Unlimited; 29.1A(flatworm): © Runk/Schoenberger/Grant Heilman Photography; 29.2: © SIU/Visuals Unlimited; 29.3A: © Biophoto Associates/Photo Researchers, Inc.; 29.3B: © David Joel/MacNeal Hospital/Getty Images; 29.4B(artery, vein): © Ed Reschke; 29.4B(capillary bed): © Biophoto Associates/Photo Researchers, Inc.; 29Ba: © Pascal Goethgheluck/SPL/Photo Researchers, Inc.; 29C: © Biophoto Associates/Photo Researchers, Inc.; Box 29D, p. 601(Bosisio): © AFP/Getty Images; 29.9: © Eye of Science/Photo Researchers, Inc.; 29E: © Astrid & Hanns-Frieder Michler/Photo Researchers, Inc.; 29.10A, B: © J. C. Revy/Phototake; 29.10B: © J. C. Revy/Phototake.

Chapter 30

Openers(HIV budding): © CMSP/J.L. Carson/Getty Images; (Kaposi sarcoma): © A. Ramey/PhotoEdit; (AIDS patient sequence, all): © Nicholas Nixon; 30.2(bone marrow): © R. Calentine/Visuals

Unlimited; 30.2(thymus, spleen): © Ed Reschke/Peter Arnold/Photolibrary; 30.2(lymph node): © Fred E. Hossler/Visuals Unlimited; Box 30A, p. 613(fever): © Larry Dale Gordon/Getty Images; 30.4B: © Dennis Kunkel/Phototake; 30.6A: © Michael Newman/PhotoEdit; 30.6B: © Digital Vision/Getty RF; 30.8A: © Steve Gschmeissner/Photo Researchers, Inc.; 30.9B: © Steve Gschmeissner/Photo Researchers, Inc.; 30.11A: © Richard Anderson; 30.11B: © Dr. Ken Greer/Visuals Unlimited; 30C(pollen): © David Scharf/SPL/Photo Researchers, Inc.; 30C(girl): © Damien Lovegrove/SPL/Photo Researchers, Inc.; 30C(mast cell): © Lennart Nilsson/SCANPIX; 31(horse): © Yva Momatiuk & John Eastcott/Minden Pictures.

Chapter 31

Openers(tiger): © Ken Cole/Animals Animals; (zebra): © Jean-Michel Labat/Peter Arnold/Photolibrary; (rabbit): © John Gerlach/Animals Animals; (wolves): © Corbis RF; 31.1A: © Arthur Morris/Visuals Unlimited; 31.1B: © James D. Watt/Visuals Unlimited; 31.1C: © Michael & Patricia Fogden/Minden Pictures; 31.1D: © Brian Kenney/OSF/Animals Animals; 31A.4: © Ardea London Ltd.; 31A.5a: © Radius Images/PunchStock RF; 31A.5B: © The McGraw-Hill Companies, Inc., Barry Barker, photographer; 31.3C(left): © Manfred Kage/Peter Arnold/Photolibrary; 31.3C(right):Photo by Susumu Ito, from Charles Flickinger *Medical Cell Biology* W.B. Saunders, 1979; p. 636(E. coli): Courtesy Centers for Disease Control and Prevention (CDC); p. 637(M. smithii bacteria): © Denis Kunkel Microscopy, Inc.; 31C: © Randy Faris/Corbis RF; 31.6: © Digital Vision/Getty RF; 31D: © Benjamin F. Fink, Jr./Brand X/Corbis RF; 31E.1: © Tony Freeman/PhotoEdit; 31E.2: © Donna Day/Stone/Getty Images; 31E.3: © Corbis RF.

Chapter 32

Openers(diver): © Buzz Pictures/Alamy; (elephant seals): © Bruce Watkins/Animals Animals; (Weddell seal): © Mark Chappell/Animals Animals; (whale): © Brandon Cole/Visuals Unlimited; (dolphin): © Stephen Frink/Corbis; 32.2(left): © Runk/Schoenberger/Grant Heilman Photography; 32.2(right): © David M. Phillips/Photo Researchers, Inc.; 32.3: © Ed Reschke; 32B(both lung photos): © Martin M. Rotker, 2010; 32B(tumor): © Moredun Animal Health/SPL/Photo Researchers, Inc.

Chapter 33

Openers(barracuda): © Tobias Bernhard/Oxford Scientific/Getty Images; (reef): © Gregory Ochocki/Photo Researchers, Inc.; (Christmas tree worm): © Espen Rekdal/SeaPics.com; (clownfish): © Dave B. Fleetham/Visuals Unlimited; (cup coral): © Jeff Rotman/Getty Images; 33A.3: © Digital Vision Ltd. RF; 33A.4: © Eric Hosking/Photo Researchers, Inc.; 33A.5: © Jason Hosking/Corbis; 33.3C(top left): © Prof. P.M. Motta & M. Castellucci/Science Photo Library/Photo Researchers, Inc.; 33.3C(top right, lower left): Reprinted from *Journal of Ultrastructure Research*, Vol. 15, A.B. Maunsbach, pages 242–282, copyright 1966, with permission of Elsevier.; 33.3C:Reprinted from *Journal of Ultrastructure Research*, Vol. 15, A.B. Maunsbach, pages 242–282, copyright 1966, with permission of Elsevier.; p. 673(doctor, patient): © Jose Luis Pelaez, Inc./Corbis, 33.5A: © James Cavallini/Photo Researchers, Inc.; 33C: © Syner-Comm/Alamy.

Chapter 34

Openers(seals): © Marc Moritsch/National Geographic Image Collection; (humans): © David Raymer/Corbis; (lions): © K. Ammann/Bruce Coleman, Inc.; (ants): © Mark Moffett/Minden

Pictures; (wildebeest): © Vaclav Silha/Barcroft Media/Fame; 34.4A(left): © AP/Wide World Photos; 34.4A(right): © General Photographic Agency/Getty Images; 34.4B(both): These photos were published in Clinical Pathological Conference, "Acromegaly, Diabetes, Hypermetabolism, Proteinura and Heart Failure", *American Journal of Medicine*, 20 (1956) 133. Reprinted with permission from Excerpta Medica Inc.; 34.5A: © Medical-on-Line/Alamy; 34.5B: © Bruce Coleman, Inc./Alamy; 34.5C: © Dr. P. Marazzi/SPL/Photo Researchers, Inc.; 34.7B: © NMSB/Custom Medical Stock Photos; 34A(both):"Atlas of Pediatric Physical Diagnosis," Second Edition by Zitelli & Davis, 1992. Mosby-Wolfe Europe Limited, London, UK; 34.8A: © Peter Arnold/Alamy; 34.8C: © BSIP/Phototake; 34B: © James Darell/Stone/Getty Images.

Chapter 35

Openers(frogs): © Hans Pfletschinger/Peter Arnold/Photolibrary; (turtle hatching): © Kevin Schafer/Corbis; (turtles mating): © Michael Patrick O'Neill/Photo Researchers, Inc.; (kangaroos): © Martin Harvey/Corbis; (whales): © Phillip Colla/SeaPics.com; p. 700(hydra): © Dr. Dennis Kunkel/Visuals Unlimited; 35.1: © Paul Nicklen/National Geographic/Getty Images; p. 701(mallard genitals): Courtesy Patricia R. Brennan, Ph.D.; p. 701(seed beetle): Courtesy Johanna Rönn, 35A(goldfinch): © Anthony Mercieca/Photo Researchers, Inc.; 35A(swans): © cupra images/Alamy; 35.3: © Ed Reschke; 35.5A: © Ed Reschke/Peter Arnold/Photolibrary; 35.6Ba: © Saturn Stills/Photo Researchers, Inc.; 35.6Bb: © Michael Keller/Corbis; 35.6Bc: © LADA/Photo Researchers, Inc.; 35.6Bd: © SIU/Visuals Unlimited; 35.6Be: © Keith Brofsky/Getty RF; 35.6Bf: © The McGraw-Hill Companies, Inc./Lars A. Niki, photographer; 35.6Bg: © Phanie/Photo Researchers, Inc.; 35.6Bh: © Getty Images; Table 35B(couple): © Vol. 62/Corbis RF; 35C: © CC Studio/SPL/Photo Researchers, Inc.; p. 710(chick): © Photodisc/Getty RF; 35.7: © William Jorgensen/Visuals Unlimited; 35.8: © Carolina Biological Supply/Phototake; 35.9A-2: Courtesy Kathryn Tosney; p. 712(frog): © Photodisc/Getty RF; 35.13B: © Lennart Nilsson/SCANPIX; 35.14A: © Neil Harding/Getty Images; 35.14B: © John Watney/Photo Researchers, Inc.; 35.14C: © Lennart Nilsson/SCANPIX; 35.14D: © Dennis MacDonald/PhotoEdit; 35.15c: © Karen Kasmauski/Corbis.

Chapter 36

Openers(buck): © Dominique Braud/Animals Animals; (doe, fawn): © Stephen J. Krasemann/Photo Researchers, Inc.; (deer running): © John Cancalosi/Peter Arnold/Photolibrary; 36.1: © David Hall/Photo Researchers, Inc.; 36.2A: © Richard Weymouth Brooks/Photo Researchers, Inc.; 36.2B: © Karen Fuller/Alamy; 36.3A(pigs): © age fotostock/SuperStock; 36.3A(rhinos): © Corbis RF; 36.7A: © Ted Levin/Animals Animals; 36.7B: © Winfried Wisniewski/Getty Images; 36A: © Frans Lemmens/Getty Images; 36.8(top): © Corbis RF; 36.8(bottom): © Ben Osborne/OSF/Animals Animals; 36B(above): © Stephen Simpson/Getty Images; 36B(below): © L. Lefkowitz/Getty Images.

Chapter 37

Openers(porcupine): © Mark Boulton/Photo Researchers, Inc.; (chinchillas): © J.M. Labat/P. Rocher/Peter Arnold/Photolibrary; (guinea pigs): © Jorg & Petra Wegner/Animals Animals; (naked mole rats digging): © M. J. O'Riain & J. Jarvis/Visuals Unlimited; 37naked mole rat queen): © Jennifer Jarvis/Visuals Unlimited; 37.1A(left): © Joe McDonald; 37.1A(right): Courtesy Refuge for Saving the Wildlife, Inc.; 37.1B(both): From J.R. Brown et al, "A defect in

Index

White-handed gibbon, 412f
White matter, 534, 540f
White pulp, of spleen, 611, 611f
White-tailed deer, 405f, 726–727, 726f, 727f
Whitfield, Arthur, 197
WHR. *See* Waist-to-hip ratio
Wild chinook salmon, 17
Wildlife, value to humans, 802–803, 802f, 803f
Wilkins, Maurice H. F., 194
Williams syndrome, 164
Wilson, E. O., 769
Wind power, 814, 814f
Winds
    climate and, 782, 782f
    ocean currents and, 784
Wine and winemaking, 134, 373
Wings
    of moths and butterflies, 210–211, 210f, 211f
    vertebrate, as homologous structure, 303
Winter solstice, 782f
Winter twig, 441, 441f
Wisdom teeth, 632
Woese, Carl, 297
Wolves, 754
Women. *See* Female(s), human
Women's Health Institute, 154

Wood(s)
    fossilization of, 443, 443f
    heartwood, 442–443
    lumber, 369
    sap, 442
    as secondary growth, 442–443, 442f
    soft and hard, 362
Woodpecker, pileated, 403f
Woody eudicots, secondary growth in, 442–443, 442f
Woody twigs, anatomy of, 441, 441f
Wrinkles, in skin, 515
Würsig, B., 754

X

X chromosomes, 155, 155f
Xenotransplantation, 236, 406, 621
Xeroderma pigmentosum, 206, 206f
X-linked alleles, 185, 185f
X-linked genetic disorders, 186, 186f
X-ray crystallography, DNA diffraction pattern, 194, 194f
X-rays, and cancer, 154, 206
Xylem, 358, 358f, 434, 434f, 437, 437f, 439, 439f, 441, 441f, 442, 442f, 446, 452, 454–455, 455f
    in angiosperms, 440f

Xylem rays, 442, 442f
Xylem sap, 452

Y

Yamanaka, Shinya, 151
Y chromosomes, 155, 155f
Yeast(s)
    budding, 372, 373f
    classification of, 372
    fermentation and, 133, 133f, 134, 373
    genome of, 241t
    spindle apparatus in, 147, 147f
Yeast infections, 374
Yellow bone marrow, 576, 576f
Yellow fever, 314
Yellow jacket wasp, 763, 763f
Yellowstone National Park, 810
Yellow trumpet pitcher (*Sarracenia flava*), 351, 351f
Yersinia pestis, 328
Yoho National Park, 282–283
Yolk, 710
Yolk plug, 711, 711f
Yolk sac, 402f, 715, 715f, 716–717
YUP gene, 55

Z

Zea mays. See Corn
Zebra mussels, 806
Zinc
    dietary requirements, 641t
    as plant nutrient, 461t
Ziram, 206
Z lines, 582, 582f
Zone of cell division, 440, 440f
Zone of elongation, 440f, 441
Zone of leeching, 462f
Zone of maturation, 440f, 441
Zooflagellates, 338
Zooplankton, 339, 793
Zoos, breeding programs at, 812, 812f
Zoospores, 345, 345f
Zooxanthellae, 793
Zygomatic bones, 573, 573f
Zygomycota, 372
Zygospore(s), 345, 345f
Zygospore fungi, 371f, 372
Zygote
    in angiosperm life cycle, 496, 496f
    development of, 710, 710f
    in human life cycle, 705
    in life cycle, generally, 160, 160f

Metric System

Unit and Abbreviation	Metric Equivalent	Approximate English-to-Metric Equivalents
Length		
nanometer (nm)	$= 10^{-9}$ m (10^{-3} μm)	
micrometer (μm)	$= 10^{-6}$ m (10^{-3} mm)	
millimeter (mm)	$= 0.001$ (10^{-3}) m	
centimeter (cm)	$= 0.01$ (10^{-2}) m	1 inch = 2.54 cm 1 foot = 30.5 cm
meter (m)	$= 100$ (10^2) cm $= 1,000$ mm	1 foot = 0.30 m 1 yard = 0.91 m
kilometer (km)	$= 1,000$ (10^3) m	1 mi = 1.6 km
Weight (mass)		
nanogram (ng)	$= 10^{-9}$ g	
microgram (μg)	$= 10^{-6}$ g	
milligram (mg)	$= 10^{-3}$ g	
gram (g)	$= 1,000$ mg	1 ounce = 28.3 g 1 pound = 454 g
kilogram (kg)	$= 1,000$ (10^3) g	= 0.45 kg
metric ton (t)	$= 1,000$ kg	1 ton = 0.91 t
Volume		
microliter (μl)	$= 10^{-6}$ l (10^{-3} ml)	
milliliter (ml)	$= 10^{-3}$ liter $= 1$ cm³ (cc) $= 1,000$ mm³	1 tsp = 5 ml 1 fl oz = 30 ml
liter (l)	$= 1,000$ ml	1 pint = 0.47 liter 1 quart = 0.95 liter 1 gallon = 3.79 liter
kiloliter (kl)	$= 1,000$ liter	

Units of Temperature

°C	°F	
100	212	Water boils at standard temperature and pressure.
71	160	Flash pasteurization of milk.
57	134	Highest recorded temperature in the United States, Death Valley, July 10, 1913.
41	105.8	Average body temperature of a marathon runner in hot weather.
37	98.6	Human body temperature.
13.7	56.66	Human survival is still possible at this temperature.
0	32.0	Water freezes at standard temperature and pressure.

To convert temperature scales:

$$°C = \frac{(°F - 32)}{1.8}$$

$$°F = 1.8\,(°C) + 32$$

Periodic Table of the Elements

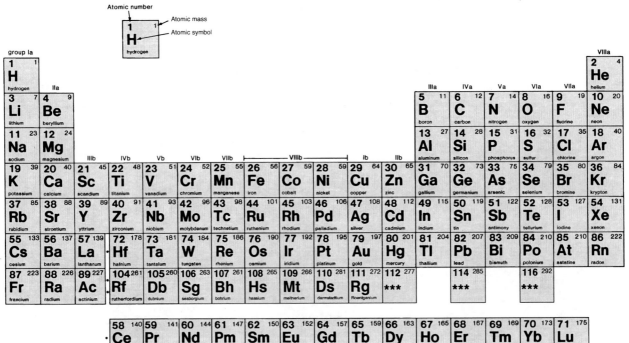